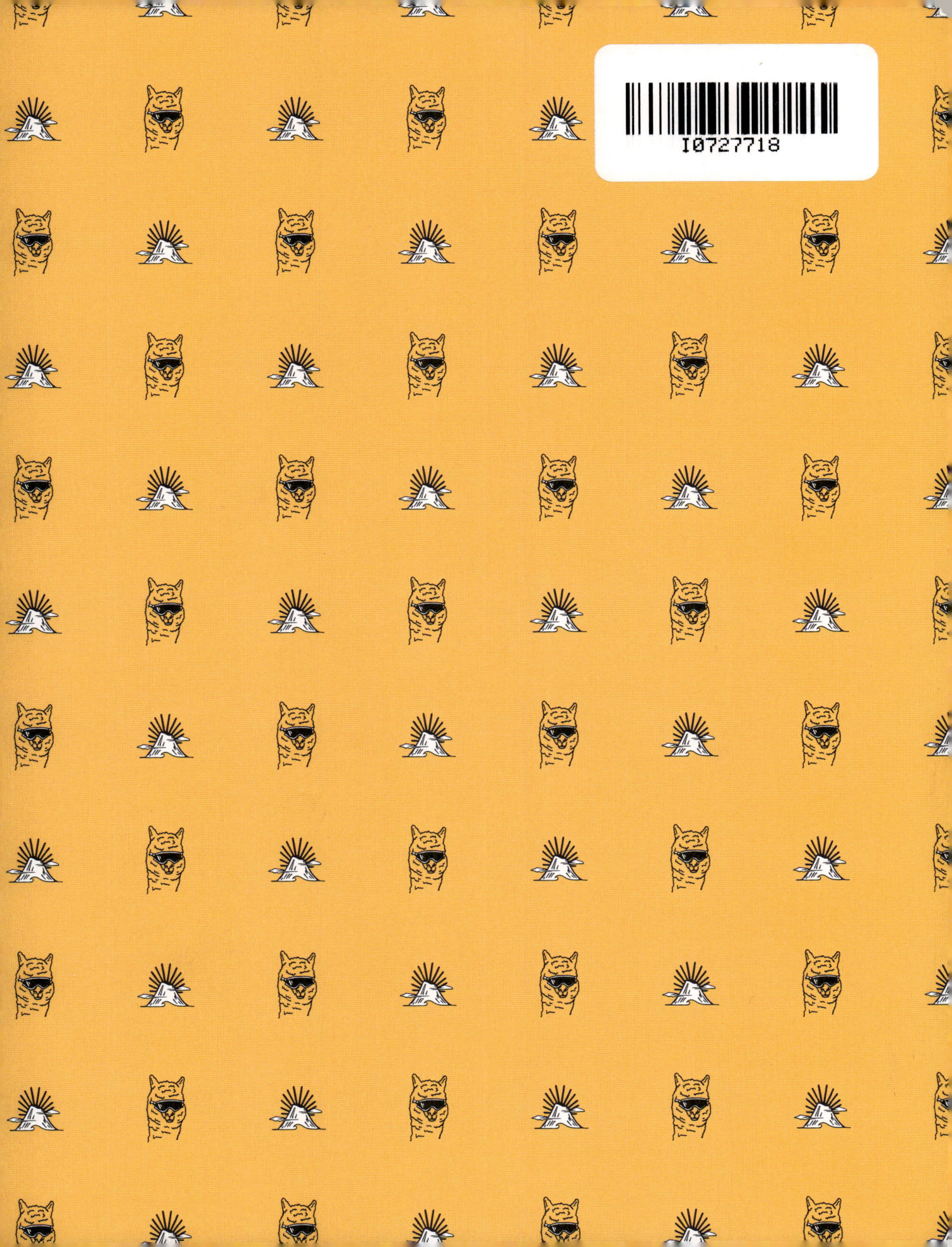

Wayward

CHRIS BURKARD

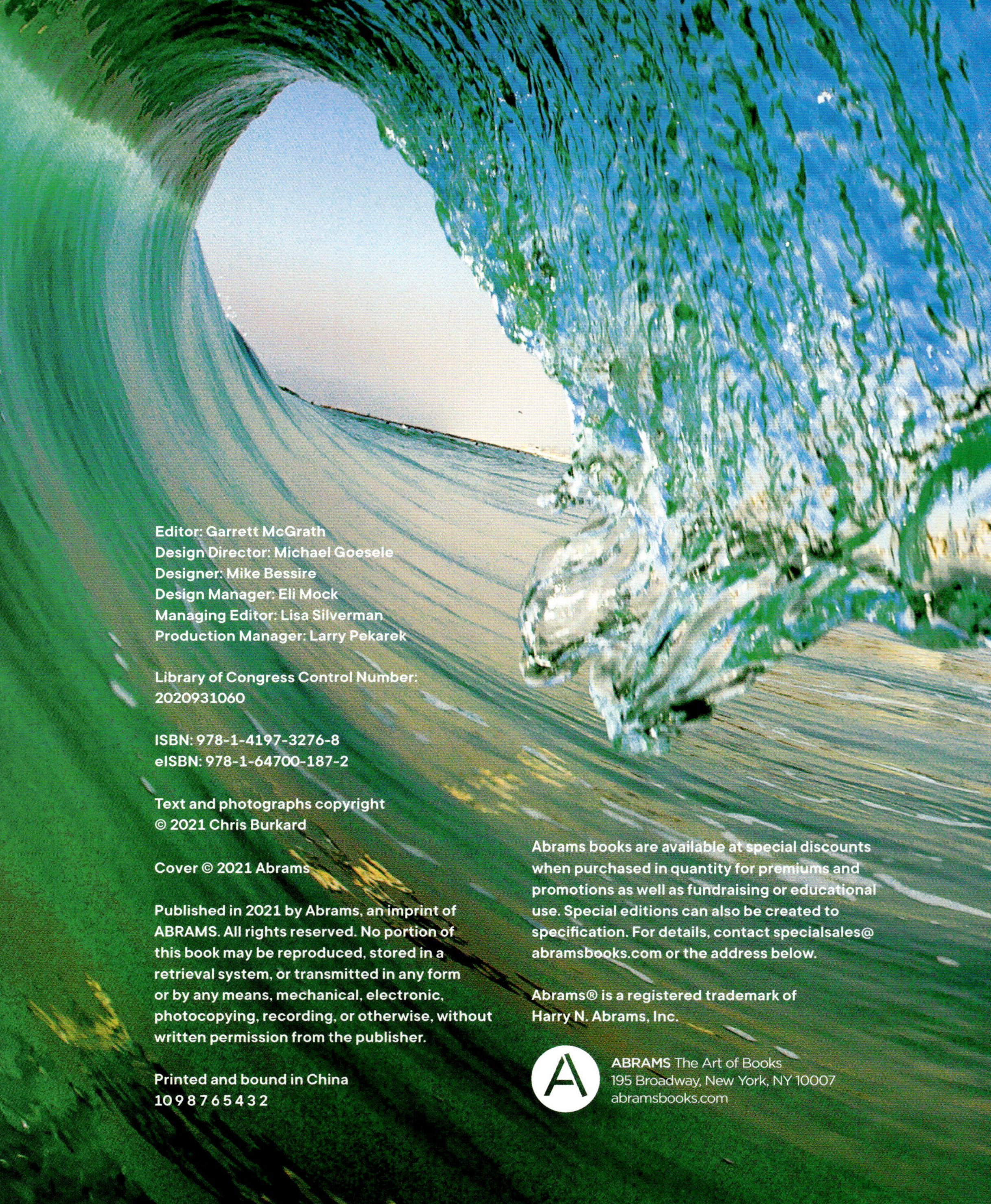

Editor: Garrett McGrath
Design Director: Michael Goesele
Designer: Mike Bessire
Design Manager: Eli Mock
Managing Editor: Lisa Silverman
Production Manager: Larry Pekarek

Library of Congress Control Number:
2020931060

ISBN: 978-1-4197-3276-8
eISBN: 978-1-64700-187-2

Abrams books are available at special discounts
when purchased in quantity for premiums and
promotions as well as fundraising or educational
use. Special editions can also be created to
specification. For details, contact specialsales@
abramsbooks.com or the address below.

Abrams® is a registered trademark of
Harry N. Abrams, Inc.

ABRAMS The Art of Books
195 Broadway, New York, NY 10007
abramsbooks.com

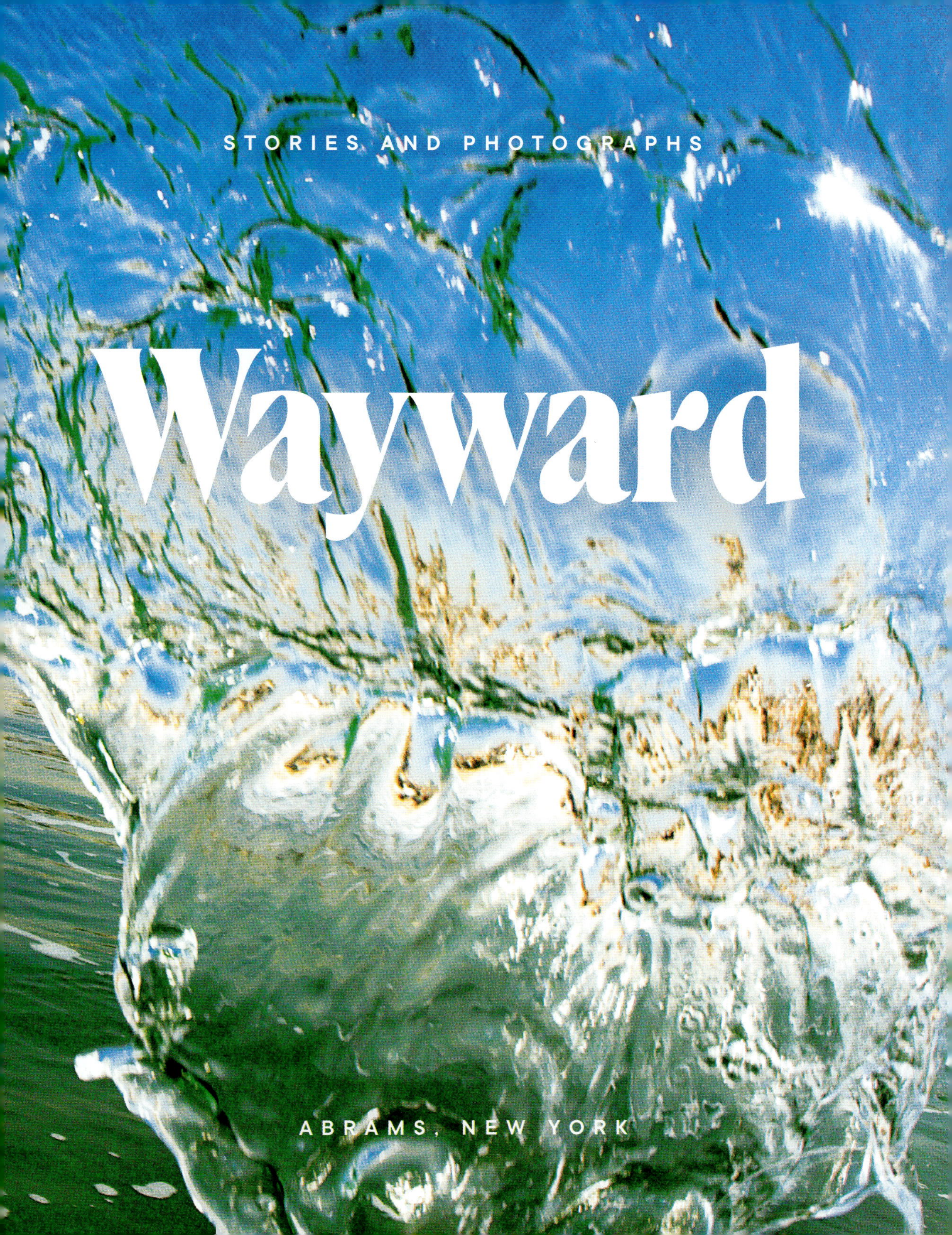

STORIES AND PHOTOGRAPHS
Wayward
ABRAMS, NEW YORK

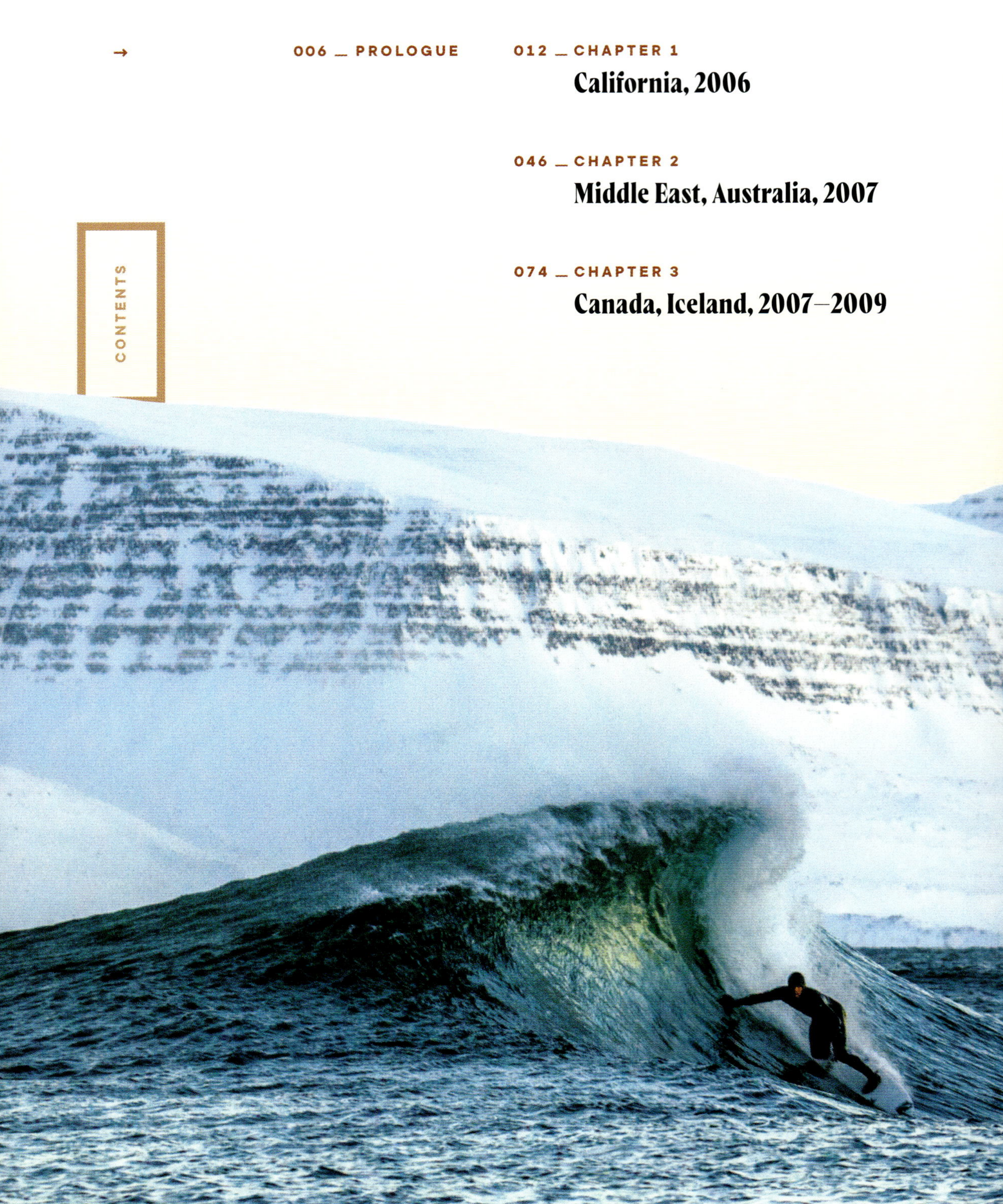

CONTENTS

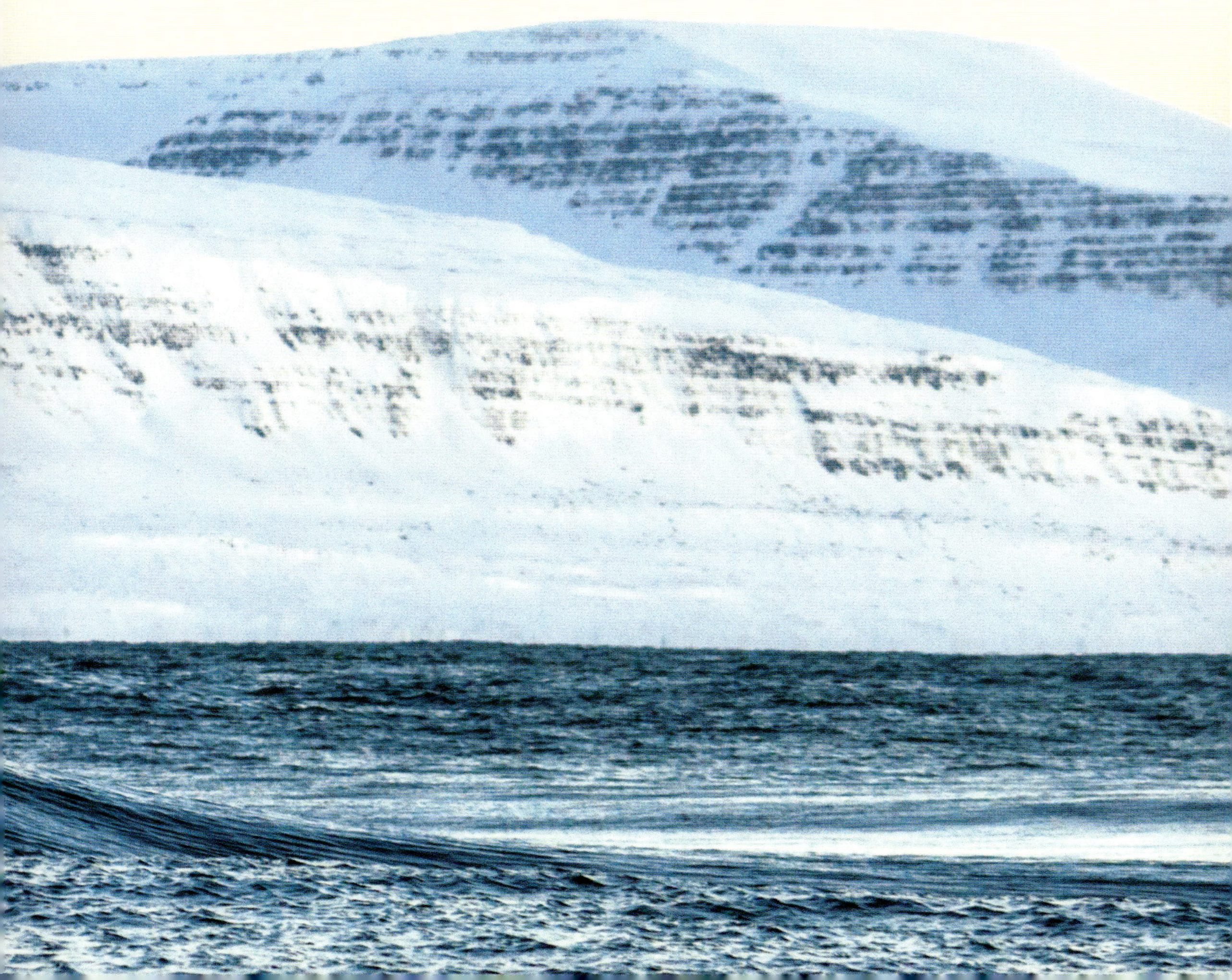

PROLOGUE

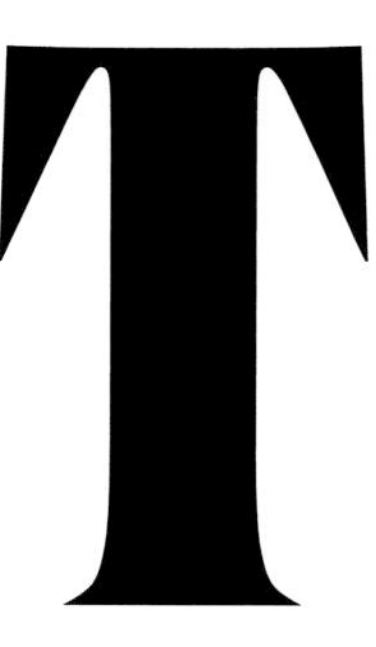

The view I had from behind the counter at Esquire News made it the perfect spot to daydream about surf. Even though I could barely make out the west swell as it was sculpted by the clean offshore winds, it was just the right angle—which is probably why my casual minimum-wage summer job transitioned into a fall job, and then an early winter job. I was nineteen years old, living in a small beach town called Pismo Beach, about thirteen miles south of San Louis Obispo, on the central California coast. I was taking a handful of forgettable "core" classes at Cuesta Community College, but what I really lived for was chasing swell around "SLO county" with a camera in my hand and a vague dream of somehow making a living taking photos. I had convinced myself that in my spare time between taking classes and shooting photos, my time would be best spent surrounding myself with the magazines that immortalized the type of photos I aspired to take—*Surfer*, *National Geographic*, *Outside*, to name a few.

Between dreaming about the surf and occasionally ringing up a customer, I would picture myself on the white sand beaches of those remote, distant shores. I figured that the more time I spent reading and absorbing these magazines, the closer I would get to actually being there, and shooting those photos ... I was pretty naive.

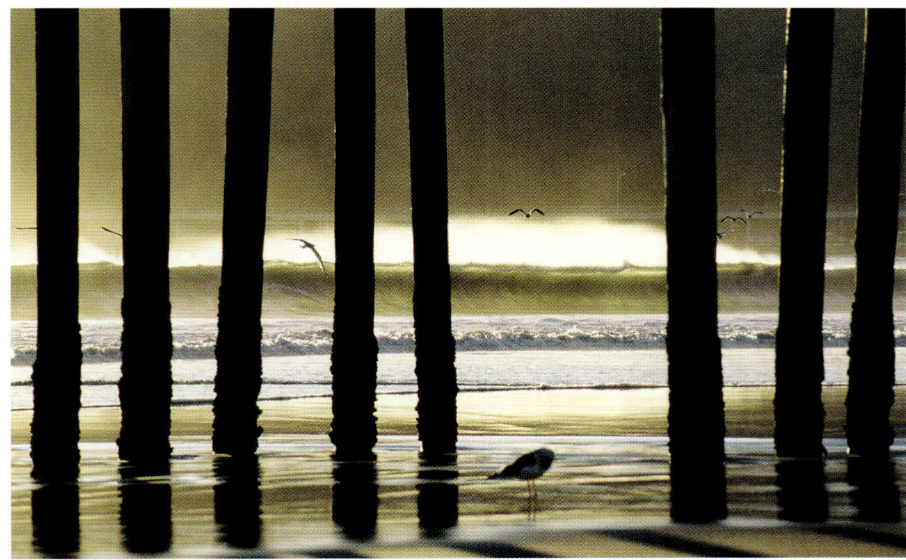

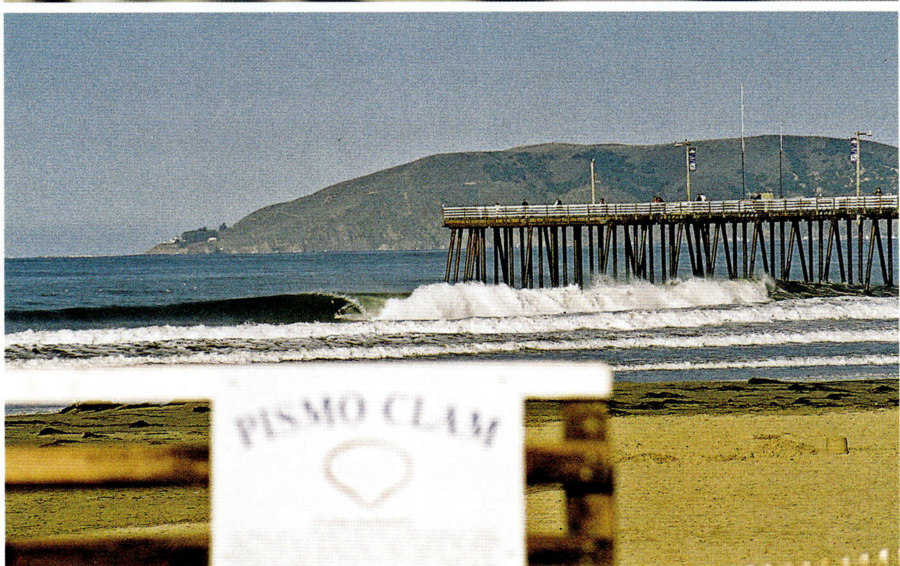

CHRIS BURKARD

WAYWARD

In reality, the more time I spent in class, or sitting behind the counter at the newsstand, the more time I was spending away from the waves, and the more angst I felt toward anything that took me away from my newfound dream. My newfound purpose. More than anything else in my life, I knew one thing: Photography had become more than just a hobby. It was my passion. And I knew this because regardless of the absolute lack of job opportunities, or even the basic knowledge of how to use my camera, I was still completely dedicated to making it work. I had to. I was impatient and ignorant, but also hopeful. And once I knew what I wanted, nothing was going to get in my way.

To be specific, the dream was to be a surf photographer. But that was—and still is—a wildly misunderstood career path. It was not about hanging out on tropical beaches getting a tan. It was about chasing long-period swells around the globe with athletes of the highest caliber, while pushing my mind and body to wield a camera in big surf, while going toe-to-toe with some of the world's most challenging waves. It was also about knowing which lens, camera, and settings were right to capture waves of unparalleled excellence, worthy of publishing in the handful of magazines that featured surf content. Then there was the unicorn of job titles: *staff photographer.* There were probably about thirty people in the entire world making a living as a surf photographer. I, on the other hand, didn't even yet own a passport, let alone a good enough camera to produce an image worthy of a dou-

ble-page spread. The likelihood of seeing this dream realized was not unlike that of winning the lottery.

But odds didn't matter to me. I felt the calling and, one way or another, I was going to make a living with my camera by my side. I had no backup plan. I began my career like a lot of photographers: senior class photos, weddings, interior photos of my friend's local skate shop—if it paid, I was in. I needed to first just prove to myself, my parents, and my girlfriend at the time that this was real and worth it. That *I* was worth it.

This book is a collection of stories that chronicle my journey. It recounts spectacular failures and naivete, as well as

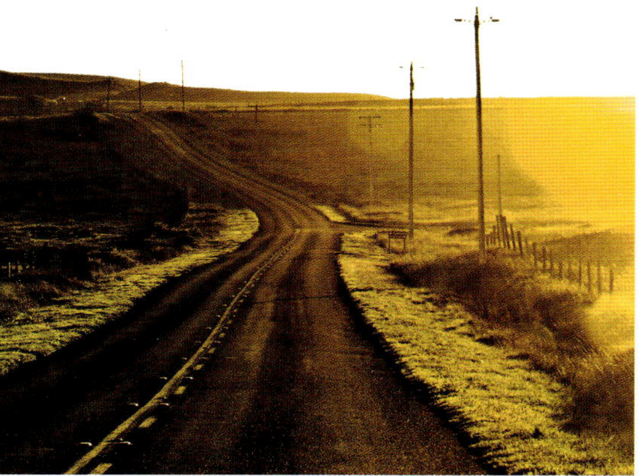

minor miracles and victories. After trying to prove myself to my friends and family, I decided it was time to test myself. I embarked on what remains one of my most defining adventures, surveying the surf of the entire California Coast, which eventually became my first book. Inevitably, the adventures became bigger and bolder, until I sort of established myself as a photographer operating on the fringes, capturing images in places that were difficult to get to, challenging to surf, and even more challenging to photograph. At remote beaches in places like Iceland and the Aleutian Islands, I succumbed to hypothermia, destroyed thousands of dollars' worth of camera gear, and spent a few nights in jail. But I also scored some amazing images—some that have even become iconic. Equally valuable to me are the memories.

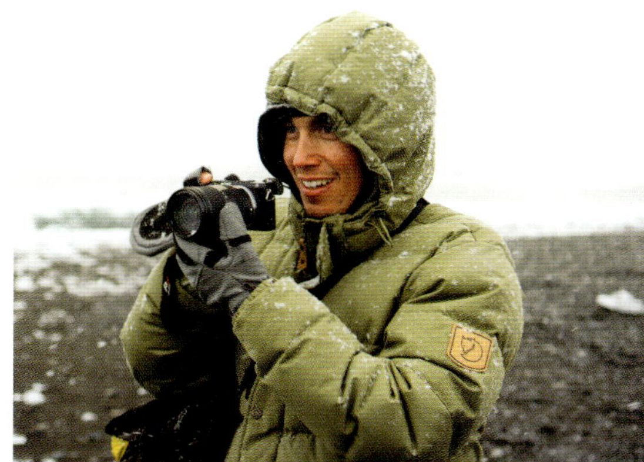

I have now made a living as a photographer for more than a decade. However, most of my stories and experiences have been expressed through someone else's lens—a talented journalist, an editor at a magazine, brand photo editors. I've always wanted to recount these adventures in my own words, dig up the images that I connected with, and share some behind-the-scenes anecdotes about how those images came to be. These are my stories, in my own words.

In October 2005, I collected my last paycheck from Esquire News and locked up after my last closing shift. After also collecting my final financial aid check—to buy film—I *unenrolled* in community college. I then went to my parents to let them know that their eldest son was now a jobless college dropout. I was terrified. I was out of my element and scared beyond belief, a foreshadowing of what would drive me in the years to come. A man with a purpose is a powerful thing, and for the first time in my life I felt like I was on a path. And like most good adventures—or, some might say, cautionary tales—my path began with little money, big dreams, a gas tank on empty, and a whole lot of luck.

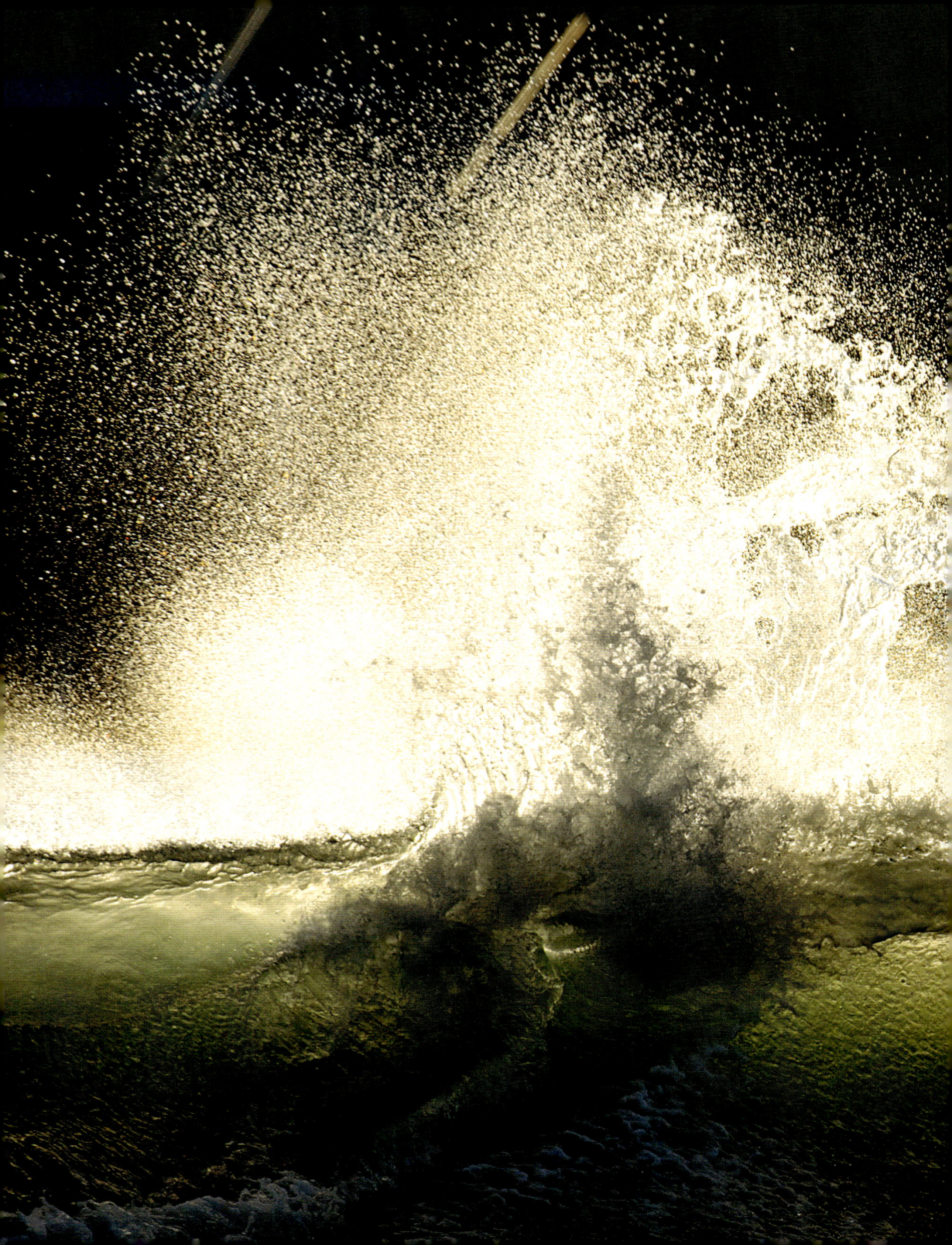

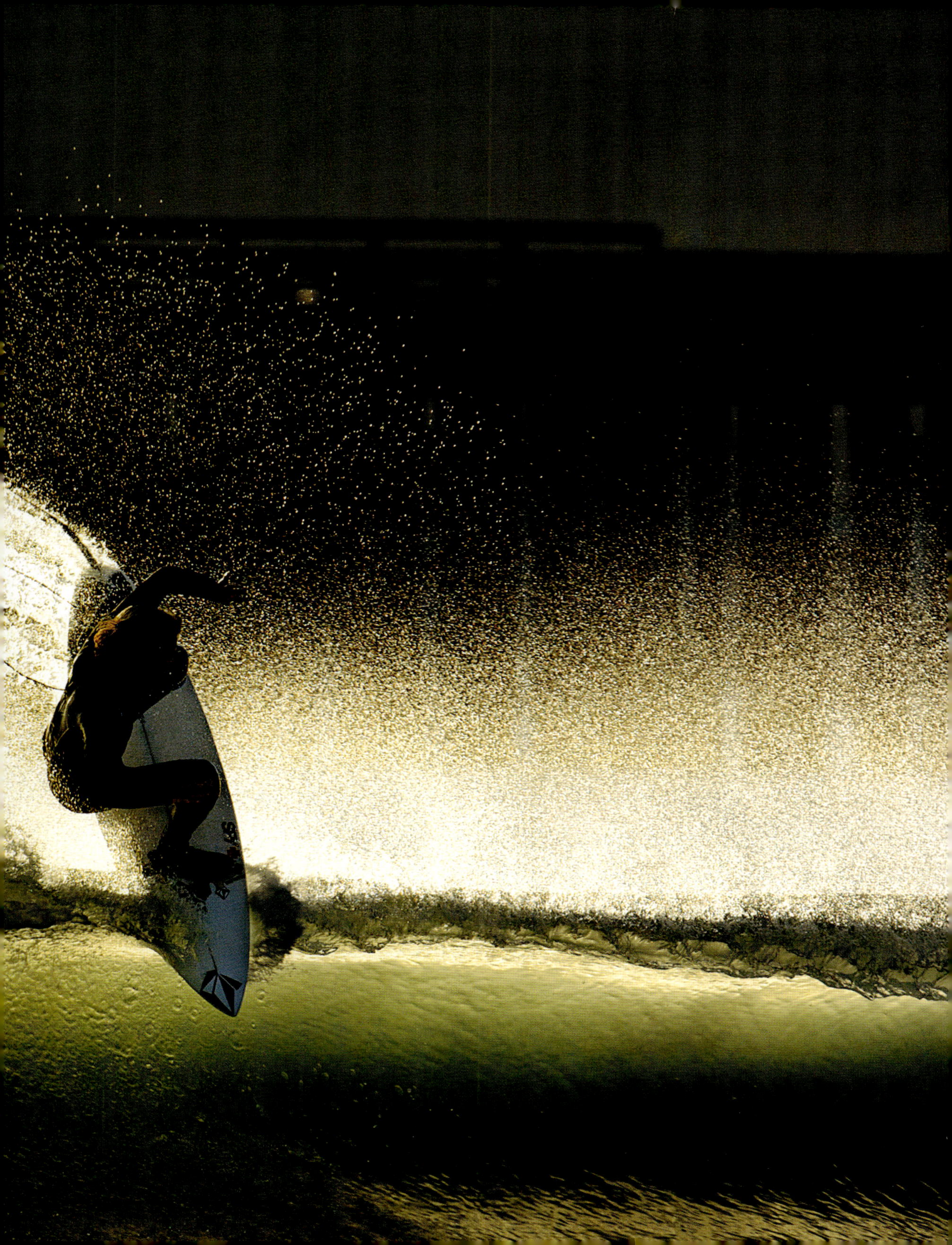

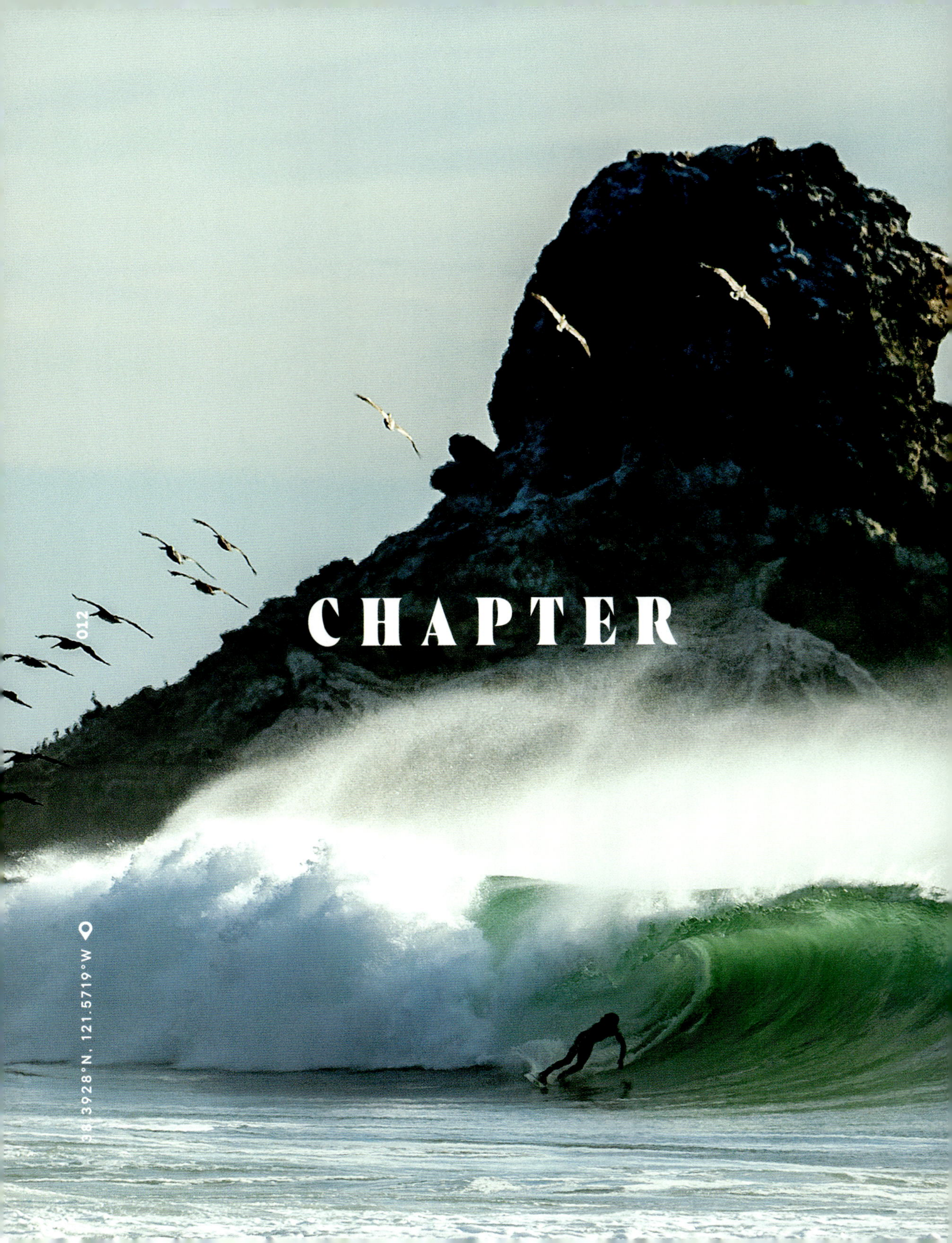
CHAPTER
012
36.3928° N. 121.5719° W

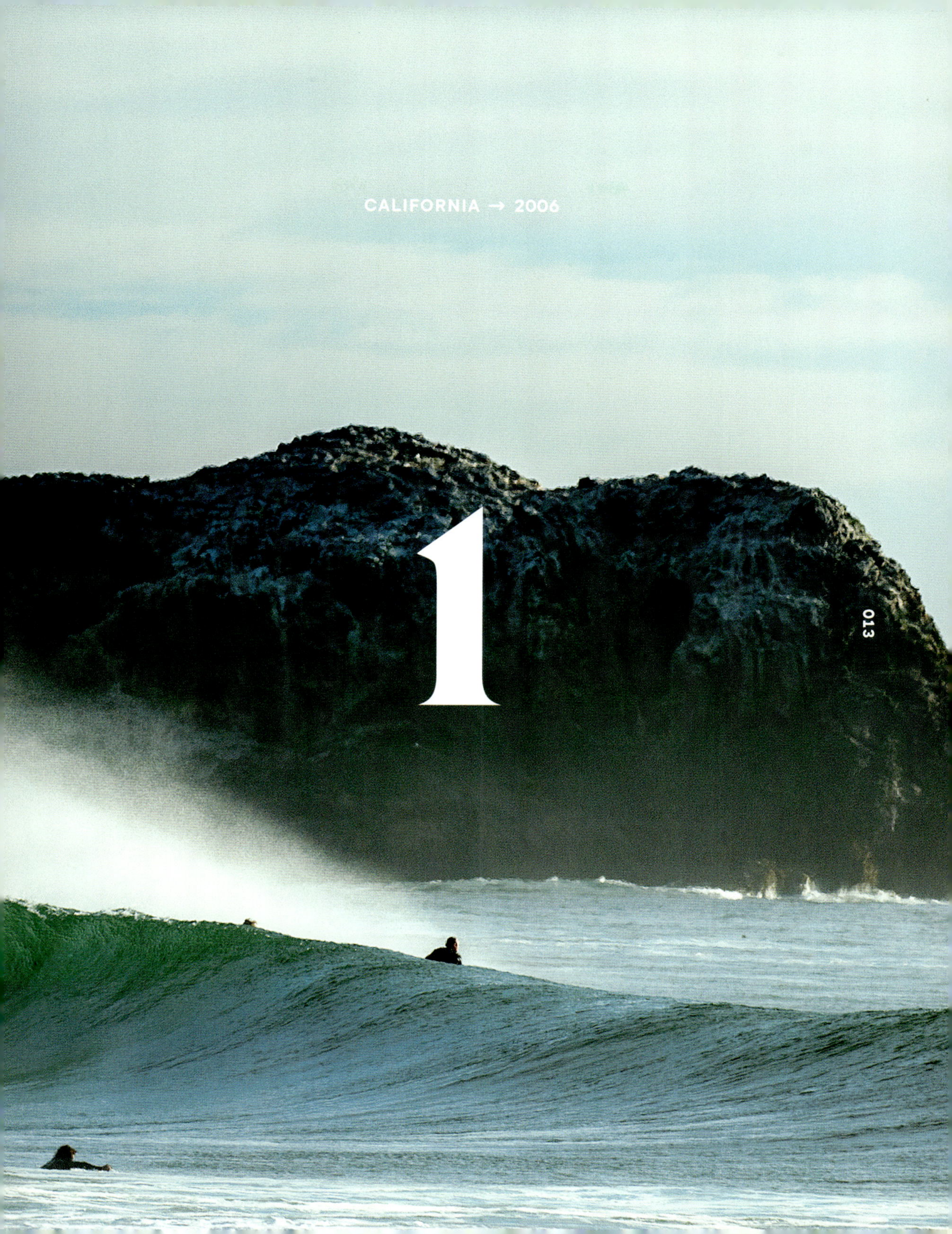

CALIFORNIA → 2006
1
013

t was Thanksgiving day when the rain finally let up. Eric and I were ten days into a fifty-day road trip down the California coast, and this was the first day we could hang our clothes to dry and air out Eric's VW bus, which had started to reek of canned tuna and stale farts. We knew the coastline between the Oregon border and Mendocino would be wet, but we had reached a level of sogginess even we didn't know was possible. By both our appearance and smell, we were morphing into wet dogs. In our psyched-up naiveté, we had strapped firewood to the roof of the bus, and it got soaked on day one; we brought musty roll-up sleeping bags purchased from the army surplus store in San Luis Obispo, and they never fully dried; and we didn't pack a single towel. For as much as Eric and I prided ourselves on spending a lot of time in nature, we had literally no clue what we were doing. It may as well have been our first camp-out as young Boy Scouts, as unprepared as we were.

However, this was a far more ambitious expedition than a simple camp-out. We had embarked on a two-month-long surf trip down the California coast, from the Oregon border to the Tijuana Sloughs, in the hope of turning our images and discoveries into a book and film—a visual love letter to our home state. Whenever we weren't surfing and photographing every mile of waterlogged coast in Del Norte and Humboldt Counties, we were cooped up in the bus, wet and irritated, at each other as much as at the weather. I had never spent so much time with another human in such close quarters—not even my girlfriend. I was on edge to say the least. When the canvas roof to my pop-top bed started leaking in the middle of the night—after we had already patched a spitting rain gutter with duct tape a few days before—the trip began to feel more like a nightmare than a dream come true. It's funny how quickly excitement and gratitude wear off when you haven't seen the sun for days and things start getting uncomfortable. "I think I'm losing my mind," I whispered from the top compartment after one too many raindrops exploded on my nose. I heard an unintelligible grunt from below and knew I wasn't alone in that thought.

But in true poetic irony, the sun finally came out on that Thanksgiving morning, showing us what humility and simple gratitude really looked like. Like caged animals freed after a storm, we ran around in circles and saluted the sun. It felt like a good omen. We were eager to get back on the road and back to work. I was so excited to finally have some warm light to shoot photos in that when Eric attempted to pull over for a leisurely coffee and bite to eat, I snapped: "No way, dude." We were on our way down to Big River in Mendocino, and I panicked at the thought that I might lose my one and only window for clear skies.

Eric's typically mellow demeanor started to show signs of wear. He lived off baked goods and hot coffee and was getting sick of my "No, let's go to the next one" trick to keep driving past a gas station or grocery store—there often *wasn't* a next one. This approach had left us without food for the night on more than one occasion. Patience really was Eric's greatest virtue, and I was testing it.

Surf adventures with Eric had always been slow and methodical. His mellow pace made me antsy at times, especially when he appeared more interested in getting to the bottom of his coffee cup than in being out in the water before the sun peeked over the cliffs. "Dude, we're gonna miss the best light," I'd nag, sounding like his little brother. "Whoa there, Burky boy," Eric would respond, in a voice like Cartman from the TV show *South Park.* "You know, Chris, you live, like, five minutes in the future—maybe even five days in the future. You need to live in the moment a little more," he finally said to me after I vetoed the pit stop.

I loved the sentiment, and I even sort of felt it when the camera was pressed up to my eye, but I honestly had no idea what it meant to live in the moment. At twenty years old, I felt like I could finally visualize my path forward as a photographer. I was too scared to slow down. Deep inside, I had convinced myself that all my opportunities were based upon forward momentum. To me, staying in one place long enough to enjoy it meant I would be moving backward or giving other people an opportunity to pass me up.

Nobody really expected Eric and me to follow through and make the book. But I had received a grant from the Follow the Light Foundation that required me to have a plan on how I would be spending the $5,000 they gave me for the project, and I'm almost certain this requirement was mostly to ensure I didn't just go out and blow the money. The details of my hopes for the grant were nothing more than a formality. But despite everyone's low expectations, I was determined to make the book a reality. The mounting pressure of delivering on my word seemed to rise to the surface on those cold, rainy nights in Northern California. I stayed up late and studied the ledger of how much money we had already spent on food and gas. Every dollar that was gifted to me felt like a promise I had to do my best to fulfill.

Eric Soderquist had always been a permanent fixture in the Pismo surf scene, one I had grown up in and, in many ways, been raised

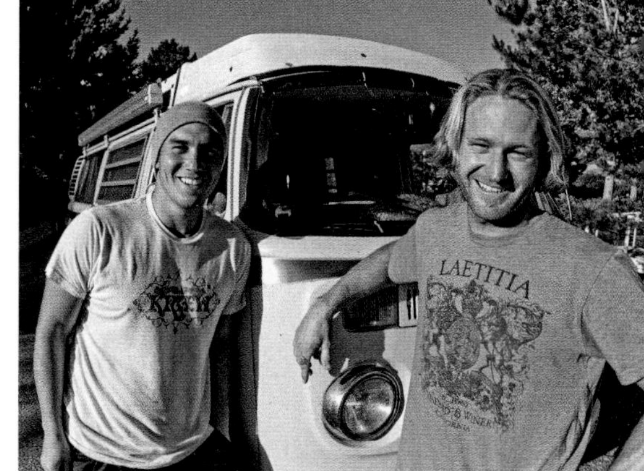

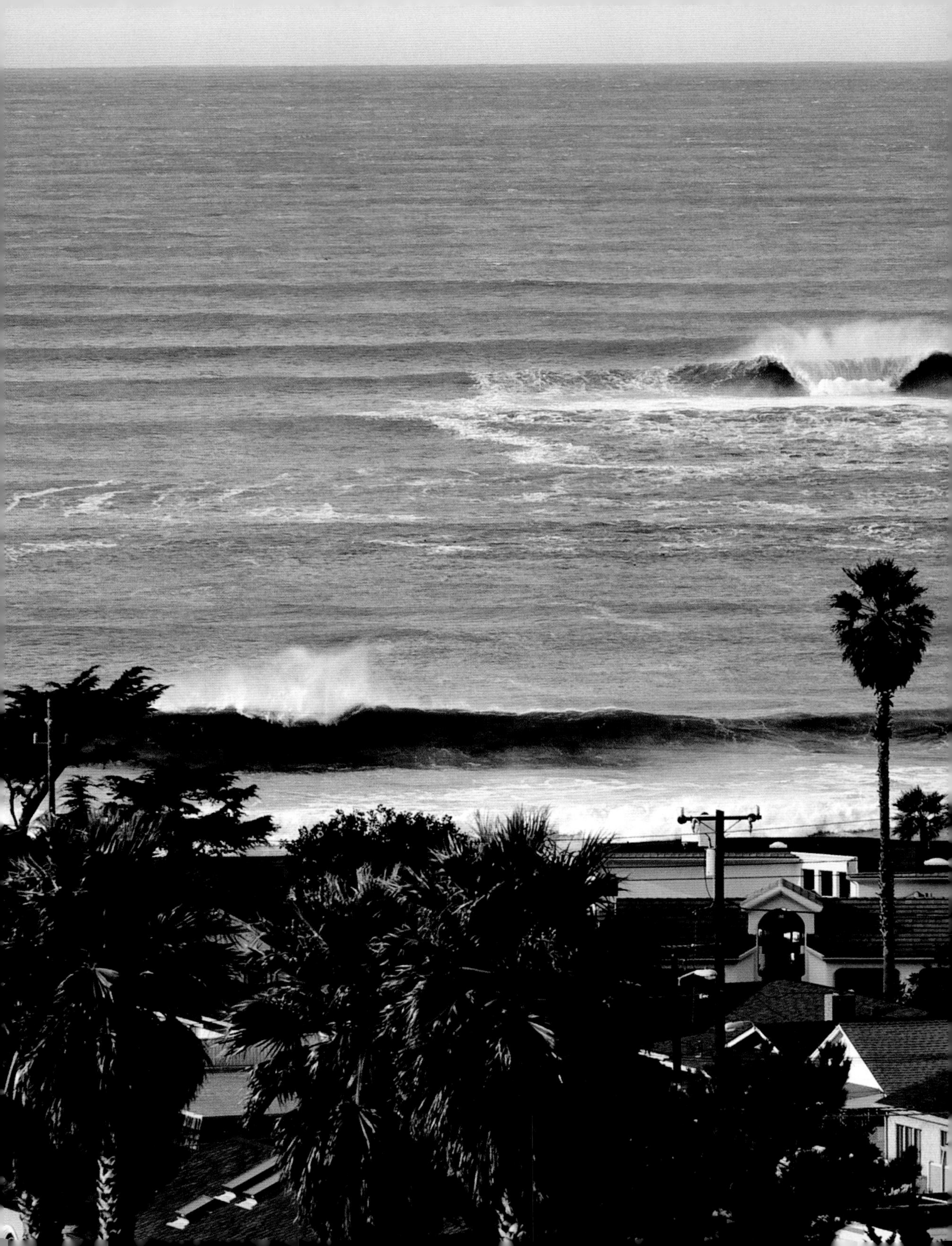

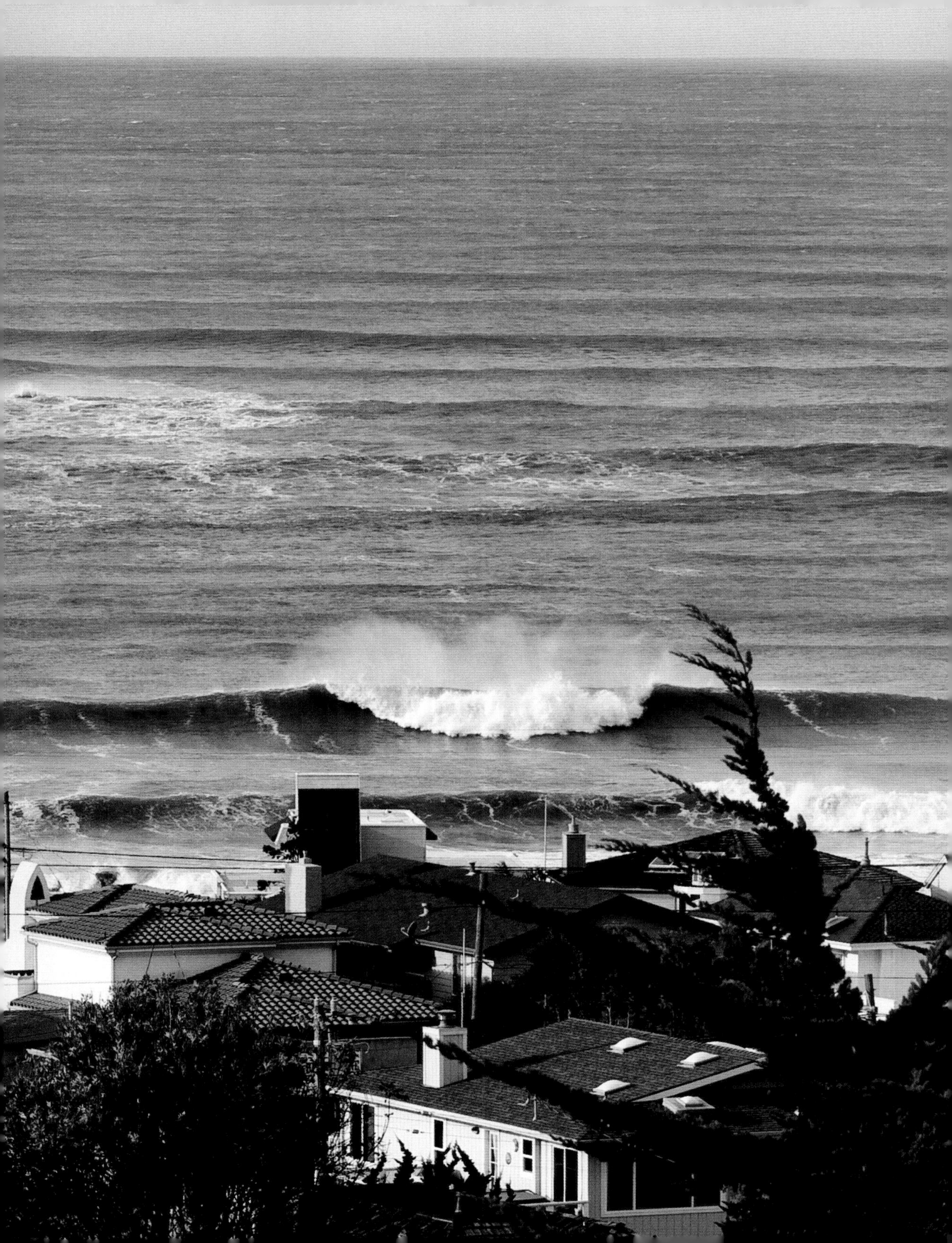

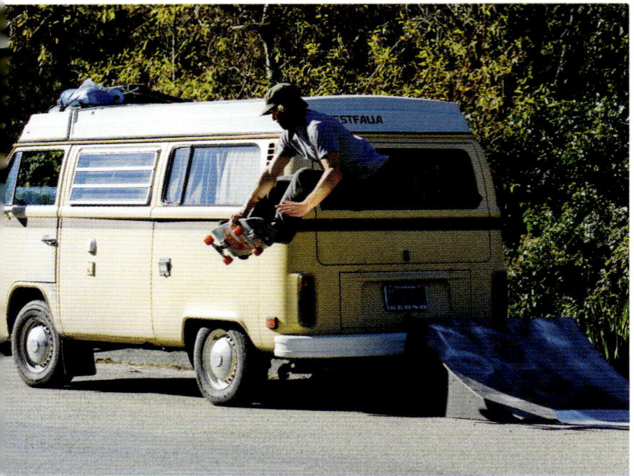

by. He always knew me as this snotty little grom, but by the time I was eighteen and attending Cuesta College, we started to plan local surf missions together. I began spending more time in the water than in class. Eric was an Impressionist painter and surfer who grew up just a few hills over from me in Arroyo Grande on the central California coast. He embodied the California surf lifestyle I always sought to capture in my photos: He was lean and bronze, with facial scruff and shoulder-length hair the color of sand. He looked iconic standing next to his 1978 Volkswagen bus, which always stood stacked with surfboards awaiting their next solo adventure. He was eight years older than me, but he may as well have lived an extra life.

Between working seasonal jobs at power plants, usually far from the ocean, Eric surfed and traveled for months on end, achieving his own special brand of freedom. He told tall tales of breaking his leg surfing Indonesia's Mentawai Islands and of camping in Big Sur during the biggest swell in ten years. I wanted to travel like Eric. I wanted to live in his stories.

Surf expeditions with Eric started in the Pismo Pier parking lot and expanded out from there. We were equally broke and stoked, and we'd make plans the night before to carpool together at dawn. The hardest decision we had to make was whether we were going north or south. It was through Eric that I found myself in the middle of the Central Coast surf scene, working with future pros like Nate Tyler, Zach Hartley, and Kilian Garland. I'd begun to consider surf photography a passion rather than just a hobby, and I knew I had to start taking things more seriously. I had to shoot people who would help me get paid.

For months I had been cold-calling every editor and magazine I possibly could, but never heard more than crickets or an auto response. Luckily, there was one editor at *TransWorld SURF* magazine who had a soft spot for the Central Coast. His name was Pete Taras. At the time, *TransWorld* was the holy grail for photographers. I emailed Pete some of my early work for feedback. When Pete replied, it was a literal answer to my prayers. After some light critiques on the photos I'd sent, he offered generic tips like "shoot with the best surfers you can" and "try to get their boards and sponsor logos in the frame." I turned his suggestions into mock assignments and obsessively hung on his every word.

One day around this time, Eric and I were hanging around Avila Beach, a small fishing community turned tourist town north of Pismo. Conditions were perfect, as a magic combination of a decent sandbar, swell, and wind collided to create the cleanest, most beautiful surf I had ever seen. As afternoon brightened to evening, the sea turned so translucent green it looked as if someone were illuminating it from behind with a flashlight.

When Eric arrived at the beach and started paddling out, I was so amped to get in the water I just about lost my mind and forgot to zip up my wetsuit. A cold cascade flowed down my back when I dove into the chilly winter shore break. The waves were the perfect size, not too big, and when they'd curl up and form a barrel, I could see the sky's blue reflection on the green mirror below. I'm color-blind—as a kid I'd often mistake the brown for the green waste bin when taking the trash out—and as a photographer I'd come to rely on contrast and tone curves for editing. But I knew the shades I was looking at in Avila that day were unreal.

Shooting with Eric was nothing like photographing sponsored surfers. Eric didn't care about the in-your-face action shots that were the trend of the moment in surf magazines and paid advertisements. He was just as fired up about a pulled-back image that made him look like an ant dwarfed by an unruly seascape. Those photos were my favorite to take—photos that add a wide landscape to a surfer or subject, showing off the rugged natural arenas that test and inspire. Even if I couldn't be a traditional landscape photographer, who said I couldn't bring a landscape perspective to surf photography? It seemed like the best of both worlds.

When I photographed Eric in the water, I learned to trust and predict his movements, especially his trademark left-hand floater. I'd let Eric surf within inches of my face, since I knew he wouldn't fall or freak out. It was like we spoke a language of hand motions and body gestures that only we understood. Our styles and energies were the perfect match, completely in sync. Together we were better than the sum of our crafts.

That night in Avila Beach, there was one wave in particular that I experienced as if in slow motion. It started off small and grew steeper as Eric tucked into its hollow emerald pocket. Water came surging back to sea from shore, crashing into Eric's tube. The wave stood up taller and I could see Eric gliding behind a liquid screen. Every droplet of water was in focus against a two-tone wave that revealed the most beautiful marriage of blue and green. I was so mesmerized I almost forgot to press the shutter button.

As soon as I got home, I imported the photos to my white MacBook laptop in a frenzy and scrolled straight to that sequence. There was still a lot of doubt among surf photographers about whether digital photography could ever compete with film, and I worried

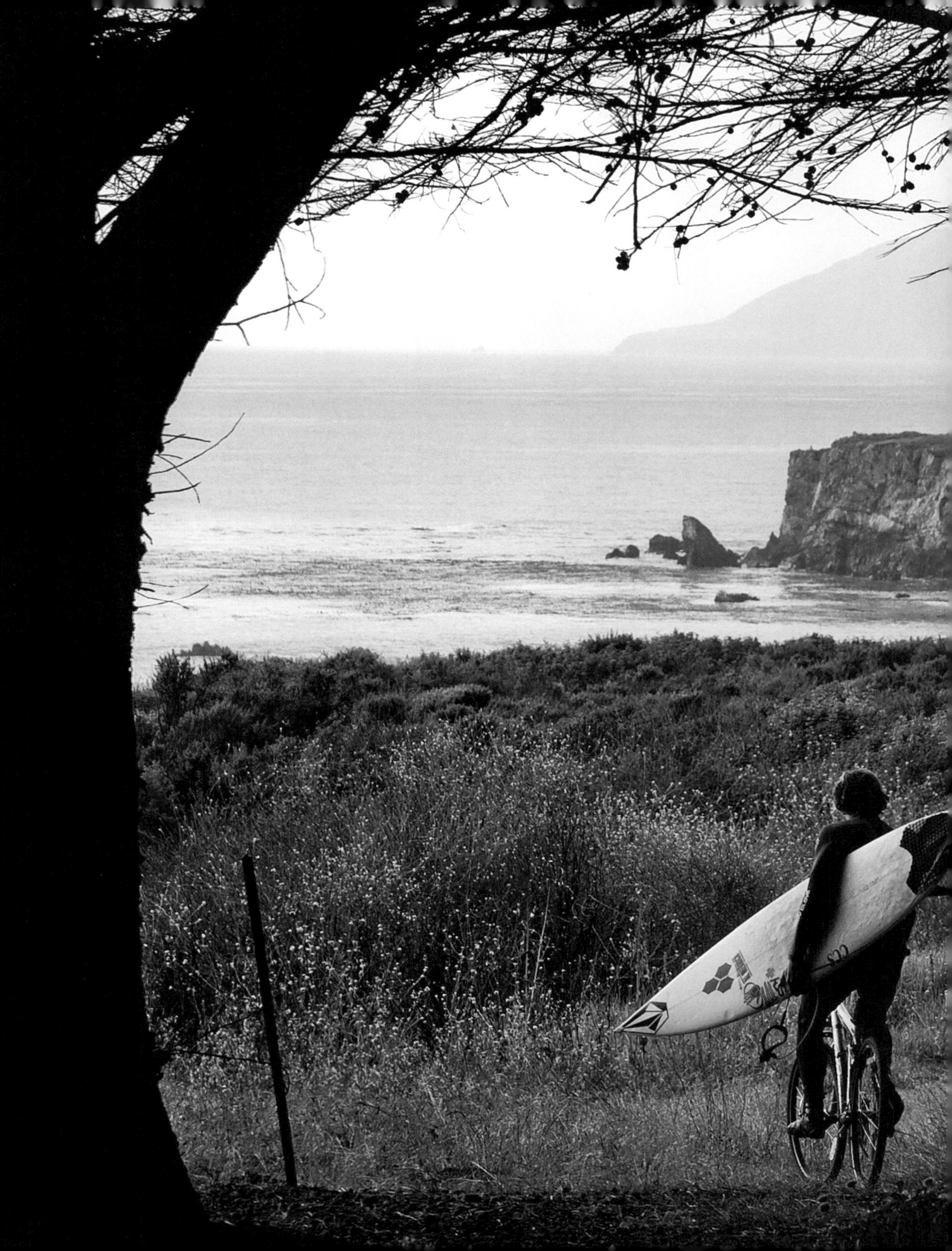

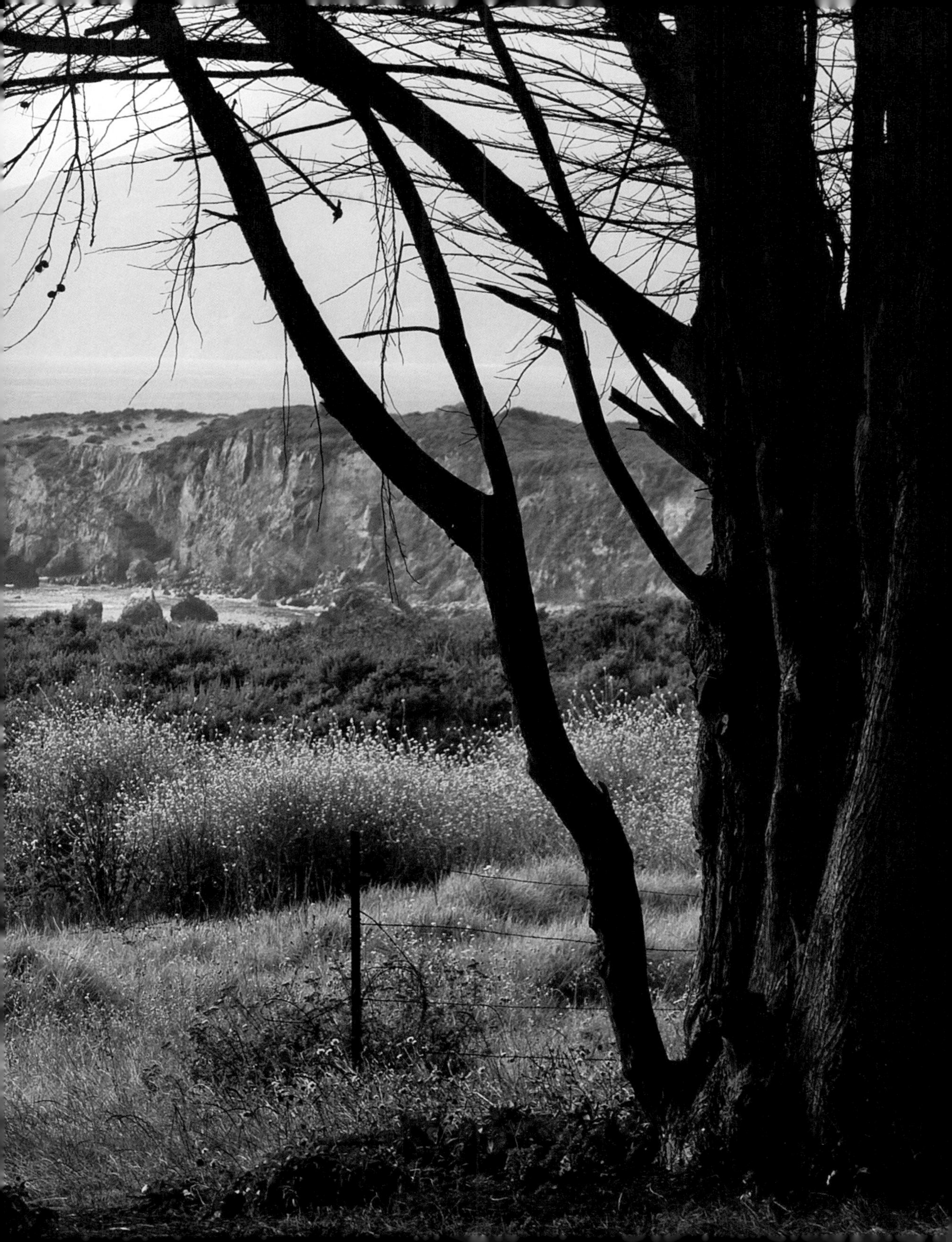

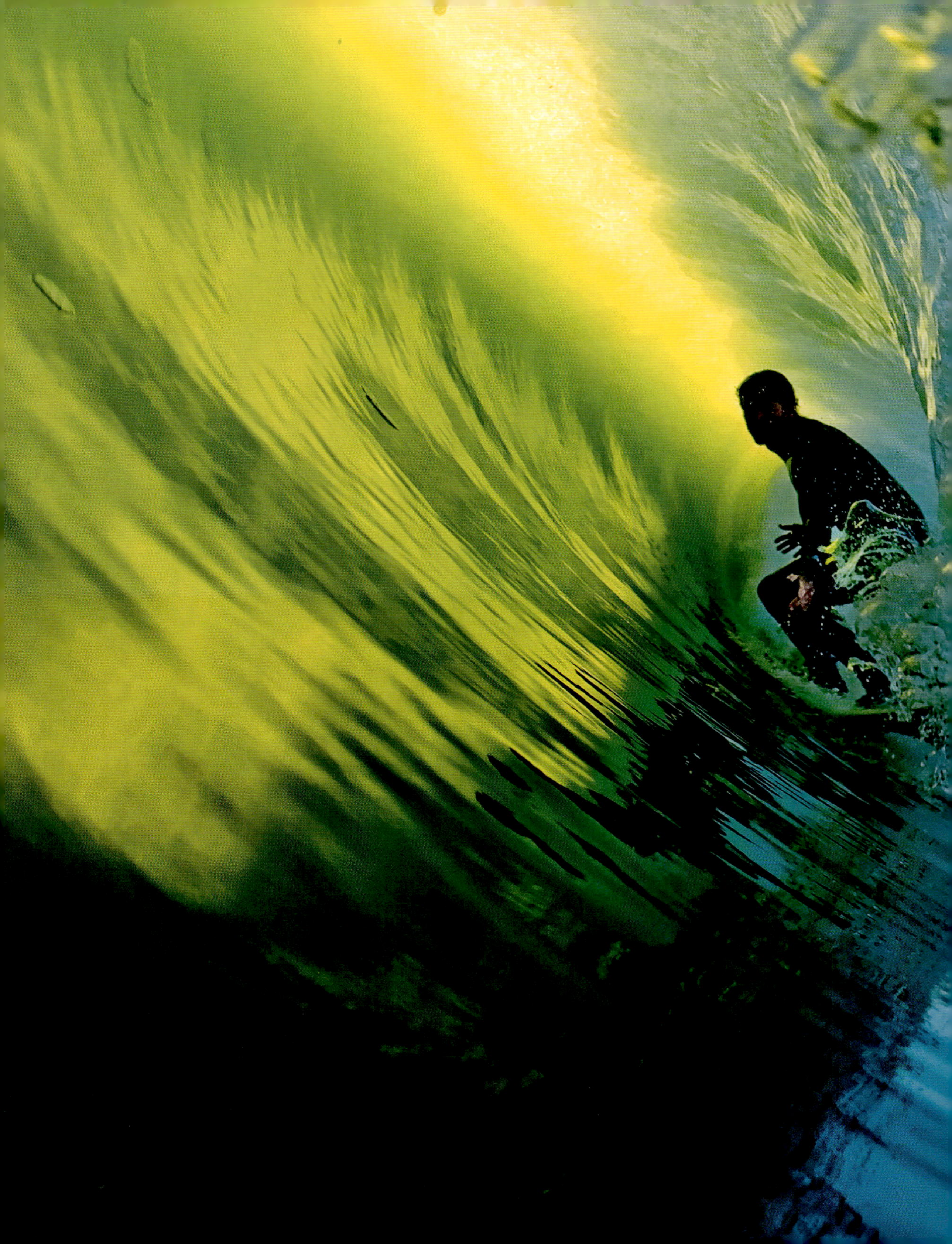

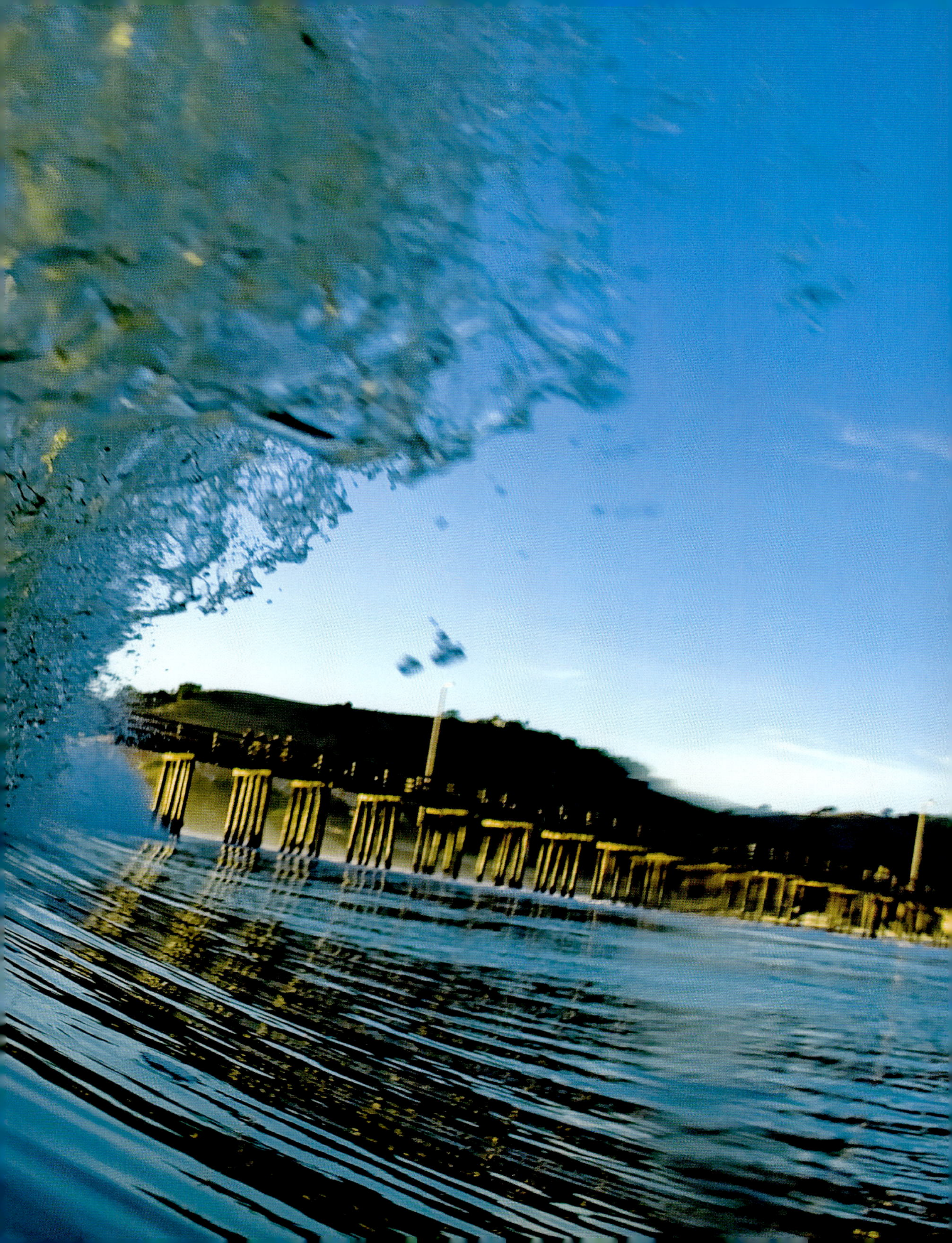

"Do You Know How to Write?"

FIRST PERSON

Eric Soderquist
Surfer & Author,
The California Surf Project

It's funny how we got the *California Surf Project* book deal with Chronicle Books. We didn't have a publisher when we did the road trip; the project started as one of the first online stories for Surfline.com that had a following. Two kids in a bus, totally naive, especially to the publishing world.

Luckily for us, Marcus Sanders from Surfline had a golden contact: Sarah Malarkey, an editor at Chronicle Books, who also happened to be a surfer. I had recently met a graphic designer who said Chronicle was one of the most artistic publishers in the business. They were our top choice, so we reached out to Sarah to set up a meeting in San Francisco.

Chris and I rolled up to this skyscraper and found our way to an office where a dozen people with dreams of getting their books accepted were all sitting nervously in the waiting room. Within minutes, Sarah opened the door. Her brown hair looked wet and disheveled from the ocean—like ours. "Hey, guys, come on back!" she said, waving us in. I could feel the stares of aspiring writers clutching their manuscripts as we walked past them into the back office. We spent that meeting talking more about surfing than book publishing; we learned that Sarah had been out in the lineup next to us that same morning at Ocean Beach. I have no idea how we walked out of her office with a book contract. I guess it pays to be part of the same salty tribe.

But then the questions started flowing in: Who was going to write the book? When I said I would write it, the editors laughed at me through the phone. At one point, it started looking like they were going to hire a writer to work with Chris, but I objected. "How the hell is anyone going to know these crazy stories of a skunk trying to get into the bus at two in the morning? I'll at least have to tell them what happened. "So you're saying you're gonna write it?" the editors asked.

"Yeah, I'm gonna write it," I declared.

"Do you know how to write?"

"Yeah, totally . . ."

At that time, in my mind, writing meant scrawling funny stories and run-on sentences with a pencil on paper. I sent them to Chronicle in the mail. "You're kidding, right? You have to type this up," Sarah said over the phone after receiving my package.

"No way!" I said. "If you saw how I type . . ."

So that's how *The California Surf Project* was written. I think we blew their minds.

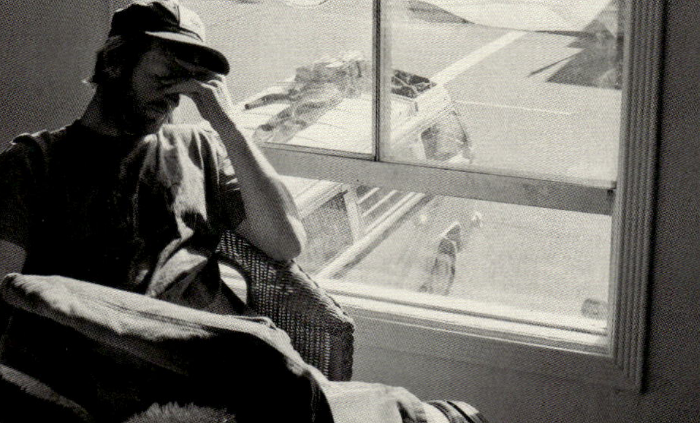

024

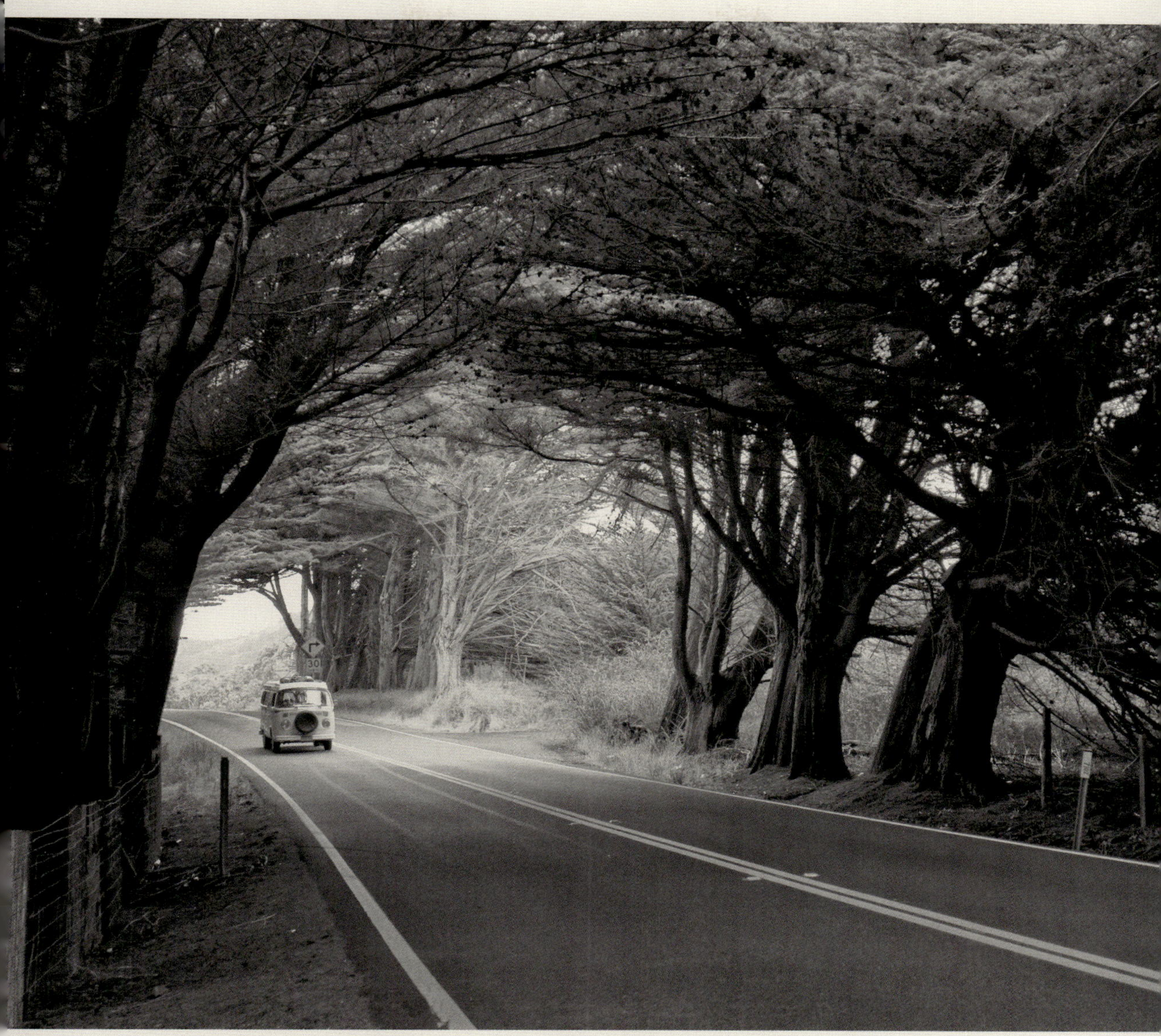

CHRIS BURKARD   WAYWARD

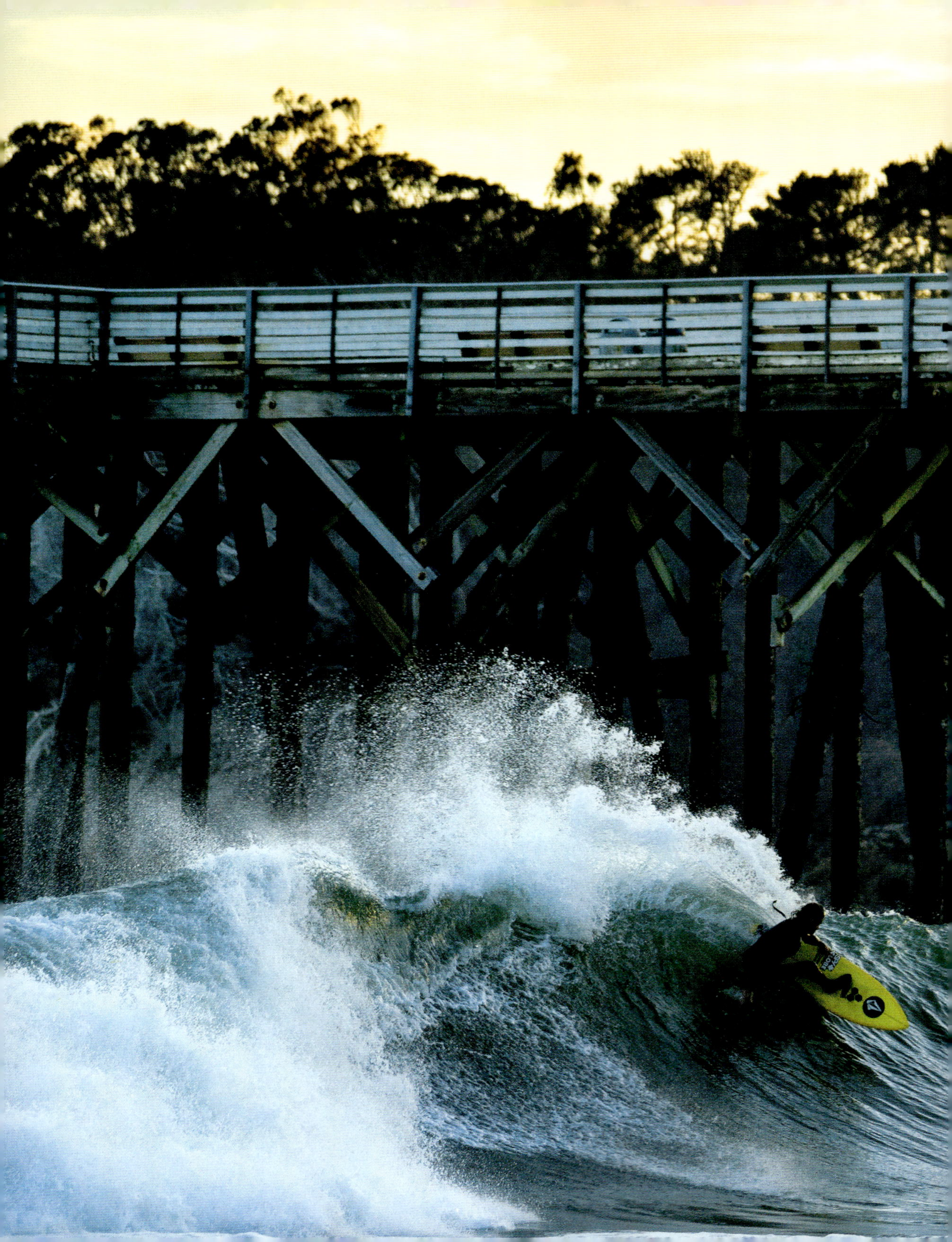

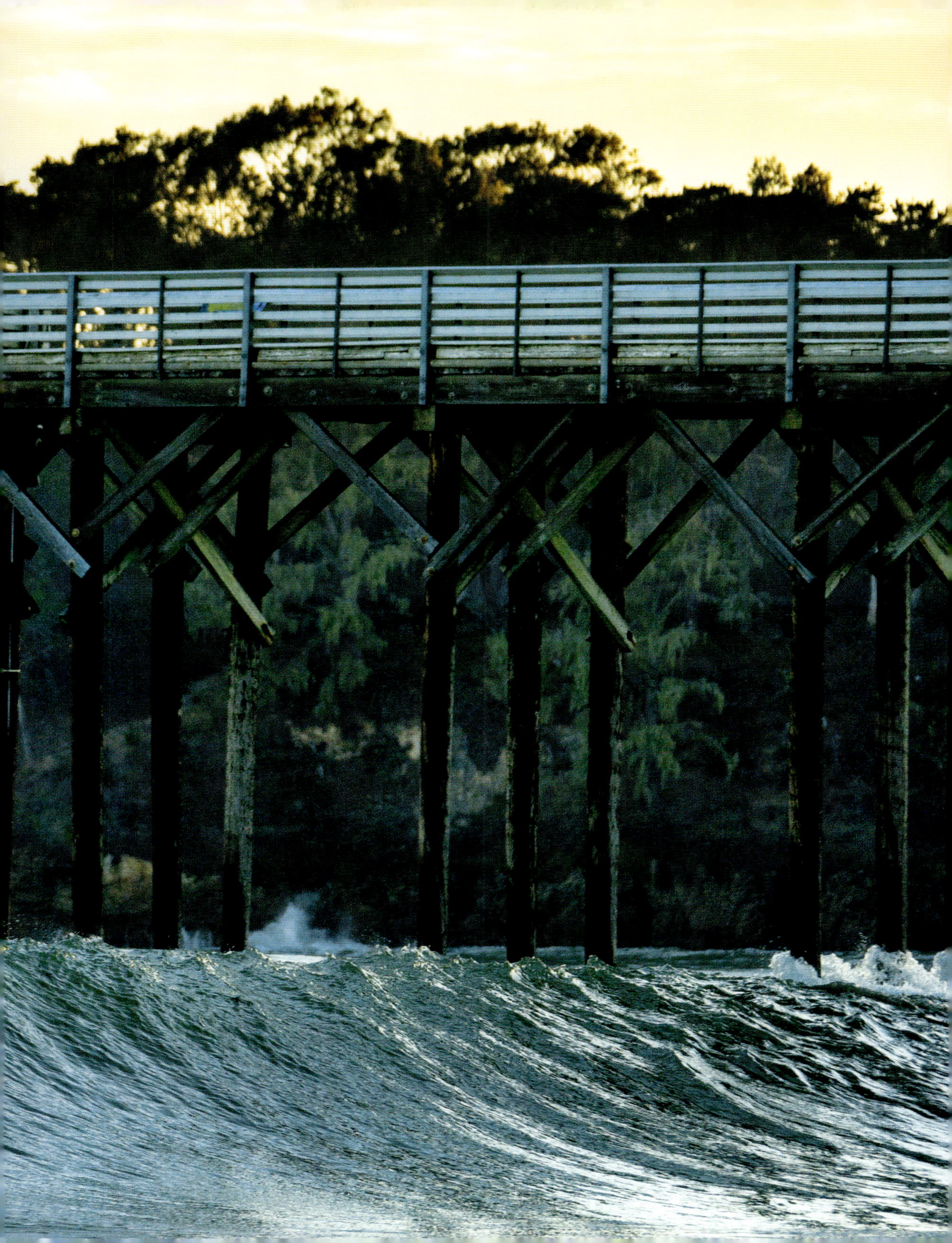

that the camera wouldn't play back the colors as vibrantly as I saw them. But there it was: Eric in that blue-green dream, proving to me that with the right lighting and a steady hand, digital could get the shot. Thanks to that one lucky night at Avila Beach, Pete Taras agreed to take me on as a summer intern at *TransWorld SURF*.

Eight months after taking that photo of Eric, I was looking at that same image projected onto a large white screen at an awards dinner. At the end of my internship, Pete encouraged me to enter the Follow the Light grant contest, which was created in honor of Larry "Flame" Moore, the longtime photo editor of *Surfing* magazine, who had recently lost his battle with brain cancer. Flame was a mentor to many respected surf photographers, and the contest was founded to finance the dreams of up-and-comers in the industry with a $5,000 grant. Eric, my girlfriend Brea, and I were there, surrounded by a who's who of magazine photo editors and industry veterans, including Bob Hurley and Surfline's Dave Gilovich. If I won, Eric and I decided we would use the grant money to pay for a two-month surf trip down the California coast from the Oregon border to the Tijuana Sloughs. We had even hoped to turn our images and discoveries into a book and film: a visual love letter to our home state.

Watching my portfolio flash across the screen reminded me of all the miles we had already driven—getting up in the dark, filling our gas tank quarter by quarter, living off salami and Ritz crackers—and how many waves and scenes we had already scored. At the end of the slide show, the judges read off the names of all the finalists—except mine. Then Aaron Chang began saying something about bad grammar in the application. My heart triggered a double beat. "And the winner is . . . *Chris Burkard*."

At the sight of Big River and the promise of waves, Eric forgot about coffee and perked up. The river was the color of jade and snaked its way out to sea. The water flowed into some fun-looking lineups peeling off a rocky headland studded with pine and cypress trees. Being the first clean surf of the trip, we quickly strung a clothesline between the bus and a tree and made a beeline for the water. The waves were head high, crystal clear, and nearly empty.

We swam and surfed our brains out all day, until Eric became a silhouette, backlit by a fiery sunset, and the water turned to liquid mercury highlighted by burnt-orange brushstrokes. On our walk back to the bus, our stomachs groaned and reminded us that during a holiday centered around feasting, we had barely eaten breakfast. As we passed a bridge we noticed a group of transients partying underneath with enough food for their own Thanksgiving meal.

"Wow, even the bums have more than us," Eric joked. Throwing me a telling side-eye, he said, "We really should get something to eat."

The loneliest days I've ever had were on special occasions spent without my loved ones, and that Thanksgiving was no different. We were both away from our families, me for the first time ever on a proper holiday, and I was missing my mom's turkey, pumpkin pie, and cornbread. Eric and I decided to drive back to the town of Mendocino to lift our spirits with a nice Thanksgiving dinner. We walked through the quaint downtown, which felt like *Little House on the Prairie* meets the California coast, in search of a restaurant without a dress code or a hefty price tag. I pressed my face against a frosted glass window and watched as a big family feasted next to a crackling fire.

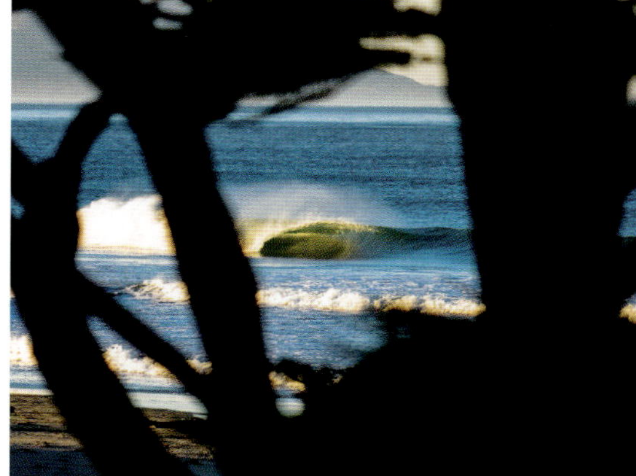

"Any chance you have a table for us?" I asked the hostess.

"It's a seventy-dollar set menu," she said, looking us up and down, pausing on our fingerless cotton gloves. Point taken.

We drove a few more miles down the road to a remote camp I knew no ranger would be patrolling. Of course, all the grocery stores we passed on the way were now closed, and I was feeling a little guilty for ignoring Eric's request to stop earlier—though the photos we got were totally worth it, so on second thought, maybe I didn't feel guilty at all. I rummaged in the back of the bus for what was left in our food bag: a few Hawaiian sweet rolls and one package of chicken Cup Noodles for the two of us to share. When I presented our sorry Thanksgiving meal to Eric, he raised his eyebrows and burst out laughing. I laughed, too. We scarfed down every last morsel until there was nothing left, not even for the mouse that had taken up residence with us in the van.

A few days later we arrived in San Francisco, where we were gifted with a heat wave and a ground swell (waves traveling over long distances from a storm). The air was eighty degrees with offshore winds, typical for fall, and the swell at Ocean Beach hovered around twelve feet—ideal conditions for surfing and photography. It was as good as it gets. We rode the epic conditions all the way to Southern California.

I had become completely comfortable with my Canon 20D and the three lenses I alternated between: a 24mm f/2.8prime (fixed focal length), the basic 18–55mm kit lens that came with the camera, and a 600mm zoom that I had borrowed from

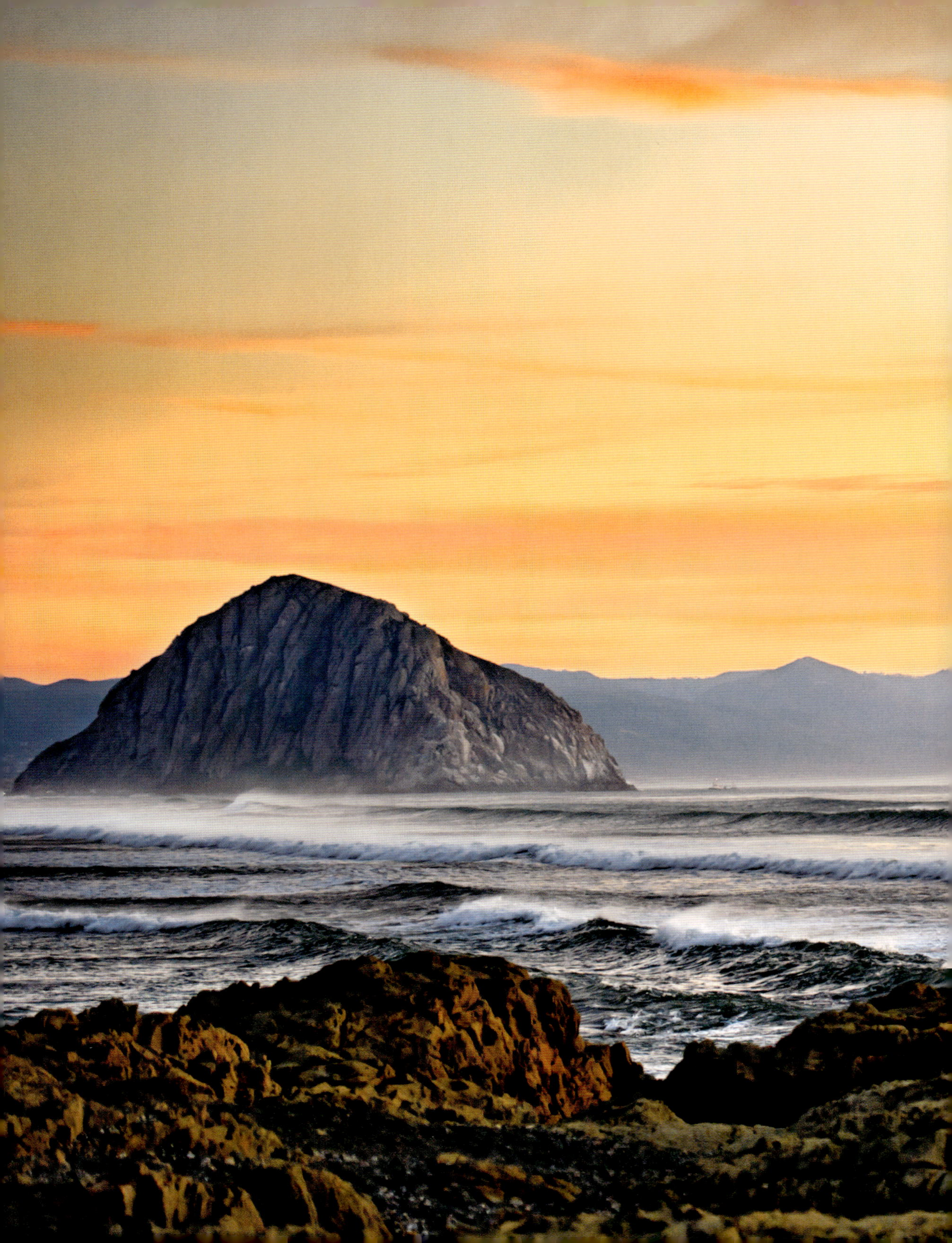

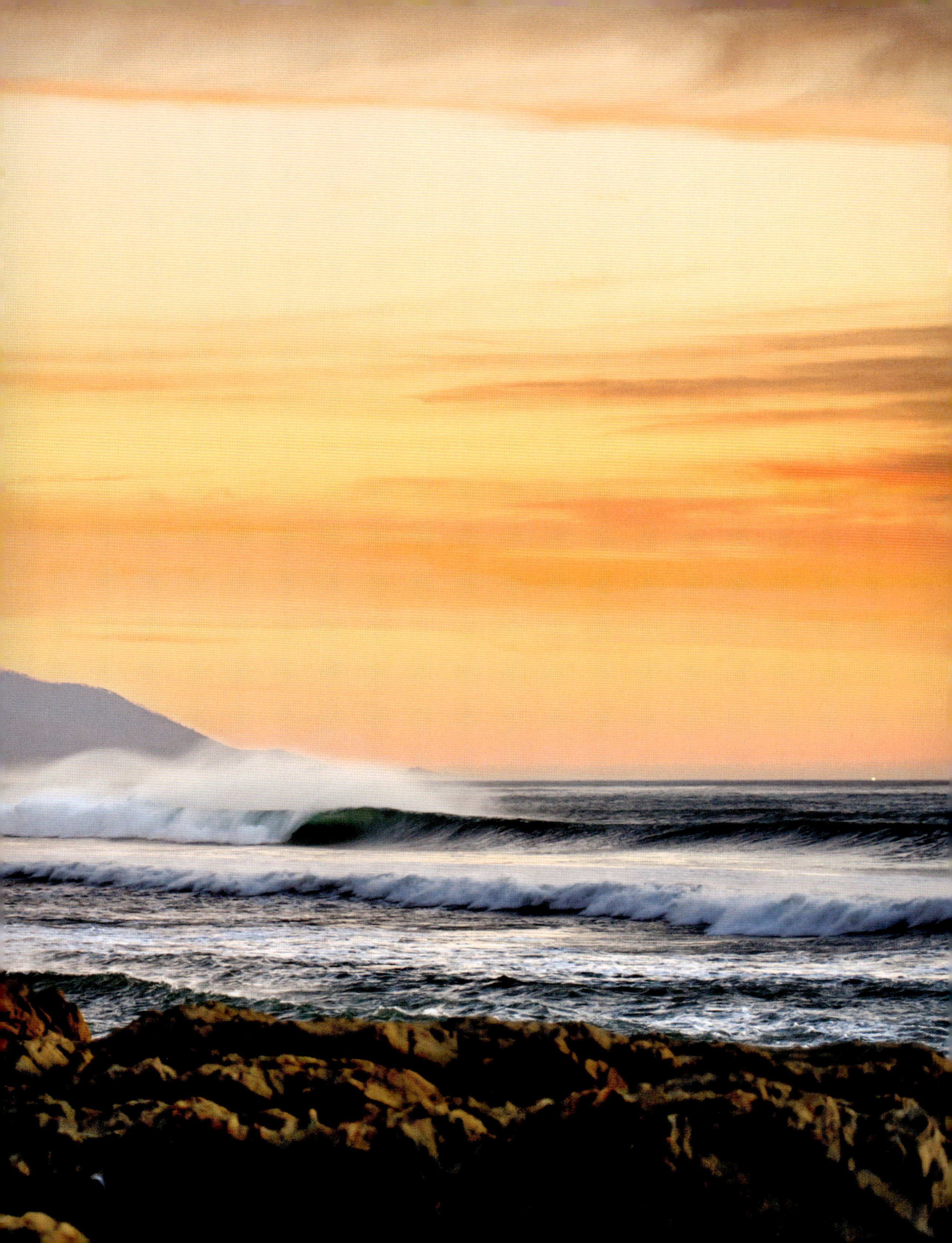

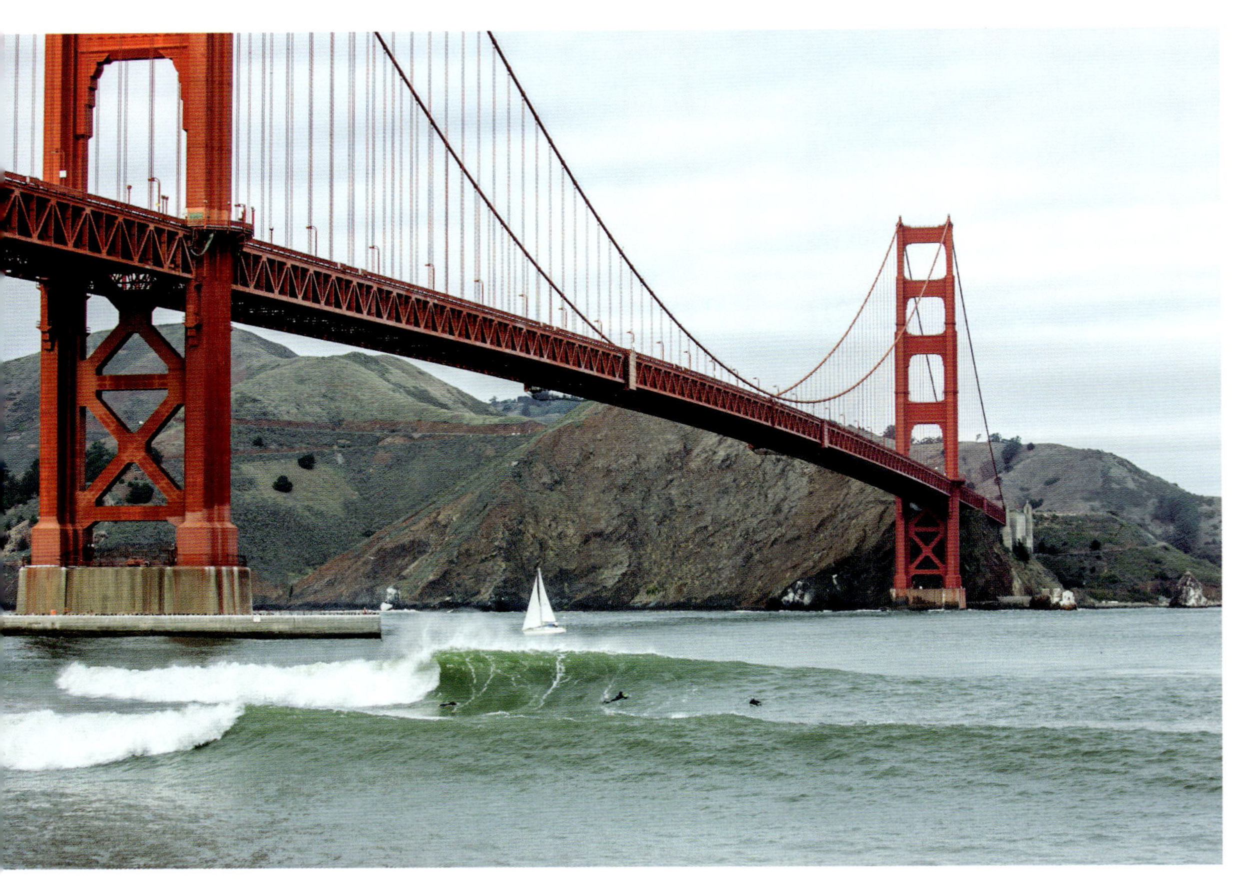

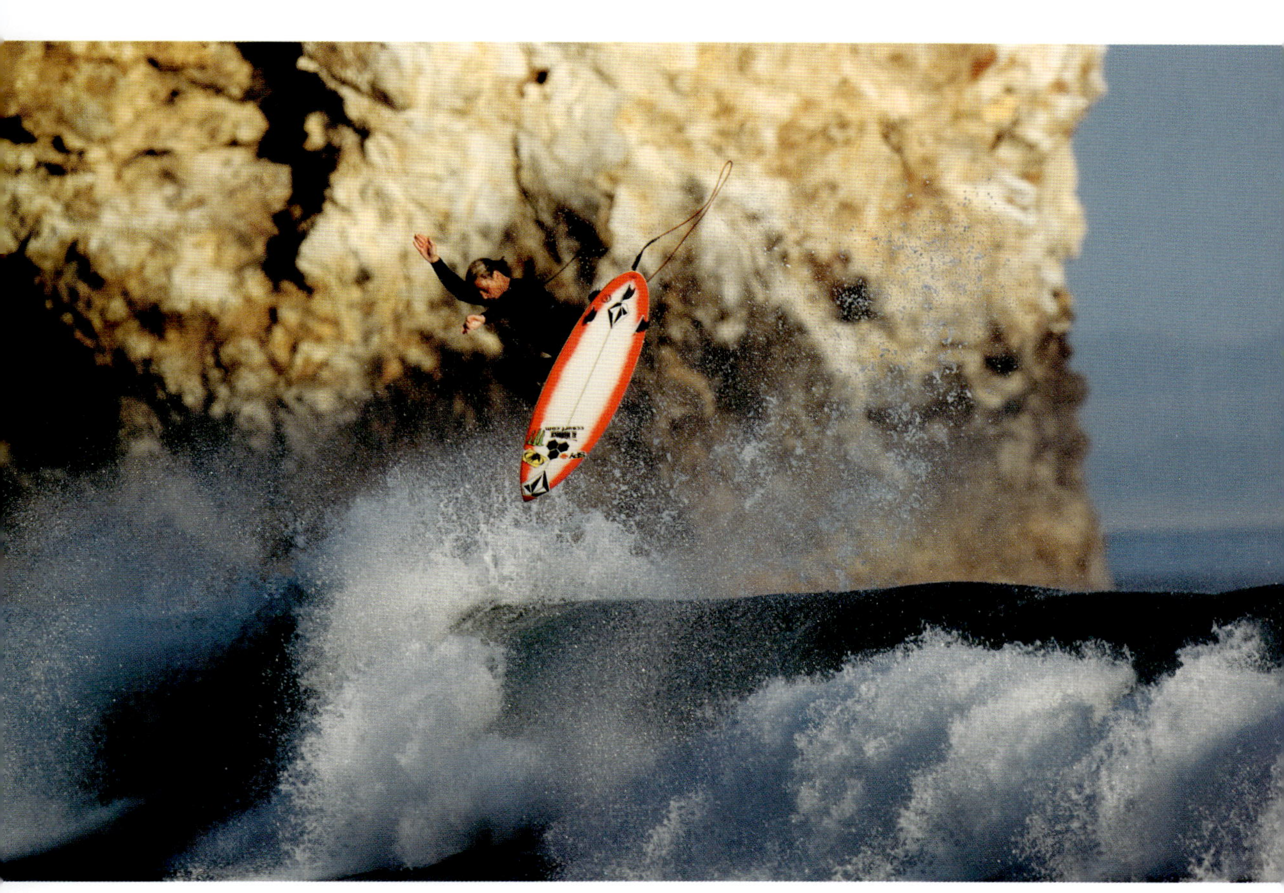

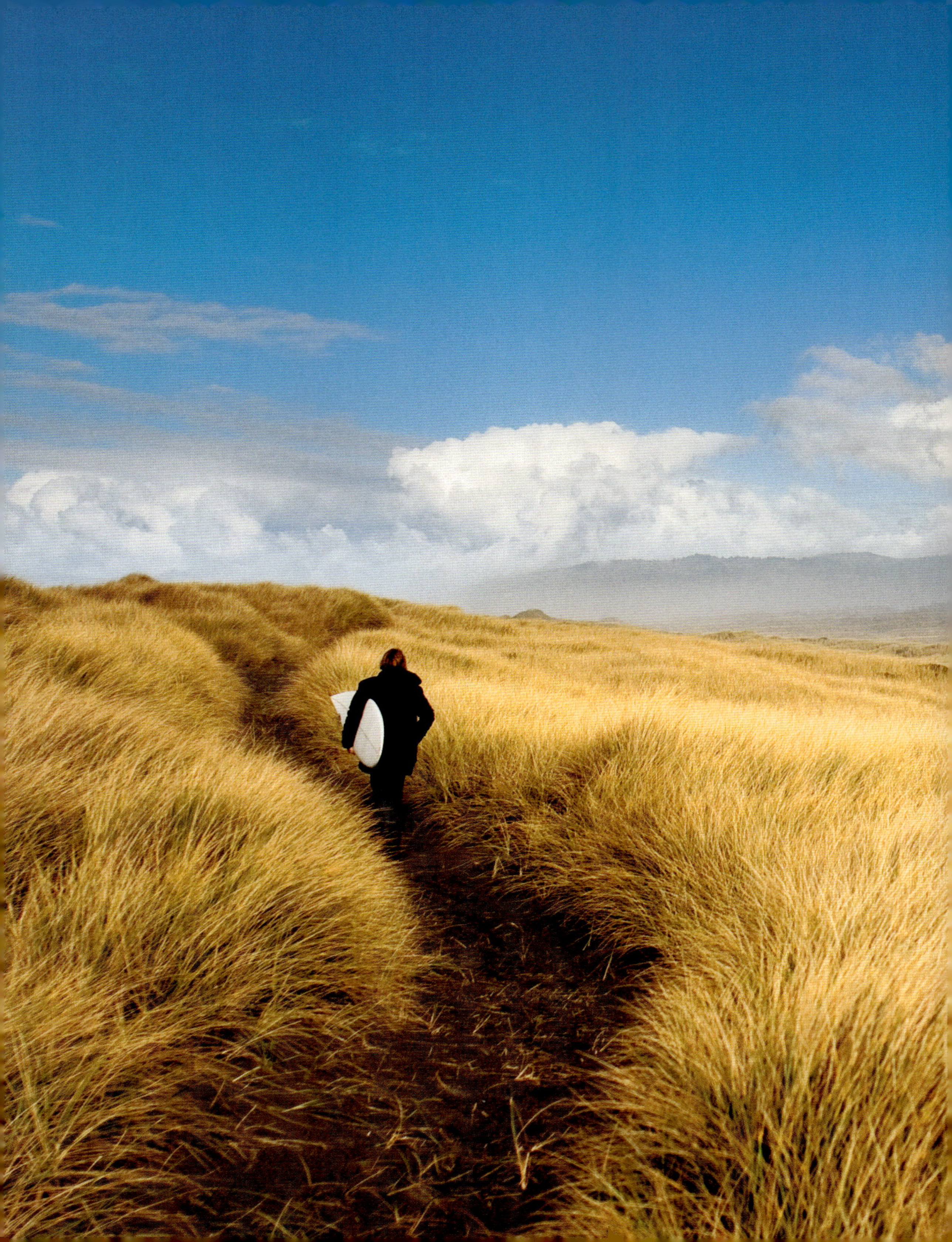

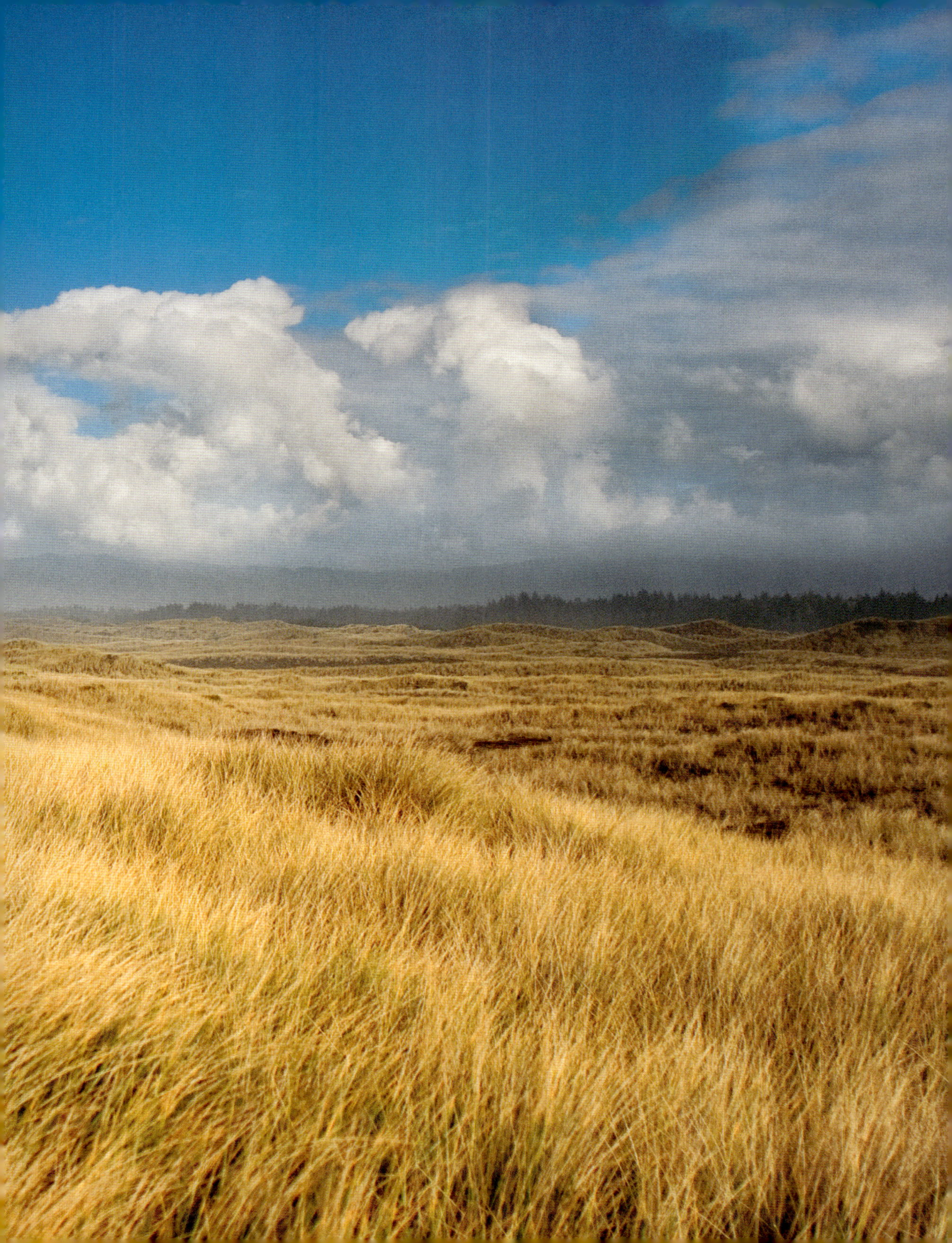

→ **The first camera I ever used was an old Nikon** film camera with a 50mm lens and a hippie strap. I borrowed it from my girlfriend's (now wife's) mom, Donna Jett, mostly as a tool to photograph the exploits of my bodyboarder friends at the beach. Compared with other artistic tools I explored while painting and drawing in high school, I found the camera so much more portable and incredibly immersive; I could take it into the mountains, into the ocean, into social settings—literally everywhere I went. In many ways, it felt like an extension of my body, especially when I was in the water. It was a revelation.

That first experience inspired me to save up and buy a used Nikon N90s film camera and the cheapest kit lens I could find. I used this prized possession exclusively for about a year. When money was tight, I'd buy expired print film from the Longs Drugs store down the street from my parents' house for twenty-five cents a pop, then shoot everything I could all day, every day. I'd occasionally splurge on slide film—Velvia, Ektachrome, or the coveted black-and-white Scala—but I reserved that for only the best waves and light, usually evening offshores in the fall and winter. I even carried around a tool to remove partially used film rolls from my Nikon if the weather suddenly required switching to a higher-quality canister, or a different ISO. Post-surf, I'd drive directly to a one-hour photo shop in San Luis Obispo, where I'd develop slide film and immediately look at my images on the light table I kept in my truck. For print film, I'd order 5x7 photos plus a digital CD from Rite Aid's photo lab. Both stores knew me by name. Such was the life of a budding photographer in the middle of the digital revolution.

A year or two later, I bought my first digital camera, a Canon 20D, off a friend I made in an intro to black-and-white photography course at Cuesta College. Digital offered someone like me, a kid who was struggling to buy basics like food and clothing, the ability to shoot all the time. I weighed the pros and cons—especially the cost of endlessly driving, scanning, printing, and buying film versus the cost of a laptop, camera, and memory cards—and digital seemed more justifiable. This was a major shift: to suddenly have an endless supply of images without having to spend all my money on film. But the romantic idea of film photography persisted, especially in surf media. So on those perfect days with epic wind and surreal light, I still leaned on film, no matter the cost. My early career was defined by experimentation on both sides of the technological divide—a theme that has continued throughout my career. —C.B.

Film Is Obsolete?

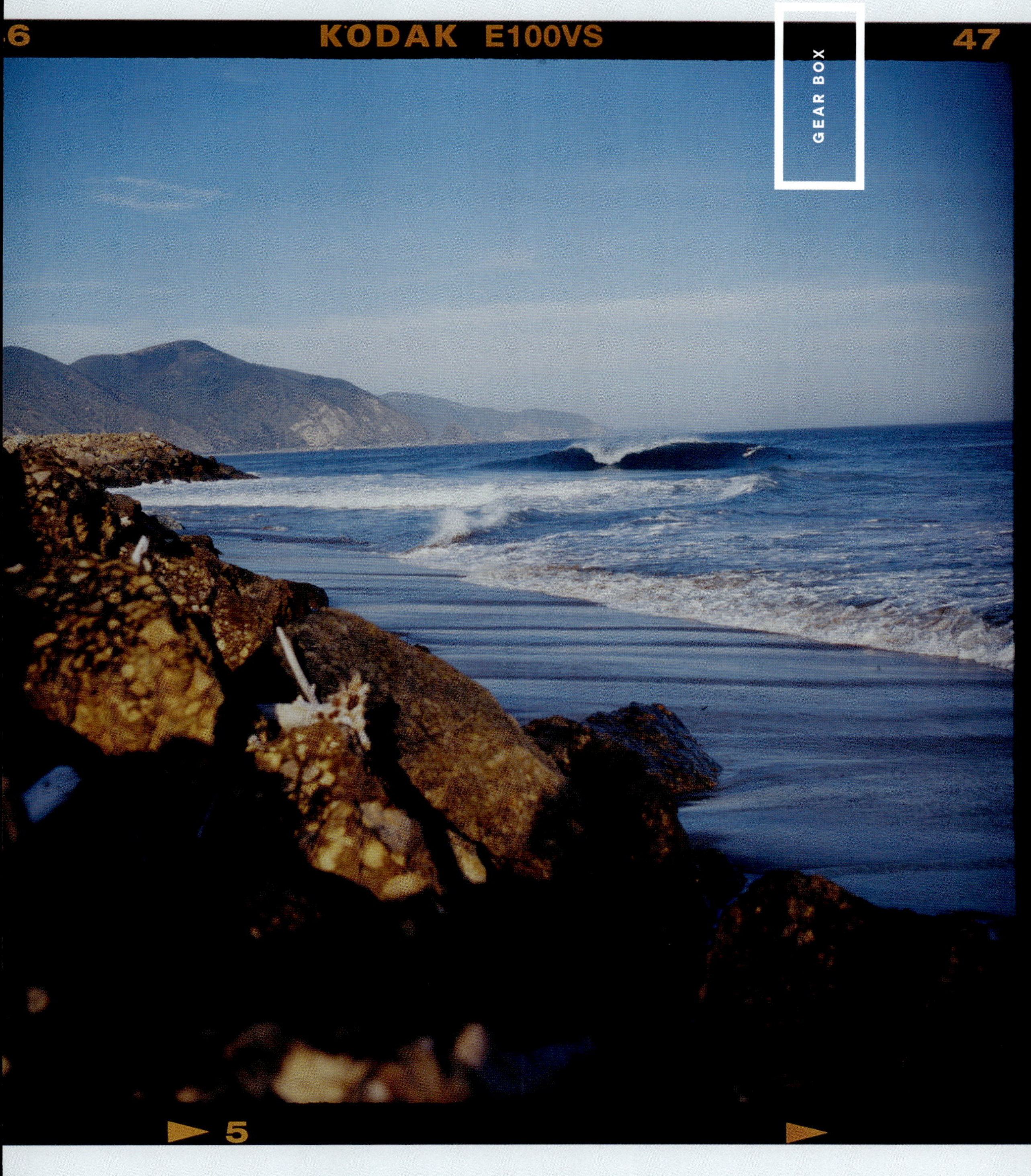

KODAK E100VS
6
47
GEAR BOX
5

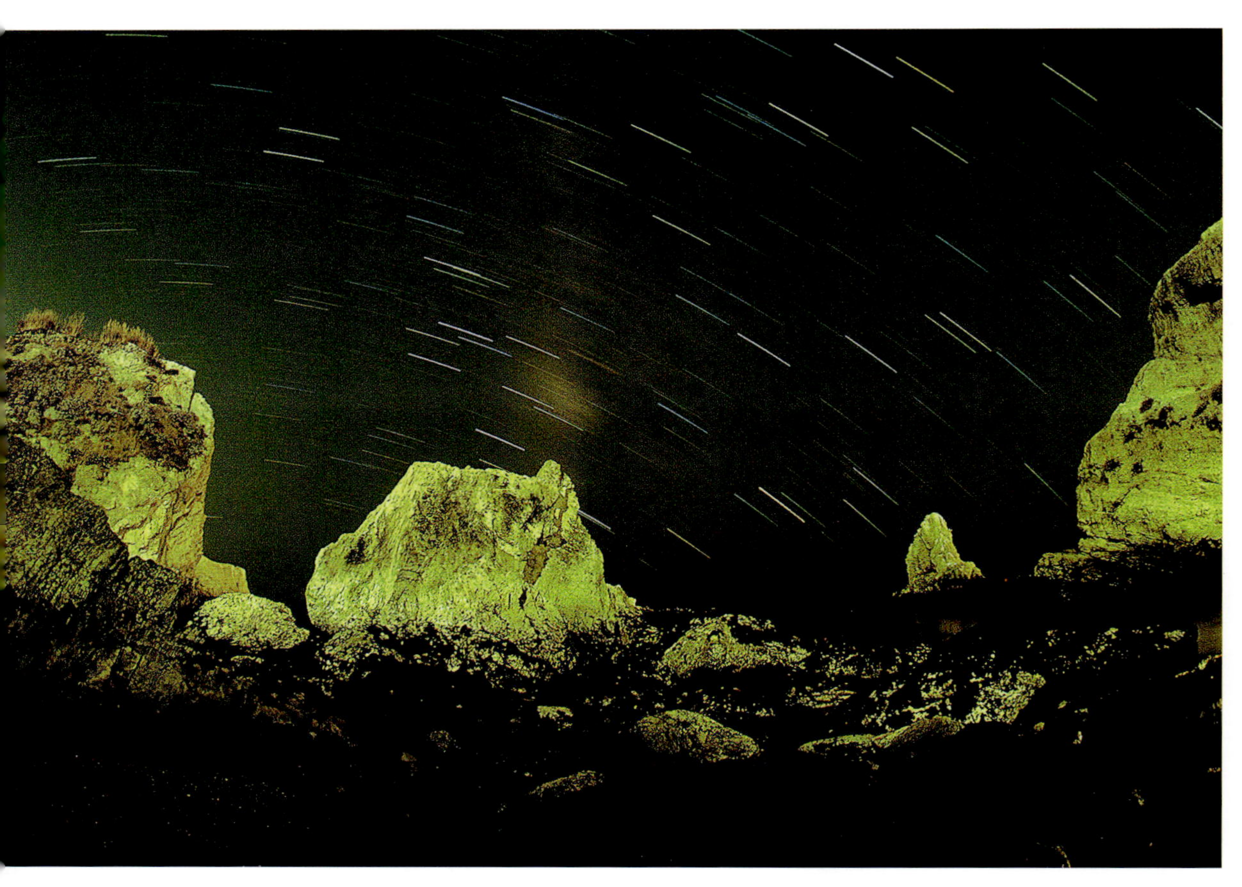

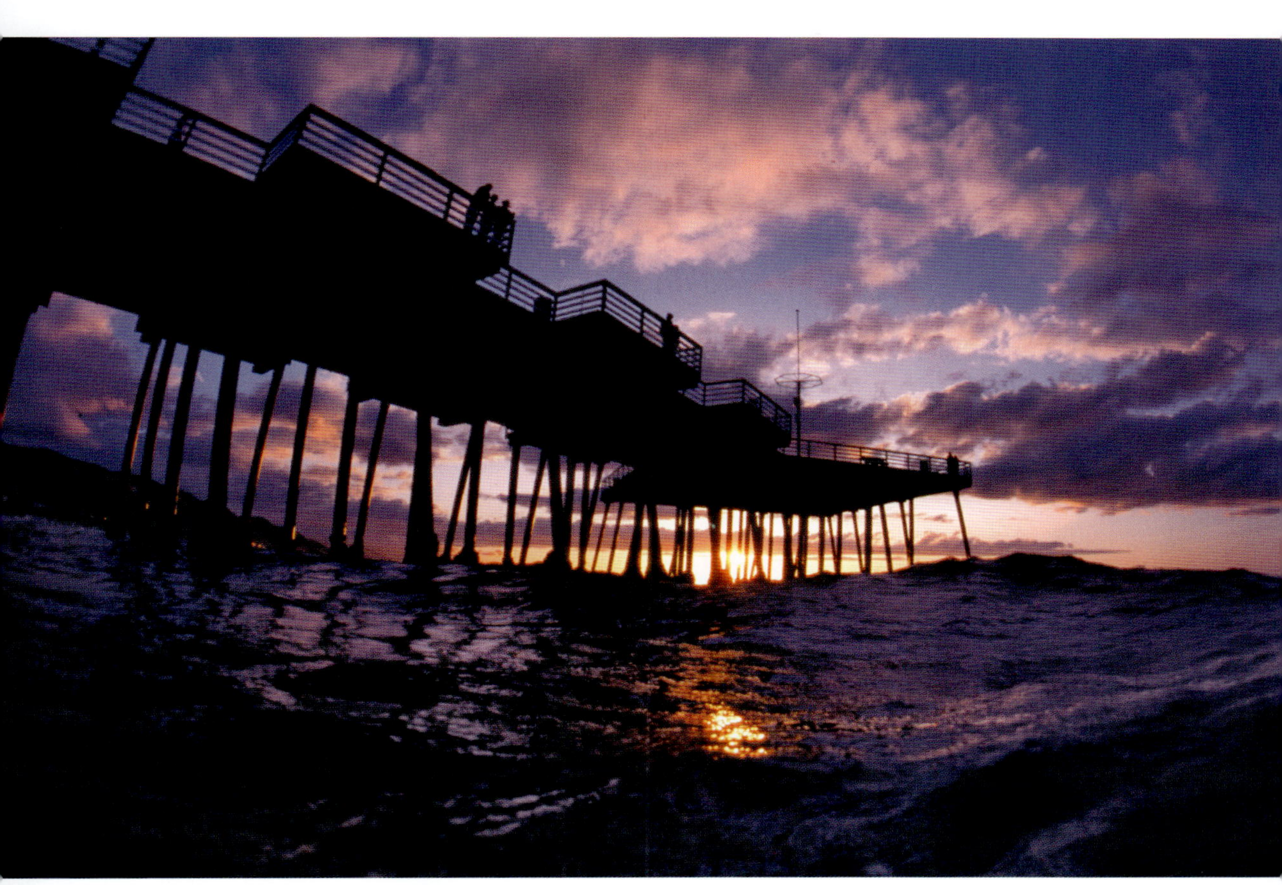

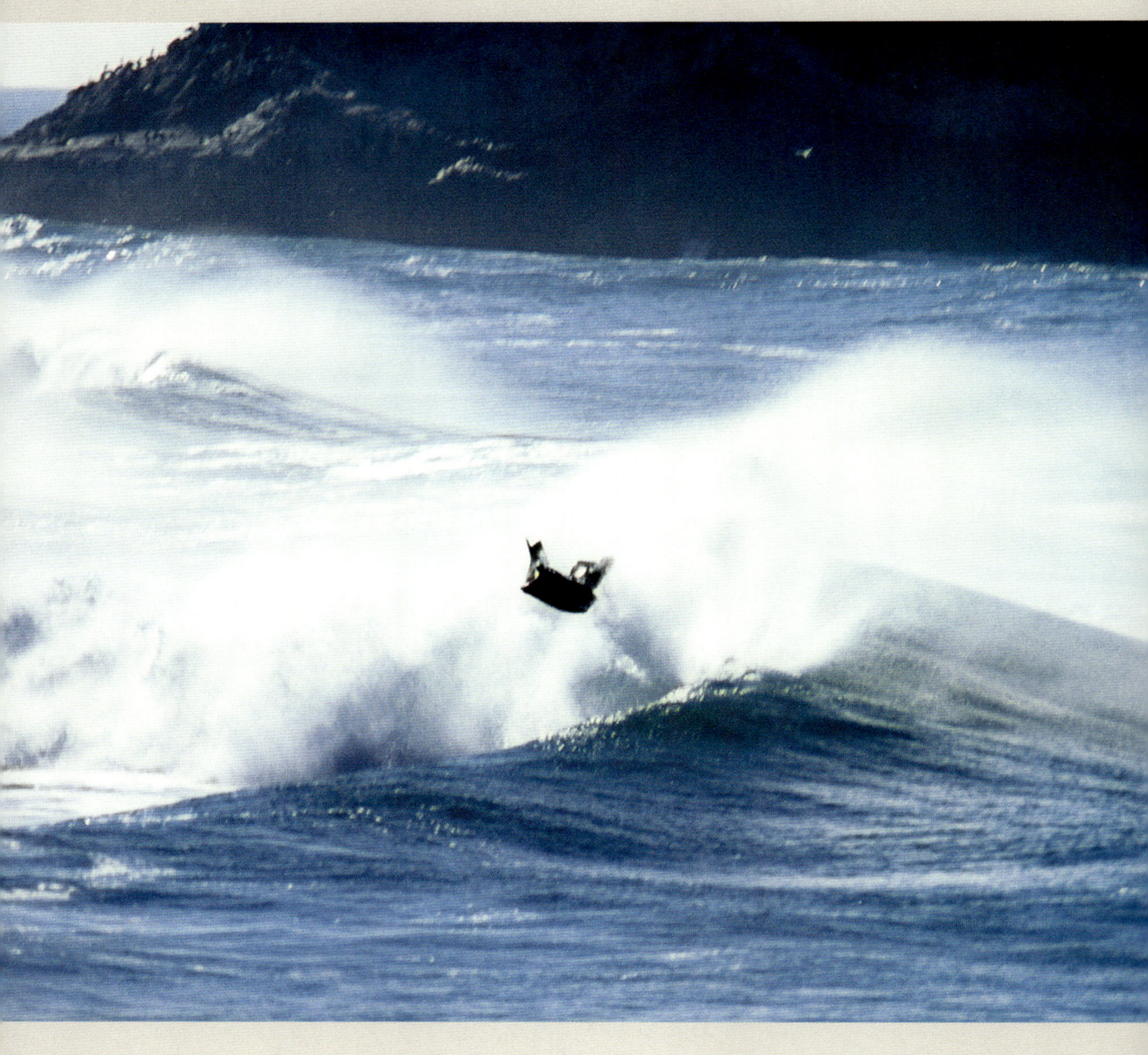

FIRST PERSON

Nick Statom
Rookies USA Bodyboarder

The Rookie Photographer

→ **By the time I met Chris, our local bodyboarding** crew, known as Rookies, was pretty tight-knit and dedicated to chasing the elusive waves of the Central Coast. We had been filming for some time, but nobody was really taking photos. I was away at college in San Diego when my buddy James Murdock called about an upcoming swell. He was like, "You've got to meet this kid Burky. He's been taking photos of us. He's a total character." Then James hands Chris the phone, and for a second I think I'm hearing static, because Chris is literally buzzing with energy on the other end of the line. I knew in that moment he would fit right in with our cast of characters.

We would end up spending many hours together, hunting swells up and down the coast. A weird guttural language emerged, based on baritone groans, acronyms, and inside jokes. But with his excitement, Chris brought real ambition. He was always pitching ideas for magazine articles and photo shoots to domestic and overseas publications. It was a drive and hunger that would eventually outgrow the antiquated bodyboarding industry.

An image of James throwing down a huge air reverse in northern San Luis Obispo County stands out in my memory. It was taken at our most frequented beachbreak, known affectionately as "The Lady." (There's a big rock that looks like a curvy lady lying on her side.) We spent so many hours in the water there chasing waves and on the sand getting chased by elephant seals. The photo was shot on slide film in Burkard's photographic infancy, but a pulled-back, cross-beach angle was his trademark even then. Early-morning light illuminates hard offshore winds, the rock in the background gives it depth, and there's not another soul in the lineup. You can be sure that I heard Burky's animated static buzz through my phone again as soon as he got that film roll developed.

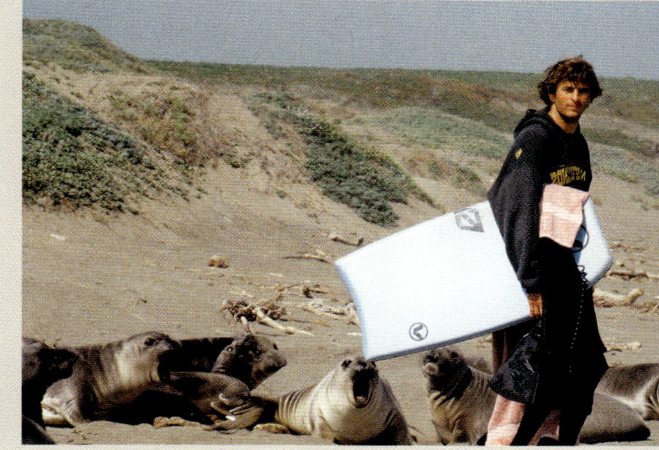

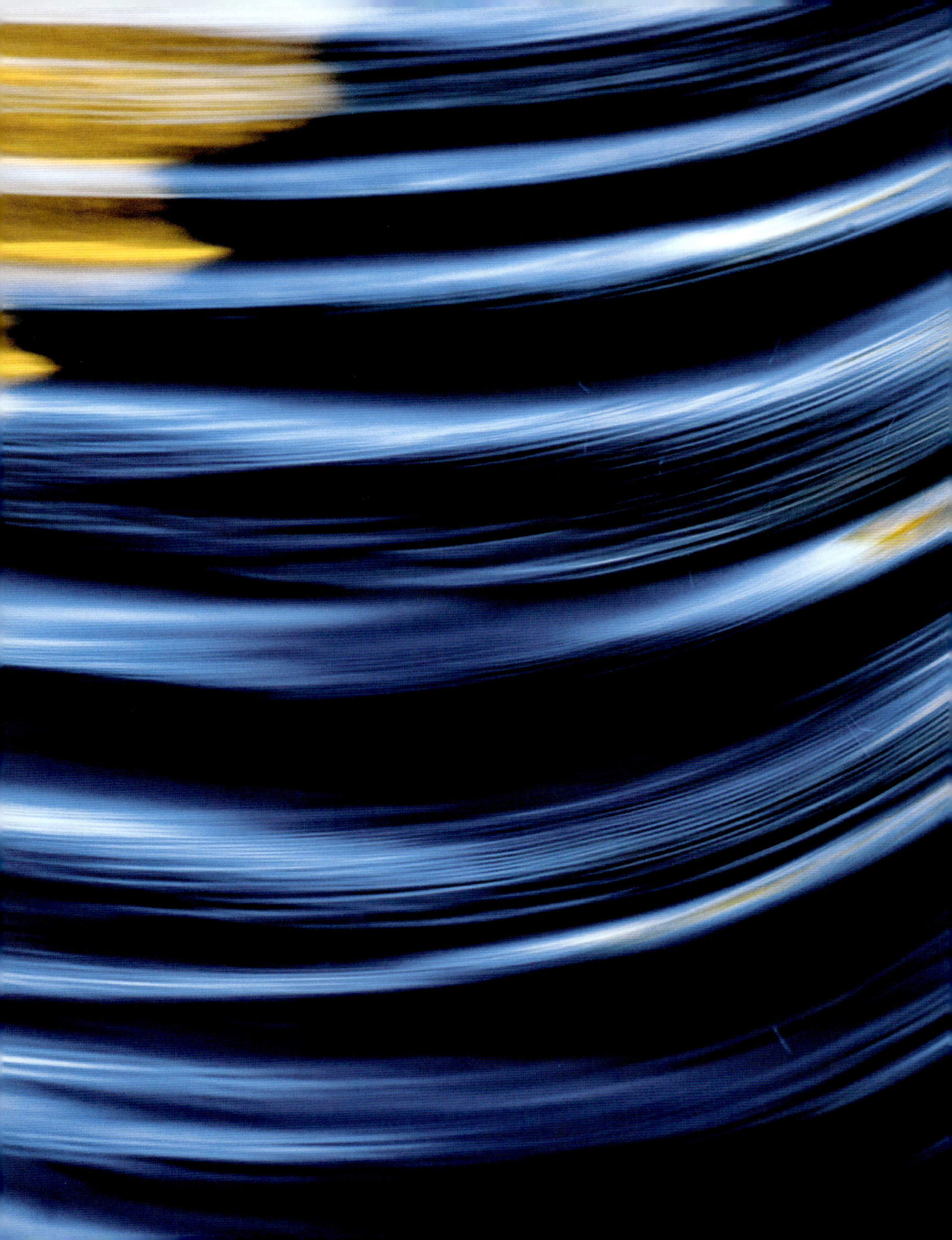

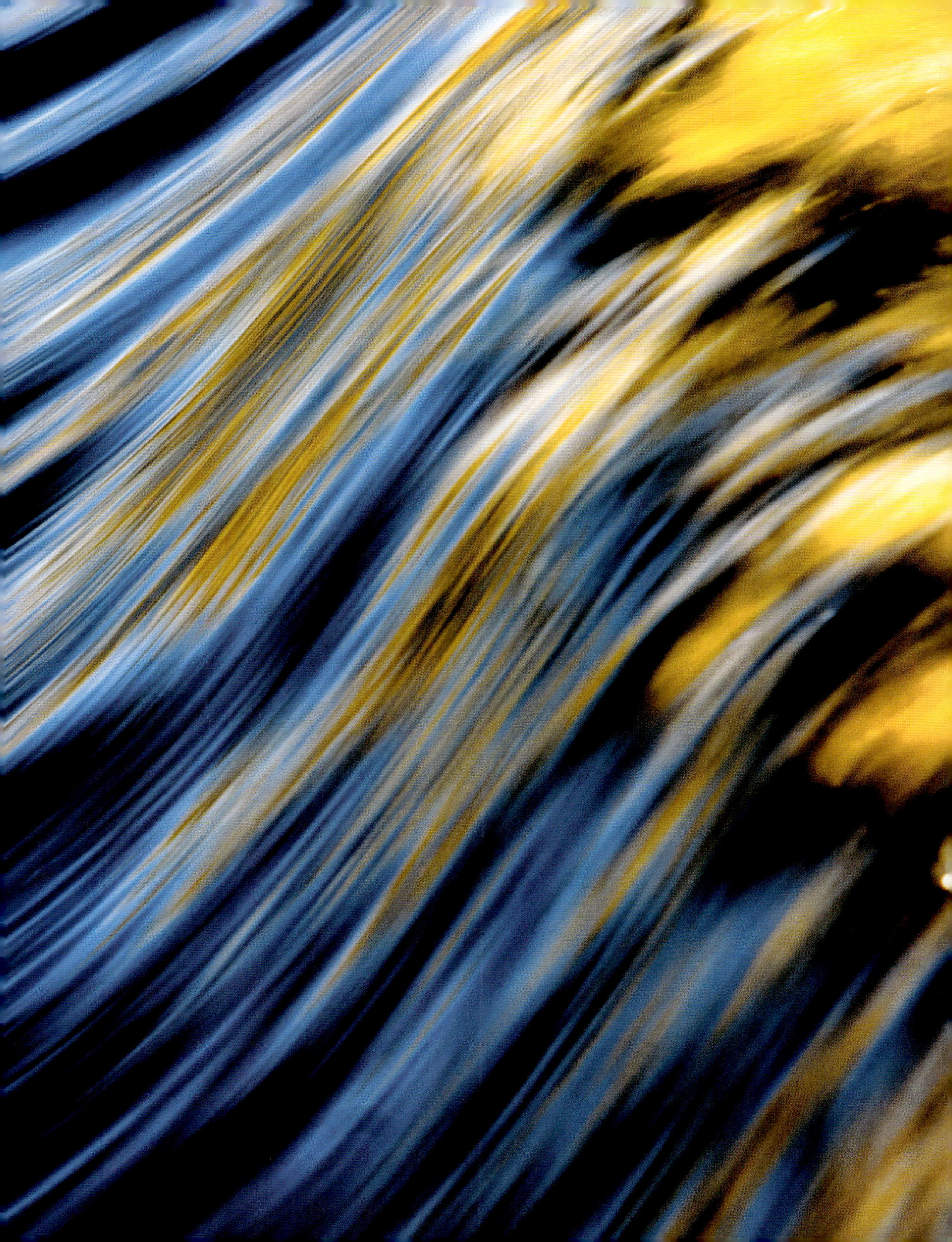

Pete Taras and *TransWorld*. Though I had been shooting for three years, I had never used my camera so consistently, from sunup to sundown for weeks on end. It was the beginning of a symbiotic relationship in which I didn't know where I ended and my camera began. Operating the settings became second nature, like driving a car or using a pair of binoculars. That habitual muscle memory allowed me to focus purely on being present and creative.

We shot mostly at sunrise and sunset, during the magic moments when the Golden State really shines. We started aiming for a style that Eric and I called "timeless." The silhouettes of surfers, foothills, telephone wires, and swaying long grasses that *anyone* who traveled along the California coast could relate to became our calling card. I wanted photos that even my mom, who had never seen this part of the coast, could appreciate. When I caught myself trying to shoot a magazine-style image, I made a conscious effort to buck the trend. We took the Hurley stickers off Eric's boards, both out of principle and to keep a low profile with locals, and I opened my lens up to wider perspectives. I opened my lenses and my eyes to the landscapes as well as the local people and culture. I realized I wasn't shooting for the fifteen- to twenty-five-year-old readers of *TransWorld SURF* anymore. I was shooting for everyone. Like the Impressionist painters that Eric tried to emulate, I wanted my scenes to last forever.

Fifty days in, we reached the town of Imperial Beach on the Mexican border. Our trip certainly had its ups and downs. On the worst days, I battled biblical levels of poison oak, which ended up spreading like the plague. We witnessed a stabbing outside a coffee shop in Fort Bragg, and Eric nearly got arrested for unknowingly trespassing on the Camp Pendleton Marine Corps base north of San Diego. That lovely run-in inspired an hours-long search of our van, but thankfully Eric had already smoked all his weed back in Humboldt.

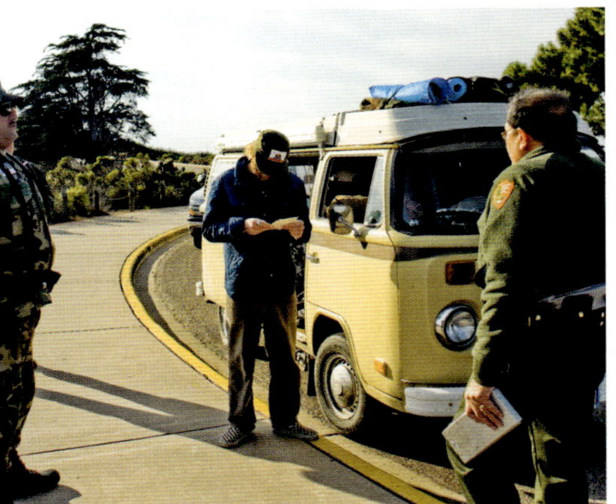

On the best days, we surfed with heroes like Dan Malloy, Devon Howard, and Alex Gray, then we sat around log fires in empty campgrounds late into the night, illuminating photos with headlamps and fire sticks until we were too exhausted to move. Most days involved push-starting the bus, listening to the Modest Mouse song "Dramamine" at least three times, and chasing raccoons away from our food stash. More often than not, we'd return from the beach to a fresh new parking ticket. (In total, we owed $2,000 dollars in parking tickets.) The trip felt like a rite of passage, the road a new kind of teacher. We discovered how wild and diverse our home state is and how liberating life can be when your commitments are replaced with simpler pursuits like exploring, surfing, and taking photos. We were just two surfers naive to the world, exercising a kind of freedom that few would ever get to experience.

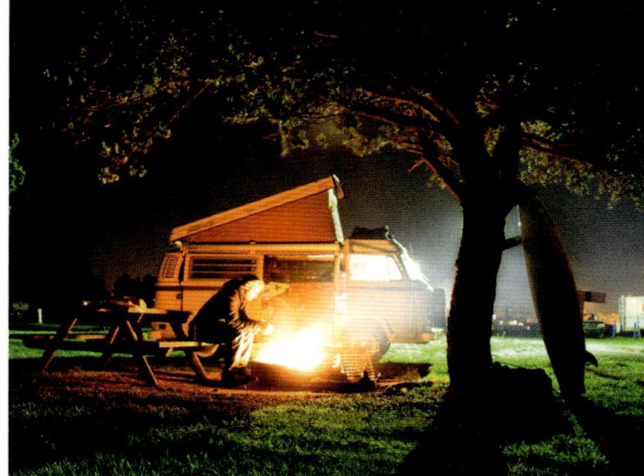

My bond with Eric during those fifty days in the bus laid the foundation for a lifelong friendship. It felt a bit like going to war together—a shared experience that could never be re-created. Sure, there were a lot of deep late-night conversations about life and its meaning, but our friendship was built mostly on a shared love for nature, surfing, and the ability to be real with each other.

One night, while we were camping along Plaskett Ridge in Big Sur, the car's starter went out. Luckily, we were parked uphill in a small pullout. We decided to sleep and find a solution in the morning, only to be serenaded all night by some sort of animal massacre—I think an eagle or an owl eating a baby pig. Emotionally scarred and twitching from the night before, we woke up to realize the only way out of this situation was to slip the car into neutral and pick up enough speed before popping the car into gear. The massive problem was that this wasn't just any hill; it was a slippery, dusty fire road that had tight turns with no guardrails, and its drop-offs led directly down to the ocean. I jumped in the front seat and looked at Eric, who was straight-faced and solemn.

"I'm doing this alone," Eric said. "If I don't make this turn . . ."

"NO! I'm coming with you," I promised.

It was a bit of a Thelma and Louise moment.

When we started accelerating toward the cliff and a tight corner with no power steering, I was definitely living in the moment, just as Eric had asked me to at the beginning of our adventure. I had learned to put my full trust in Eric, because I knew he always had my back.

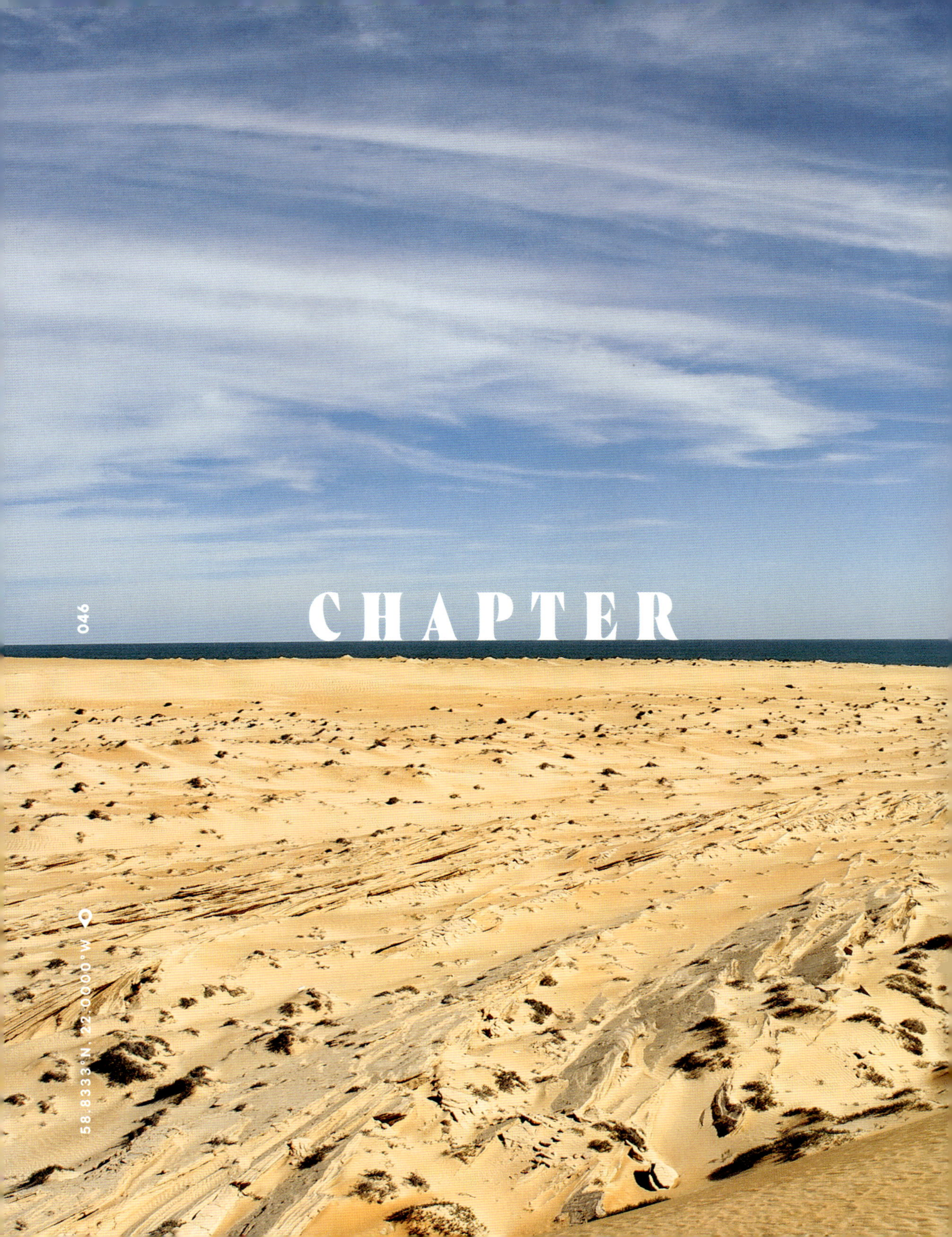
CHAPTER
046
58.8333°N 22.0000°W

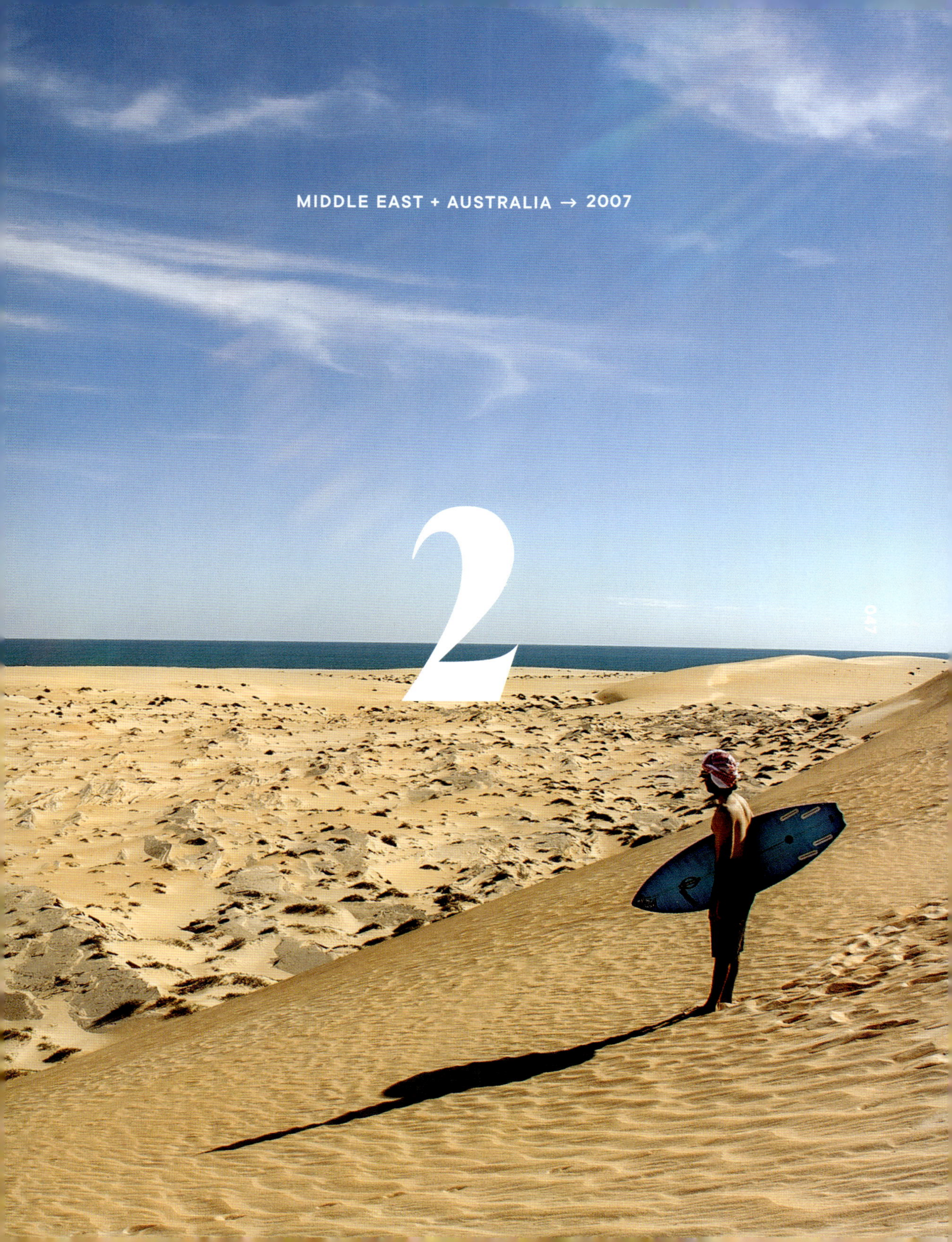
MIDDLE EAST + AUSTRALIA → 2007

2

047

returned to the Central Coast feeling restless. I was expecting a feeling of accomplishment and contentment. Instead, life back in my old routine felt full of excess and rigidity, and I felt constricted after so many unstructured days on the road. Coming home after living out of a backpack and the back of a van brings up these feelings. You've stripped away some of the BS and are left with only the things that matter. Our California surf adventure actually inspired me to become a minimalist.

All I could think about was my next trip. It felt as if I had developed an addiction to the rawness and unpredictability of life on the road. And with these feelings came a certain amount of clarity. The simplicity of living in a bus made me realize how little I needed to be happy. I thrived living out of a suitcase. I signed up for my next adventure without a second thought.

I was approached by a filmmaker named Dana Morris, who invited me on a surf trip to the Middle East to shoot stills that would help promote a 16mm surf film he was working on called *Beneath the Surface*. We would be visiting Dubai, Oman, and Yemen, and it was the perfect opportunity to put off reentering the real world for a little while longer. Eric and I had only just gotten home on Christmas Eve, and one week later I departed on my first real international trip.

We arrived in Dubai on New Year's Eve. It was Dana and me and a group of surfers that included Nate Tyler from the Central Coast and Josh Hoyer and Justin Hugron from Southern California. We stuck out like a sore thumb in the futuristic blossoming Arab country. We stuffed the elevator full of surfboards and camera gear to ascend the twenty-seven floors to our furnished apartment in a mega high-rise downtown. From our window we could see the under-construction Burj Dubai, now known as the Burj Khalifa. It is still the tallest skyscraper in the world.

Outside, dust and the smell of doner kebabs swirled through the city, which was an international melting pot of the ancient and the cosmopolitan. People dressed in cloaks and head scarfs as well as business suits. Outdoor bazaars sold everything from spices and hookahs to designer bags, and a giant mega-mall housed an indoor ski resort. I was shocked by how much money was put into imitating outdoor experiences. "Discover Nature, Space, Harmony, Tranquility," a towering apartment building advertised.

Not only was this the farthest I had ever traveled from home, but it was also my first time navigating a huge, burgeoning city—one that didn't speak my language or share my culture. When I closed my eyes, I couldn't understand the conversations around me or the intonation, which was equal parts thrilling and terrifying. At the airport, our copies of *TransWorld SURF* got confiscated for their risqué REEF ads. I was told by our guide, Ali, whom Dana knew from college, that I couldn't snap photos in grocery stores or point my lens toward women without their husbands' consent.

It had been a little more than five years since September 11, and friends of ours in the military had warned against traveling to the Middle East, especially to Yemen, where there were ongoing religious conflicts. Personally, I felt most of these arguments were bullshit, mainly because I wasn't about to let opinions based out of fear keep me from my goals. I don't mind taking risks in my life, as long as they are calculated, and Dubai in particular sounded totally safe.

Our SUV was topped with an oversized surfboard bag that cried "tourist" as loudly as a fanny pack and floppy hat. Luckily, our tourist beacon tended to be more a point of curiosity for locals than a point of contention. For most of that trip, I attempted to travel without any preconceived notions, knowing I couldn't continue to just get my opinions from the news or my parents. If I was going to be a photographer, I needed to see the world through my own eyes.

The surf in Dubai never got that good; the best we found was some East Coast–style wind swell breaking near the luxury hotels of Jumeirah Beach. During down time, I walked the streets in search of locals to photograph. I was nervous, but at least I had my camera as a way to filter this unfamiliar world. I started with a few construction workers but quickly felt intimidated by their stares. I followed the sound of laughing kids to a group of teenage boys playing soccer. Soccer was my sport of choice growing up, so I was excited there was some common ground we could share. I pointed at my camera to ask permission to take photos. They struck sporty poses and then crowded around me, giggling when they saw the playback.

I took a few more shots, but I realized that every time I held the camera over my face, I was putting up a barrier between myself and these kids. It may have felt safer to hide behind the viewfinder, but what I really wanted was to engage, not create distance. I set the camera down and kicked the soccer ball back into the field to play.

A few days later, after crossing into Oman and briefly stopping in the capital, Muscat— and unsuccessfully scouring Masirah Island for surf—we drove an otherworldly highway through the undulating dunes of the Wahiba Sands. A little way down the highway we

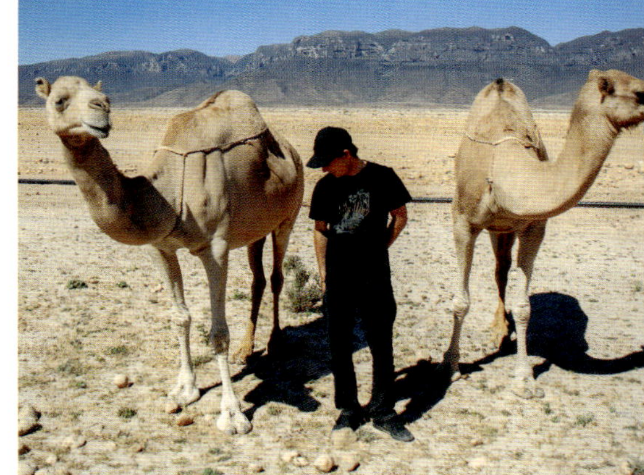

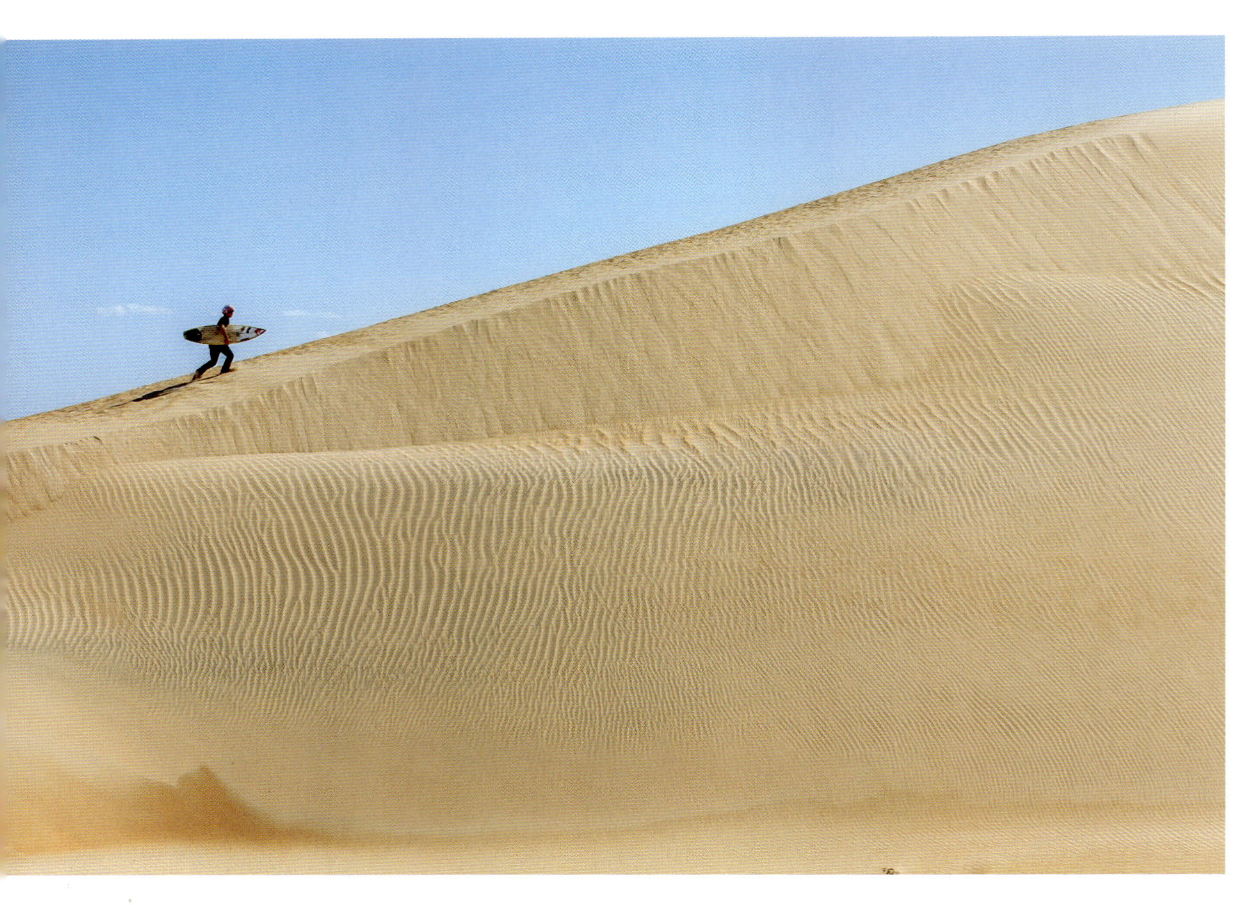

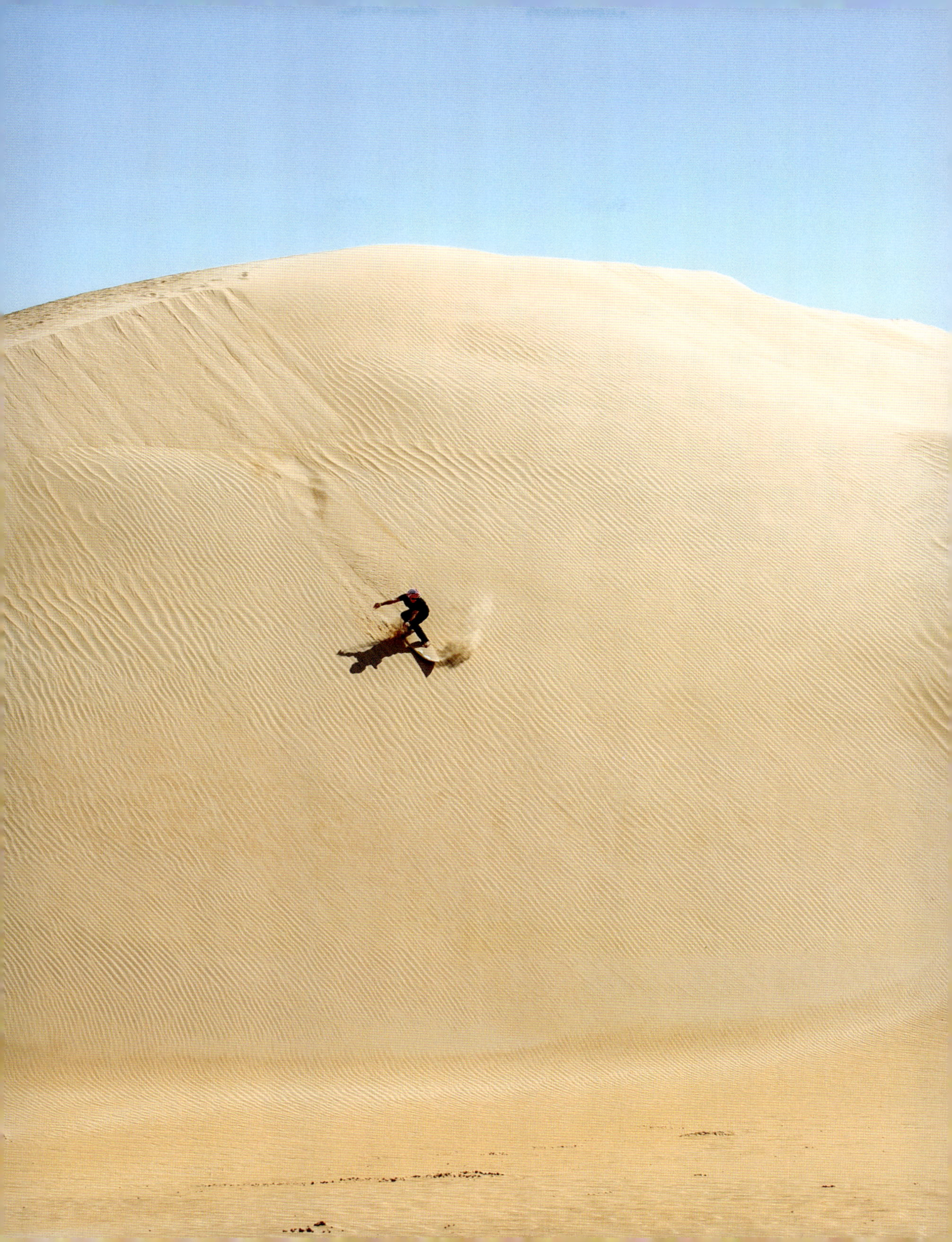

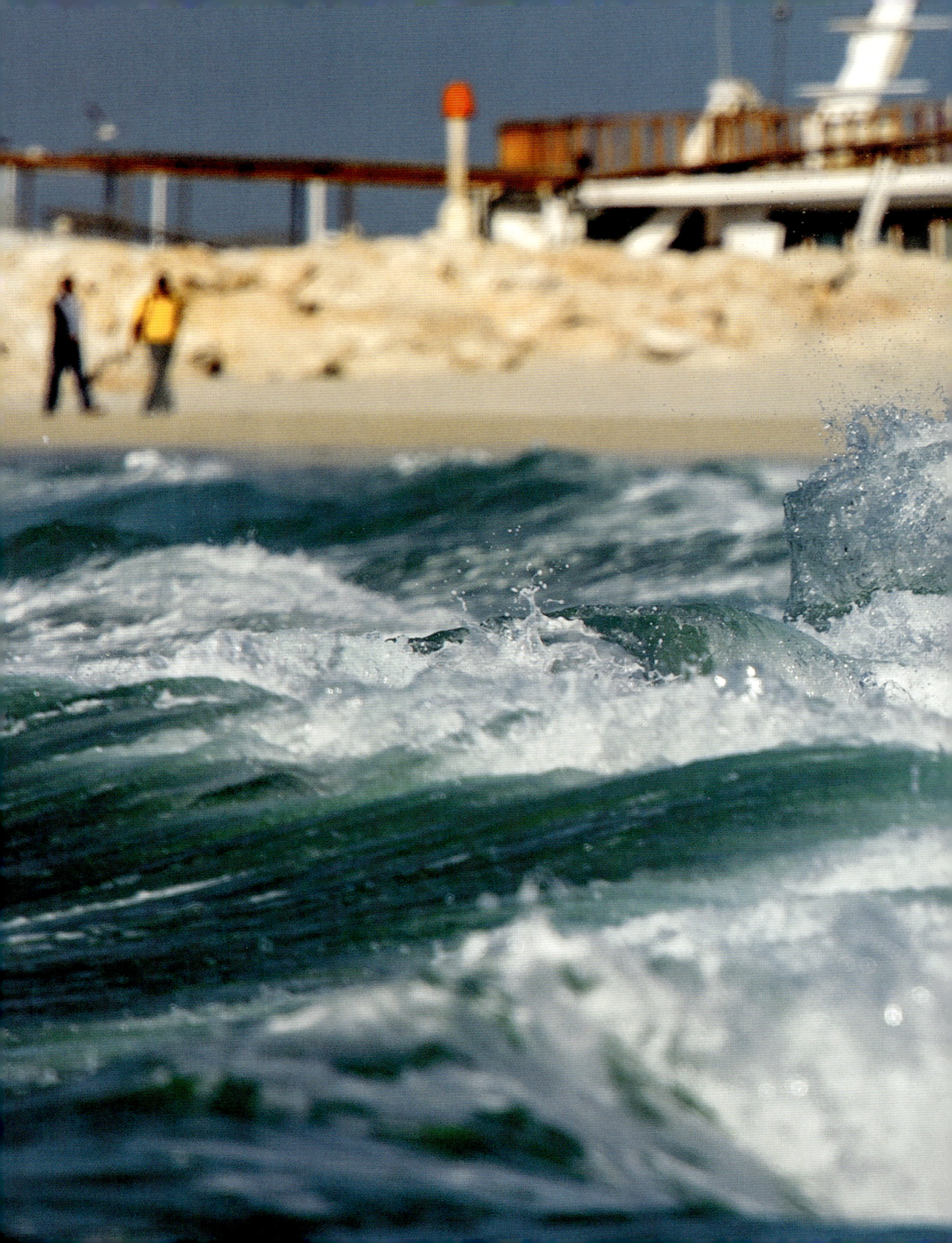

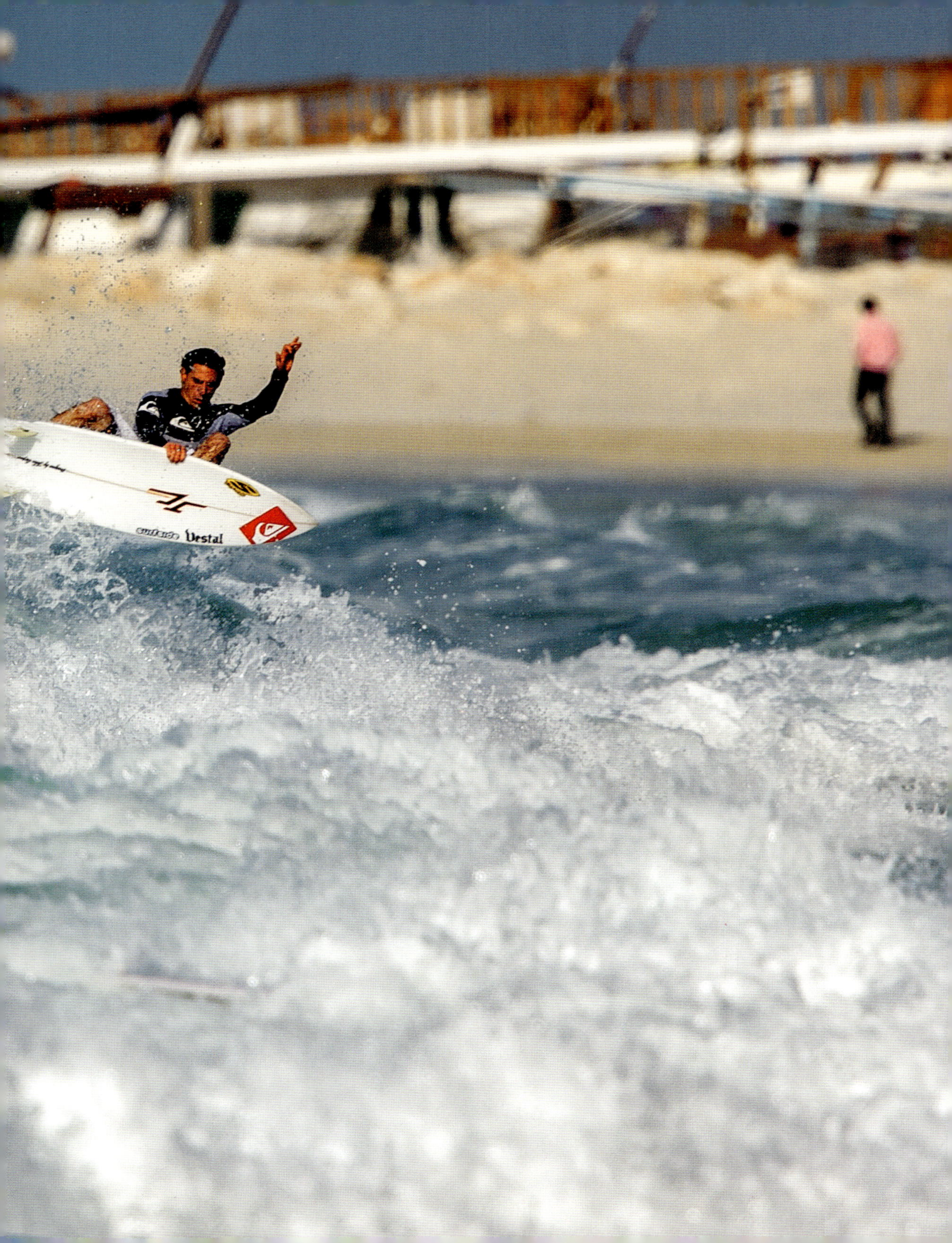
Vestal

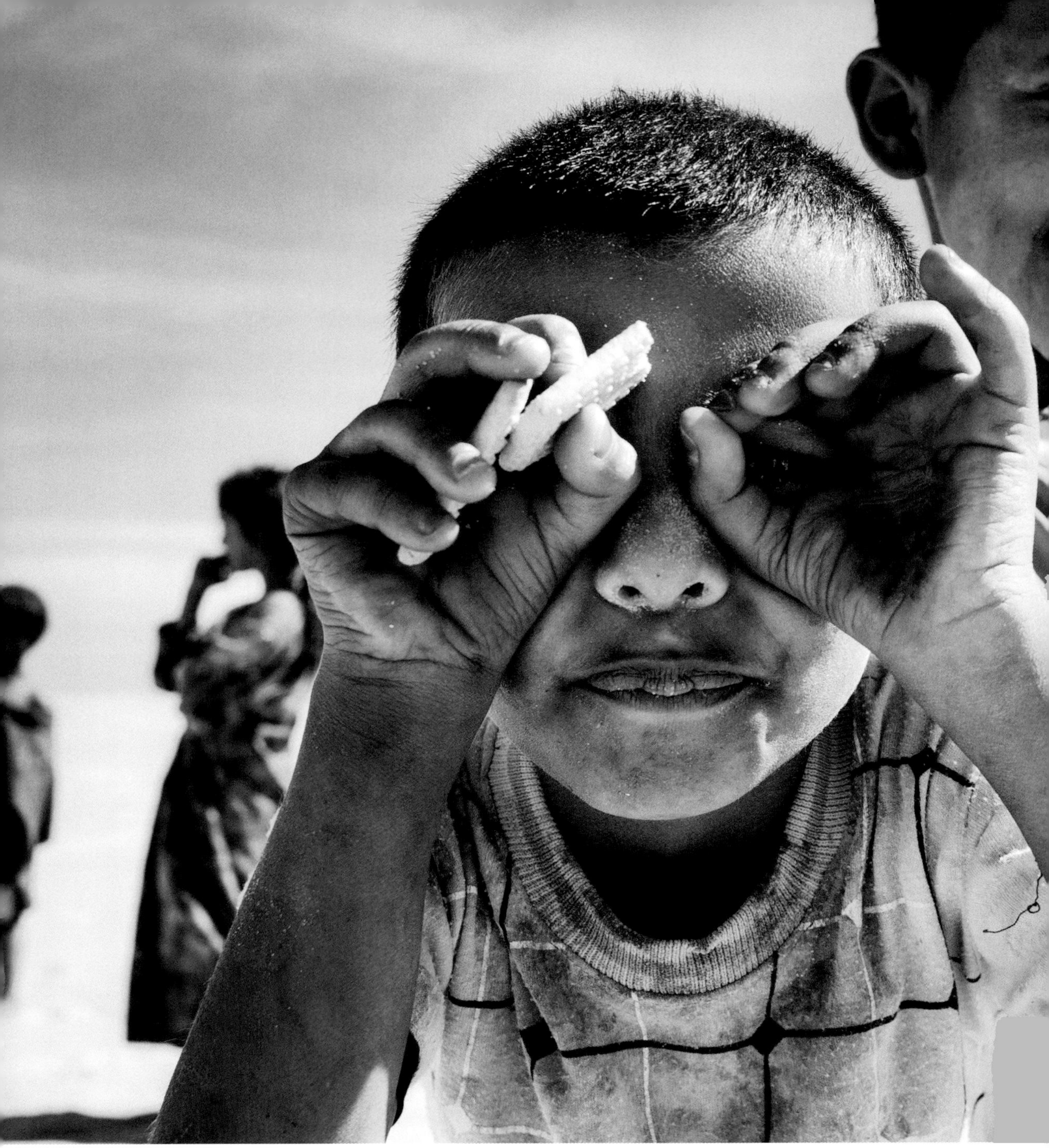

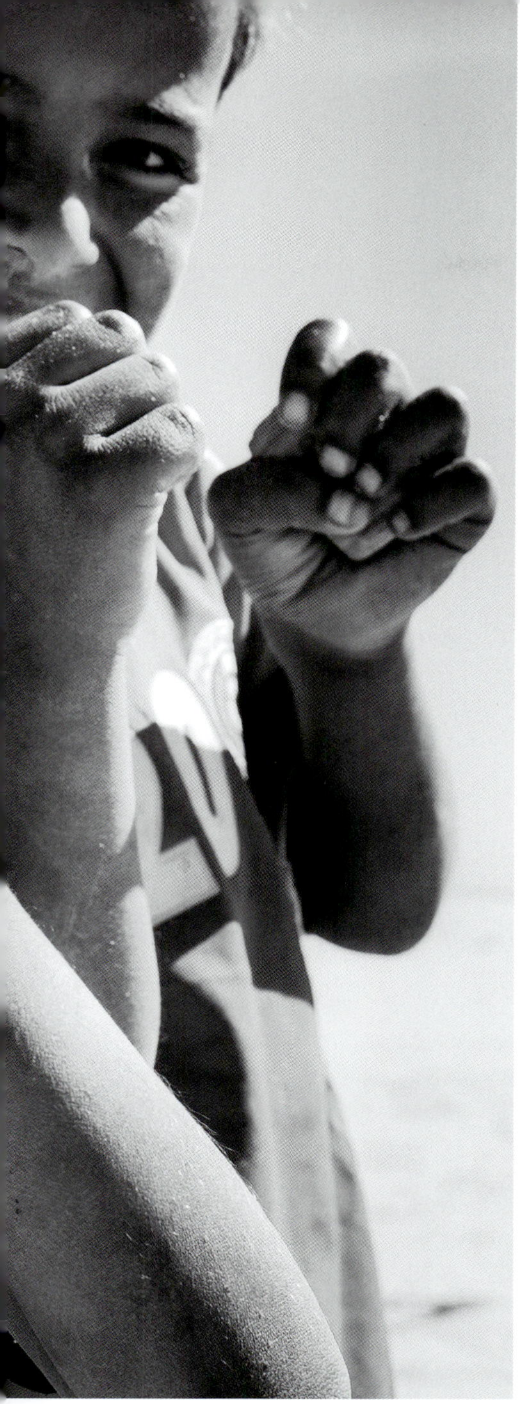

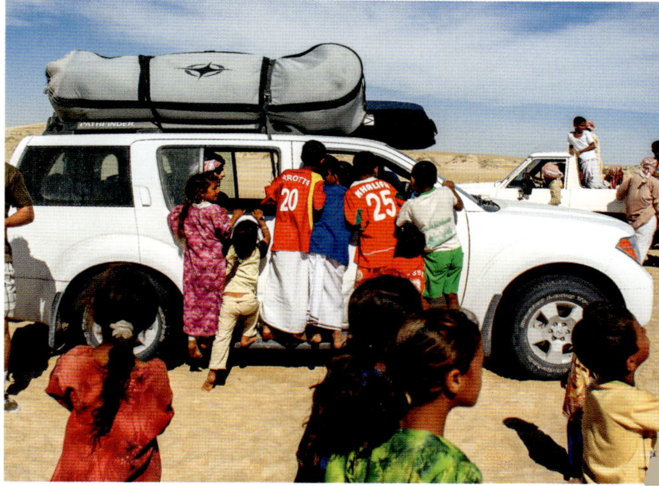

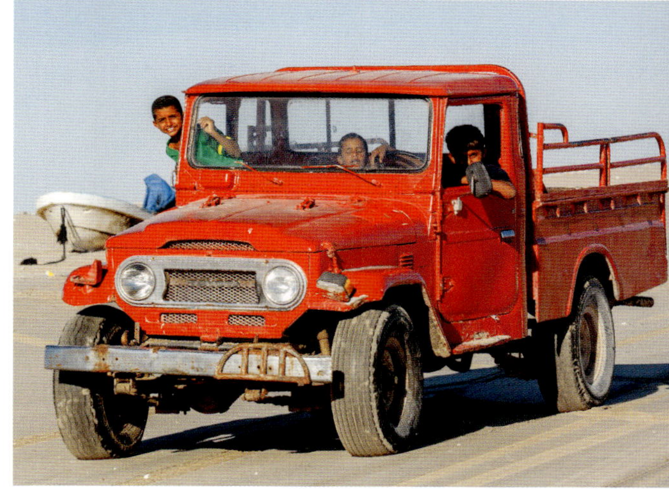

CHRIS BURKARD

came across a ramshackle village where homes were tied together with tarps and fishing nets. Bedouins lived here with a mini ark full of camels and goats.

The kids of the clan ran up to our car. "Biscuit, biscuit?" they asked. Fortunately, we were armed with cookies, which we placed in their henna-stained hands in exchange for pictures. Treats in one hand, crumbs in the other, a young boy cupped his eyes as if mimicking binoculars and stared at his reflection in my lens. I snapped the shutter button, trying to immortalize the moment. This is why we travel, I thought—to connect with foreign cultures in remote places you'd never read about in an in-flight magazine. Even when you don't have much in common, you can share a smile, or a photo, or a biscuit. You can leave a little piece of yourself behind in exchange for the photos and stories you bring home.

Once again, when I returned home to my small town, I had trouble sharing my experience with others and translating how transformative it was. But I felt empowered after facing discomfort, poverty, and even a little danger. I felt as if there was nowhere I couldn't go. For the first time, I had experienced something my parents hadn't. And although my parents were proud of me, to them, this job was still plan B.

Not long after that trip, I received my dream job offer: to become the first-ever staff photographer at Surfline. I was twenty years old, my girlfriend, Brea, and I had just gotten married, and I was desperate for a steady paycheck. And yet, the contract went unsigned for days. It just sat there on my cheap green desk, which was connected to a bookshelf where my water housings, hard drives, and camera lenses each had a designated space.

My office was shabby but functional, the place where I worked tirelessly to attempt to become a provider. After we got married, Brea moved in with me, into the cottage below my parents' house. I was now navigating joint financial decisions: Could I really afford new camera gear when we didn't have insulated windows or a washer and dryer? It had been a little more than six months since we had gotten married, and as I looked at the Surfline contract on the desk, I knew it could help . . . a lot.

Digital surf media was on the rise, and the Huntington Beach company, most famous for its surf reports and live video streams, was

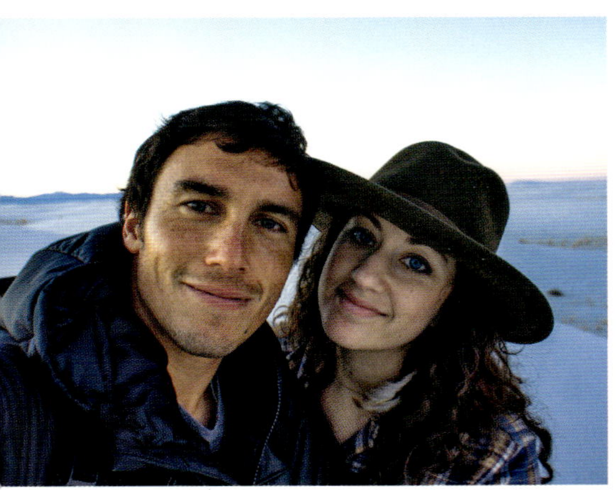

expanding its editorial coverage of swells, contests, and surf lifestyle. I got connected to Surfline through the editor Marcus Sanders, whom Eric and I first worked with on a three-part photo series about our California road trip. In fact, it was Marcus who put us in touch with Sarah Malarkey, an editor at Chronicle Books who helped us transform our crazy idea into a published coffee table book: *The California Surf Project*. I continued shooting for Marcus between magazine work, and at some point, it must have dawned on him that Surfline could save a bit of money by offering me an $1,800 monthly retainer instead of paying for every photo I submitted. Surfline had quickly become my go-to location for submitting new imagery, specifically for the swell features they ran frequently during the winter months.

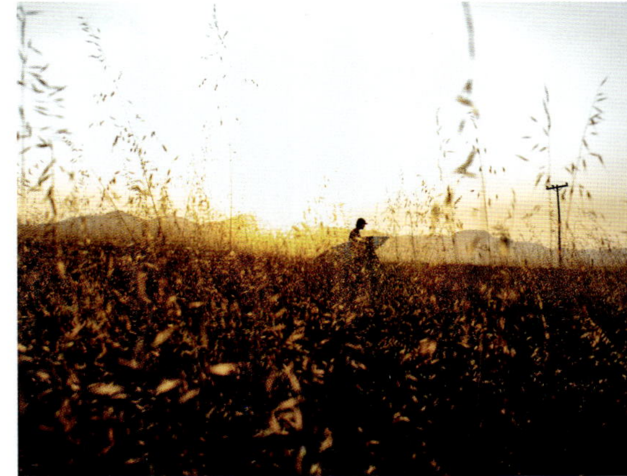

But I was also worried about the fast-paced nature of digital surf photography and the backlash I'd received for one Surfline interview I had done that described stealthily shooting a territorial break in Northern California. Readers weren't happy that an out-of-town photographer was exposing their turf. I wondered whether working for Surfline might damage my relationship with the public as well as with magazine editors.

On the creative side, though, Surfline owned *Water* magazine, a high-end quarterly in the glossy mold of the *Surfer's Journal*, so I'd have a built-in print audience combined with massive web exposure. Some photo features were getting fifty thousand to seventy thousand hits, way more than traditional surf magazines. Here I was, barely scraping by, and an opportunity landed on my desk for a steady income plus millions of views. I grabbed a felt-tipped pen with my left hand and scrawled out a signature in my caps-cursive style. I didn't know where this decision would take me, but I prayed it would be somewhere good.

Surfline had come a long way since it was founded in 1985 as a call-in forecasting service. Anyone who paid fifty-five cents to dial 967-SURF ("the Surf Line") could hear a ninety-second swell report, powered by forecasting pioneer Sean Collins and his scrappy string of Southern California dawn patrollers. These surfers would check conditions every morning and relay them back to headquarters—via beach pay phones—before the rest of the world woke up.

Ten years later, the website launched, with written surf reports published alongside

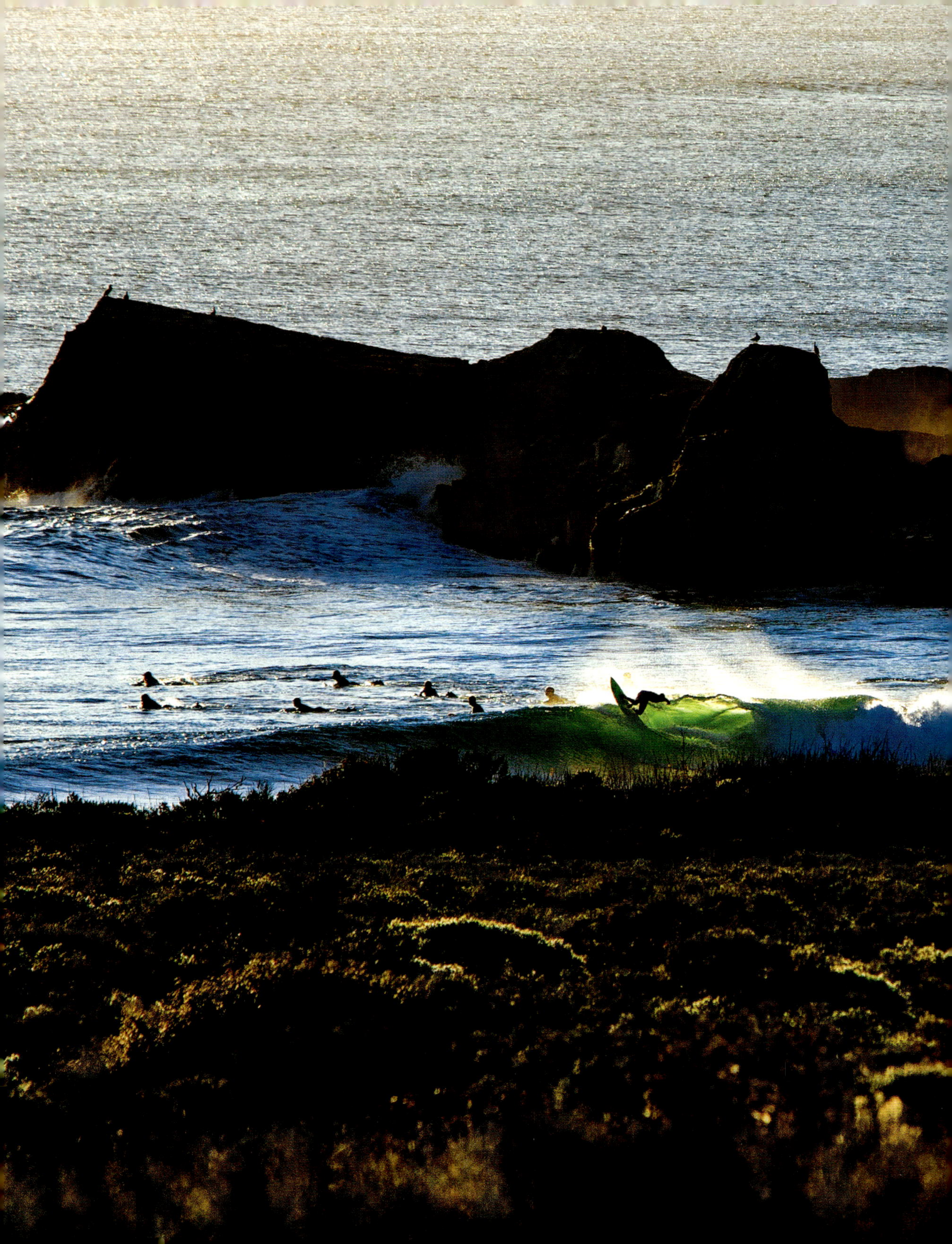

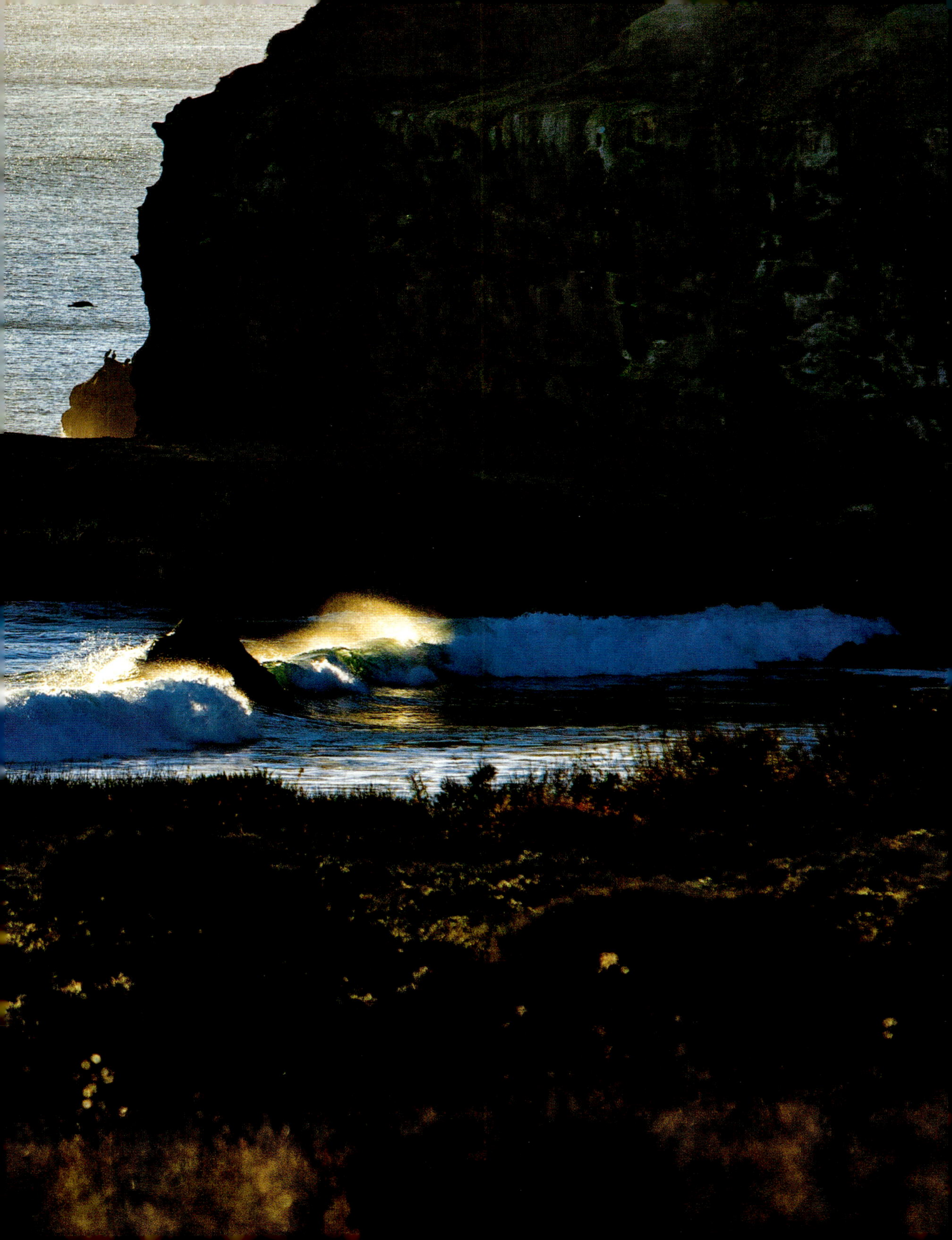

live footage from security cameras that had been repurposed as "surf cams" the company installed from Hawaii to the Hamptons. By 2008 the staff was churning out cutting-edge photo and video features for its audience of seventy-five thousand daily (or one million monthly) web visitors—the biggest of any surf media outlet in the world. Surfline was tapping into America's insatiable appetite for immediate online content. I was now responsible for the eye candy.

In practical terms, this meant being wherever the waves were, documenting surf culture, and spreading the stoke, especially about swells—Surfline's M.O. When it came to covering swells, the forecasting department would predict them, I'd go out and shoot them, and the editorial department would curate a digital photo gallery within a day or two to showcase how good the waves were.

The job felt like payoff for all that I had been working toward. But the Surfline opportunity also came with an unexpected challenge, one that would further fuel my desire to get as far away from home as possible: localism. Localism in surfing is basically a pecking order that rewards ability, ego, social status, and time spent at that particular break, ideally since birth. And with this came unwritten rules about not publishing photos with obvious landmarks (a recognizable jetty, an iconic lighthouse) that could give such a spot away. I knew these rules well, and I respected them. But simply bringing a camera to the beach made me an easy target. My lens was the one now intruding in surfing sanctuaries.

I grew up with localism and understood most of the reasons for it, from crowd control to making beginners (aka "kooks") watch and learn before causing bodily harm to themselves or others. And yet, the landscapes I mostly wanted to shoot—remote and wild beaches— were the same landscapes people wanted to protect from the masses. In surf-impacted California, where all the media and brands were based, these final frontiers were starting to feel endangered. I didn't blame people for fighting back. What I never quite understood, though, was how an unnamed and nondescript photo that I'd take—one that showed only surfer, wave, and sky—would make someone want to do me physical harm.

Once, while checking waves at a spot just down the highway from my house, I noticed a middle-aged guy with a five o'clock shadow and strained beady eyes staring at me from close behind. When I turned around, he was cutting an apple with a pocketknife. He brought a slice to his mouth then waved the knife so it glinted back at me. He looked at the knife, looked at me, wiped it off, and cut another slice. I put my camera down and left.

The in-person altercations increased. I was veered off the road near Big Sur and belligerently harassed by a surly local at a parking lot in Cambria. "This place isn't yours to exploit for money or fame," one local shouted at me. Words sting more when you feel a sliver of their truth. Although fame was never my goal, making a living was. People wrote nasty comments below digital stories of mine, and some even googled my name to find my contact information listed on my website. I received an email with the subject line "Britney Spears" that accused me of being a sellout and a "whore of the industry." There was even a short-lived website called Surf Sheriff that published the license plate numbers and descriptions of photographers' vehicles—including a post on my truck and all of its identifying features. One winter day, I was sent to photograph a swell at a localized beach break in Ventura County and saw the words *Fuck Chris Burkard* massively painted onto a huge drainpipe.

The times when I could shoot my friends and just be stoked to share their golden moments were long gone.

I remember driving home from Ventura that day in a rage, jealous of the other photographers strictly shooting for magazines like *Surfer* and *Surfing*. None of them would ever receive the flack I did since it would take two to three months for their images to be published, a stark contrast to the instant galleries that Surfline put up. I had a target placed on my head and Surfline advertised it to the world.

I preferred to shoot in wilder, secluded spots, and I was always going to these places with locals, but I started to run out of options. The episodes started affecting my mood so much that I seriously considered quitting photography altogether. There had to be better places to photograph that wouldn't put my life in danger, I thought. I had to stop letting other people dictate my path and my worth.

One of the things that made Surfline's job offer too good to refuse was the travel budget. My run-ins with California localism were making me more and more eager to take assignments farther away, even if they were just to places my editors wanted me to go. I was inspired to see the world, and I didn't want to get pigeon-holed as a California photographer like so many others. Plus, travel could also be an escape from my day-to-day reality.

Not long after being hired by Surfline, I got what I thought I always wanted. I was asked to travel to the Gold Coast of Australia to cover the Hurley Pro Junior competition. Even then, I knew this wasn't exactly the kind of place, or the kind of subject, I liked to shoot. But it certainly felt like a great opportunity, and I justified the trip,

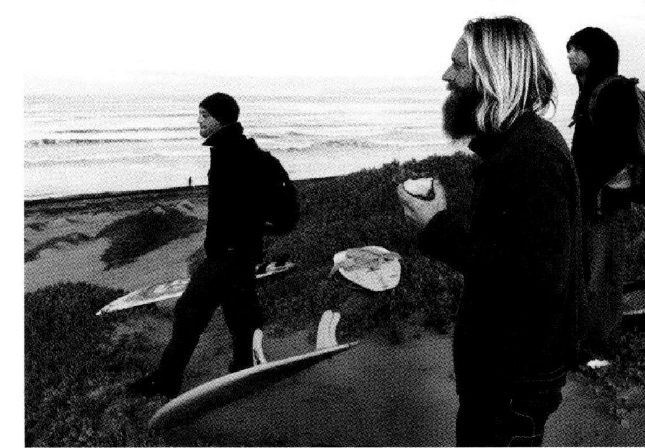

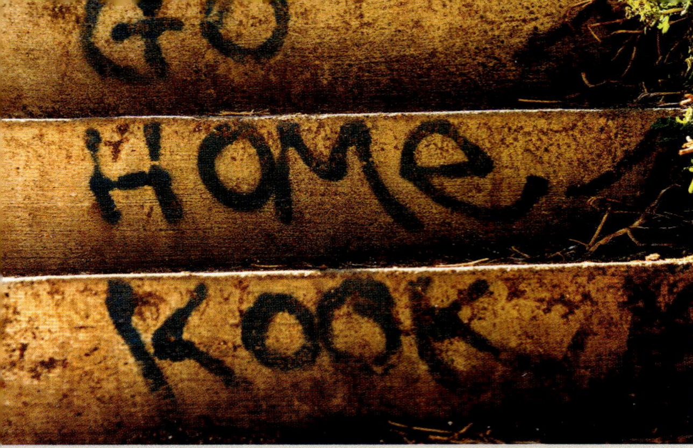

Localism: Territorial practice whereby resident surfers in a given area try to exclude nonresident surfers through threat, intimidation, and occasionally violence; a predictable, if rarely defensible, surf world response to overcrowding.

Localism wasn't named until the late 1960s, but the practice itself predates World War II. Visiting California surfers Gene "Tarzan" Smith and Tom Zahn were both harassed, even beaten up, by Hawaiian surfers in the '40s during their visits to Oahu, and a Surfer magazine letter writer in 1963 noted that Honolulu surfers were "always fighting" with nonnatives. Two developments set the stage for localism's wider disbursement. First, post–World War II changes in board design encouraged the surfer to perform turns while riding at a tight angle across the wave, and to do so he needed to ride alone. Whereas surfers in previous decades often rode in congenial groups of five or ten or more, "one surfer/one wave" became the new performance requirement, and put a higher demand on wave resources. Second, and more important, by the late '50s the sport began attracting hundreds, then thousands, of newcomers, which marked the beginning of an exclusionary "we were here first" attitude at some of California's better breaks.

As noted in a 1969 issue of Sports Illustrated, a professional surfing competition at Steamer Lane was sabotaged by a group of Santa Cruz locals—reasoning that the contest and the ensuing media coverage would bring new surfers to the lineup—who shoved an unmanned judges' stand over the beachside cliff onto the rocks below. Localism hit an apogee of sorts in Southern California during the 1970s; fights were relatively uncommon, but verbal harassment was rampant, and theft and vandalism were widespread, as nonlocal surfers had their car tires slashed, their windshields broken, or their wallets, boards, or wetsuits stolen. "If you don't live here, don't surf here," "locals only," and "go home" became popular graffiti slogans.

While California and Hawaii are both less localized than they were in the '70s (in part because the fight against crowds is now seen as hopeless), territorial pockets remain. Lunada Bay in southern Los Angeles County is generally recognized as the surfing world's most localized break, and in some instances—in Oxnard, California, as well as Lunada—law-breaking local surfers have been convicted of assault charges. Localism has been condemned for the most part by the surf press, who often refer to it as a "plague" or "cancer," but at a basic level it's proven to be an effective practice; fervently localized surf breaks such as Lunada are in fact less crowded, while nonlocalized spots (Malibu, for one) are overrun with visitors.

L Is for Localism

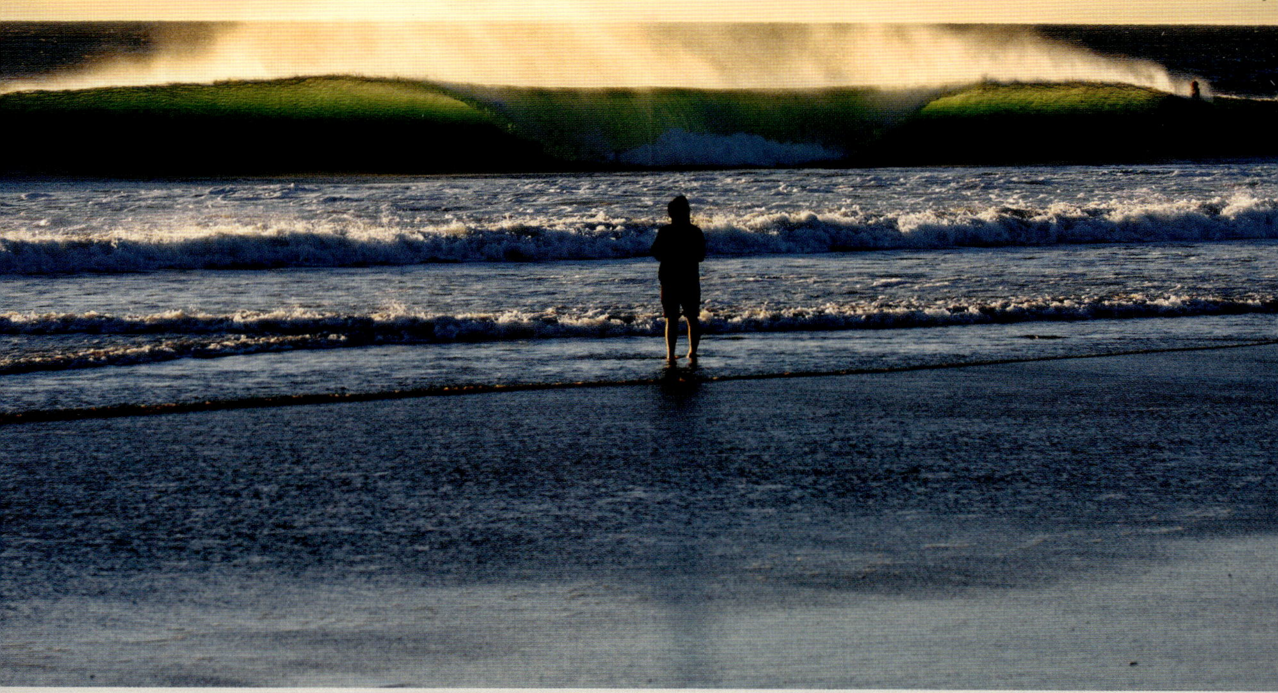

knowing it would make my editors happy and keep my paycheck secure. But that first real international assignment for Surfline taught me an unexpected lesson that would shape the rest of my career.

The Gold Coast of Australia is an overdeveloped string of resort towns south of Brisbane that's like a southern hemisphere fusion of LA, Miami, and Las Vegas—I started to feel like Bill Murray in the time-loop plot of *Groundhog Day*. I was traveling with Mike Cianciulli, Surfline's upbeat, shaggy-haired staff writer, and some of the best young American shredders, including Conner Coffin, Nat Young, and Evan Geiselman. We were joined by Mitch Crews from the Gold Coast and Kai Barger from Hawaii; at eighteen, they were older than the others and of legal drinking age in Australia.

With that much unbridled testosterone brewing and a lack of supervision, the fifteen- and sixteen-year-olds grew more feral by the day. I was used to traveling with older surfers, and I found it strange to be thrust into the role of "chaperone." I was barely legal myself. But even though I was only a few years older than these guys, I was in a completely different stage of life. The dynamic left me feeling lonely.

Every day was some version of the same routine: get the teenagers fed and out to the Hurley Burleigh Pro; dodge bluebottle jellyfish while shooting at another local break like Surfers Paradise (though it was far from it); try not to fry under Australia's vanishing ozone layer; cruise around in our rented red station wagon competing in farting contests and talking about hot chicks; then party back at the house—everyone but me, that is.

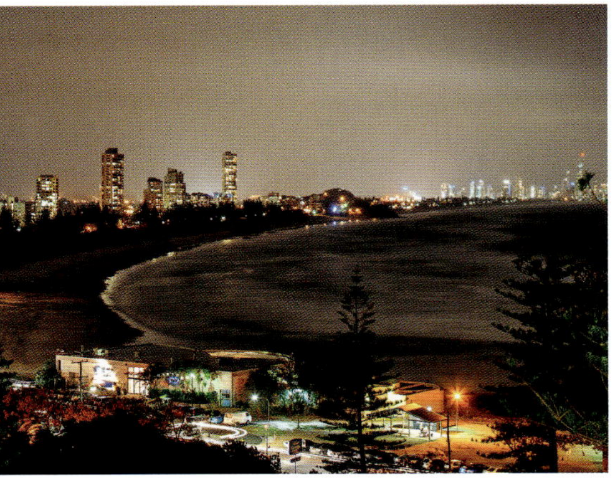

The highlights of this trip for me were things like climbing giant fig trees in the rain forest and hiking to a remote beach. The first and last time I drove the red rent-a-car involved turning onto the wrong side of the road during a nighttime tropical downpour.

"Burky! Are you trying to get us killed?!" the terrified teenagers in the back seat screamed at me.

The only headlights were far enough in the distance that I had time to right my wrong, but the gang didn't let me live it down. I was a rookie at traveling and deserved the reminder.

Australia marked the beginning of a frenetic few years, saying yes to just about everything that came my way. After my first trip to Dubai, Oman, and Yemen in early 2007, I ended up traveling like crazy, adding enough stamps to my passport to make up for the fact that I didn't even own one until I was twenty. I went to Bali and the Mentawais in Indonesia, and Kiribati in the central Pacific. I had survived questionable levels of safety in Yemen, drunken debacles in Australia, and tsunami warnings in Thailand. I was racking up stamps in my passport, blinded by quantity over quality. Surf photography became my ticket out of my small town, and in the span of a few years, I had actually gotten out.

But the more I traveled, the more I felt a dull pain in my heart, like a splinter hiding beneath the skin. I was going through the motions and wasn't finding the adventure I had envisioned when I started down this path. I began noticing a pattern: These were all warm, heavily touristed destinations where the barrier to entry was low and the resulting experience was shallow.

The Australia trip drew a line in the sand for me. I decided I no longer wanted to travel to traditional surf destinations rife with tourism and Wi-Fi, privilege and partying, just because they're good at pumping in swell. Places like France, Spain, Mexico, Costa Rica, Bali, Thailand, and Indonesia were no longer my dream adventures. In photographs these places looked empty, conveying the illusion of adventure, when in fact they were full of cameras, chain hotels, cellular coverage, and half-naked Westerners drinking on the beach. The worst part of it, though, was using my creativity to help sell these superficial experiences, rather than using whatever gifts I had for something more meaningful. The sliver kept poking through to remind me that I wasn't living my purpose. I didn't know exactly what that purpose was, but I knew this wasn't it.

I wanted to travel to become a better person, to grow wiser and stronger. Growing up, I felt the most peace when I was pushing myself physically and mentally. My most powerful memories came from experiences like hiking fifty miles as a Boy Scout, shoulder to shoulder with my friends and brothers, losing myself in my surroundings. My mind is often such an intense place to be that I am only able to tap into the simple gifts around me once I exhaust my body enough to do so. The more active I was, the quieter my thoughts became. I found the exact opposite of what I needed in these tropical "paradises" where I was bombarded by the man-made world colliding with the natural one. Stagnant and stuck in one three-foot spot on the sand for hours at a time, my body craved to be doing more. There was no silence, no place to be alone, no place to feel small.

I longed to use my creativity, not just my camera, and to push my mind and body to reach unridden waves in harsh places like Canada and Iceland. Although I came to this revelation fairly quickly, it would take another two years before I would finally make the change and begin my crusade against the mundane.

065

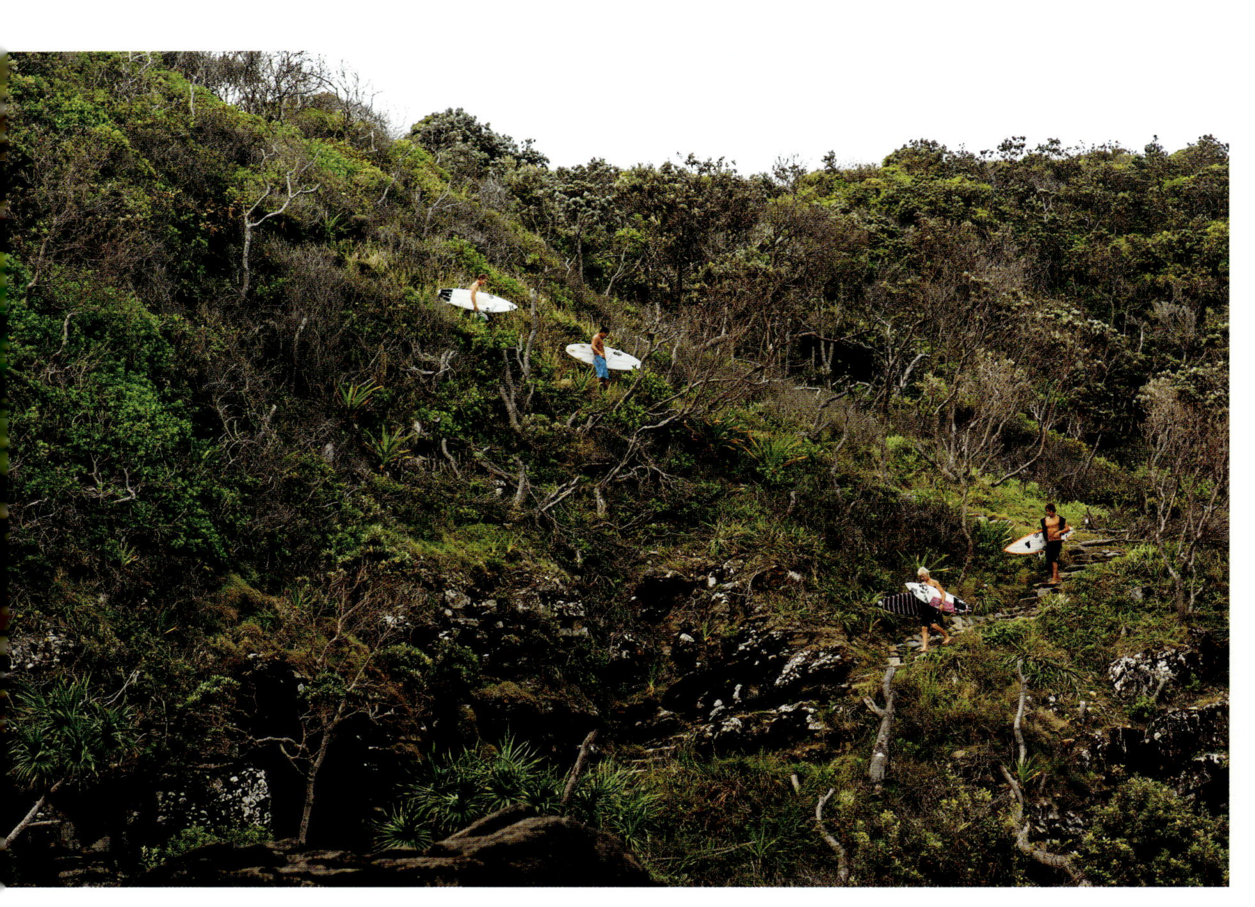

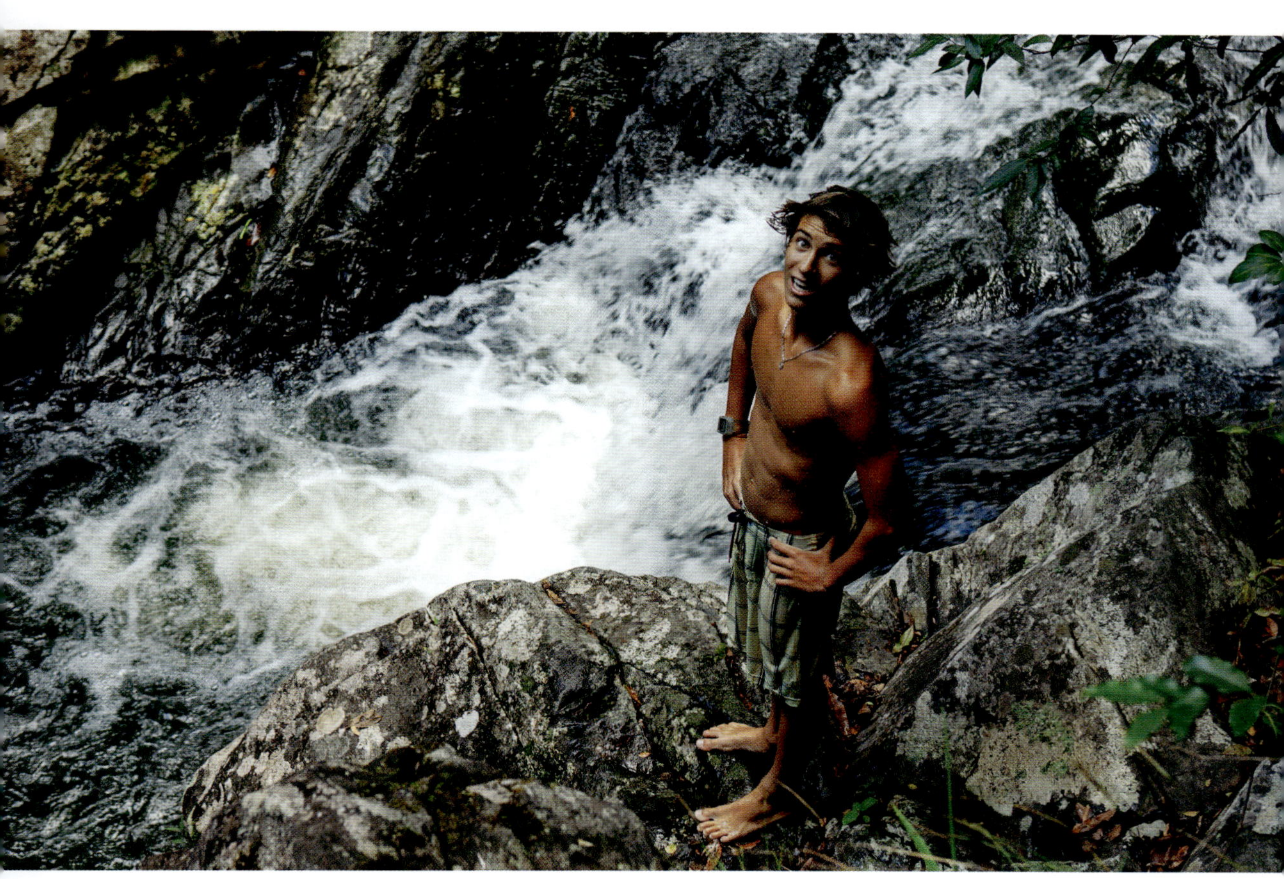

Find Your Focal Length

→ **I laugh now when I think about the two-month-**long road trip I took early in my career that culminated in the book *The California Surf Project*. I carried one camera body (my Canon 20D) and three lenses: a 24mm f/2.8 prime, an 18–55mm kit lens, and a borrowed 600mm zoom—the lens of distinction for professional surf photographers—which I borrowed from my photo editor at *TransWorld Surf*, Pete Taras. I couldn't justify bringing more lenses, in part because it was highly inefficient to change them all the time, and I didn't yet know myself as a photographer with a preferred focal length (the measure of how much of a scene will be captured and how magnified the individual elements will be).

Weeks after the road trip, when I finally

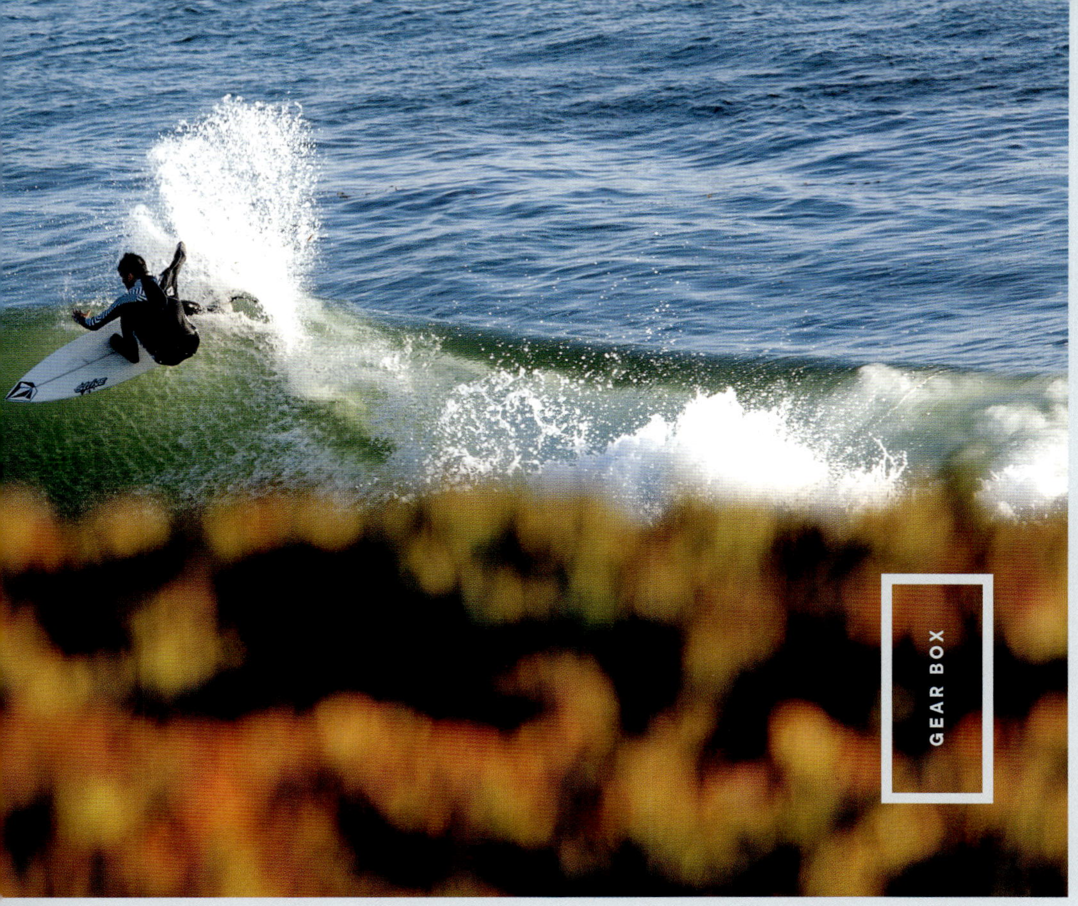

edited down the eighty thousand photos I took over those fifty days, I discovered something valuable: 90 percent of all the images I shot were on the 24mm f/2.8 prime lens. It could have been because it was the sharpest lens I owned, but most likely it was the ease of use and the fact that it was always the one attached. I realized I probably could have gotten the job done with that single camera-lens combination alone, and it helped immensely going forward to know my preference for pulled-back images that convey a wider scene. Nowadays, my favorite lens has a 16–35mm focal length, but I still find myself shooting primarily in a sweet spot of around 24mm to 35mm.

One of the benefits of using a prime lens (with a fixed focal length that doesn't zoom) is the way it forces you to walk forward. You should hold it within a few feet of your subject, which pushes you out of your comfort zone and into someone else's personal space. Shooting with a prime lens, especially one this wide, encourages you to connect with your subject and create images that are, in many ways, more intimate. That moment of connection is really where you're going to get the most unique expressions and postures. One of the best pieces of advice I got early on was to shoot with a 24mm prime for a week, to understand all the intricacies of that one focal length, its advantages and disadvantages. If you're anything like me, that lens might have a prized place in your camera bag forever. —C.B.

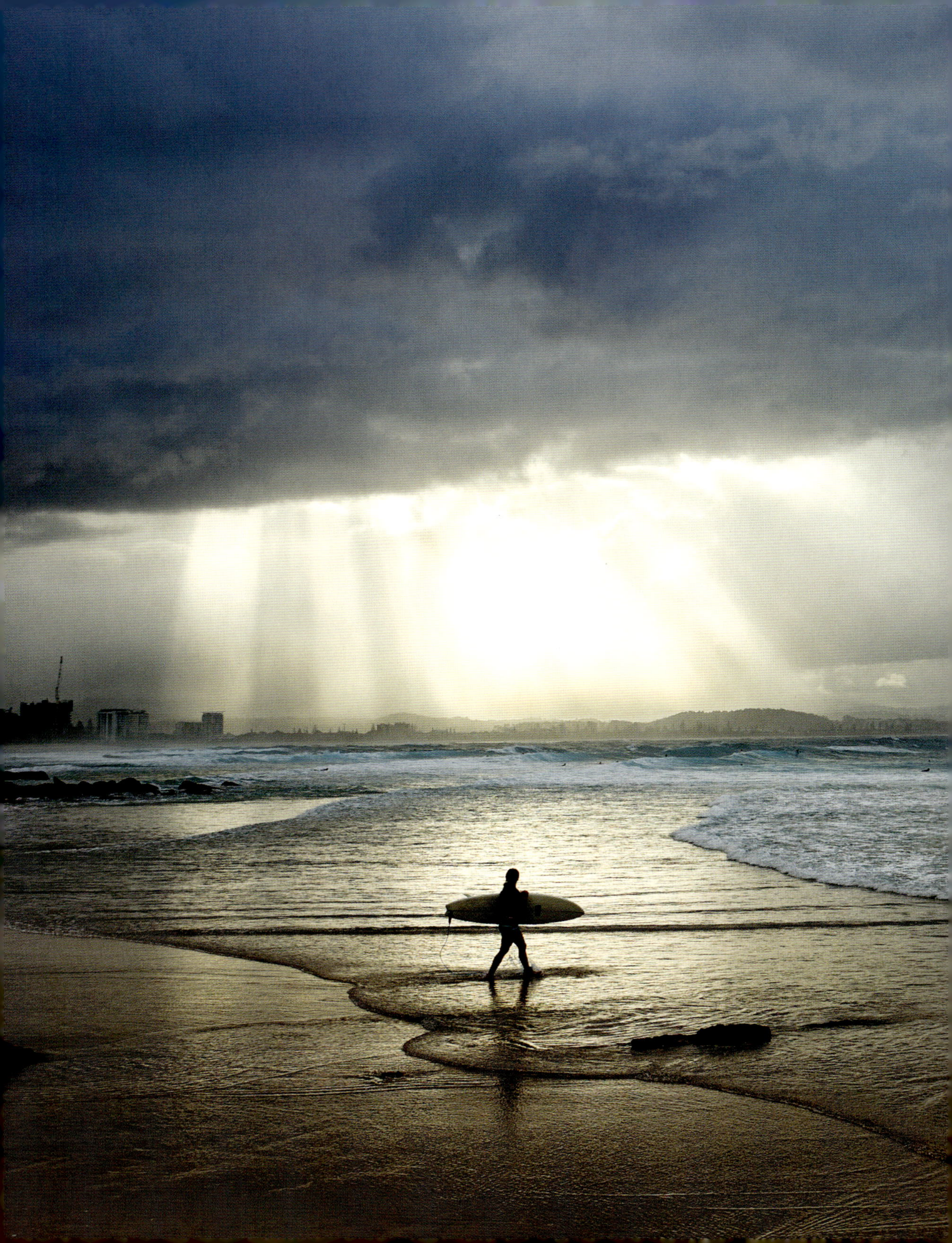

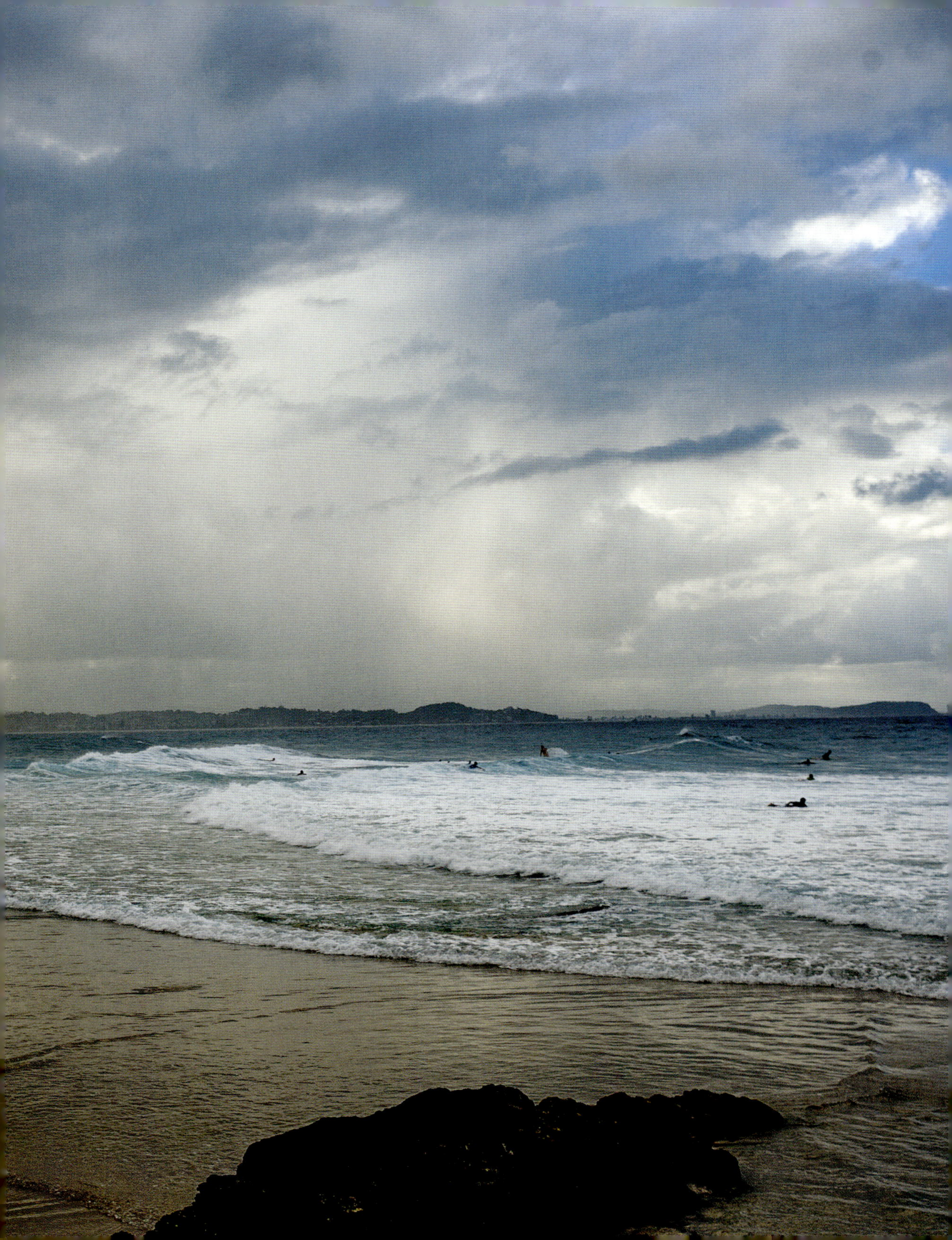

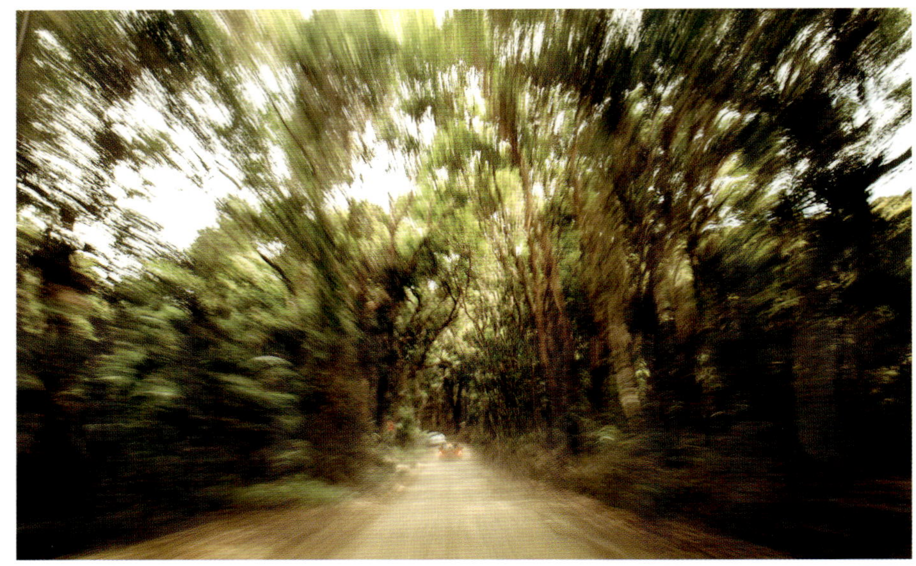

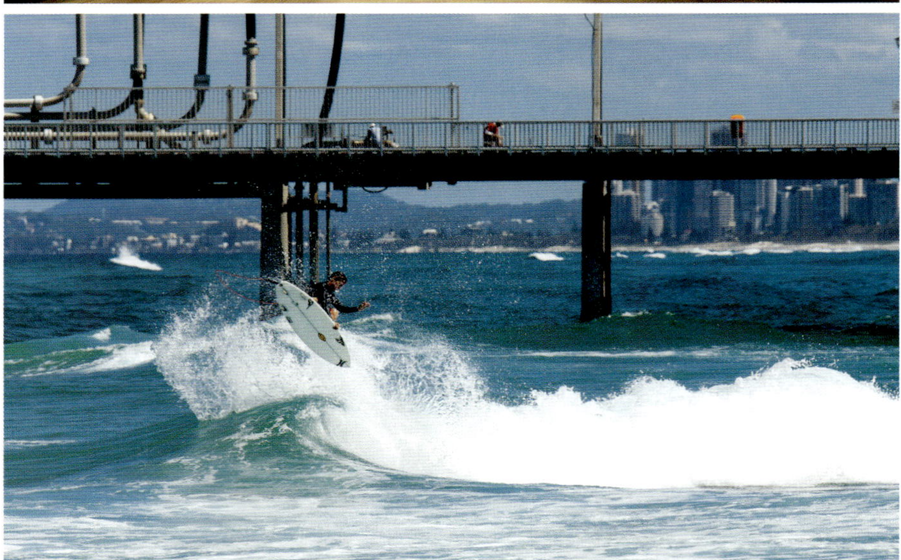

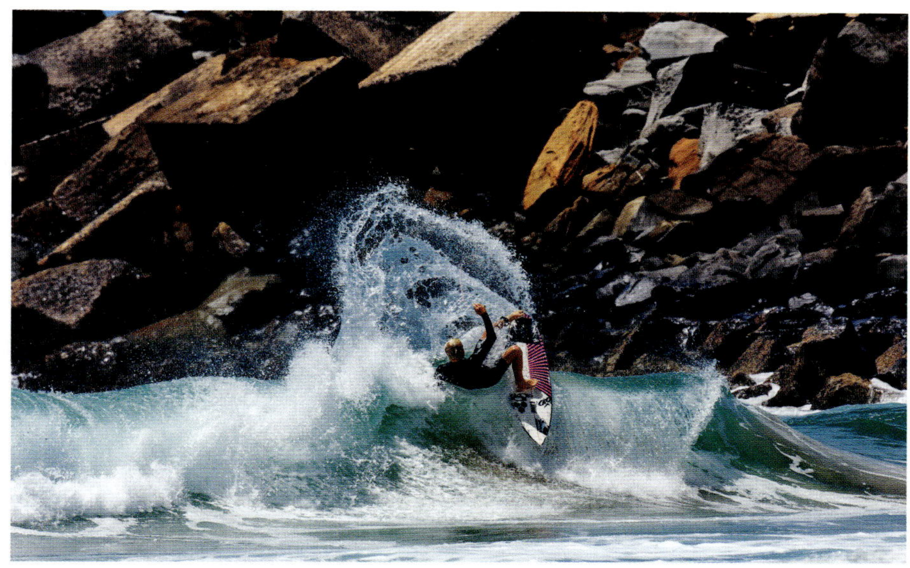

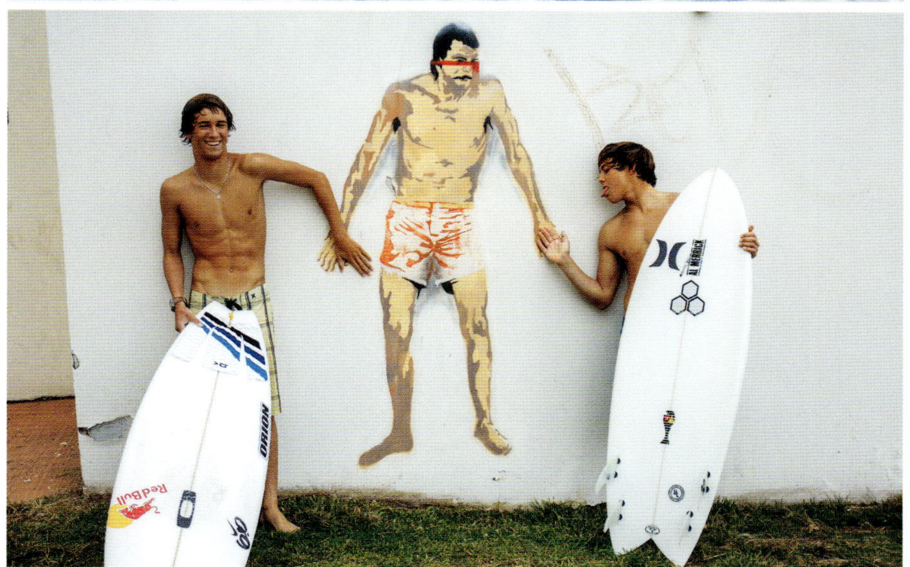

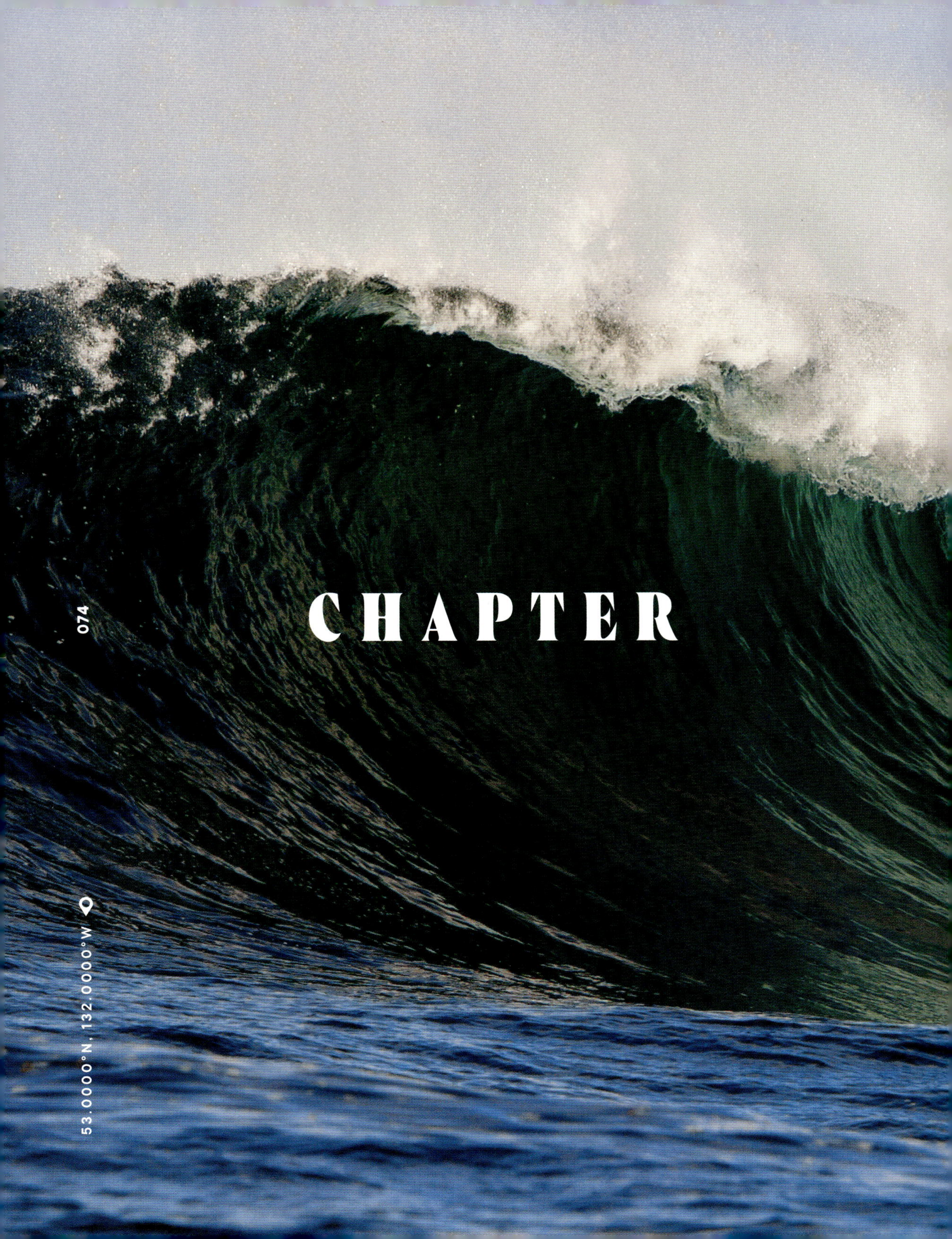
074
CHAPTER
53.0000°N, 132.0000°W

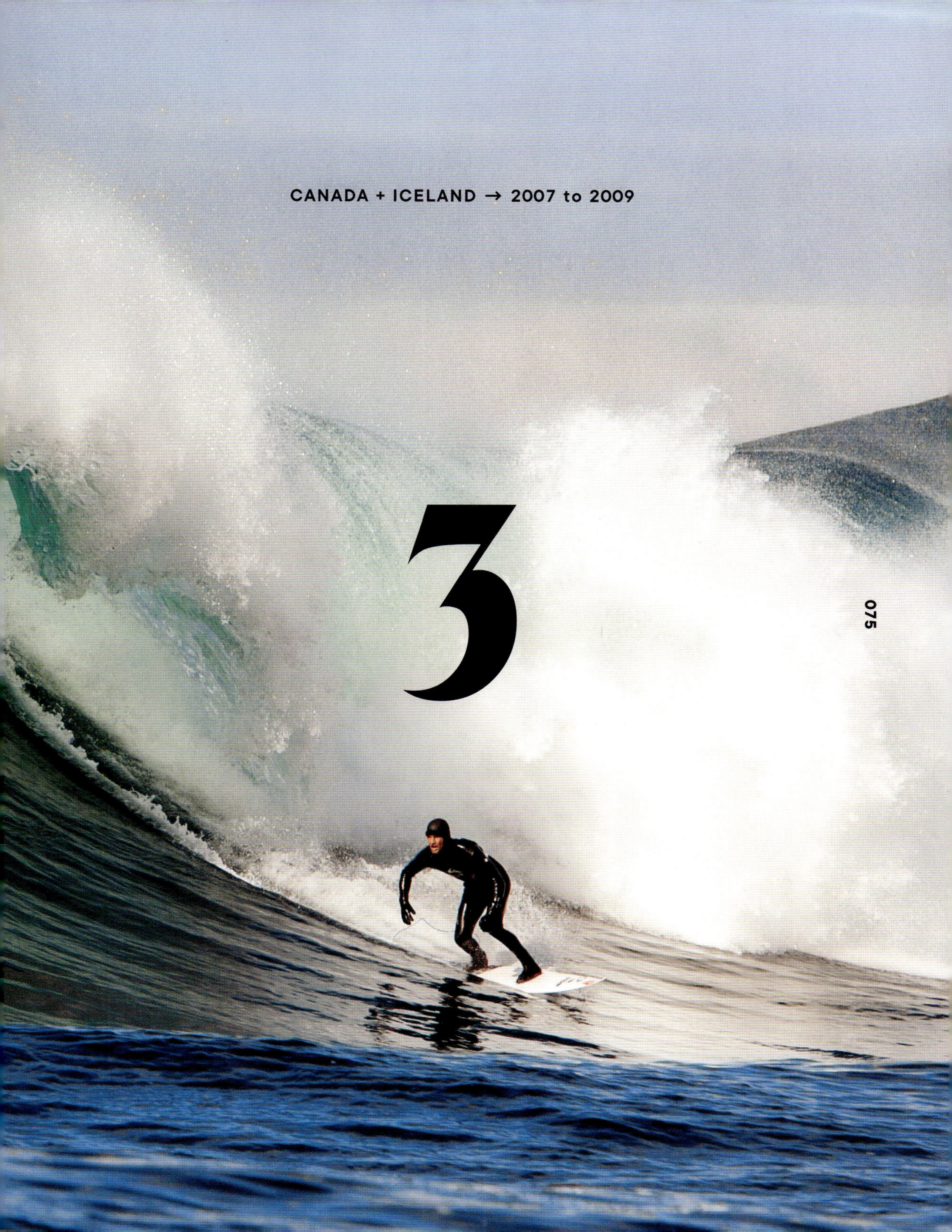

CANADA + ICELAND → 2007 to 2009
3
075

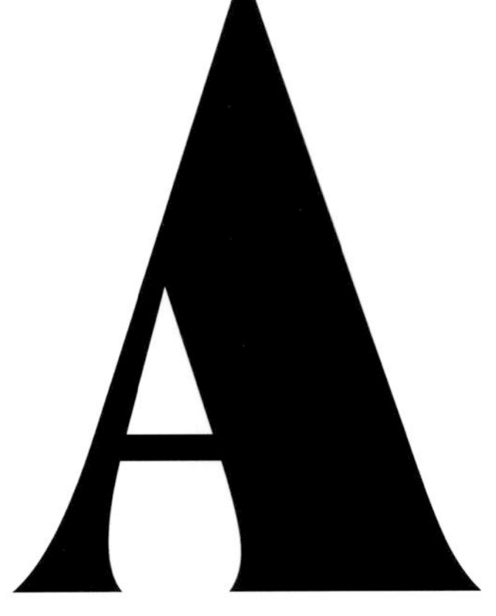

After two long years of burying my own dissatisfaction in order to please my bosses—people who had first given me a chance and continued to provide me with a steady income—the cracks inside grew too deep to ignore. I could sense that I was only reaching the surface of what was possible. There were places that were calling to me, and I felt driven to answer. If I waited for these opportunities, they'd never come. I knew the only way to break free was to start planning my own trips. I also knew that this would require me to make pitches so good and well-thought-out that there was zero chance of them being turned down. My secret weapon was delivered to me in the form of a prolific writer and magazine hustler named Michael Kew.

Michael Kew combined the free spirit of Jack Kerouac with the build and sun-kissed mop of Laird Hamilton. I used to call him "mini Laird." He was like a mad surf-exploring scientist. By the time I met him at the *TransWorld SURF* office in 2006, Kew had already spent five years surfing and atoll-hopping around forgotten specks in the South Pacific. But even a trade wind–loving creature like Kew was getting jaded by equatorial warmth and perfection.

Shortly after I met him, Michael shared with me an idea he had cooked up to head to Haida Gwaii (formerly known as the Queen Charlotte Islands), off the west coast of British Columbia. I felt honored and excited when he offered to bring me along for the ride. We were both craving cold and the uncertainty that came with it. I had finally found someone just as crazy as I was, and I needed the backup when it came time to convince surfers to join us. That trip to the wild, rugged coast of British Columbia was our first adventure together.

I had been fascinated by B.C.'s potential ever since I'd seen an article about it in *Trans-World SURF* years prior. It was frigid and remote, and many parts of it had never been surfed before. We enlisted a hardy crew of surfers willing to trudge through snow and windswept sand to camp among driftwood and paddle out in forty-two-degree water, sheathed in five-millimeter wetsuits plus neoprene hoods, gloves, and booties to brave the ferocious seas. Suiting up for sessions like these feels a bit like going into battle. It ignites a primal part of you, where fun and survival work in instinctual harmony.

If I was going to have any luck delivering the type of photos I had envisioned in this environment, it would only be possible with a passionate crew. Our group included Josh Mulcoy, a lone wolf from Santa Cruz who worked as a landscaper and ditchdigger when he wasn't exploring empty lineups in the Pacific Northwest, Alaska, and Norway; Tyler Smith, another Santa Cruzan, who's been a top competitor at Mavericks—making him one of the best big-wave riders in the world; and Raphael "Raph" Bruhwiler from

South Chesterman Beach in British Columbia's wood-shingled surf town, Tofino. Raph was Canada's first professional surfer.

We arrived on the island to unrelenting blasts of raging wind. The forecast showed gales hitting forty to sixty miles per hour for the next three days. Swell would not be a problem here—West Coast buoys measured thirty-foot faces—but access would be. The few logging roads that existed were covered in snow and dead-ended at wide inlets, steep mountains, and dense rain forest. We all took turns piloting the vehicle and chasing surf-able leads. "Let's see what's down that road" became the ongoing joke of the trip. The truth is, most of them led to nothing but empty logging roads that progressively got less and less drivable. But every so often, one would take us to a remote beach or viewpoint that at least revealed the island's surf potential.

Ultimately, after a lot of trial and error, we realized that the most exposed parts of the coast—with the best potential for waves—were going to require a boat. Raph actually had a specific wave in mind. His brother-in-law, who ran a fishing charter, told him about a "big breaker" (typical fisherman talk for massive surf you want to keep your boat far away from) that he once saw rumbling in near Rennell Sound.

You'd think chartering a boat in a fishing village would be easy, but we had a hard time convincing anyone to chauffeur us on our wild goose chase. Then we met a coast-guardsman named Chumma who had bought a new Boston Whaler that needed to get wet. A few days later we met Chumma and his deckhand Gary at the docks at 5:30 A.M. The treasure hunt started with a sunrise journey down the narrow Skidegate Channel and then on toward a fishing lodge. The details were all there in stick figures on Raph's map, hand-drawn on a disintegrating napkin.

Shrouded behind overgrown green foliage, the weather-beaten wooden lodge finally revealed itself to us. And just beyond the lodge, a quarter mile off the beach, twenty-five-foot sets were angling around a sea crag. The Native name for Haida Gwaii is Xhaa-idlagha Gwaayaai, which in one translation means "islands coming out of concealment." Seeing this mythical wave felt like a gift from the Native spirits that inhabit these lands.

Raph and Tyler quickly sprang into action and were the first ones to dive off the

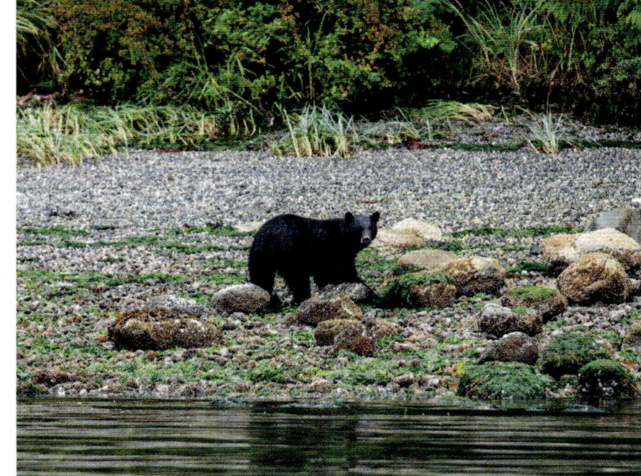

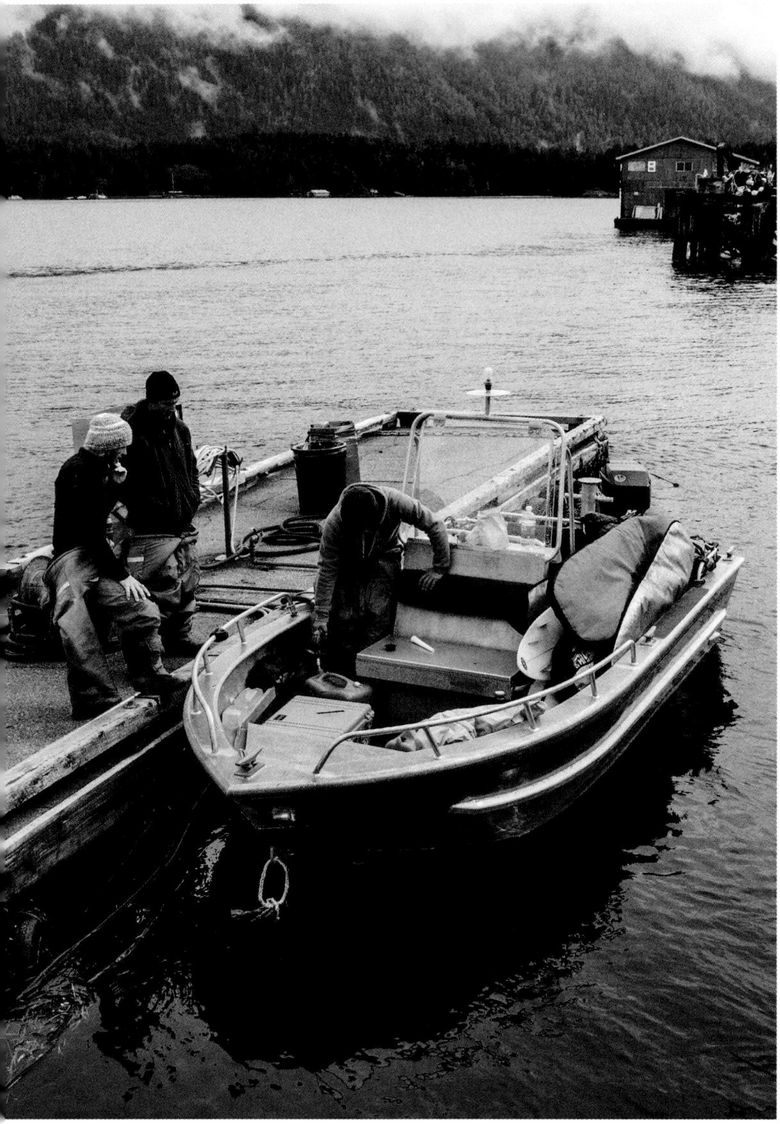

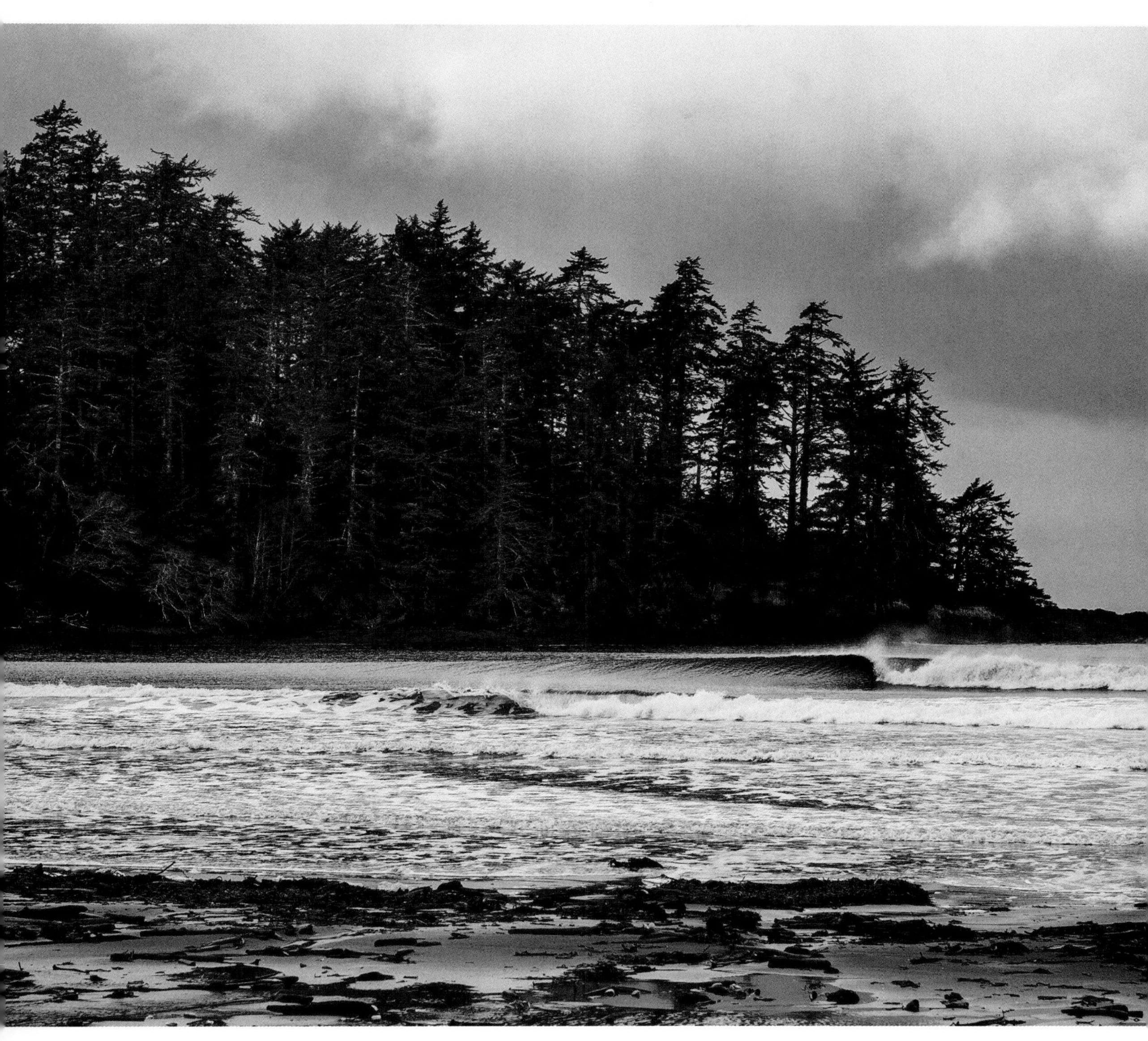

CHRIS BURKARD
WAYWARD

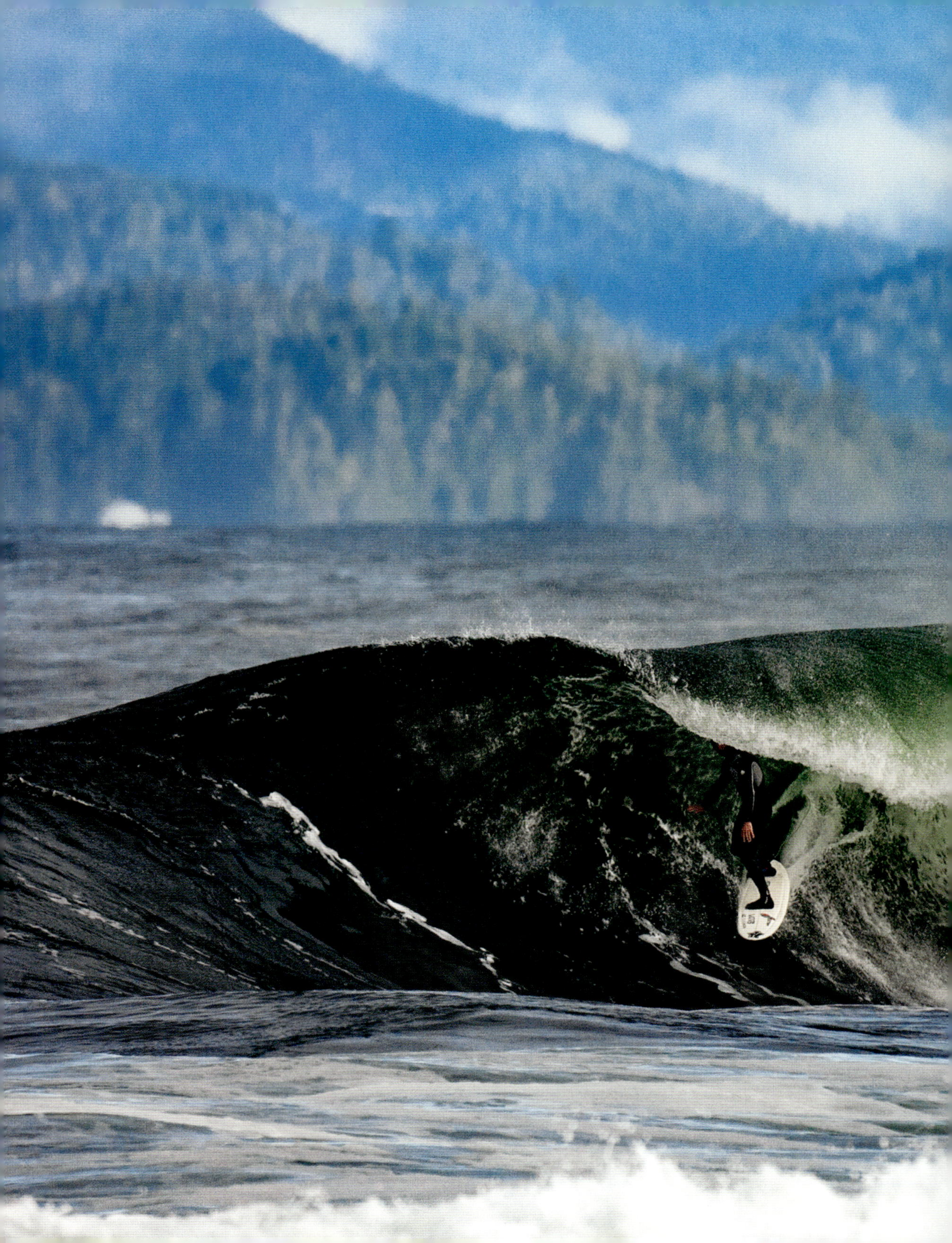

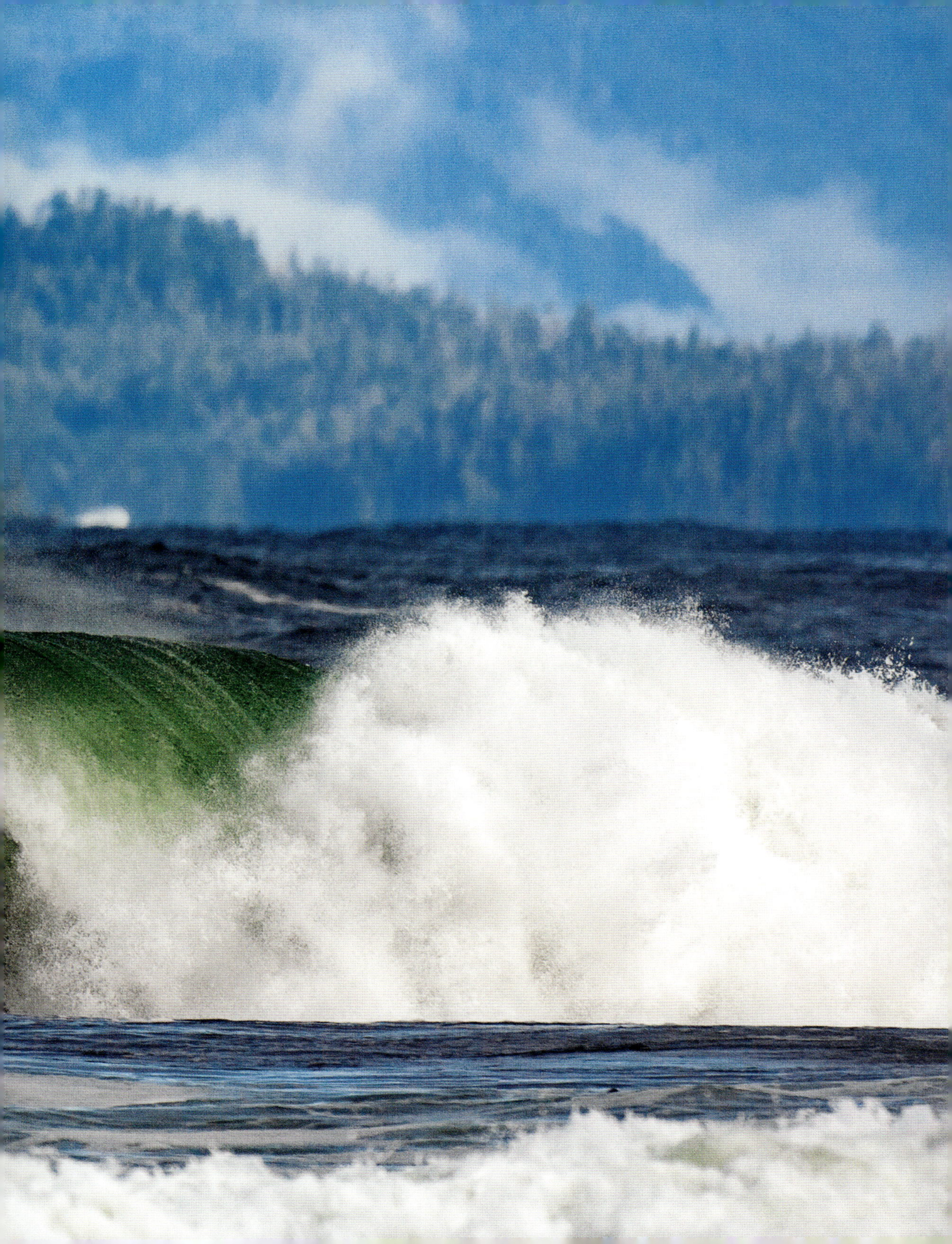

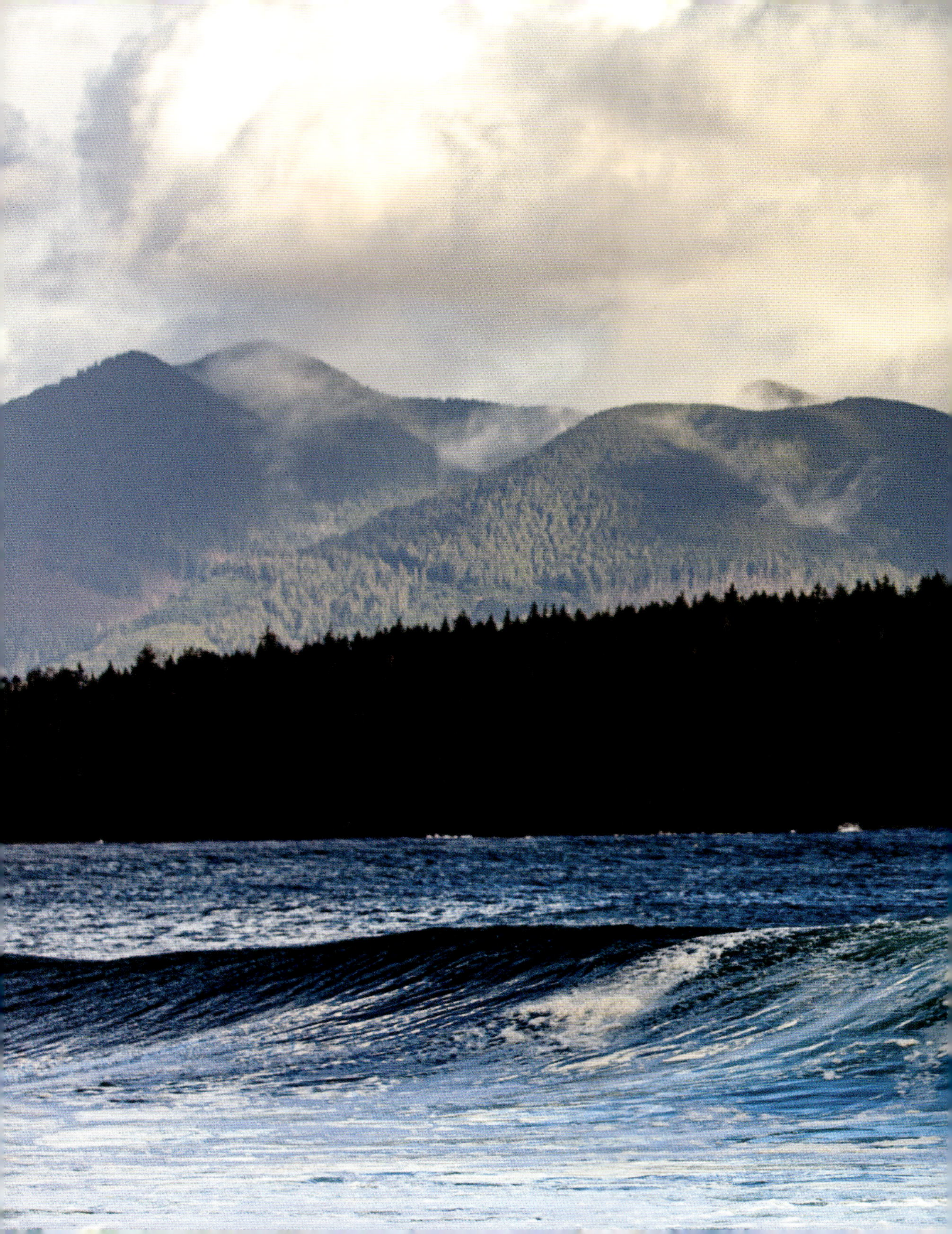

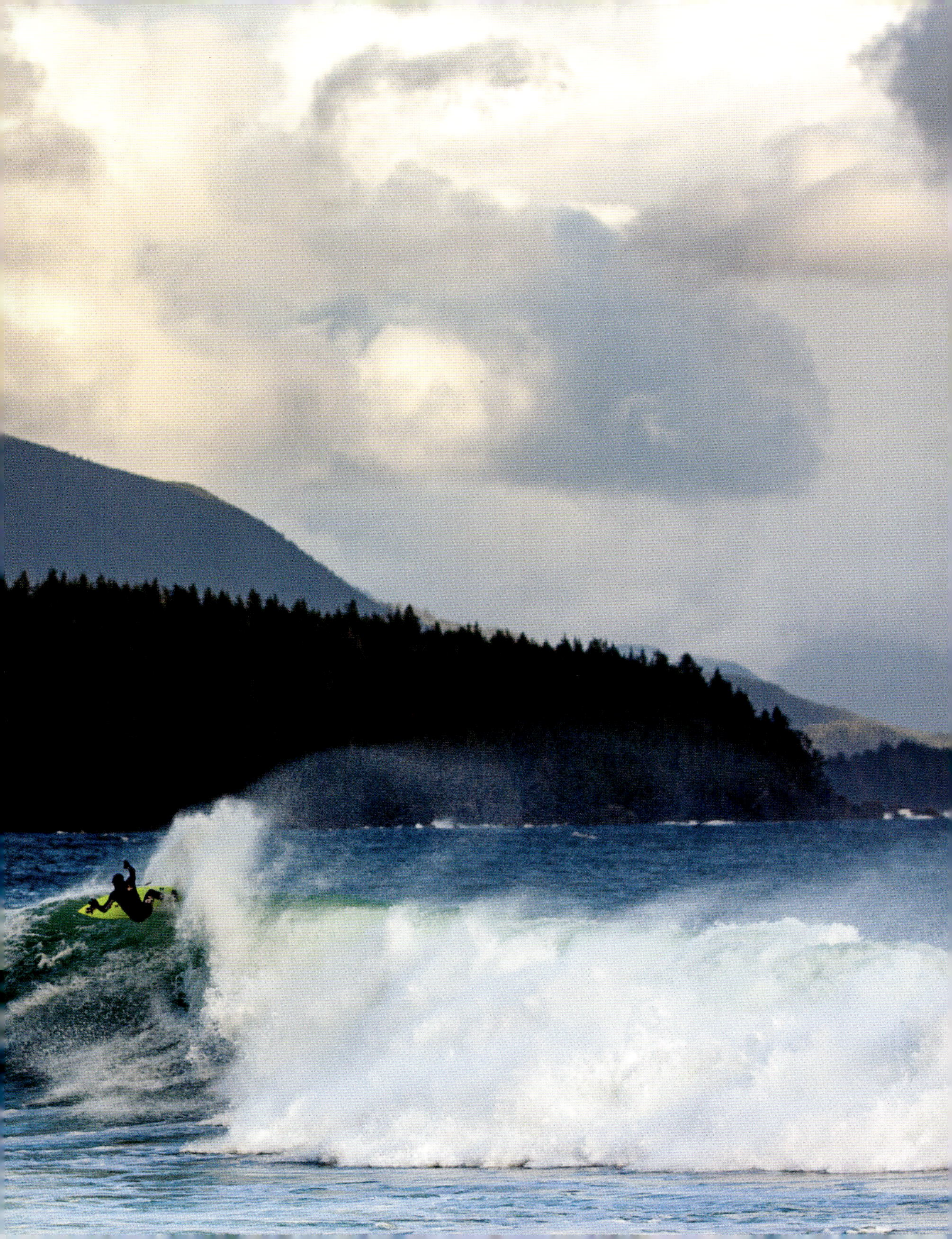

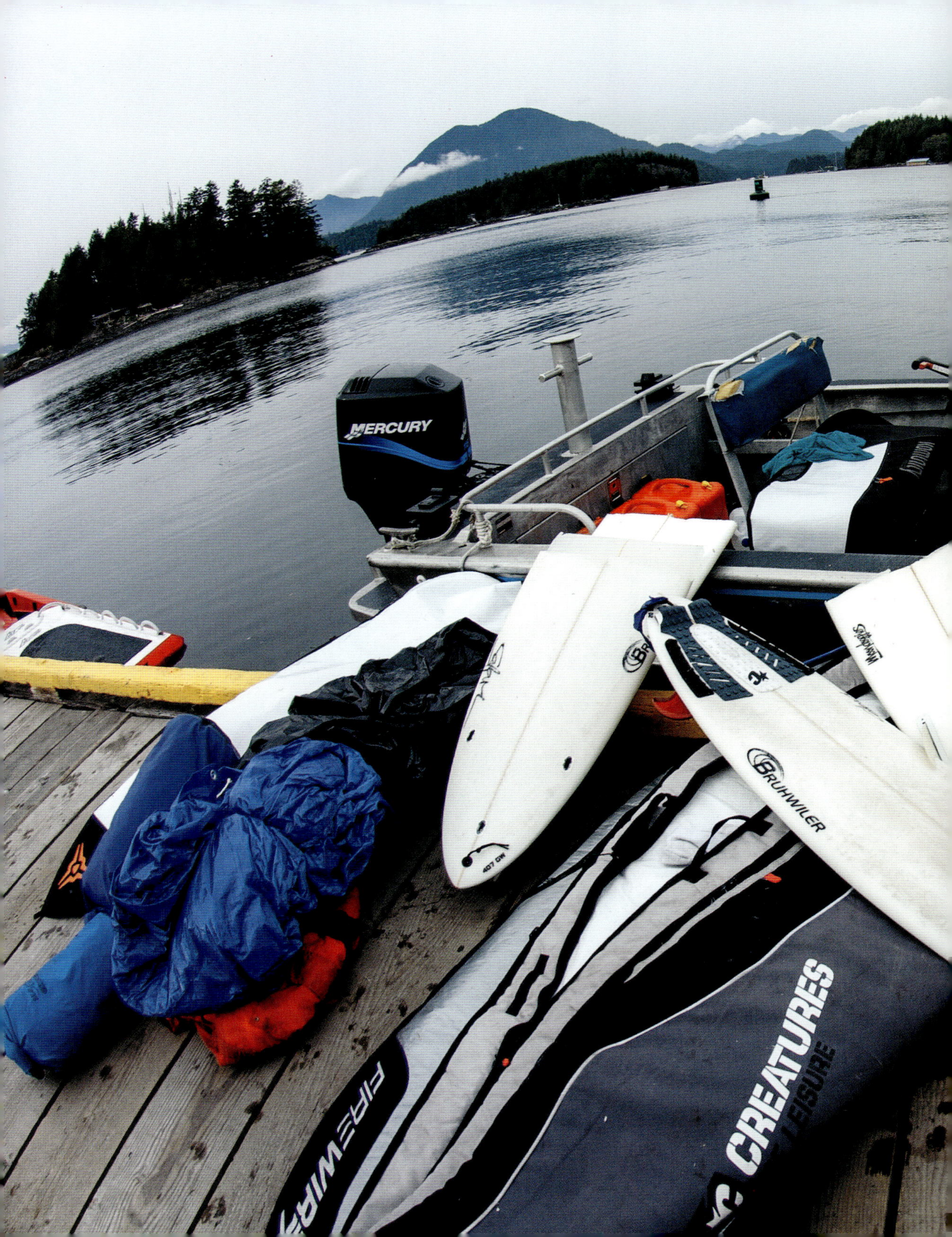
MERCURY
CREATURES
LEISURE
BRUHWILER

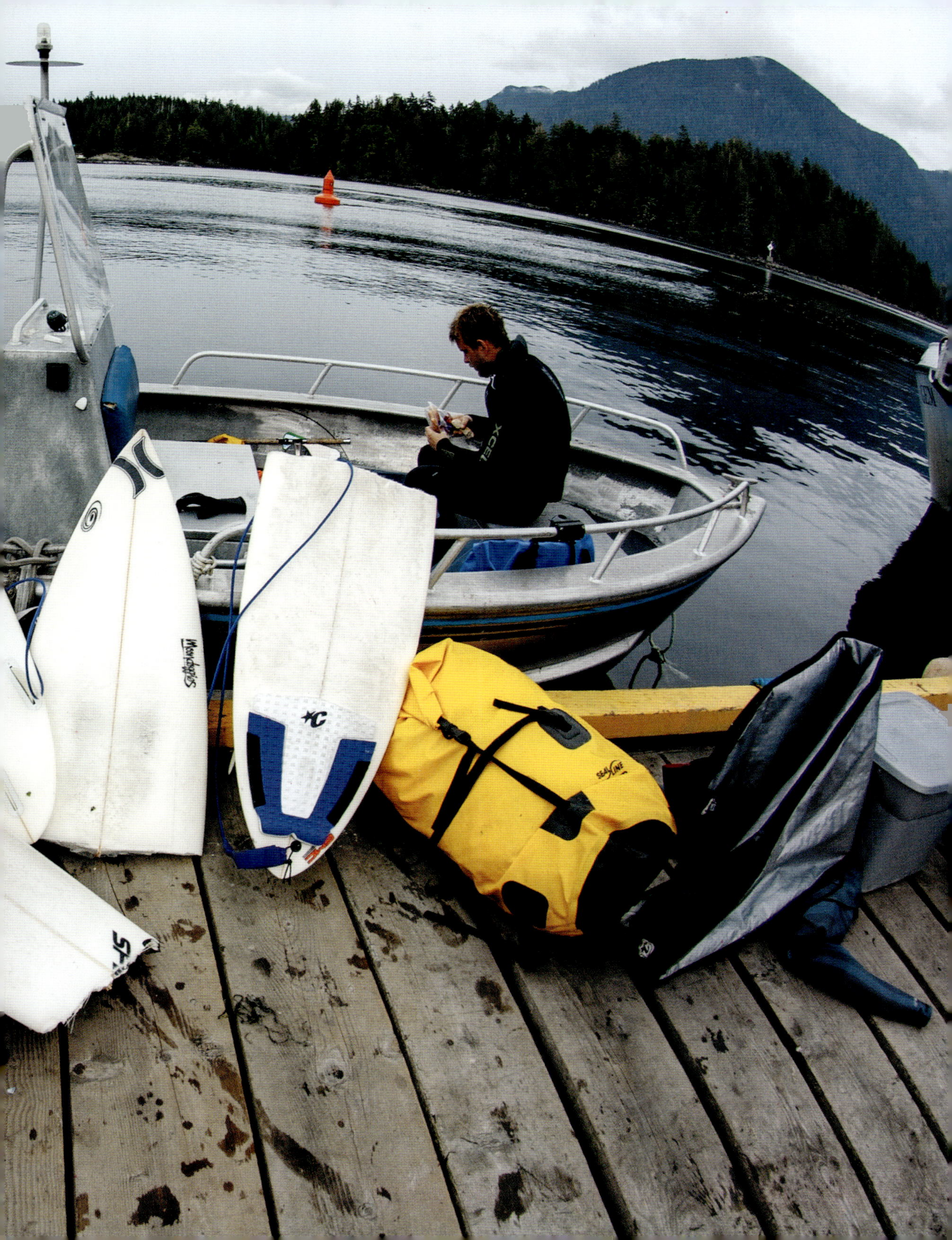

boat with their boards. Josh moved at a methodical pace until the second he hit water, and then he morphed into a freakishly fast amphibian. With expert skill, Chumma and Gary anchored us into a nice sightline on the shoulder of the wave, clearly proud to have played a part in delivering our dream. I spent the next few hours grateful I didn't easily suffer from motion sickness as I bobbed back and forth, shooting until my fingers cramped and my feet went numb.

The sun shone all day long, warming our spirits in a way that can only really be appreciated after a week of relentless rain, wind, and darkness. Never had I felt so alert and alive. In that moment I thanked my lucky stars that Raph was just as much of a conspiracy theorist as the rest of us, believing in his wrinkled-up piece of passed-on folklore. The session culminated with a photo of Raph edging into a bomber set that, at the time, was the biggest Canadian wave ever documented.

I wondered how many other myths I had heard whispers of that might also turn out to be true.

Canada set off a chain reaction in my professional life. I now had a list a mile long of next potential adventures. I had new hunting grounds to explore and felt more focused than ever. I was hungry to search for more untouched surf folklore, the colder the better. The more the potential for suffering, the higher the chance of growth and reward. And as if I willed it to be, I received a magazine assignment that was everything I could ask for.

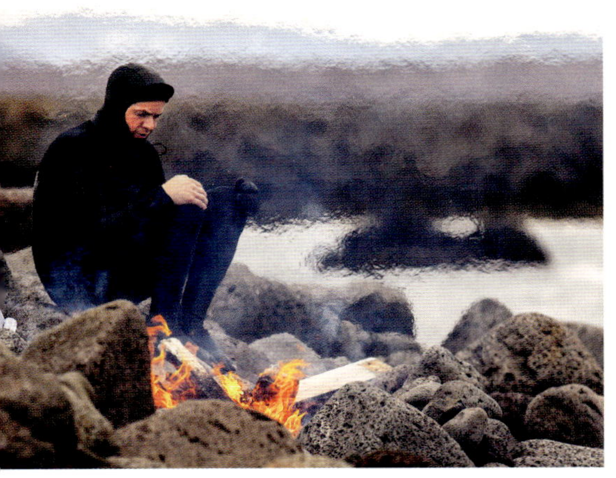

Men's Journal hired me to travel to Iceland to photograph Huntington Beach surfer Timmy Turner. Timmy and I had shot together all winter back on the Central Coast, and he mentioned my name to the magazine's photo editor. Timmy went out on a limb, trusting a hungry young up-and-comer like me to help document and share this opportunity with him. It's because of Timmy and people like him that I was awarded most of the best experiences of my career.

Timmy was a walking miracle. The fact that he was alive and chasing waves, let alone Arctic ones, was surreal to say the least. It had only been a few years since Timmy narrowly survived a horrific medically resistant staph infection that put him into a coma. The deadly bacteria ate through a big chunk of his sinus cavity, brain, and skull. Most of the left side of his skull was removed and later reconstructed. Sewing it back together created the gnarliest scar you've ever seen, which runs from his right ear up to his widow's peak and then loops back around his head like the stitching on a baseball.

Because of this ordeal, Timmy could no longer surf in tropical destinations, since the risk of reinfection was too high. But rather than feeling sorry for himself like most people would, Timmy dove into cold-water surfing with the same fervor that he had brought to the tropics. In true Timmy fashion, his mental and physical road to recovery involved chasing down frigid waves in Alaska, Ireland, New York, and now Iceland. He was documenting the experience for his fifth surf film, *Cold Thoughts*. This film would become the sequel to his 2004 movie *Second Thoughts*, about a feral experience surfing and living in the bush of West Java. This was a film I spent countless hours watching and rewatching with my friends in high school. I never could have guessed I would play a part in its follow-up.

Timmy lived for simple and savage experiences. Following the advice of his friend and surf photographer Dustin Humphrey, who had recently traveled to Iceland and scored, Timmy planned a spring adventure around the unexplored northern coast. His dream was to camp in the snow and ride heavy Arctic barrels, far from the already discovered reefs of the Reykjanes Peninsula.

Iceland is an island in the middle of the North Atlantic that literally gets pounded by swell on all sides. With only a handful of local surfers, most of the island hadn't even been explored for surf at this point. The possibility of discovering new waves no one in the world had even experienced yet was what dreams were made of. Unfortunately, for all of its crazy surf potential, Iceland also holds its fair share of deterrents and obstacles. It was the most expensive trip I could dream up, with pricey flights, ridiculous gas prices, and limited options for lodging. Despite being on my radar for years, it just seemed unattainable, which made the magazine assignment such a gift. I decided to invite a couple of other surfers, Josh Mulcoy and Sam Hammer, and turn it into an exploration of the country and its surf breaks.

Despite feeling strangely familiar, landing in Reykjavík was like landing on another planet—one covered in lava rock, every type of moss, and more waterfalls than you could possibly count. We weren't even ten miles past the airport before we found perfect waves. An old naval base had recently opened to the public, providing us with safe access to the beach where there previously wasn't any. We cleverly dubbed the new wave "Airport Slabs." Shocked that we found surf so quickly, we prayed this luck would follow us for the remainder of the trip.

We spent the next two weeks driving treacherous mountain passes through

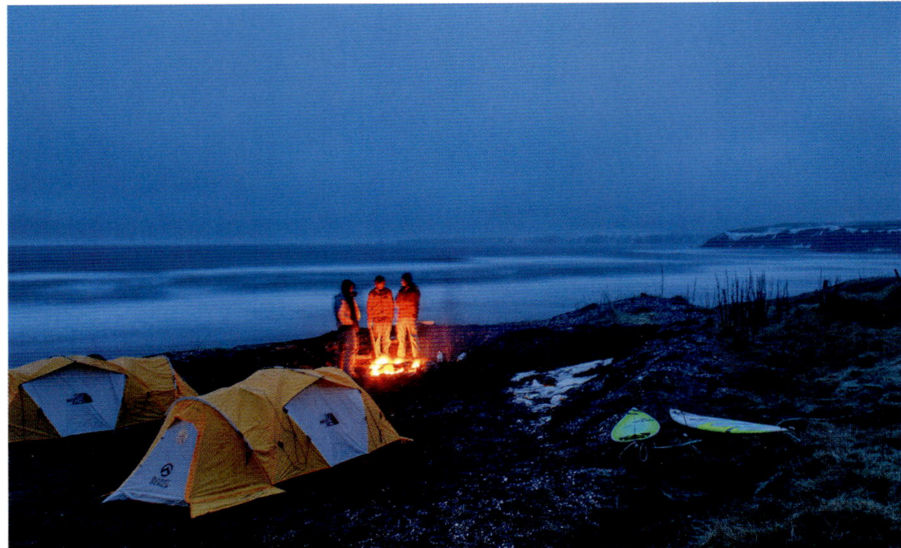

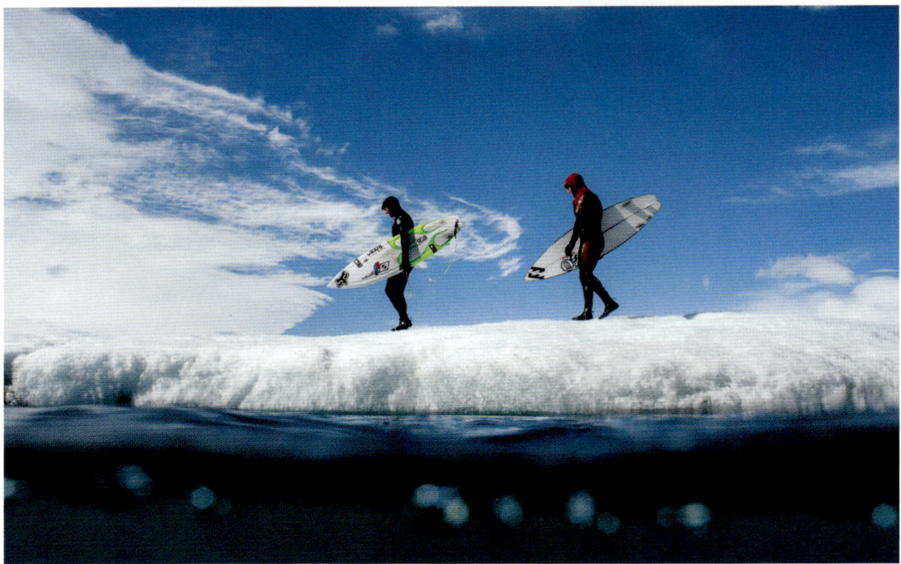

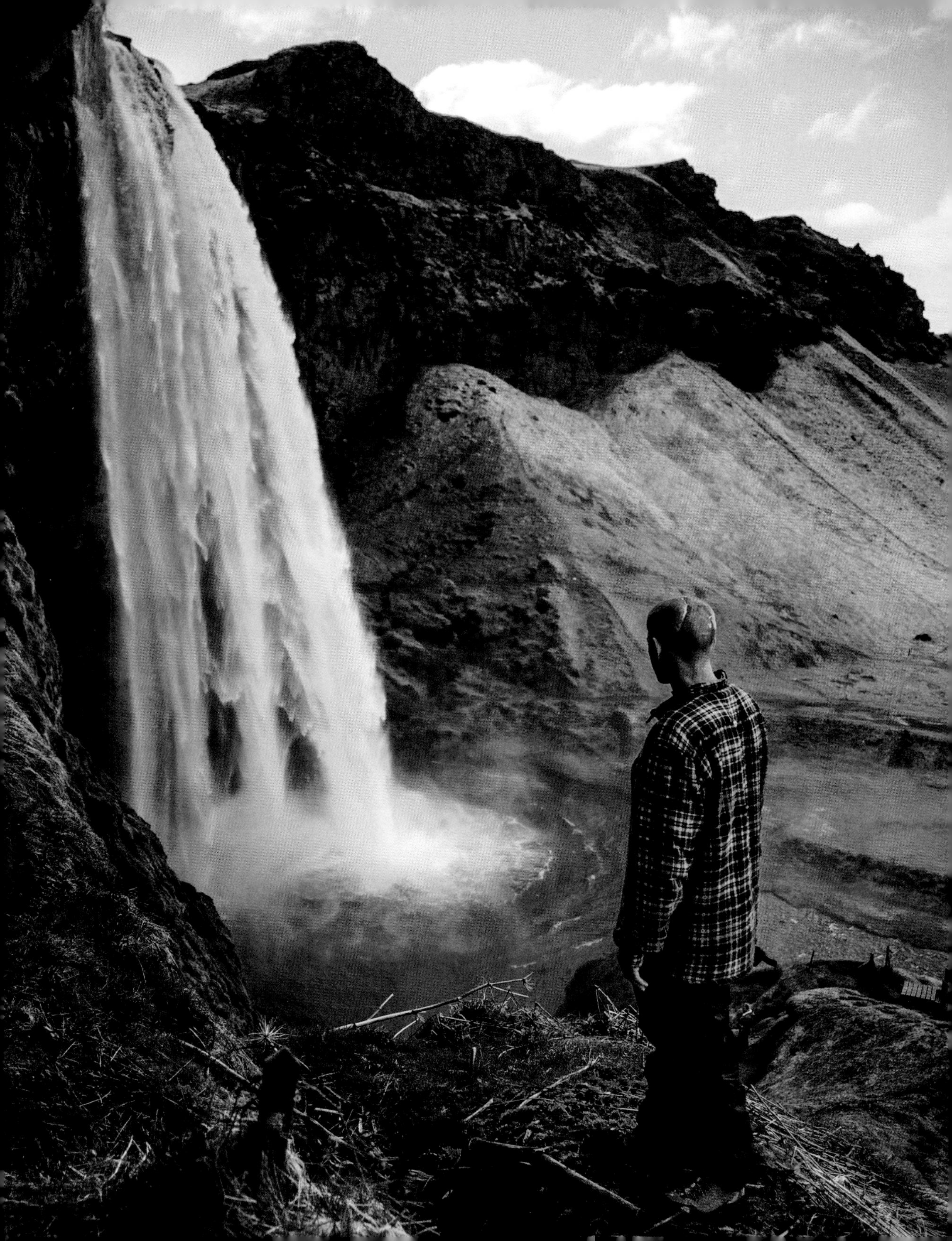

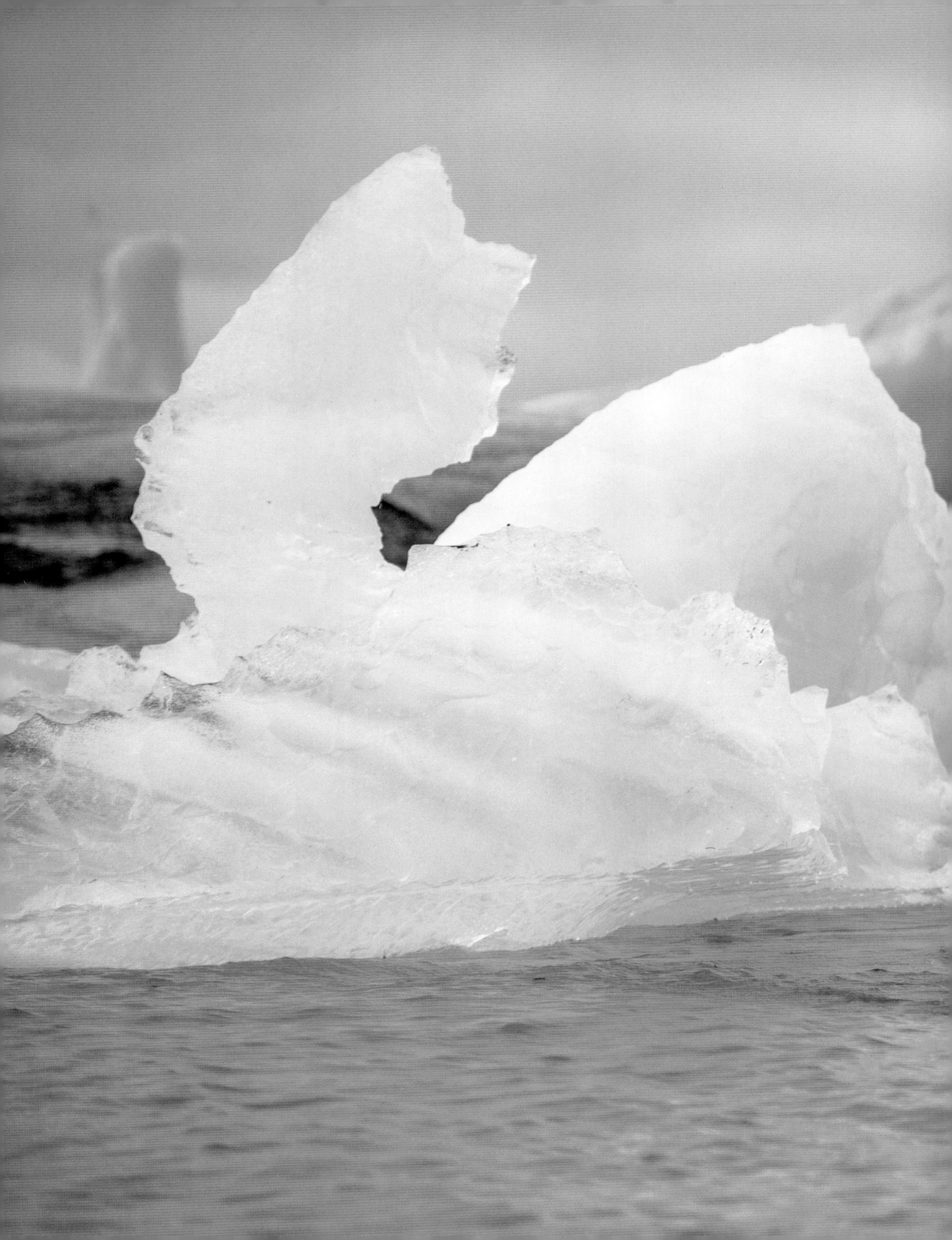

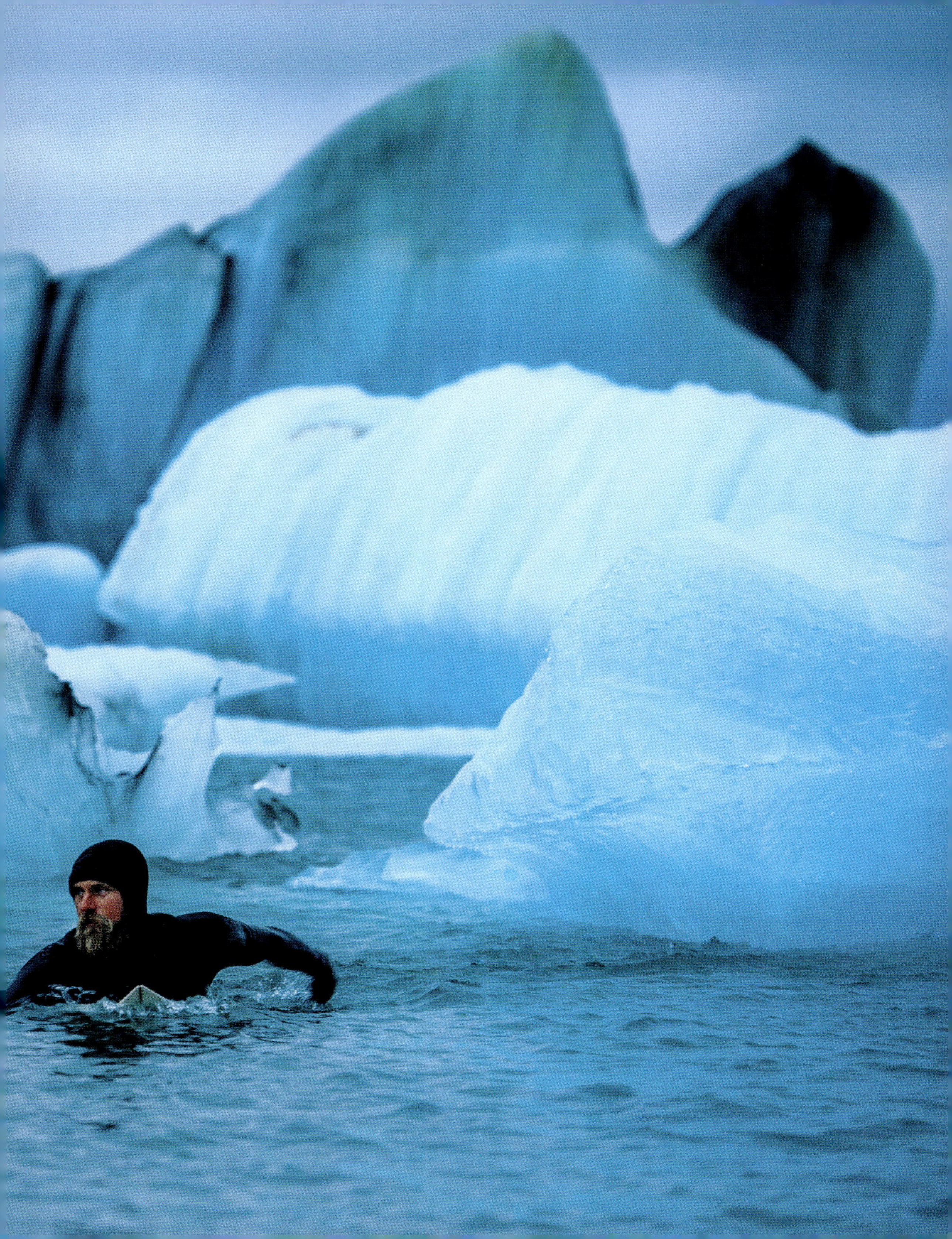

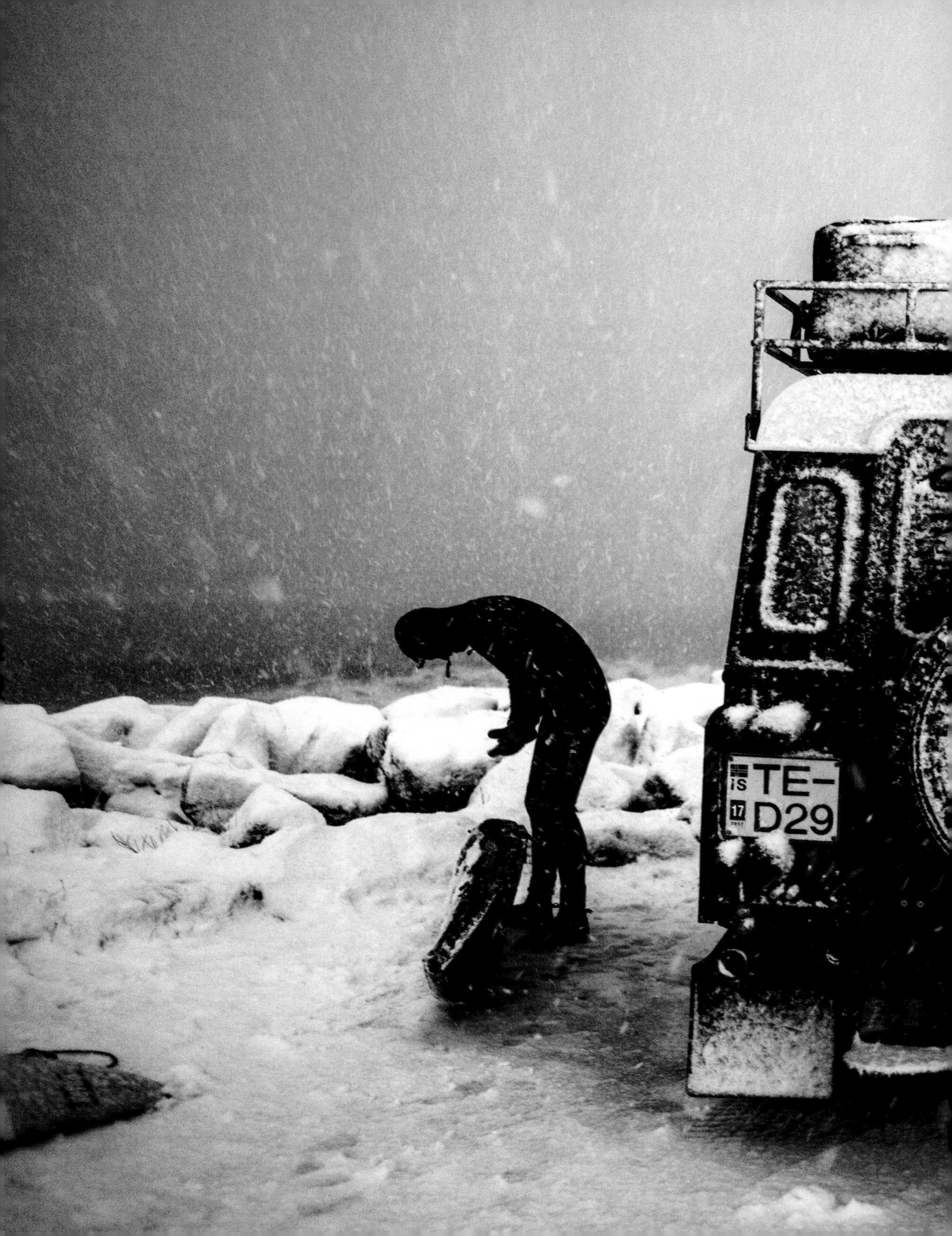

iS
TE-
D29

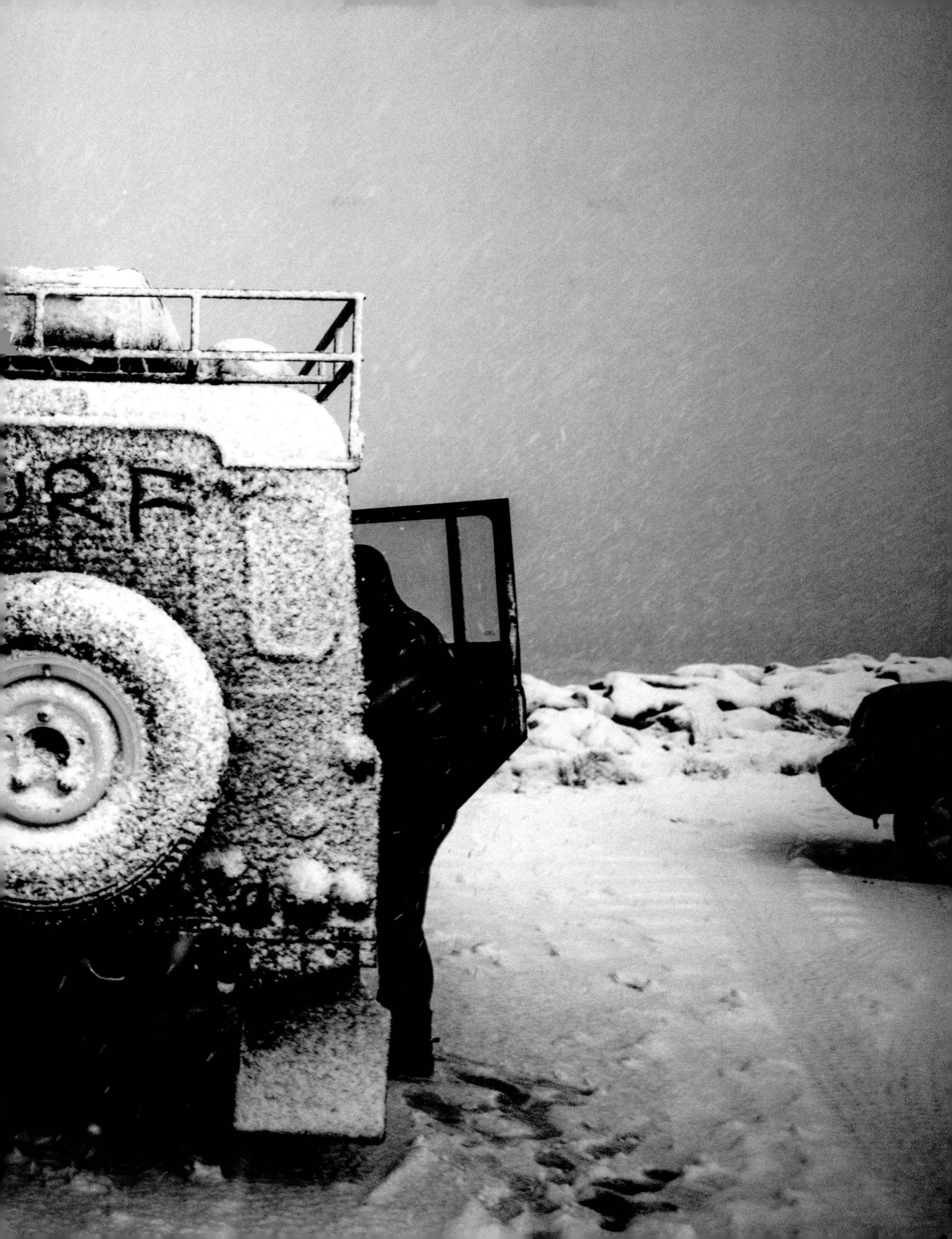

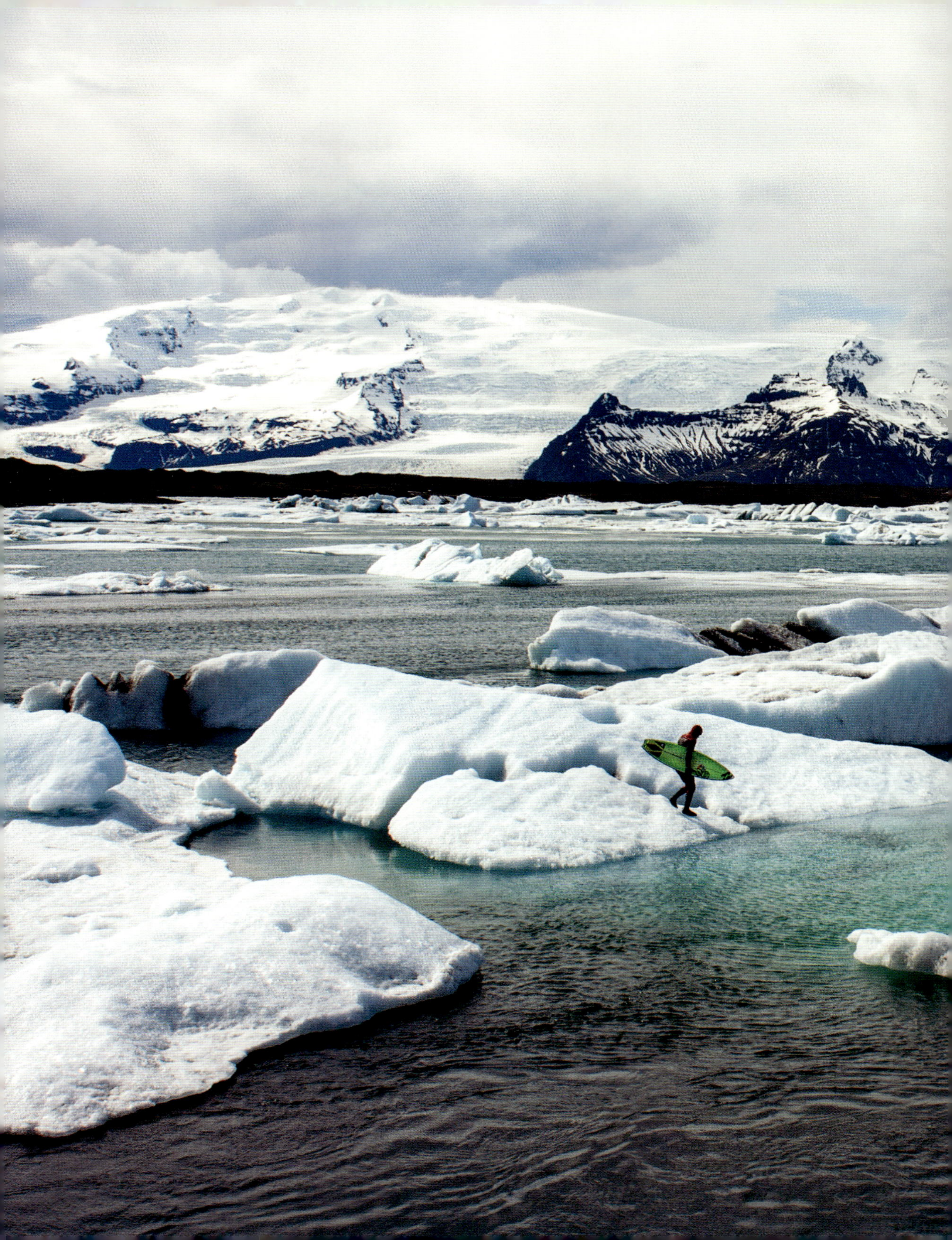

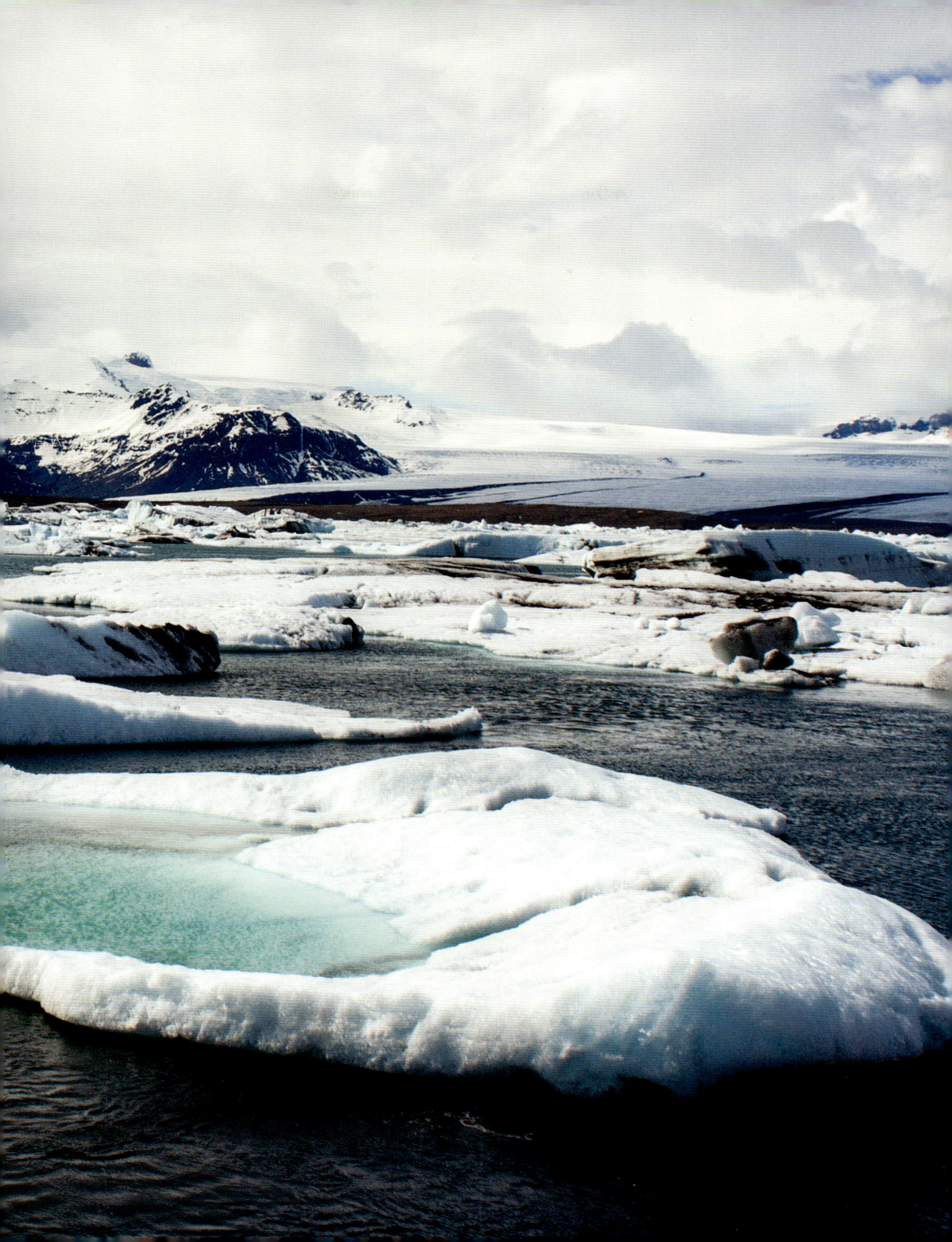

spontaneous storms and camping on frosted beaches, where we'd wake up to fresh surf and snow. Just when the gray sky and April chill would start getting us down, a friendly local would invite us to use their sauna and eat some Arctic char. The spirit of the people cast as strong a spell on us as the landscape had. To solidify our enchantment, there were no other surfers or tourists in sight, just bleating sheep and cracking waves.

We circumnavigated much of the 3,700-mile coastline and found so much more than swell. I couldn't get enough of the light shifting across barren moonscapes backed by rain, rainbows, snow, wind, and waves. I honestly didn't know so much untamed beauty could exist in such a small place, and a spark ignited in me to document it. Iceland was far and away the first country I had been to that felt truly wild. A part of me woke up there, a part I hadn't realized was sleeping. In the far corners of these Arctic fjords, I felt I had found one of the world's last quiet places. If Haida Gwaii was my gateway drug, then Iceland began my full-on addiction to cold-water surf travel. It was as if the shared trauma of freezing water, harsh weather, and dramatic problem-solving brought me closer to myself and to the friends I was traveling with. Iceland had changed me in those few short weeks, and it had the power to change anyone who gave it a chance.

Even Timmy succumbed to its call to grow and let go. Completely unannounced, he pulled over at a gas station to shave his head. He had been growing out his hair to cover his scar, and in the middle of one of our marathon drives, he decided he couldn't stand hiding it any longer. There was no premeditation, just an overwhelming urge. Outside in the snow, while the temperature hovered around fifteen degrees Fahrenheit, he seemed unfazed with the hair that blew off his freshly shaved scalp into the cold wind. Hopping back into the car, we all looked at each other and then back at Timmy, who seemed much calmer without the weight of his hair or his hiding.

The biggest blessing of having Timmy along to experience Iceland with me was that he attacked it with the passion of someone who wasn't going to take a single second for granted. In the eerie calm of a rare windless night, he and I decided to camp under the stars, which is unheard of in Iceland in

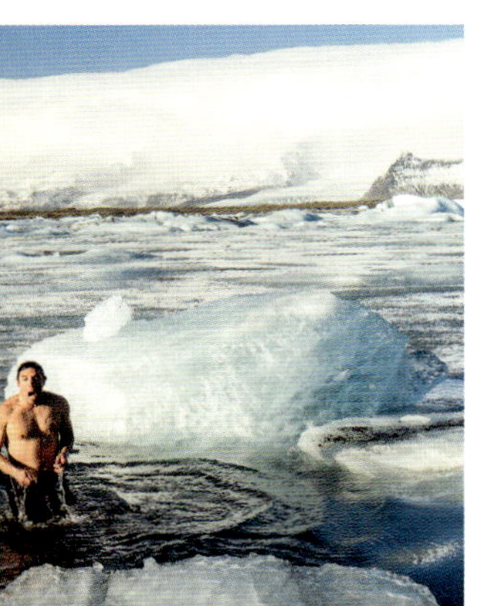

early April. The landscape was barely easing out of winter, but something just felt right. If Timmy was going to do it, I sure as heck was going to do it with him. The other guys decided to sleep in the van, so it was just Timmy and me who lay in our sleeping bags with no tent, beside a dimming fire.

Given that it was late in the season, I was silently considering the dwindling likelihood I would see the northern lights on this trip. With few words between us, I watched the sky and connected the blanket of familiar stars like I had a million times before. Then, out of nowhere, this celestial body that had always looked so familiar and stable suddenly began transforming and taking shape. For the briefest of moments, I felt com-

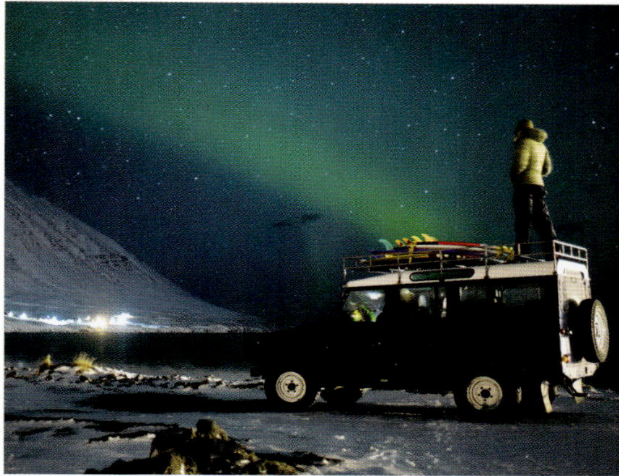

pletely out of my body and scared. Seeing those first green lights start to dance was as perplexing as if the sun didn't rise. My heart was racing, but I didn't even reach for the camera. Not only did I not have a clue how to photograph it, but I also didn't want to miss a single moment. Knowing how fleeting the northern lights can be, I surrendered to the spiritual experience and decided to just take it all in.

We have no idea how long it lasted—it could have been minutes or hours—but as the flow of lights started to die down, Timmy and I reflected on our own insignificance. He expressed how grateful he was to be alive, and I was grateful to him for reminding me that I was, too.

When I returned home from Iceland, tunnel vision set in. I put every ounce of focus I had on getting my next fix of cold, uncharted surf. My passion turned quickly into obsession, and in a matter of a few short months my goals for the future had shifted. Night after night, I would kiss my wife good night and retreat back to my corner of the barn to study Google Earth, blogs, and WannaSurf forums for intel. It wasn't uncommon for me to get back to bed around 2:00 or 3:00 A.M. with bloodshot eyes and a nagging sore neck. My tiny office nook began to look like a conspiracy theorist's den, with pixelated printed photos and a plethora of random website and GPS coordinates scrawled on highlighted sticky notes.

I found it liberating to just look at a map and start to dream about what might exist beyond those distant shores. And the only way to find out was to go.

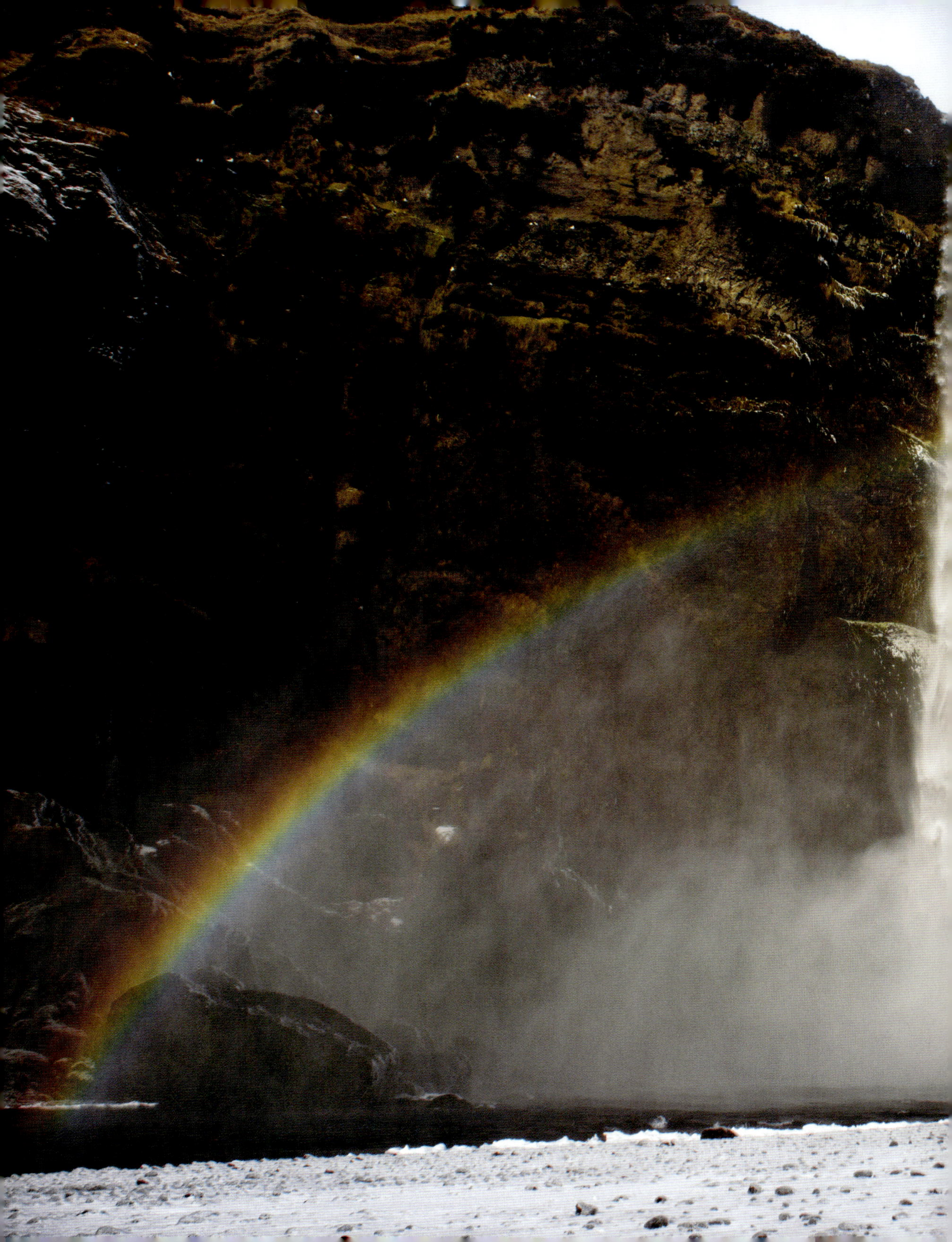

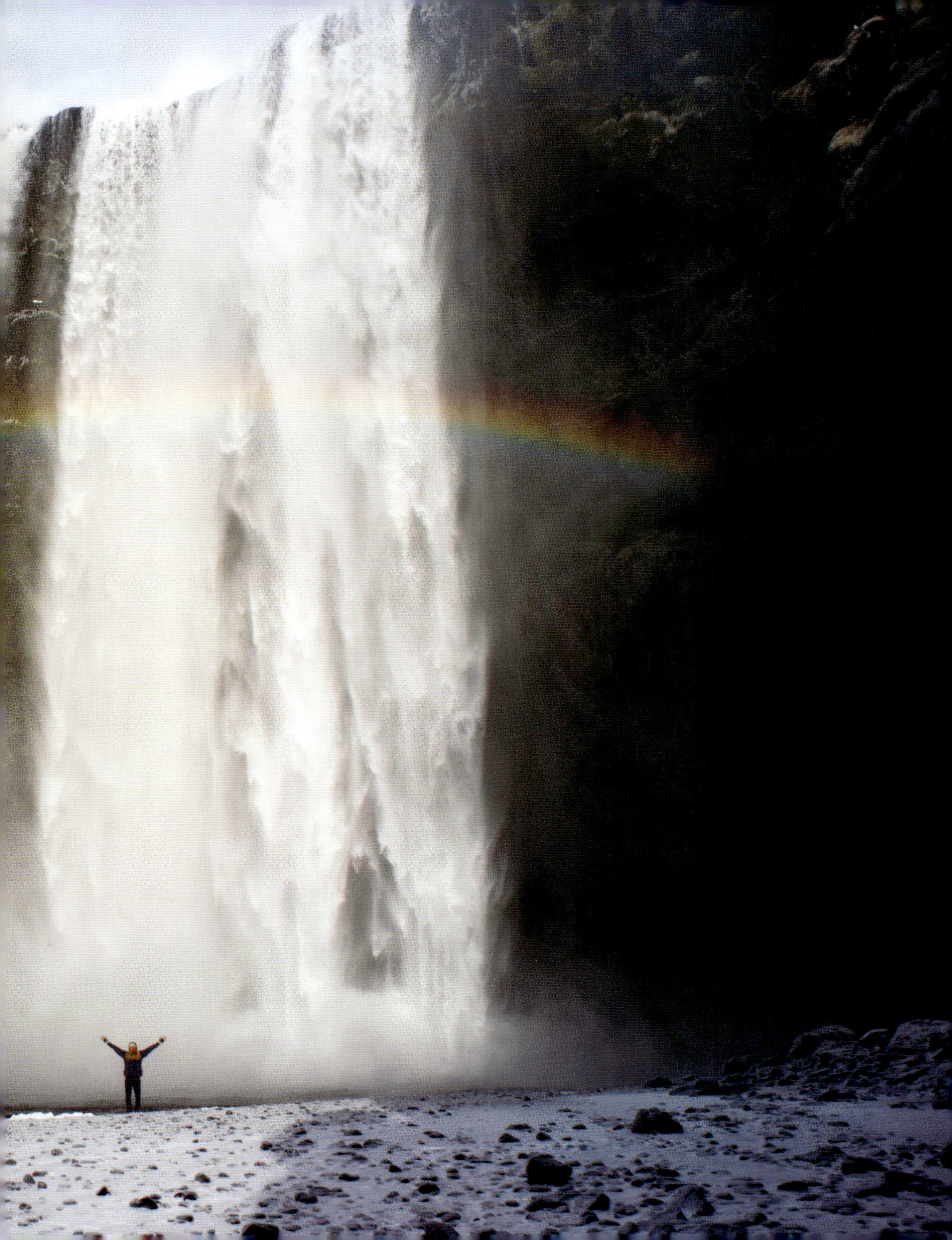

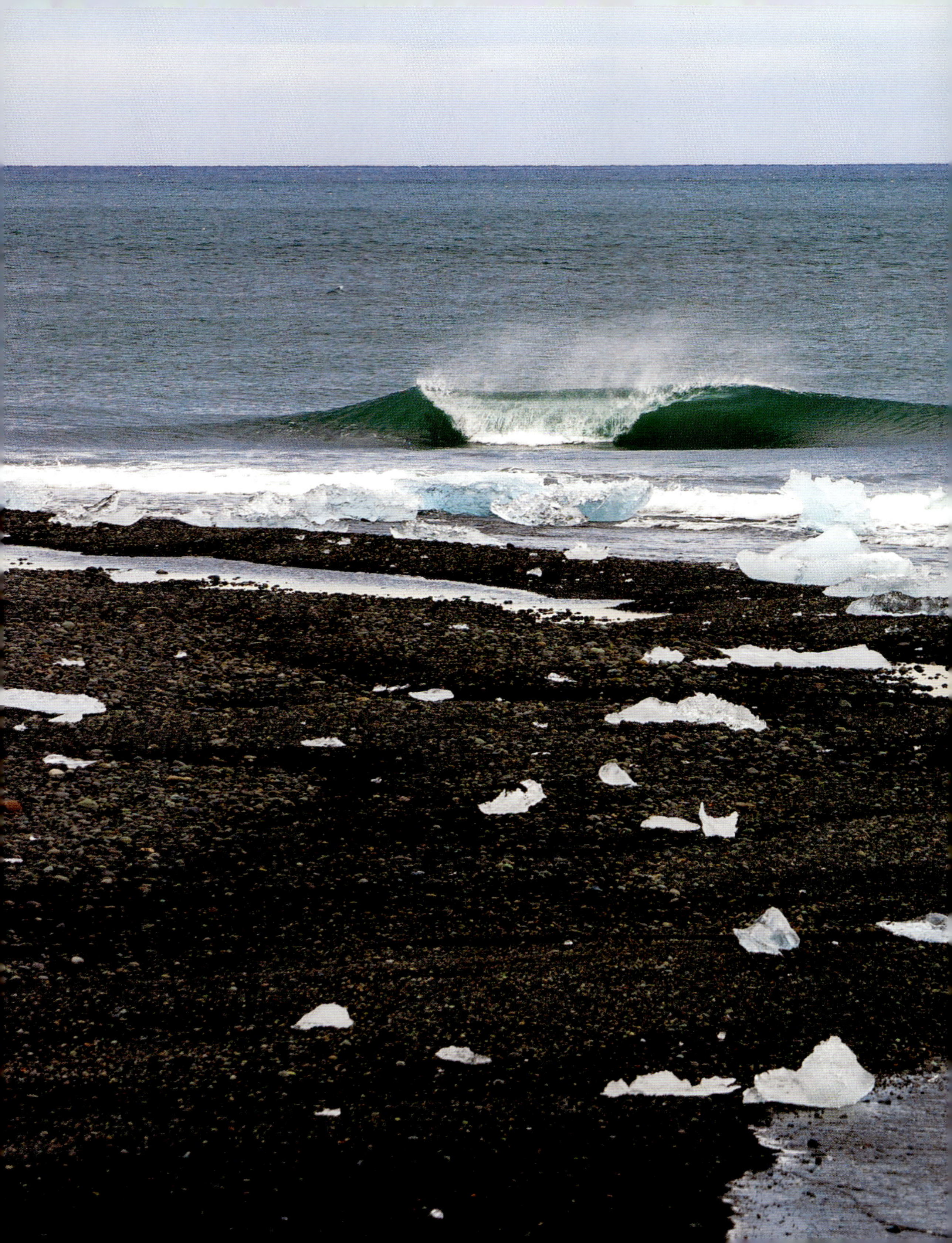

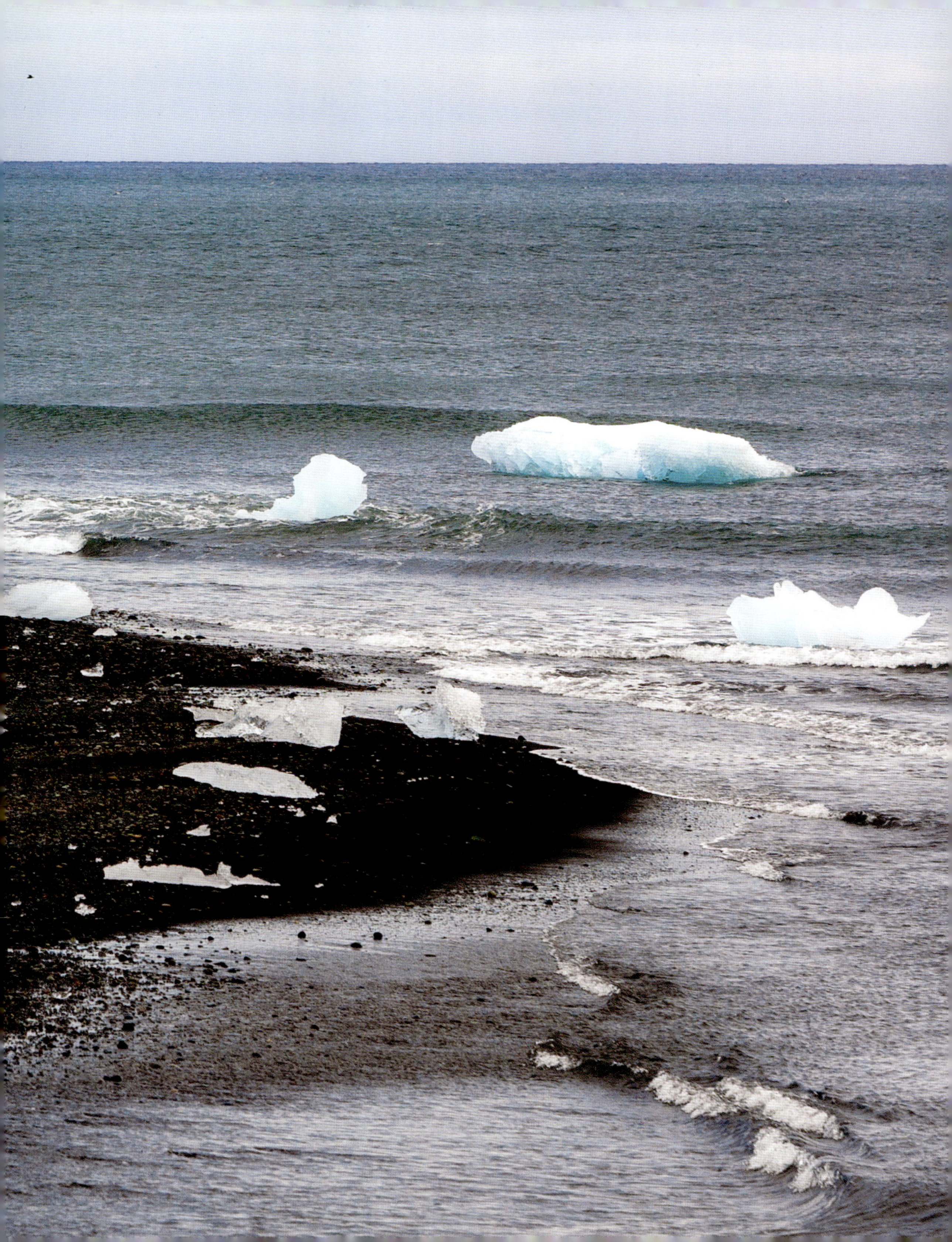

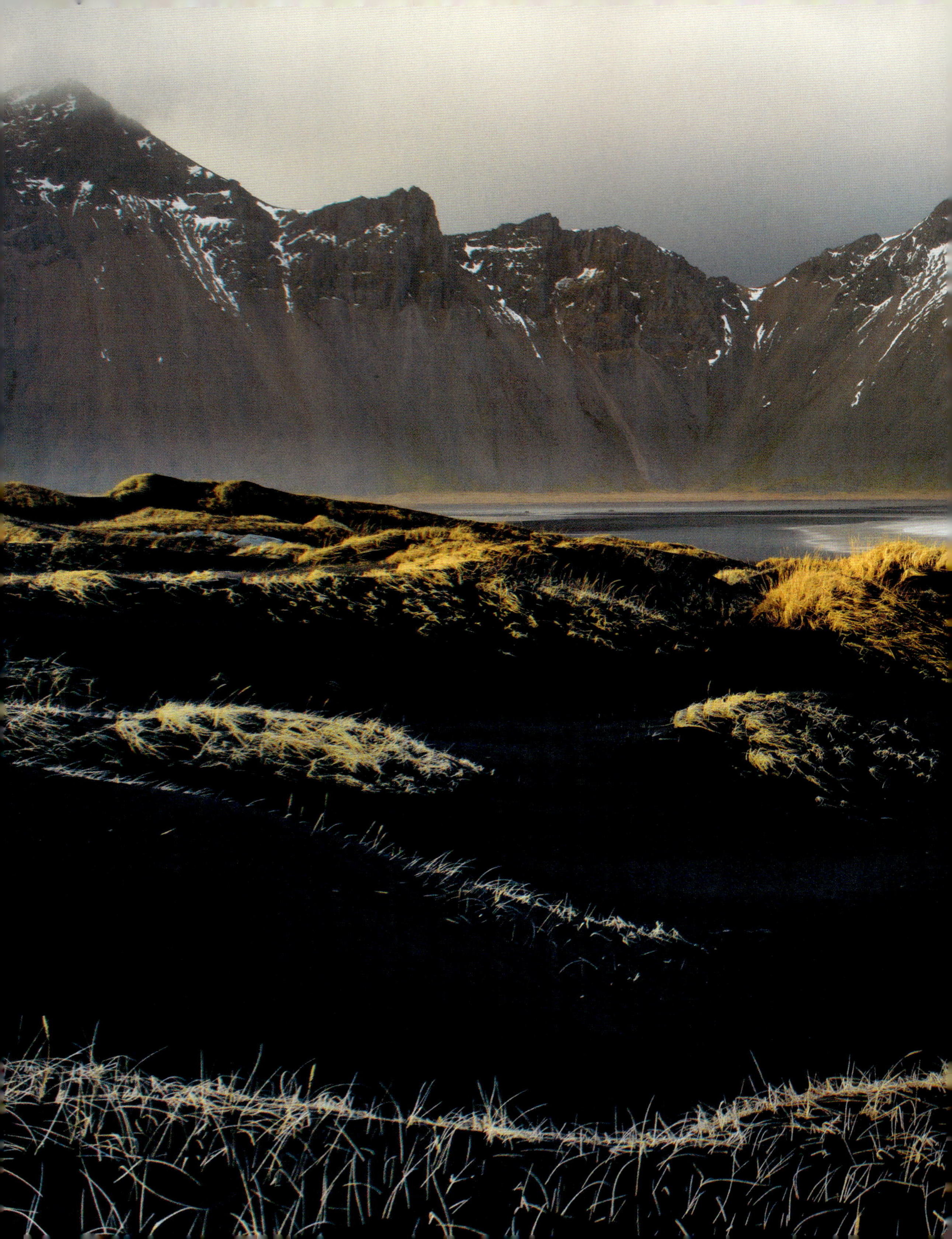

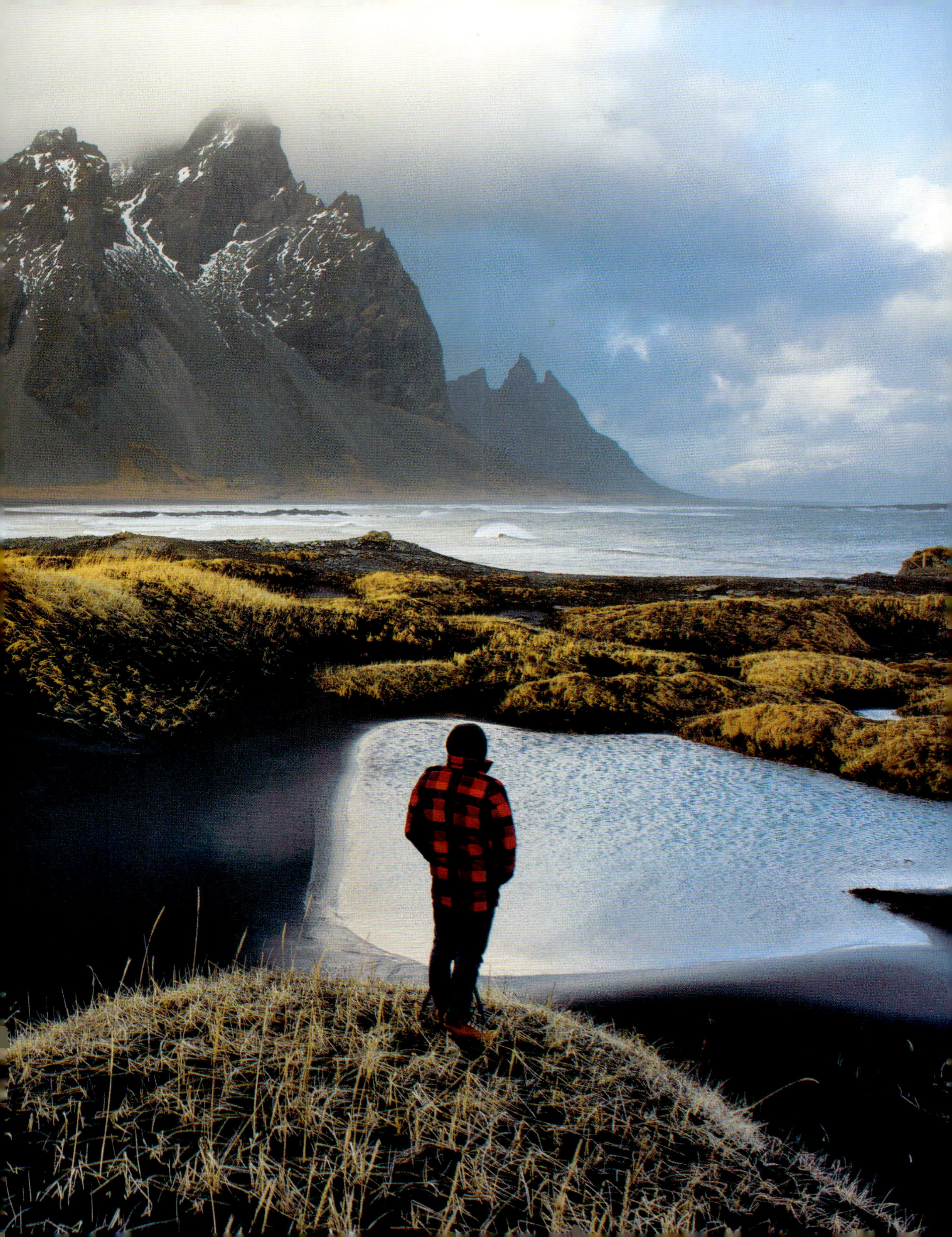

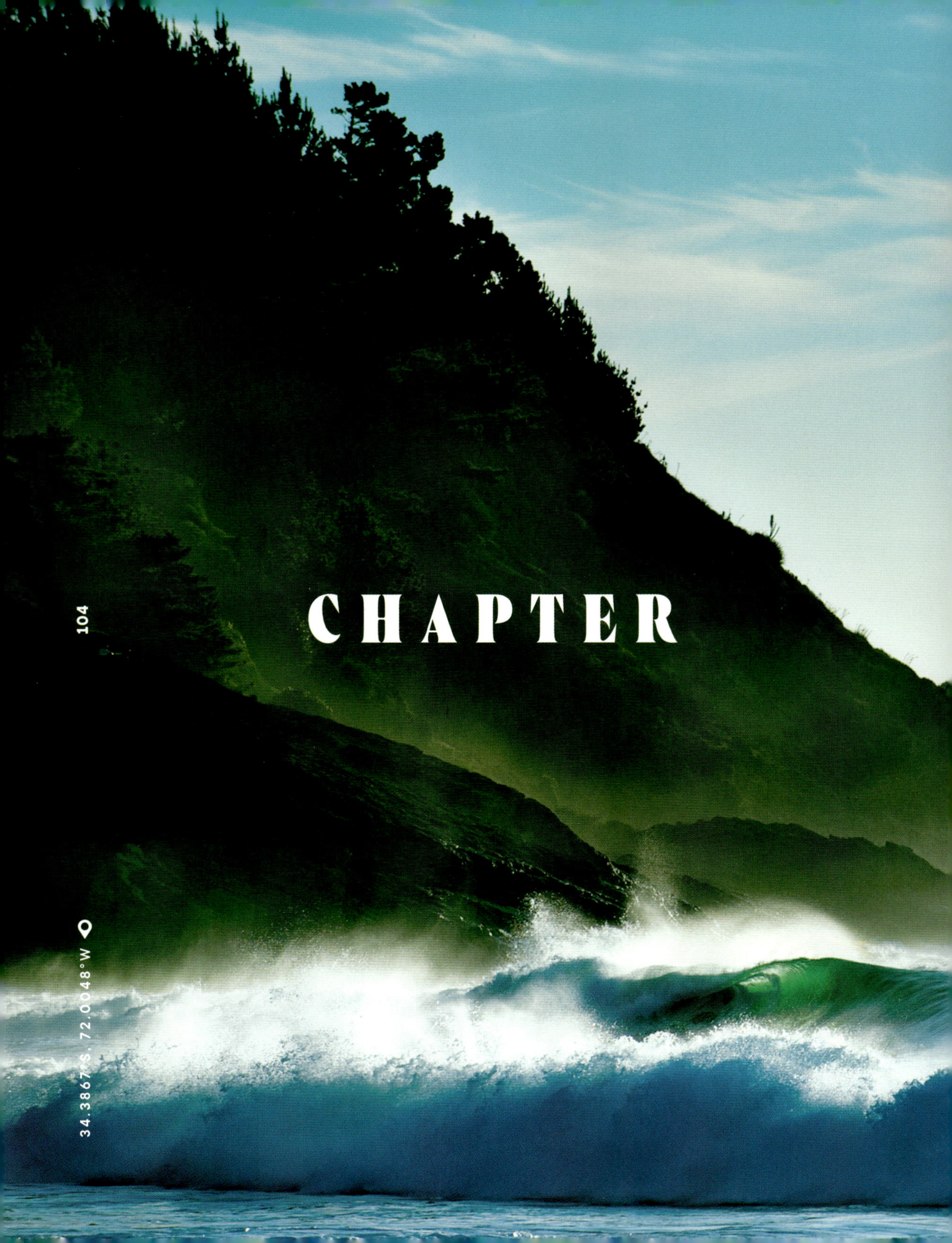

CHAPTER

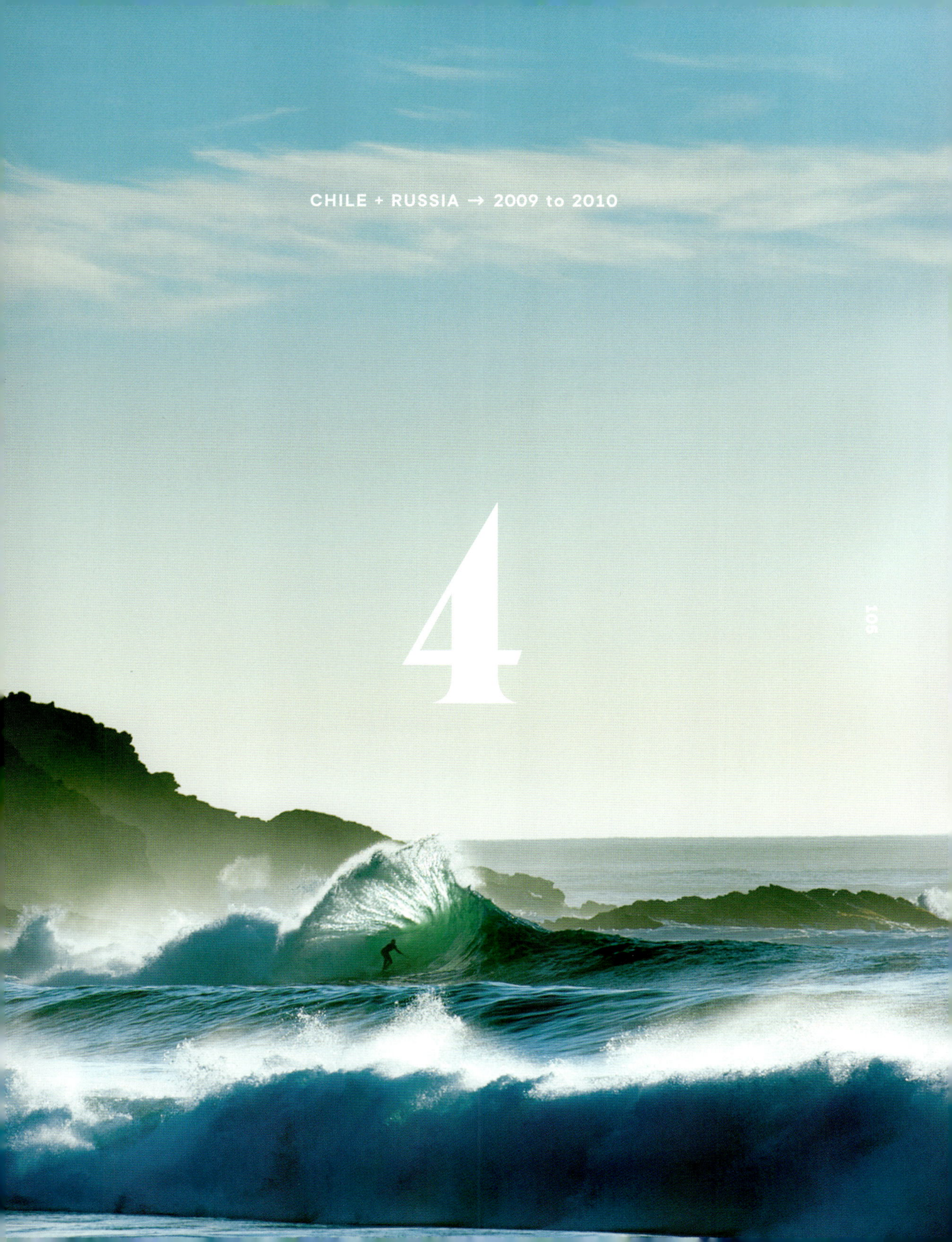

CHILE + RUSSIA → 2009 to 2010
4
105

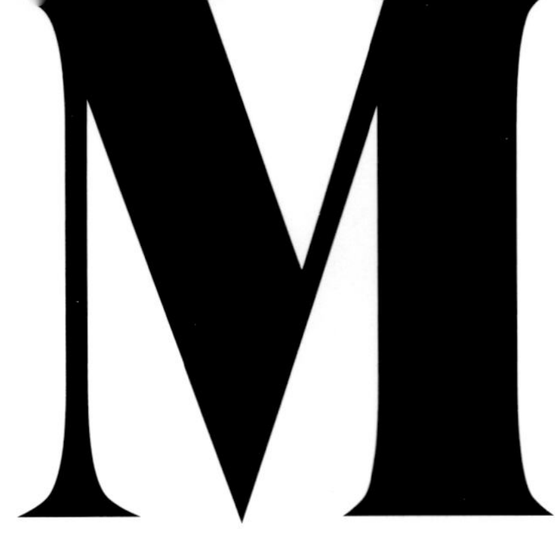

y position at Surfline allowed me access to state-of-the-art swell forecasting, enough funds to think big, and an open-minded group of editors. So I started pushing my geographic boundaries to colder coastlines farther from the equator. I also started handpicking my crews, developing an *Ocean's Eleven*–style approach to assembling the right mix of A-list free surfers. Surfers who don't compete on the pro tour were usually more enthusiastic about exploration and the prospect of finding something unique as opposed to something perfect. Their careers depended on photo and video incentives, which required scoring the best waves possible, and they treated each one as a gift. This kind of surfing took grit, experience, and usually a lot of luck to pull off. The high likelihood of failure is what made these assignments so raw and real. Just as cold-water adventure became my new escape, risk became my new addiction.

One of the first trips I exclusively designed for Surfline was an exploration of the left-hand point breaks of central Chile, between Santiago and Lebu. Since left waves (which break in a left-hand direction from the surfer's perspective) are favored by goofy-footers (surfers who ride with their right foot in front and therefore face a left-breaking wave, the preferred position), I picked the following team: Nate Tyler from my home region, a powerful goofy-footer known for big aerial maneuvers; Florida free surfer Peter Mendia, also a goofy-footer who specializes in deep tube-riding and crazy cutbacks; and Hank Gaskell, "Hana Hank," a regular-footer (left foot in front) from Hawaii who's most comfortable inside thicker, heavier tubes, like the ones Chilean point breaks could offer. Then we reached out to two of the best Chilean chargers, goofy-footers Cristian Merello and Diego Medina, who really helped make the trip possible. If there was one thing my early days of shooting taught me, it was to look to the people who know the region best. I was always turned off by the typical tourist experience, but having epic local surfers guiding you to their best waves was a guaranteed way to get off the beaten path. It was really because of Cristian and Diego's invitation and encouragement that this entire trip came together the way it did.

With a young surf scene that had only been growing since the seventies, Chile was still fairly uncharted territory. None of us Americans had been there before, and surf tourism and related localism were still emerging down the four-thousand-mile serrated coastline. Unlike in places like Dubai and Oman, I could actually find surf shots of Chile online and see the visual potential. Websites like WannaSurf served up grainy photos of feathering lineups backed by towering headlands and sea stacks—it was like Big Sur on acid. Gray-brown sand framed teal-blue barrels that turned hollow and backlit at sunset. Some waves looked twenty-five feet plus. Flying into Santiago, I actually had a faint vision in mind of the exact image I wanted to compose. The only question was whether everything would fall into place to make it possible.

Ignoring the salt-encrusted Atacama Desert to the north and the saw-tooth pinnacles of Patagonia to the south, central Chile reminded me of California, especially if the Golden State were inverted. The latitude of Santiago is close to that of San Clemente, and the climate is similarly Mediterranean. Unfolding out the car window between the Andes Mountains and the Pacific Ocean, wooded hills and low-lying shrubs blurred into citrus and avocado groves, cabernet vineyards, cow pastures, and wildflower meadows. Road signs listed the distances to names I recognized: Santa Cruz, San Fernando, Los Angeles.

When we reached the coast near Pichilemu, the rugged headlands and wraparound point breaks looked familiar, too. It was just as I had imagined . . . except for the storm clouds. No matter how much you research in advance, weather is the one outlier you can never predict. Just as we set up camp, the sky broke open, and we were blasted with rain.

Over the years, I have come to appreciate the access, immersion, and of course the affordability of camping, so the tents and sleeping bags were my idea. Luckily, I had come a long way in a few short years from those unprepared nights with Eric drowning in the van. Being able to unzip a nylon door to a beautiful beach or mountain range, and fall asleep to the roar of waves and rain, was the recipe for my dream trips. Regardless of the rain, we did exactly that for our first four nights in Chile. Whether the other guys shared my enthusiasm, I'm not so sure.

During one especially gusty downpour, we took shelter in the car as our tents got a lashing. With bleached-blond locks dripping onto presoaked T-shirts, Peter and Nate gave me a look that said, "What the hell did you get us into?" I didn't say anything back audibly, but I was thinking, *Isn't this part of the fun?* I'm sure they were beginning to question why they followed such a frothy young kid down this wet rabbit hole, but to me these kinds of experiences made everything worth it. My enthusiasm didn't really matter, though, because I was going to be the one to blame if things didn't turn out well. I wouldn't just be letting down the magazines, but I would lose the respect of all these surfers I admired. It was still early in my career,

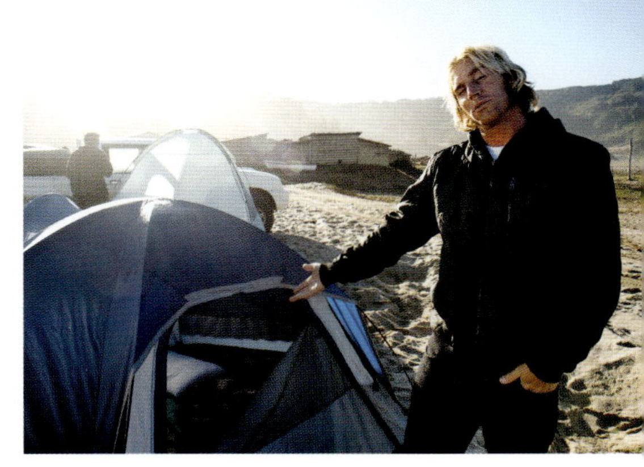

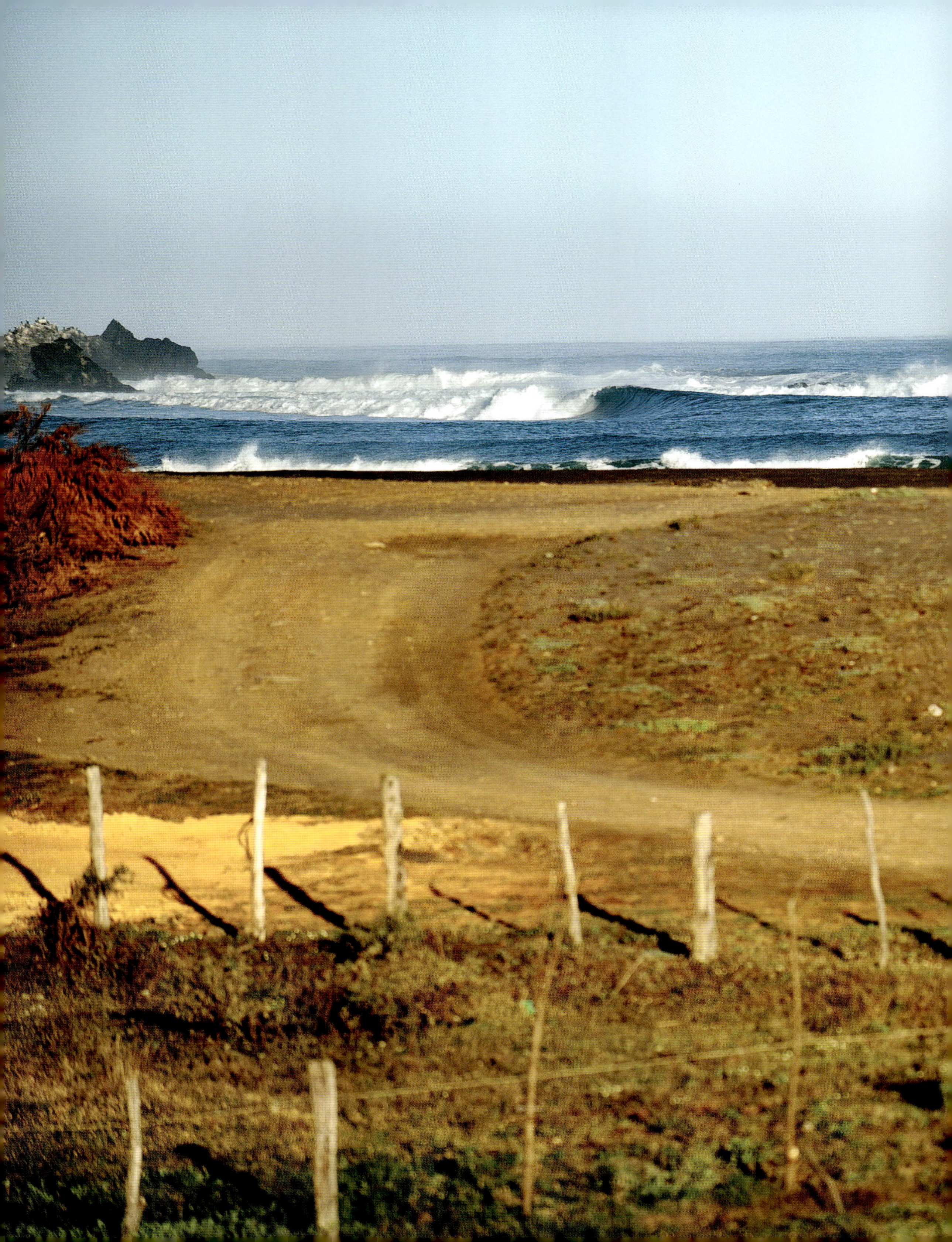

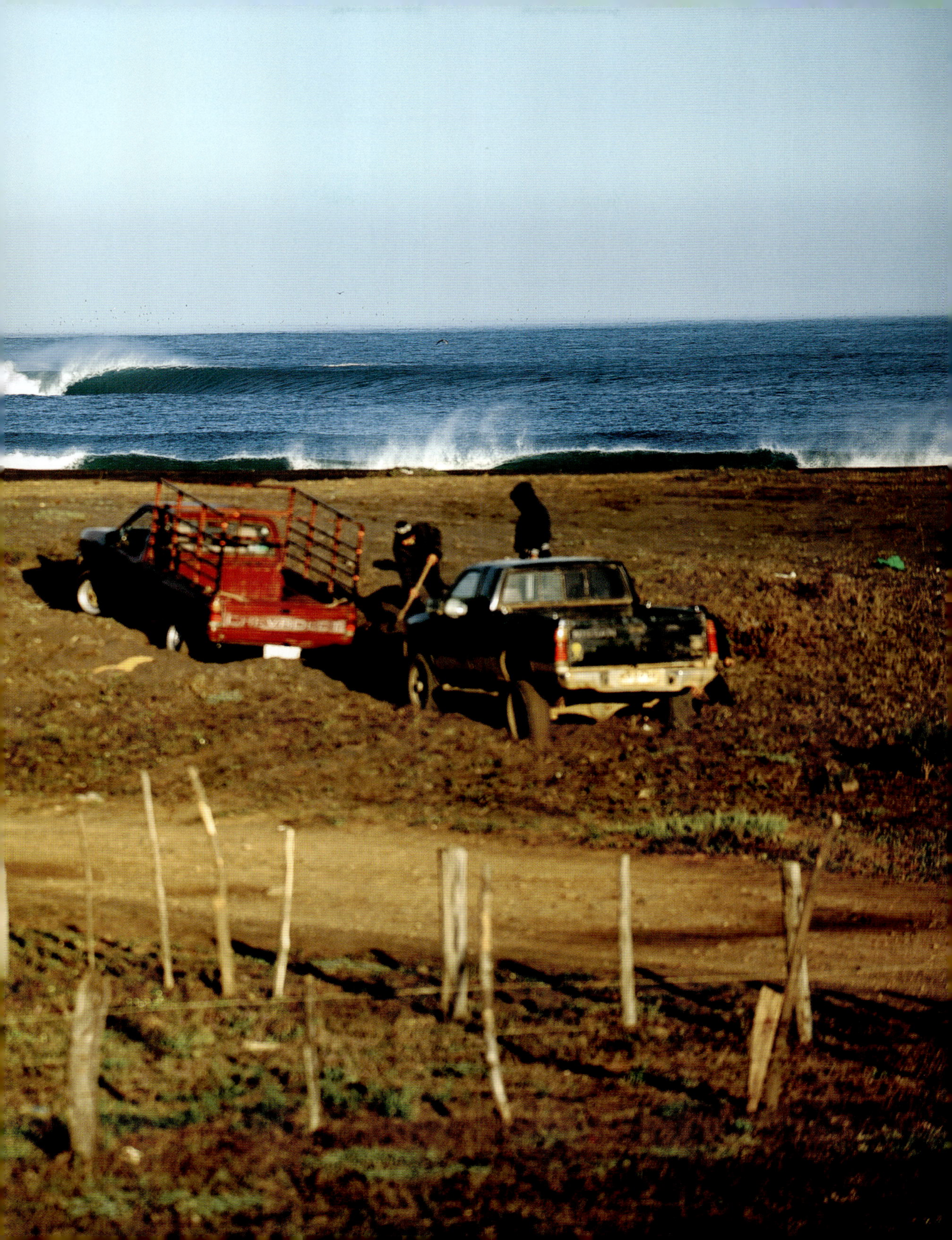

→ **Chris came into my world just as we were putting** together Patagonia's photography book *Unexpected*. Most of the photos were Patagonia classics, but Chris's image from Chile of a wave exploding was one of the newer selections we put in the book. To me, it was a standout photo—received from a surf photographer, who took the time to make that photo, versus a photo of a surf star or a performance shot. The image makes you want to be there, to hear the waves crash, smell the ocean.

What sets Chris apart is that he takes advantage of what the day brings. His photo submissions were often quite varied from what you'd expect a surf photographer to send you. This photo focuses on the natural environment and has a completely different point of view from sport photography. It's a special moment, a split millisecond when the wave opened up and had a burst.

This exemplifies why an assignment and "spec" photography can result in such different bodies of work. You can't predict the swell, conditions—or life! Patagonia mostly works with photographers "on speculation" (without a prior contract that promises payment or publication). It's an unorthodox and intensive way to procure photography, but I think it sets Patagonia's photos apart. In the case of the Chile photo, that wave opened up at that moment, and someone was there to click the shutter button.

A
New
View

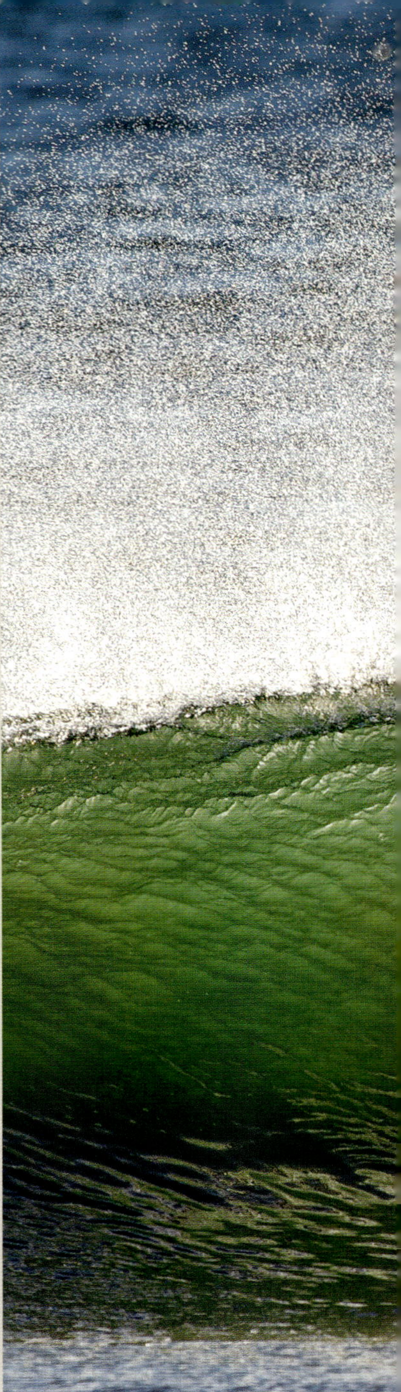

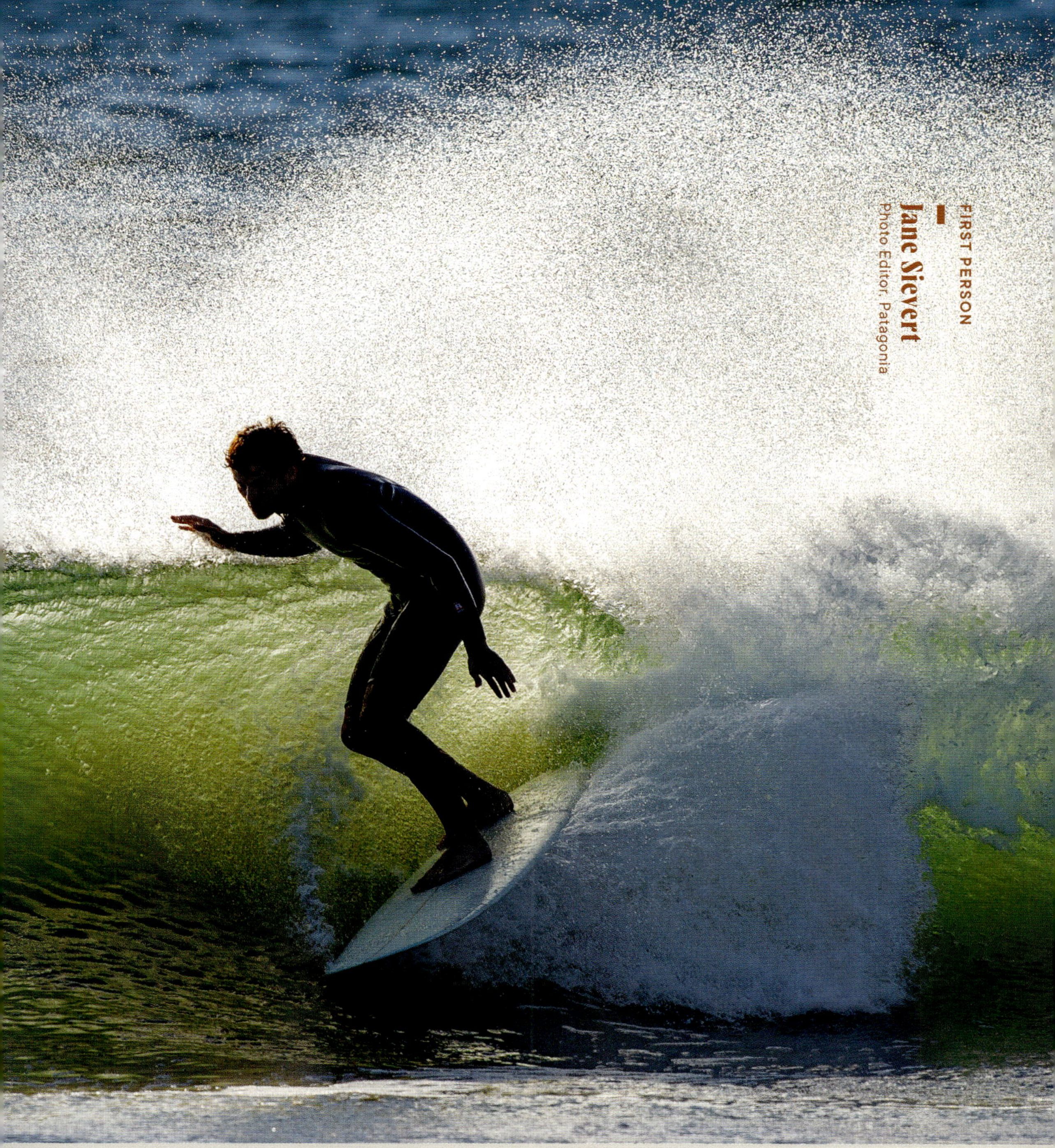

FIRST PERSON
Jane Sievert
Photo Editor, Patagonia

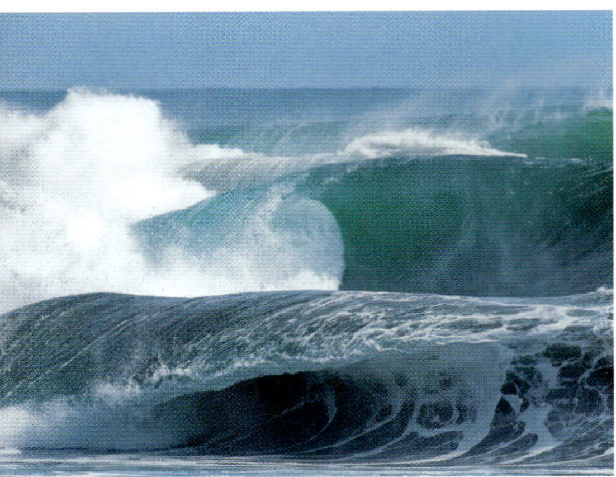

and no one would trust me if I didn't deliver. This was strike one.

The next morning, all was quiet. When I unzipped my tent door, the view was frosty but clear. Beyond the vapor of my breath, I could see the details of the landscape that had been blotted out for days. The scene was like a Polaroid that had just come into focus. Dew-covered grass and pines gleamed against volcanic rock. Radiating around the rugged point was the most incredible wave setup I had ever seen. It was as if the ruler-edge lines I once drew on my high school notebook had come to life as groomed sandbars. I watched the swell lines pinwheel around the point, then perk up and barrel straight in my direction.

All five surfers scrambled to pull on their half-frozen wetsuits while I paired Nikon lenses to camera bodies. Then, like rabid dogs, the guys ran to the water as fast as they could and started doing laps on glassy gray lefts that pitched and peeled before petering out away from the impact zone. When everything lines up in a setup like this, the energy grows frenetic. You forget about everything else, and the only thing that matters is how to capture every moment.

With the excitement of kids on Christmas, the guys paddled—or got out and ran—back to the rip current that sucked out along the rocks like a conveyor belt, and then did it all over again. One by one, the waves glided in and then unloaded right off the point. The Americans and Chileans took turns free-falling, locking into position, and crouching down to counteract the force of overhead waves. Walls of liquid curled, piped, and shot them out faster than my Nikon's burst mode of seven frames per second could capture. With my camera dangling around my neck, I ran up and down the beach, laughing, hooting, and shaking my head in wonder. When the guys finally got out of the water for lunch, they couldn't stop smiling.

"I don't think I made a single turn," Peter said. "That was like three straight hours of tubes!"

Morale was restored, and Chile had more than delivered.

Those three straight hours of perfection continued for six straight days. There's a rule in surfing that says you never leave a break when the waves are good—the tide and wind shift so frequently that you're likely to get skunked at the next spot. Every new point we drove to—at the risk of ruining our surf karma—looked better than the last.

When we pulled into the lookout at another fairy-tale point, the image I had been dreaming about before the trip began moving from fantasy to possibility. Pencil-like pine trees and colorful houses led my eyes to mythical sea cliffs that tumbled down to the point. At their base, eight-foot waves were firing beneath a setting sun. Everything was falling into place, so I grabbed my camera bag as fast as I could, shotgunned some water, stuffed a chunk of bread in my pocket, and took off running down the shore. The guys must have thought I was psycho as they watched me sprint till I was nearly out of sight.

From a distant vantage point, I zoomed in with my 70–200mm lens to locate the surfers, then I expanded the focal range out to 140, 120, 100, and then 70. With each turn of the lens, more scenery came into view—barrels stretched into long, drawn-out waves; the rocky point rose into cliffs—until the playback revealed a complete picture. The shot I envisioned was starting to materialize as the sun dipped low enough to light up the sea spray from behind like a golden halo. The only problem with my setup was the rising tide. It came with fierce backwash that caused explosions of foam when it crashed into oncoming waves. I looked around for higher ground. Some elevation would have helped me get above the shore break, but there was no option in sight.

Lessons from my years interning under Pete Taras and landscape master Michael Fatali came bouncing around in my mind: "Creating a level of separation between your layers will help make the image feel more three-dimensional." But I was stuck with everything important in a one-dimensional plane. I racked my brain and paced around in the sand. I started dreading the conversations with Nate, Peter, and Hank about how they were hidden in my photos because I was shooting at a 70mm focal length halfway down the beach on flat sand. But just as real panic started to set in, I noticed that the surge of the set waves occasionally washed up the cliff face and rushed all the way to the sets out back. The shock waves created these amazing backlit flares that reached above the shore break. I wondered if my camera could catch a surfer right inside the burst.

I adjusted my framing and zeroed in on Nate paddling for a set. It hollowed out super steep, and he backed off at the last second. My heart sank. Hope was restored when Peter then angled into a wave that looked like it might collide with the backwash. He dropped in and got in position just in time for the shock wave to hit. The frames flickered back at me like a film reel: the silhouetted surfer slides into a glowing green barrel; barrel erupts open into a giant liquid fan; water falls back down, closing the wave; surfer disappears.

Had it really happened? I feared watching the replay on my camera in case my eyes had invented that barrel burst. But deep down I knew they hadn't. This must be what French photographer Henri Cartier-Bresson meant by a "decisive moment," when "inside

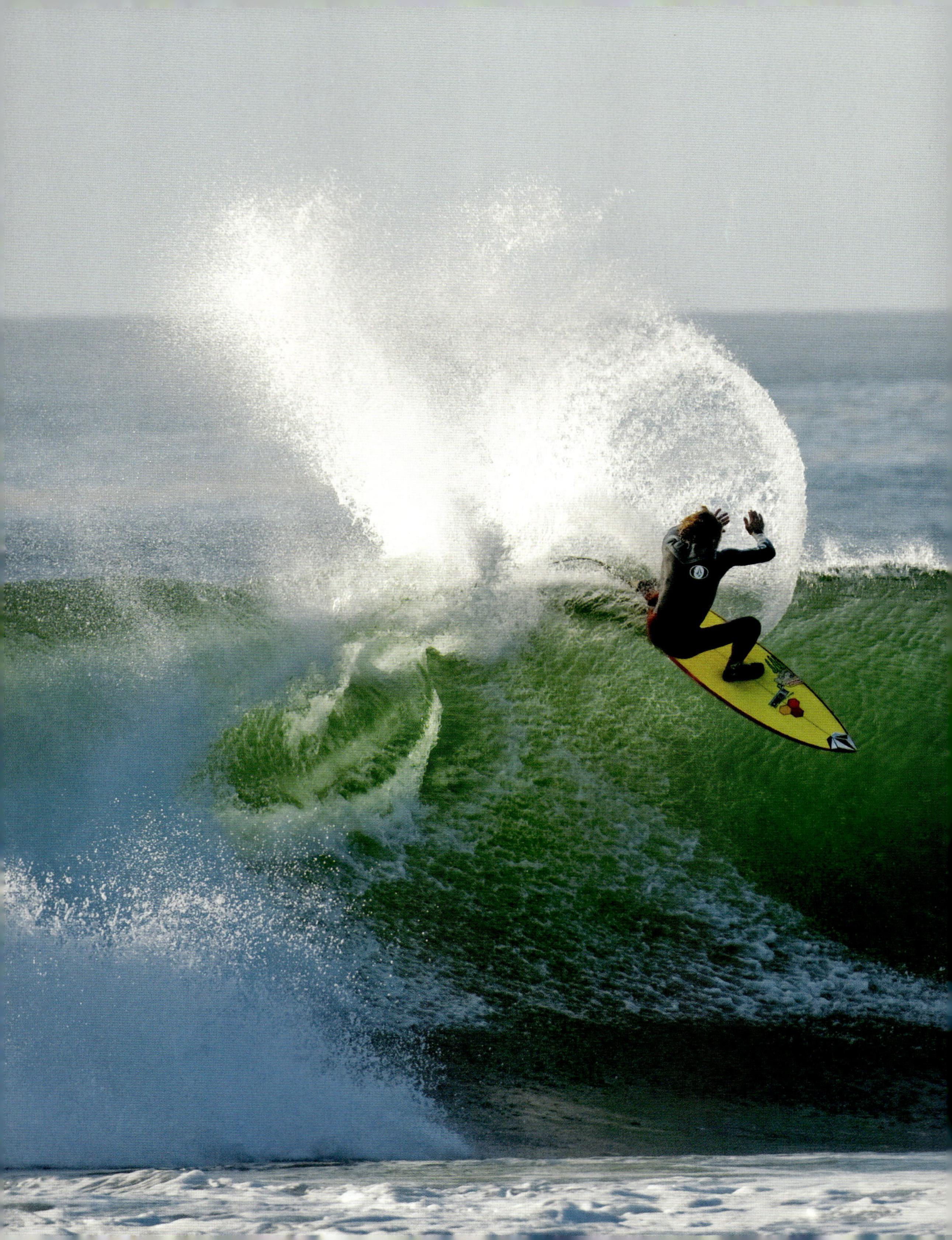

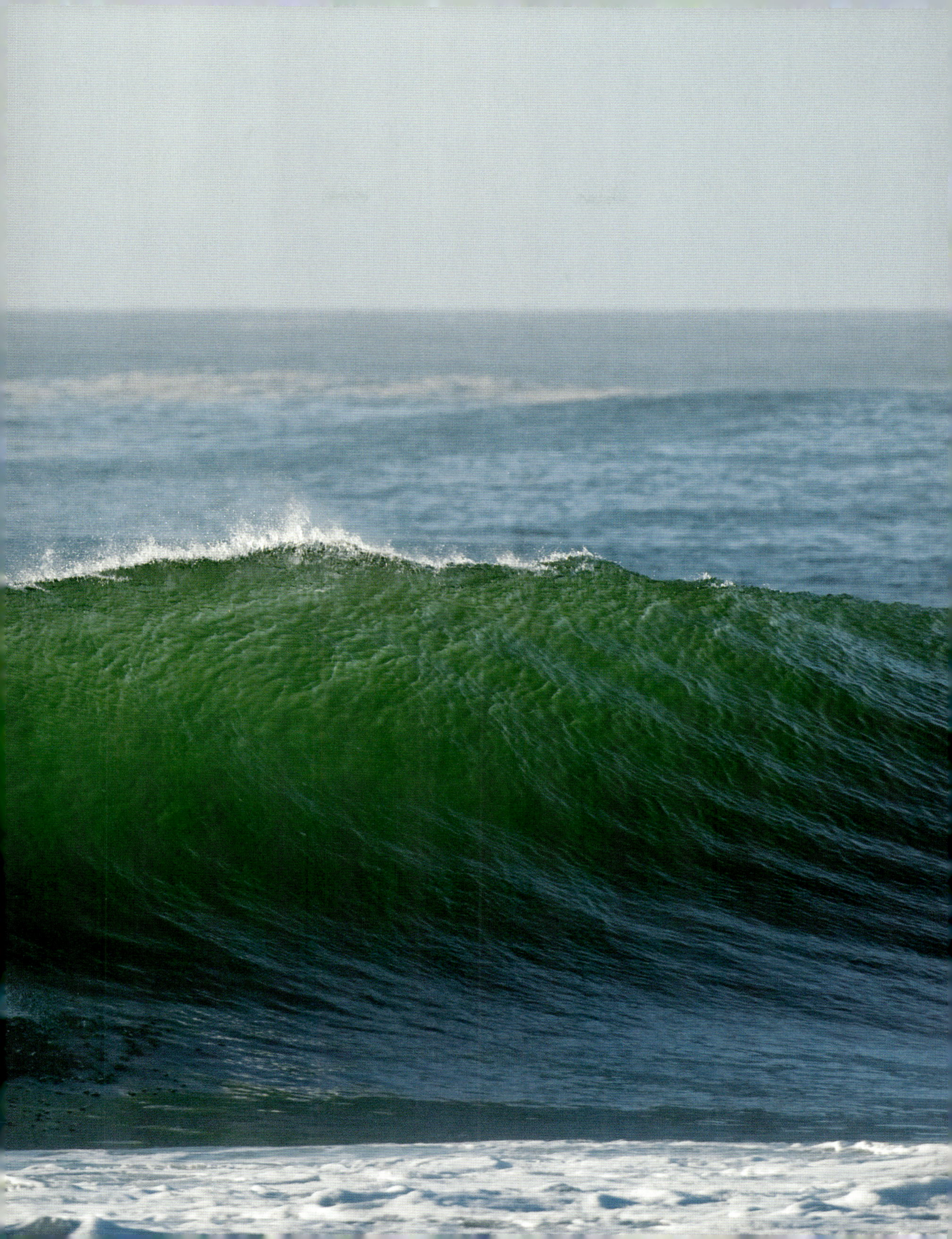

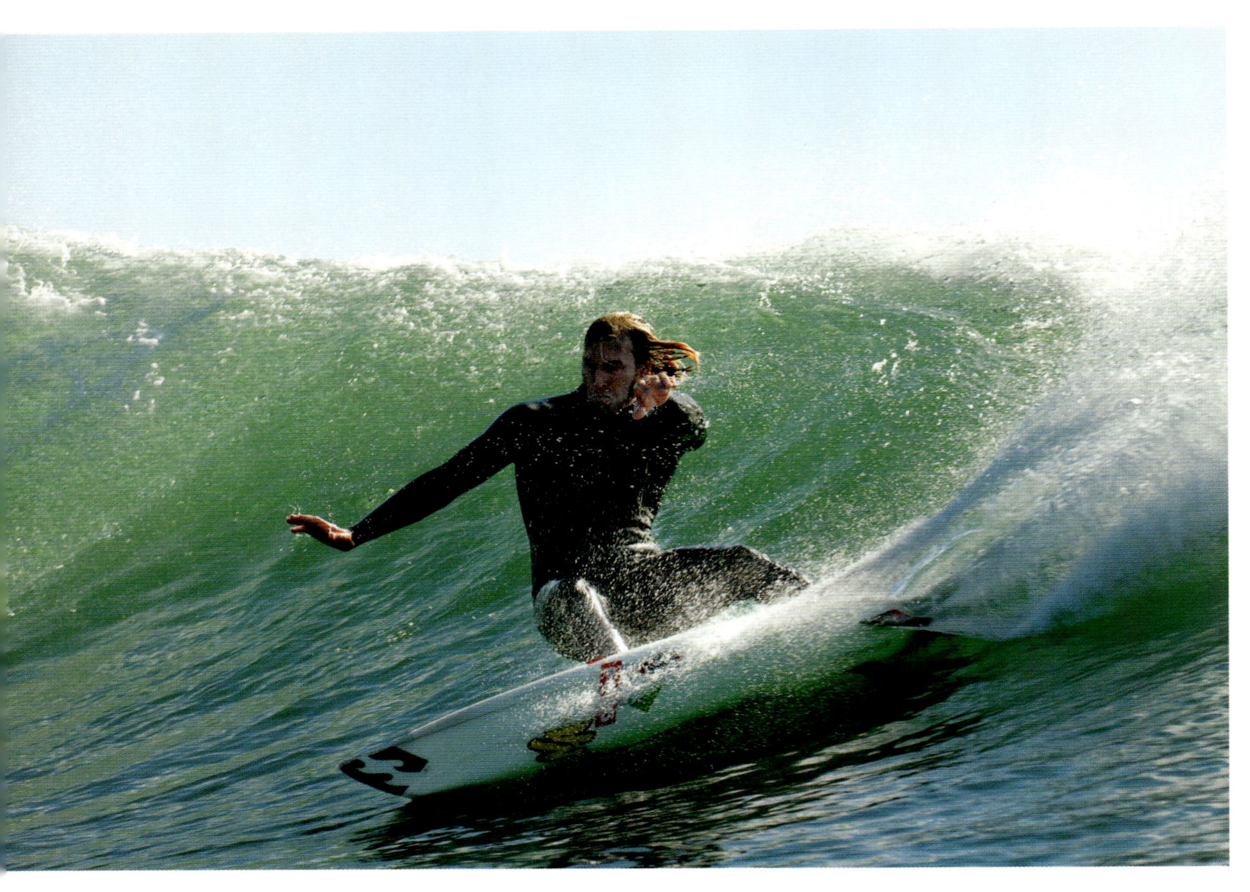

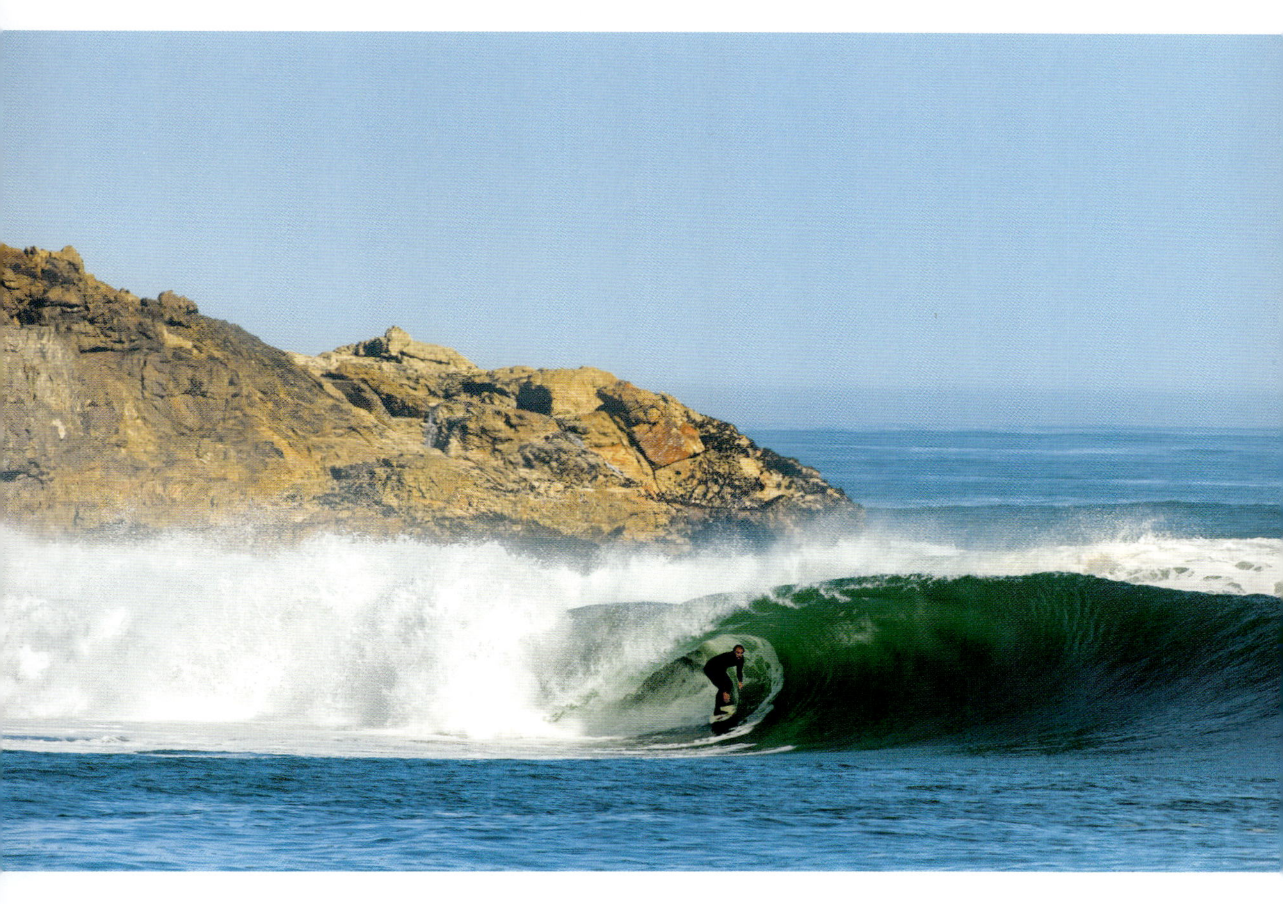

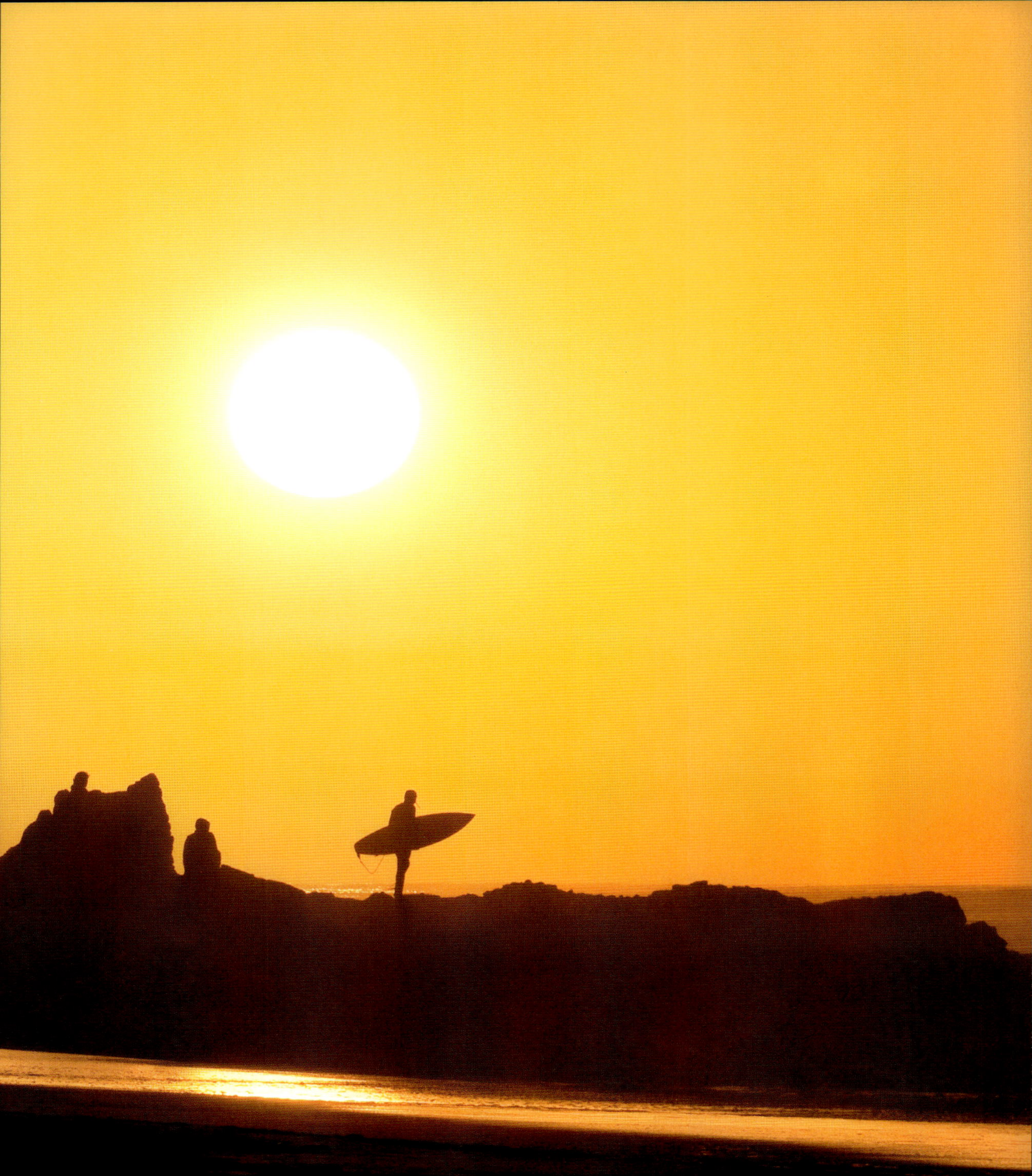

movement there is one moment at which the elements in motion are in balance."

I didn't know how I had managed to freeze-frame that magical millisecond. All I knew was that it had happened—and it felt significant.

Upon my return from Chile, I felt more in control of my own destiny than ever. My first book, *The California Surf Project,* was finally published two and a half years after my trip with Eric. Publishing a book, I realized, is a truly glacial process, and it was never quite the moneymaking venture I thought it might be. Nevertheless, I was surprised at how quickly it started to pay off in other ways after it was released.

Chronicle Books managed to place *The California Surf Projec*t everywhere from Barnes & Noble to Urban Outfitters. I began receiving inquiries from wineries, clothing companies, and lifestyle brands about print sales and image licensing. I was completely out of my element. Negotiating image sales felt like I was listening to a different language. I didn't know the difference between "in perpetuity" and "digital buyout." I did my best to wing it.

It wasn't long before my favorite outdoor company, Patagonia, got in touch about buying an image for a catalog cover. I was starstruck just talking to the photo editor over the phone. They offered $4,000 for a slow-shutter photo of the ocean's surface at sunset, which was way more than any magazine was paying at the time. I had no idea how that stacked up in the retail or corporate world, though, so I began a phase of business research. I wanted to become fluent in this new language.

However, Surfline remained my bread and butter, and I was learning that surf expeditions were still very crucial to my career as well as my psyche. After experiencing Haida Gwaii, Iceland, and Chile, I felt compelled to raise the bar. I wanted to go to colder and more remote destinations—even though I may not have been quite ready to. Michael Kew would mention ideas in passing, sometimes even jokingly, and I would begin obsessing over them. As they say, I was so busy trying to figure out if I could, I forgot to stop and ask if I should. Russia became one of these obsessions—and even I was surprised when it became a reality.

Michael Kew and I had been talking about going to Russia for more than a year. Kew had even been communicating with a woman named Olga on the online comment forums of WannaSurf.com. Olga lived in Vladivostok, where, apparently, there were a dozen or so breaks along the mountainous Primorsky Krai coast, which is just above North Korea. To Olga's knowledge, no foreigners had ever surfed there. The only problem? Primorsky Krai was inside the Sea of Japan and only funneled in swell on a few freak days per year— typically in early fall.

I vividly remember the meeting at Surfline when I first pitched the trip. My PowerPoint presentation was straight out of my high school tech-lab class, and included the best Flickr

→ **There's a reef that breaks way off the port in** the town of Lebu, Chile. We could see the swell wrapping around the headland when we arrived just before sunset, but the wave was too far for my 200–400mm lens to make out clearly from land. We needed a *panga* (motorboat). Luckily, this town was full of *pangas*.

Early the next morning, we scoured the harbor and found a fisherman willing to take us to the reef. I packed all the gear I had with me—the big tele-photo lens, plus two camera bodies (a Nikon D700

Flooded

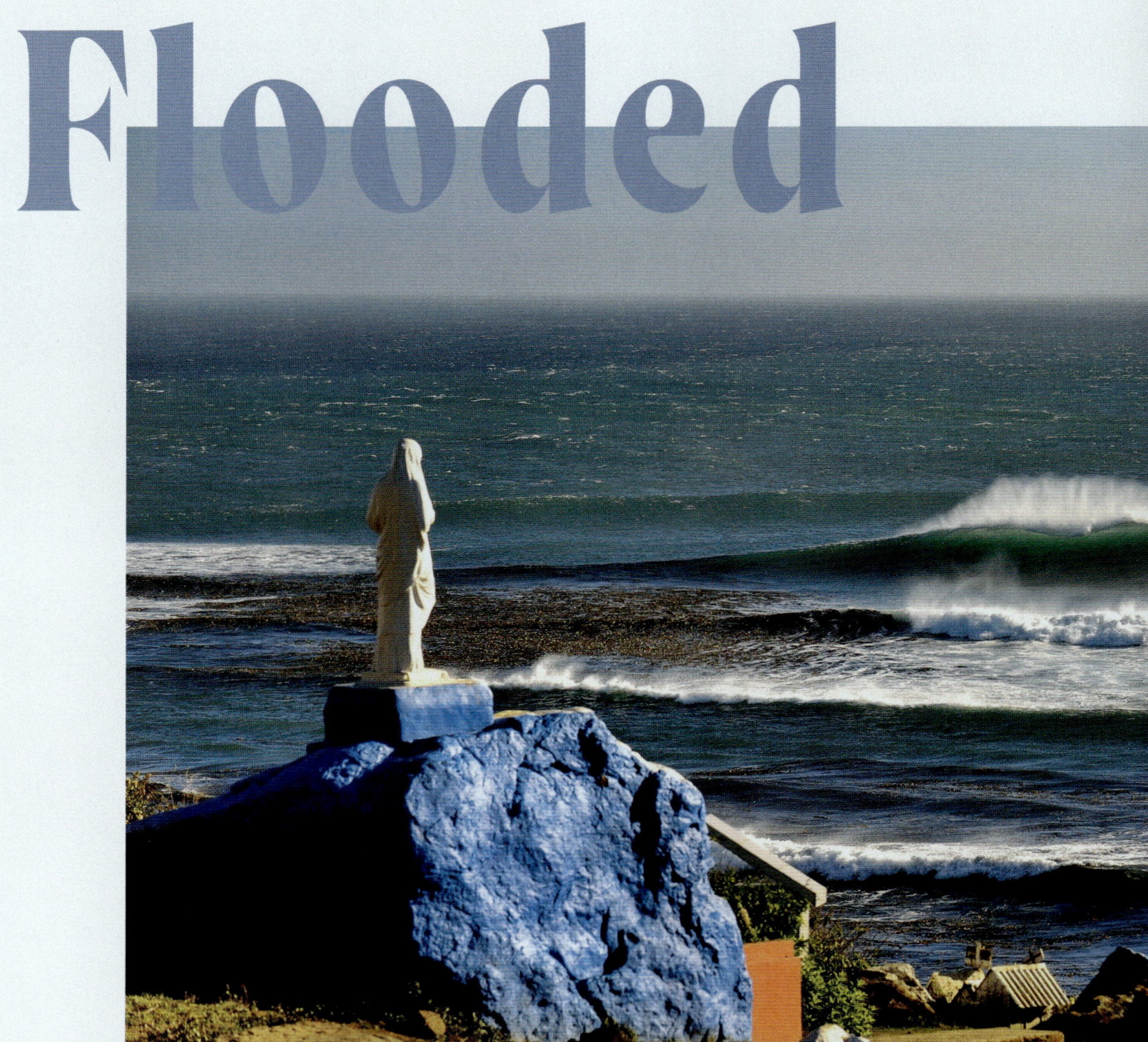

and a Nikon D300S), plus small lenses and a battery grip—into my camera bag and loaded it onto the boat. The fisherman looked tired, as if he had just woken up. His eyes were swollen and bloodshot. I could smell a hint of pisco on his breath. But whatever hesitation I felt about our boat captain was outweighed by my excitement and sheer determination to access this wave. Peter Mendia and I boarded the *panga* and motored out to the break.

Walls of water came pulsing into A-frames before making unexpected turns to the left. They were hard to predict, but we managed to make it safely to the wave's shoulder. Once we got there, I saw a ripple forming on the horizon, but not where the others had been . . . This thing was two hundred feet farther to my right—way outside, and huge—as it wrapped hard against the reef and headed straight toward us. Our boat was positioned with its bow pointed at the headland, ready to take this monster wave to its side (the worst angle in boating as well as in surfing). The fisherman quickly reoriented the bow toward the oncoming wave. The bow is where I was sitting, holding my prized Nikon D700 and a 200–400mm zoom lens worth $7,000 in my lap. I shielded my gear, expecting to receive a light splash on the back, when the rogue wave literally crashed over me, drenching everything in its wake like Shamu at SeaWorld. With all that gear, I must have weighed down the front of the boat to the point that we nearly submerged into the exploding whitewater.

Once the shock wore off and the fisherman moved us to safety, I lifted my camera. Salt water gushed from its cracks. *My career is over*, I thought. *I just flooded $30,000 worth of camera gear*. I pulled out the memory card and battery and futilely tried to dry them on my soaked T-shirt. Did I back up that incredible sunset shot of Peter from the previous night? My one saving grace: I had.

Neither Nikon would turn on back at the house. I opened every orifice, buried the cameras and lenses in rice, and blasted the heater in the bathroom to try to dry them and absorb some of the moisture. By some miracle, one camera eventually came back to life, but I didn't have enough working gear to continue the trip. This is the only time I've ever changed my ticket to head home early. The adventure was over.

In the end, I filed an insurance claim worth $18,000. My "all perils" insurance policy became just that. It was an expensive reminder about packing and waterproofing, as well as two important lessons I should have paid more attention to as a child: Don't turn your back on the ocean, and think twice before trusting a stranger. —C.B.

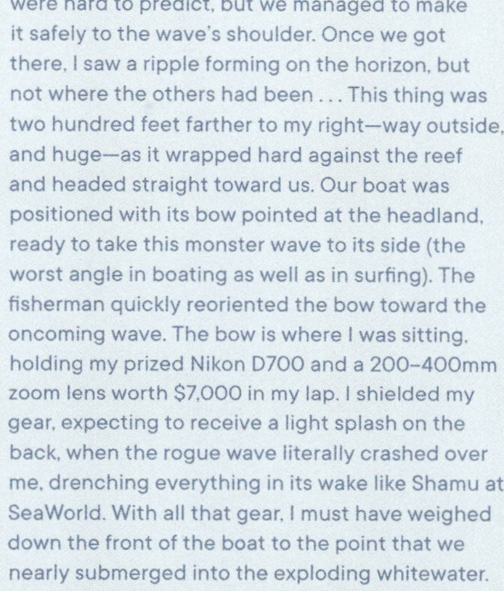

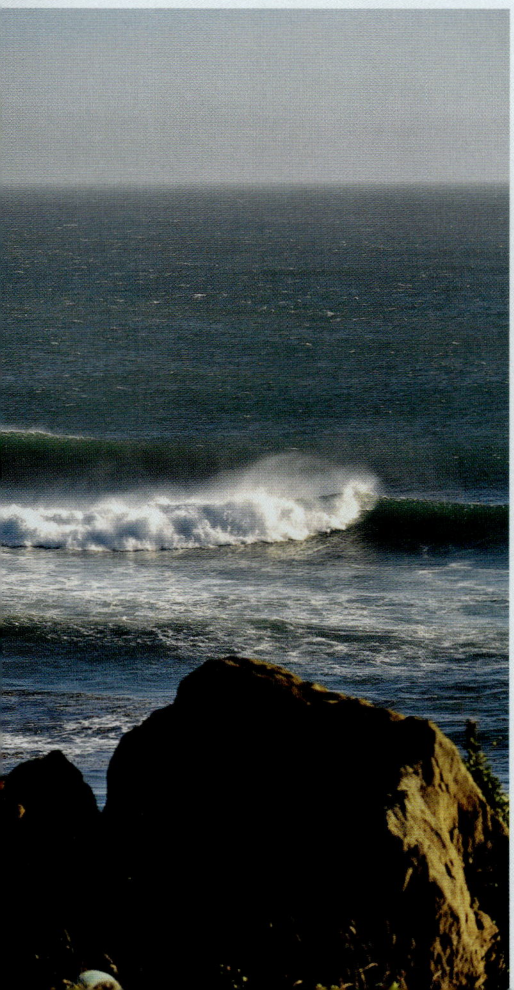

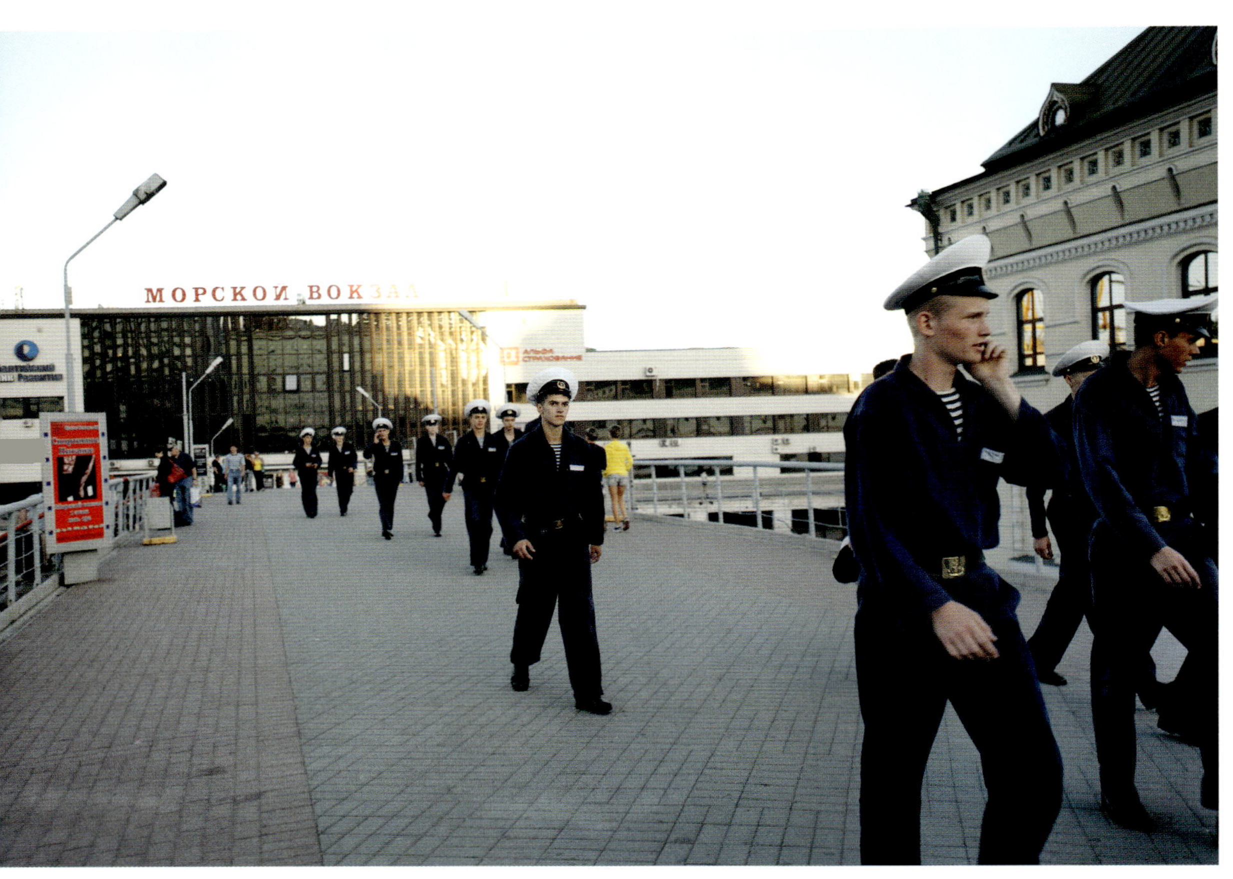

МОРСКОЙ ВОКЗАЛ

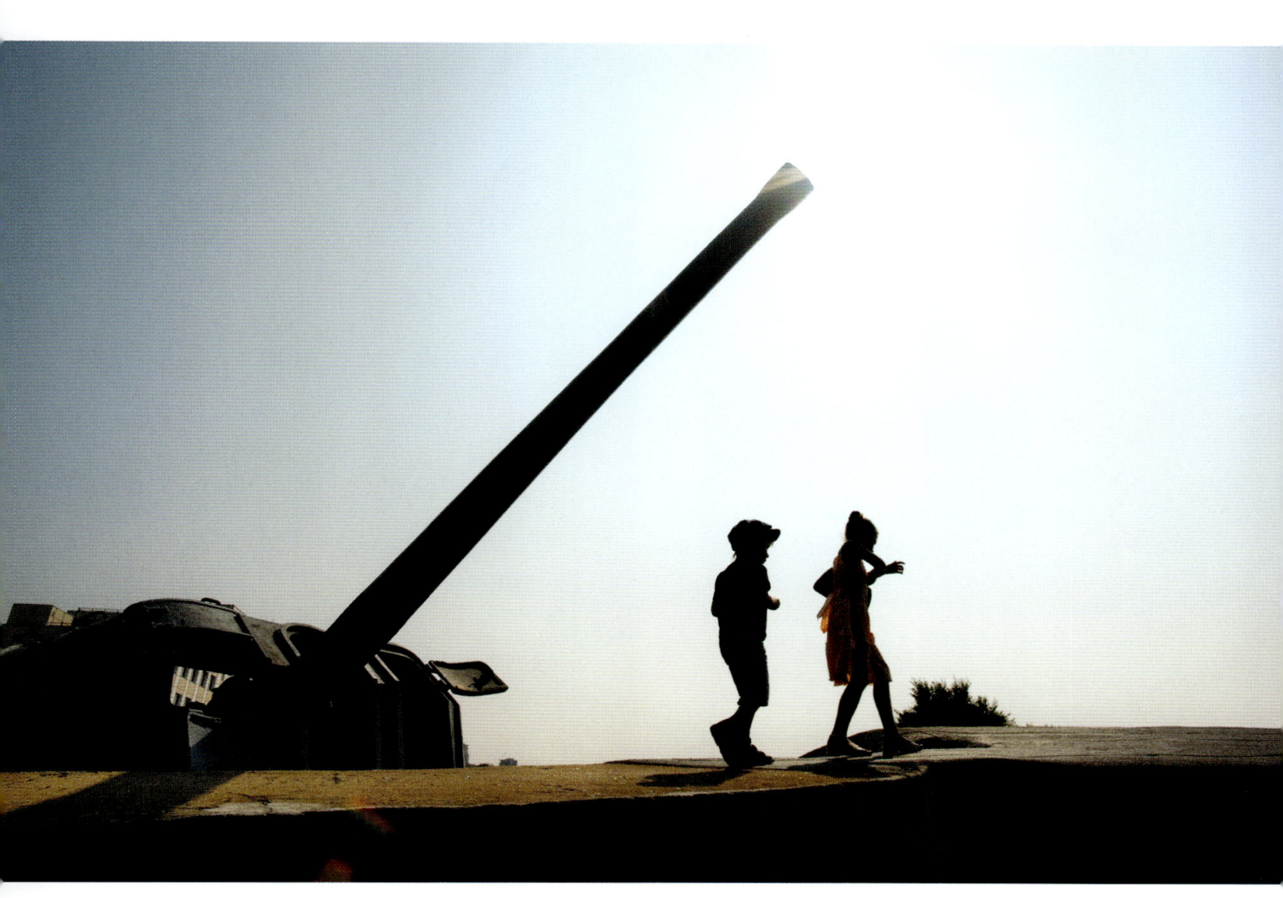

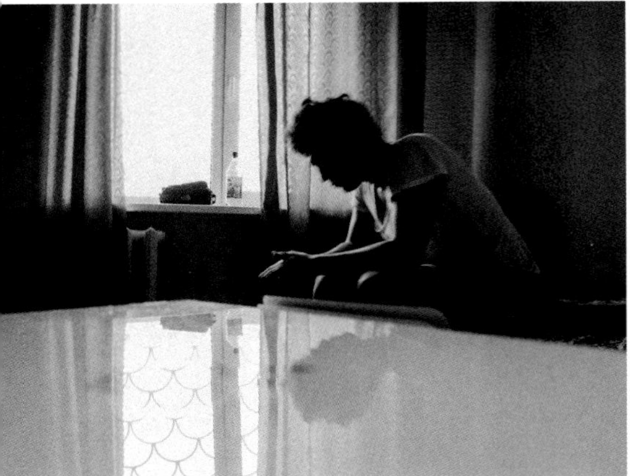

photos I could find of the local waves and primeval scenery of an obscure spot called Zolotoy Bereg, which loosely translates as "Gold Coast" in Russian. It wasn't enough. Having caught on to my naive inexperience, Dave Gilovich and Marcus Sanders looked at me with time-proven skepticism from more than a decade of working in surf media.

I came back to them after doing a few more weeks of research. I found out that August through October—Japan's typhoon season—was our best window. I even organized two different crews of surfers to cover our bases and mapped out the entire itinerary. Kew and I would depart in late August with one crew and stay for twenty days, overlapping our time with a second set of surfers to maximize our chances of getting surf. For unproven zones like this, the waiting game was just what we needed to increase our chances of success. Surfline reluctantly signed on, but added a dirty little caveat at the end of our initial assignment meeting.

"If you get waves, we're in," they said.

In other words, Surfline wasn't fully committing to pay for the trip—it would all be out of pocket if I failed. Perhaps my success in Chile was obscuring my judgment a little.

BAM BAM BAM. A knock at the door of my jail cell pounded in my chest, jolting me back to the room.

"Who's there?" I asked.

The hunchbacked guard who had been monitoring me from outside leaned in. In lieu of English words, he motioned roughly for me to follow him. I pointed to my bag as if to ask, *Am I getting out of here?* He shook his head with impatience. NO. I had never even made it past immigration. Minutes after landing in Russia, I was whisked away to a holding cell for a visa violation—my visa had been stamped to begin the day after my arrival, and they were insisting I leave the country and return the following day.

My mind bounced between thoughts of confidence—our *fixer will get me out of here*—to anger, thinking of the woman at the Russian embassy back in the States who mishandled my visa paperwork. How did she manage to print the wrong entry date on just my visa? Why did the rest of the crew get in no problem? I was the one who submitted all our passports at the EXACT SAME time, with the EXACT SAME information . . . yet they're out there doing God knows what and I'm stuck in here? This is HER fault. Definitely her fault. But reality loomed. *You're gonna get fired for this.*

The holding cell was dank. The bed was a deflated box spring laid over a rusty base. There was a steel table backed against sad, grandma-ish wallpaper with yellow stains and curled-up edges. Above it, scalloped curtains tried, but failed, to hide iron window bars. The only sound was the drip-drip of the toilet, which was feeding the shallow tributary seeping across the cement floor toward my duffel bag.

Igor stood in the doorway, motioning for me to follow him. We ended up in what looked like an operating room, but it was in fact a kitchen, like a military mess hall with a long steel table. He pointed to a folding chair. I sat. He left for a moment to go into a pantry and returned with two white plastic cups. One contained a brown mush that resembled watery lentils; the other had dried cucumber drizzled in mayonnaise. Not eating didn't seem like an option, so I took a sulking bite of mush.

Unfortunately, no amount of negotiating with the Russians or begging the embassy to intervene could save me from being deported to South Korea. I started dreading my flight to Seoul. All my fears and doubts floated to the surface. I felt a heaviness in my chest as I worried about letting my colleagues and editors down and began doubting my abilities and readiness for pulling off the tougher trips I was interested in.

After almost twenty-four hours of travel, ping-ponging from Russia to South Korea and then straight back again, the customs officer stamped my passport and finally allowed me to walk out into the thick, diesel-scented air as a free man. Never had afternoon light looked so bright and beautiful than after forty-eight hours of detainment indoors and traveling in airports. As I power walked my way out of the airport, fearing they would change their mind, our translator-fixer Olga showed up in her small LADA hatchback.

"There are waves!" she said excitedly when I opened her car door. "One of the best swells this year!"

When we parked at the beach, throngs of Russian couples and families were tanning, dancing to Euro techno, and bodysurfing three-foot waves crowned by offshore wind. Not exactly the solitude I was expecting. I spotted Mike out in the A-frames, exploiting every ounce of wave energy and busting airs between swimmers. I took a deep breath; there was no time to waste.

I ditched my backpack with Kew and Josh, who looked a little hungover on their beach towels, and set up my water housing like a shell-shocked soldier loading a gun.

The questions started pouring in: "Dude, what happened in there?"

I was too stressed to answer. *This might be the only opportunity for waves in this fickle, godforsaken place,* I thought. The only comfort in that moment was picking up my camera

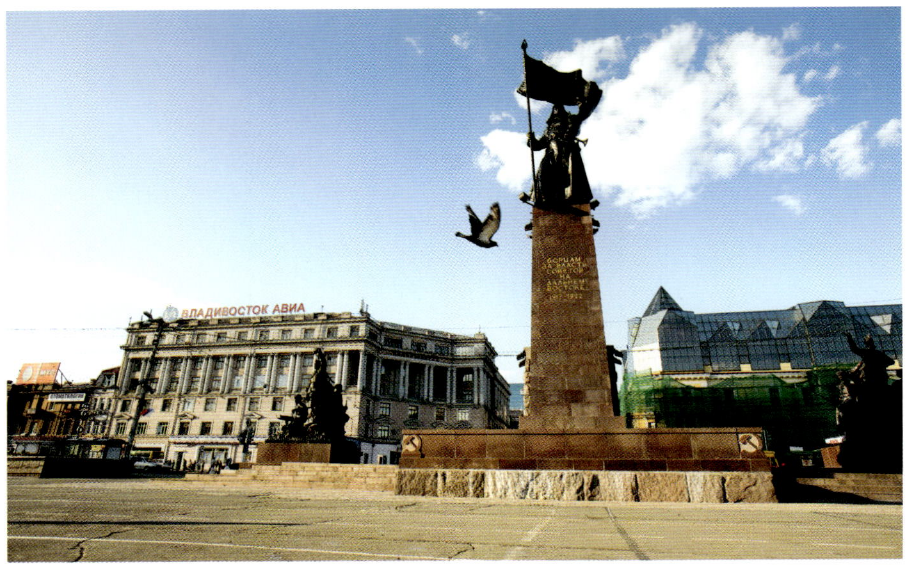

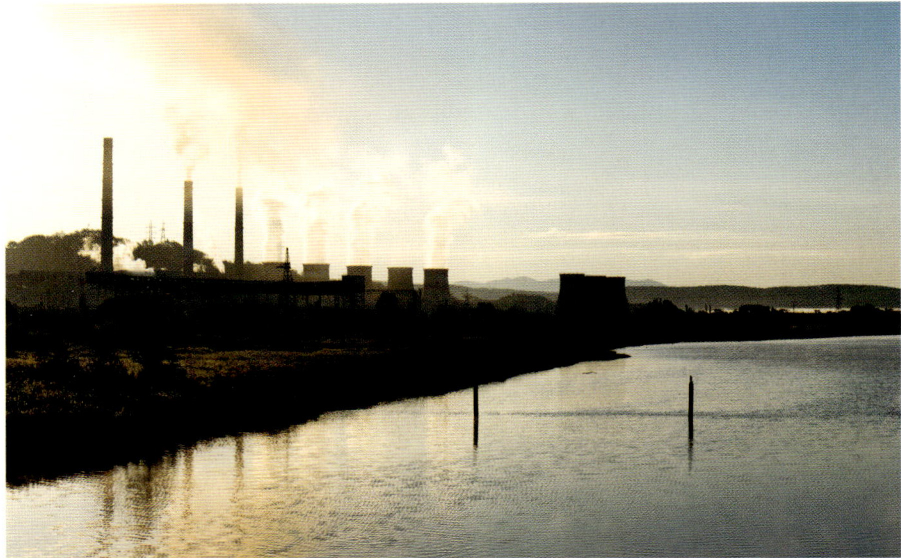

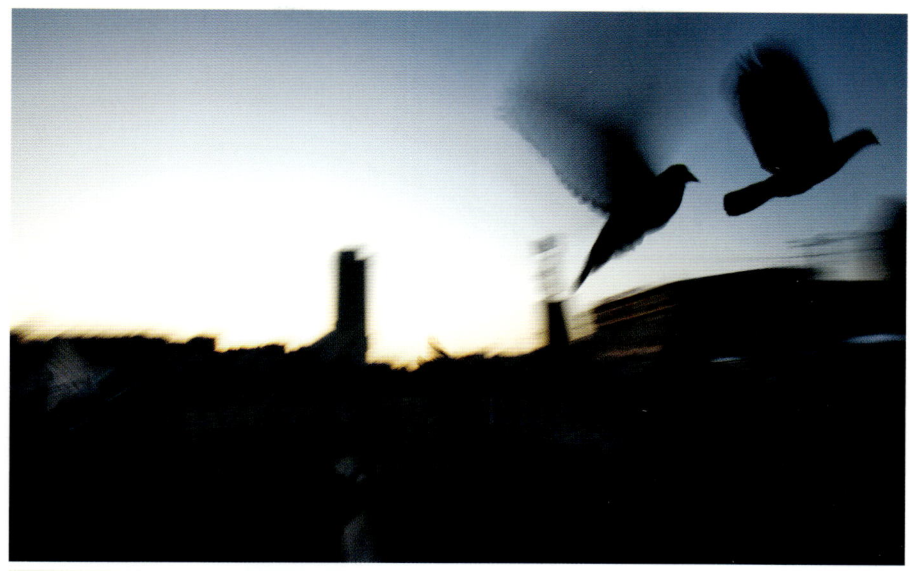

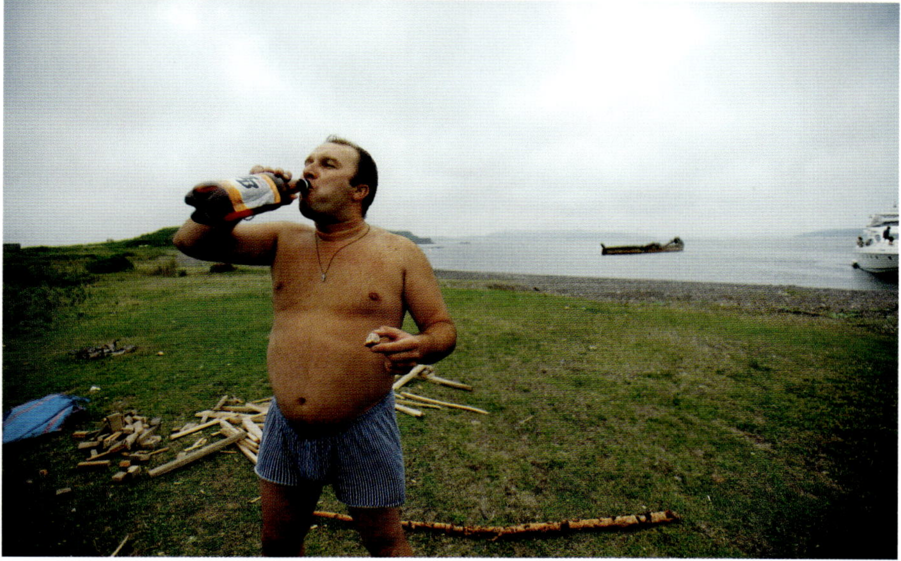

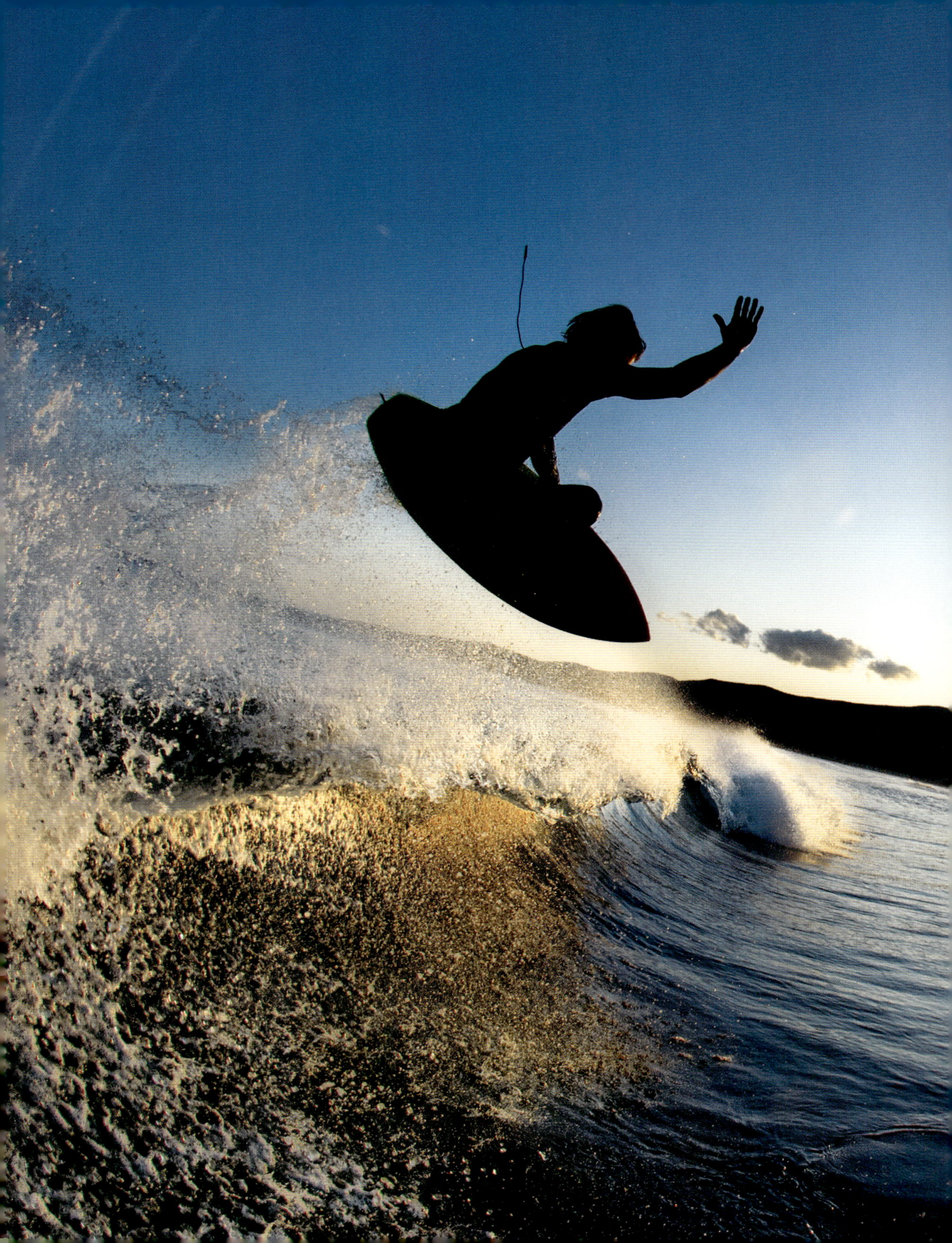

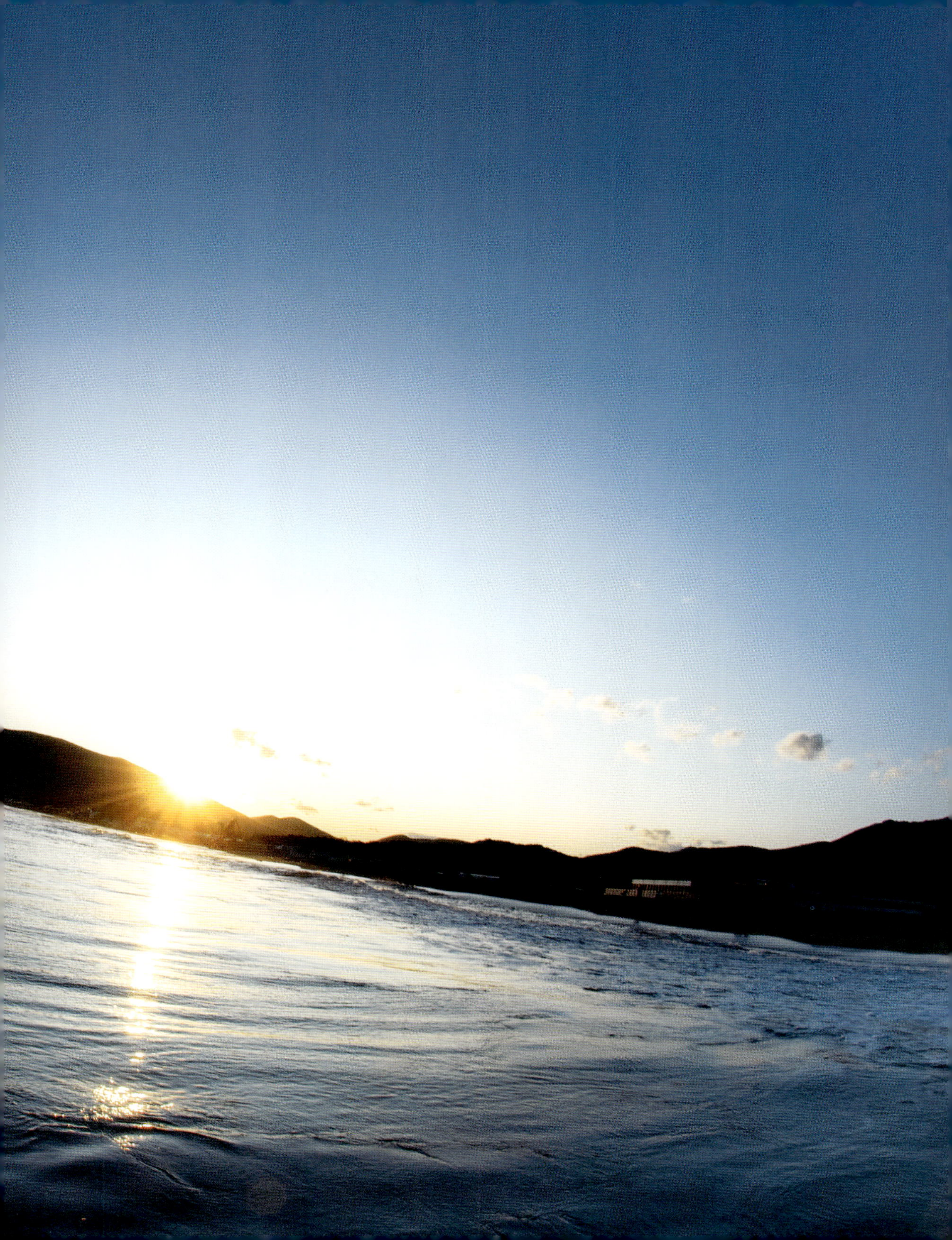

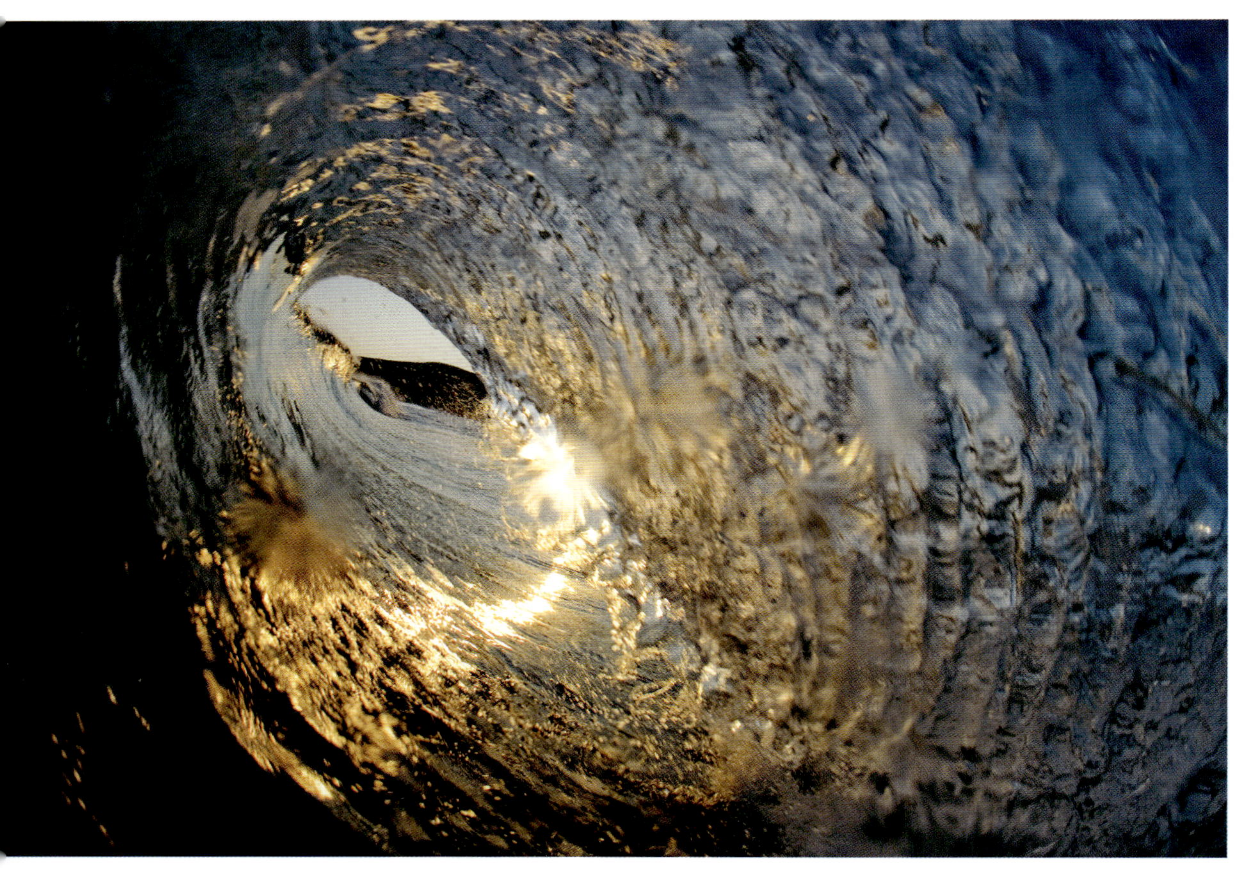

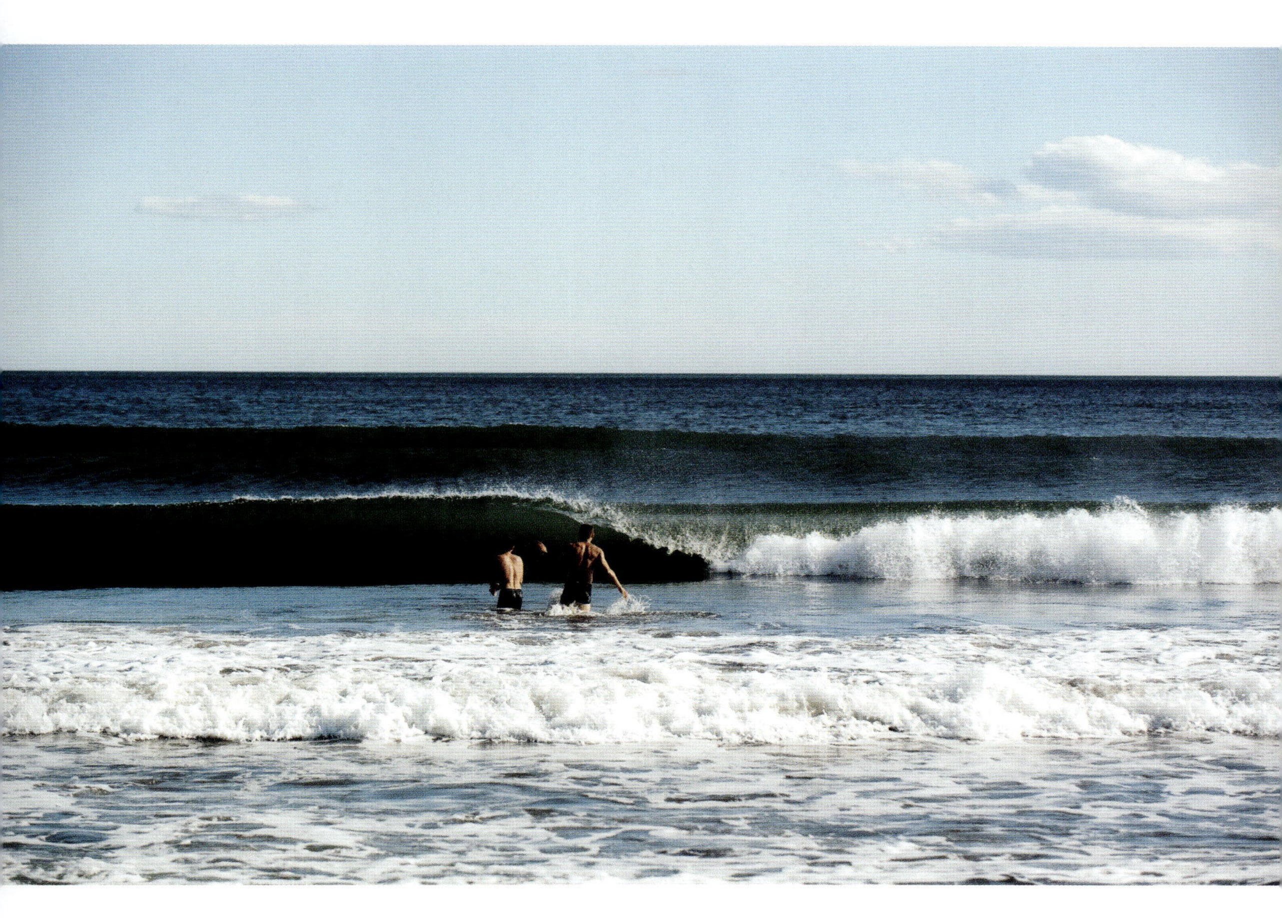

CHRIS BURKARD   WAYWARD

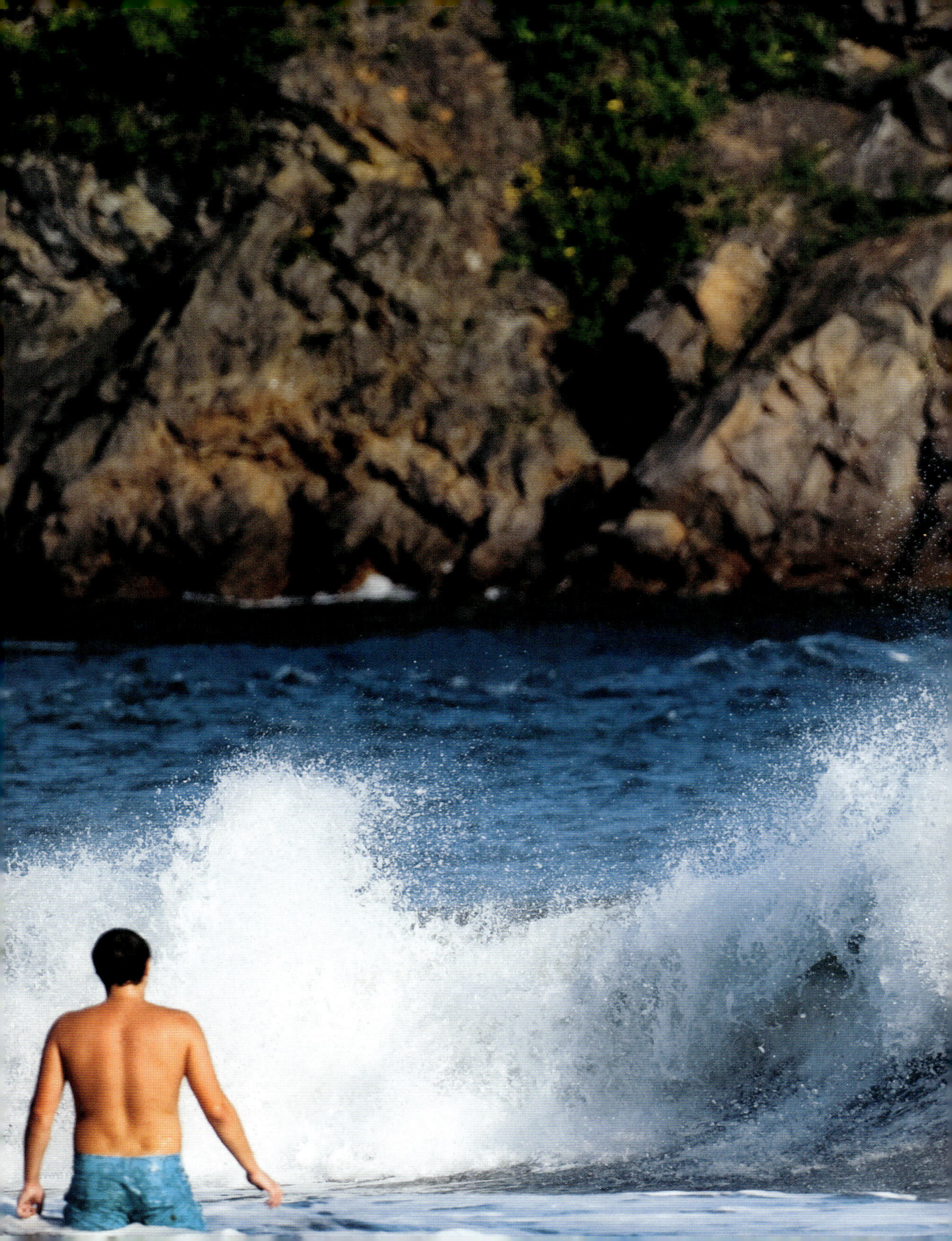

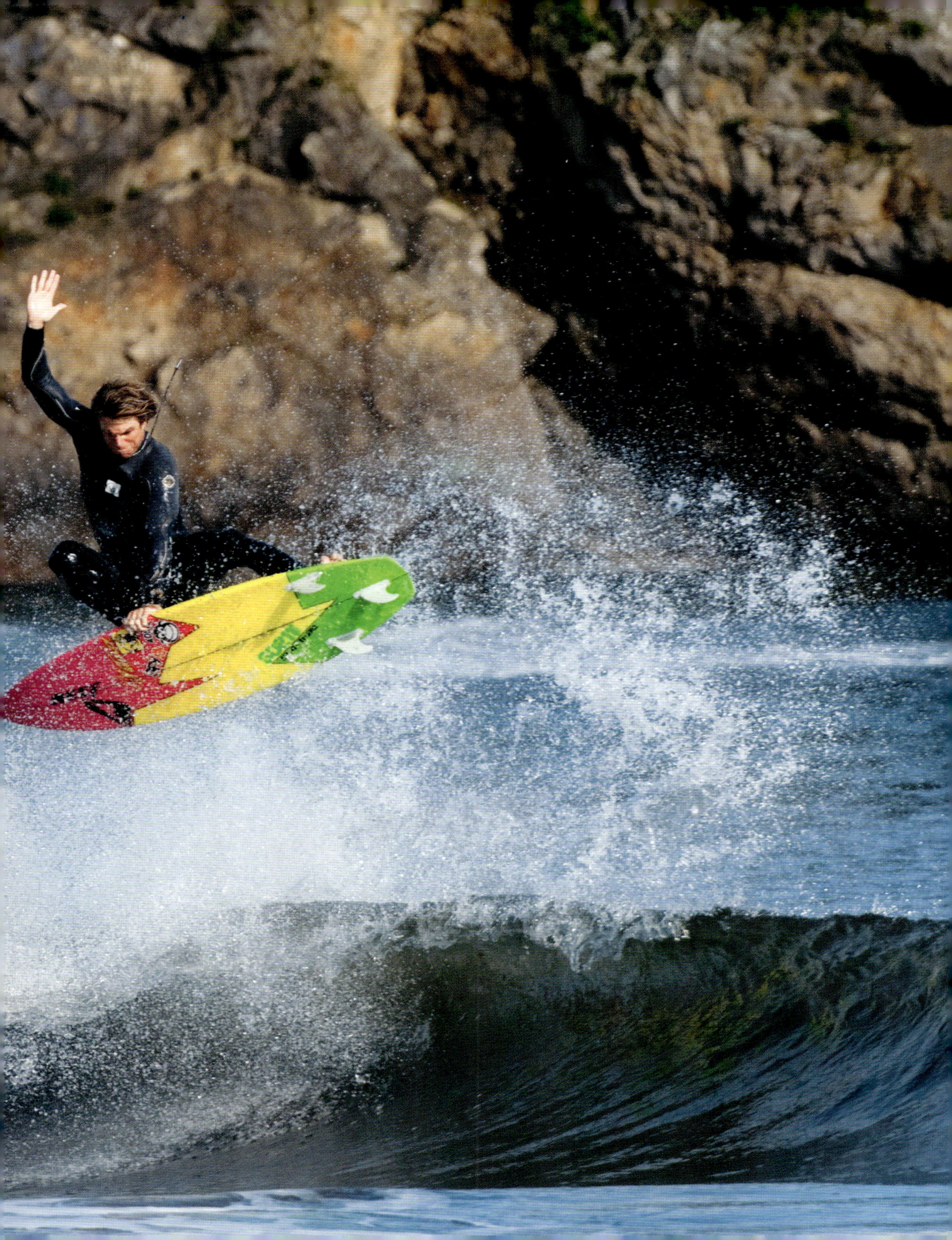

and getting to work. Seeing those wedgy offshore waves brought out an emotion that I had managed to suppress this whole time: the joy of finally seeing surfable waves.

As I sloshed into the shore break, cold water pricked my hands and feet. I dove through a wave crest and felt a shudder ripple from my skull down through my spine. The sun dipped behind the mountains, darkening the scene except for a shaft of white light shining toward me. I gripped the handle of my water housing tight and aimed my camera at the reflection. As I held down the shutter button in burst mode, Mike pumped his neon board in the path of the sun ray and launched himself clear into the clouds. He landed with a splash and a "Yeeew! Burky, you made it!"

A few months after the trip to Russia, I found myself sitting at a table at the 2010 Red Bull Illume awards ceremony in Dublin, Ireland. To my complete surprise, my sunset photo of Peter Mendia scoring that backwashy barrel in Chile was selected from among thousands of other images as a finalist in the "Illumination" category.

My foot was tapping at an alarming rate when my wife, Brea, reached over to calm my jitters. Completely subconsciously, when I'm feeling my most nervous, my body betrays my inner turmoil with an incessant need to move. I took in a deep breath as we sat in contemplative silence inside the historic Trinity College dining hall.

Event organizers had transformed the Hogwarts-style space into something more like a nightclub. While the other contestants mingled over red wine or Red Bull, I was sipping water, picking at my fingernails, and praying that my sweat stains weren't starting to show through my flannel shirt.

It's not every day that you're chosen as one of the forty-eight best photographers out of an international pool of five thousand. The Red Bull Illume photo competition is free to enter, and nearly 22,800 photos were submitted in total. I knew that image of Mendia in Chile was special, maybe even great—there was no doubt those backlit barrels and wind plumes were beautifully illuminated—but I worried the image might be too pulled-back, and too focused on the landscape for a hard-core action sports audience. Up until this point, it had only ever been published on Surfline.com, and it had never even graced the page of a magazine.

An Irish TV host named Síle Seoige took the stage, introducing the event in her thick accent. The winning images were selected by a panel of fifty-three judges, she said, deepening the suspense. The top fifty images flashed across a screen. The first two winning images were both surf shots by Australian photographers—I doubted another surf photograph could win a category. Just like trying to solve an episode of the TV show *24*, I started to strategize statistical probabilities and find any potential clues that would point to the winner of my category.

It seemed as if they held off showing that final photo and name for a good thirty seconds longer than all the rest. I was mentally racing through so many possibilities that I almost didn't hear my name. Síle's accent shortened the second syllable so *Burkard* sounded a little like *burger*.

As I made my way back to my seat, I had no chance to really celebrate, because my mind quickly moved on to my new odds of becoming the overall winner: one out of ten. But with three surfing photographs now in the mix, not to mention some images that really pushed the envelope when it came to technique, lighting, and creativity, it felt like one in a million. The level of talent I was up against was humbling. Several of the final photos were more technical than I had experience with in my own career. A fair amount were more like studio shots set up with strobes and backdrops—which, unbeknownst to me, had become common in action sports photography. This style made it possible for scenes to be controlled, manipulated, and perfected. I wondered what surf photography might look like if we had any say over how the ocean behaved.

My photo was different. It was about being in the right place at the right time to capture a beautiful moment. It was a special, fleeting moment. A moment frozen in time that combined a perfect swell, wind, and tide, all synchronized with the most important component of all: the athlete. Honestly, it couldn't have been duplicated even if I tried. The image told the story of a place, a trip, and a rare interaction between man and nature—I named it "Perfect Day." I just didn't know whether a photo like mine deserved this prestigious award.

Before any more doubt could worm into my mind, Síle answered the question for me. "And the winner is . . . Chris Burgert." Standing outside in the courtyard afterward, my photo appeared in a slideshow alongside some of the most powerful action sports photographs out there: a sunset sequence of Canadian surfer Peter Devries in Tofino shot by Jeremy Koreski, and the climbing photographer Tim Kemple's now-iconic photo of Tommy Caldwell and Kevin Jorgeson hanging in a portaledge during one of their historic attempts of Yosemite's Dawn Wall. All I kept thinking was: *This must be a fluke.*

A burden had been lifted. For so long I had felt at odds with my editors about shooting landscape-style surf photography, but the Red Bull Illume was confirmation that I was on the right path. My Chile photo was an example of what was possible; the Illume was the ultimate validation. It also seemed to solidify a mission statement, of sorts, for what I was hoping to achieve with my photographs. Maybe that was the purpose of my work, I thought: to reflect the rawness and wonder of nature and seek out those quiet moments when the earth really speaks to you.

FIRST PERSON

Michael H. Kew
Author, Crossings

Russian Reflection

→ **One morning we drove far to the north, to a** spot with excellent swell and wind exposure. En route we were nearly arrested for having breakfast in a military town. "And zere are no waves in zee forecast," our driver said slowly while we sat in his car at the surfless but scenic cove that took six dirt-road hours to reach. "Zis is bad." He chuckled. He was serene Valera, Vladivostok's first surfer, excited to have witnessed Mike Losness and Josh Mulcoy surfing the previous day. They were the first foreigners to ride waves near his hometown. Excited, too, was the lovely blonde Olga, the city's first wahine, our trusty translator and overall fixer. More than anyone, though, Valera knew his zone's requirements for rideable swell, and throughout the rest of our trip there were enough false-start days to kill even the strongest optimism. The much-needed typhoon never happened. The wind blew lightly and the sun cooked, and Buoyweather.com lent no hope. When the East Sea went flat, it went f-l-a-t.

Warren Smith, C. J. Kanuha, and Sam Hammer arrived later but could not wet a rail. Instead we killed time in Vladivostok, where we could dissolve and lose ourselves among oceans of cheap vodka, cigarettes, hookahs, close-at-8:00 A.M. nightclubs, new friends, good food and music, and—for the unmarried among us—the world's most beautiful women. "Let's drink vodka together" became a theme. Eventually time distorted and the city's soul was unveiled, yet Russia's subtle intelligence was no match for the stubborn East Sea. It was an act of restraint before the annual winter freeze.

Burkard was shattered. He'd flown all that way, endured detainment and deportation, and was emotionally and financially drained, and, with us, he watched nearly a year of planning evaporate into the sunny Siberian sky. Russia was truly a tough place to ingest—huge, stoic, unpredictable. The East Sea's typhoon season was in premature hibernation, its gates sealed. We surrendered—the Soviet surf trip was done.

136

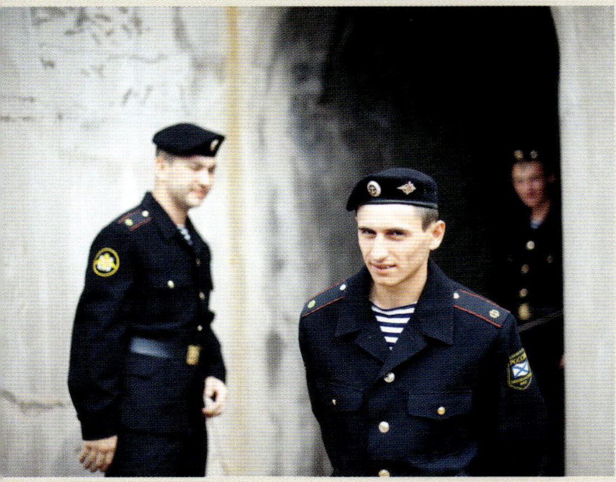

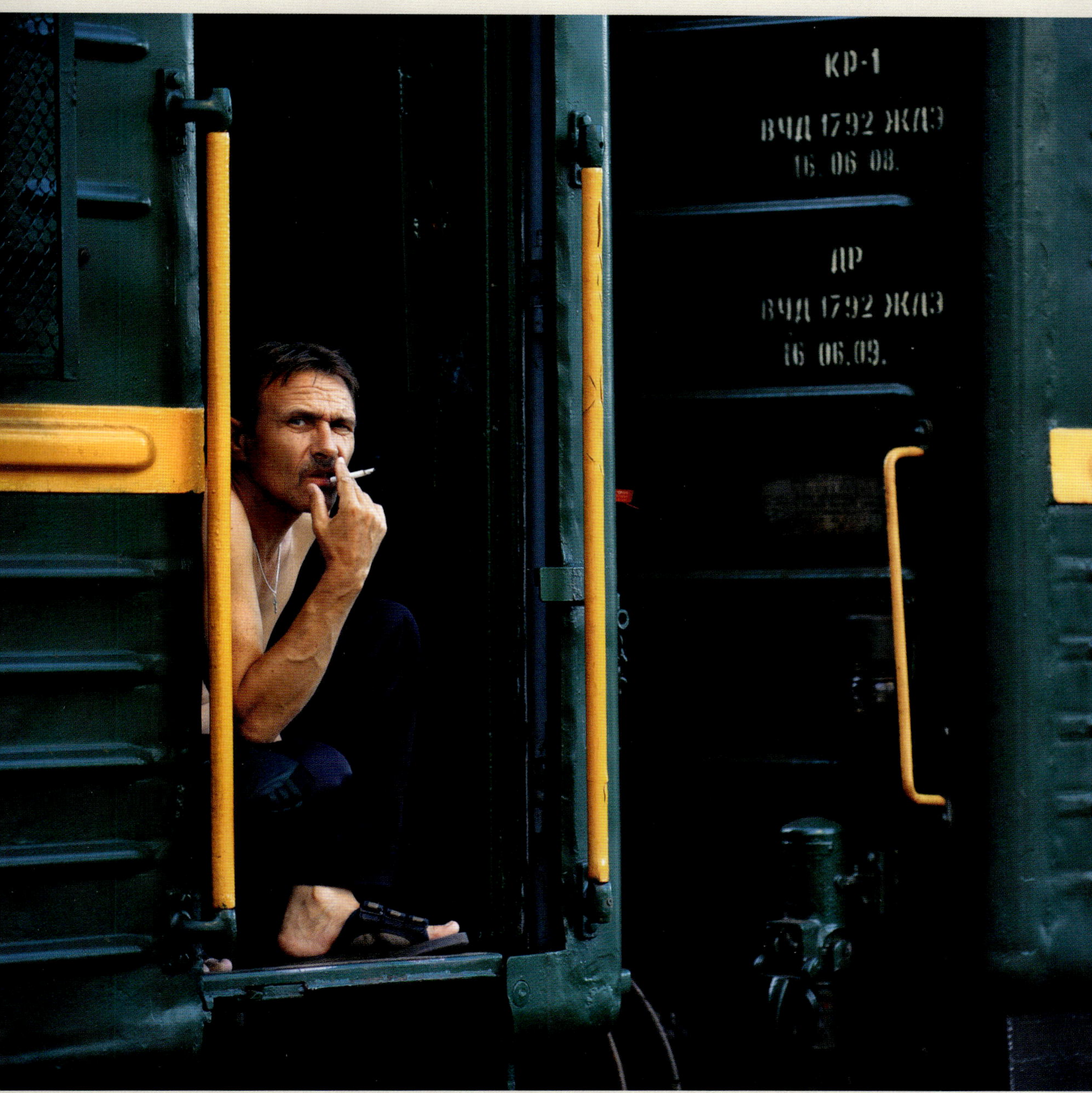
КР-1
ВЧД 1792 ЖЛЭ
16. 06. 08.

ЛР
ВЧД 1792 ЖЛЭ
16. 06.09.

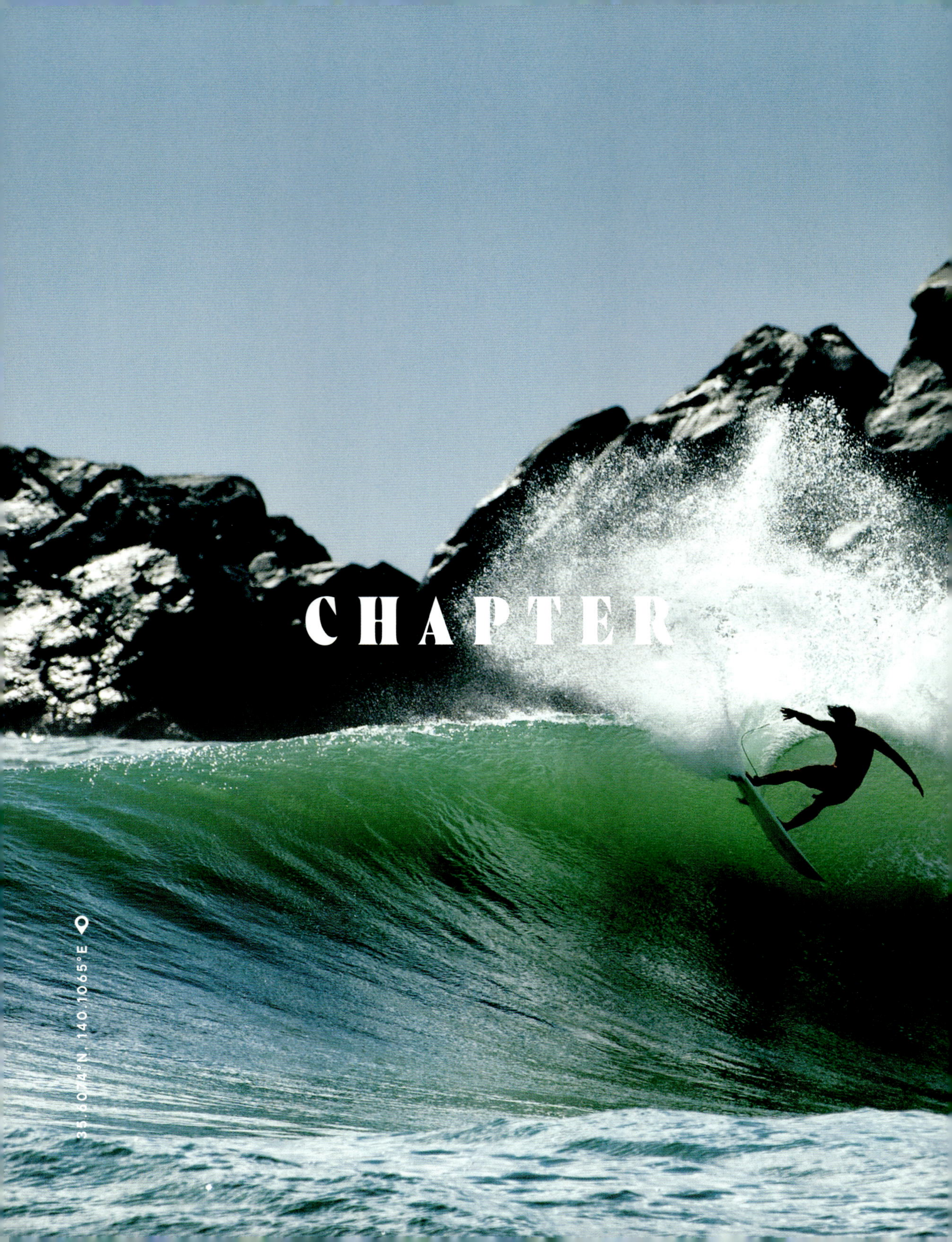

CHAPTER

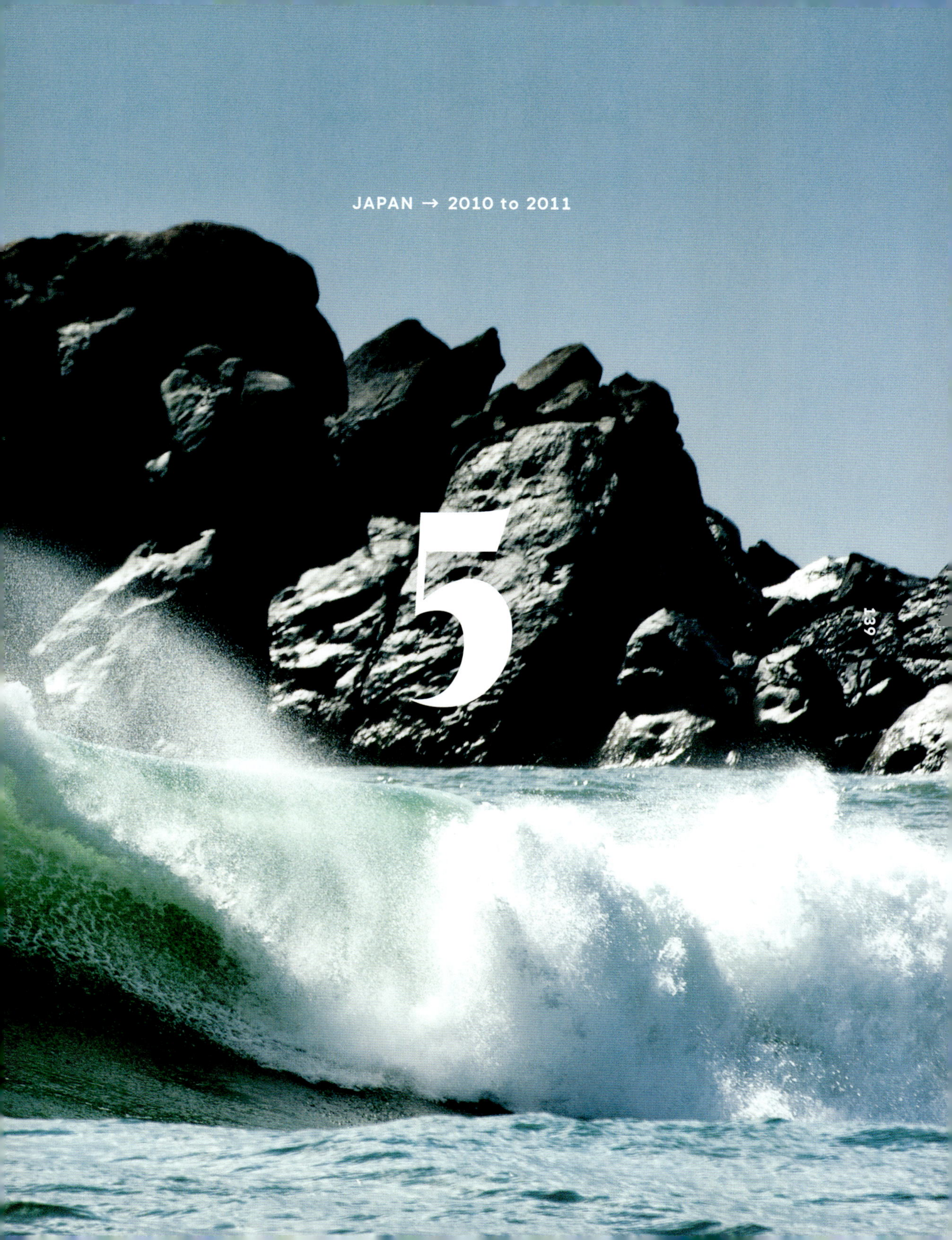

JAPAN → 2010 to 2011
5
139

I first started working for Patagonia in 2009, but by 2010 it had become one of my most reliable clients. As a kid, I looked at this progressive outdoor clothing company as a brand that made gear I could only dream to afford. As I grew older it wasn't just the clothing I admired, but its stable of world class athletes. I was in awe of Patagonia-sponsored legends like Gerry Lopez and the Malloy brothers and their exploits with raw undiscovered surf breaks. I began looking forward to getting their quarterly coffee-table-worthy catalogs, and I think I spent more time looking at them than I did *National Geographic* (one of my all-time favorite print publications).

By 2010, the company was big—1,265 staff members and $315 million big—and this was even two years into the Great Recession. Not only were they growing monetarily, but their reputation and ethical business practices were garnering respect and admiration from anyone who loved the outdoors. More importantly, it coincided with a time in my life when I was exploring outdoor adventures other than surfing—climbing, skiing, backpacking—and the synergy was undeniable. Other than working for *Surfer* magazine, which I had been doing for a couple of years before officially getting hired as a staff photographer, my only other photography goal in the early days was to shoot for Patagonia. By 2010, I was working for both.

Patagonia and *Surfer* were a dream team. Patagonia was excited about cold-weather surf expeditions and was willing to provide the durable down, wool, and waterproofing to keep me warm and dry on assignment. The company also took a photojournalistic approach to adventure photography, which offered a creative challenge and style that perfectly suited magazine work. Patagonia would help pay for some trips, and I could publish photos in brand catalogs, books, ads, and websites, as well as in *Surfer* magazine, since Patagonia was an advertiser, not a competitor.

The extra paycheck was liberating, but so was the brand diversity. Patagonia's roots are in rock climbing and surfing—the two biggest passions of founder and CEO Yvon Chouinard—but it also makes gear for skiing, fly-fishing, mountain biking, and every outdoor pursuit in between. My work in surf photography was geographically limited to the coast and weather-dependent, but now, if the wind and waves weren't on, I could photograph any other activity under the sun—or snow. Looking at the categories on the Patagonia website, I realized all my hobbies, everything I loved, could be an opportunity to explore new avenues of my career, as well as to earn income.

Pete Taras, my editor from *TransWorld SURF*, once advised me against being a surf photographer altogether. He sat me down for a meal at Wahoo's Fish Taco one day and warned me of the dangers of limiting myself creatively. It didn't take long for me to understand what he meant: Your specialization and skills prepare you for one thing and one thing only, to get easily pigeonholed in one style of photography. At the time my ego didn't allow me to accept Pete's words during that tense lunch meeting. But it was his wisdom that I leaned on only a few years later, that helped me realize the incredible opportunity Patagonia was providing when it came to my future.

At *Surfer* I was hoping to follow in the footsteps of visionary lensmen like Ron Stoner, Art Brewer, and Tom Servais. At Patagonia I was simultaneously looking up to adventure photographers such as Jimmy Chin and Corey Rich and finding encouragement to pursue the gritty editorial style that the company helped pioneer. Patagonia's photo editor, Jane Sievert, had a strong eye for the raw, unplanned experiences that make adventures so memorable. She valued those moments or mishaps worthy of *National Geographic* caught on a climbing or surfing expedition.

Jane told me the story of the image that launched Corey Rich's career: a grainy flash photo of Corey's friend Tom getting a penicillin shot to the ass during a surf trip in Mexico. Out of a couple hundred slide sheets that Corey sent in, it was that photo that Jane pulled from the bottom of a box and ultimately turned into a full-page Patagonia ad that ran in *Outside* magazine. Jane called it "the lucky snapshot." For me, it was the Illume-winning photo of Peter Mendia in Chile that first got Jane's attention. She selected it as one of the newer images for the Patagonia photo book *Unexpected*. I was floored that I didn't just get to work on their catalogs, but now my photo would be immortalized in one of their epic hardback books. Proving why she was an expert at what she does, she caught on to the spirit and reality of the photo immediately.

"You couldn't set up that shot," Jane explained. "You had to be there at the right time."

Maybe it had something to do with the fact that all of my earlier mentors were men, but with Jane, I felt safer than with all the rest. She was the first photo editor who was purely an editor and not a fellow photographer. Every other editor I worked with was also contending to run their own work in the magazines, which created an obvious undercurrent of competitiveness. With Jane I didn't feel an overwhelming urge to prove myself. I knew she was there to support the art and the artist. I looked up to her just as much, maybe even more, than bosses I'd had before. I was inspired by the way Jane looked at images on slide sheets and in print. I'd often walk into her office and see her tilting ponytail as she was getting a different perspective on a scene, rotating horizontals into verticals. Never looking at a photo in a linear way, she saw what most others didn't. I felt something of a kindred spirit in her—she had high standards and didn't shy away from very direct critiques, yet her intentions seemed pure. She simply wanted me to be the best I could be, and she offered her support to help get me there, just as she had done with photographers Jimmy Chin, Jeff Johnson, and so many others before me.

It was Jane who invited me to LOOK3, a photography festival founded by *National*

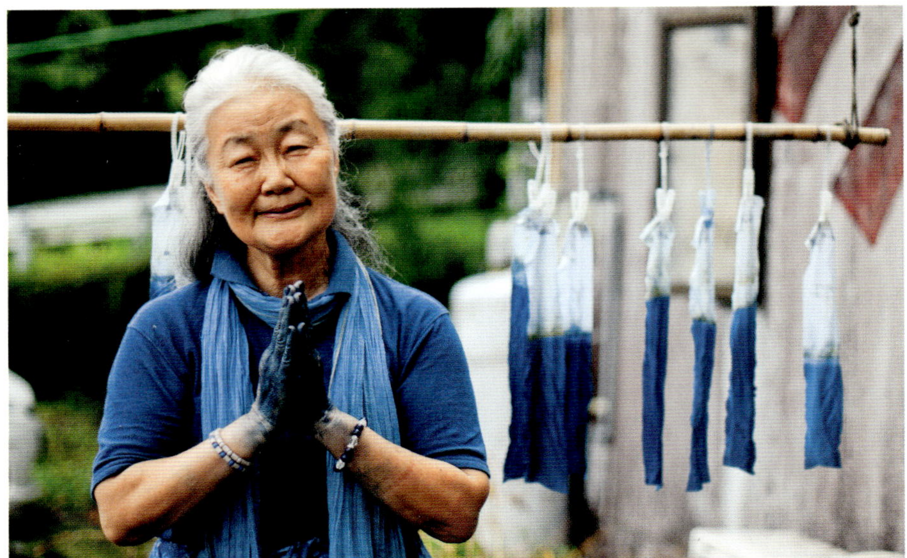

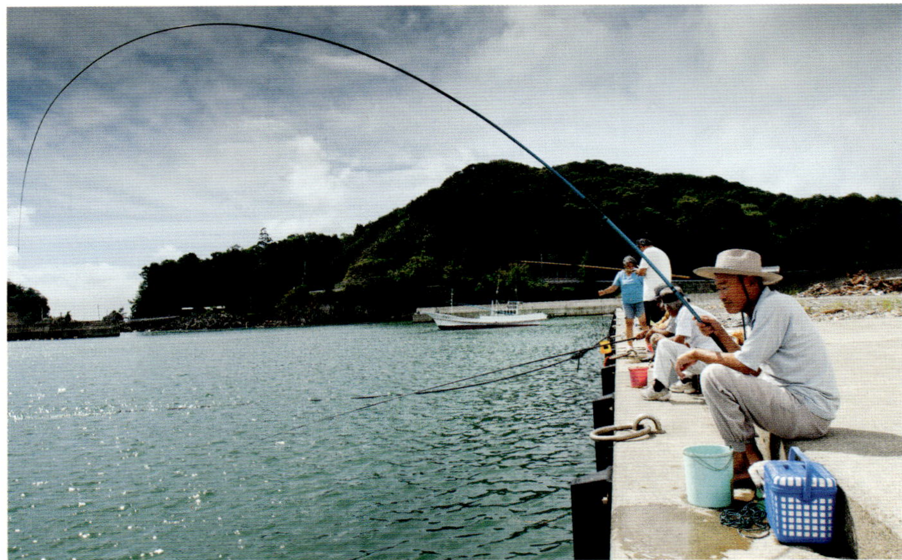

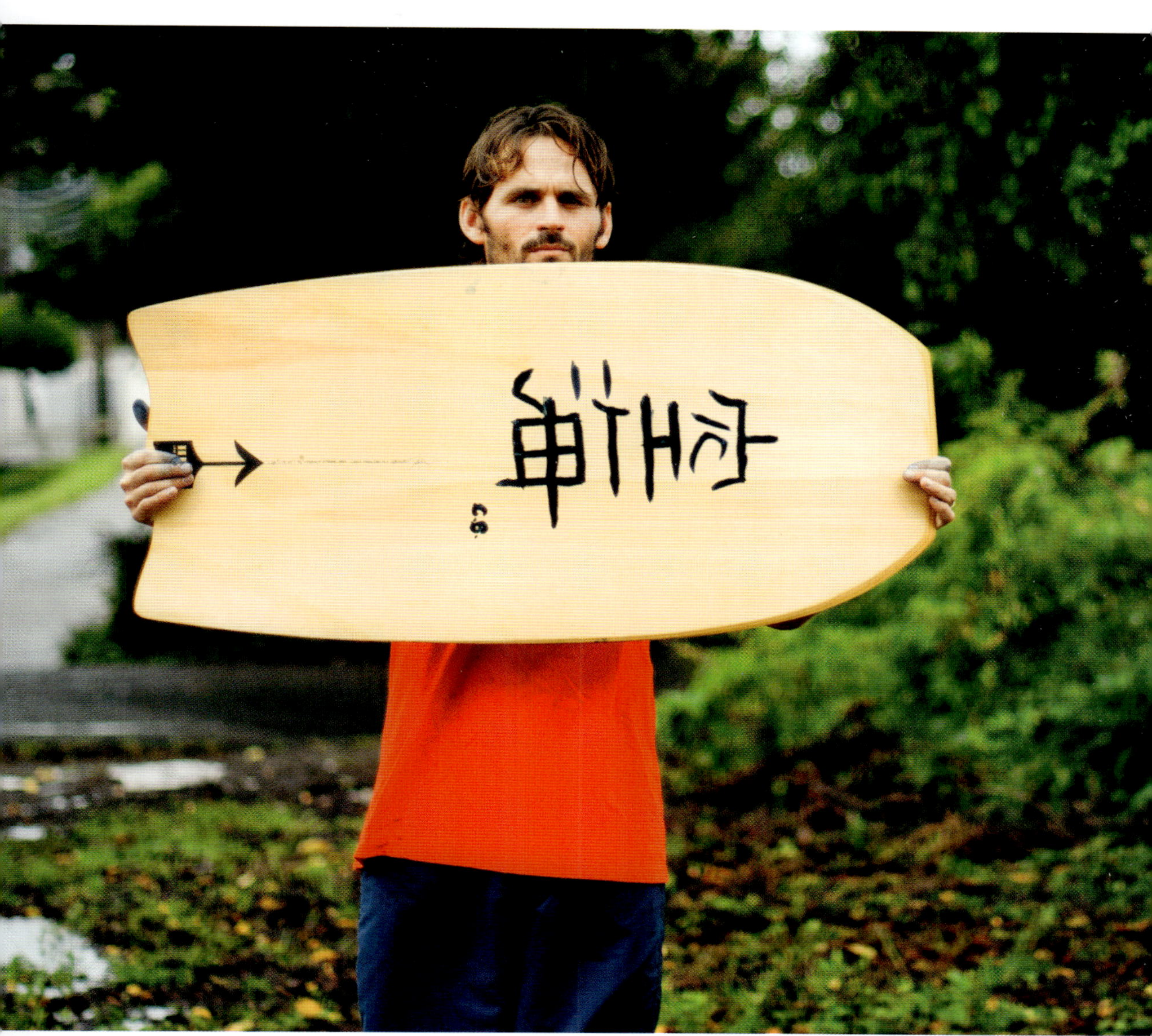

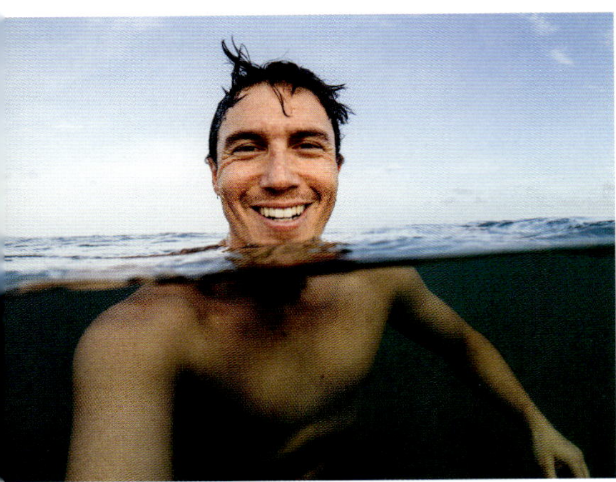

Geographic photojournalist Michael "Nick" Nichols in Charlottesville, Virginia. In 2010 the festival debuted an event called LOOKbetween, which was a mentorship program for early-career photographers. When asked for nominations, Jane picked a Canadian ornithologist turned nature photographer named Steve Ogle and me.

LOOKbetween was like adult summer camp, complete with live music and fire twirlers. After sunset each night the crowd assembled on a grassy hill overlooking a pond to watch video projections by some of the one hundred invited photographers, including myself. There was a photo essay on living with Arctic hunters; a series that documented a national park every day for an entire year; and a project about the antelope migration and wildlife corridors of western Wyoming, shot by a young biologist-photographer named Joe Riis.

I started to feel self-conscious about what I had to offer. *Why am I here?* I began to ask myself. I may have had a bit more experience working with magazines and brands, but my photography felt kind of shallow compared with these portrayals of animals and humans fighting for their lives in remote places.

Later that night in my hotel room I couldn't get the pictures out of my head. Here were all these other subjects I could, or maybe should, be covering. Sure, I had moved away from postcard-perfect surf images, but surf photography itself felt frivolous compared with these deeper stories about human and environmental trials. Looking back on the experience, I wonder if Jane was showing me that this was what real photography was; this was what art was—without having to outright say it. She was teaching me what could come from deeply listening and witnessing the world around me.

The festival ignited a deep surge of inspiration, but with it came some new doubts and fears. There was a clarity that came with realizing most of my work felt truly surface level; it forced me to take a step back and take mental stock of what I wanted most. I knew deep inside that I wanted to create images that expressed deeper emotion and told a more humanistic story of struggle and connection to place. I even slowly started visiting destinations where I could combine a surf adventure with some photojournalism, like southern India, Cuba, and Nicaragua. But I often felt uncomfortable documenting people, especially those in destitute situations. I didn't have any of the confidence I had pointing my camera at the throat of a giant breaking wave. I couldn't shake the feeling that my images would do nothing to improve their lives.

It was during a month laid up in bed after contracting MRSA (a medically resistant staph infection) in Tahiti that I decided to watch a documentary called *War Photographer*, about the legendary photojournalist James Nachtwey. Over and over I watched a completely composed Nachtwey walk into various hellacious scenes of human suffering. Whether in Rwanda, Kosovo, or Palestine, he'd dodge bombs, cover his face with a bandana to protect himself from toxic gas, and get within feet of corpses and grieving mothers with his Canon film camera. Despite how much I admired his grit, I realized I could never do that, no matter how altruistic and noble it seemed. If I needed one more reality check, this was it. These experiences did sharpen my purpose somewhat, but mostly because they revealed my limitations and showed me where my comfort level truly was.

And it left me wrestling further with the idea that my work, no matter how adventurous it was, was shallow and unfulfilling at times. I felt compelled to marry my love of travel and exploration with something of more substance. And it would actually take years until I began to see and define my *purpose*.

Oddly enough, the next trip I signed on for after recovering from my bout of MRSA—and my photojournalism fantasies—was neither gritty nor gut-wrenching. It was just another surf trip. But its poignancy was in the fact that it was just a simple surf trip, a sort of reminder that unforgettable and iconic moments can come from anywhere, at any time.

It was 2011 and Patagonia invited me to Japan with surf ambassadors Kim Diggs and Dan Malloy, one of my surf heroes, as well as "Mr. Pipeline" himself: Gerry Lopez. It was a PR trip to attend a store opening in Chiba, just outside Tokyo, as well as a meet and greet with Gerry and Australia's counterculture surf legend, Wayne Lynch. And it would turn out to be yet another turning point for my career.

After fulfilling our obligations at the Patagonia store opening in Chiba, we were eager to start the surf portion of our trip. Kim, Dan,

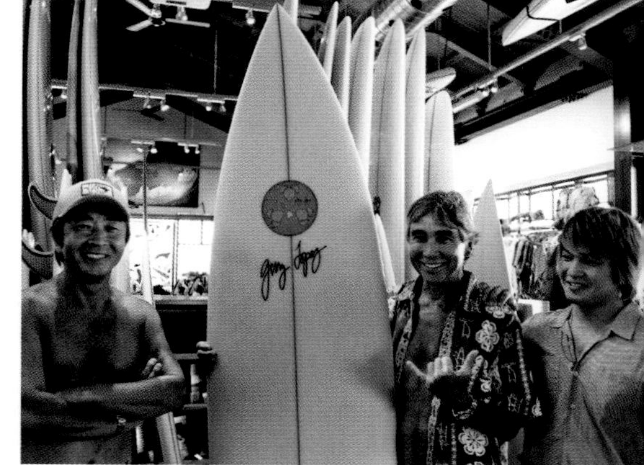

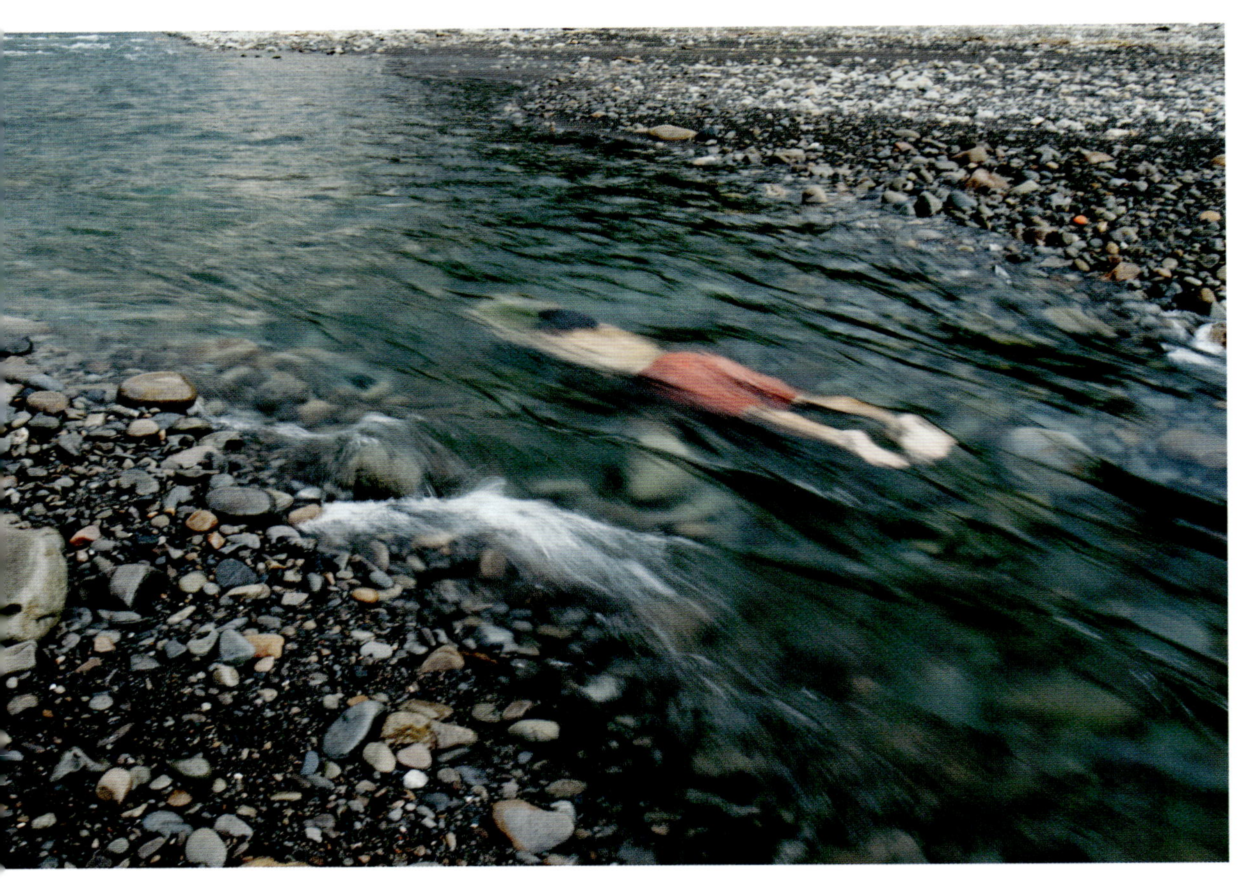

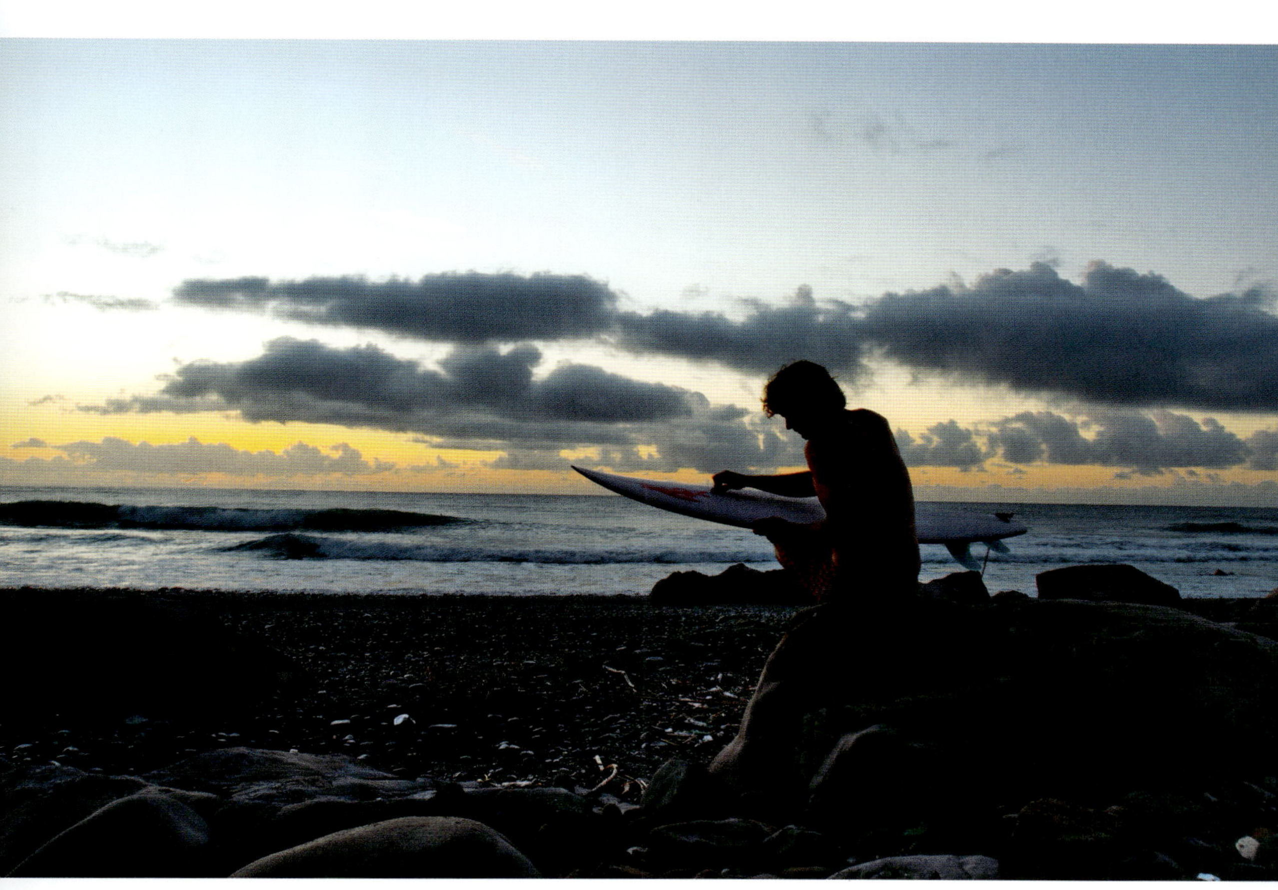

CHRIS BURKARD   WAYWARD

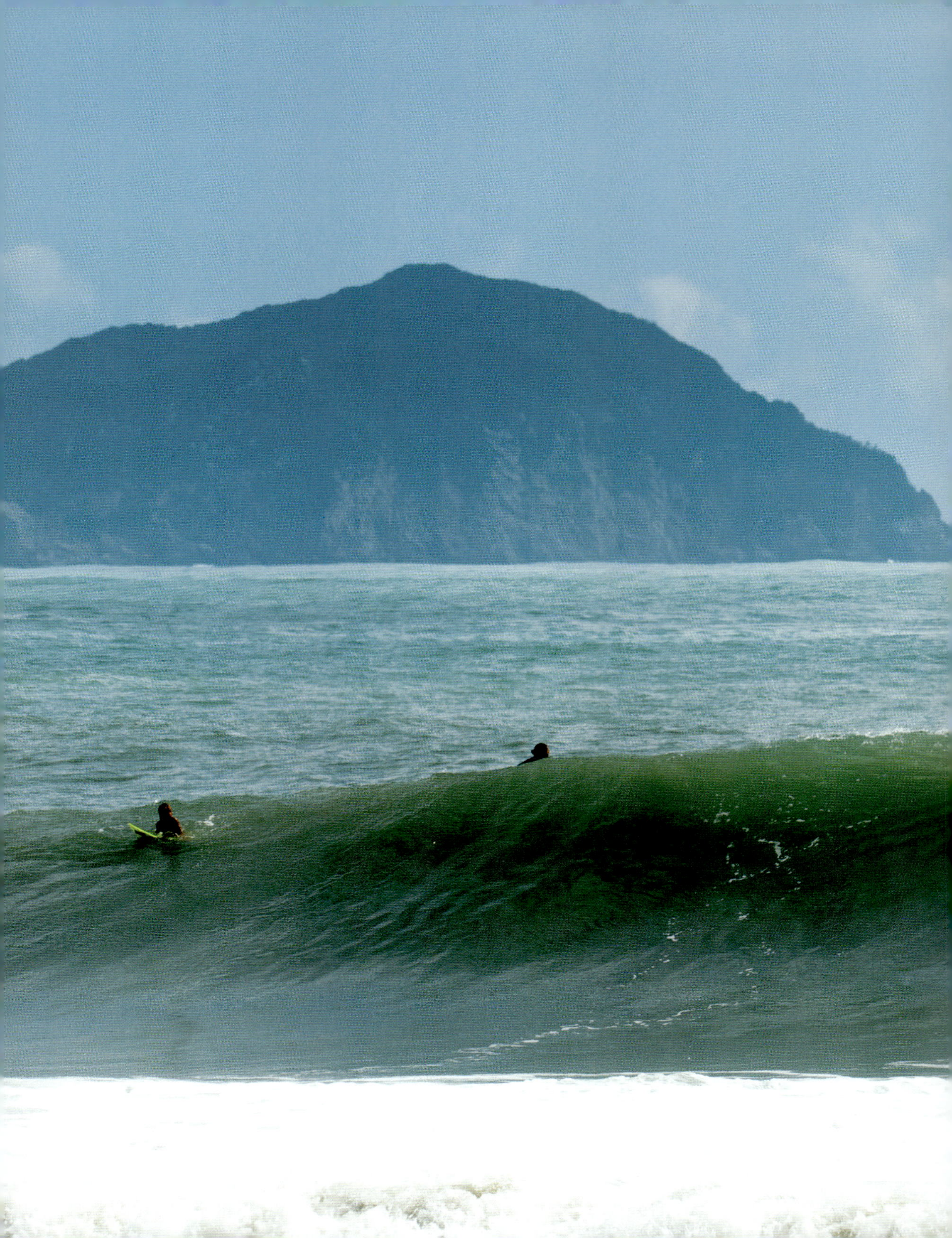

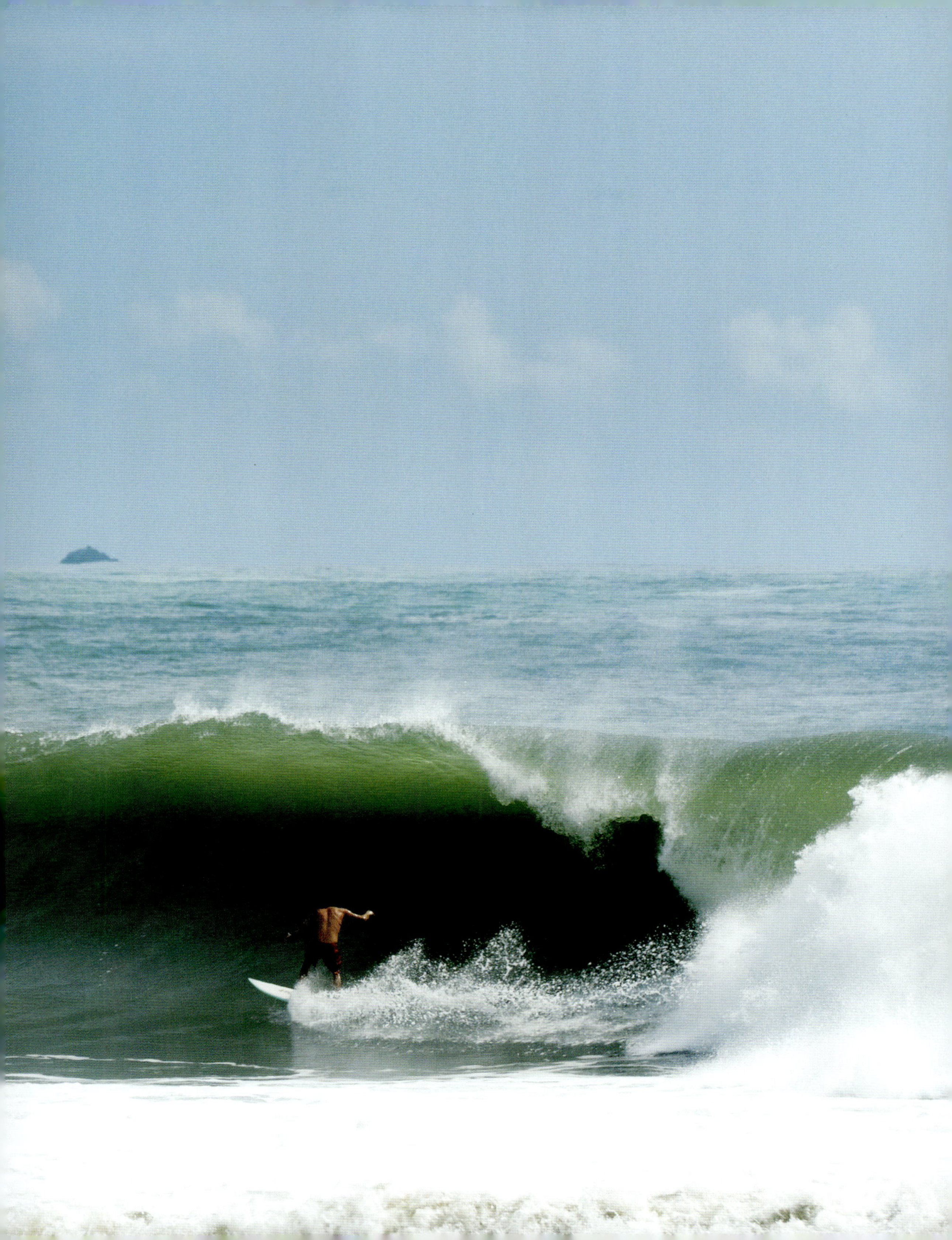

and I had a goal to catch some typhoon swell and hoped to produce a story for *Surfer* magazine from it.

Gerry told us to find his friend Kohei, saying, "He will show you everything you need to know." Kohei had a surfboard company called 303 Surfboards, and he was by all accounts the Japanese version of Gerry Lopez, a stylin' Zen master with perfect teeth who everyone knew and loved. Having no idea how to find him, we trusted in Gerry's magic and simply hoped we would.

As often happens in the irony that is my life, the swell didn't hit until the day we were headed to the airport. Dan left one board and a pair of board shorts unpacked just in case of this very scenario, and we decided to drive up the coast on our way back to Tokyo, stopping anywhere we saw as much as a watery lump along the way. About thirty minutes north of where we were staying, Dan and Kim squeezed in a short sunrise session at a beach break, which at least gave us a few more surf shots for Patagonia in some nice pink light.

Feeling somewhat deflated, we drove back toward this river mouth that we had checked around twenty times before. On each attempt there had been either too much wind or not enough swell. But as we approached the jetty this time, we got a glimpse of something a bit different—something we hadn't seen all week: offshore wind plumes spraying up like geysers behind the breakwater. I tapped Dan on the shoulder and saw my own mania reflected in his crazy gaze.

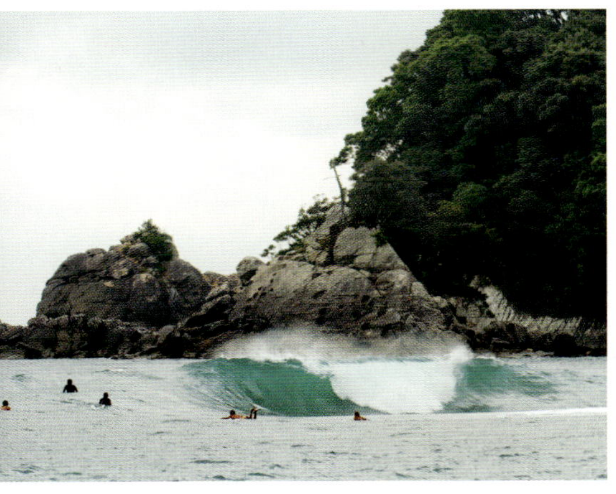

Dan threw on his trunks and grabbed his shortboard in record time, then ran down the jetty, jumped off the rocks, and paddled right to where the double-overhead waves were spiraling. Sure enough, there was Kohei, the local legend Gerry Lopez had told us about, also taking advantage of the conditions.

Dan channeled years of surfing California point breaks into an incredible thirty minutes. I followed him down the jetty fast enough to see him catch his first wave. I got a decent photo but immediately realized I was too high up and that Dan was surfing the right-hander peeling away from me. The angle wasn't doing justice to how epic the wave really was. I needed to find a lower vantage point so I could look up to see the row of big black boulders I was standing on, which would perfectly contrast against the wintergreen waves. Random computations were running through my brain of how far and how elevated I needed to be. Anxiety started to pour over me as I looked down at my watch. I was literally racing against the clock, and I only had one more shot to make the image happen.

Looking over at our well-worn rental car, I had a brilliant idea: drive over the bridge to the smaller jetty. It had already been ten minutes, and I figured I might lose ten more, but I knew it was worth the risk. I'd rather fail at trying to get the best photo than settle for a mediocre result. Dan probably only had time for one or two more waves anyway.

After I made it across the bridge, I ran as fast as I could down the beach with one camera and one lens strapped to my body. I quickly climbed over a dune of sand littered with wood and buoys to find my angle. Once in position I was a good half mile away. I spotted a surfer I thought was Dan and started photographing a nice-looking section. Upon studying the playback, I realized the surfer didn't have Dan's style or anywhere near the skills I'd studied the millions of times I'd watched him before. The sun was shining right in my face, so the guy was just a black silhouette. Not Dan's silhouette. I was sure of it. Kicking myself for not picking up on the clues sooner, I knew time was almost out.

Another surfer dropped into a second set. This time there was no question I was looking at Dan Malloy. He rode out the steep drop and did a Tom Curren–esque bottom turn that brought him back to the lip. Then he cracked the tightest, most forceful cutback I had ever seen, drawing a smoking C shape in white spray. The energy flowed from his right to his left arm, which perfectly mimicked the arc of the wave. Dan's entire figure fit under the glowing curl. He was almost anonymous, except for his speed skater–like lean and a left arm as graceful as a dancer's. Frame to frame, the sequence was flawless, and I felt like I had experienced the entire ride. I had never seen a more perfect turn, and whether Patagonia was going to use it or *Surfer* was going to run it, I knew people needed to see it.

"This is one of the best turns we've ever seen," said Joel Patterson, the editor of *Surfer* magazine, as we looked at Dan Malloy on the cover of the February 2012 issue that released five months after my Japan trip. At the end of every article in the magazine, there's a tiny icon of a surfer shaped like Tom Curren, and Joel suggested maybe he should change the emoji to Dan. "This is an iconic photo," he said. My heart swelled.

This was my third cover for *Surfer* magazine, but it was by far my most significant. I had dreamed of seeing my name below a cover image of Dan Malloy, never expecting it would actually happen. Holding the magazine in my hands, I couldn't stop looking at my last name printed on its glossy card stock.

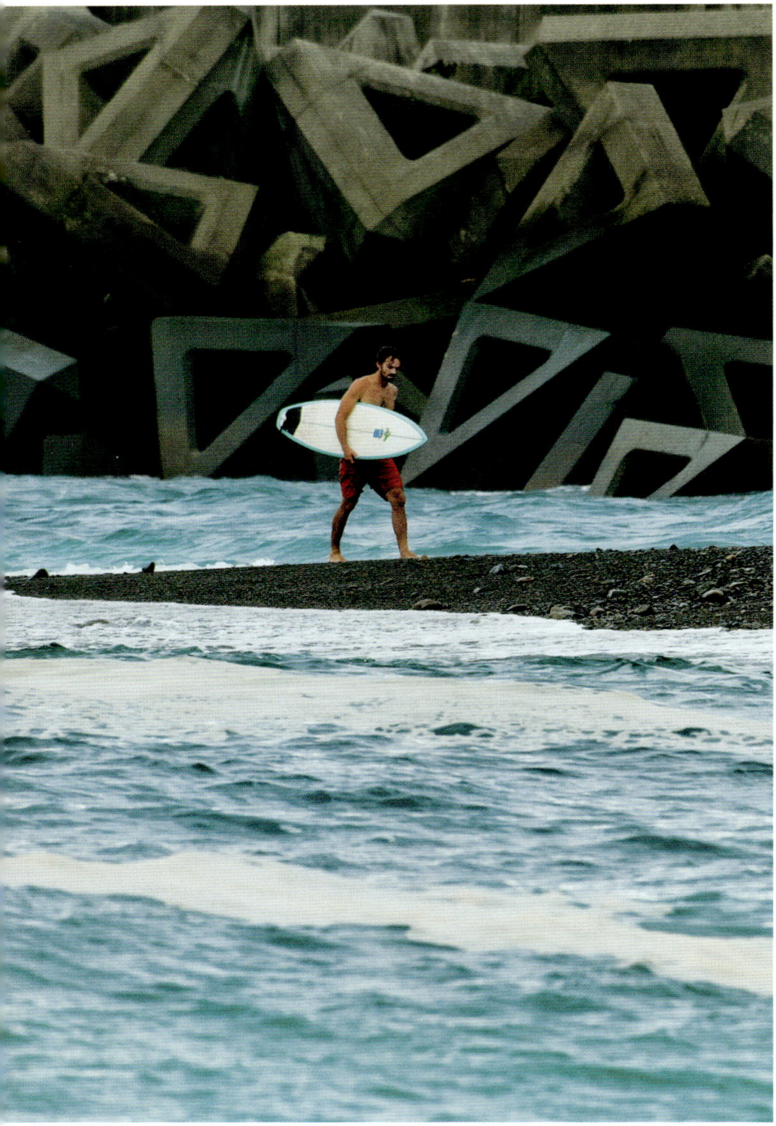

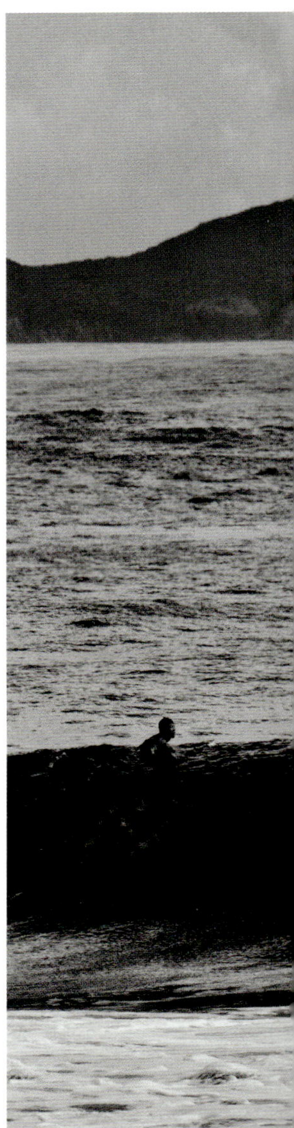

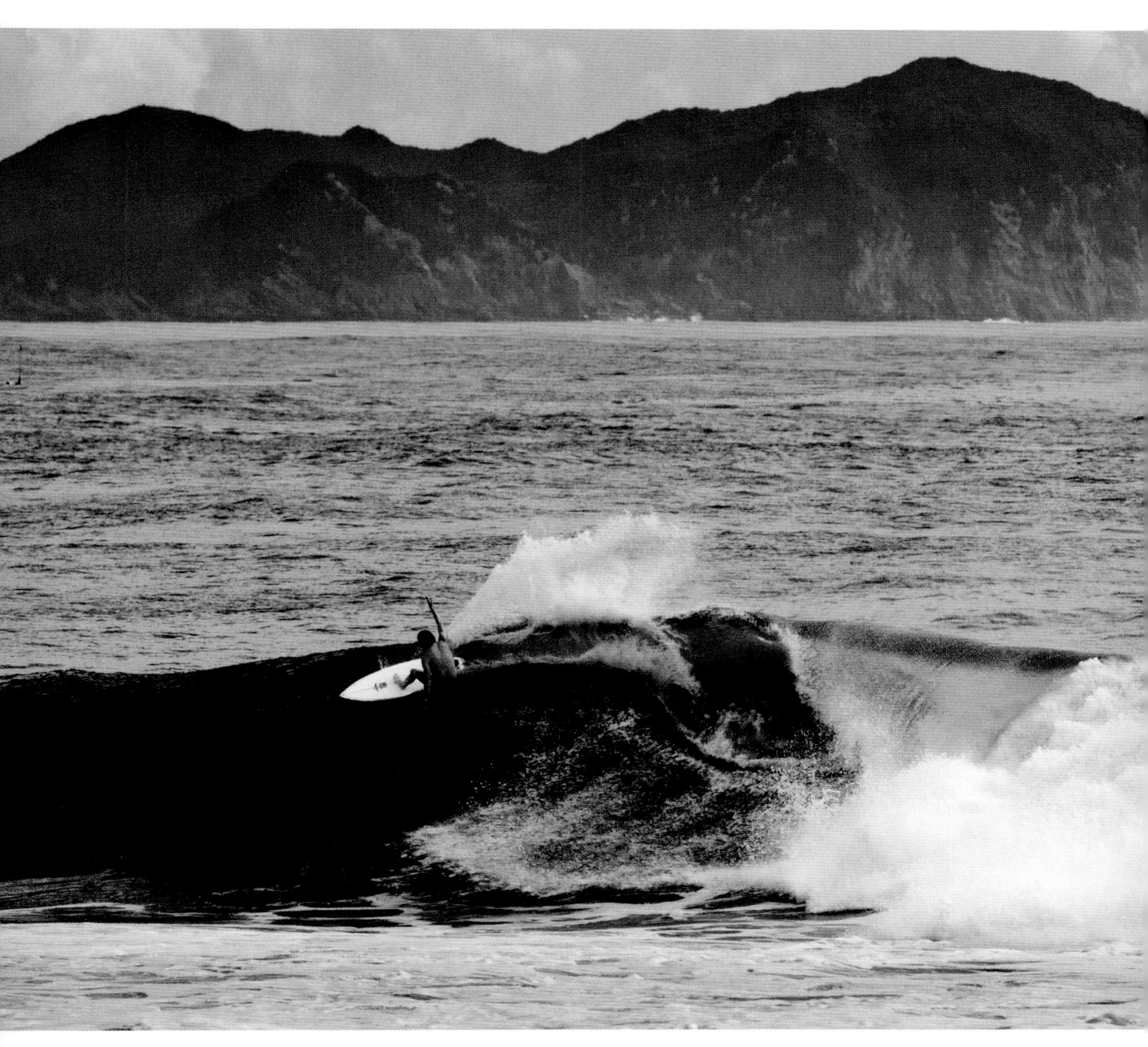

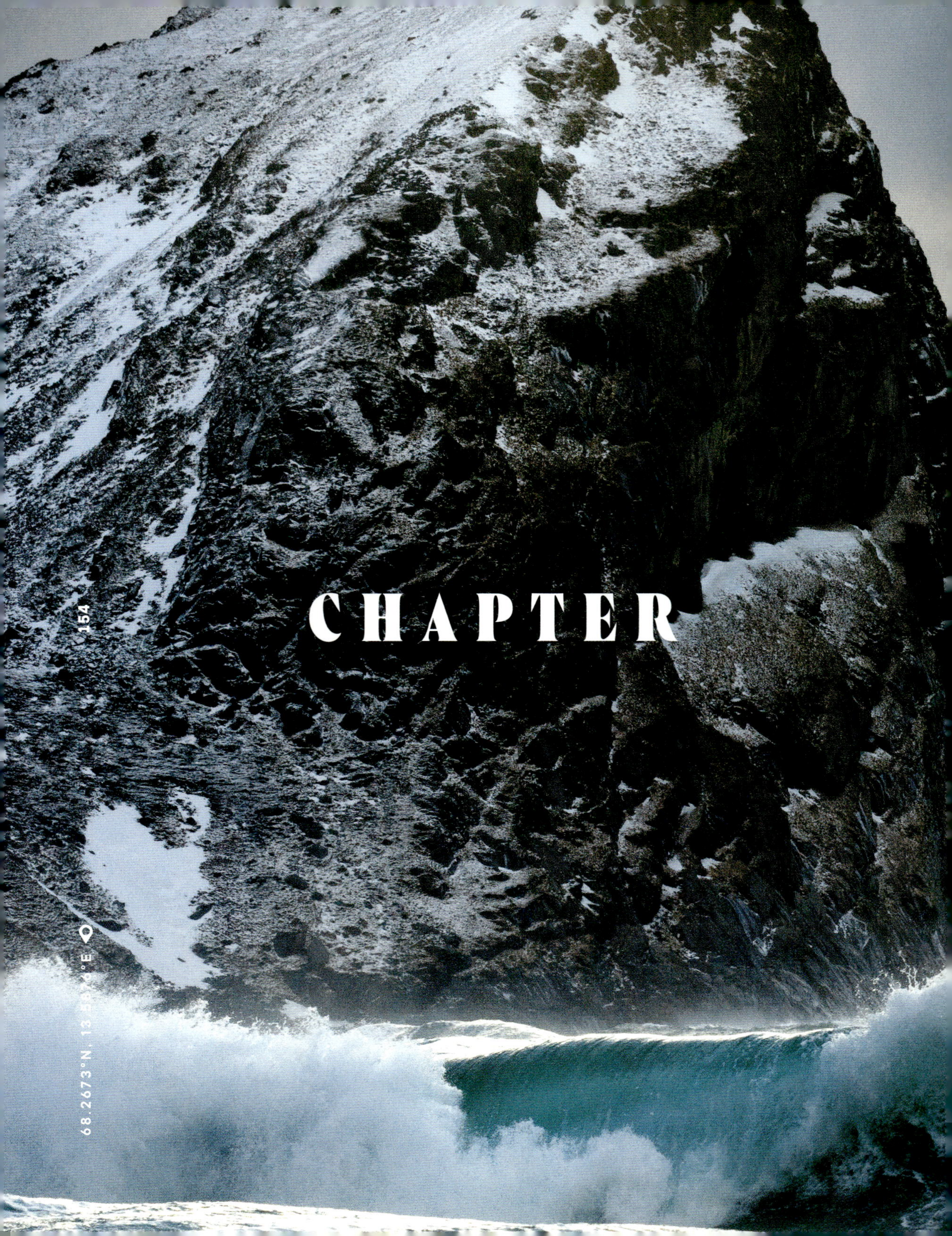

CHAPTER

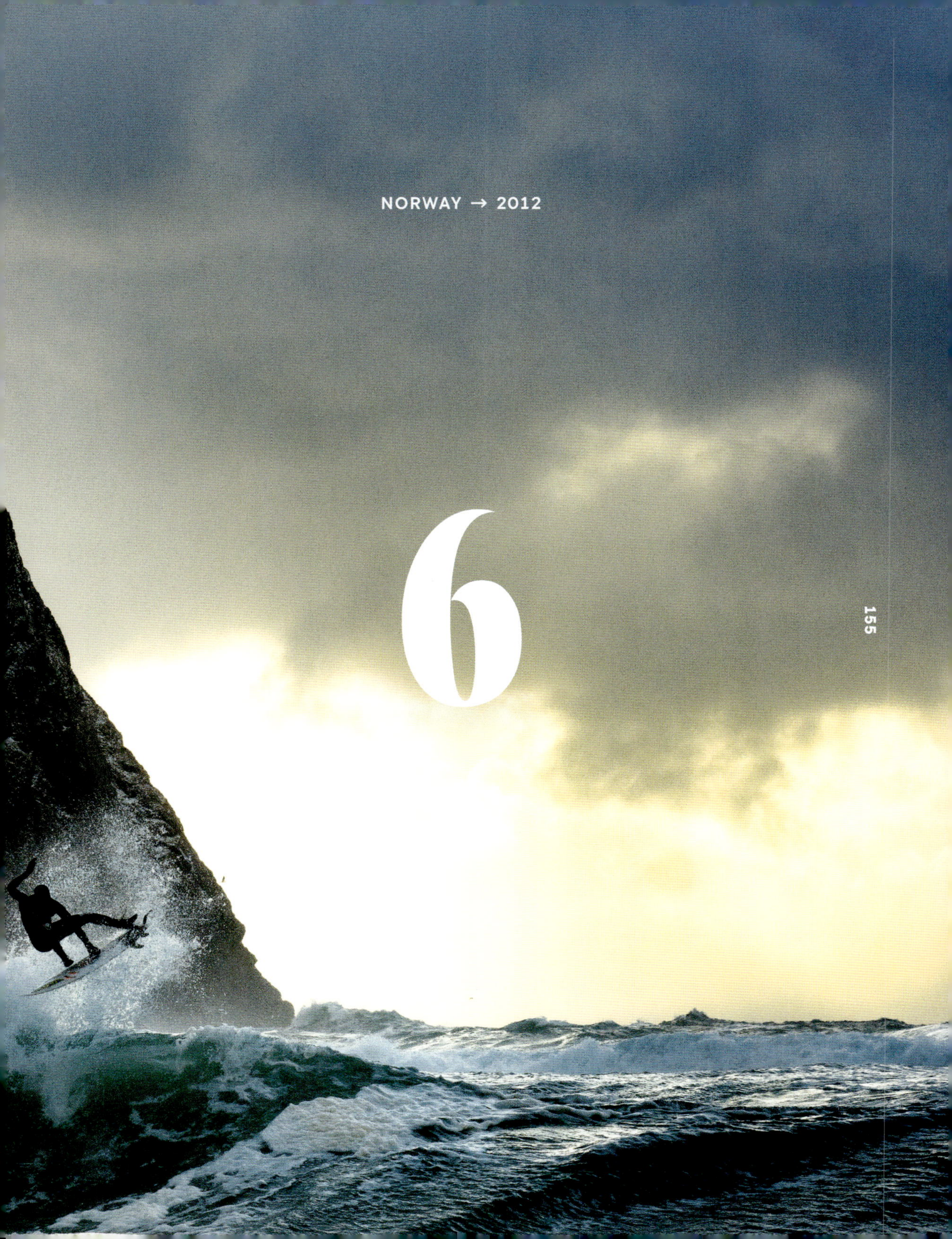

6

I was starting to sweat in my five-millimeter wetsuit and seven-millimeter booties, but I couldn't make myself open the van door. Instead, I watched through the foggy window as Keith and Dane scrambled over snow-dusted boulders and paddled out to the left-hand wave at the far end of the bay. It peeled from left to right, clean across the steamed-up windshield. Booming offshore gusts feathered off the six-foot faces. I sat squinting, stalling, soaking up every last ounce of warmth from our rental van, which shuddered in the wind like a sedan being shaken by a speeding semitruck. *Even the cars here shiver*, I thought.

March is the coldest month for ocean temperatures in Lofoten, Norway, which range from about 35 to 41 degrees Fahrenheit. (For seawater to freeze, it needs to be at a temperature of 28.4 degrees.) But with ice forming on your wetsuit hood and around your face, you don't need a thermometer to know it's cold. Ironically, the water is actually balmy compared to the external climate. When the wind picks up, the already below-freezing air temps can plummet to −10 degrees.

You hear the ominous howling before you feel it. It swoops down from the jagged peaks into the Unstad valley and blasts the sea with intimidating power. I've heard stories of sheep being blown off hillsides, old ladies getting knocked down, and cabins flipping over like toys. We were nearing the end of our three-week Norwegian odyssey, and we had seen sunlight crack through the clouds for a total of maybe an hour.

I held my neoprene gloves up to the car heater and angled the vents so the hot air blew down the hand holes. Then I cranked up some Euro techno on the radio to psyche myself up. *This is why you came here, to get out of your comfort zone.* I shook my camera from a towel on the back seat and set the ISO to 400 (to counterbalance the gray sky) and the settings to shutter priority (Tv) mode with a speed of 1/800 of a second (to capture fast-moving surfers). Shutter priority would basically put the camera on autopilot, since my fingers would soon be numb and turning dials would be impossible.

Then I started the tedious process of protecting my hands; despite numbness being likely, they still are the most important appendages of the water photographer. I stretched on a seven-millimeter "lobster claw" mitten, sliding my outer digits deep into one compartment and my index finger and thumb into two others until my left palm looked like a black rubber cactus—not a configuration that looked ideal for swimming. I meticulously tucked the base of my hand inside the wrist seal of my wetsuit to prevent cold currents from rushing in. Over my right trigger hand, I pulled on a three-millimeter glove so I had the dexterity to press the shutter button and change my camera settings if need be. That wouldn't have been possible through a seven-millimeter pincer, but now my right hand was guaranteed to suffer. Resistance was futile; it was not a question of *if* I would freeze, but *when.*

I already had a few nice surf landscapes in the bag, but it was time to get in the water. I felt nervous about getting out and swimming in the menacing swell. Just about every local we talked to had a story of a friend of a friend getting swept out to sea and drowning. I had tried to train for Norway by doing endurance exercises to increase my blood flow, taking cold showers, and working on techniques to control my breathing, since the ocean there likes to steal it away. But life at home had been an onslaught of birthing classes and redecorating, so needless to say I didn't get in as much practice as I had planned.

I attached the camera to my left wrist with a two-foot leash and tucked my rubber swim fins under my armpit, which was radiating body heat. When I grabbed hold of the door handle and pushed, it caught the wind and flew open, nearly hurling me off the driver's seat and pulling my arm out of its socket. Scanning the charcoal sea, I located the rip current that I would ride out to the lineup, where Keith and Dane were already giving everything they had. *It's go time*, I thought, like a soldier going into battle. *Now the timer starts.* Thankfully, I couldn't have had a better crew.

My obsession with Norway dates back to around the time I met Ben Weiland, a computer ninja turned surf writer and videographer who fast became my cold-water co-conspirator. I first reached out to Ben in 2009 after discovering his blog, *Arctic Surf*, during one of my many nocturnal research sessions. I would spend hours on Google Earth zooming in and out of remote beaches and reefs, looking for any kind of whitewash that might resemble a wave. Ben's website documented his re-search on wave riding, specifically in places written off by mainstream surf culture; his posts on locations like eastern Russia and Alaska's Aleutian Islands were some of my favorites. I would scour the maps, satellite images, and webcams he posted, dreaming of a future adventure.

Soon Ben became my surf-scheming pen pal, and it wasn't long before we were meet-ing up at a nautical-themed diner called SC Cafe in San Clemente to share our obsessions in real life. He was the first person I had ever reached out to via the internet—it felt like a trippy blind date, but for surf junkies. When he walked through the door, I was greeted by an unassuming graphic designer type with a

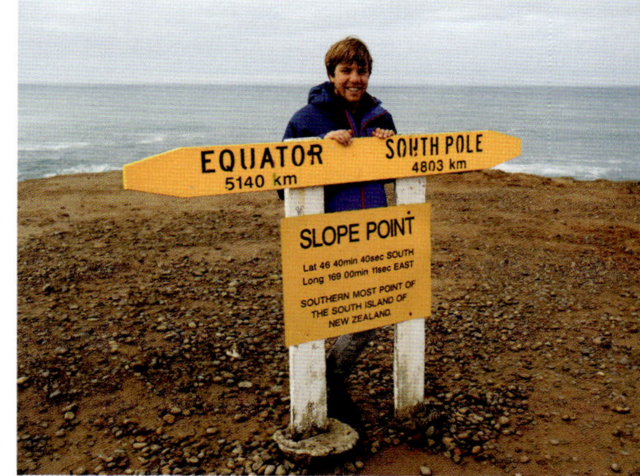

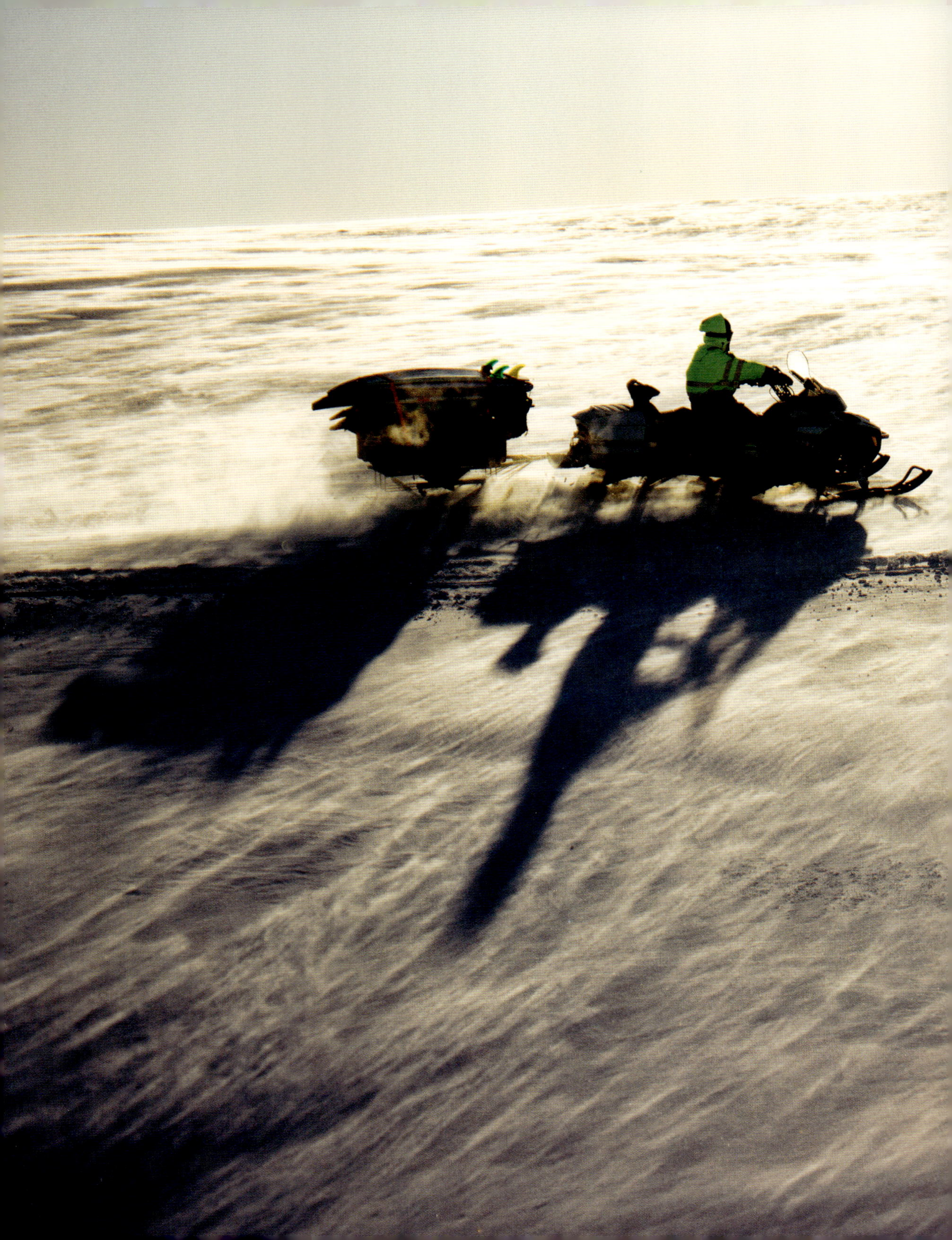

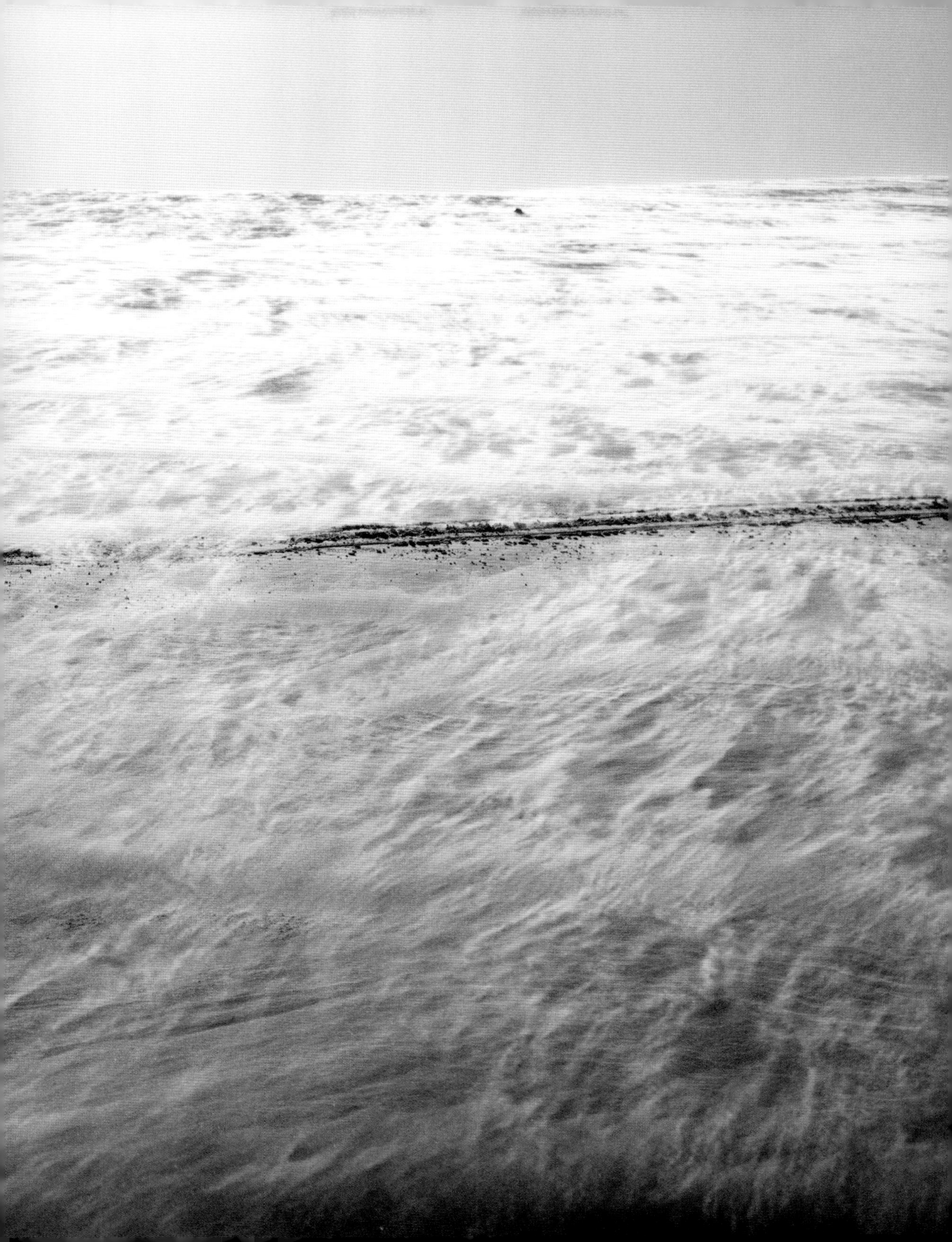

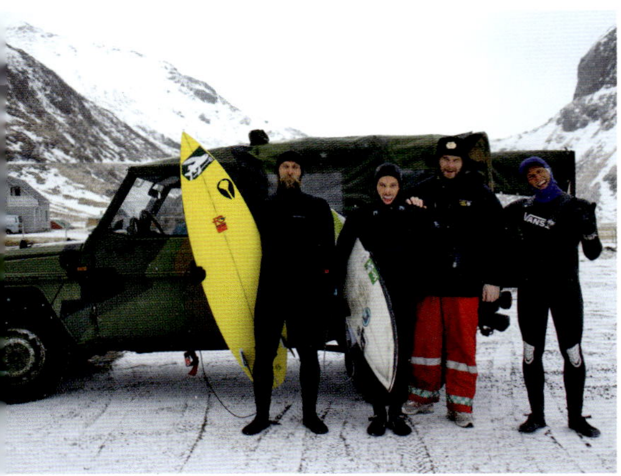

giant toothy grin. Ben came from a family of skiers and climbers, and it was obvious that he was an adventure junkie with Arctic exploration in his blood. We both dreamed big about freezing our asses off while finding mythical waves. Our breakfast meeting transformed into a mind meld that lasted for hours, carrying over into afternoon doughnuts. We had a mutual love for research and fantasizing about our dream surf trips. That day laid the foundation for years of travel and friendship to come.

One of the first times Ben and I worked together was an excursion to the South Island of New Zealand during winter. We produced an article for *Surfer* magazine that drew widespread support and interest. Norway was also on both of our bucket lists, and we wanted to step it up. One of the biggest luxuries I was afforded once I became more established in my career was being able to handpick who I went on trips and worked with, and Ben was often my favorite collaborator.

If I had my chance at making an all-star surf lineup, first on my list would be Dane Gudauskas. Hailing from Southern California, Dane was a hippie shredder who beamed positivity and was always down for any of my crazy plans. Next up on my all-star roster would be Keith Malloy. Keith and his two brothers Dan and Chris had given up competitive surfing and a long list of sponsors to work with Patagonia and live a lifestyle more in line with their ethics. They didn't want to be billboards for brands and products they didn't believe in.

I developed the closest relationship with Keith. We both shared an affinity for getting out in the water, and it didn't matter the vehicle or tool we chose to do it with. He was the stoic middle Malloy and the quietest of the clan, despite standing out with his tall stature and bushy beard. He is arguably one of the most well-rounded watermen in the world. Rounding out the crew were New Jersey's Sam Hammer and Floridians Alek Parker and Peter Mendia, three East Coast workhorses who I always knew could perform in any type of waves, from two to twenty feet, offshore barrels or sloppy beachbreak; they would always pull through with a great image. The magazines had no problem financially supporting boat trips to consistently pumping places with high-profile sponsored surfers, but an unproven high-risk exploration with a relatively under-the-radar crew took some convincing. When asking for $3,000 to support this trip, the more we could offer in return, the better. We knew the website and video content were a huge part of *Surfer*'s distribution model in addition to the magazine, and we wanted to provide more than just images and words. Ben was to produce a story from Norway for *Surfer*'s annual "Big Issue" while also shooting video and putting his supercomputer brain on some of the travel logistics, as I handled the athletes, backup research, and gaining additional sponsorship from Norway's tourism board. Logistics were Ben's territory, and I handled the business and monetary pieces. But even with all of the research we did, nothing prepared us for the immediate and literal roadblocks we faced upon the first leg of the trip.

Shortly after arriving, we were all more than a little caught off guard to find out that the coastal road Ben had planned for us to travel from Vardø to Hamningberg was blocked by a five-foot wall of snow. Going to the extreme northeastern tip of Norway is not something you can just do on a whim. One of the things Ben hadn't accounted for was a particularly harsh and late winter that left the highway—which we expected to drive for ten days around the very northern part of the Norwegian mainland—completely impassable.

But one of the reasons Ben and I thrived on these kinds of trips is because they test your mental capabilities as much as your physical ones. A trip like this can take you back to surfing's roots of raw, unfiltered exploration. Together we were resilient and resourceful, taking our combined lifetime of skills learned from Mom and Dad, brothers, Boy Scouts, and ski trips and putting them to the test. We were now faced with simply trying to sort out the logistics and budget for how we were going to access the remote coastline we had planned to explore. I even had to front the money myself and figure out reimbursements later. In my desperate attempt to salvage our expedition, I relied heavily on the pity of locals.

Word travels fast in a small village where everyone knows each other. After we spoke with Sven, our tourism liaison, he leapt into action and put his network to good use. Knowing we needed to access a portion of the national park typically only visited by tourists during the summer months, his first solution was a few teams of sled dogs. After all, there were more sleds than cars in the village. But we had too large a crew and far too much equipment.

Sven then introduced us to Roy, who owned a few snowmobiles, as well as a cabin in the exact area we were hoping to surf. Ben and I left the crew behind as we rendezvoused with Roy in his fifth-floor apartment to negotiate details. Roy was built. He had more weights than furniture in his living room. He had just returned from Russia, where he worked as a miner; he was only home for a brief leave. Feeling more like a late-night

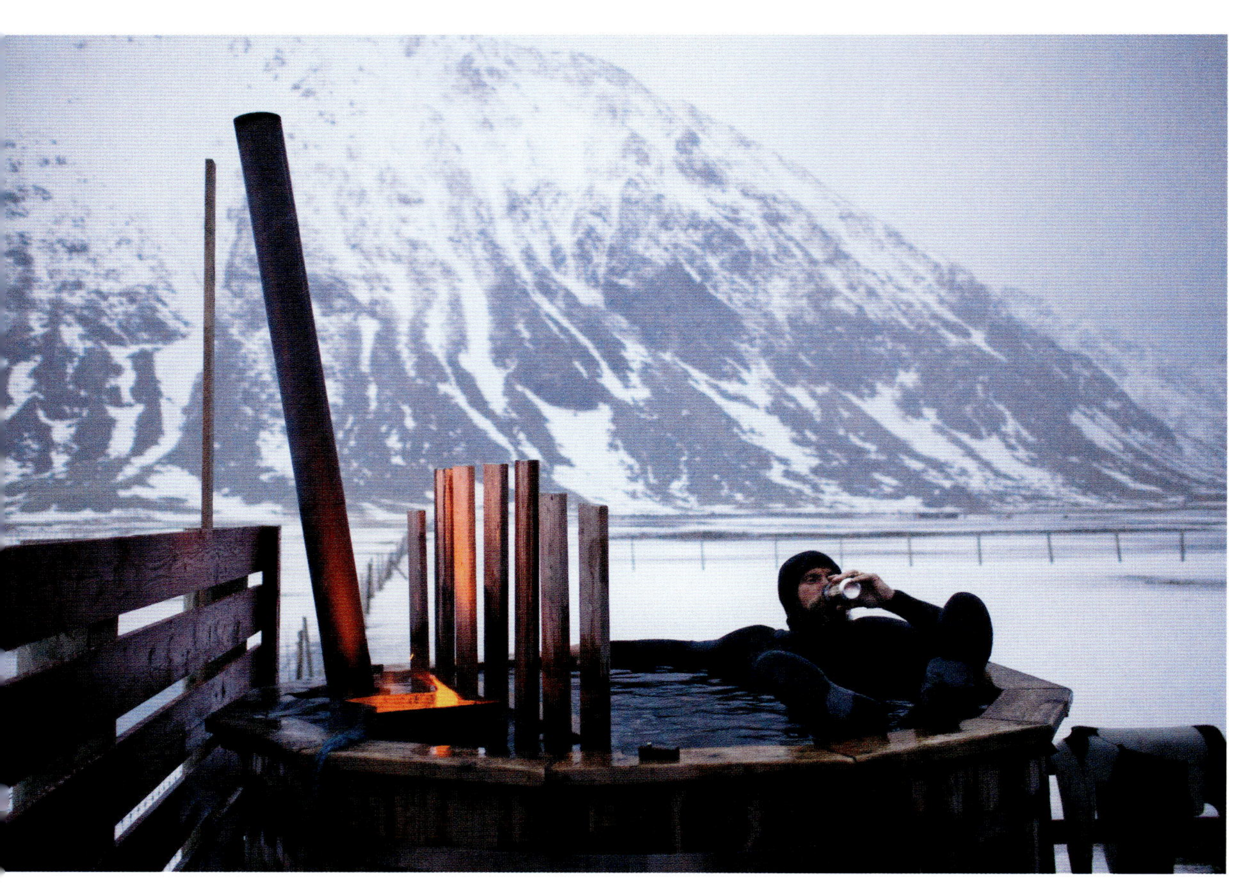

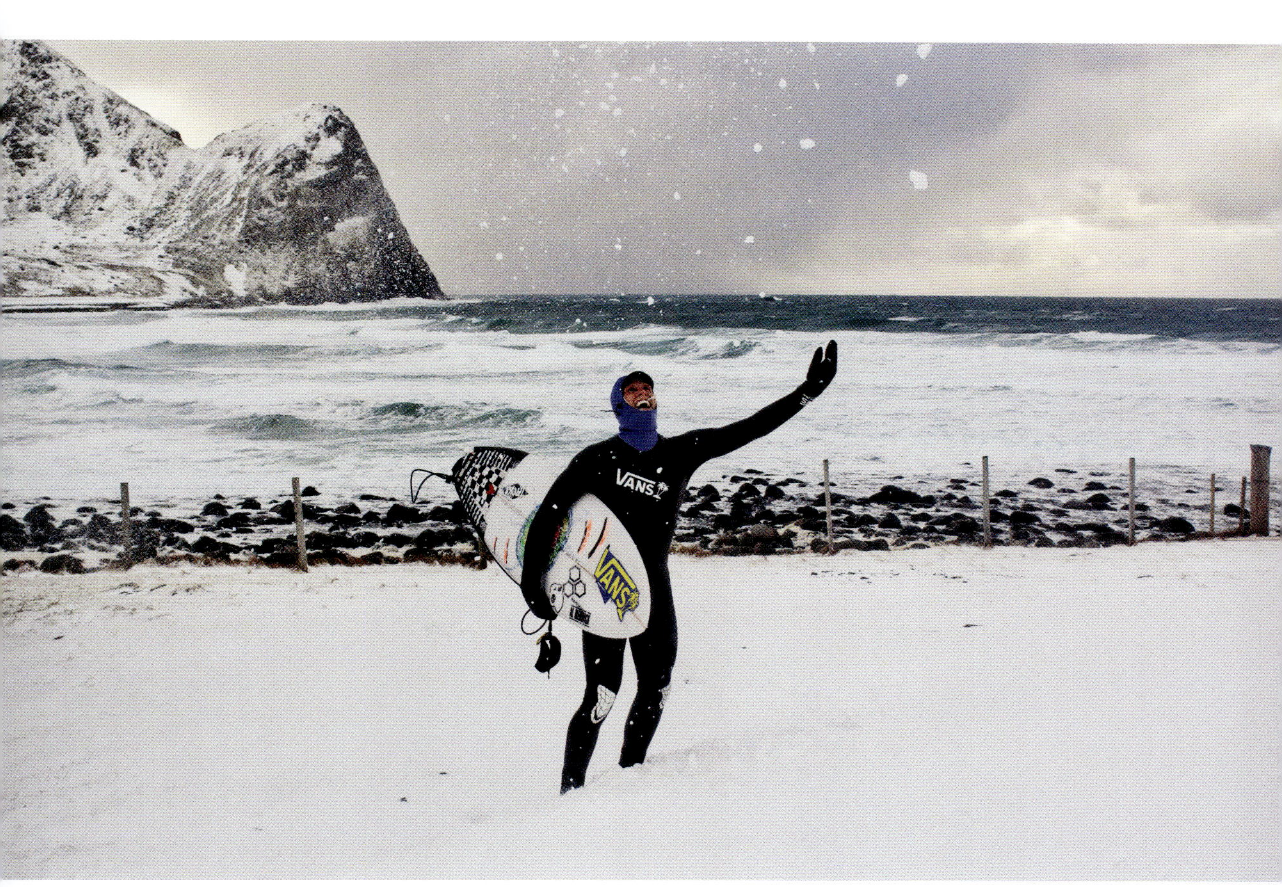

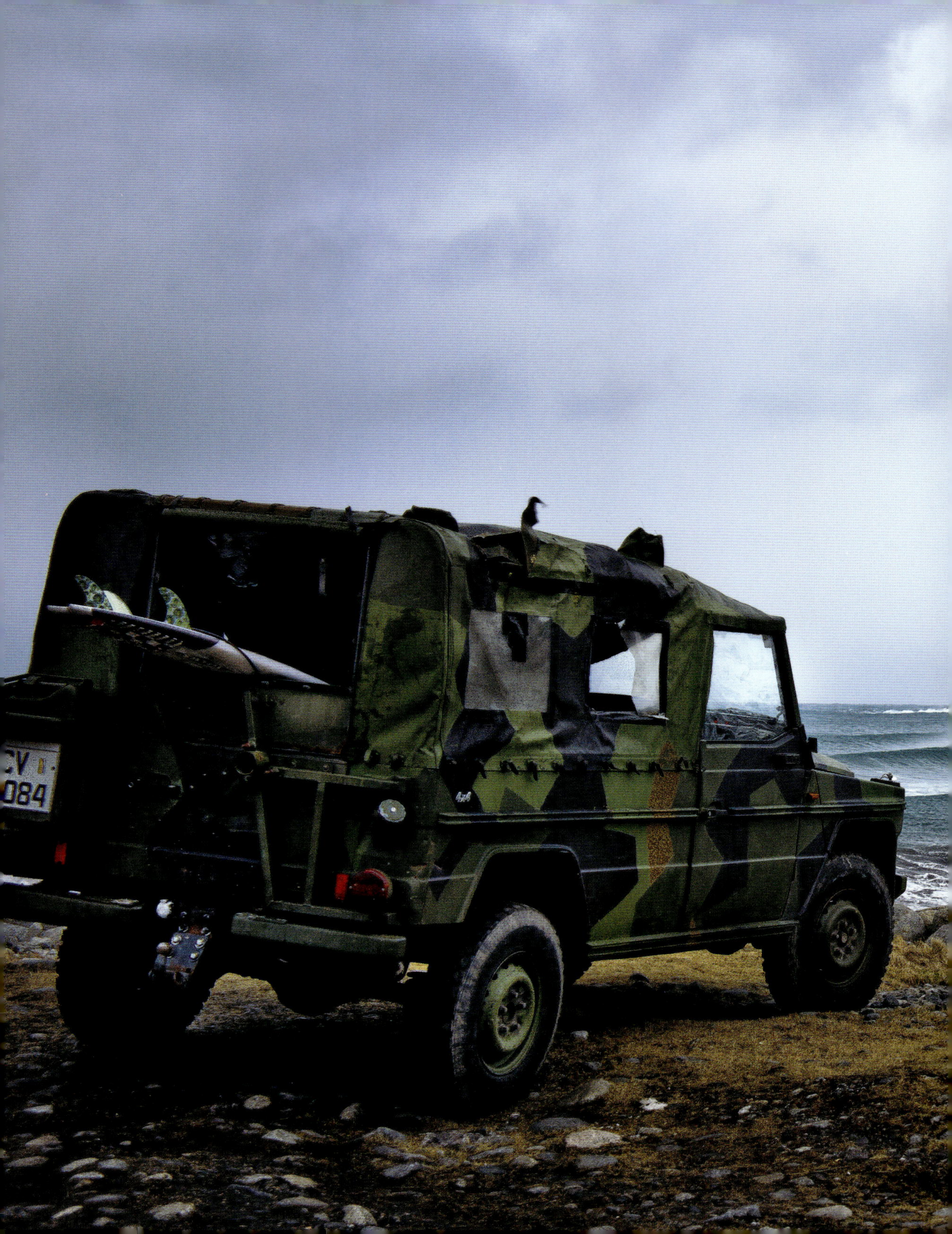

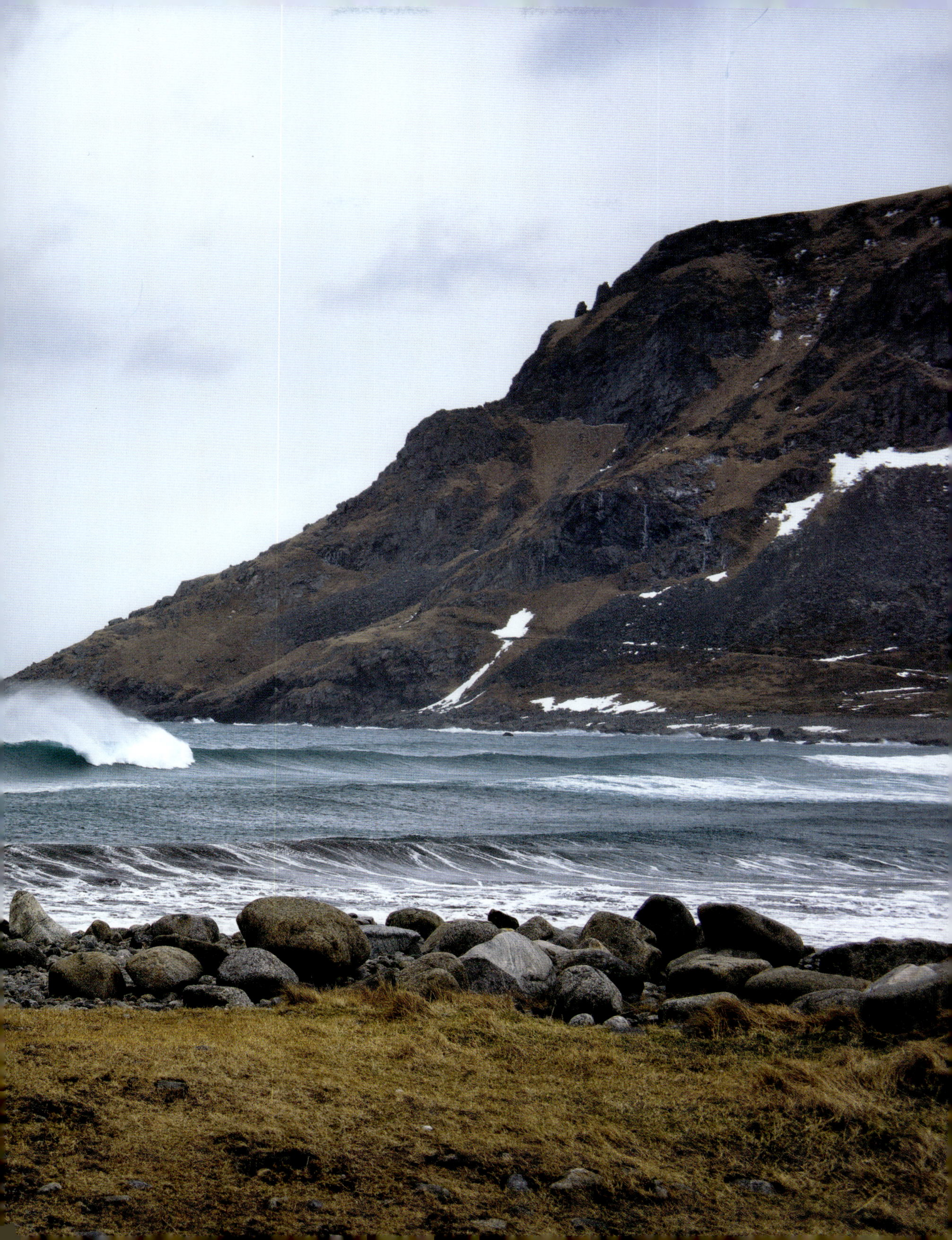

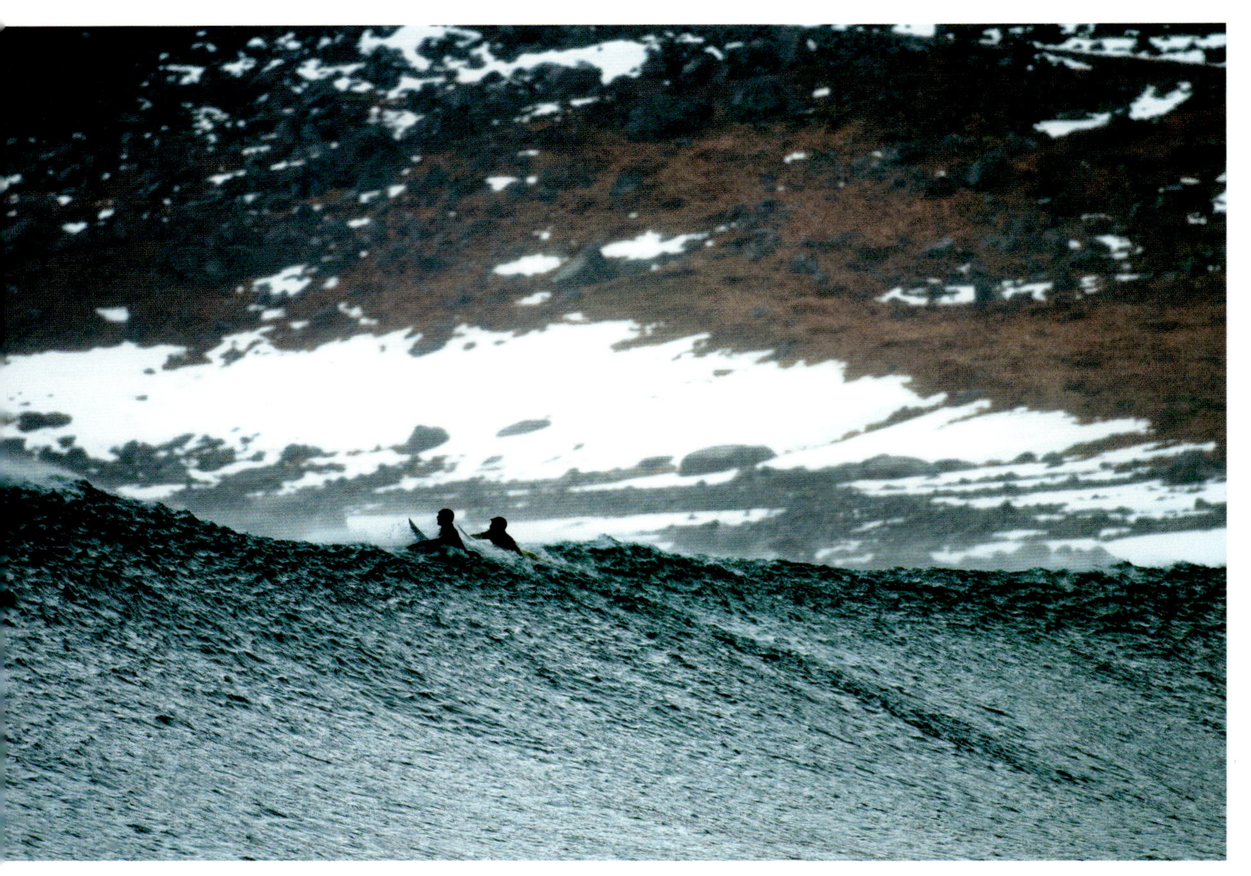

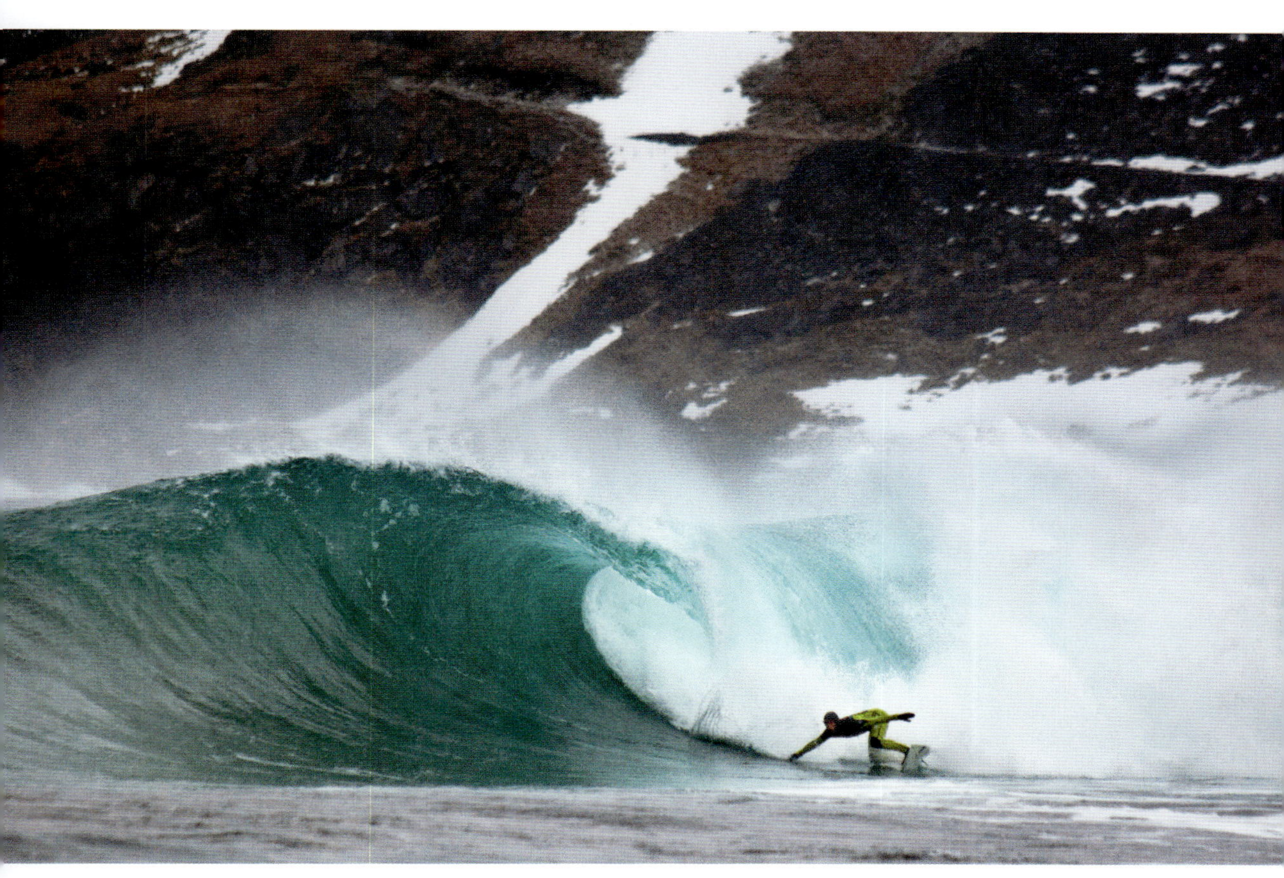

CHRIS BURKARD

WAYWARD

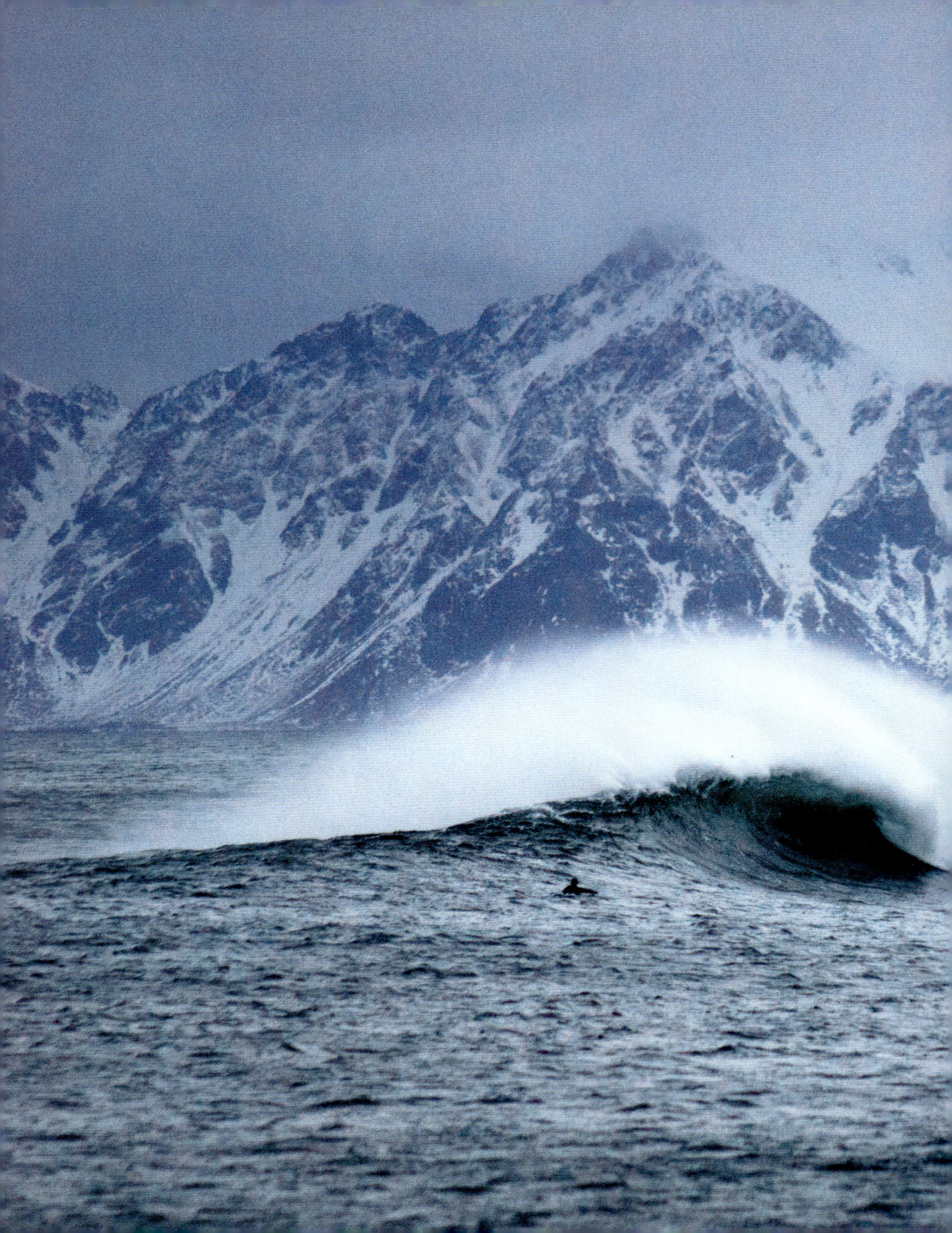

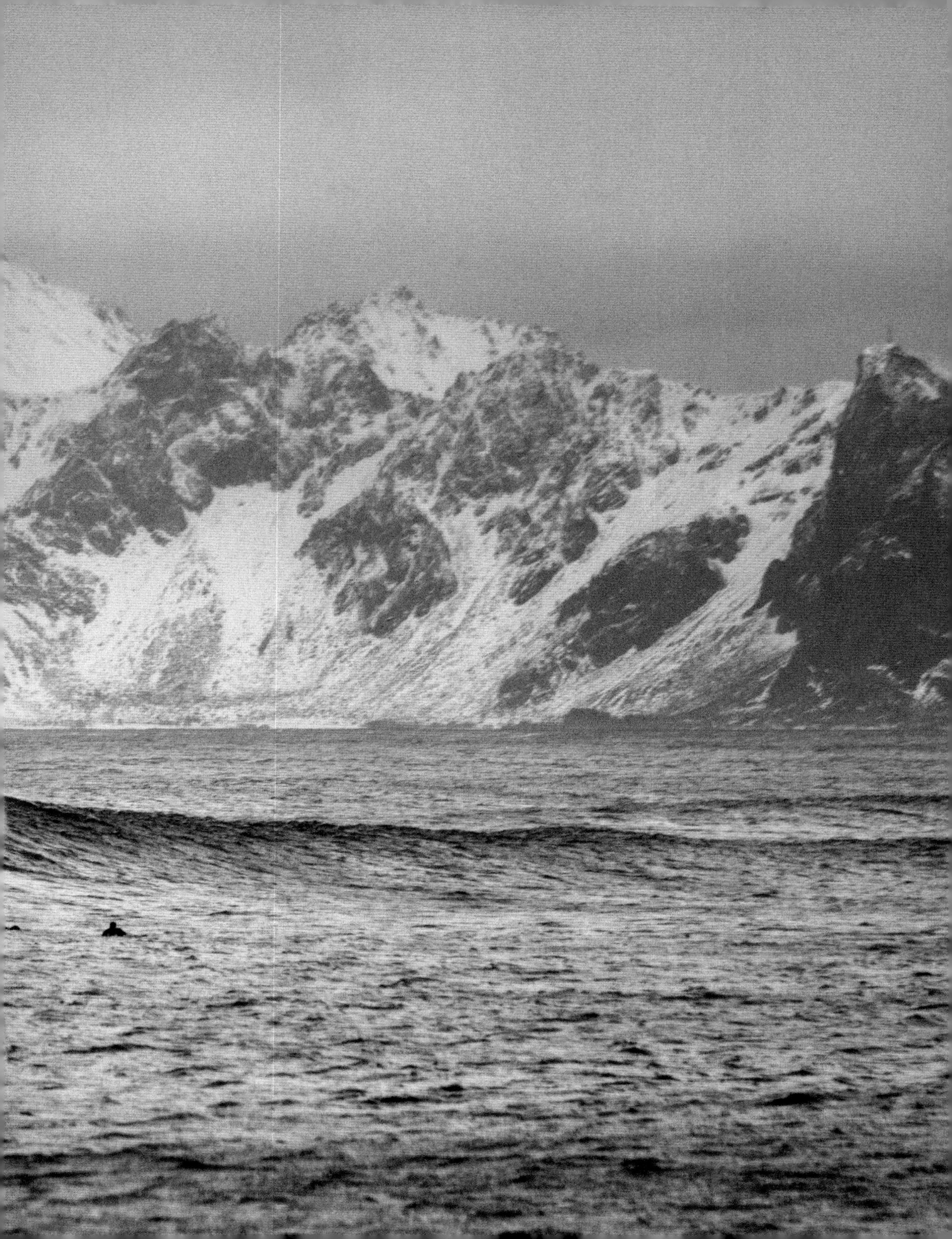

drug deal than an agreement on a vacation rental, we agreed on terms for his services and shook hands.

As we began preparing for the trip, we were notified that wearing our own snow clothes would never be sufficient while traveling the tundra at high speeds. Anything less than borrowing their survival suits and astronaut-grade helmets could mean death due to hypothermia. We were headed to unmarked backcountry trails that had no gas stations or businesses to stop at along the way. If anything went wrong, or if we ran out of gas, we would be stranded, frozen, in the middle of nowhere. To say my crew were doubtful of my leadership is an understatement. Sam Hammer, Alek Parker, and Peter Mendia were designed for much warmer weather, and now I had to convince them that strapping on borrowed gear and riding for hours on the back of strangers' snowmobiles was our best bet.

After hours of riding through uncharted terrain, we arrived at the cabin, starving but grateful to be alive. Thankfully, the Norwegians came prepared—stuffed in a bin hauled at the back of one of the snowmobiles was an entire carcass of a reindeer. That night we enjoyed a gamey feast of stewed reindeer that had been hunted by the chef who prepared it for us. As we grew more comfortable with our new acquaintances, our hosts broke open their prized store of beer and vodka. Before long the Norwegians were wielding knives of various sizes from an impressive knife collection and were showing off feats of daring and strength. Things got weird enough that Ben, Sam, and I locked ourselves in our room and started a restless attempt at sleep.

As the house awoke the next day, the mood was tentative. When sunlight hit, we saw that we had missed the best window for swell. We decided to at least test the conditions and hopped on snowmobiles for the icy drive to the beach. The waves were mediocre but still managed to break the awkward tension between us. Our hosts graciously made a huge bonfire on the beach so the guys could warm up between sets and have some heat to change near.

Roy and the rest of the Norwegians were entertained watching a bunch of crazy surfers bobbing like ice cubes out in the ocean while they sat next to the cozy fire. While the waves that day didn't fully deliver, they revealed a definite potential, and I found myself planning a return trip before we had even left.

Arriving back in Vardø, it felt like we had been alone in the wild for weeks, but only two days had passed. We bid farewell to our guides and began trying to figure out how we would access the other locations on our Norwegian hit list. Our best and only option turned out to be a local cruise ship that traveled the northwest coast.

The plan was to check out as many remote surf setups as possible over the next few days. By boat it would only take about five hours to make it to our next stop. In a village just a little farther south there was a converted lighthouse that would serve as a base camp until, ultimately, we would make our way to Unstad.

We set up a makeshift weather station of phones and laptops in the lounge of the boat and monitored the swell. We also imagined the light station illuminating the un-ridden waves of our dreams. Outside, the gales continued to chop up the black sea. Our computers slid back and forth on our laps. Around midnight, static took over the ship's intercom, and a deep voice announced, "Mr. Chris Burkard, could you please come to the reception desk?"

I nervously made my way to the main control room, where blinking lights and weather forecasting charts were pinging with the rise and fall of the boat. It was there that I received the bad news: We would not be disembarkng at the lighthouse tonight; the weather was too rough to harbor. The first mate gave me a glimmer of hope, offering to continue on all the way to Lofoten, where we wanted to end up. But it would cost us.

I relayed the information to the guys, who consulted their forecasts while I consulted my bank account. A huge swell that had just hit Ireland would soon be surging up the North Atlantic and into the Norwegian Sea. It was scheduled to arrive in Lofoten in two days—just in time for us to meet it there.

It was early morning by the time we reached Unstad and found ourselves in a small village of colorful cabins and barns, surrounded by a granite rock amphitheater bathed in silver light. The beauty of the landscape was second only to the reassurance I felt when I saw the sea. Out front was the most picturesque bay I had ever seen—like gray-blue corduroy with mythical mountains on both sides. I hadn't slept in far too many hours, but my depleted energy tank was immediately refilled upon arrival. I couldn't believe we had actually made it to a place that I had read about and studied photos of for so many years. The surf was small, but it was perfect, and as clean as it gets. In a trance, I shot empty lineups all morning while the guys slept awaiting the swell.

After hours of shooting out in the elements, I stumbled to the cabin too cold to speak and fumbled with the lock on the door. I tried to sleep, but I was too wired from being in Unstad. I kept looking out the window at the snow-covered peaks with a permanent smile.

Unstad Bay, in Norway's Lofoten Islands, is shaped like a lefty's catcher's mitt. From above, it looks more like the bottom jaw of some ancient sea creature with mountainous molars jutting up on both sides. Any North Atlantic swell left over after being gobbled up by Iceland, Scotland, or the Faroe Islands wraps around the left-hand point (the thumb of the catcher's mitt) or the rest of the landscape (the fingers) farther north. The far-left point, also known as the Garbage Dump, can grind like Mundaka on the right swell, while

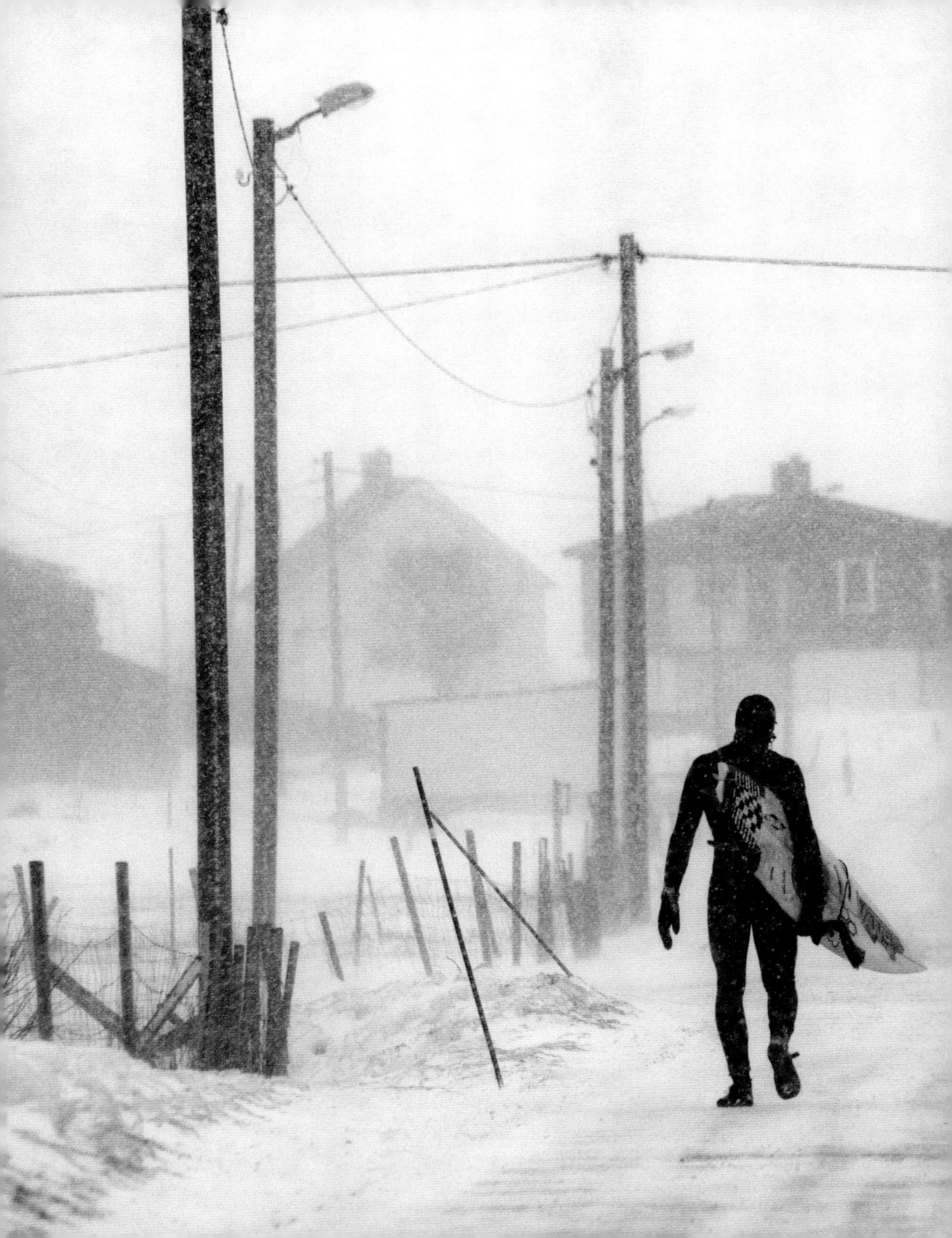

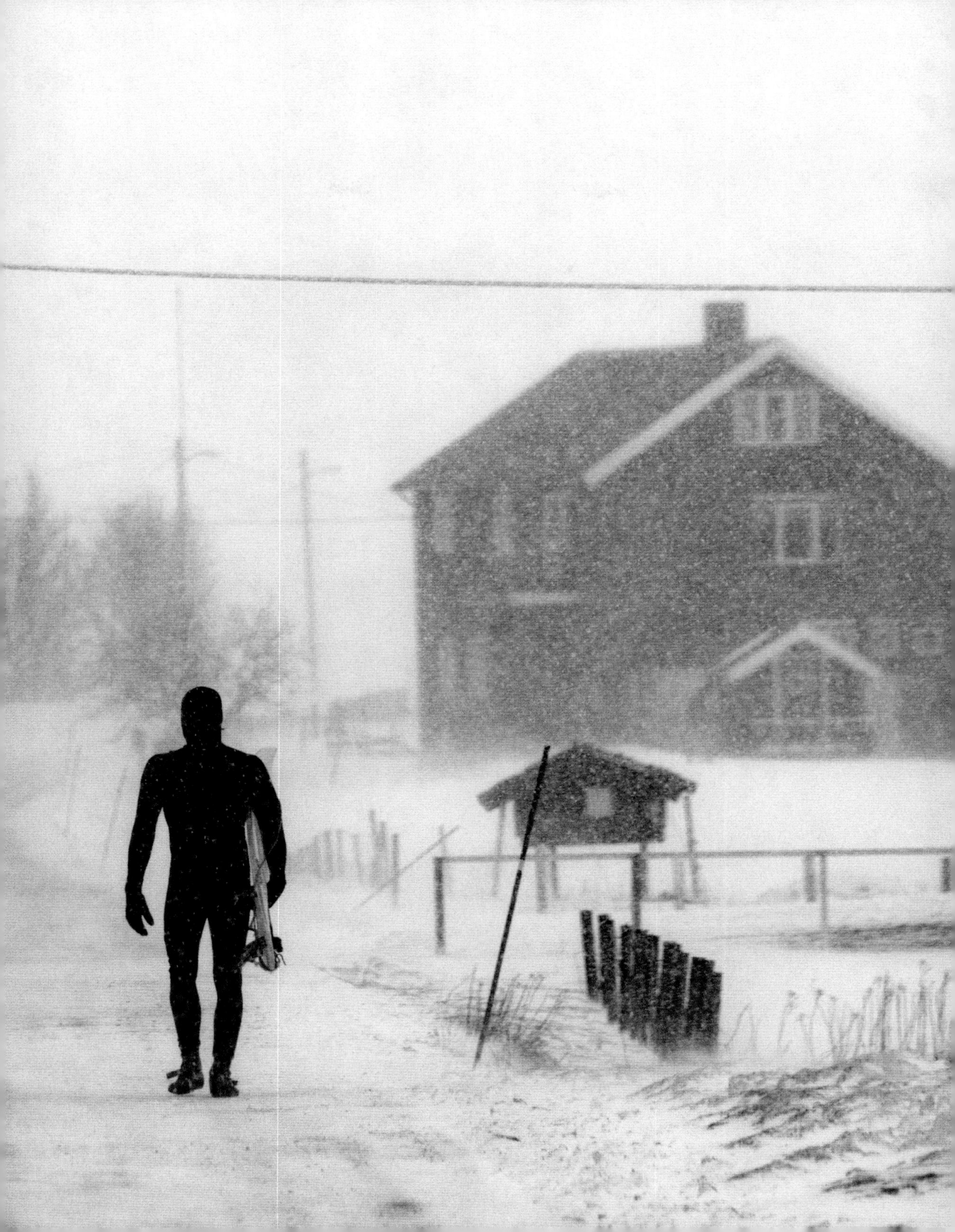

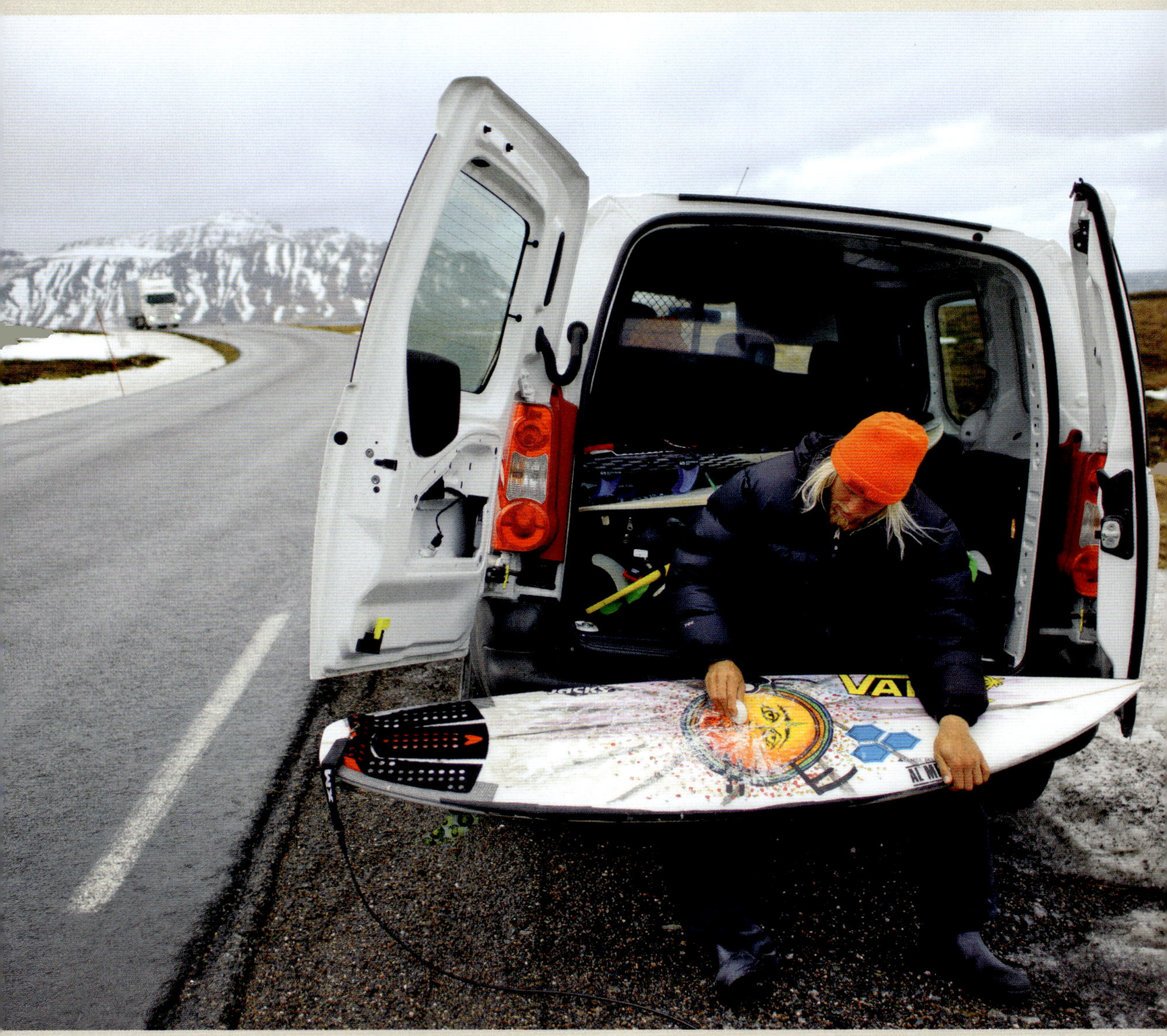

VANS
AL ME

FIRST PERSON

Ben Weiland
Director and Cinematographer

Car Casualties

→ **When we walked into the airport in Vardø,** Norway, a representative from the town's tourism board handed Chris the keys to a small white rental van, a generous favor that would transport us up the coast for the next few days.

Or so we thought. Because the surrounding area had zero road access, our tiny van was useless. Even worse, there were no waves. Our local host mentioned a lighthouse farther north, where the coast was more exposed to swell. We could take a ferry up, stay in the lighthouse, and drive actual roads along the shoreline. Chris began to look hopeful.

That night we made our first real drive, onto the car deck of the boat, and we crashed on ferry bunks for the overnight journey. But a storm rapidly descended, and the captain announced that we wouldn't be harboring at our destination. Instead, the ship would steam deeper into the Arctic. For hours, Chris and I debated what to do. Could we carry on with the ship and take it all the way to the Lofoten Islands, nearly five hundred miles away? How would we return the rental car? The draw of Lofoten proved irresistible. We decided to leave Vardø, kidnap the van, and hope that somehow it would all turn out okay.

Back on land, in the Lofoten Islands, we got stuck in the snow many times during the long drive to Unstad. In one situation, a local farmer had to pull us out. Another time, a gust of wind bent one of the doors back on its hinges so it would no longer close properly. Later in the week, surfer Pat Millin and I were fueling up, and we carelessly put gas in the diesel tank. On our way back to the coast, the van ground to a halt. It was toast.

We had to get towed home. (Cue heckling.) But miraculously, we were able to turn it in to the rental company and get a new one, no questions asked.

When Keith Malloy arrived, Chris went to pick him up at the airport. On the way back, he had to fuel up in the new van, which was not diesel but gas. Another vehicle wrecked. More heckling ensued. At this point, the vehicle situation had turned into comedy. When our host in Unstad, local surfer Tommy Olsen, heard of our plight, he produced an old Norwegian military truck to drive us from our hostel down to the water.

In spite of all our ill fortune and stupidity, we scored in Unstad. Days of swell brought perfect surf conditions. But the part about the lost vehicles and the trail of destruction . . . well, I left that out of the magazine article.

175

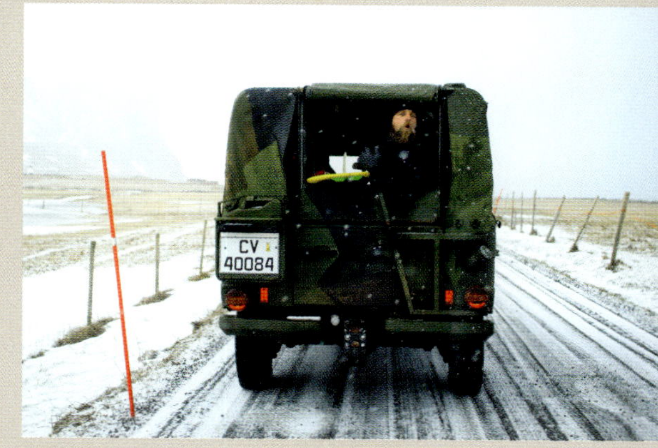

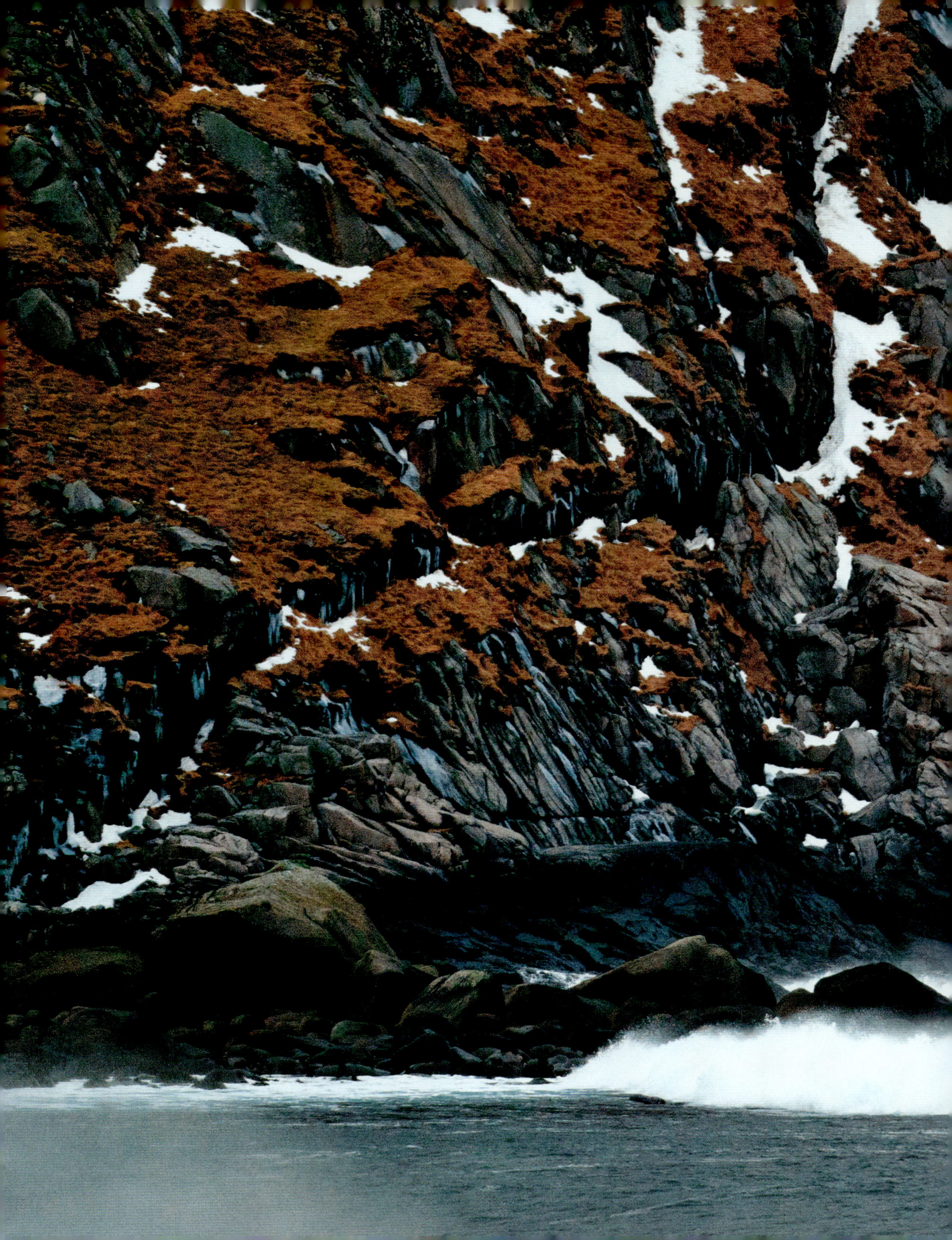

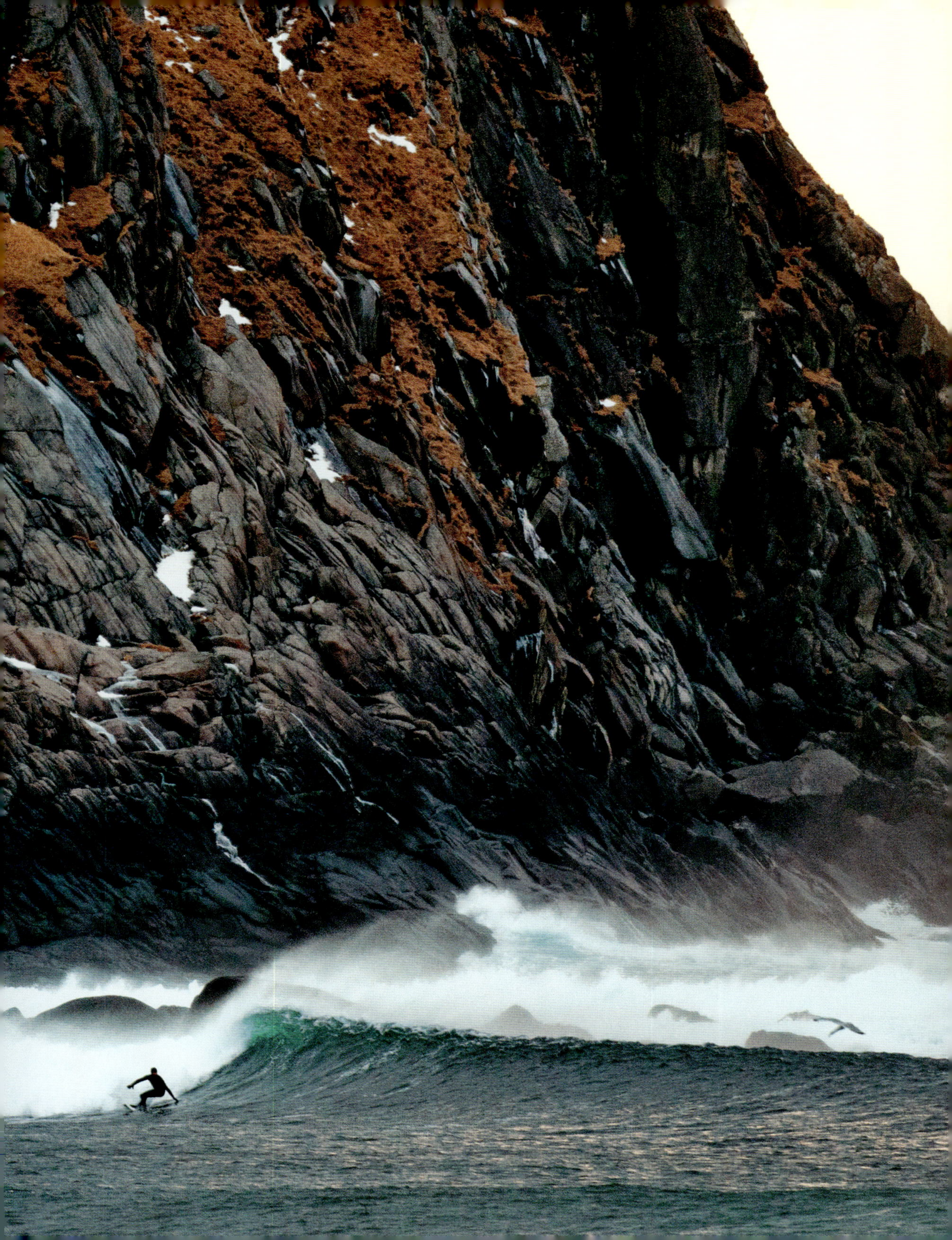

the more sweeping right-hander is a frigid version of Honolua Bay. But this was neither Spain nor Maui. It was the Arctic Circle in Norway, almost the sixty-ninth parallel, some six thousand miles north of Hawaii, in mid-March.

This must be how Thor Frantzen and Hans Egil Krane felt when they first surfed Unstad Bay in 1963. The story goes that Hans Egil discovered surfing at Bondi Beach while working on a ship in Sydney, Australia. When he returned home to Lofoten, he told Thor, "We have to try this." In the absence of boards and wetsuits, Thor and Hans Egil built a surfing plank out of foam from a 1950s refrigerator and coated it in polyester resin and fiberglass. The design was inspired by the white board with blue stripes on the cover of the 1963 Beach Boys album *Surfin' Safari*. On their first session, the intrepid Norwegians paddled out in only their bathing suits. They lasted fifteen minutes. Later they discovered that wearing wool sweaters under rubber diving suits could increase the length of their sessions.

Unstad remained a relative secret until the 1990s when a small crew of Norwegians, led by Kristian Breivik, came up from Stavanger with *Surfing* magazine and scored a monster swell. Meanwhile, Thor's daughter, Marion, who had grown up surfing Unstad, was simultaneously inviting surfers from around the country and around the world to experience the legendary waves just inside the Arctic Circle. In 1999 the surf film *E2K*, starring British wave riders Sam Lamiroy and Spencer Hargraves, put Unstad on the global surf map. It inspired Thor and his wife, Randi, to open a few cabins, a café, and a board rental business to cater to the new influx of summer surfers. A few years later, Marion and her husband, Tommy Olsen, a former wind surfer, bought the business from her parents and rebranded it Unstad Arctic Surf, which now receives visitors year-round.

But in March 2012 it was a ghost town. There were moments that were clear and calm, and you could hear your echo bouncing across the steep granite walls. But a minute later, dark clouds would get sucked into sharp mountain peaks and pop, dumping snow on the town. Our little red cabin was no match for the wind. It would blow the doors open and send fresh powder skating across the floor.

Along with reading the wind, figuring out the surf here required a watchman's level of

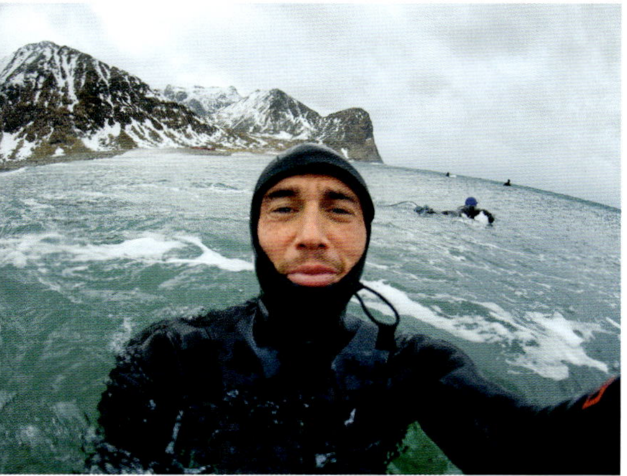

commitment, plus a lot of trial and error. We began the process of getting to know the break immediately. Our first afternoon, Peter paddled to the outside left and wrestled a beefy barrel while Alek just barely made it out of the hollow right-hander before it smashed against the rocks. Meanwhile Sam was repeatedly getting spit out of head-high tubes at the central beach break. California's Pat Millin, who had surfed Unstad before and met us the day after we arrived, showed the guys how to paddle into the sets at the top of the left point and shred all the way down the line. Keith Malloy and Dane Gudauskas flew in a few days later but were up to speed in no time, especially on the inner left. As soon as the tide dropped, Keith spotted a draining double up on the inside and dove in hard, as if he'd been surfing there all week.

Dane and I picked a shifty sandbar on the right side of the middle beach break, and before I was done setting up my angle, Dane was out there. I chose a focal length of 90mm, which could just fit Unstad's triangular southern monolith in the background like some Himalayan wonder transported to the coast. It seems to almost double in size when you compressed it with the 90mm lens. I used my Sony APS-C camera because I wanted as much of the scene as possible to be in focus: the foreground, the background, and Dane.

In an instant, a ball of sunlight blasted around the crag beneath the smoky storm clouds, sending a shaft of light across the whitecaps. Dane dropped in, pumped down the line, and launched himself off a bumpy ocean ramp into a giant front-side air, the spray glistening off his board with the contrast of the dark sky. I looked at the playback on my camera screen and admired how the minty color of the ocean perfectly complemented the orange haze of the sun and the navy-blue clouds.

Once we got acquainted with the swell and the arduous process of snow surfing, we fell into a good rhythm. We would wake up to a few feet of fresh powder, shovel the driveway, scarf down toast, bacon, or any fatty food available, and light the wood-burning hot tub on the deck. The most essential conclusion to our day would require the tub to be properly steamy by the time our frostbitten fingers and toes really needed a post-surf thaw.

The following day was my birthday, and, unbeknownst to me, our kindhearted host Marion had a dinner party up her sleeves. Inside the dining area, which was formerly the schoolhouse mess hall, we were offered a buffet of fried cod, roasted halibut, potatoes, farm-fresh goat cheese, and even some stewed and grilled minke whale, a local delicacy and, to the Norwegians, a gift for their guests of honor. Food was, and remains, a special way to connect with people.

Tommy and Marion had become more than just our hosts; they opened their doors and truly invited us in. They were always there to provide a surf report, bandage a few stitches, or preheat the sauna after a long, cold session. Seated beneath Norway's original

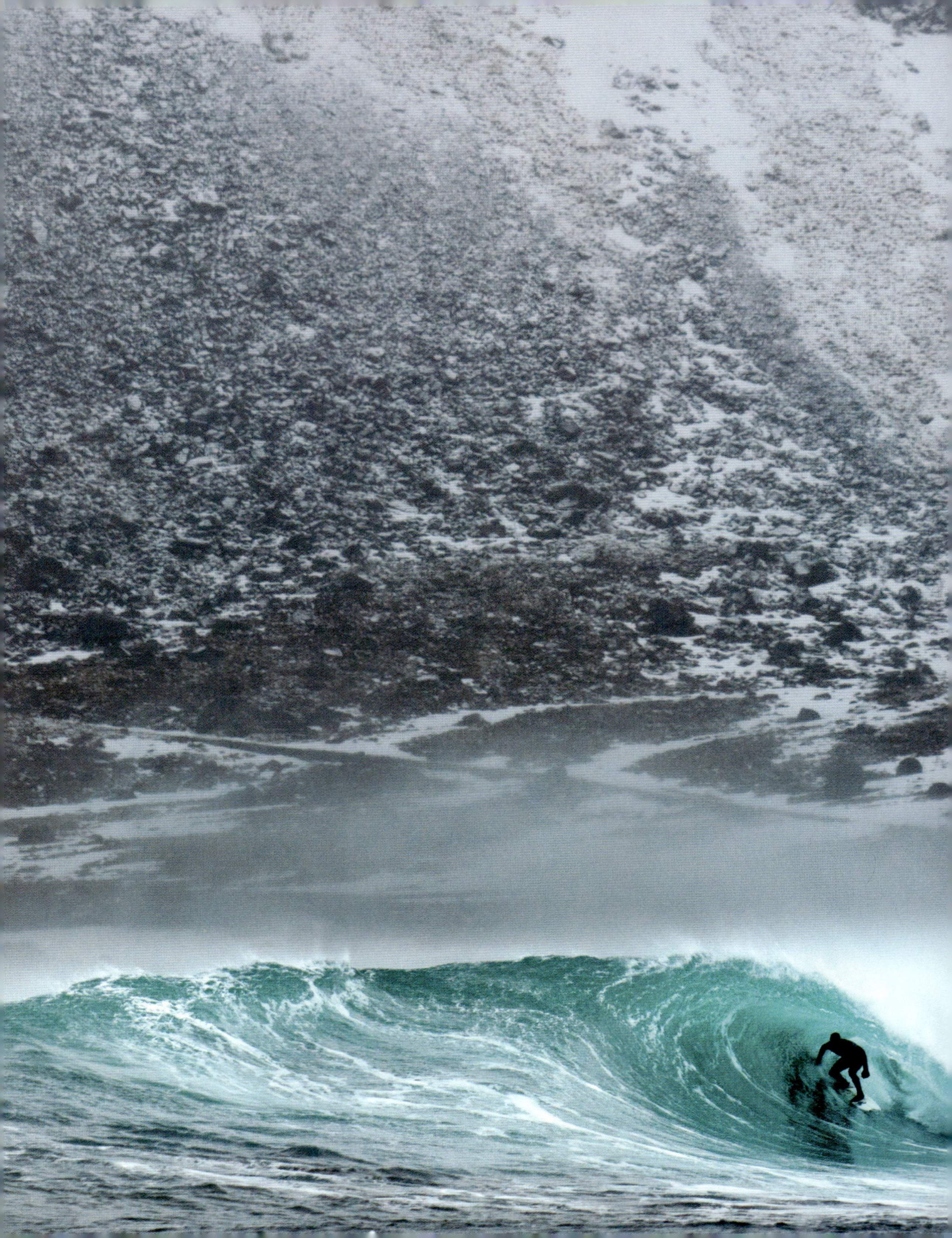

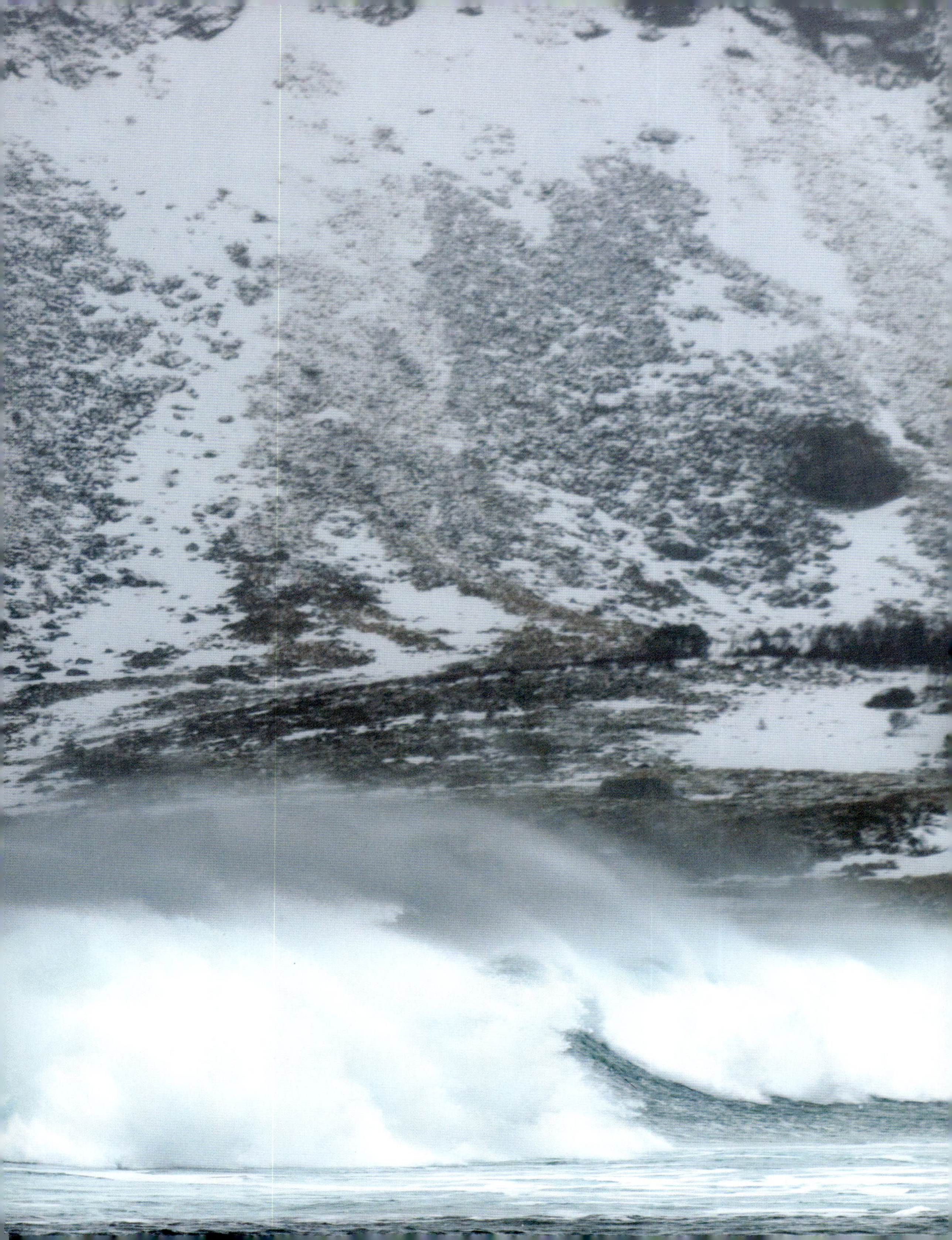

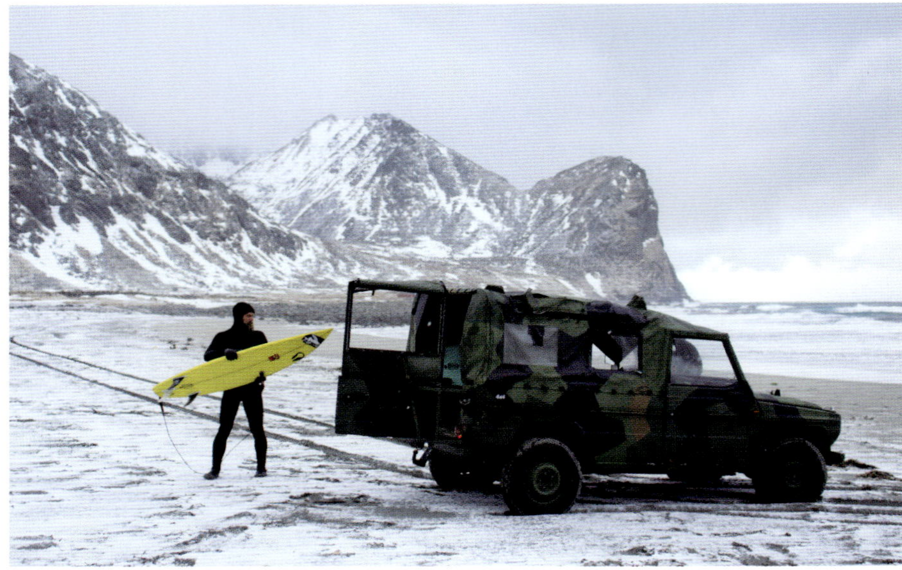

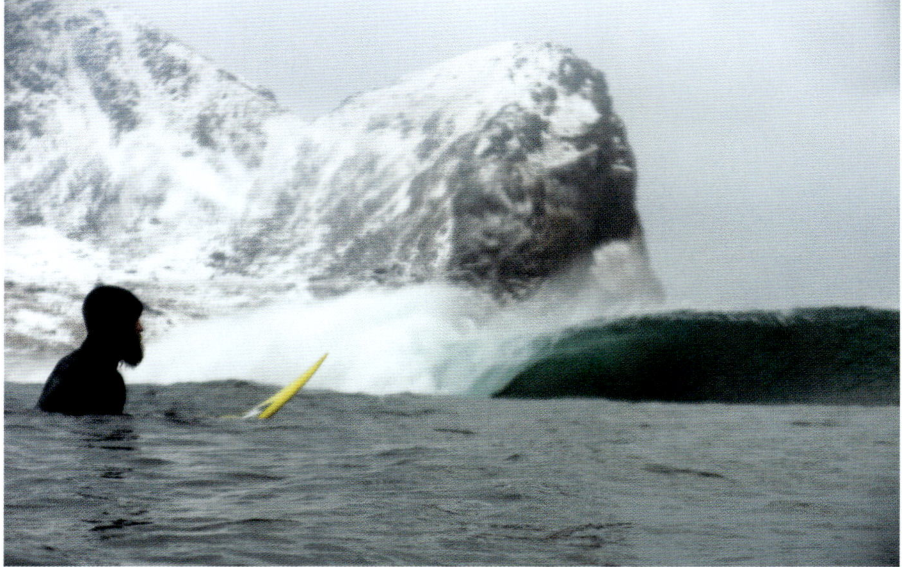

surfboards, including that white-and-blue refrigerator foam relic and another yellow-and-black specimen that Marion's dad, Thor, called "the Banana Board"—we discussed the history of the sport in Unstad and plans for the surf camp's future. Then, as we scraped the last morsels of fish and potatoes from our plates, the lights went off. The room turned pitch dark, and out came Marion holding a cake with a single candle.

"The waves are firing," I could barely hear Dane yell over the howling of the wind as we approached the water's edge the following morning. I stuffed ten pounds of camera gear under my left arm and sat in the numbing whitewash to pull my swim fins over my thick booties. A trickle of water seeped through my crotch seam, shocking my body with a scrotum-searing surprise.

Struggling to fit my fins over my booties, I realized I should have gone a size up to account for seven millimeters of extra rubber. I immediately lost circulation to my toes. The first few waves that splashed over my head were actually a relief after all that time sweating in the car. Cold water has a way of snapping your mind awake so you're aware of all the sensations. I attempted some deep yogic breathing to generate some heat in my core while swimming sidestroke with my left arm.

After about ten minutes in the water, Dane paddled for a set wave. I held my camera up, ready to snap the sequence, but I couldn't see through the viewfinder. It was completely fogged up. *Oh no. Not now!* It wasn't uncommon to have a fogged-up water housing. All that time sitting in the heated car must have built up condensation on the inside of the plastic. The only way to clear it out was to open the housing to let cold air in—that, or wait a couple of hours for it to clear on its own. I didn't have a couple of hours.

I glided back to shore with my feet up like a capsized rafter floating down a riverbed. When I reached the rocks, I ditched my flippers and monkey-crawled to the car. I threw the door open, pulled off my gloves, cracked the water housing open as fast as I could, then ducked behind the car door to hide from the bite of the wind. As the housing cooled down, so did my core temperature. Soaking wet and exposed, my body started shivering. My insides began to ache. I jumped in place with my hands shoved into my armpits. When that didn't work, I breathed warm air onto my knuckles and bit my white fingertips. There was no time for the car heater this time around.

On my second swim, the ocean felt like cold molasses. I moved in slow motion. Every oncoming wave punched me with an ice-cream headache that turned into a migraine, sinking deep beneath my brow bones. I focused on my breathing and the surf, which managed to get better during that whole foggy intermission. By the time I found a safe spot on the shoulder of the wave, Keith and Dane were taking turns blasting toward me on a barrel that doubled up and re-formed on the inside. I dipped my camera in the water,

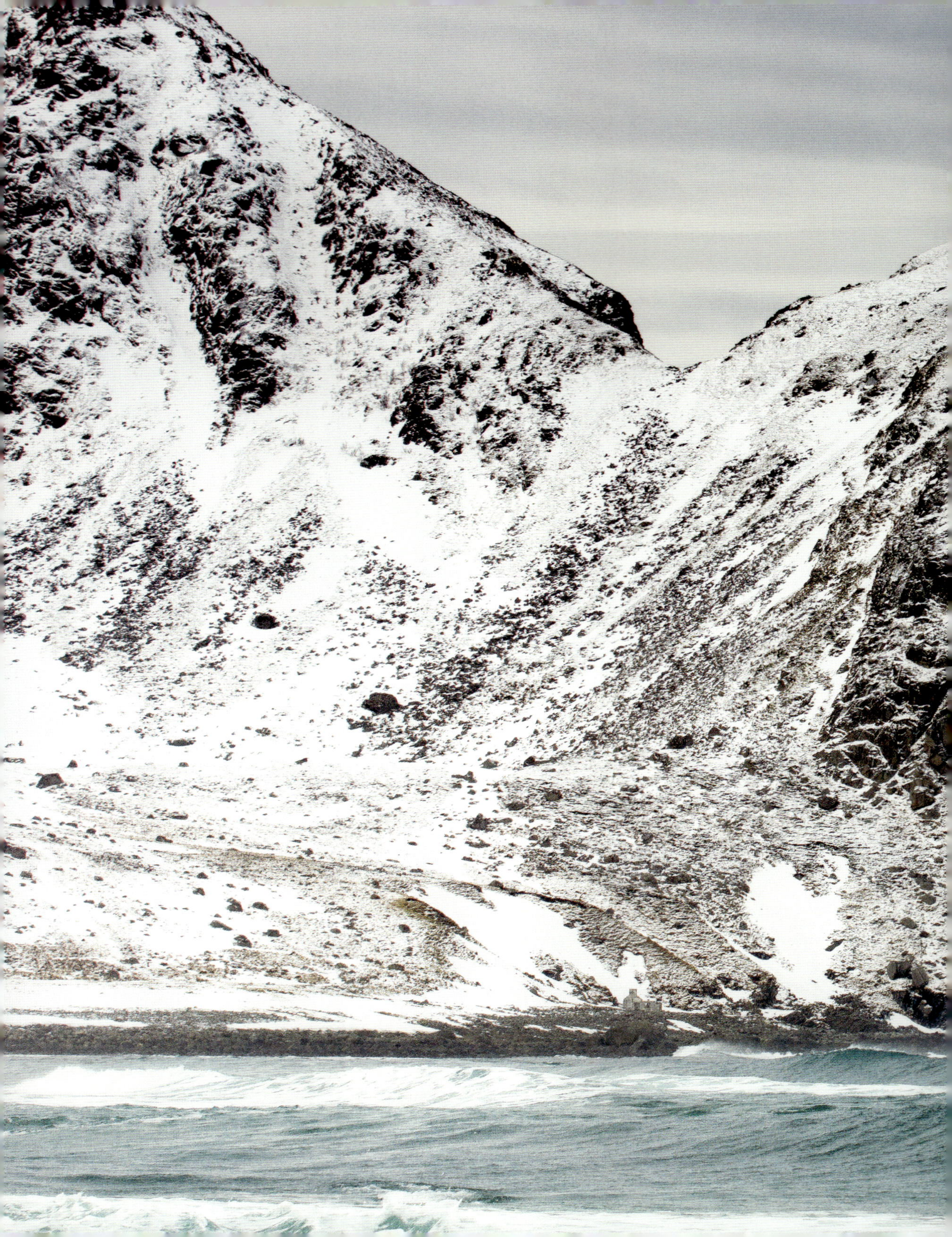

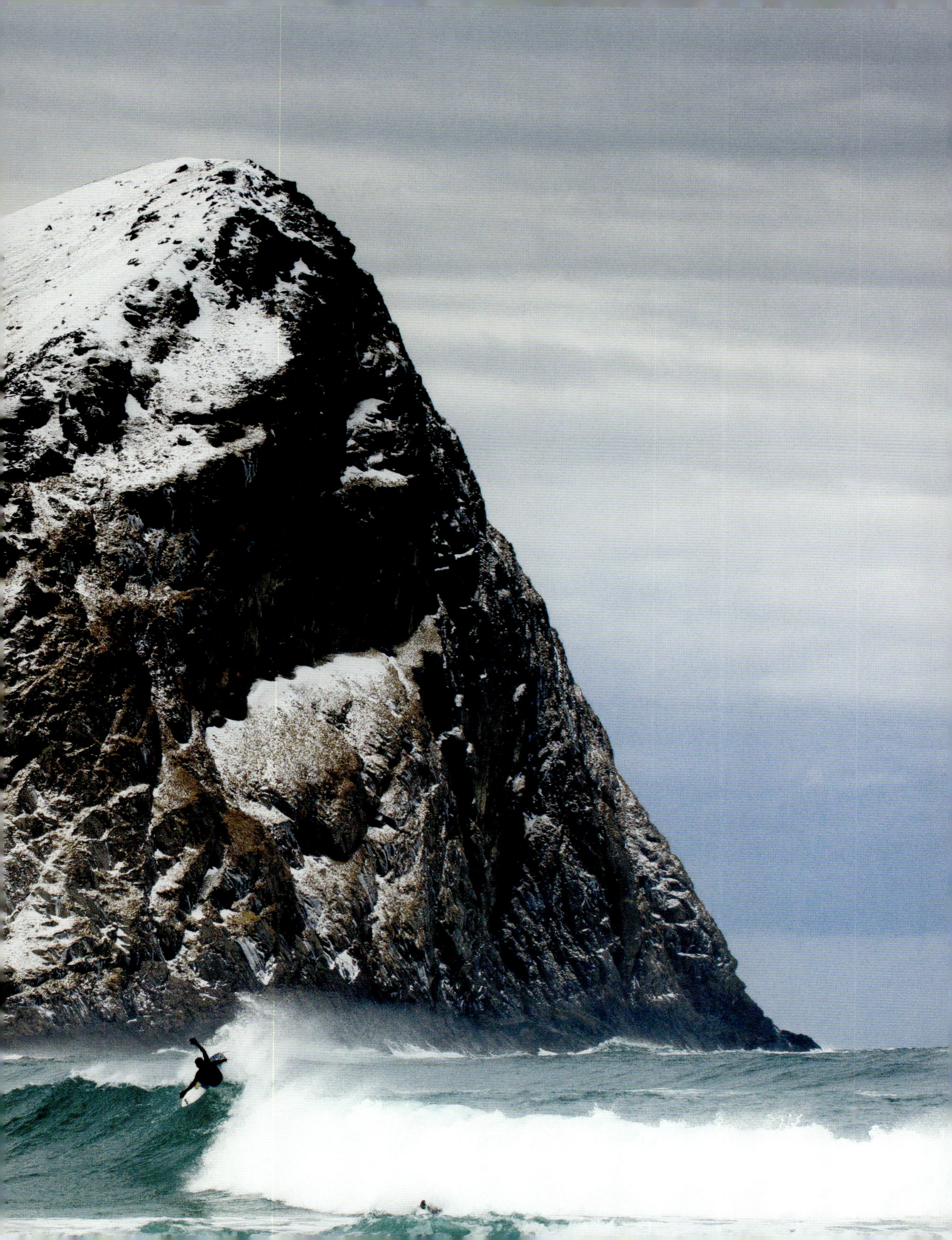

let the beads fall off, and held it up to my eyes. I could see. I held down the trigger on Dane until the last moment, when I had to submerge myself into freezing cold hell to get out of the impact zone. Then it was back into position again.

Every time I would line up to shoot a section, I would get swept away in the fun of it all, completely forgetting my cold ache, only to be reminded of it when the wave ended and I had to painfully wait for the next set. "I'm so cold right now," Dane screamed with a huge smile, over waves and wind that crashed like shattering glass.

Then for a few seconds the wind stopped and all was quiet. I sipped in a few breaths of relief. Keith caught the next wave and looked like a bearded mountain man surfing a milky-blue ice cave. I tried to whistle to share in the stoke but could barely move my lips. The tiny oval circling my eyes, nose, and mouth was the only part of my body entirely exposed to the elements, and I sensed it getting puffy. Soon I could no longer press the shutter button. My index finger was so cold and cramped I thought maybe the nail had been ripped off. I had stayed out a good thirty minutes longer than I should have.

"Hey, guys, I'm heading in," I tried to yell, but no sound came out. I turned to the horizon and started kicking toward shore, doing a weak backstroke without my arms. *Keep breathing, keep moving*, I told myself as I stared up at the white sky. A seagull was struggling against the wind and snow, just like its human counterpart in the water. I tilted my ice block head down to find the horizon line and realized the seagull and I both were headed out to sea. Not the shore.

Disorientation is an early sign of hypothermia. Luckily, after a few moments of disjointed thought, my adrenaline kicked in. I slowed my breath back down and one-arm backstroked as hard as I could, alternating arms that were as lifeless as metal poles. Finally, my butt started dragging along bowling-ball-shaped rocks, and I knew I had made it to shore.

"Dude, your face is beet red! Why are you smiling?" Dane said as he helped me to the van. My lips were too swollen to respond. I felt like I'd been worked in a boxing match; everything was sore and achy. But I sensed the smile, and I felt the satisfaction. I had pushed my body for this and might have even managed to get a few good water shots of each guy to share. It was the kind of reward and accomplishment that can only come from overcoming pain, fear, and uncertainty. It was something akin to pure joy.

Dane drove us back to the cabin, and I stumbled straight into the sauna to take off my suit. As soon as the faintest bit of feeling returned to my fingers, I stripped down naked and cranked the shower to hot. I put my hands under the steaming water but couldn't feel the heat. I tried dousing my head and body but everything was numb. I stood there with the water beating down, waiting for the feeling to return. Then, all of a sudden, my blood rushed back, like a sledgehammer slamming the heartbeat into my hands and feet. Nausea followed, making me double over and dry heave. I didn't know what exactly drove me to go to such an extreme just for a photograph, but I knew I would do it again in a heartbeat.

On my last night in Norway, I was all alone. Keith, Ben, and Dane had already boarded their flights home, and I was up late packing and cleaning before my departure the next morning. Snow had been showering down all night, so I went out to shovel the driveway. After I had worked up some warmth, I noticed tinges of green trying to break through the black sky. The hazy tentacles grew brighter and brighter, taking on the color of a glowing swimming pool. The northern lights. I put the shovel down and ran inside for the camera I had just packed away.

I tried to photograph the lights glimmering over the mountains, but there was too much glare from the cabins and the road to do them justice. I decided to walk to the beach. The aurora continued to grow more intense. The ocean was a lake. I lay on the boulders and looked up at the sky. I stared at the white mountain that had been my favored backdrop all week and watched as fluorescent green beams lasered around it like snaking searchlights.

I set up my tripod and took a sequence of photos at a thirty-second exposure. The playback showed undulating rays straightening into spotlights and then a single brushstroke that arced from the horizon to the heavens. The reflection on the snow and water lit up the whole scene, allowing me to shoot like it was daytime. I had never seen such a bright or dramatic demonstration of the northern lights, nor had I ever seen them flare up from the horizon so close to the sea. That was rare even by Norway's standards. On a night like this, I could only imagine what it might look like to see those perfect reeling lefts we surfed earlier in the week breaking under the northern lights. To document something like that would be truly incredible, but perhaps impossible.

I thought I had seen all sides of Unstad— from its most serene sunsets to its angriest storms—and then I was given this, like a gift saved just for me. I had appreciated this spot when it was drab or dangerous just as much as when it was perfect. I simply watched and listened until the last bursts of light dimmed out.

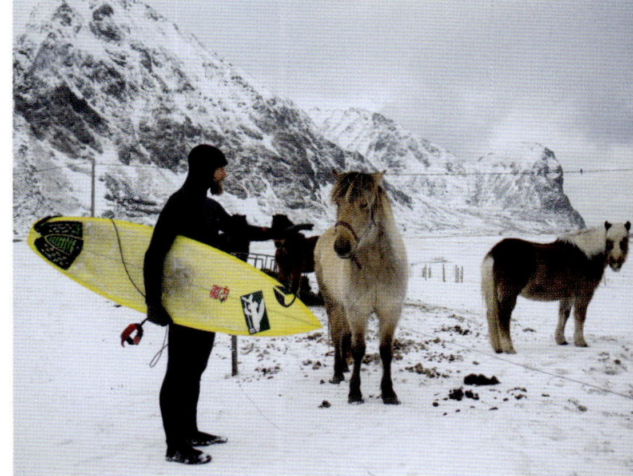

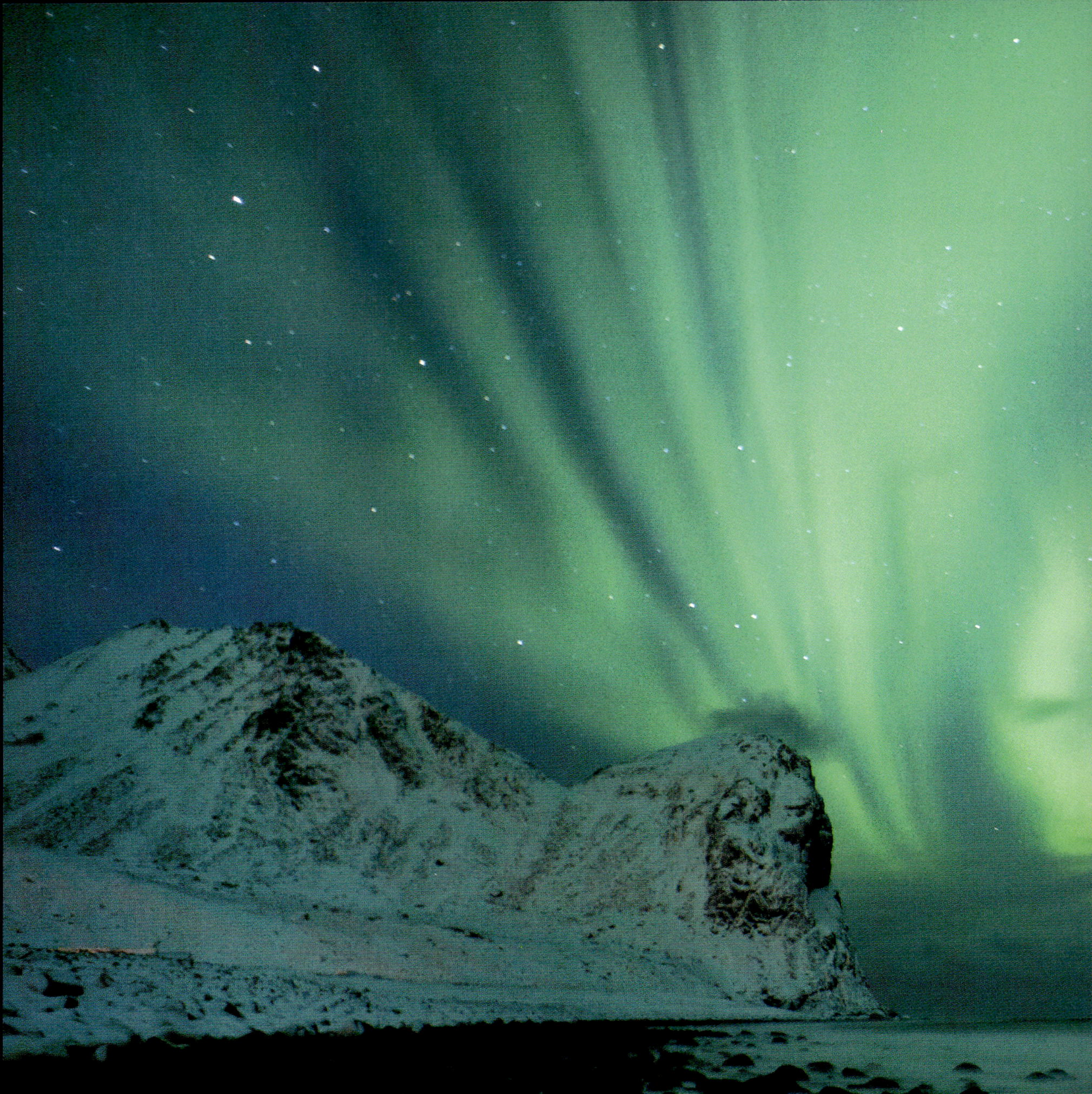

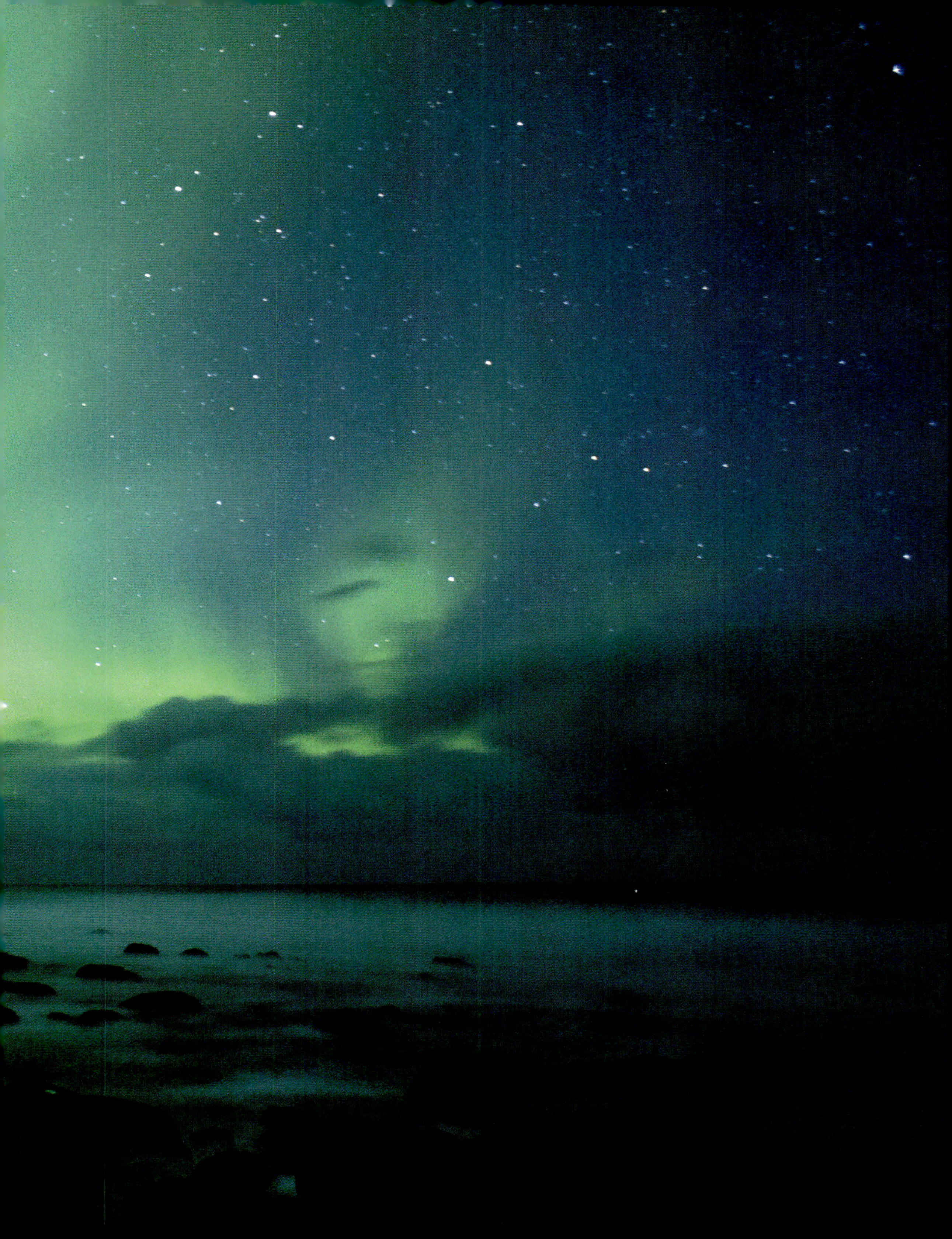

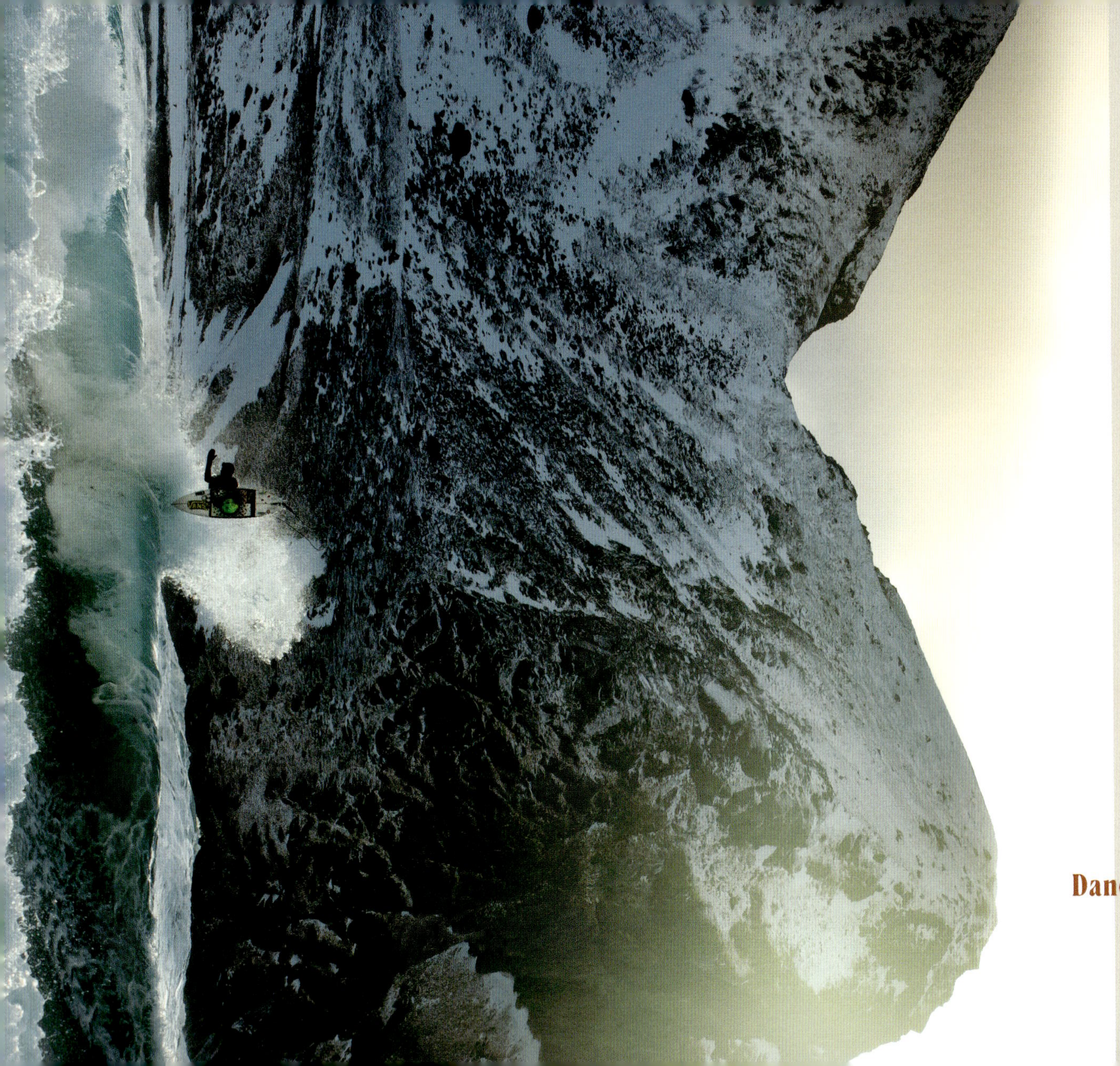

Dane Gudauskas
Surfer

Flyin' Frozen

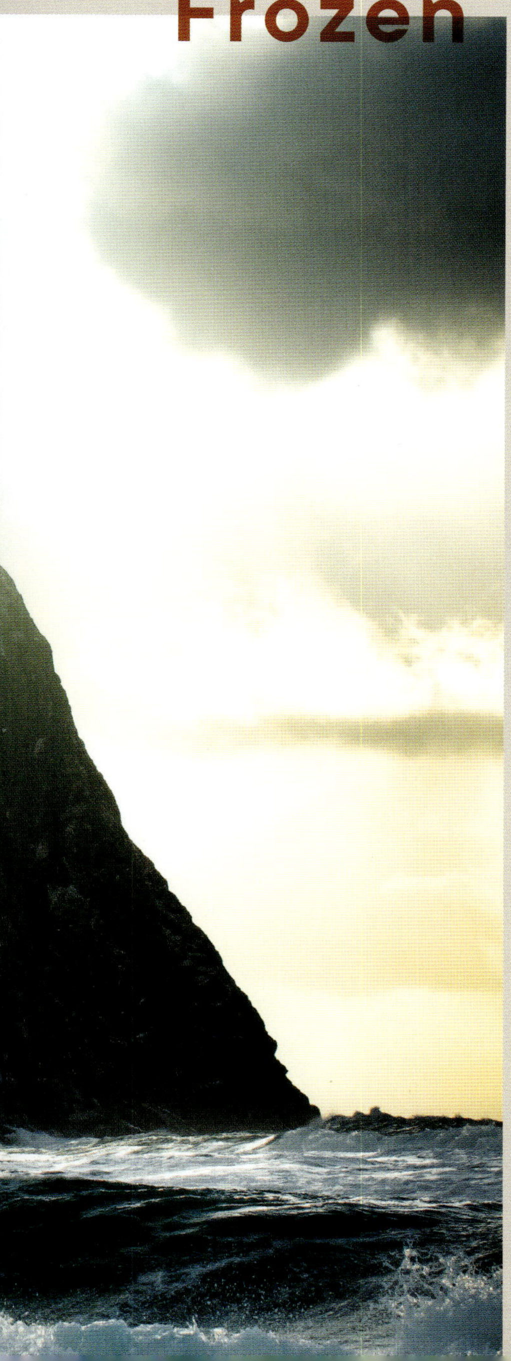

→ **The winds were blowing forty to fifty miles an** hour, straight into the left-hand break at Unstad Bay. The waves were six to eight feet on the face, surrounded by backwash and riptides. It looked like a nightmare. Like Victory at Sea.

Chris, of course, was super excited to shoot. It was kind of snowing, with big dark clouds. Moments of brilliant light broke through the darkness. We were up against this valley, and there were all these massive snow-covered cliffs. It looked so insanely dramatic, and I wanted to go out there and try to launch a couple of airs. I knew Chris would be in the right spot, where it would look crazy if everything came together. My air ability is probably not as high as other guys'—I wouldn't say it's my strong suit—but when the wind is forty miles an hour, it makes it easier to fly.

I was the only person in the water, in a place I never thought I would be. I saw Chris as this little black dot across the bay—he'd been wearing the same black setup for weeks. Ben was right behind him with his video camera, in a pair of jeans that got soaked through from snow. Out in the lineup, the water was churning, and so freaking cold. You can only really take five or six waves on the head in succession until your body starts shutting down, and your head feels like it's going to explode. It was getting dark and stormy, and I was thinking, *God! This is not coming together like I thought. This is chaos!*

All of a sudden, this orb of colors began shining through. Elsewhere it was so dark that everything appeared polarized. I focused. *Okay, this is your moment. I got to find a little wedge and really go for it*, I thought. Literally, a couple of opportunities came together right in that five-to-ten-minute window. I couldn't feel any part of my body, and I was exhausted after all that paddling and duck diving. But when the light came out, I was able to get some big airs. That session showed me what I was capable of enduring and experiencing. It opened my eyes to a whole new environment that I now love.

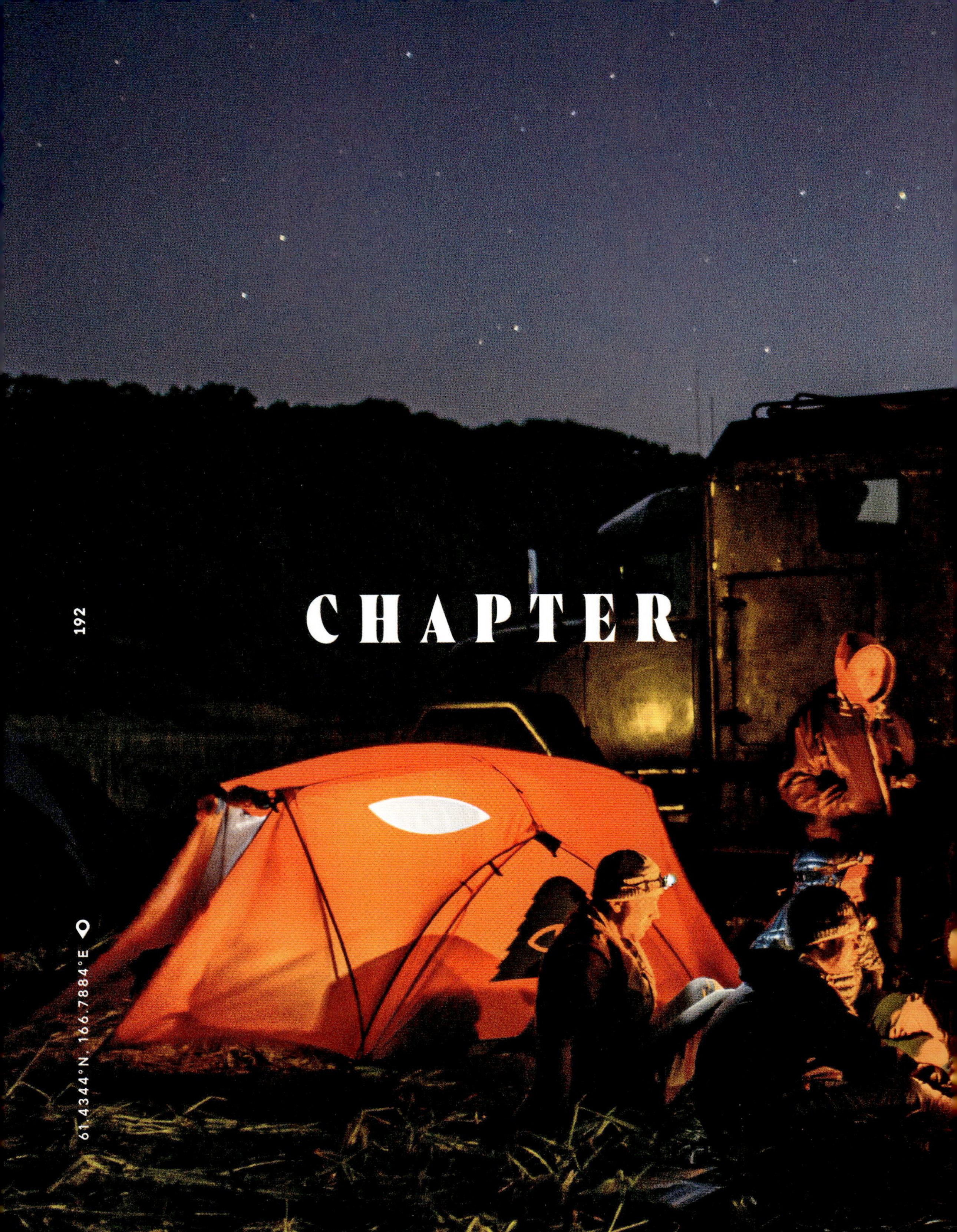
CHAPTER

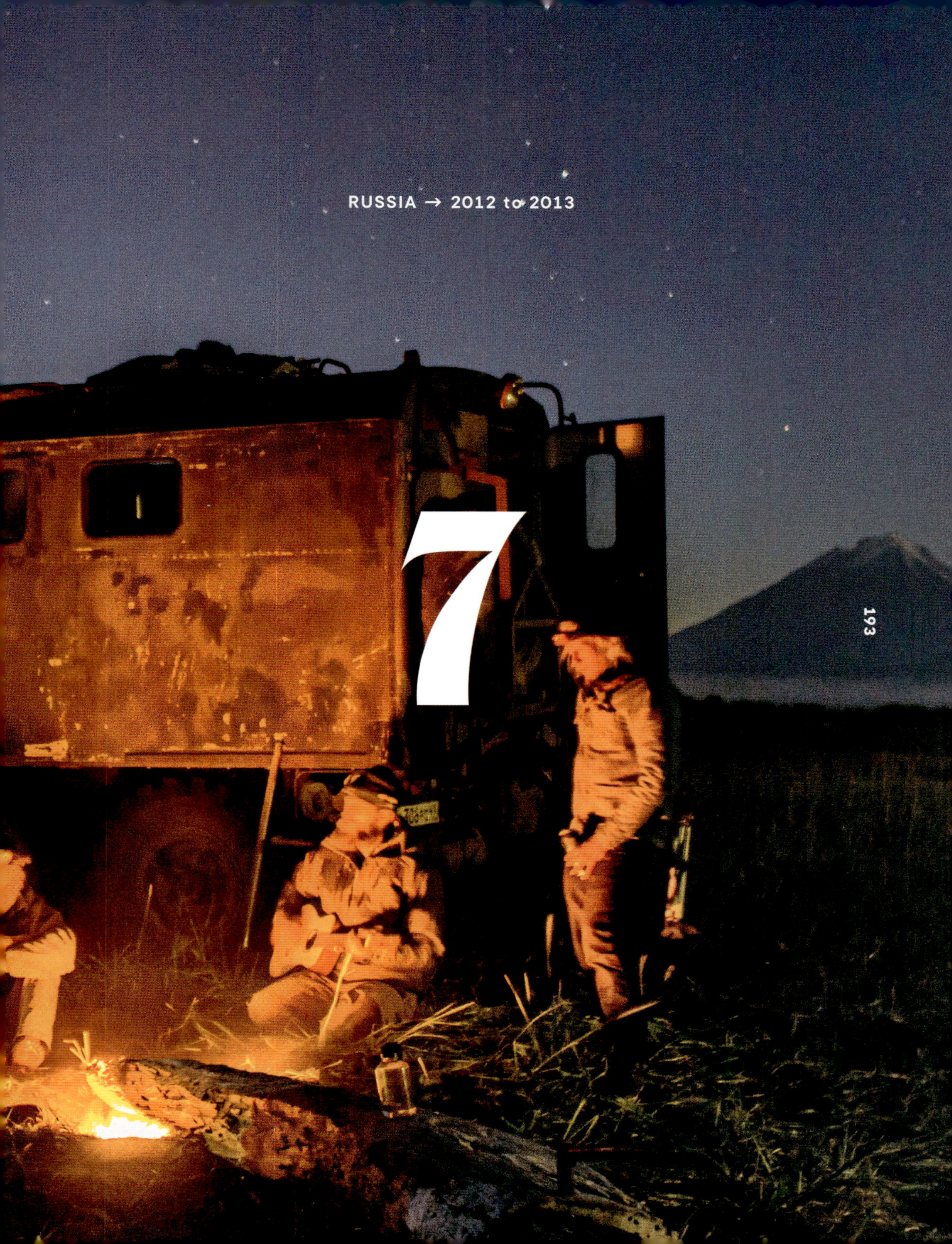

RUSSIA → 2012 to 2013
7
193

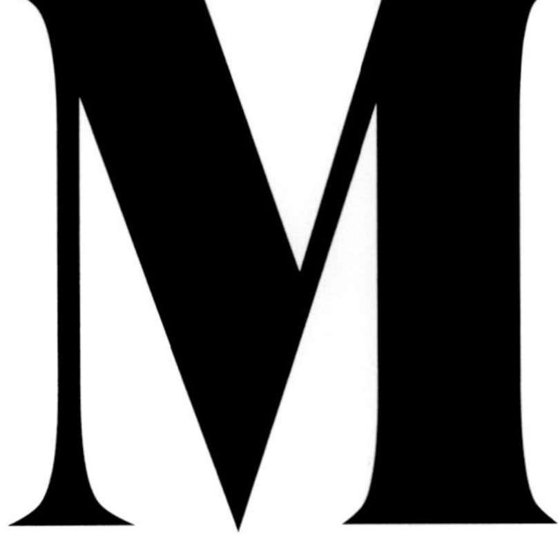

y time in Norway erased whatever doubt I had left about whether the trips I was taking were worth it or not. The images and stories from our time there appeared everywhere from Patagonia's wetsuit catalog to Yahoo! News's trending stories. The issue of Surfer magazine that featured our Norway adventure was one of the bestselling issues ever. Norway cemented my place in the early cold-water surf movement, and my expeditions were becoming a signature of sorts, opening new doors—including opportunities to do bigger and bolder trips.

This coincided with the birth of my first child in 2012, and I now had an entirely new set of responsibilities at home. While I wanted to be involved and present every second of my son's earliest years, my wife and I both understood these trips nourished me. I even believed—and still do believe—they made me a better father and husband. In fact, the recent memory of Norway was like a beacon in the storm. I had a need, almost a compulsion, to document the beauty and joys found in nature. Solace was waiting for me in the wild places on this planet. Solace and clarity. Even though I knew part of me was running away by returning to life on the road, I also knew it was the only way that I could find clarity. My wife and I agreed we would figure out how to fit my trips into our lives.

Ever since my first dicey visit to Vladivostok in 2009, I had been craving a Russian redo. Russia was unfinished business, and I wanted to redeem myself. But this time I had my sights set on the Kamchatka Peninsula, nine time zones from Moscow and across the Sea of Okhotsk. Kamchatka held the promise of more wilderness, fewer people, and hopefully more waves.

Ben Weiland and I had been studying the landmass through online forums and Google Earth for years. Satellite images of the serrated eastern coastline fronting the Pacific showed broad bays that stretched for miles, interspersed with smaller coves cut between headlands that stab the sea in every direction. Plus, we could tell that the peninsula's interior, which borders Siberia, was dotted with swirling pinches of uplift—massive volcanoes—many of which are active and would help create some otherworldly photo backdrops. We saw endless possibilities.

We also knew that Tom Curren and Brian Toth had scored waves somewhere on the conch shell–shaped peninsula in the early 2000s with Australian photographer Ted Grambeau. Trips instantly became an easier sell once we knew there were pioneers who had succeeded before us.

Kamchatka is a northern link in the Ring of Fire, one of the most volcanic regions on the planet. Somehow, an abundant array of wildlife has managed to survive in

Kamchatka's explosive ecosystem, from otters and eagles to a quarter of all wild Pacific salmon, as well as one of the world's largest populations of oversized brown bears that consume them.

Surfers, however, were not so plentiful. Kamchatka was not cheap or easy to visit; no roads connected the peninsula to mainland Russia, and tourism had been strictly off limits until after the Soviet Union collapsed in the early 1990s. This mission felt reminiscent of genuine surf adventures from decades past. We'd be just the second international crew after Curren's first-ever group to surf the peninsula; we'd tent camp in bear country, fly-fish teeming salmon runs, and off-road or ride a Soviet helicopter to hard-to-reach waves.

But the stakes felt much higher for me this time. There was a lot of added pressure to make sure this experience was as productive as possible to justify the time away from my family. I hustled hard to assemble the right team of athletes, sponsors, and media partners. Patagonia and *Surfer* magazine agreed to cover some of the expenses, which we could exclusively tap into for travel, and travel only. That money was only guaranteed, of course, if we produced usable photos and an article. In addition to our initial support, I made small deals with Clif Bar, Poler apparel, Goal Zero portable chargers, and HDX Hydration Mix to just try and break even. All in all, the trip would cost around $5,000 to $6,000 per person. The only way it became feasible was because we worked a deal with Yakutia Airlines to cover our flights.

This trip was definitely not going to be a moneymaker. If I was lucky, we would get an article in the magazine that would pay out. The amount of compensation depends on the size and quantity of photos run, usually anywhere between $800 and $2,000. The ultimate goal would be adding a cover, which would round the total up to somewhere around $3,000. On top of that, I could hopefully sell a few images back to our partner brands on top of what I already owed them. Of course, everything depended upon us actually getting good surf.

But more than anything, I was hoping for this trip to be something memorable that could allow me and Ben to create a film and maybe even a small zine of our own. If we were really successful, we could make some supplemental income while also bringing more exposure to both of our careers.

These were also the early days of Instagram, which we planned to utilize, unsure of how it would be received. I had just started posting on the platform a year prior and was trying to navigate my way around using it as a complement to the surf trips I was doing, without giving away the entire story. We would also be updating the Patagonia blog, *The Cleanest Line*, to allow people to follow the adventure in real time and to tell a more inclusive story.

When word got out that we were assembling a crew to go to Kamchatka, there was

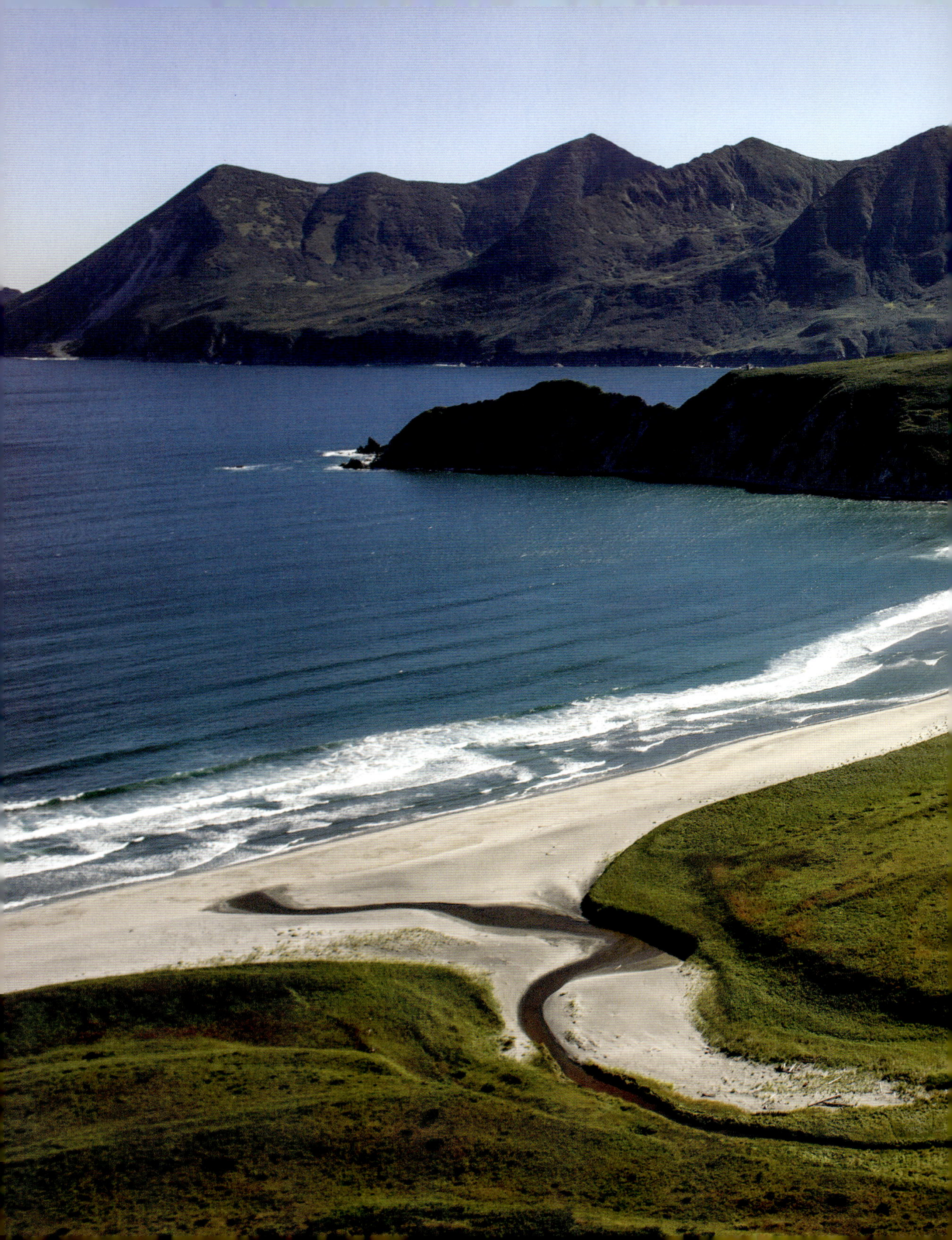

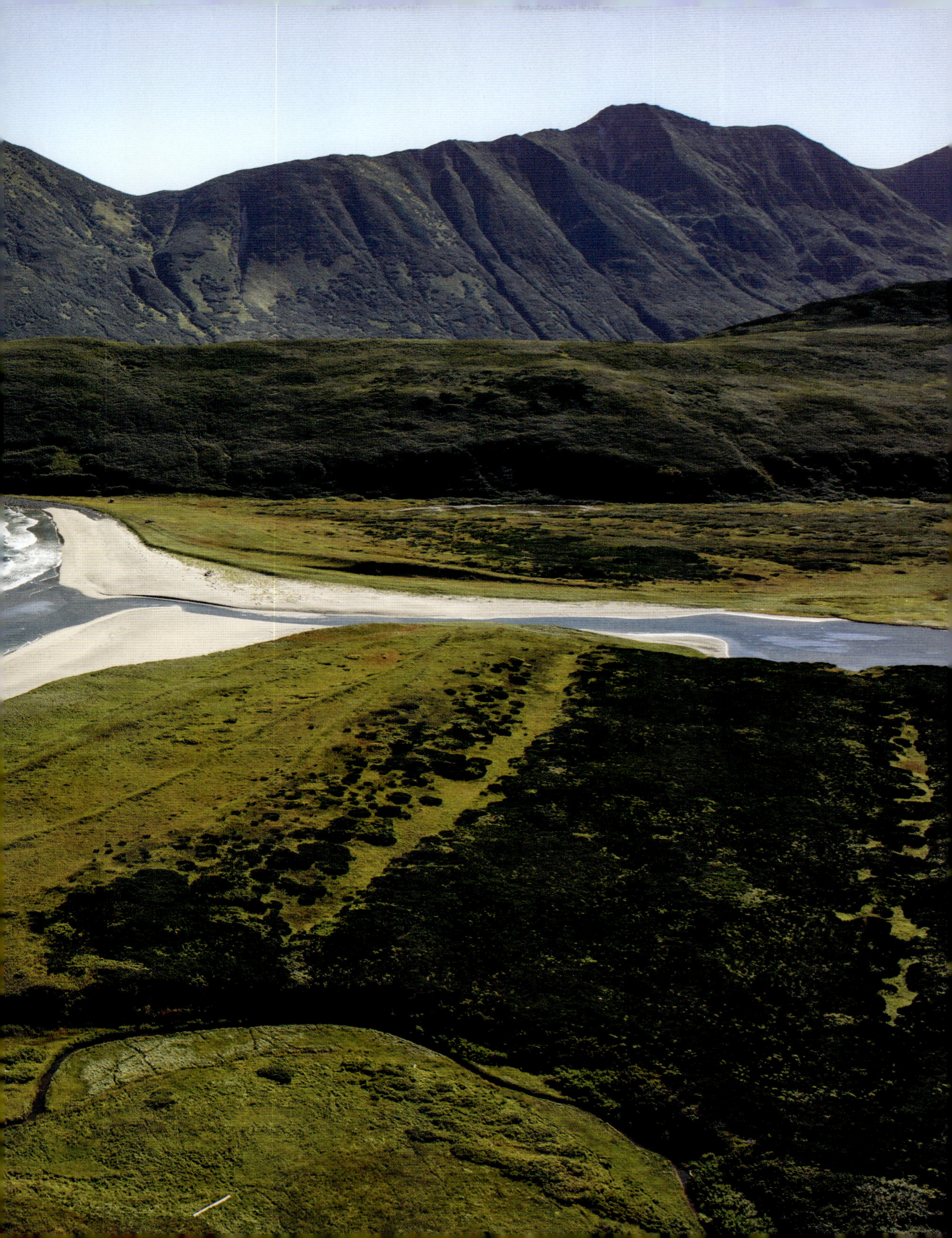

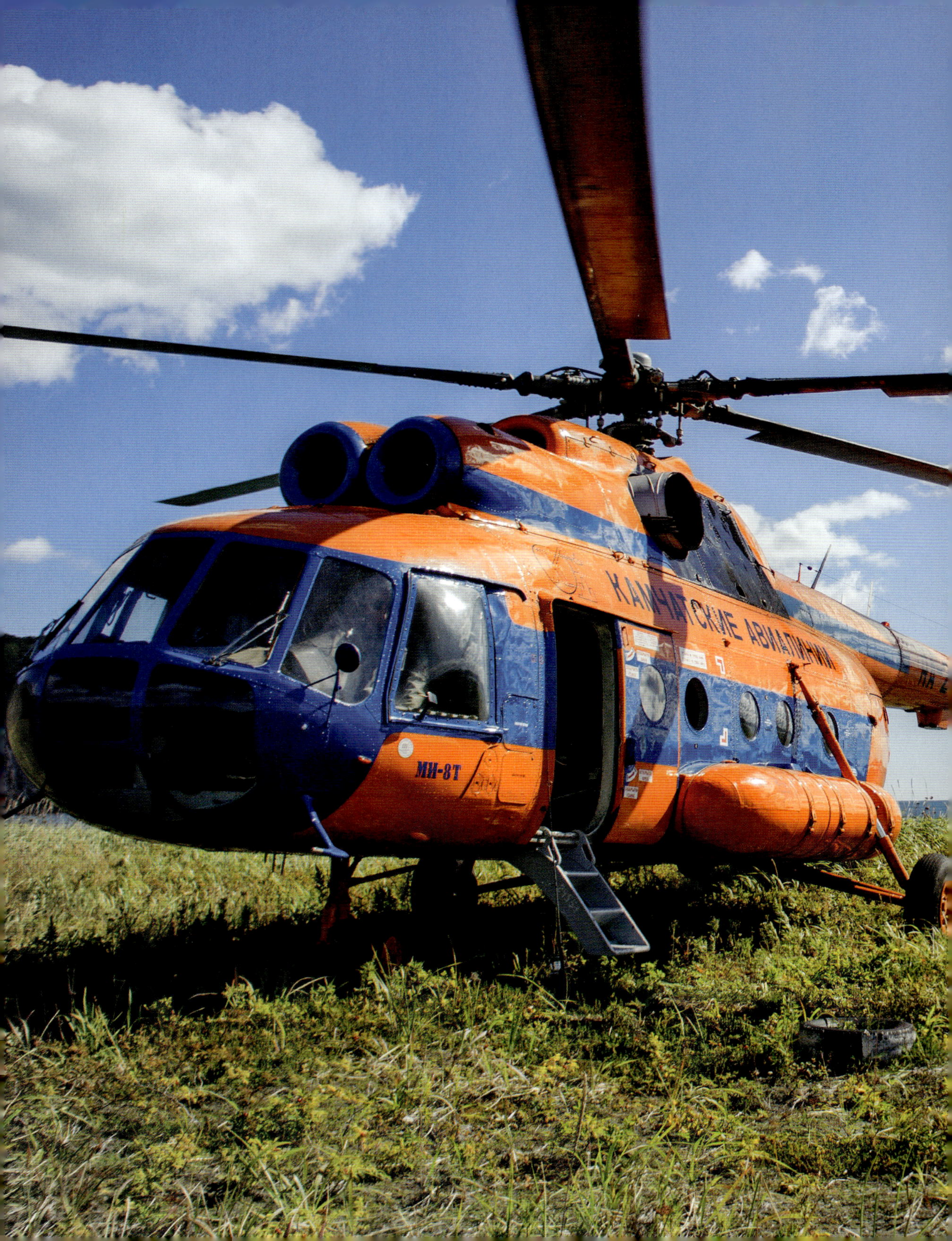
КАМЧАТСКИЕ АВИАЛИНИИ
МИ-8Т

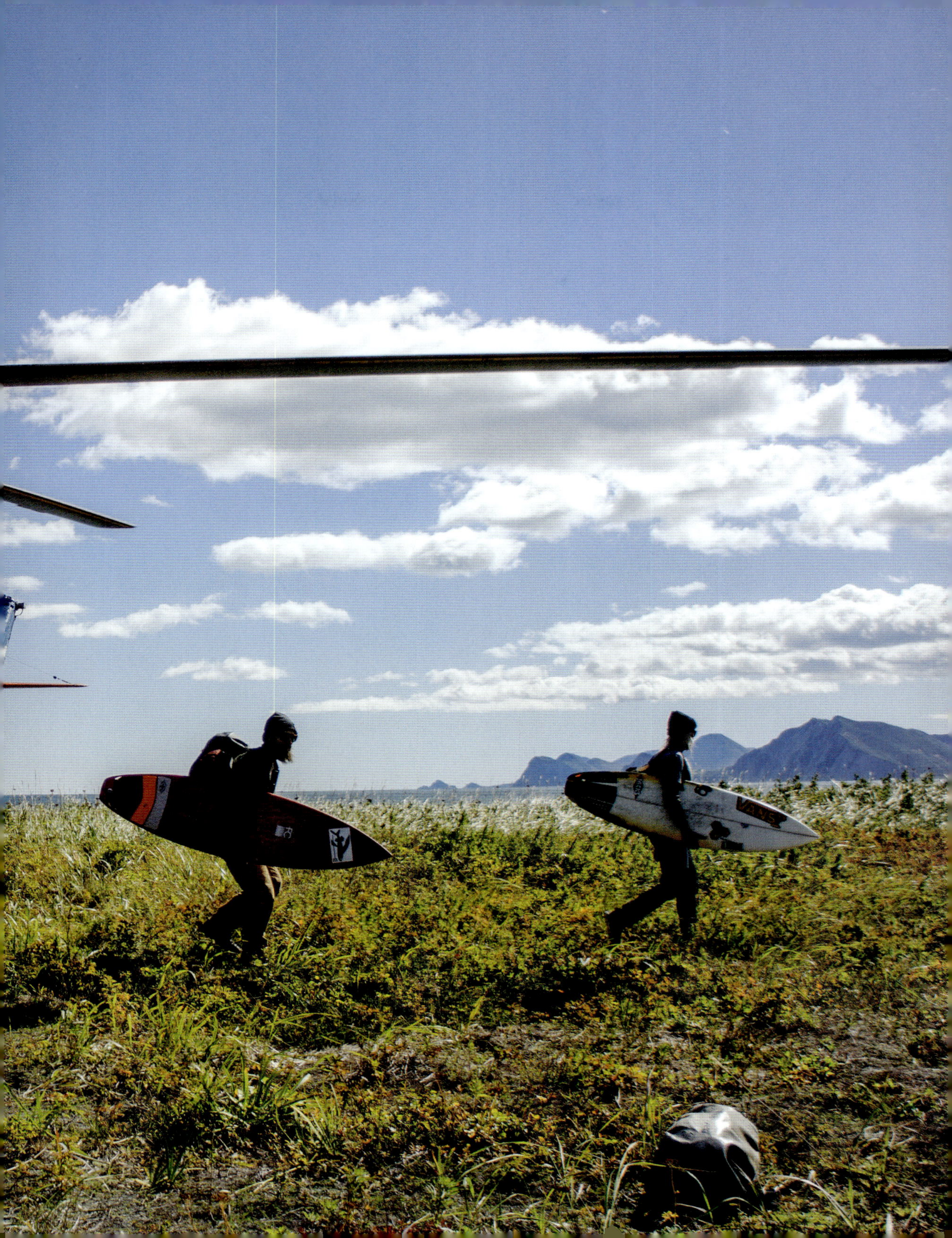

interest from a lot of surfers. The eventual lineup included Patagonia ambassadors Keith Malloy and Trevor Gordon; cold-water convert Dane Gudauskas; surfer, filmmaker, and Korduroy.tv founder Cyrus Sutton; and "van life" pioneer Foster Huntington, who was working as Patagonia's social media manager at the time. He was also the crew member with the largest Instagram following in 2012—at least a hundred times larger than my twenty thousand followers. Foster and Trevor then cleverly invented the hashtag #kamshaka so surfers and travelers could live vicariously through our photos and updates sent via Wi-Fi hotspots and satellite phone. Little did we know #kamshaka would become one of the most effective and popular hashtags of its day.

Our flight was the last Yakutia Airlines departure of the summer from Anchorage, Alaska, to Kamchatka, Russia. After a brief stop to refuel and wait out the fog in Siberia, we arrived at the airport in Petropavlovsk-Kamchatsky, the administrative and population center of the peninsula. Flashbacks of my visa fiasco from 2009 made my palms sweat, but our fixer, Lena, assured me that she triple-checked our paperwork and there would be no problems this time.

Traveling across the country was extremely challenging. However, when a twenty-one-person troop carrier rolled up to pick us up, we knew we were in good hands. This thing was a beast, but it definitely wasn't designed for speed. All our childhood dreams were being realized as we loaded into the oversized tanker. It was G.I. Joe meets Hot Wheels, and simply hopping inside made us feel like we were on a legitimate expedition.

Getting to our first destination would take a five-hour drive, which none of us minded, since we were all accustomed to surfing road trips—just never quite like this. We traversed volcanoes and descended into valleys. The paved highway gave way to rattling gravel and then hellish forest roads that we bounced through in our six-wheeled military tanker. When we finally reached the coast, it was socked in by fog and getting dark. You couldn't even hear the waves, which were muffled by the dense haze. We set up camp in the long grass and huddled under a tarp to stay dry.

When we awoke the next morning, it was still cold and misty. The entire coastline remained shrouded in mystery. We began to question whether we had made the right choice. But then the mist slowly burned away to expose the landscape that was hidden behind it, revealing that this was a place worth waiting for. The fireball sun eventually exposed volcanic cones dusted in snow and head-high sets.

Meanwhile, a fun California swell began to take shape, so the guys suited up. The ocean was numbing, even in a hood and booties, yet you could barely walk barefoot across the beach come midday when the black sand baked in eighty-degree heat. Despite the cold, we surfed twice that night thanks to our proximity to the North Pole and long summer days.

Cyrus easily caught the best waves of our first surf session. The glassy peelers were a perfect fit for his yellow single-fin. At the end of his session, Cyrus slid into a spraying tube, crouched under its thick lip, and reached his right toes for the nose. Every single one of us watched his finale in shared excitement, whistling in support. With arms counterbalancing his feet like a praying mantis, he locked into a translucent tunnel and glided into shore. He was most likely the first person ever to do so at this beach.

As I photographed him, I thought about how ironic it was that we had traveled halfway across the world to find waves that looked like Oceanside, California—only icier and surrounded by purple pyramids, lush forests, and bears. But maybe that's what made the place so special. It was wild and remote *and* it had waves as good as California's.

Walking back to camp, I was reminded just how wild this place was. Uninhabited and expansive, Kamchatka felt like the Wild West. These beaches hadn't even been accessible to the rest of Russia until the nineties, and they continued to remain remote and secret. Every other step along the black sand revealed sharp-clawed bear prints the size of dinner plates. Our only defense on this isolated beach would be an electric wire that our guide Sergei hooked up to his truck battery and ran around the perimeter of our camp. One night I accidentally hit the wire on my way to take a leak and felt nothing stronger than a vibrating text message.

"You didn't bring any guns?!" I asked Sergei.

"Guns? We have no guns. We love bears," he muttered in a thick Russian accent.

A few days later, we checked a wave near the city and were surprised to find another car topped with boards. The driver introduced himself as Anton and said he ran a surf school in the area. Anton explained that he was inspired to try surfing after Tom Curren's visit in 2004. He went on to share tips on local tides, swells, and surf spots, including one that he and his friends affectionately called Curren's Point.

"Who we gotta make friends with to surf that wave?" Dane probed, jokingly.

"You can't surf it anymore," Anton said unequivocally. "It's inside a military base."

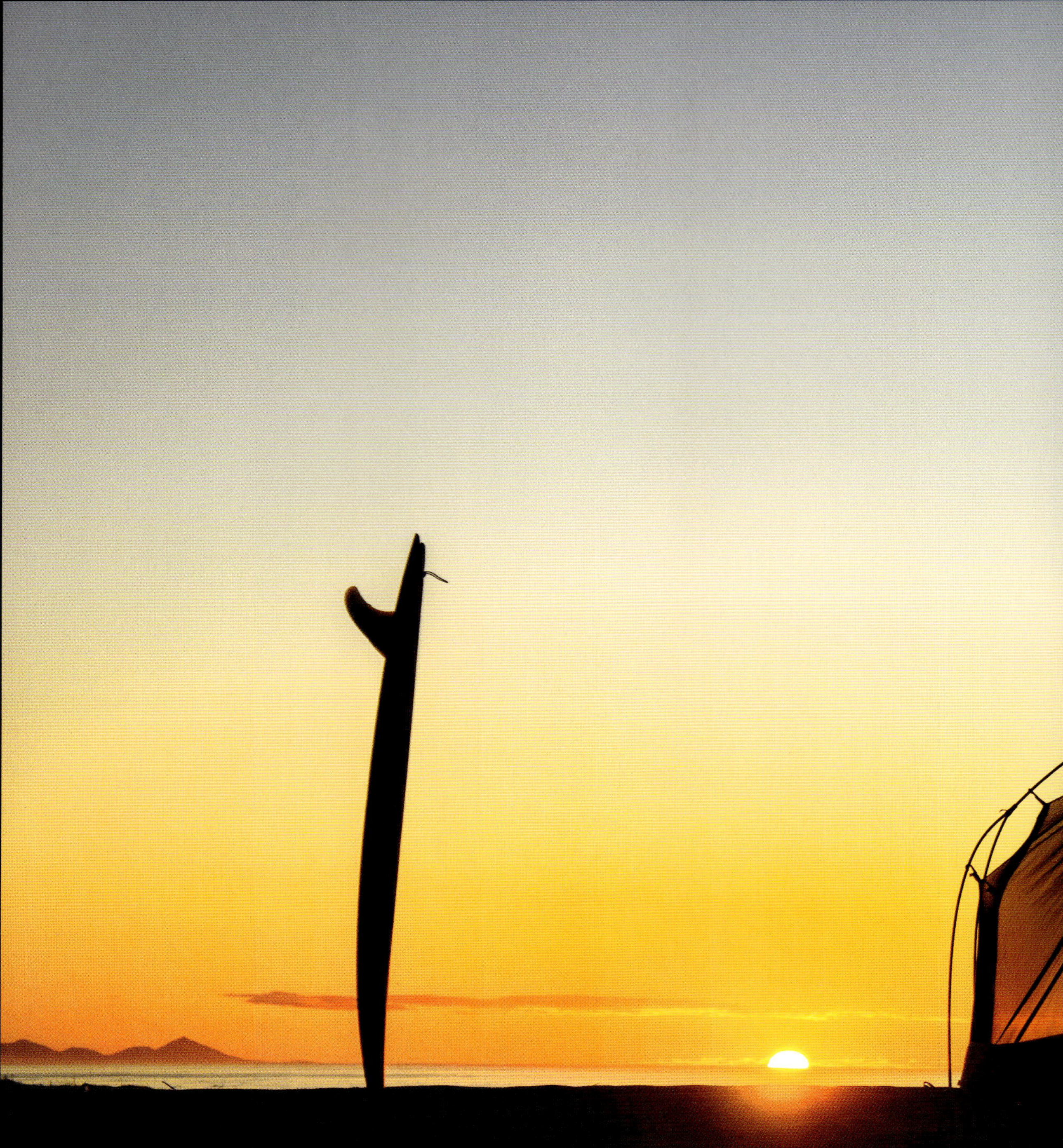

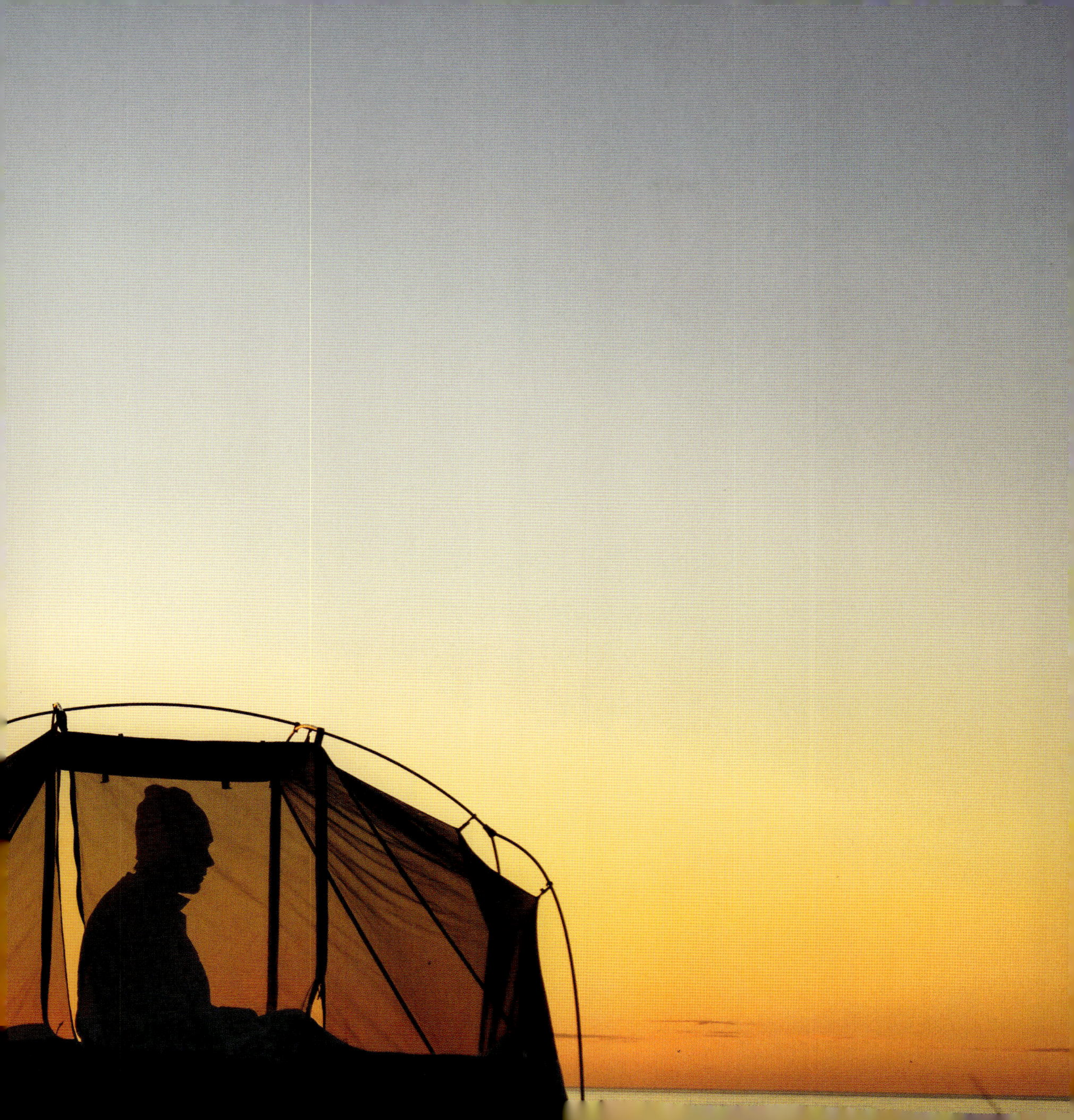

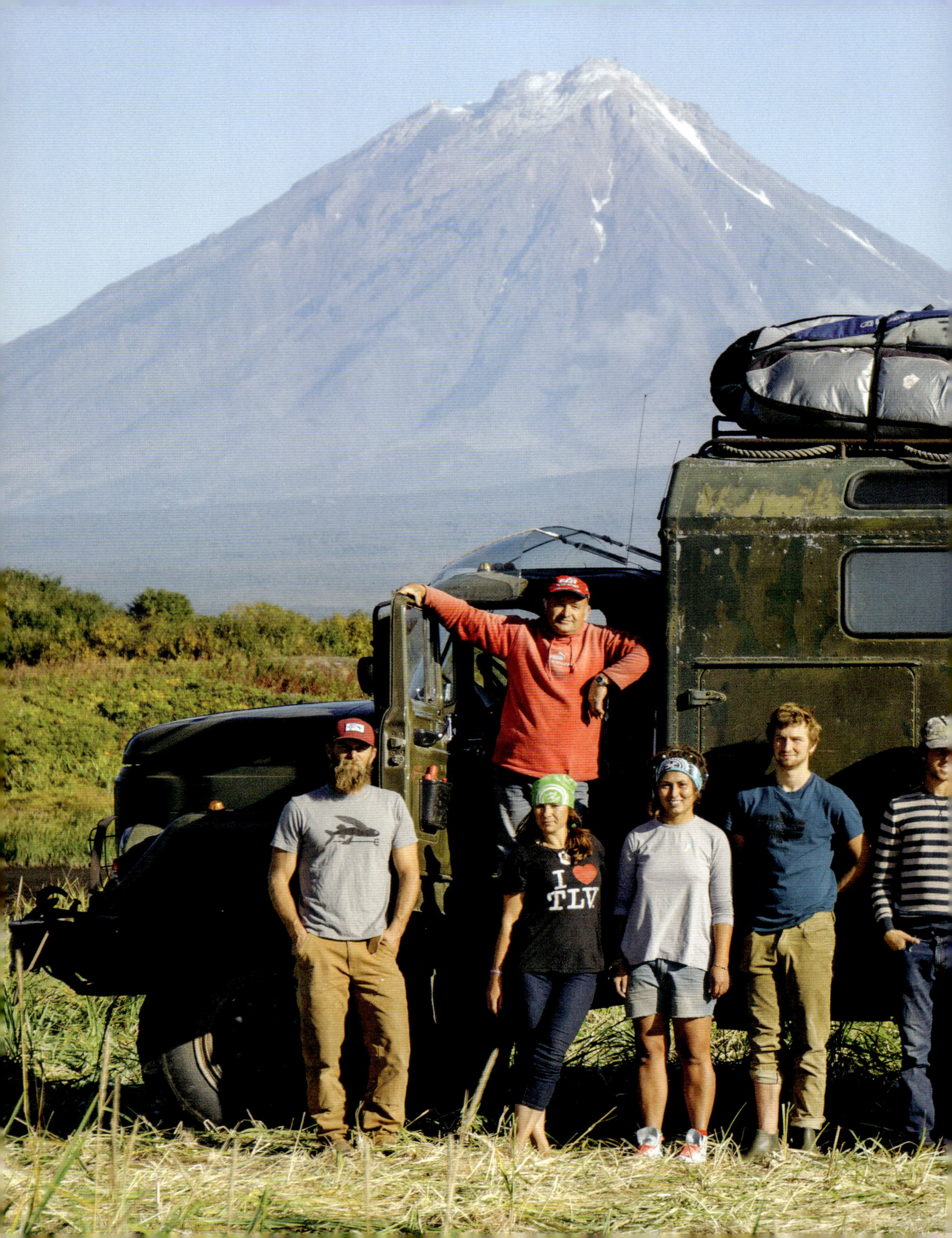

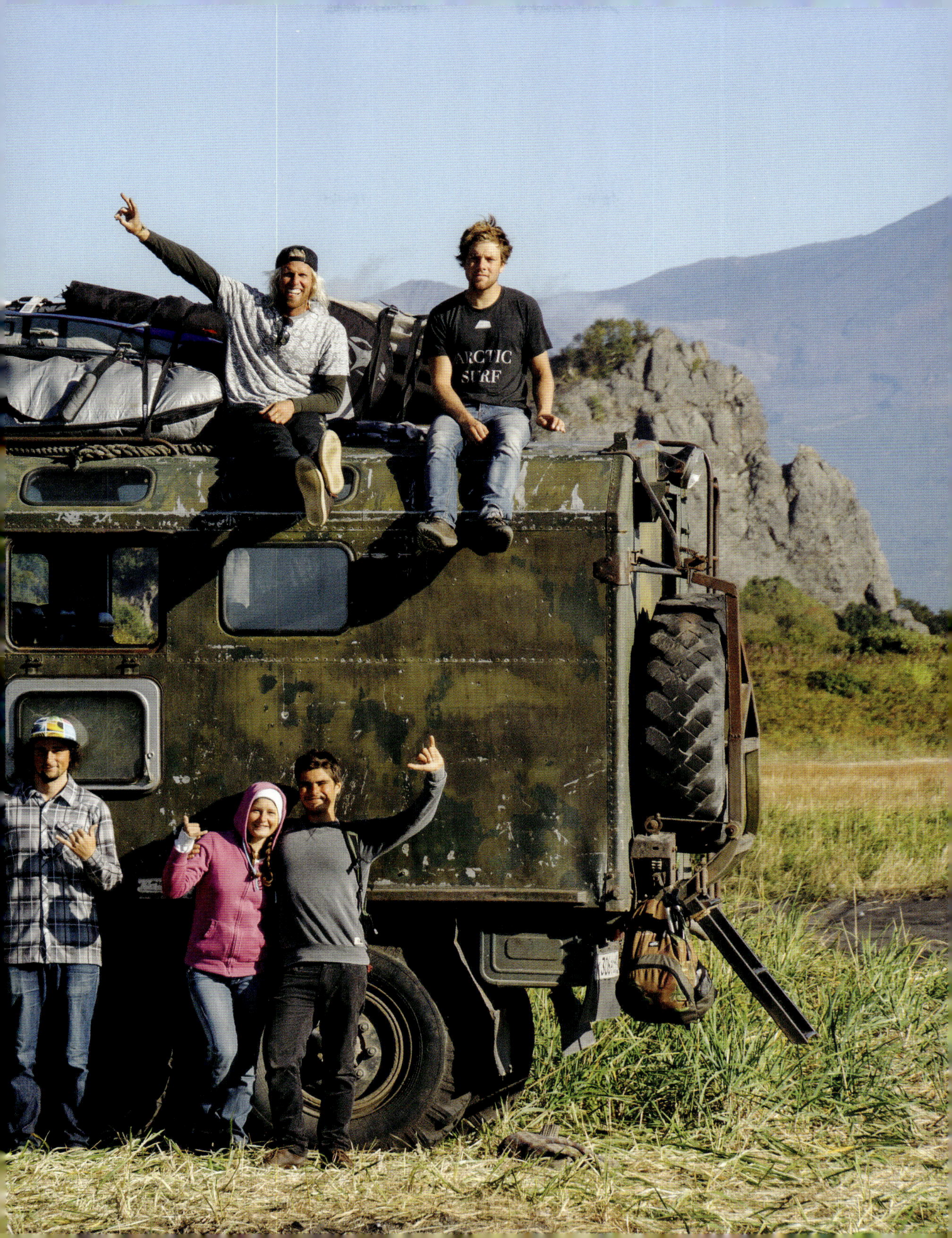

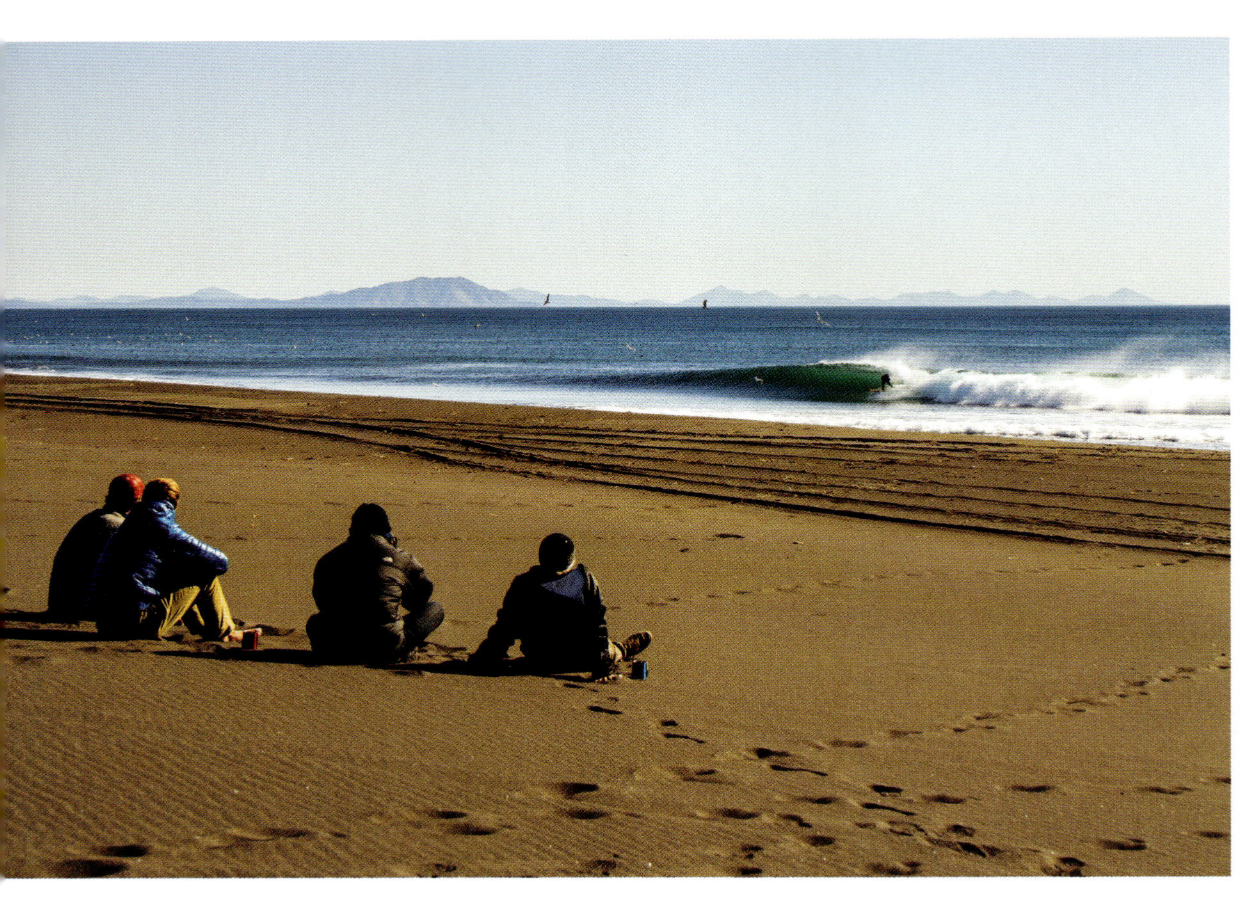

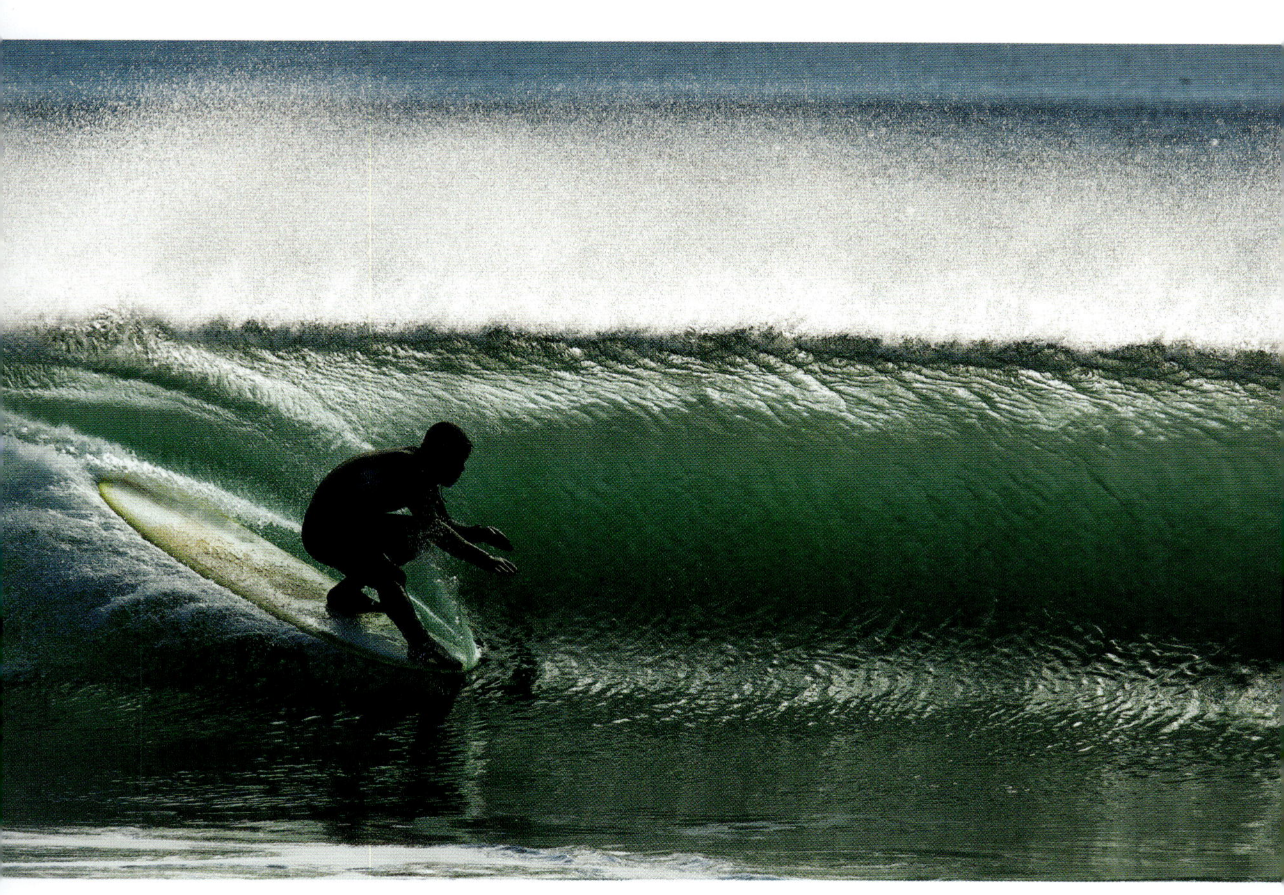

CHAPTER—7

CHRIS BURKARD   WAYWARD

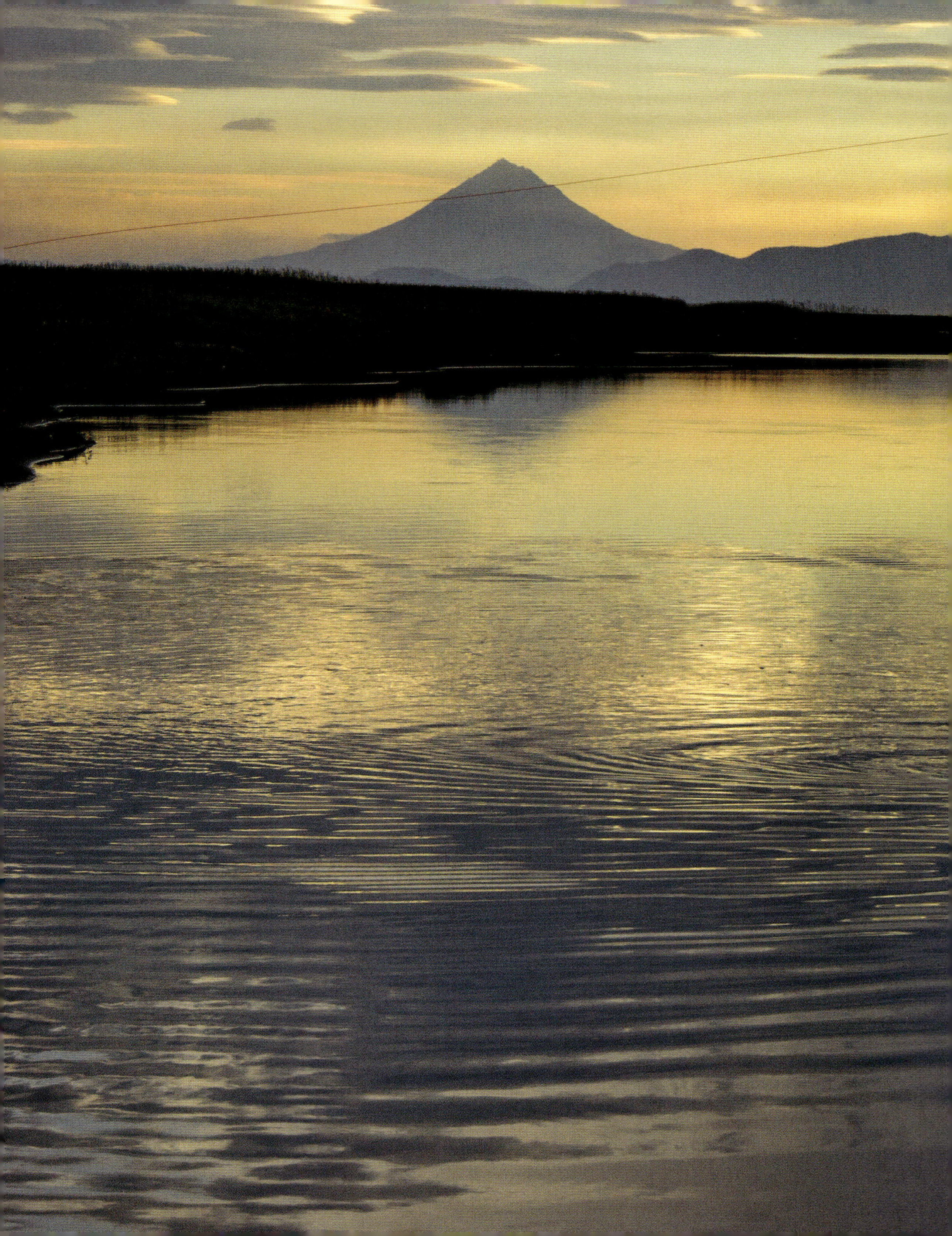

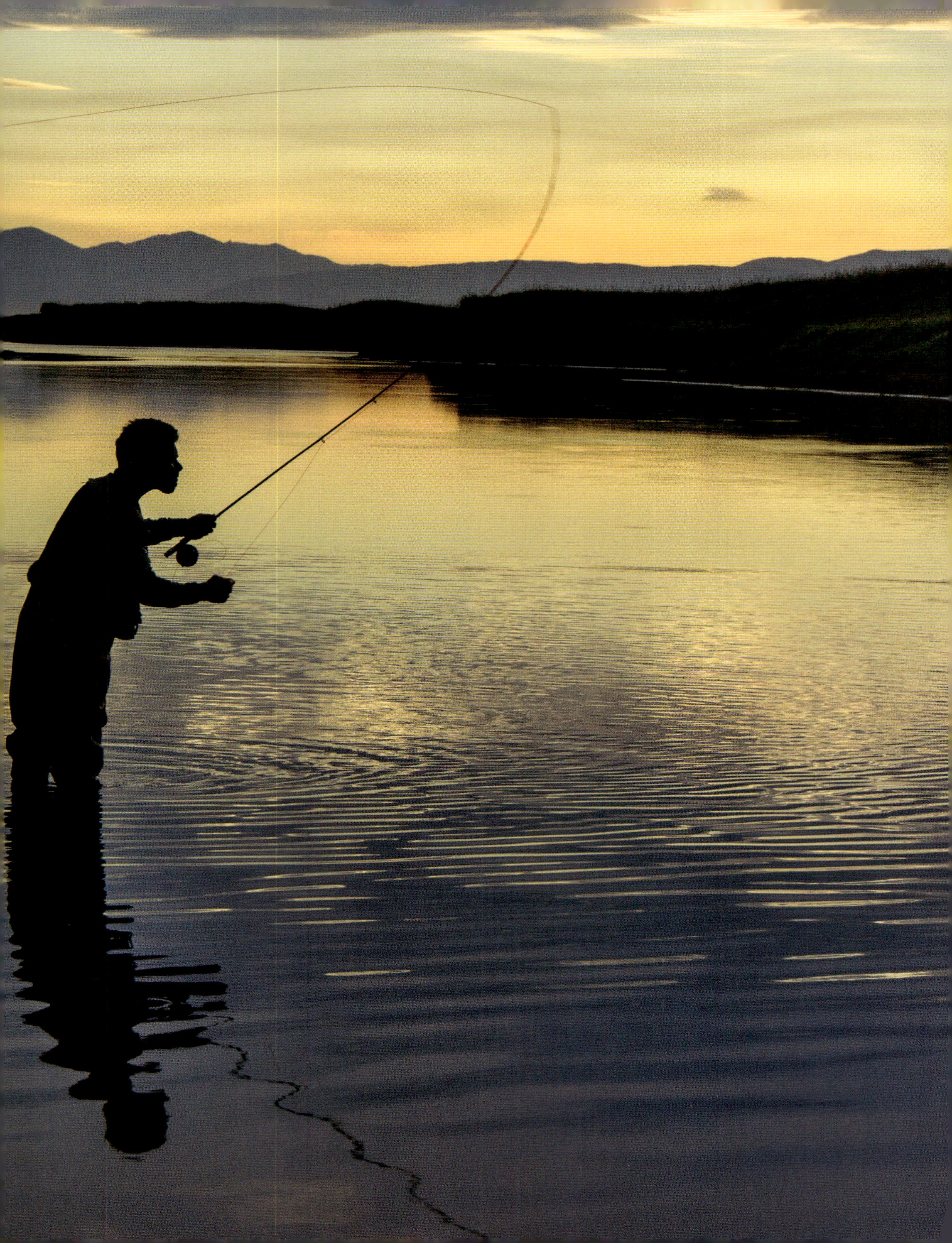

Instead of deterring me, Anton's word of warning rang as a challenge in my ears. The very next day, I set off to find the point, curious if its legends would prove true. The potential for great waves and images overshadowed the risks. From Kamchatka's main beach, Khalaktyrsky, I trained my binoculars across the river where giant satellite dishes and antennas sprouted from a distant headland. I asked Sergei for a confirmation that what I was seeing was truly off-limits.

"Military base," he reiterated.

But my mind was made up.

I asked the rest of the group if anyone was coming with me. They all declined.

It would have to be a solo reconnaissance mission. But through my long lens I saw all the classic signs that what was happening down the beach was worthy of further investigation—including barrels. I took off toward the headland about a half mile away.

For most of the walk, my view was obscured by a mound of dark sand, but as soon as I climbed it, reeling offshore tubes came into focus. They were the best waves I'd seen all trip, glowing against a black cliff backdrop. *The guys are never going to believe me unless I take some photos*, I thought. With sniper-like precision, I shot for twenty minutes as the waves got cleaner and cleaner. I was so absorbed in the scene that I almost forgot where I was.

The G-Wagen–style SUV that appeared about a quarter mile down the beach snapped me back to reality real quick. I had been mentally strategizing about this moment from the time I set foot on this dune. I decided that if anyone showed up, I would just start walking away. Two guys wearing military fatigues emerged from the vehicle, but they hadn't noticed me. They walked around the car and pulled out a fishing net. They seemed occupied enough for me to go about my business, so I raised the camera to my eye again and freeze-framed a few more waves. But I was pushing my luck, and when I swiveled back toward the fishermen, they were waving and pointing into my viewfinder. I looked up from the camera, and they were running straight toward me.

I had to think quickly. The last thing I needed was to get sent to another Russian holding cell. My first thought was memory

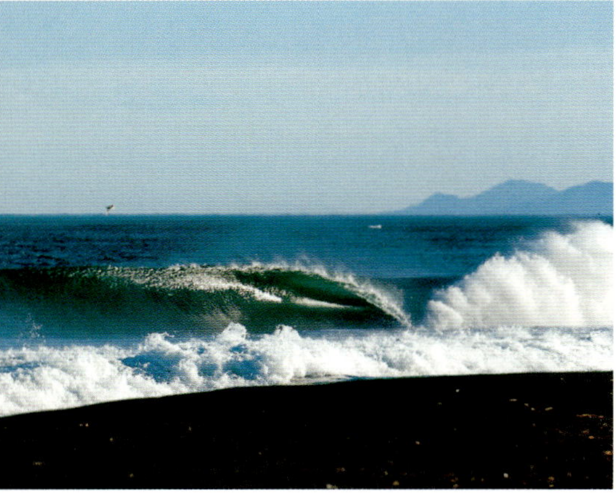

cards. I ejected the SD card from one camera and then the second and grasped both of them inside clenched fists. I briefly considered shoving them into an open orifice but I opted for the back zipper pocket of my pants instead. Then I ran. If I could make it to the river, and Sergei saw me in trouble, he could explain in Russian why I was there with my camera.

But more time had passed than I'd realized, and the river had swollen massively from the incoming tidal push. I had to wade chest deep through frigid water holding my camera bag over my head as the current threatened to sweep me off my feet. Once I made it across the river, I turned back to find the guards standing on the opposite bank. Luckily, they weren't shaking guns at me, only their heads.

While the incident scared most of the crew off, when a peak started forming across the river a couple of days later, Ben, Dane, and Trevor couldn't resist. Sure enough, the moment we set foot on forbidden sand, a military guard was trailing us. Ben walked over and introduced our group in German before asking politely if we could check the waves farther down the beach. The guard answered with a resolute shake of his head. Ben tried a second attempt, explaining that the waves were far better down the shore. He shook his head again, but this time more slowly. *Ah, persistence is key.* With a little extra pressure from me, the guard gave in.

Down near the point, water sucked up into tall peaks that spilled over themselves. Dane and Trevor sped through a couple before the waves smashed on hard sand. And just like that, our time was up. The light was fading, signaling the guard to end our surreal session together.

The trip to Kamchatka was my first real introduction to social media as a tool, and it was enlightening. At first it felt jarring to gather images and jot down thoughts to try and share in quasi "real time" for media updates, but soon I fell into a rhythm. In magazine photography, it was completely off-limits to reveal images before they were published. It wasn't until the Kamchatka trip that I was taught the value of sharing behind-the-scenes footage and anecdotes to tease a final product. In fact, I became convinced this resource might even complement the final product. It was invigorating to keep the magazines, the world, and my family back home apprised of what was going on. I came from the school of "never looking at what you shot until the end of the trip," but doing daily reviews and editing images helped me consider what I was missing, and what I needed to shoot more of. I became my own photo editor and could analyze and improve my approach for the rest of the trip.

The response our crew received from the Kamchatka trip solidified the idea that maybe what we were doing could actually reach people and inspire them. Unlike with

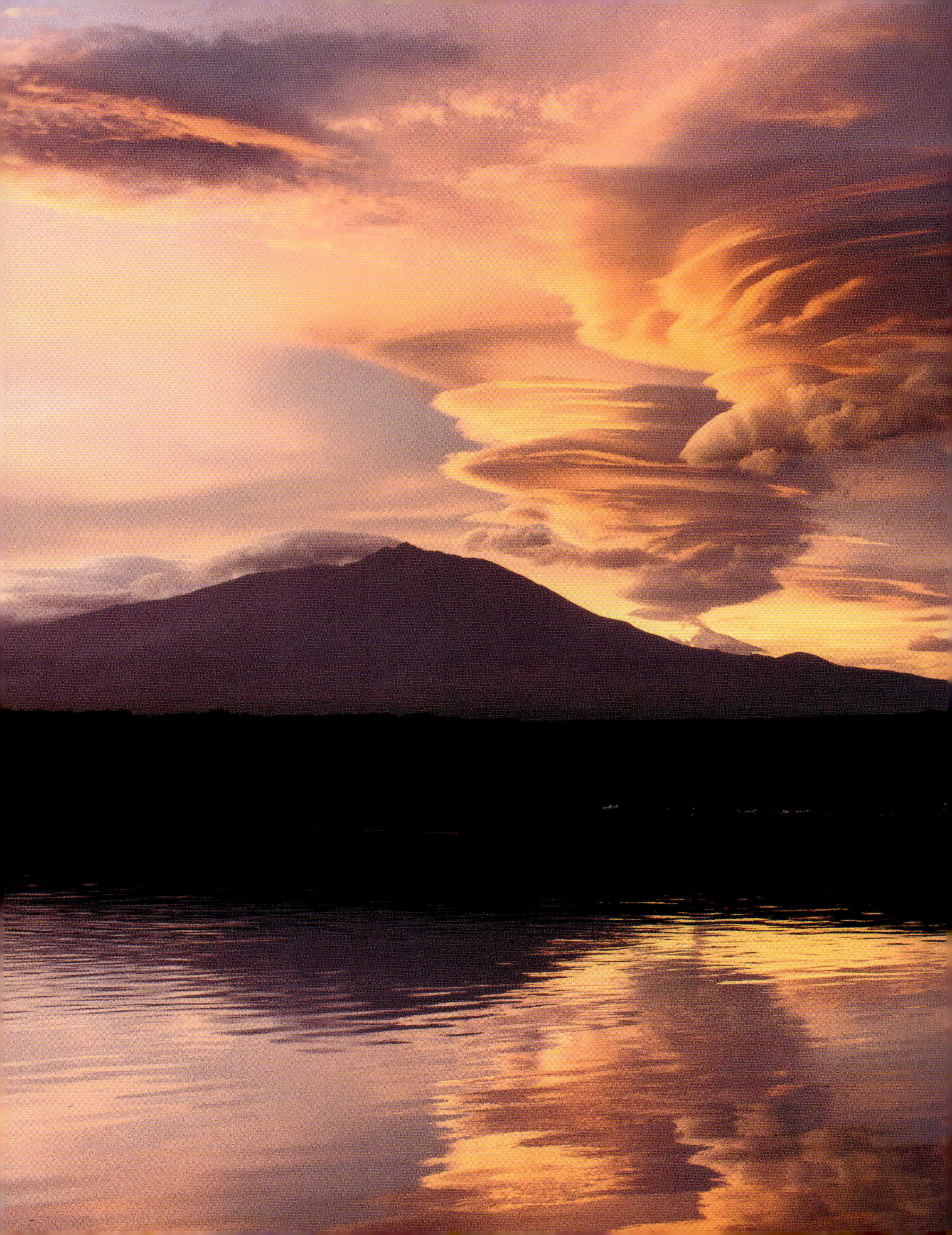

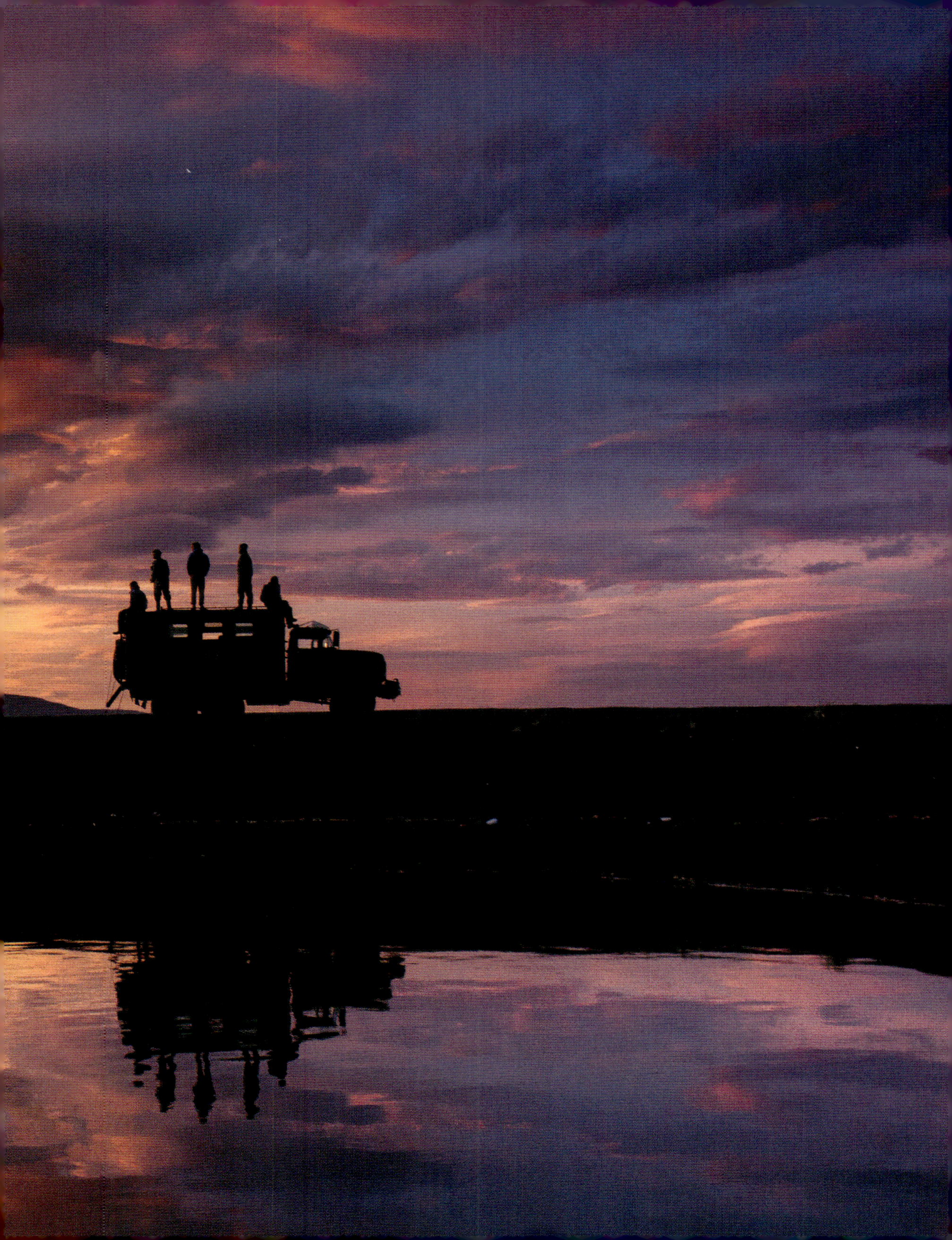

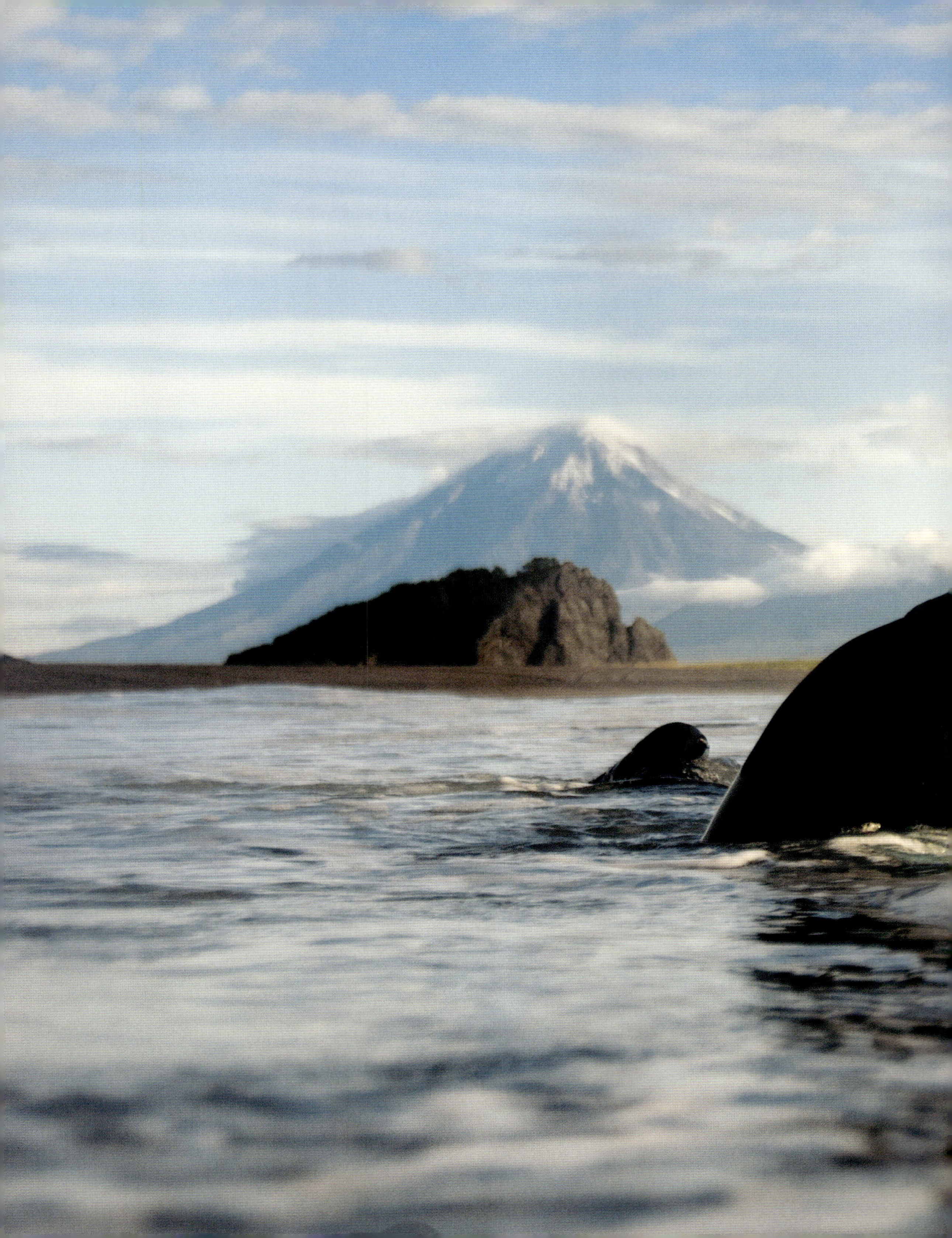

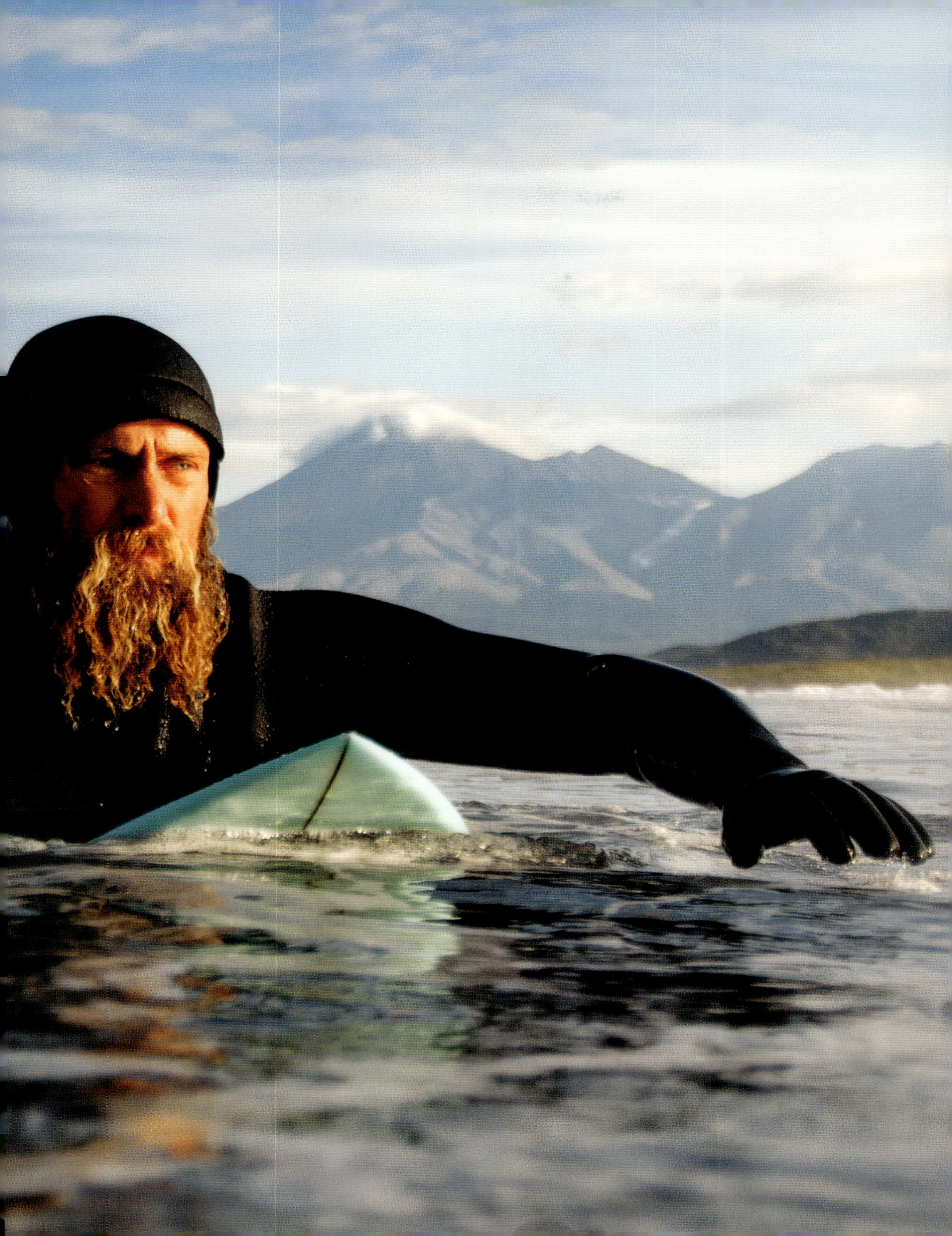

previous projects—which rarely generated any feedback outside my immediate circle of friends, family, and editors—each of us was getting comments in person and online from perfect strangers about how the journey had moved them.

It was the first time I had ever traveled professionally with other visual artists, aside from Ben. Partnering with brands and athletes took on a whole new meaning now that we had a social media strategy. Using Facebook, Instagram, and Tumblr, we could maximize exposure for our assignments and for each other. There was an obvious pinball effect that resulted from using each other's handles and hashtags and cross-posting to multiple accounts. After the trip, people started following me who weren't from my immediate circle. I was interacting with thousands of people I had never met in real life.

Soon I shifted from sharing mostly behind-the-scenes images to featuring selections of my best work after it was published. It was amazing to share unpublished outtakes, unearth old projects, and include my personal reflections on Instagram, which seemed designed for landscape photography. I had spent years compiling images that never ran and thus had never seen the light of day. It dawned on me that instead of relying solely on magazine articles—written by others and often cut down due to space constraints—I could now speak with my own voice and connect with my own audience.

Social media in many ways is what helped me realize what it meant to be a storyteller. These locations I traveled to challenged me and made me a better person, and I hoped that by sharing them with the public, I might inspire someone to go out and find that for themselves.

Video was another form of storytelling that became increasingly appealing after Kamchatka. Though still photography would remain my first love, I felt inspired to bring characters and emotions to life in 3-D. Not to mention that videos unequivocally proved the quality of written-off waves, like those found in the northern latitudes, better than any photo ever could. When our magazine article about the Kamchatka trip dropped in the January 2013 issue of *Surfer* magazine, we released the short film *Hidden Sea and the Pyramid of Fire* alongside an online photo gallery, setting our favorite scenes and memories to music and garnering thousands of views.

But Ben and I always had a goal to also make a longer version of the film. We eventually produced the film *Russia: The Outpost Vol. 01* to enter into festivals, screen in our local communities, and sell on iTunes accompanied by a zine-style book. That film felt like my greatest professional accomplishment to date.

Russia: The Outpost Vol. 01 and the accompanying zine set off a chain reaction of opportunities. Ben and I toured the film all over California's coast and, stop after stop, heard the same reaction. People were craving this type of intimate storytelling that they could connect with. Kamchatka opened my eyes to the concept of working smarter, not harder.

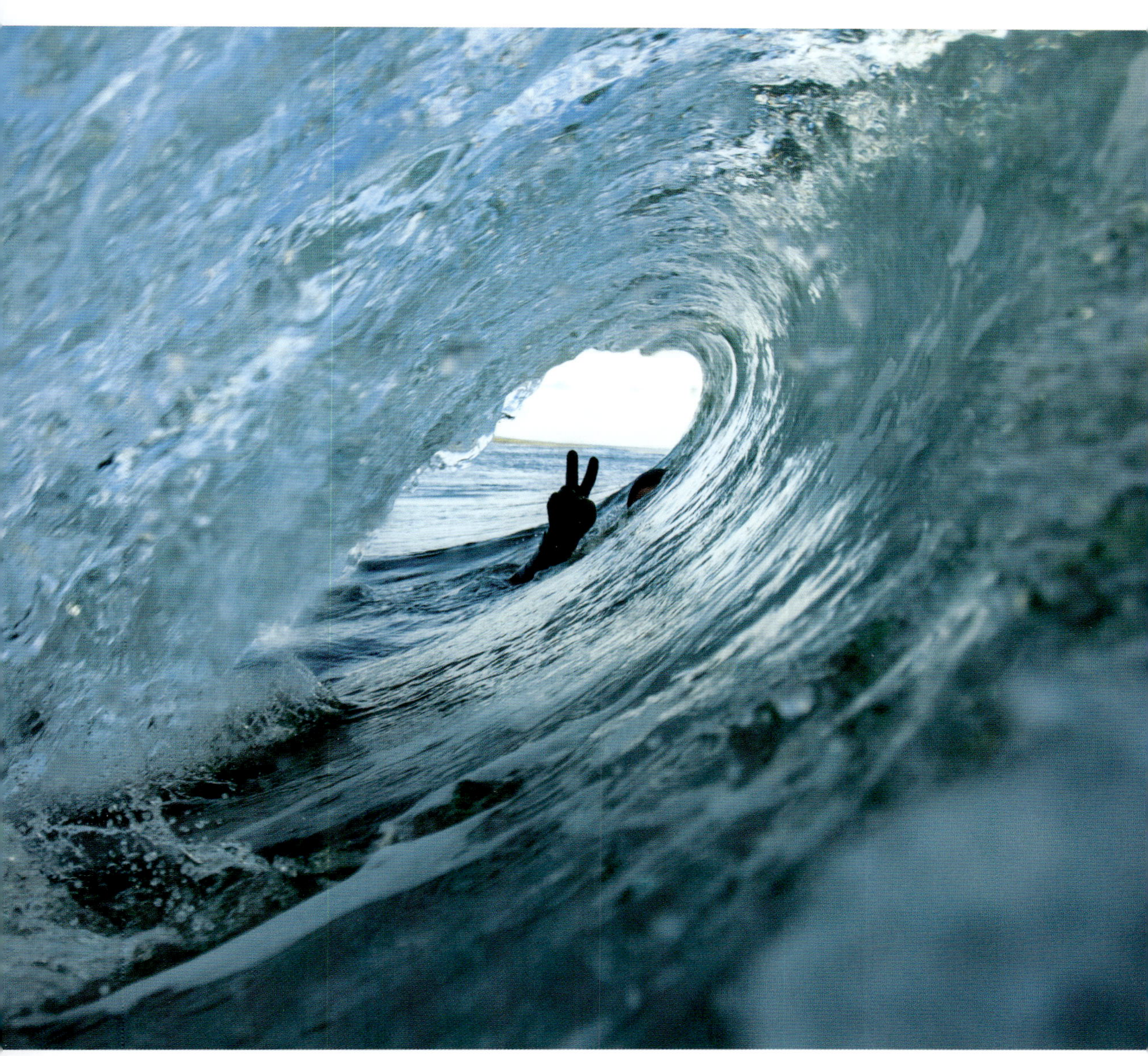

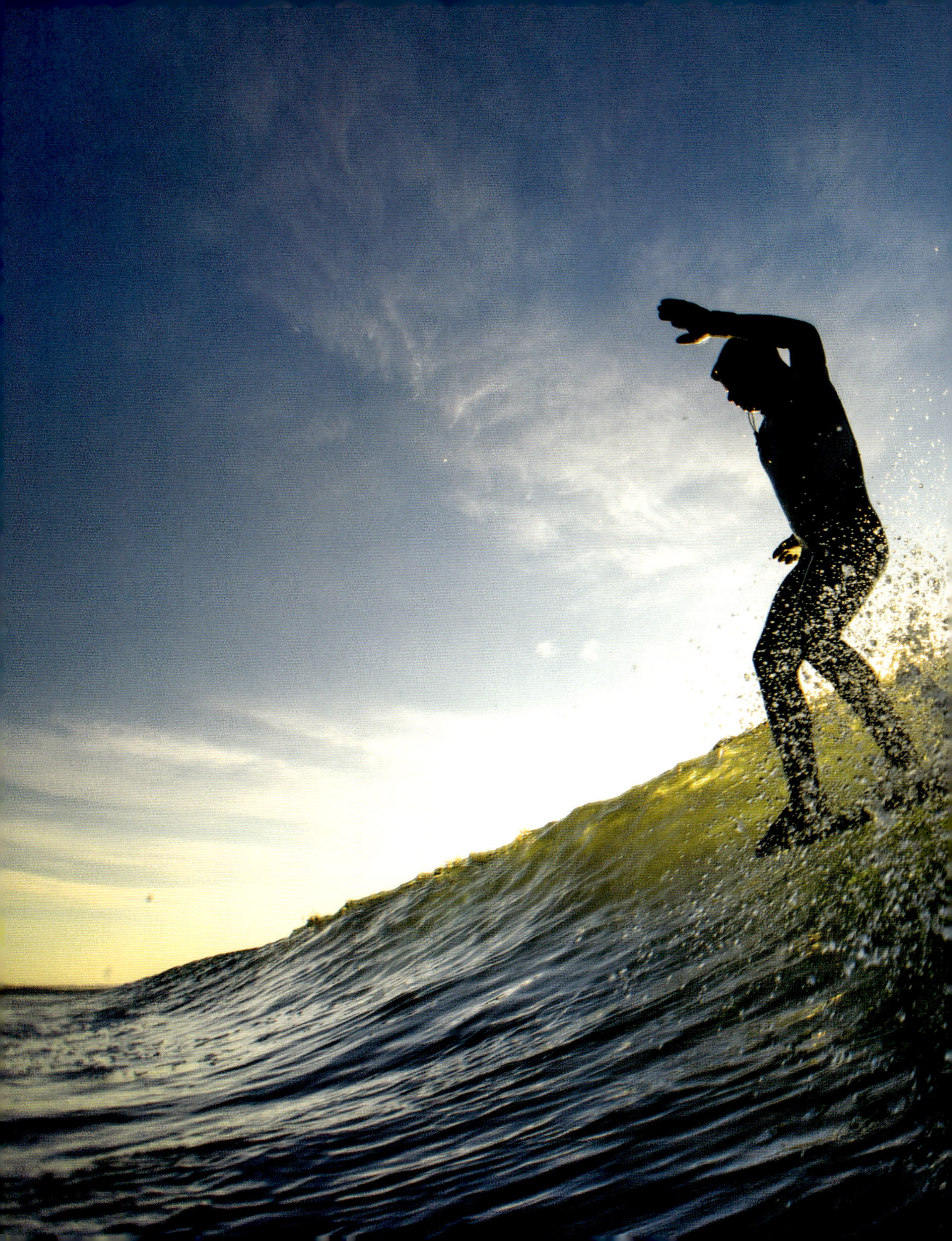

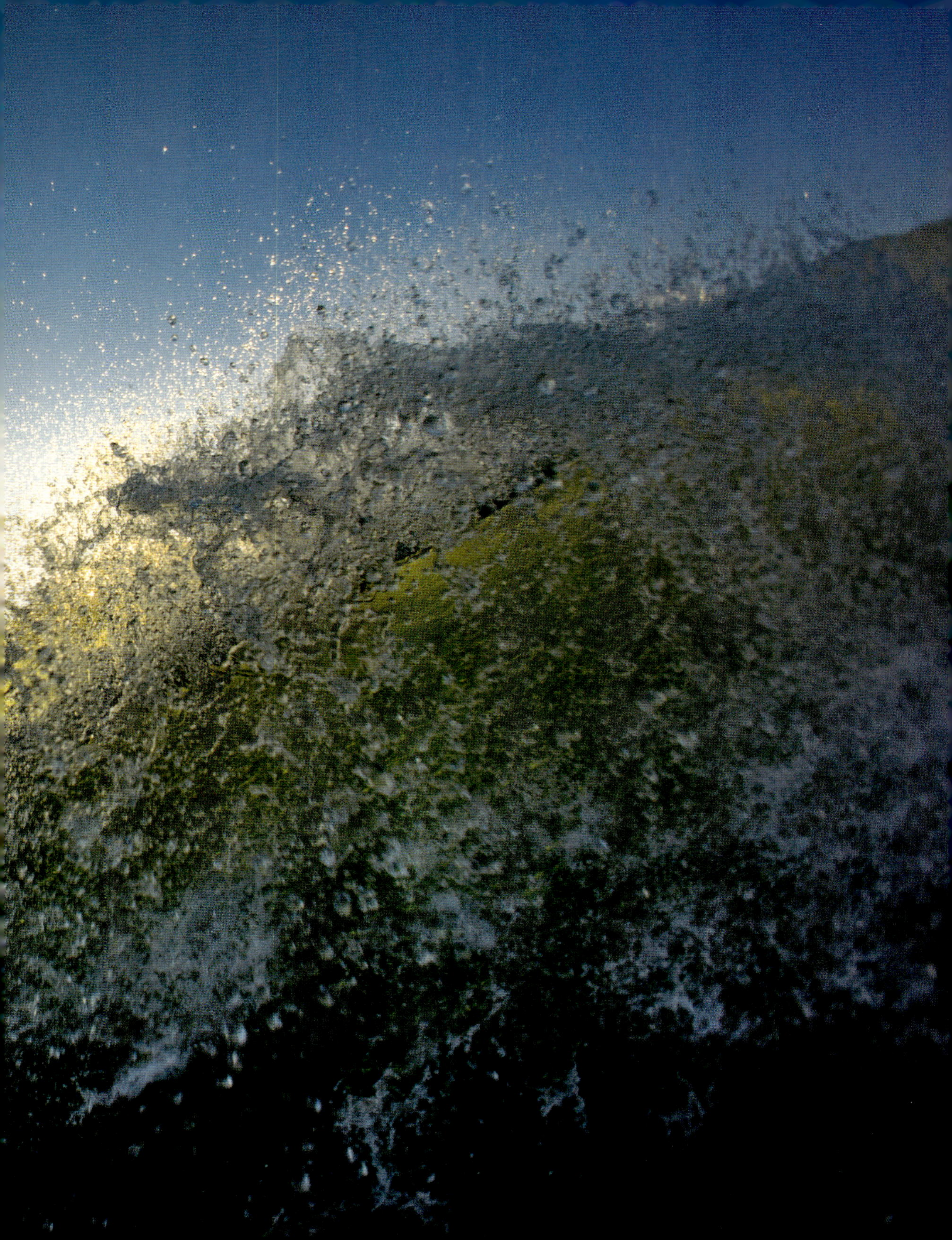

Deal with the Devil

Chris would show up to the *Surfer* magazine office with these absolutely wild ideas. I would always take the meeting with a mixture of excitement and dread. I'd be like, *Oh, God, what are we in for now? How much money is this going to cost?* Chris would say things like, "I want to rent a fishing boat and go to the end of the Arctic and try to surf off an iceberg." I would respond, "Why? Why would you want to do that?"

Most of the time, we didn't have the funds in our editorial budget to do some of his more ambitious trips, but Chris wouldn't take no for an answer. If we didn't have the funds, he'd go find someone else who could help him get there. The Aleutians trip—which we subsequently turned into a movie and the *Surfer* magazine cover of Josh Mulcoy and the volcano—was a similar thing. Crews had gone there before, and the wave quality was average at best. So when he pitched the idea and told us the cost, we couldn't really figure out why we would want to back that.

But Chris proved us wrong, showing that the confluence of nature and being there at the right time is always part of making any photograph. To an end user it may seem like Chris has some sort of deal with the devil—the clouds part and the weather gets amazing right when he's there. But that hides the reality, which is that he and his crew sat in a little shack for days on end waiting for the storms to pass, so they could experience that moment they were after.

When he came back with the photos, the video footage, and the story from that trip, I couldn't believe it. If it were a piece of fiction, it wouldn't have been better than what they were able to pull off on that trip. The wave quality was the best we'd ever seen from that area of the world. Them cruising out on ATVs and freezing themselves half to death to surf these waves. It was just a remarkable surf adventure—probably the most remarkable surf adventure of my tenure at *Surfer* magazine.

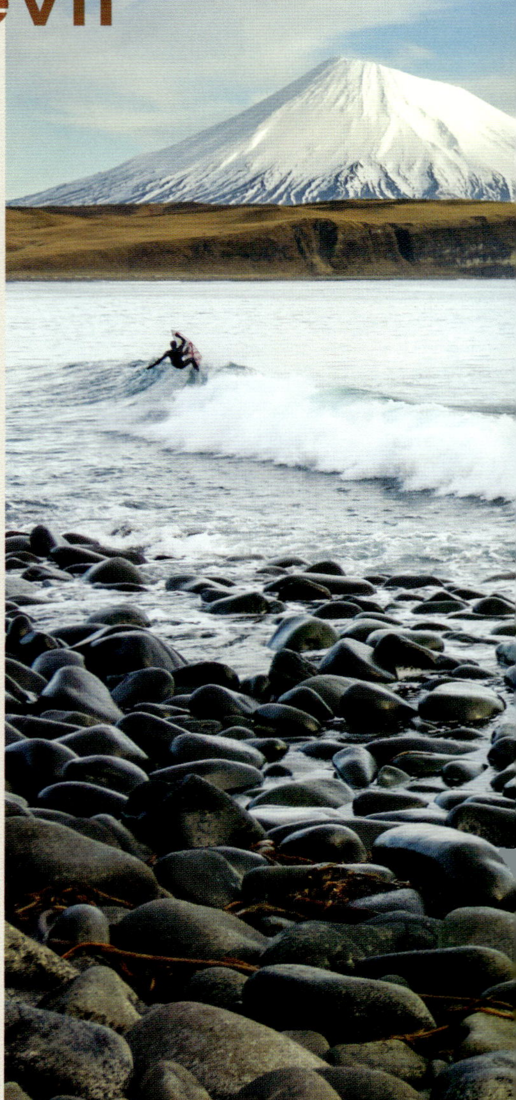

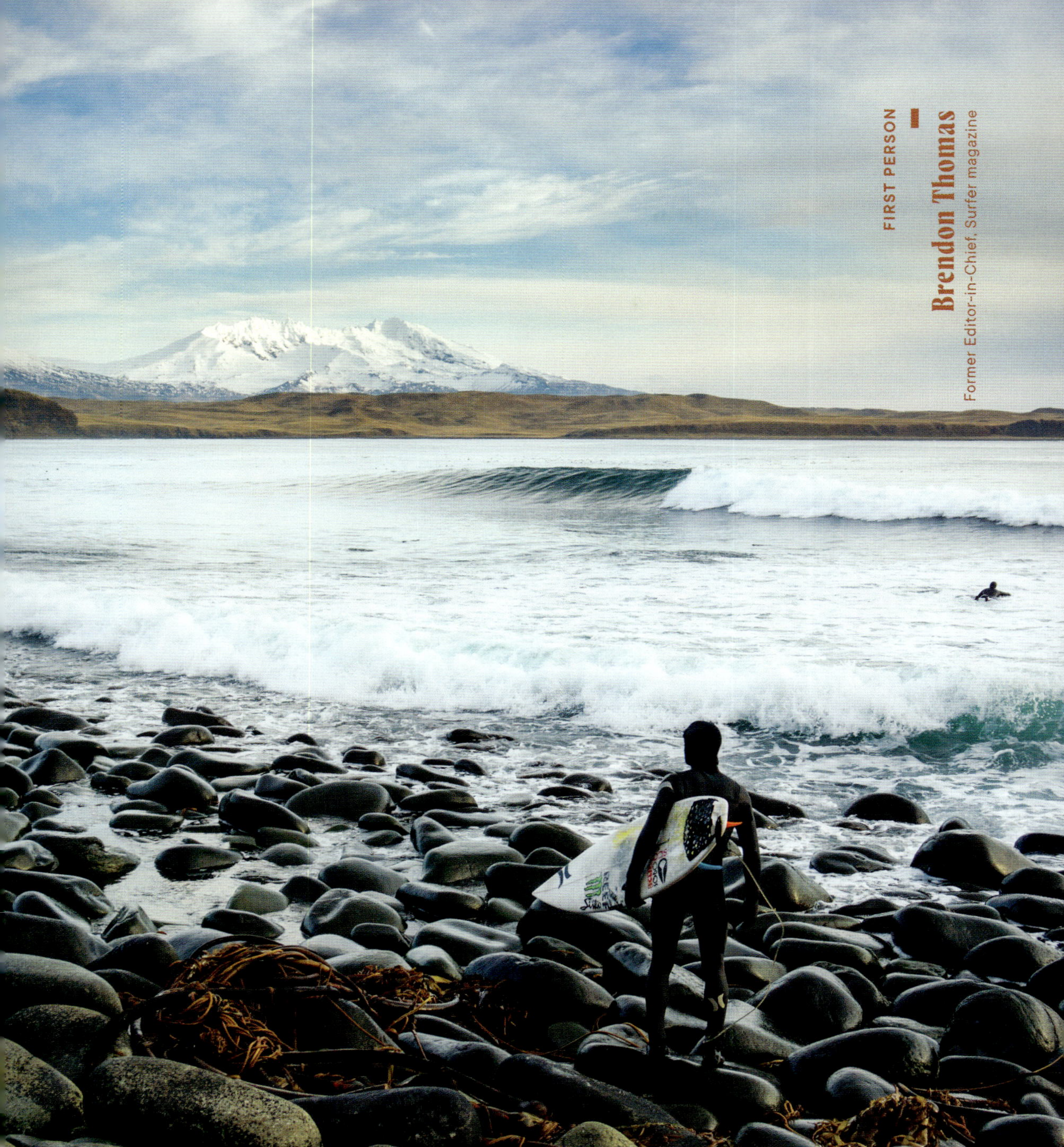
FIRST PERSON

Brendon Thomas
Former Editor-in-Chief, Surfer magazine

CHRIS BURKARD

WAYWARD

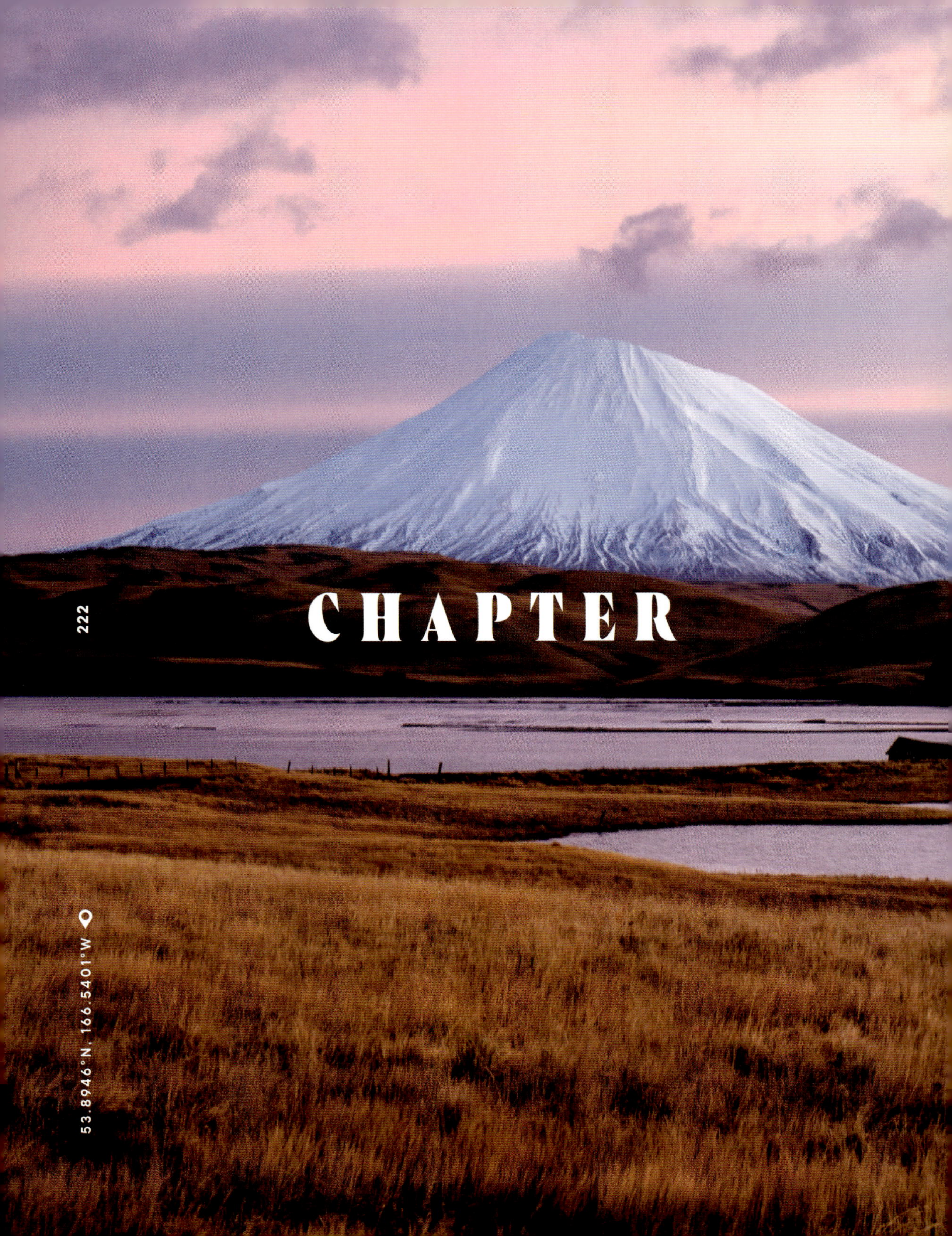

CHAPTER

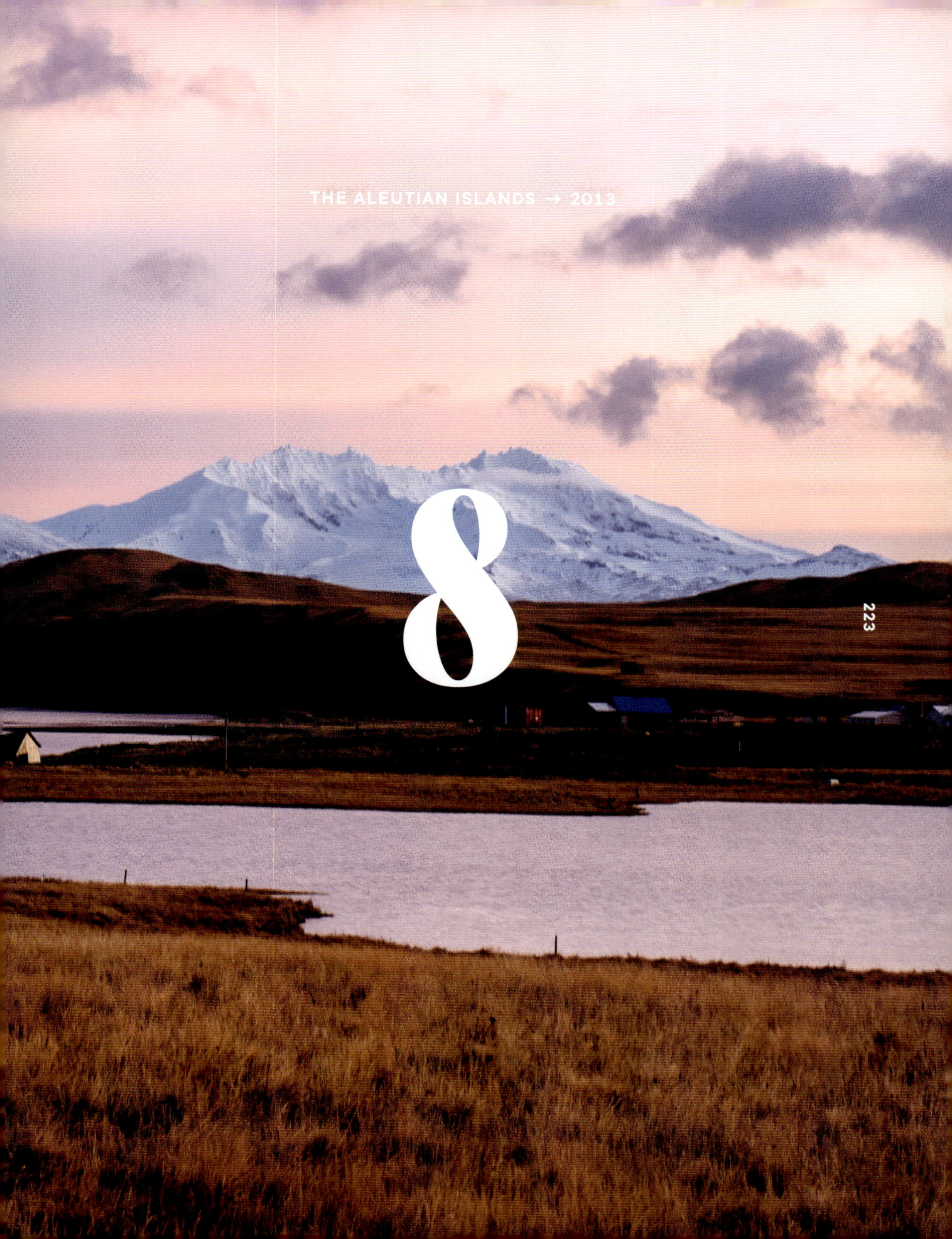

THE ALEUTIAN ISLANDS → 2013
8
223

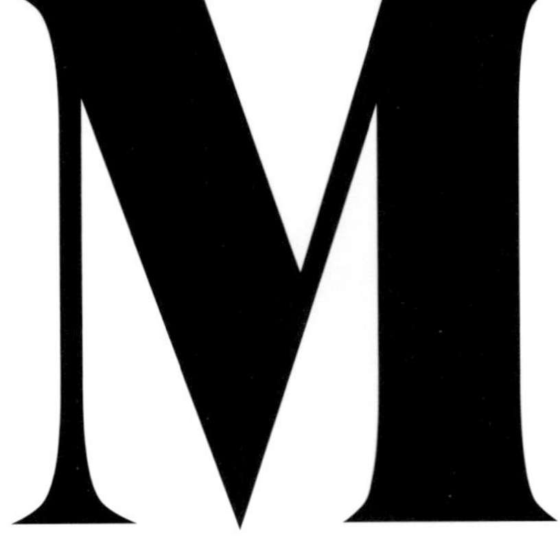

y first official studio was hidden within a brick building on Front Street in Grover Beach, nestled next to the train tracks. For years Brea and I would drive past the small development of business offices, and I would casually mention how epic it would be to have my own studio there. So when we started moving into the space in July of 2012, my wife said I "manifested it."

But I was uncomfortable with the idea of expanding my business and hiring official employees and bookkeepers; heck, this place even needed a cleaning service. It was almost as if I worried that by having a physical representation of my growth and success, I would scare it away.

It was the first public face of Chris Burkard Studio, a modest gathering space where friends, clients, and members of the community could stop by. The two-story space was spare and white, with hairless gray carpeting and a particleboard ceiling, like a surf-themed doctor's office. Downstairs was the waiting room gallery, while upstairs was where we worked and where the day's hottest debates took place—usually about who had control over the playlist. Our back room housed gear and a small kitchen where the wood divider doubled as a mini climbing wall.

The motivation for hiring my first employees and eventually moving the office out of my garage was a combination of necessity and opportunity. By the end of 2010, I realized I had taken on double the assignments of the previous year, and deadlines for photo submissions started getting lost in the new bulges of my Yahoo! account. In my mind, there aren't many things worse than squandering an opportunity, and I had no excuse now that I was bringing in more income. Disorganization is my true trigger for anxiety. When life gets increasingly chaotic, order helps me make sense of it all.

Around this time I was also beginning to have people approach me, asking whether I was hiring, or hoping to gain some insight into the industry. I felt overwhelmed and inadequate at the thought of being an authority on any subject, let alone photography. I was still trying to navigate my own career and had no clue what gave me the credentials to guide anyone else on this path. But I've always appreciated being able to connect with fellow artists, and I genuinely enjoy helping other people make their way.

At first I would agree to meet interested photographers for a meal or a quick smoothie to chat business and share tips. But when I started noticing fellow surf photographers working with assistants, I considered the benefits of assembling a team. Fellow photographers Dustin Humphrey and Nate Lawrence showed me how much was possible if you had the right people surrounding you. I watched their assistants support them in the logistical side of their businesses and provide backup support on larger, more demanding photo shoots, which then gave Nate and Dustin freedom for more creativity.

It was time to hire a part-time assistant and, before long, a full-time employee. I trained my staff to navigate my photo archive and follow my critical and obsessive process for edits and submissions. By 2013 I had three employees plus an intern all helping me juggle new commercial clients and prepare for trips. This made me feel much more productive and helped me stay on top of work, especially when I was on a trip and out of range. In a lot of ways, the studio became a rotating door for up-and-coming photographers to gain experience, make connections, and support my growing career.

I was transitioning from mainly creating editorial and surf lifestyle photography to running a full-blown commercial studio. Our focus became image licensing, print sales, and a growing list of non-surf clients. I also started working with an agent for the first time. Thanks to the exposure from *The California Surf Project*, I began getting requests and inquiries for print and commercial work. But being hired by brands and companies instead of magazines and editors was foreign territory for me, and an agent could act as a sort of translator between the art and commercial worlds. Once I began to understand this side of the business a little more, there was one particular pre-agent gig that still haunted me.

I was approached by a marketing agency to shoot a gig for a wine label that had been developed by a popular musician. I was overeager and excited to have a chance to work for someone I had paid to see in concert numerous times before. Wide-eyed and ready to jump as high as they wanted me to, I agreed to my first commercial shoot for $4,000. Feeling on top of the world, I showed up to set feeling as if it were the first day of school. With only my camera gear as my assistants, I walked into a scene I'd only ever seen before in movies. A full film crew of about fifty confident professionals—all easily ten to twenty years my senior—greeted me with an air of expectation. I must have looked like a lost puppy, not sure where I was allowed to be, sniffing my way safely to the catered food service tent.

When it came time to actually get to shooting photos, I quickly understood that my position in this assignment was the lowest on the totem pole. Since they were shooting video assets, I was to be neither seen nor heard, which was nearly

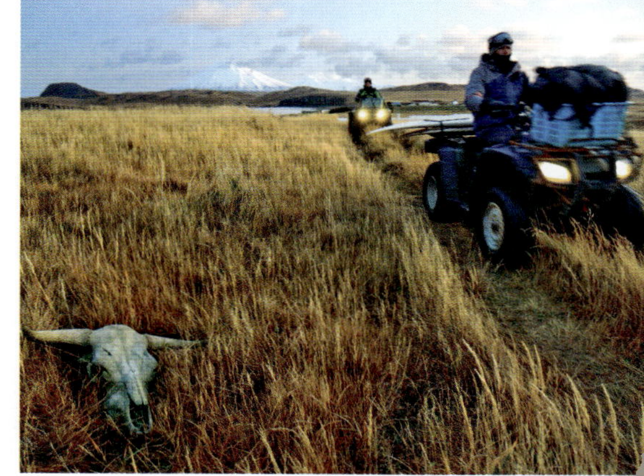

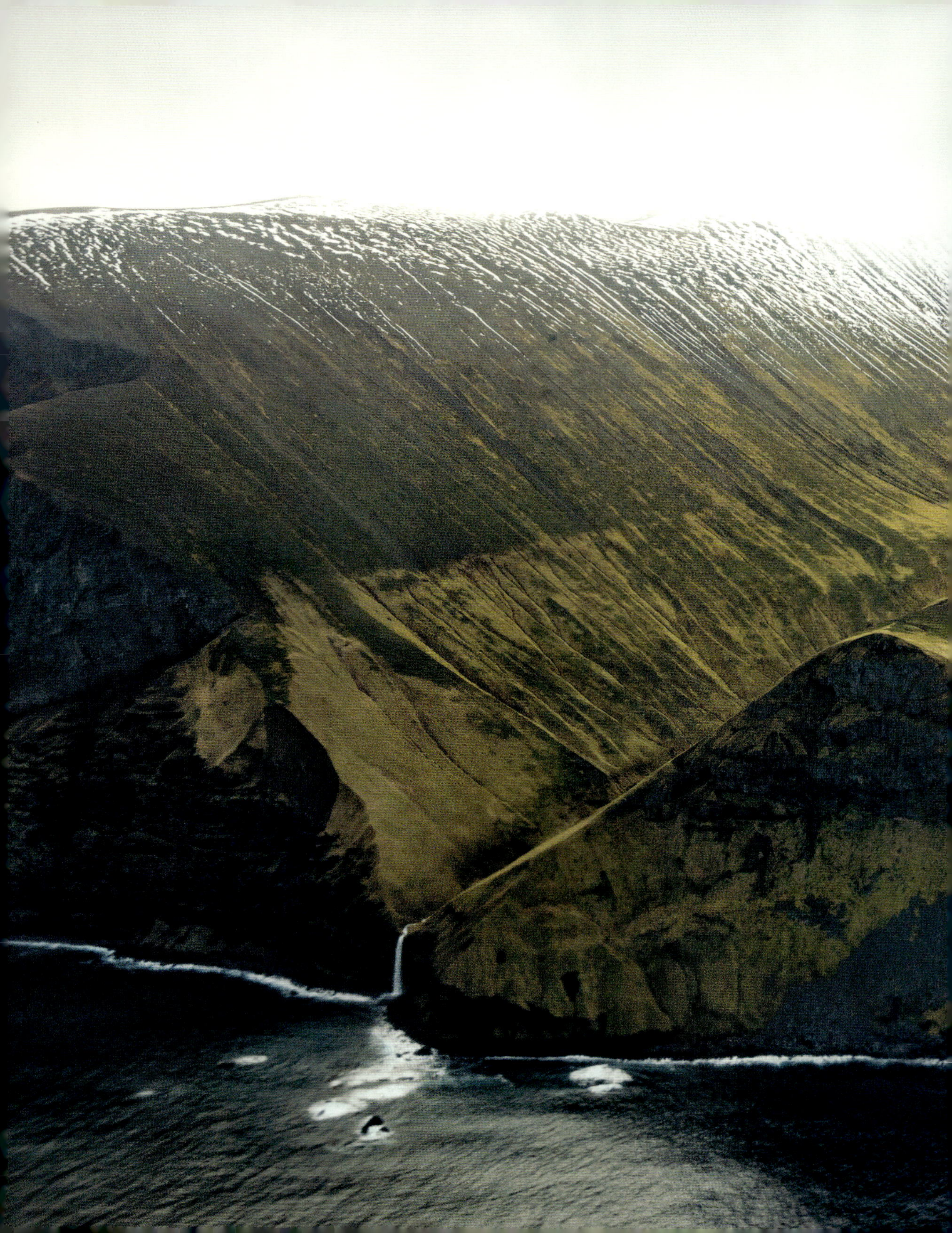

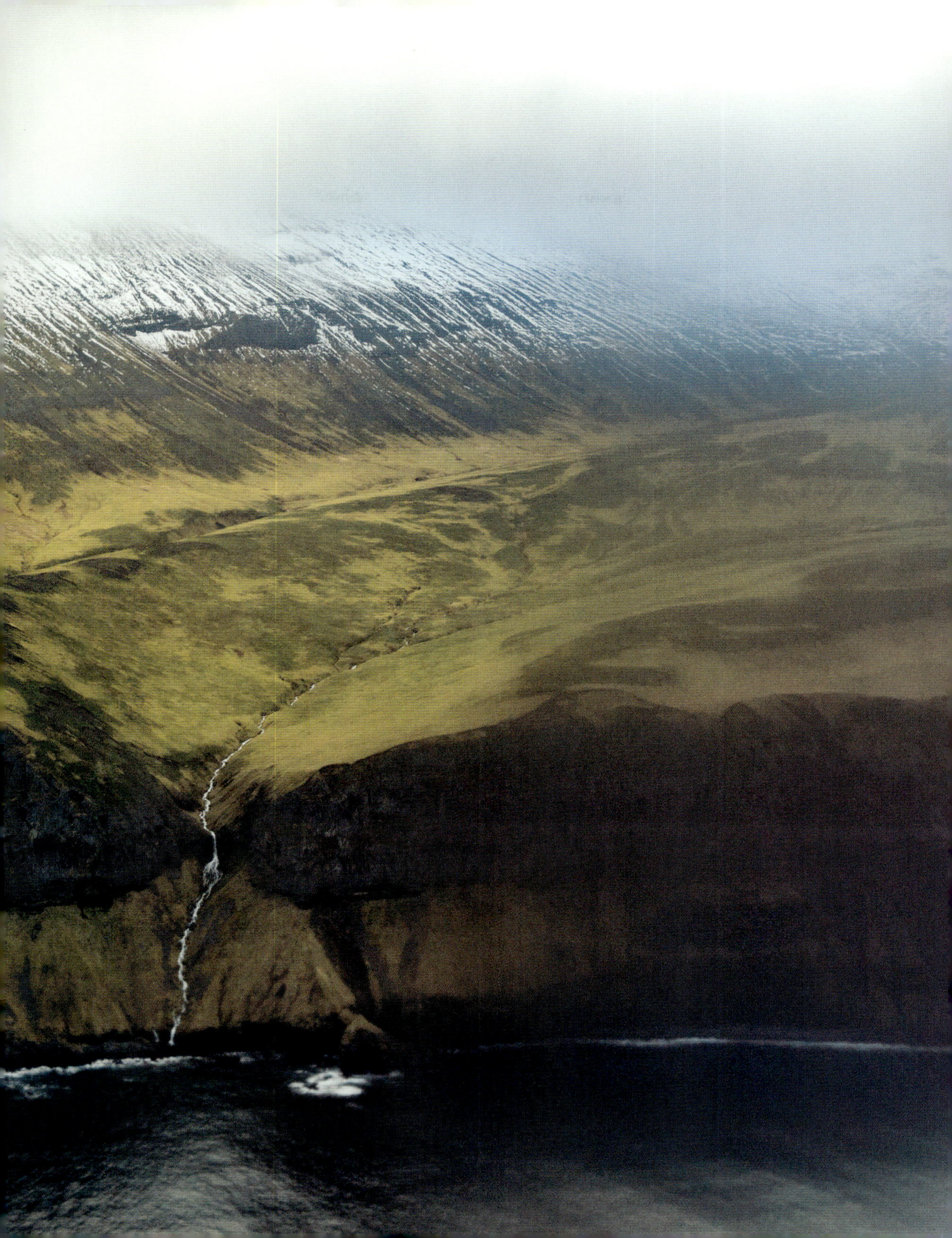

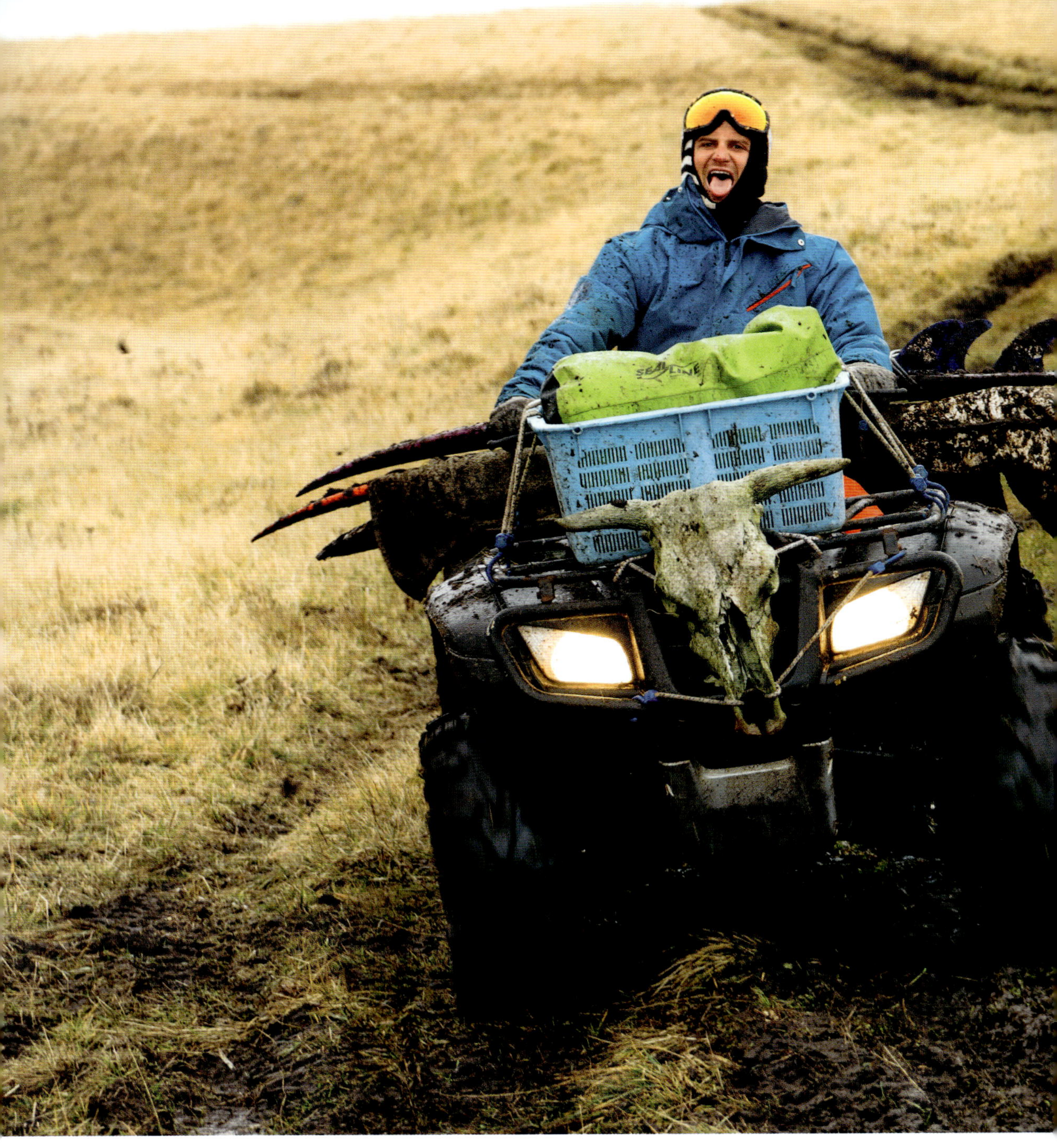

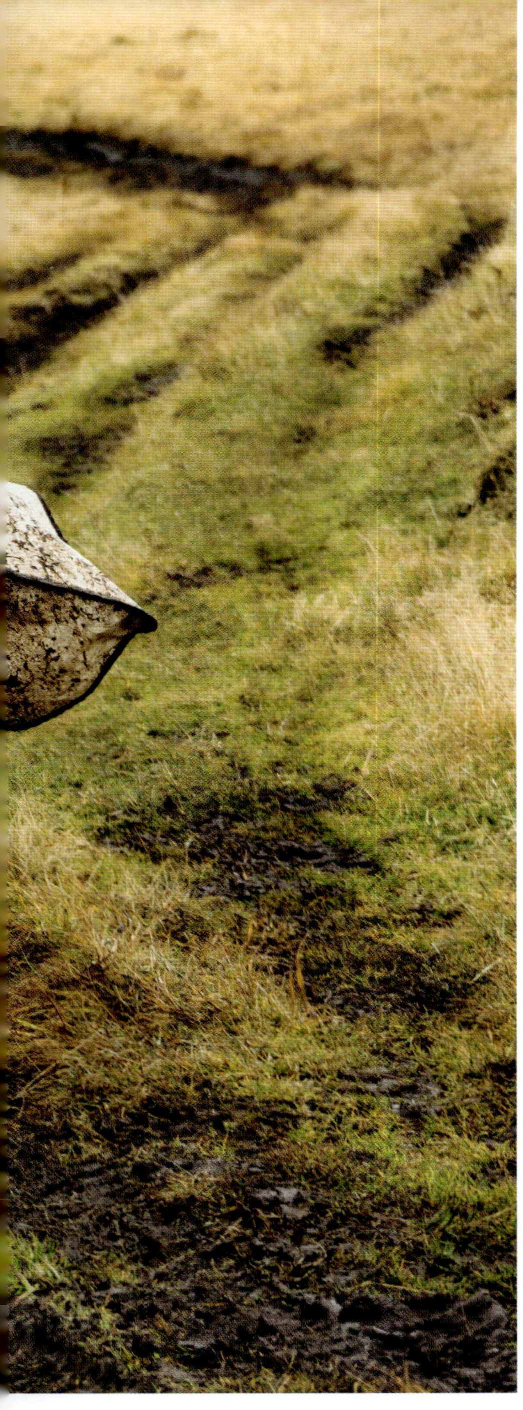

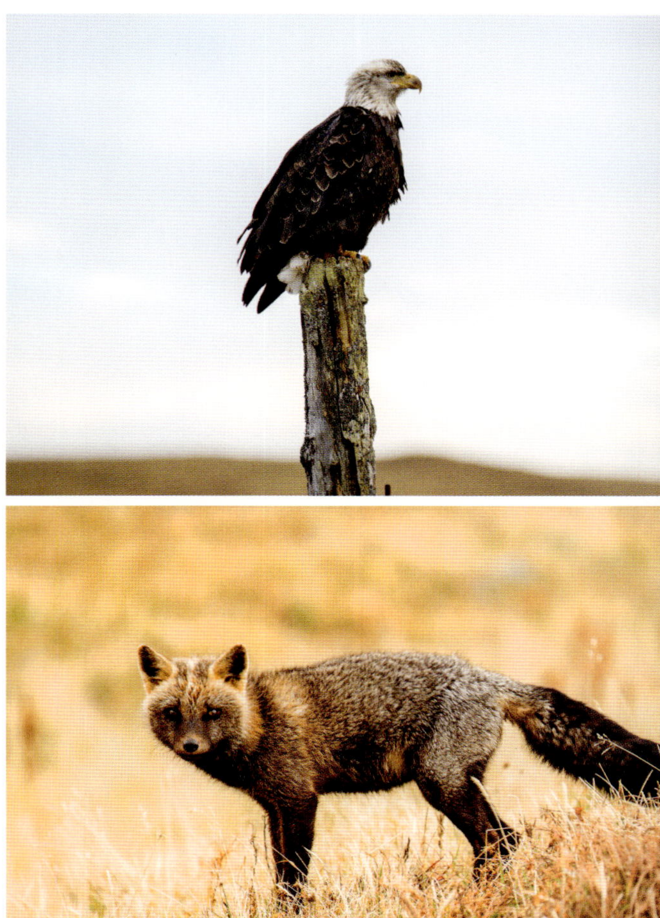

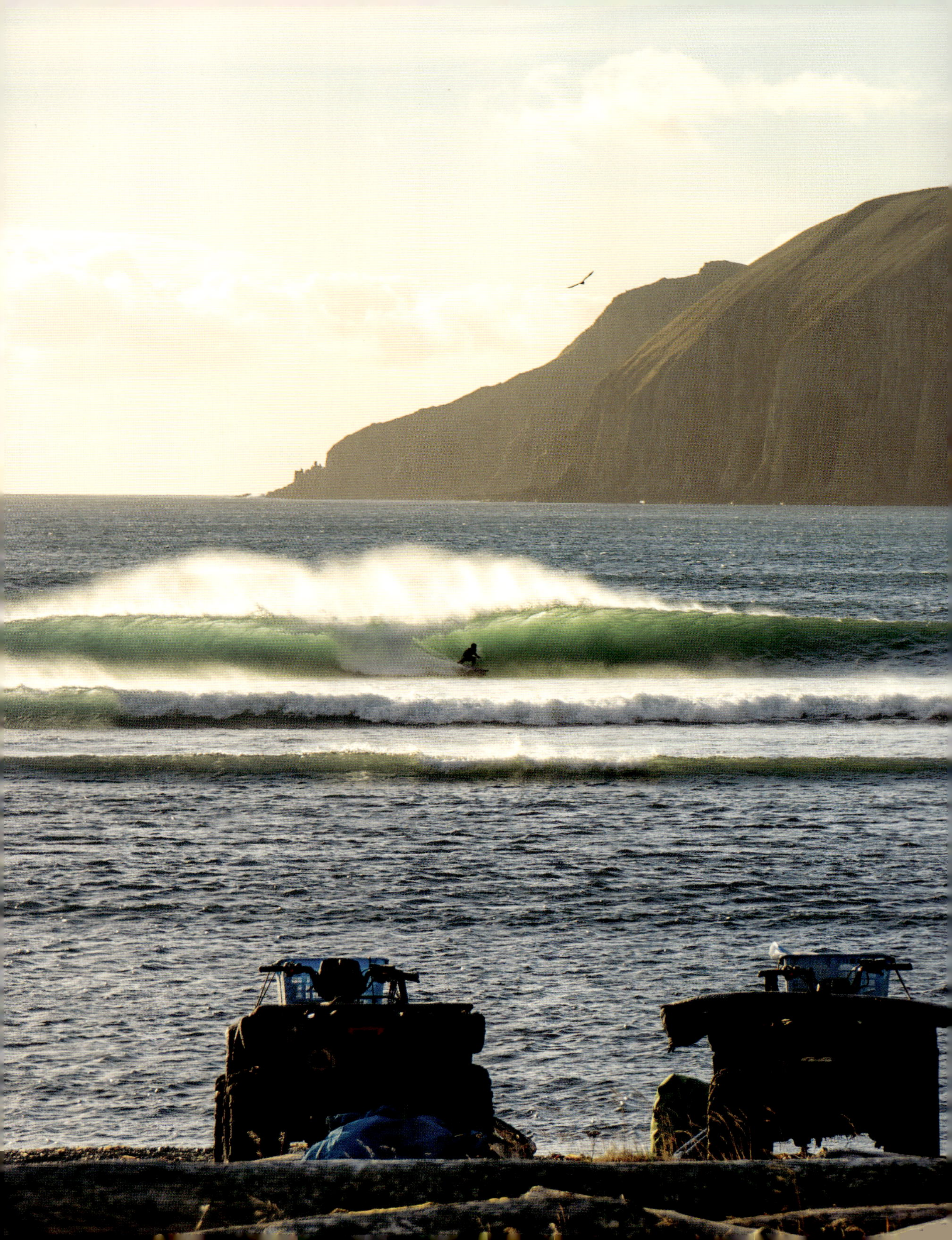

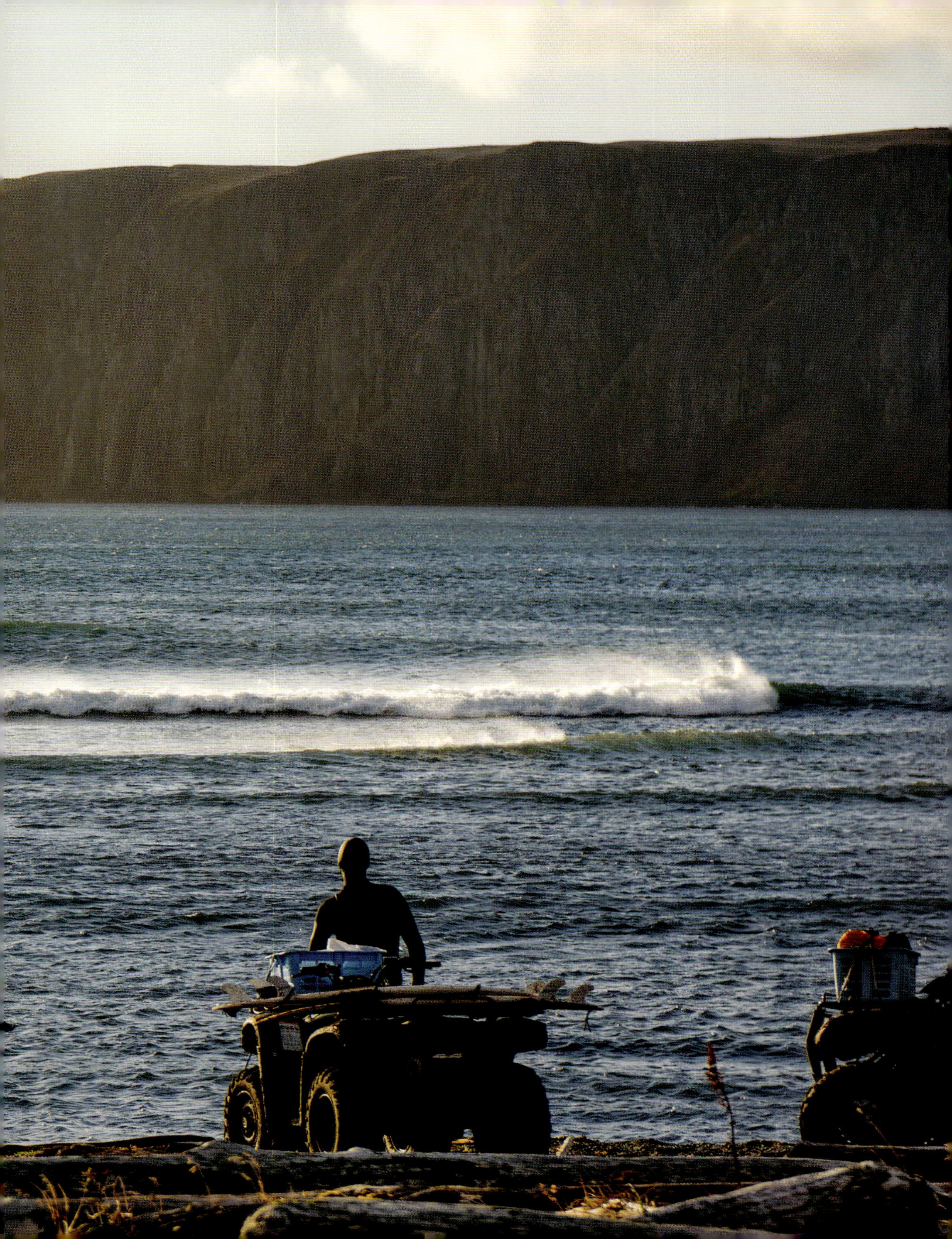

impossible—cameras weren't silent in that day and age. Every click of the shutter sent death glares my way, so I resorted to my surf photography experience, shooting from a distant angle and settled into my spot perched like a sniper in the trees. Negotiating how to fulfill my responsibilities with a giant film crew while also trying not to impose on or inconvenience the talent was intense and overwhelming. It was because of foundational experiences like this that I learned to develop a determined and assertive approach to commercial settings. No one was going to look out for me or the work I needed to get done, so if I wanted to be hired again, I would have to fight for my position.

After my first shoot I spent the entire month editing an endless mountain of photos. The only thing I could compare it to at the time was shooting the biggest wedding ever. During those hours upon hours of sifting through images—a little thrown off by the fact that I left the shoot with a tip of an additional $1,000 from the creative agency that hired me—it began to sink in that I had probably underbid the job. It wasn't until I started asking my peers if tips were normal that I realized how sorry the team must have felt for my ignorance. When I was approached a second time by the same company, I apologetically admitted I would need an increase in pay due to the workload, and to hire an assistant. Then I asked for a whole $2,000 more. They didn't bat an eye and even offered to cover travel expenses.

Years later, my agent asked me if I was interested in selling those images in perpetuity to the brand. I had almost forgotten about these photos. When he told me I could charge anywhere between $80,000 and $100,000, I spit out the water I was sipping. When I reluctantly admitted what I had charged for the initial assignment, my agent explained I easily could have gotten three times that price. In fact he probably could've charged them $60,000 to $70,000 for the initial shoots, in addition to this final buyout. I quickly understood the value of having proper representation, to ensure I wouldn't be undervaluing myself any longer.

Jobs like this led to more meetings with editors and ad executives and gave me a basic education in how to make photography a viable long-term career. Using an agent and assistants helped me relinquish control and simply focus on the job I was being hired for.

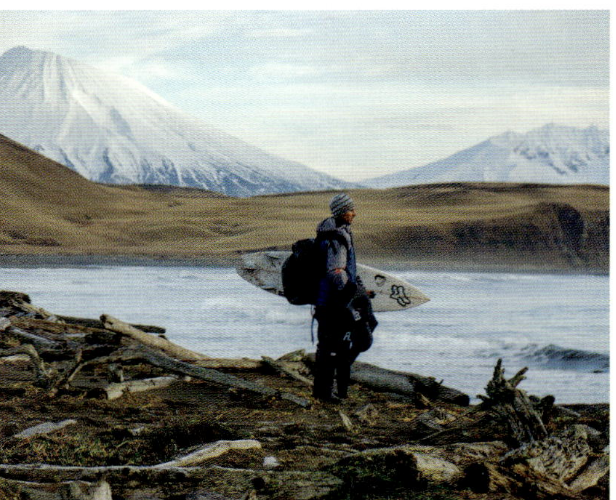

By 2014, I had built an extensive new commercial portfolio made up of dream clients like auto companies such as VW, Toyota, and Land Rover, and tech companies including Apple, Google, and Microsoft.

I learned how to fine-tune this new type of photography mainly through trial and error, and basically through saying yes to everything. Although my tools were the same ones I had used on remote beaches, it still felt like learning a new language when I entered the commercial space. I was insecure about shooting products and brands outside my wheelhouse, but I was determined to gain new experiences. In a few short years, I went from knowing little beyond small slices of the surf, skate, and outdoor industries to having a much wider view of my commercial worth and opportunities, which felt almost endless. Once again, I could focus on the parts of the job I loved most: telling stories.

Despite these cushier commercial gigs, cold, inhospitable surf trips remained my North Star. They defined me. Which is why Ben and I were once again spearheading another Arctic adventure in October 2013, this one to the Aleutian Islands of Alaska.

Once again, I brought in some outside brands and sponsors to create buzz and help offset the costs of the trip and another film, this one coinciding with the debut of Surfer Films. The region is similar to Kamchatka geographically, climatically, seismically, and in its inaccessibility. But whereas swells often fizzle out by the time they reach Kamchatka, the Aleutians are where most swells are born. Some even call it "the cradle of storms."

The Aleutian archipelago is a chain of more than 165 islands between the Bering Sea and the North Pacific that hooks North America to Russia. In 1998 big-wave riders Mark "Doc" Renneker, Peter Mel, and Jay Moriarity explored the area around Unalaska with former *Surfer* magazine editor Steve Hawk and photographer Tom Servais. They were met with sunless skies, raging winds, freezing temps, and impressive albeit temperamental surf, which Tom relayed to Ben over a cold call. Tom was supportive but vague about the details, encouraging us to keep the spirit of exploration alive. By all accounts, the odds were in our favor for swell in October and early November. The challenges, as always, would be weather and access.

Canadian surfer Pete Devries and fellow cold-water veteran Josh Mulcoy were our first picks for the team. Both had surfed in Alaska before; Josh may have even been the first ever to do so, and Pete surfed in the Aleutians six years prior, but only for a day with bumpy ankle-slappers. We added on Southern California–bred Alex Gray as a wild card. We knew Alex had the surfing chops and stamina for the trip, but this would be his first experience surfing cold water, and it would be one of the longer-term expeditions he'd ever participated in.

There are no paved roads, let alone surf cams, on Umnak Island. All our surf checks

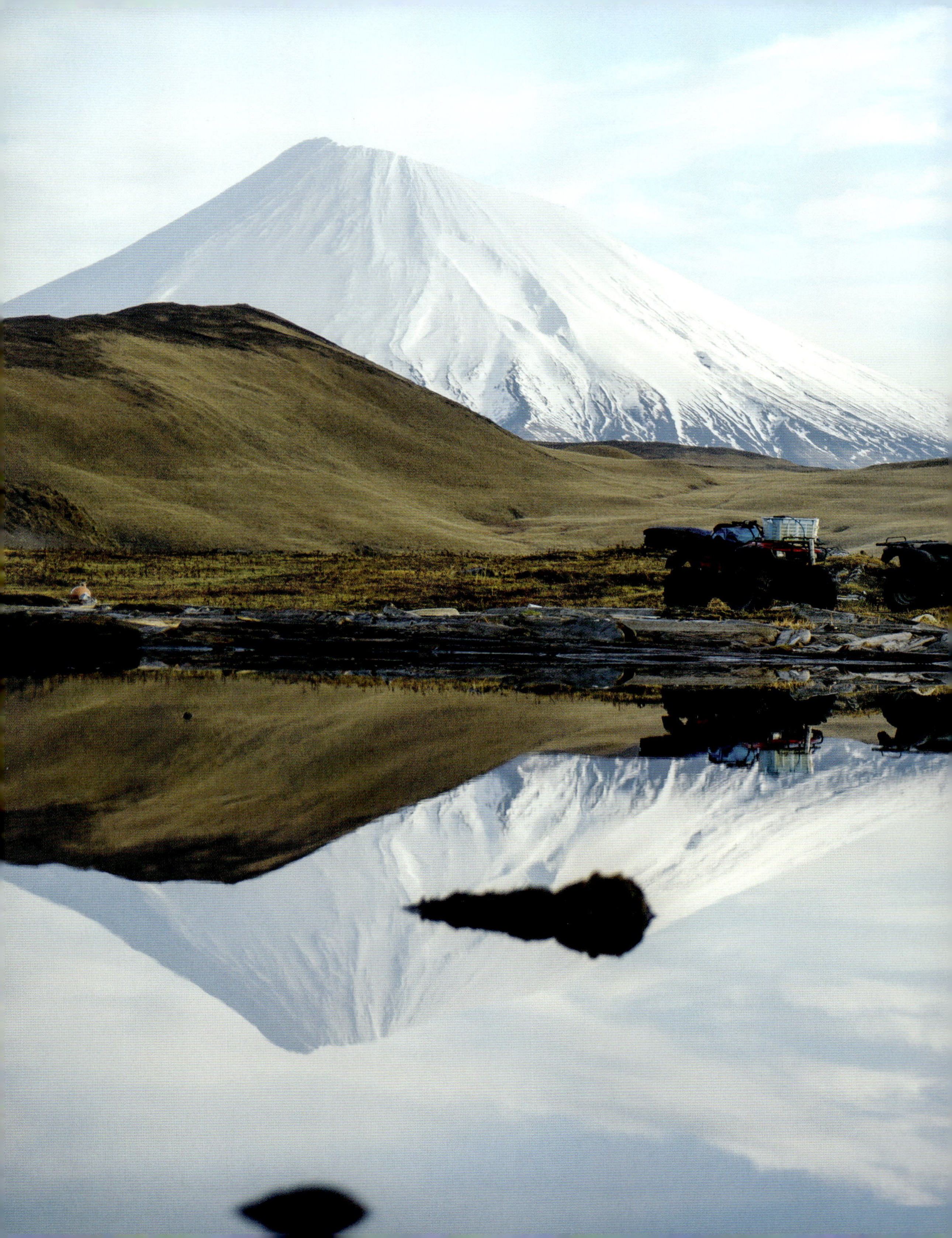

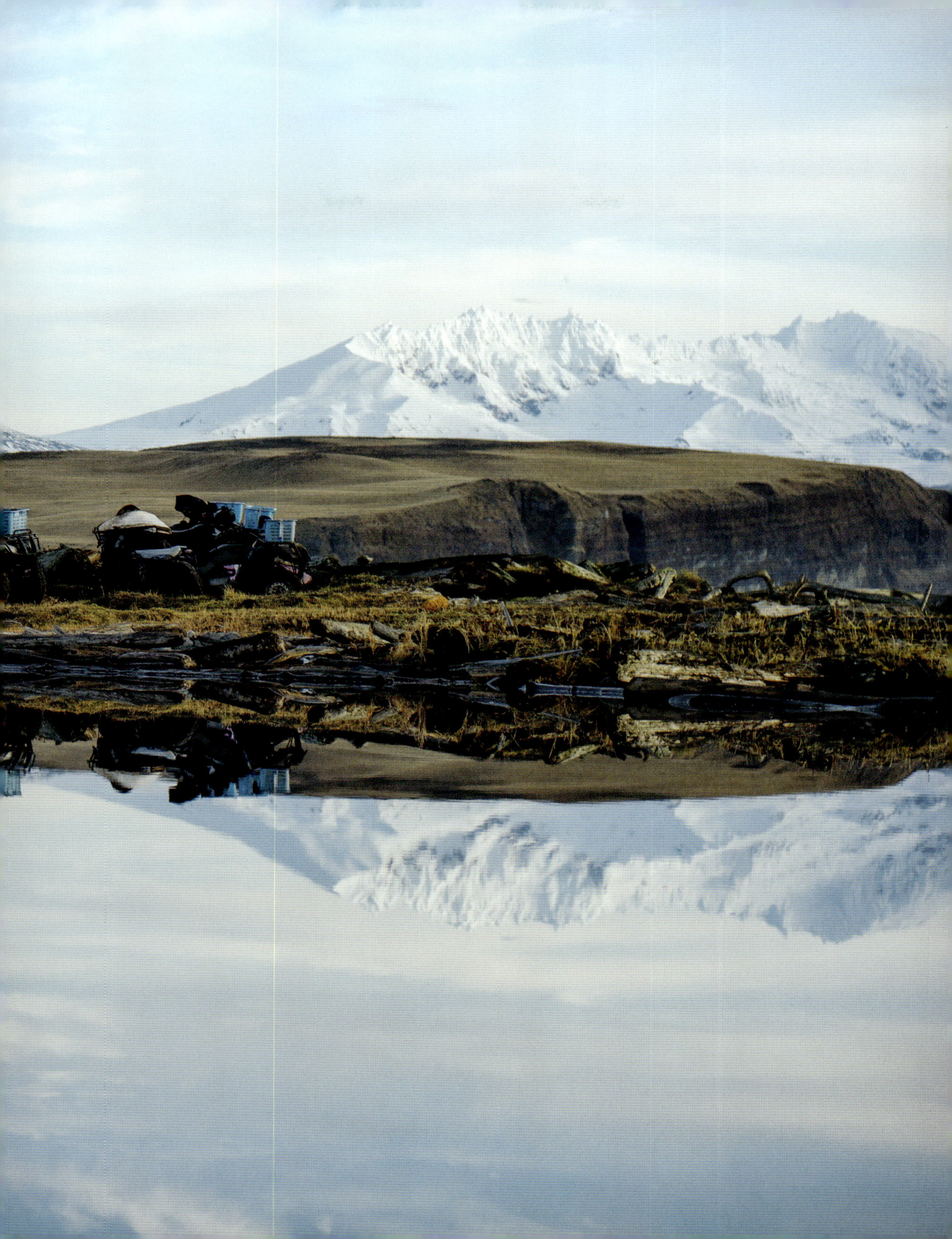

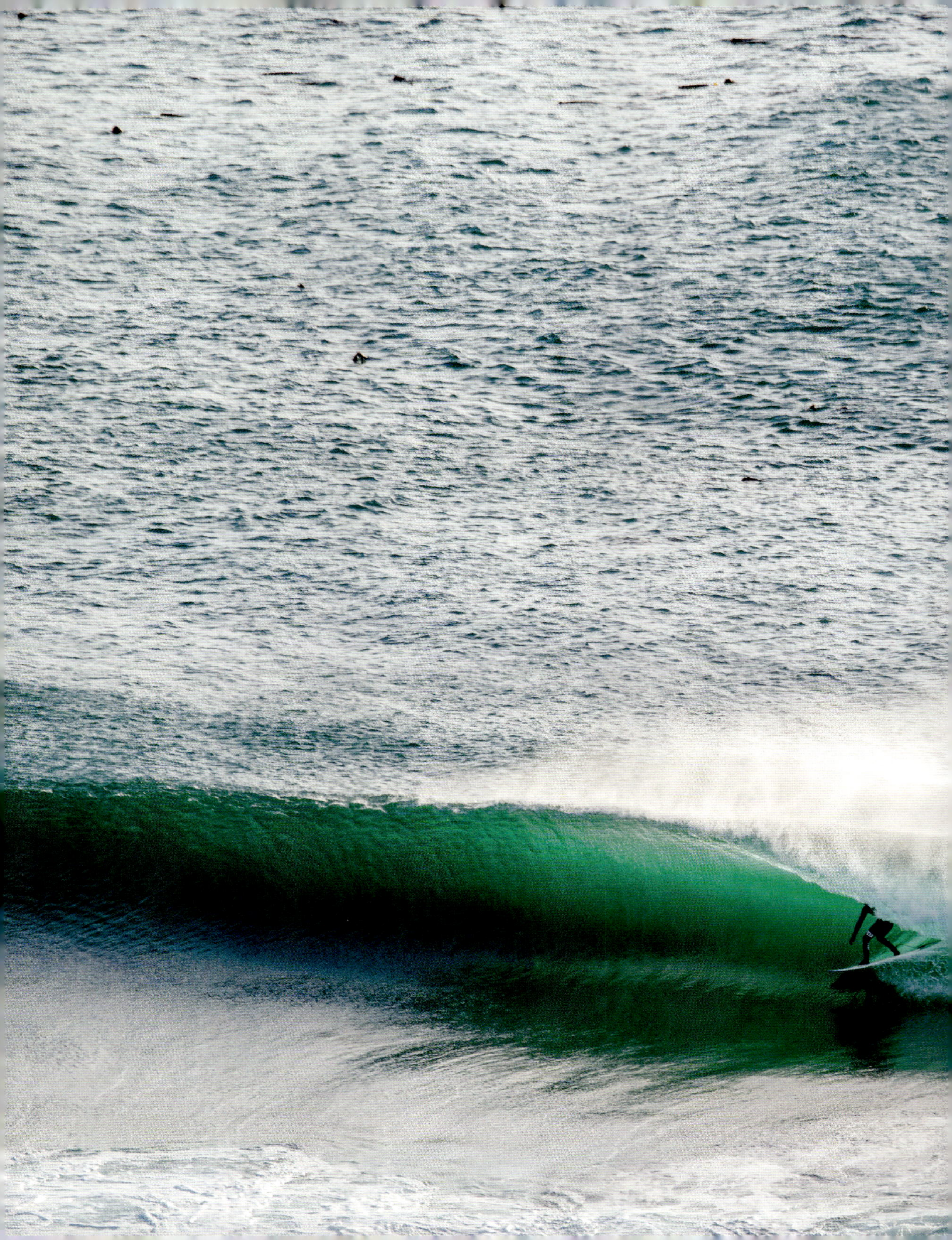

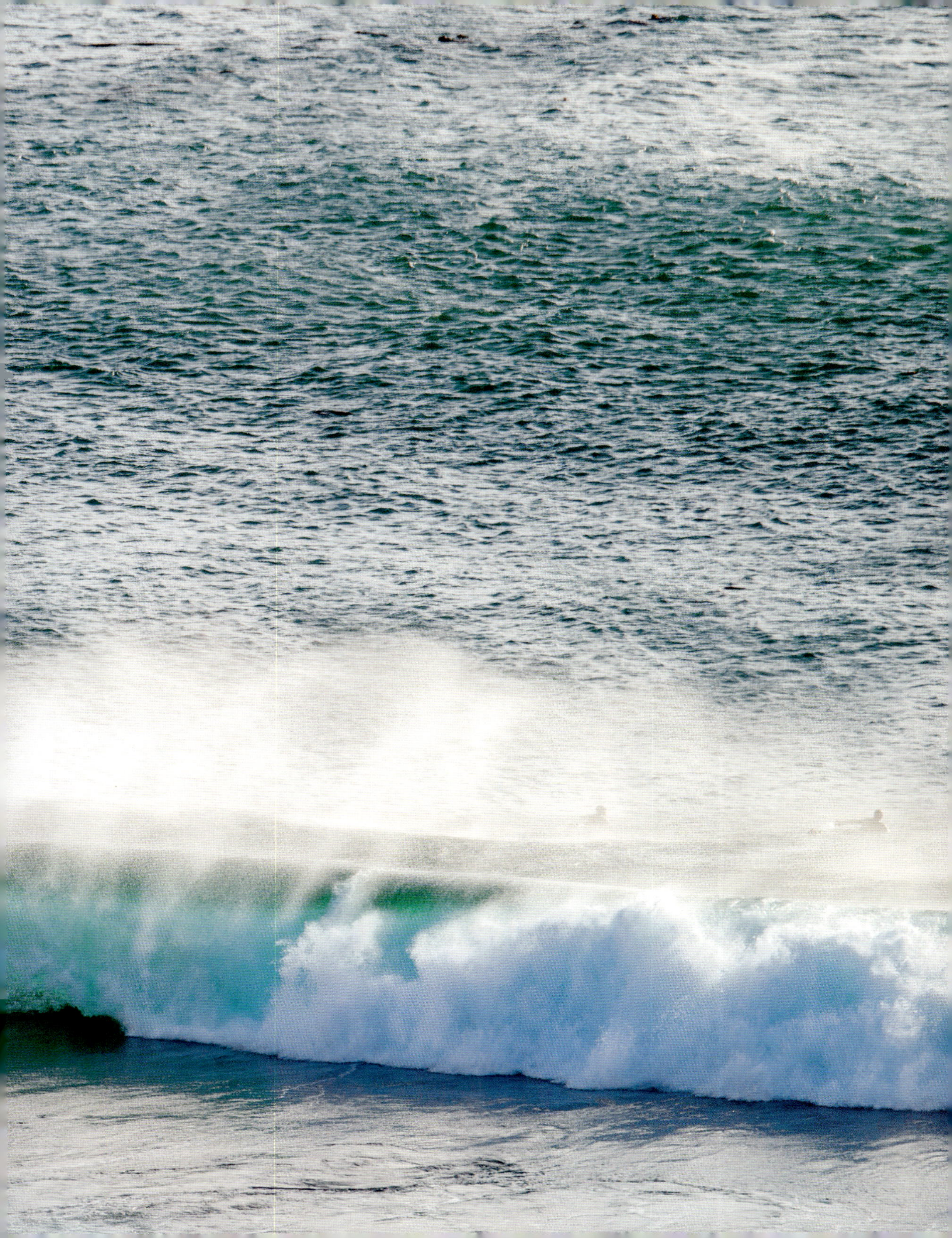

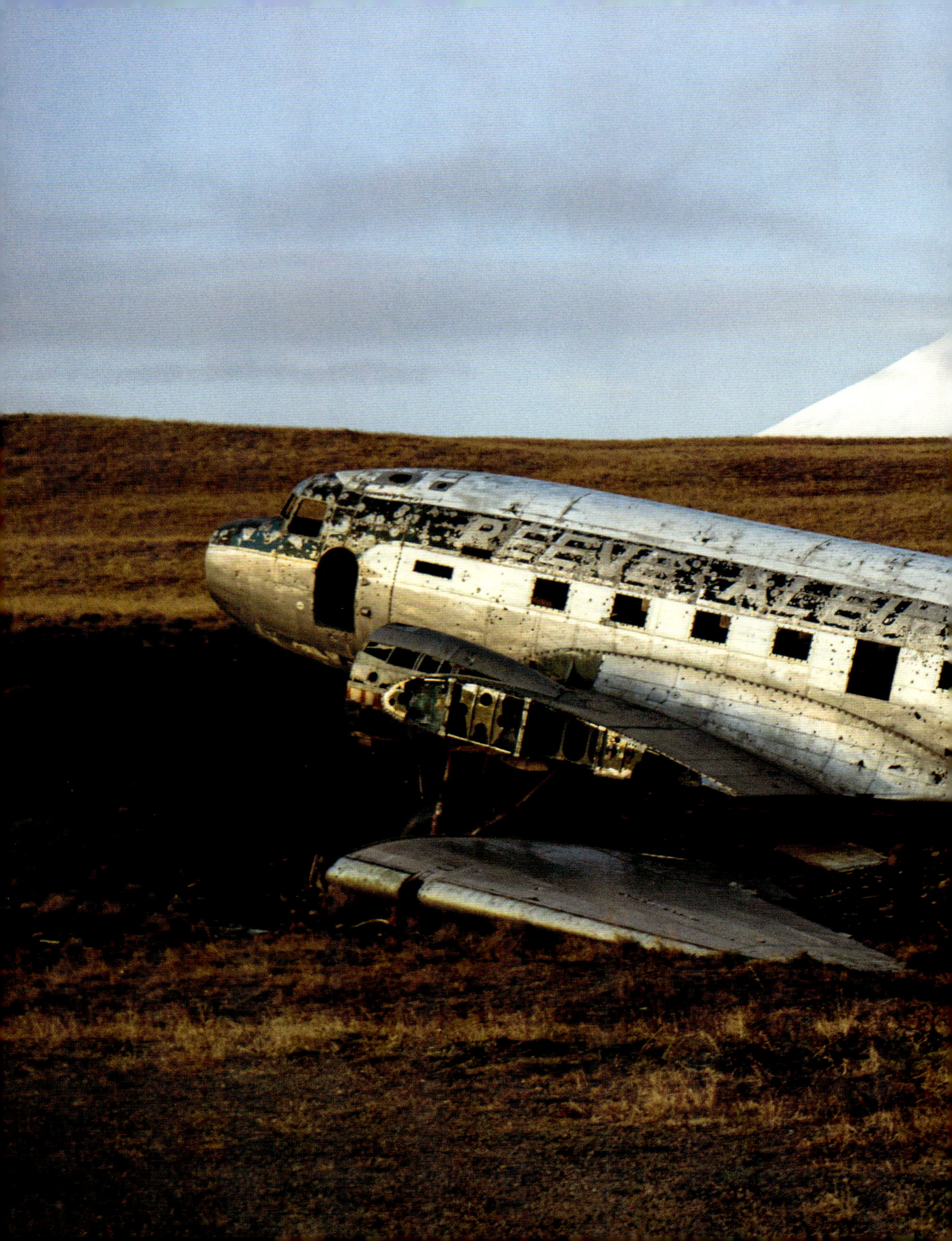

REEVE ALEU

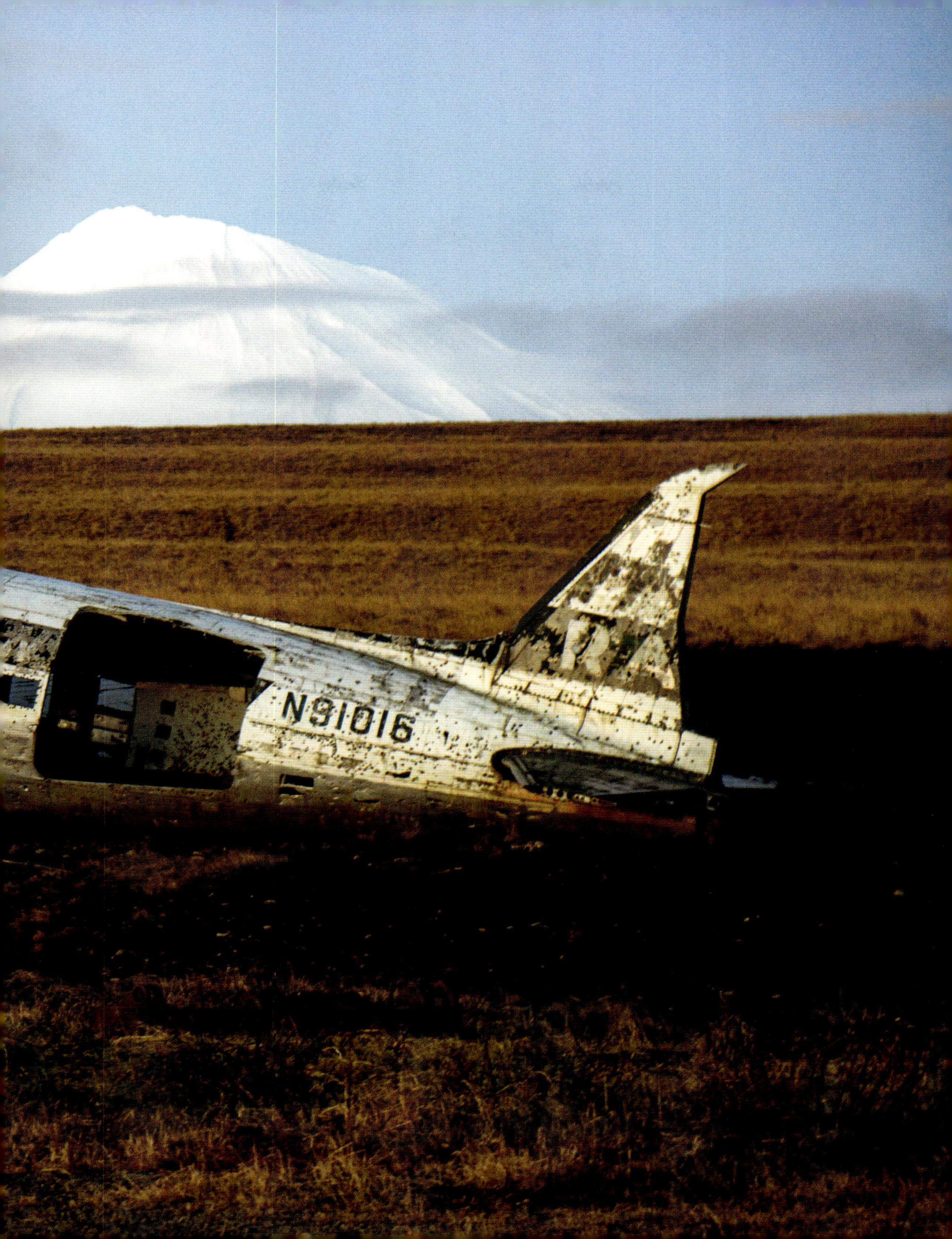

N91016

Is This Photoshopped?

→ **There's never a moment when something just happens.** If you're prepared, it's not luck. Simply charging a camera battery and being organized enough to have the thing with you means you were in some way prepared. That was certainly the case in the Aleutian Islands when a volcano that had been cloaked in haze for days finally came into view. In the predawn light of our only clear day, I could make out its entire shape, from the slightly broken tip to its snow-covered slopes angling in perfect symmetry. The blue sky and soft clouds in the background looked as if they had been brushed on by an Impressionist painter.

Once at the beach, we found a right-hander that was surfable, providing the most incredible foreground for our emerging volcano landscape. Between the reeling wave and the snowcapped peak, it was the burnt-orange tundra in the middle that provided all the separation of layers that I needed. I knew instantly that the magazine cover I had been waiting for was coming together. I just needed to move about twenty feet forward and down for the action shot.

But which camera to use? The question weighed heavy. Over one shoulder, I had a full-frame Sony A99V with a wide-angle lens, ideal for capturing a two-page spread; on the other was my backup Sony NEX-6 set to a 100mm focal range. I needed to get low to the shoreline to create those three layers—ocean, land, volcano—and I didn't expect much time before the clouds rolled back in. I could see a set peak out the back and Josh Mulcoy starting to paddle for it. In a split-second decision, I chose the NEX-6, reasoning that the APS-C crop sensor—which focuses on a smaller area—would bring out greater detail, depth of field, and dynamic range throughout the scene without having to change the settings; most important, the ISO. I knew that to achieve the same image in my full-frame camera would require changing my lens and adjusting my f-stop and ISO to attain a similar depth of field without sacrificing the fast shutter speed needed to capture a surfer in action. The end result would be a photo with a lot more noise. So I picked the APS-C, as if all my previous wars had prepared me for one last battle. I instinctively chose the weapon with the least room for error.

I've often thought about how I made the right decision. But the reality is, I did. It's why people often ask me if the image has been Photoshopped. The scrappy bodyboarder in me also feels some pride. I produced one of my most successful images ever on a consumer-level camera that cost $1,000 when it came out. As someone who once relied on used film and hand-me-down gear, I've always been grateful for high-quality cameras that anyone can afford. It just goes to show that putting yourself in the right place and knowing your gear are more important than having the latest and greatest technology. There may be fewer barriers than you think. —C.B.

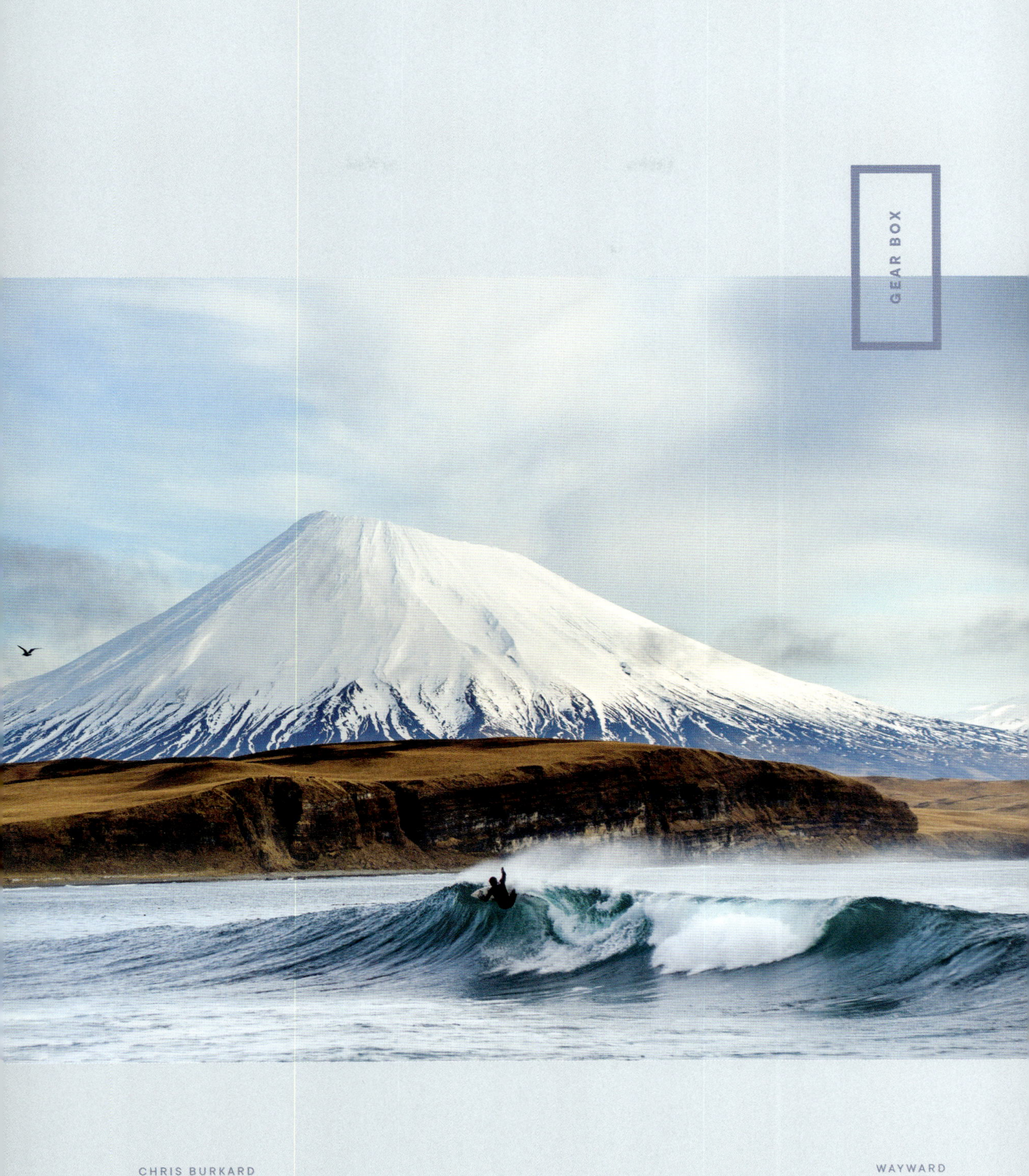

CHRIS BURKARD   WAYWARD

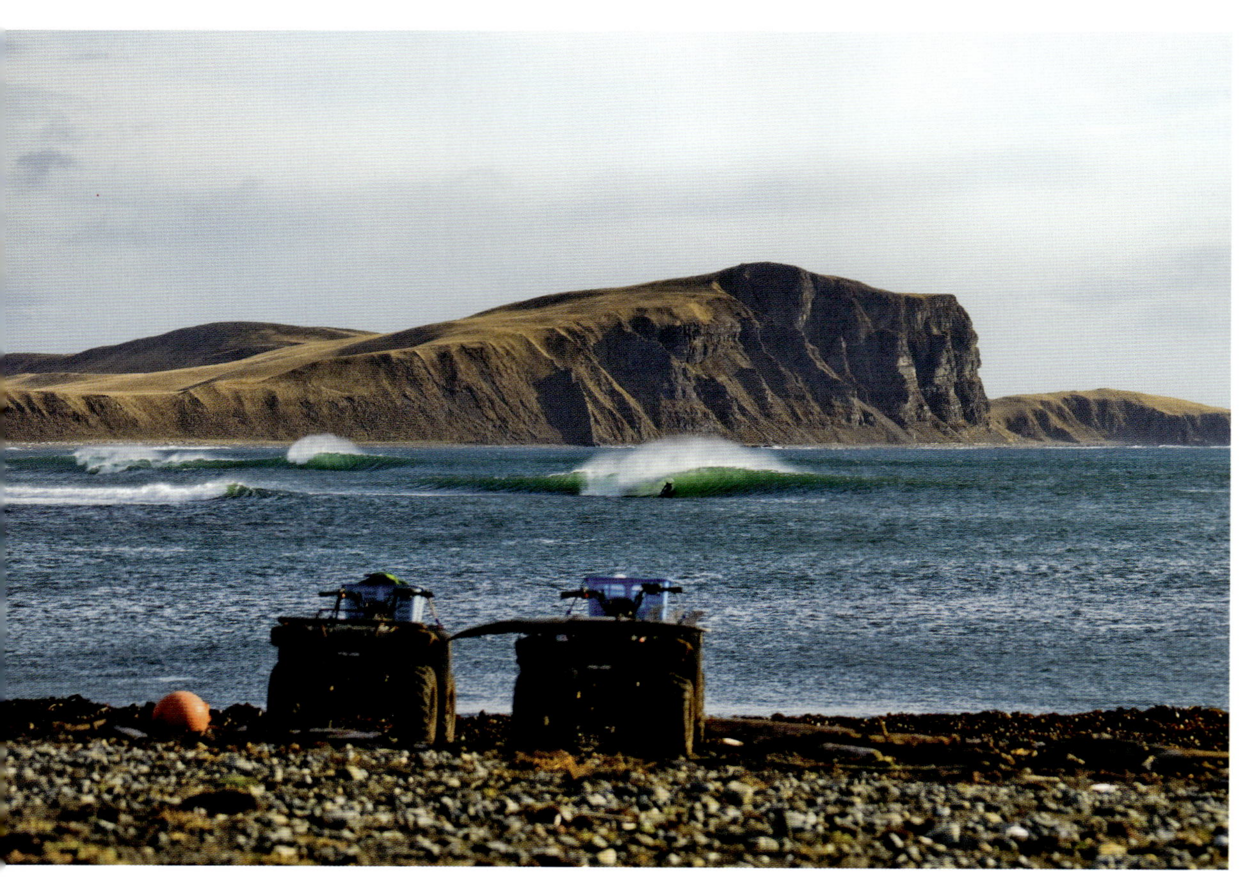

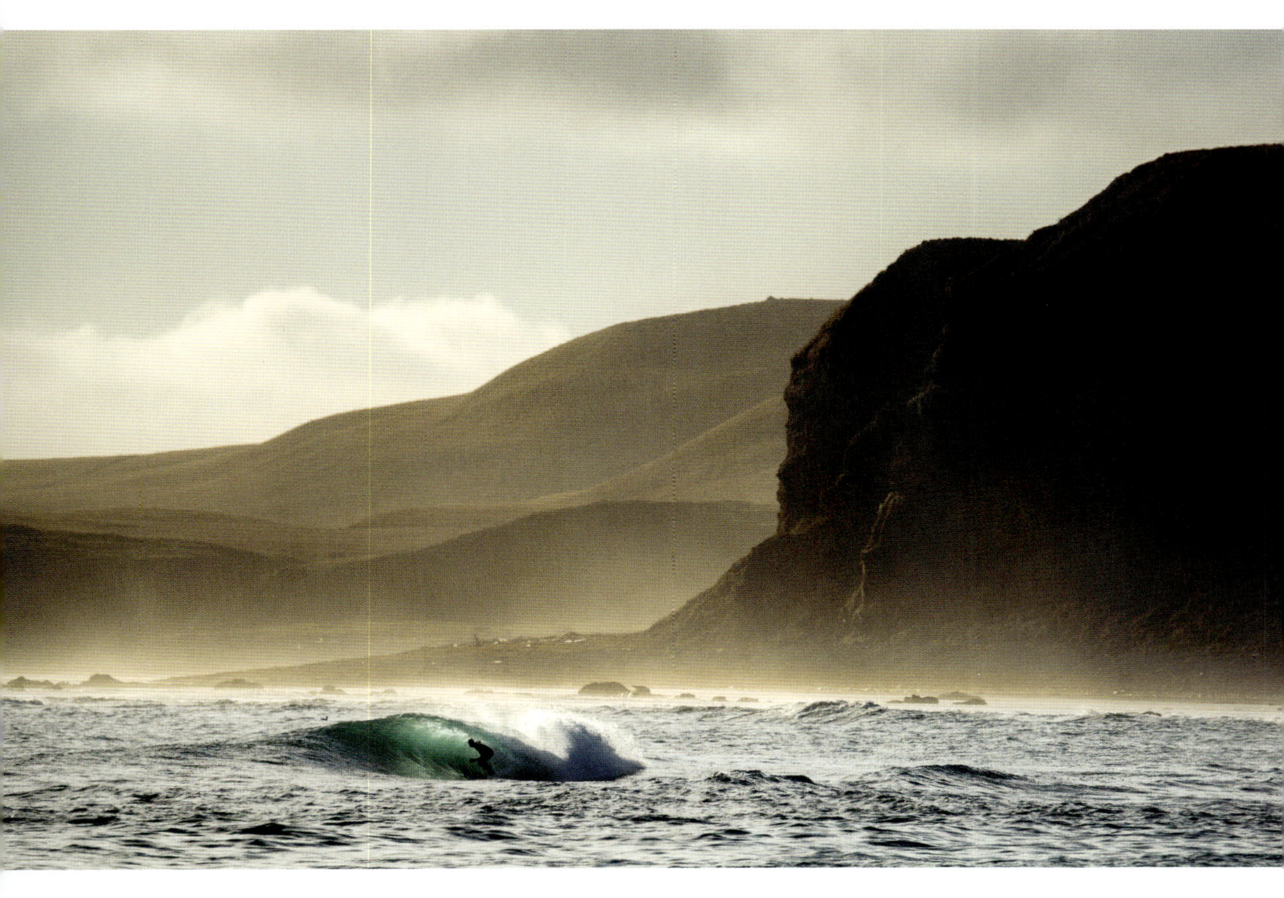

were done in person via ATV, even in the hurricane-force winds. We spent a few freezing hours each day navigating treacherous tundra, laden with frosty grass boulders, mossy driftwood, and sludgy pools. Animal carcasses and reindeer antlers threatened to puncture our tires or send us somersaulting over the handlebars. On day three, heavy clouds rolled in, casting a shadow over the island and unleashing a torrential downpour that created waterfalls out of rain gutters. The Aleutian Low, a collision of Arctic and tropical air, was notorious for creating massive cyclones here. The storm pulsed against the glass window like an anxious heartbeat. We were trapped inside the hunting lodge for two days as a monster cyclone blacked out the sky, pushing the swell report over twenty-five feet, washing the entire weather map purple.

Alex was growing antsy inside the lodge. Every time we got a streak of weak Wi-Fi, he was checking surf conditions in Hawaii, like a vulture stalking food. For Alex, early November always meant Hawaii. The start of winter at Pipeline is the biggest stage a surfer can perform on. I wasn't very concerned about losing him simply because the options to fly off the island were extremely limited and expensive. Little did I know he was secretly plotting his escape through an outgoing mail plane. I had to convince him to stay just a couple more days.

The next morning, not a breath of wind rustled the grass. Behind a fun-looking right-hander, the area's most iconic volcano was on display in high definition. The landscape was coming to life as if in answer to my prayers. All of us, including Alex, were there to see it.

"It's like a unicorn," Josh said before heading out to meet it.

Tendrils of white snow cascaded from the mountain's broken summit, pushing the honey-colored headland into relief, which is exactly what I needed to give the proper perspective. The golden foreground was everything in this moment; without it, the whole photo would just bleed together.

I had a brief thirty-minute weather window to capture all the elements that were playing perfectly off each other. I was frothing with excitement by the time I got my gear in order. Pete was scanning the conditions in the foreground, while Josh paddled back through the impact zone. Alex was pulling a cutback on the inside.

As I took in the 180-degree view in front of me, it was one of the few moments in my life my vision turned into a wide-angle landscape format. I could see the cover and two-page magazine spread clearly, and I knew if I didn't work quickly, it would be gone.

All my senses were firing. I thrive in crunch time and live for the excitement that comes when it feels like the clock is ticking faster. With two camera straps crisscrossing over my shoulders, I alternated between full-frame wide-angle setups and my crop-frame setup. My weapon of choice was my Sony NEX-6 paired with a zoom lens, which offered extra zoom and helped achieve better focus across the image. I knew this scene had cover potential—there's nothing like a snowy volcano to give a surf story a sense of place and adventure. The only other time I felt this type of fleeting sensation was with Peter Mendia in Chile. I just had to make sure the background was as clear as the surfers.

I scrambled over rotting driftwood and slick boulders toward the shoreline to compress the ocean, headland, and volcano all into a single frame, and then I held my trigger finger down in continuous shooting mode as the guys alternated waves. I maximized the capacity of my camera's burst rate of eight frames per second, hoping to capture every micro-movement of the peak action sequences. At one point, when I pressed the shutter button, I noticed Josh fanning across the lip of a wave right as a seagull flew into view.

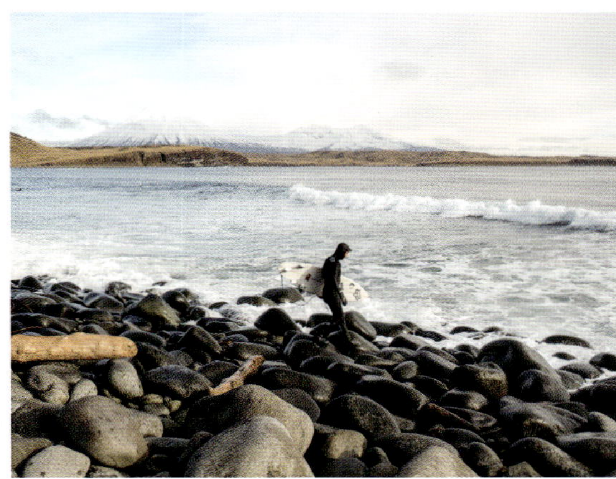

As we made our way back to the cabin, we all sensed the magic in the air. I immediately stashed one of my memory cards away in my storage wallet. There was plenty of room still left on it, but I felt so protective of what I had just captured that I stowed it away for safekeeping. I avoided the typical routine of everyone huddling over my shoulder to review the playback on my small camera screen, too nervous to relive the moment on anything less than my high-definition laptop.

As soon as we walked in the cabin door, I exiled myself to my room to upload the card. I couldn't wait to find out if the photos lived up to the actual experience I had just witnessed. As soon as the shots started materializing on my computer, I felt relief and gratitude. What I saw in front of me was Josh Mulcoy, my longtime surfing mentor—who had helped pave my way in this industry and always treated me with more patience than I deserved—immortalized in one of my photos. Josh was perfectly centered in the best surfing landscape I had ever observed. That session made my trip, and later my career: It would end up to be my favorite cover of *Surfer* and my most recognizable image to date.

But in that moment in the cabin, I simply hoped this image could maybe serve as a humble thank-you to Josh for all the years of traveling and sharing these wild rides together. Seeing the smile on his face when I showed him the photo was all the approval I ever needed.

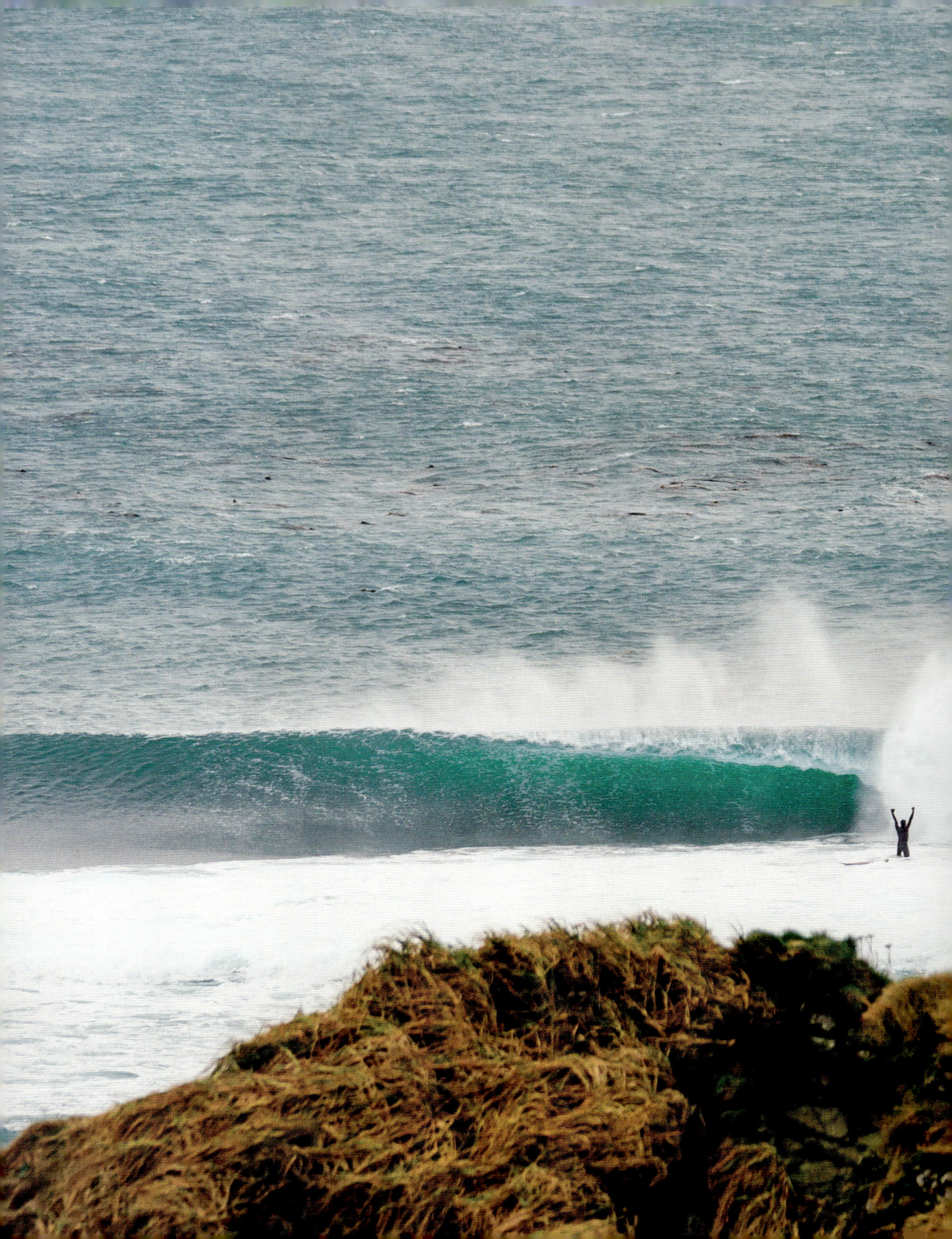

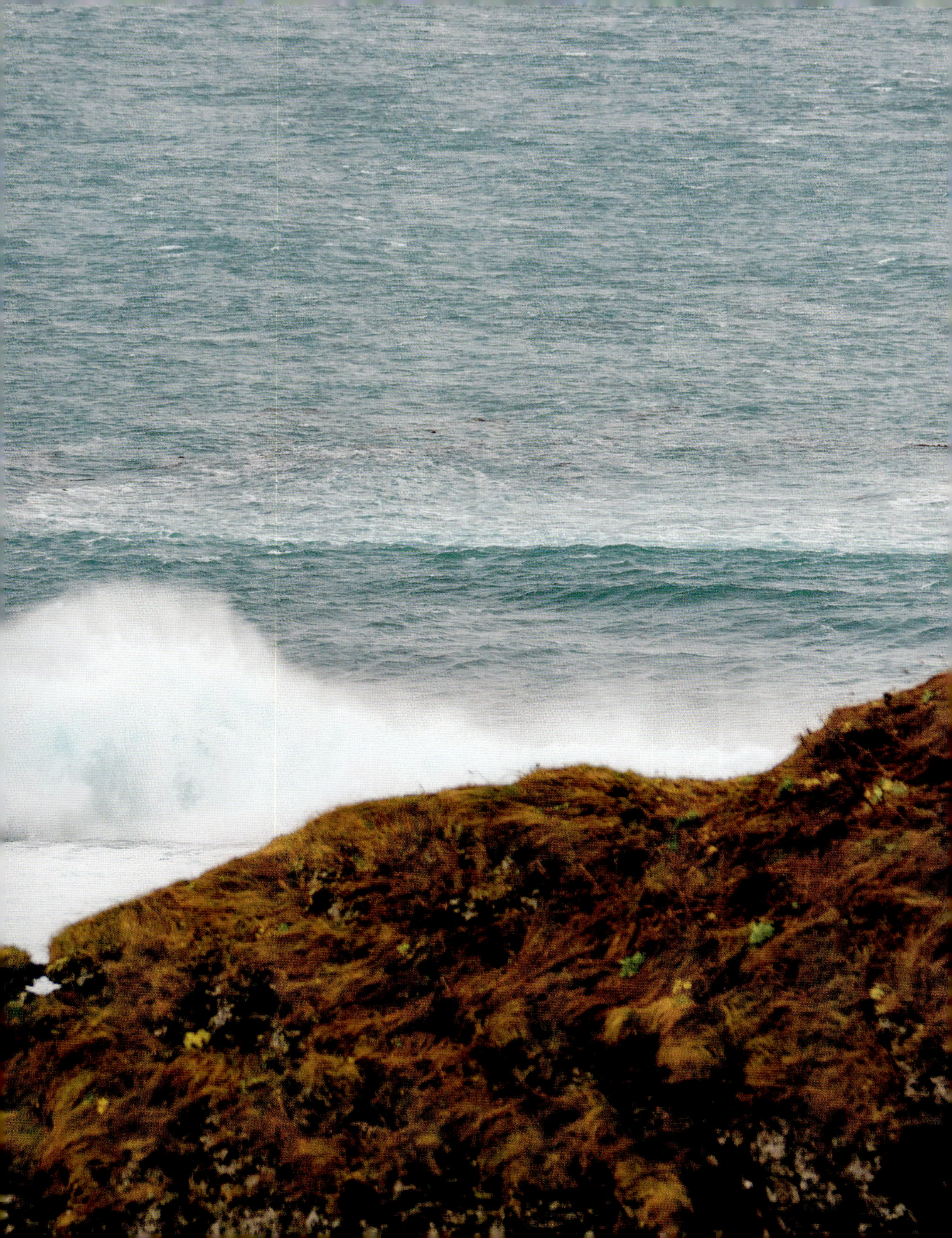

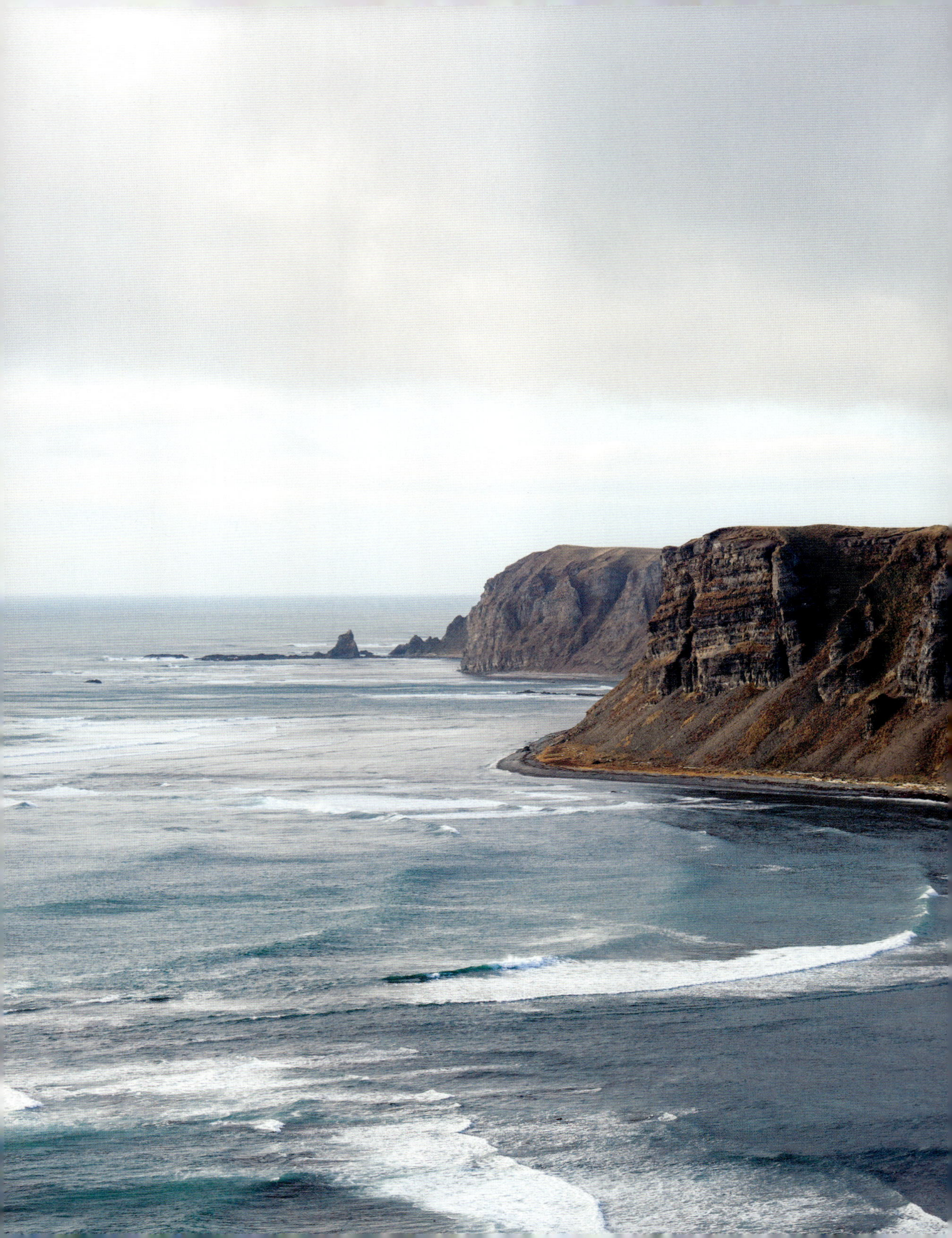

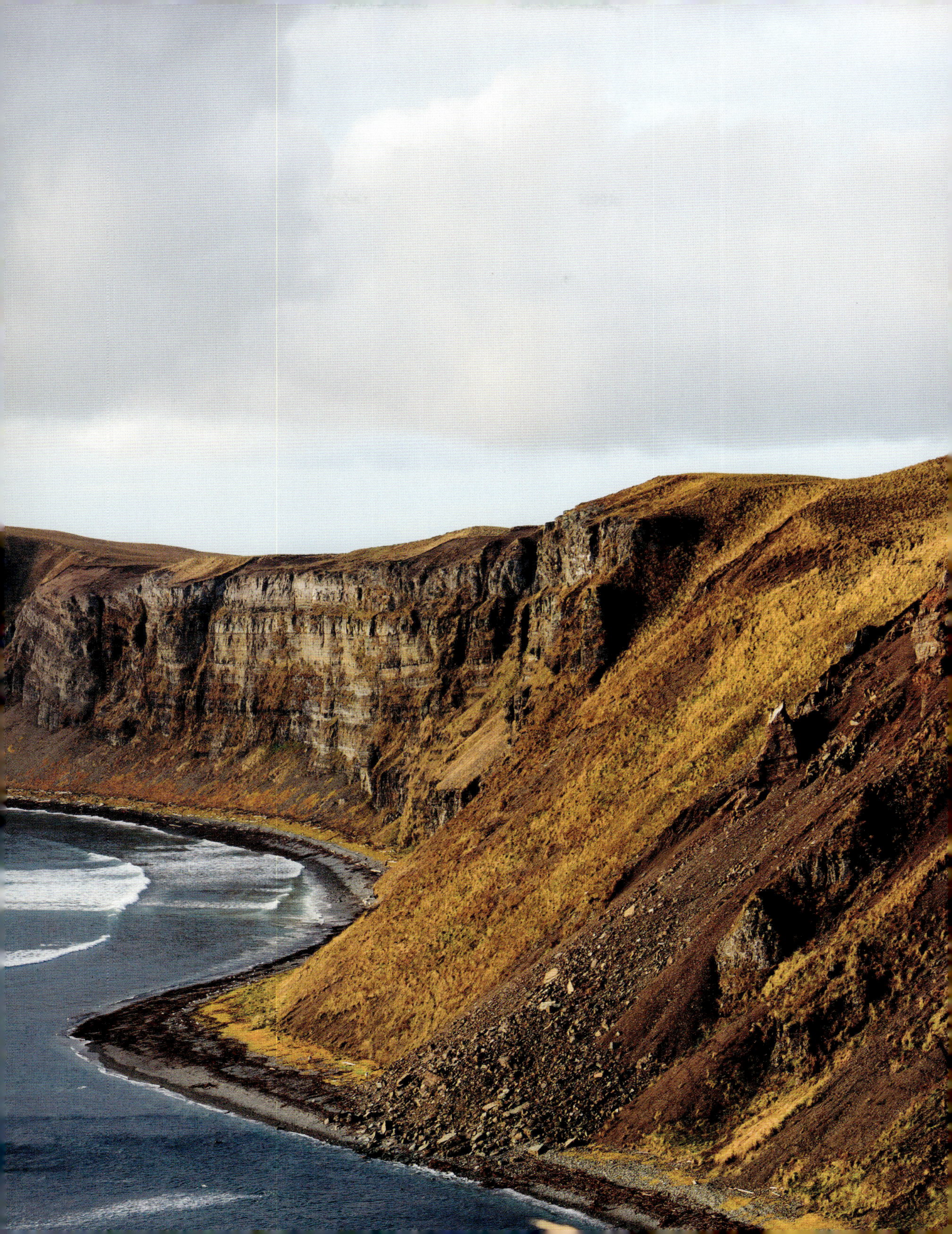

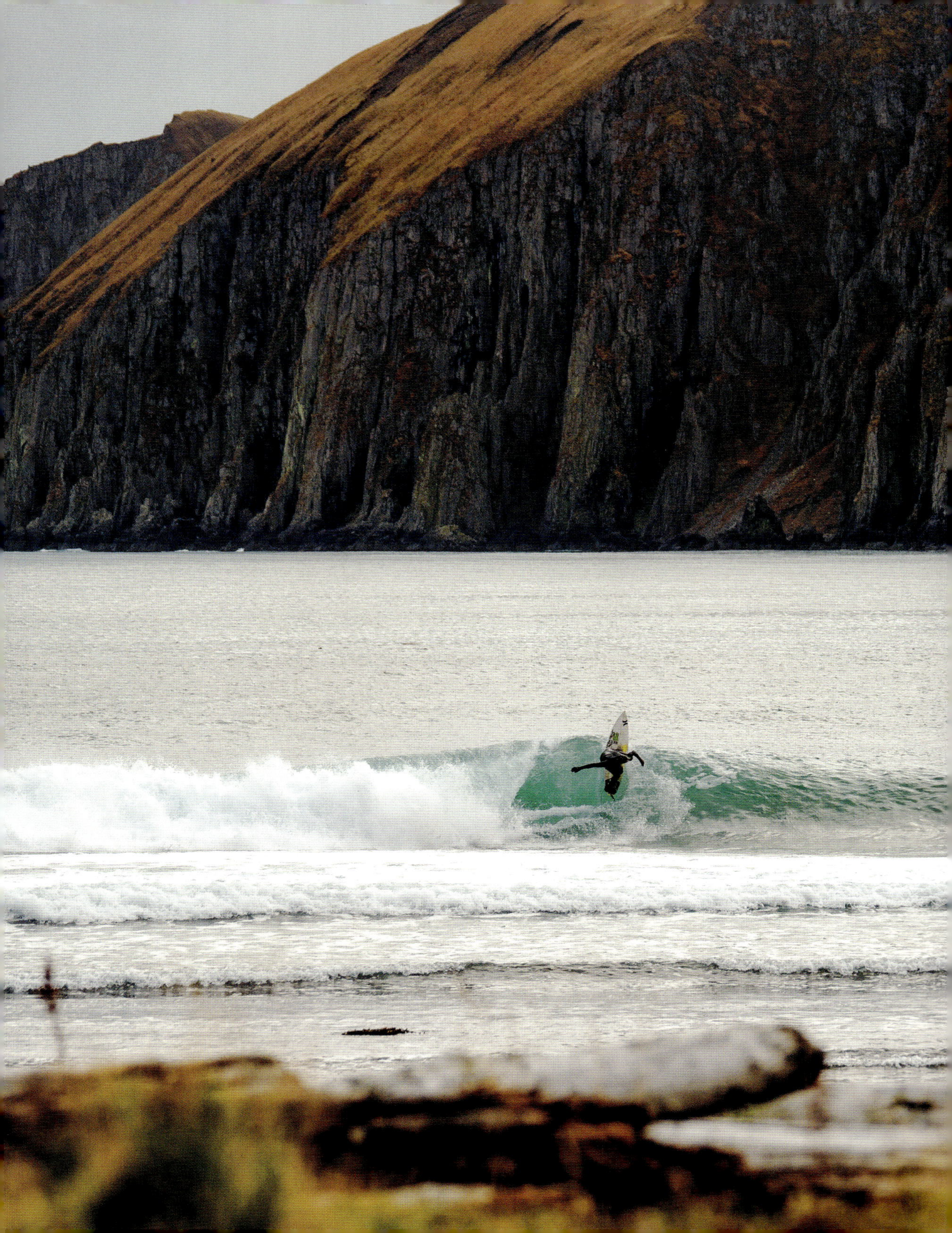

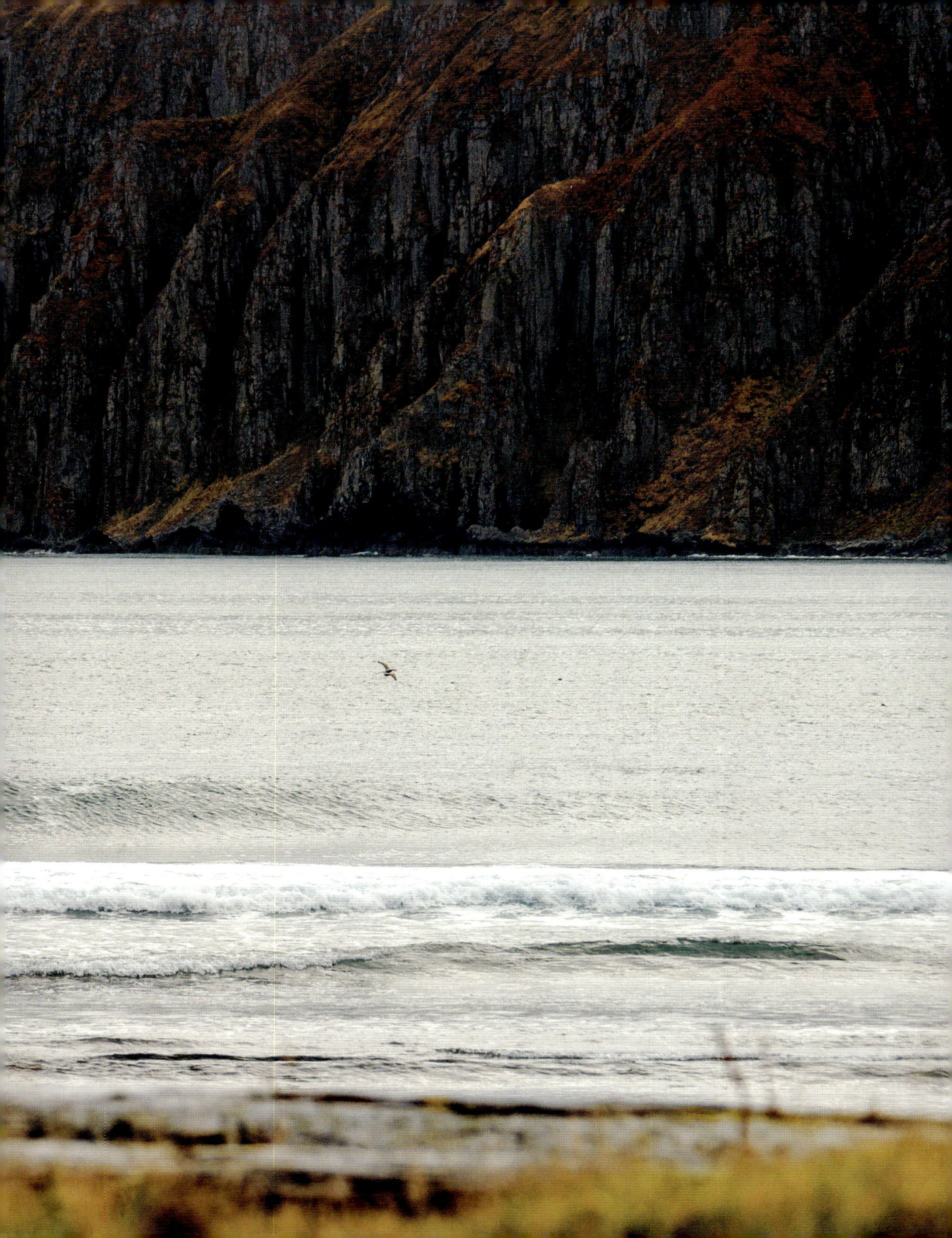

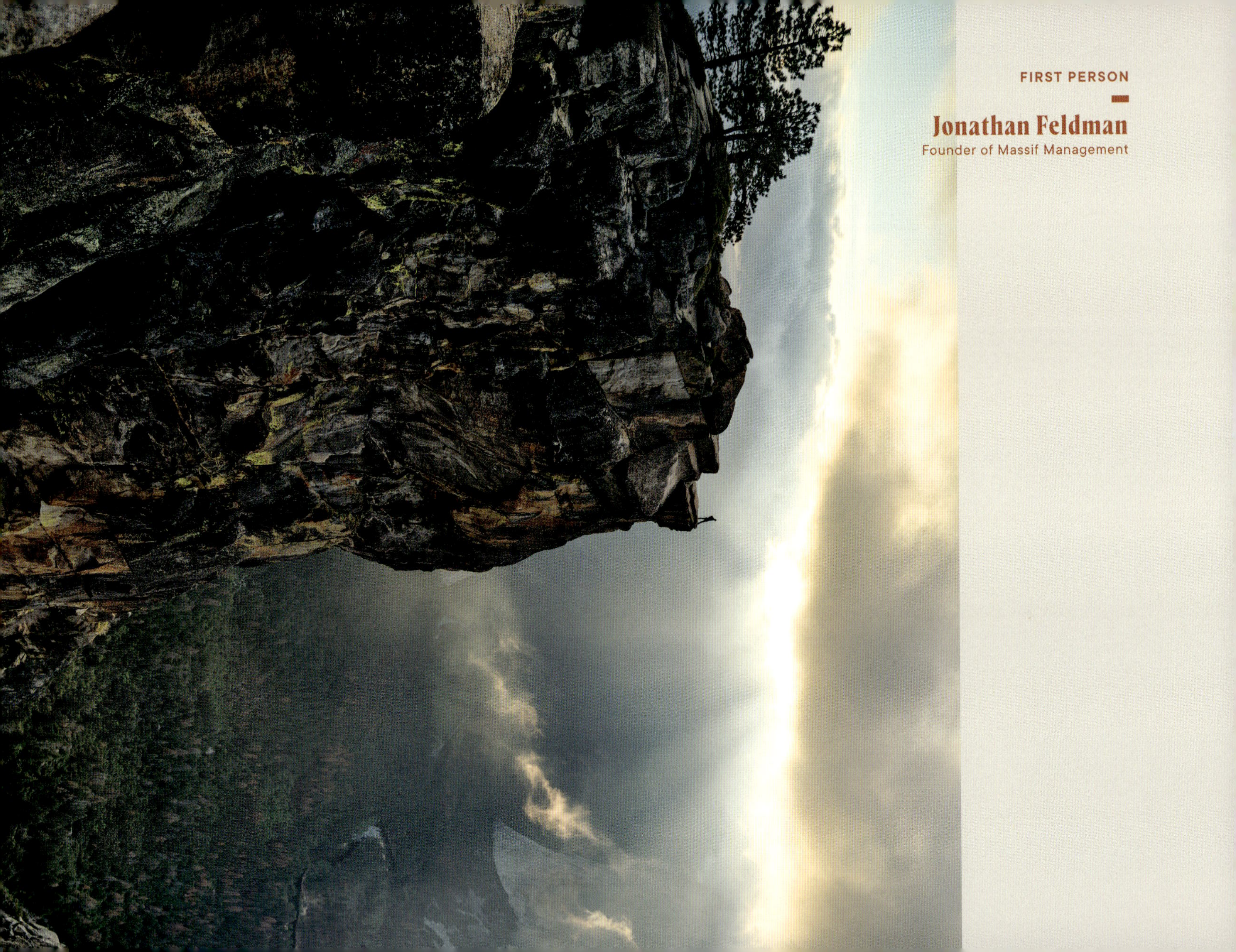
FIRST PERSON

Jonathan Feldman
Founder of Massif Management

The Aesthetic Sublime

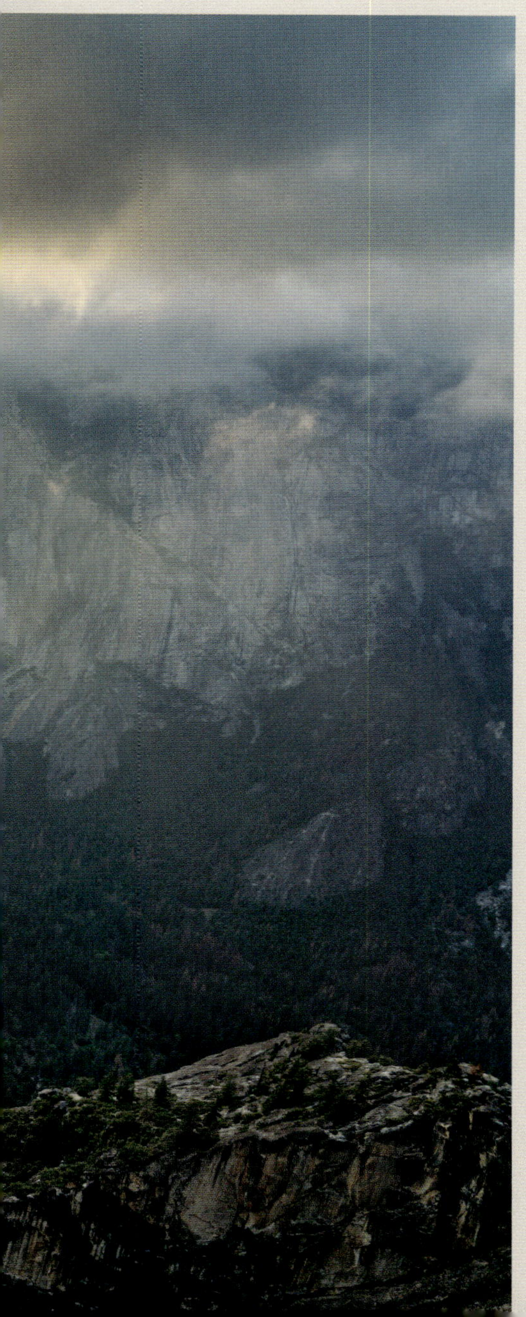

→ **I don't think it's too much of an overstatement to** say that Chris invented a new pictorial language—or at least that he's been in the forefront of developing a new kind of landscape photography. No such language is ever purely original, but I think what he found a way to do was lead the viewer into the landscape through a surrogate of some kind, typically another human figure. By identifying with the figure in the frame—the figure in the landscape—the viewer is compelled to imagine herself present in the scene.

And typically, for Chris, that scene, or that landscape, is sublime—in the specific way that that term was developed in eighteenth-century aesthetic theory by writers like Edmund Burke, Immanuel Kant, and G. W. F. Hegel. Put simply, and acknowledging important differences in the way these thinkers approached the subject, the viewer's encounter with a representation of nature (or the actual experience of being in a landscape, especially the mountains) nearly overwhelms one's sensory faculties. It has something to do with scale and it carries a hint of violence, such that nature produces terrifying psychological effects. But only up to a certain point. The sublime is felt in the presence of an imminent threat that never actually realizes itself.

I think Chris may be working in this tradition of the aesthetic sublime, especially as developed by nineteenth-century landscape painters. Chris's images of a figure standing on the diving board–like outcrop of Glacier Point in Yosemite are one example. The valley is beyond, underneath, and on all sides, so there's a real sense of what climbers call "exposure." This is the sublime. And some of Chris's aerial photography of Icelandic glaciers also approaches the sublime. These images offer a relationship between the viewer and the scene through a surrogate, such as the wing of a plane or another plane flying beneath his own. There's a way in which the viewer is interpolated within the frame. It is a tradition that is both hundreds of years old and entirely new, especially as Chris deploys it within social media.

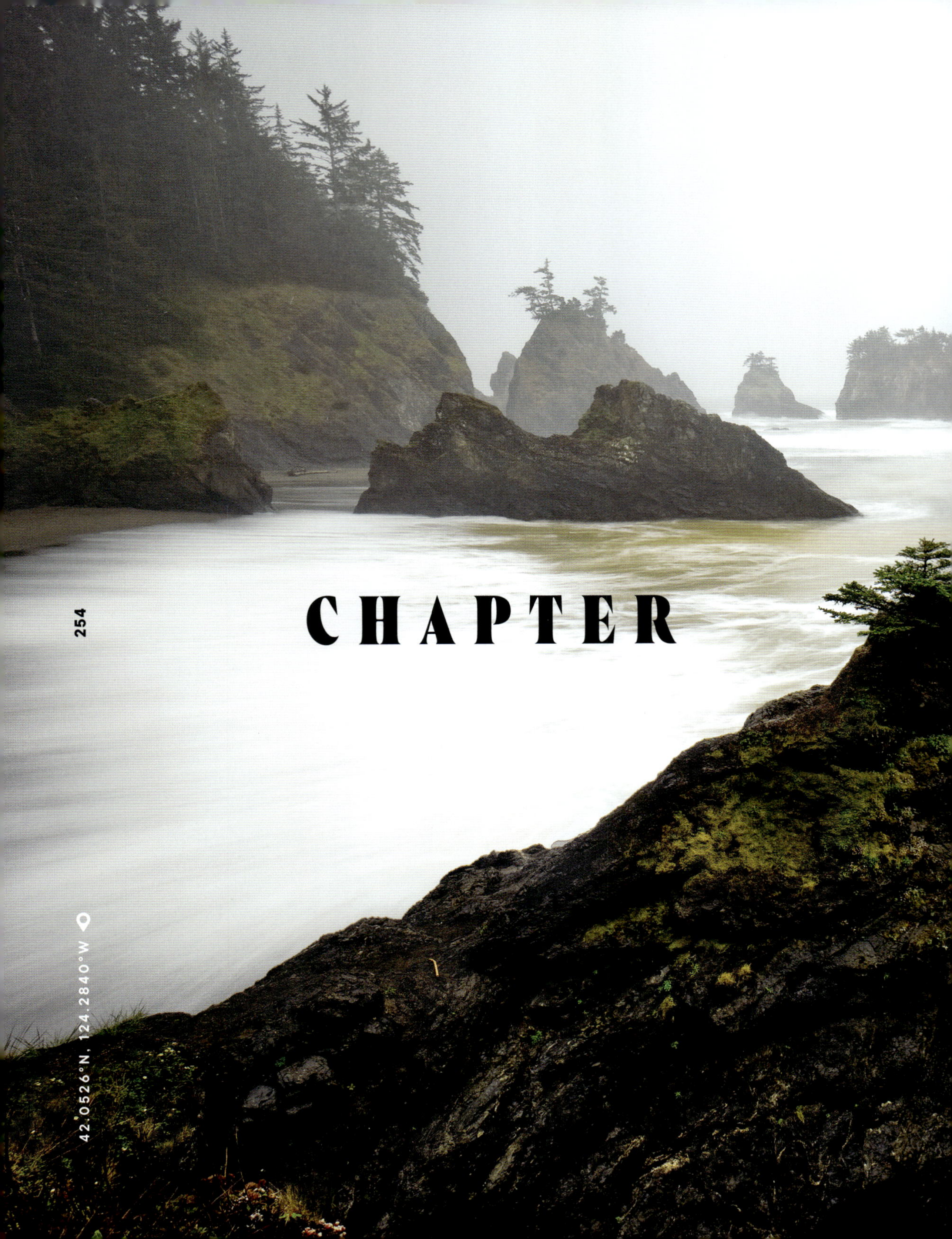

CHAPTER

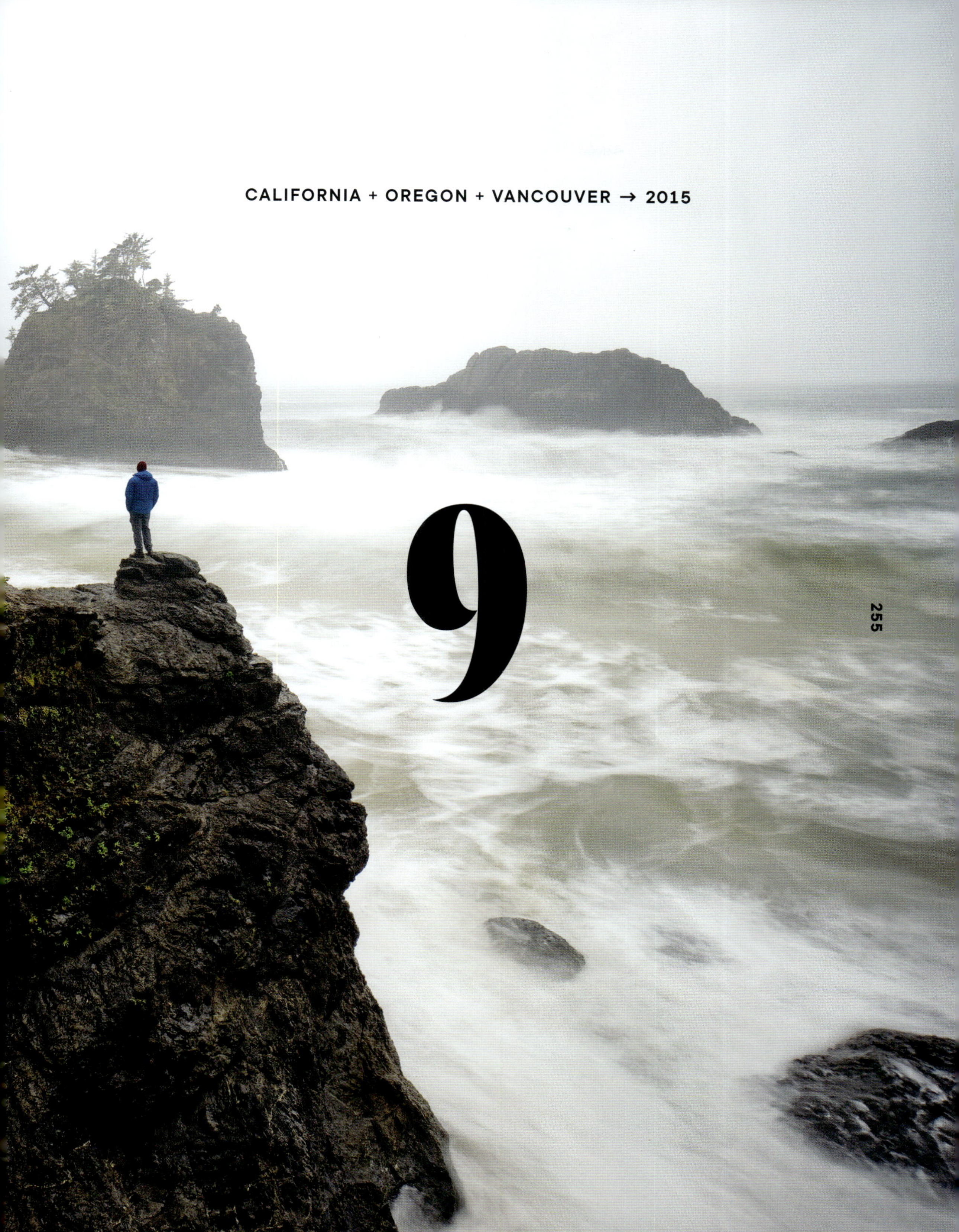
CALIFORNIA + OREGON + VANCOUVER → 2015
9
255

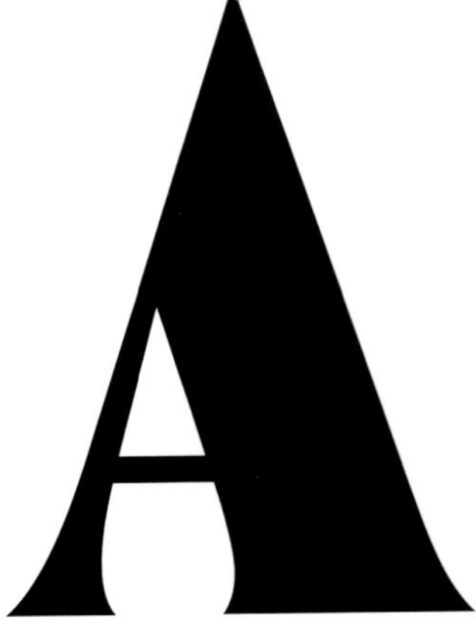

nyone who knows me knows how little numbers mean to me—number of followers, number of likes, even the number of stamps in my passport. But our trip to the Aleutian Islands was actually predicated on the idea of reaching as many people as possible, and in real time, whenever possible. And this set in motion a relationship with social media that has grown more valuable to me every year since.

Our team in the Aleutians was one of the first to take advantage of several different channels—including film, Instagram, blogging, digital storytelling, and print—to tell our story. And this was at a time when print editors would still disown you if you leaked an image before it was published. Once again, I was out of my comfort zone and ultimately my realm of understanding, but it was an exciting time as projects became more three-dimensional. The film about our trip became the most successful *Surfer* magazine film of all time.

And this is why when I talk about the growth of my business, I can't ignore the rise of Instagram. My profile on the social media platform grew from about 30,000 followers in 2013—when I took my first gig with Toyota—to more than 650,000 by early 2015. It was a perfect storm that made landfall all at once. But I'm conflicted in my feelings toward social media and the power that it has. It automatically triggers an internal eye roll, even from me. I talk about it now as if it were a living, breathing thing, and in many ways it is alive. It has grown and evolved over time, fed and nurtured by its consumers. It's almost as if by addressing it, I am forcing everyone to admit to the shared guilty pleasure so many of us partake in. But I also have to appreciate that it's partly because of this digital entity that I have had access to so many opportunities.

It's not sexy to talk analytics, engagements, and algorithms, but it's those features that helped bring me to where I am today. When ruminating on the influence of social media, I can't subscribe to the theory that it dangerously disconnects us from one another. I have found that it has a tremendous capacity to do the opposite. It all just depends on the way we use it. I thrive when connecting with people, whether digitally or personally, and if you don't enjoy communicating with people, this platform simply isn't for you. Some of my most meaningful adult relationships are thanks to a direct message or a *follow* button. These digital connections have translated into personal face-to-face experiences, which has been one of my favorite gifts from Instagram. Virtually all my employees, my greatest creative counterparts, artistic inspirations, and friends are all thanks to social media.

To see the kind of growth I had in such an intangible space was strange, though. I had nothing to compare it with. Was it like comments under an online article? I was getting constant real-time feedback, which sometimes felt like I was drinking straight from a fire hose. Those first few years experiencing Instagram lit up the part of my brain that's fed

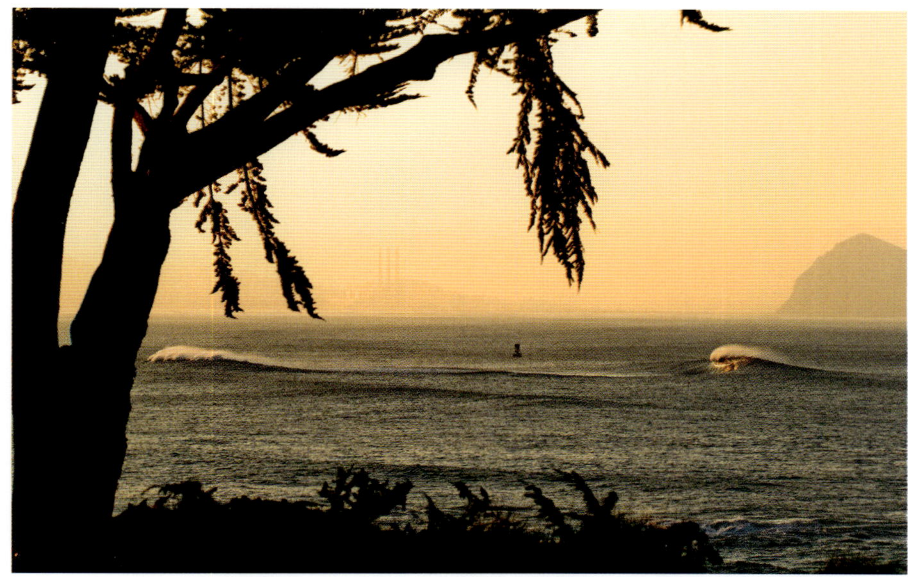

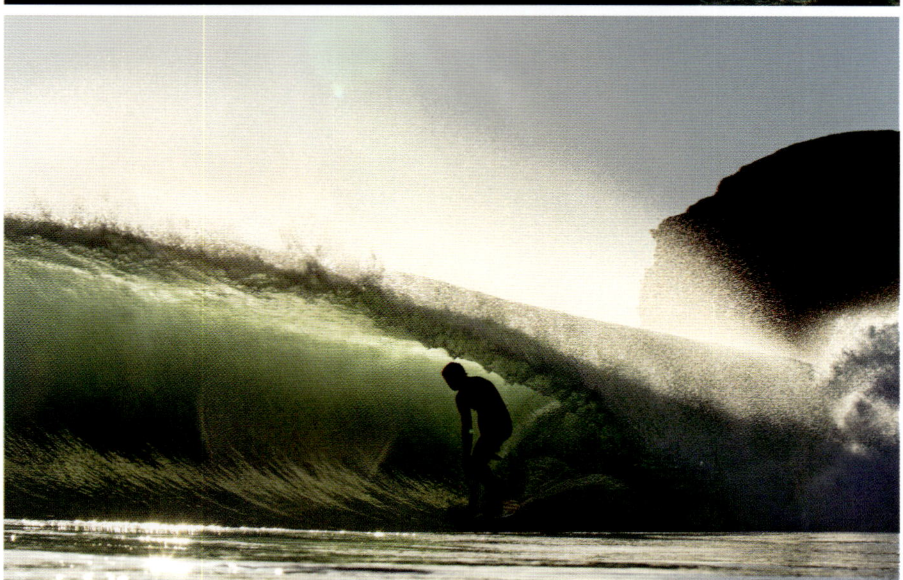

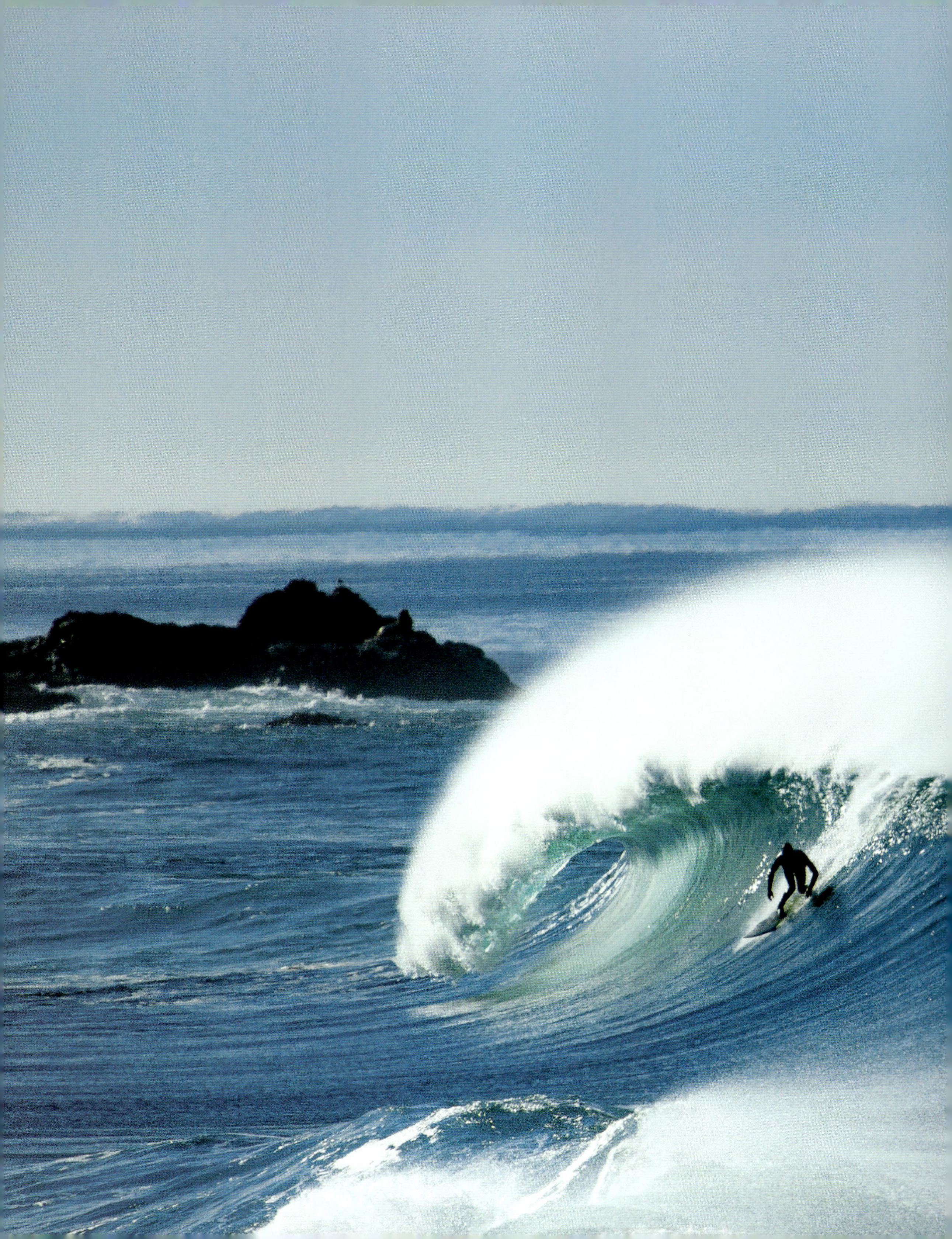

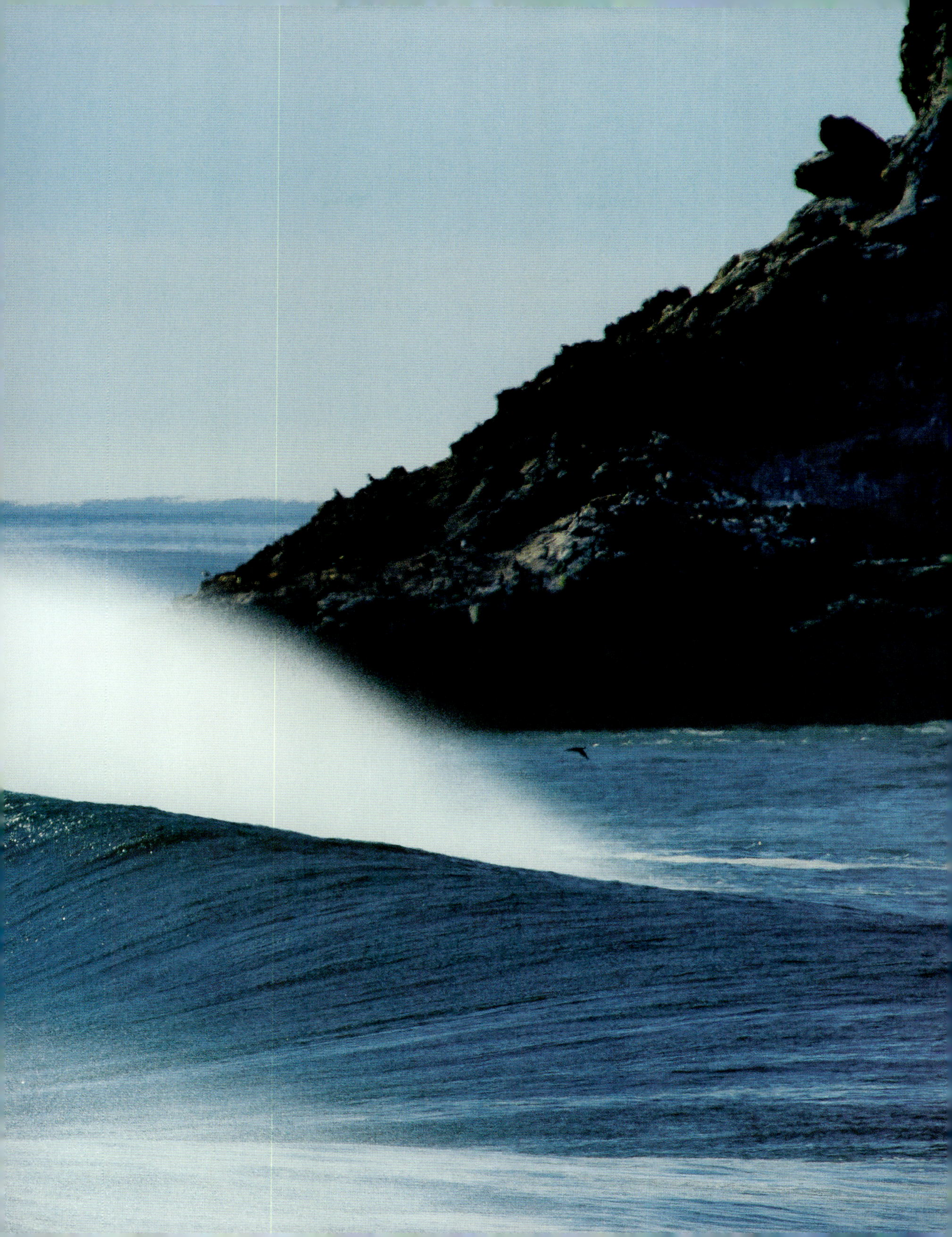

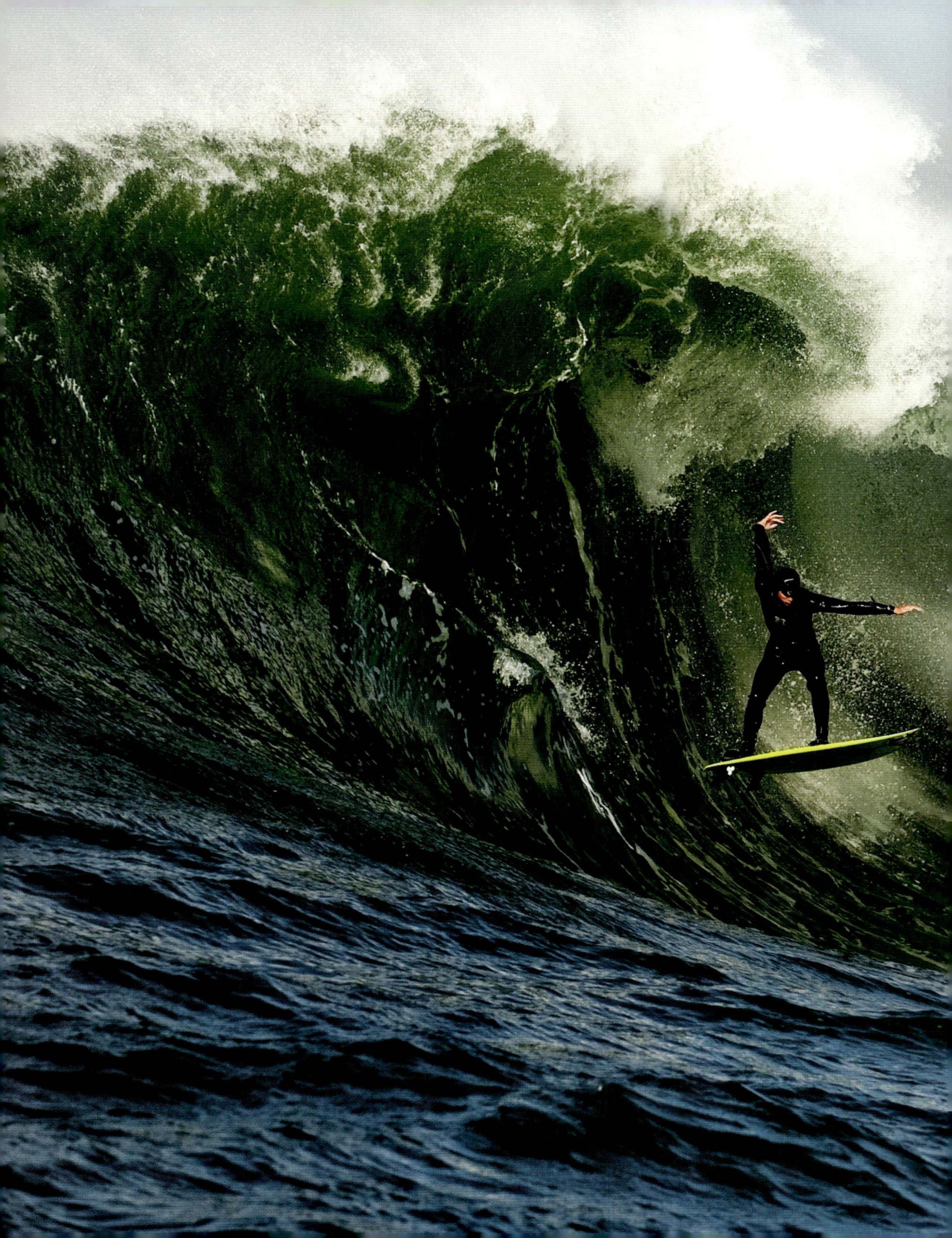

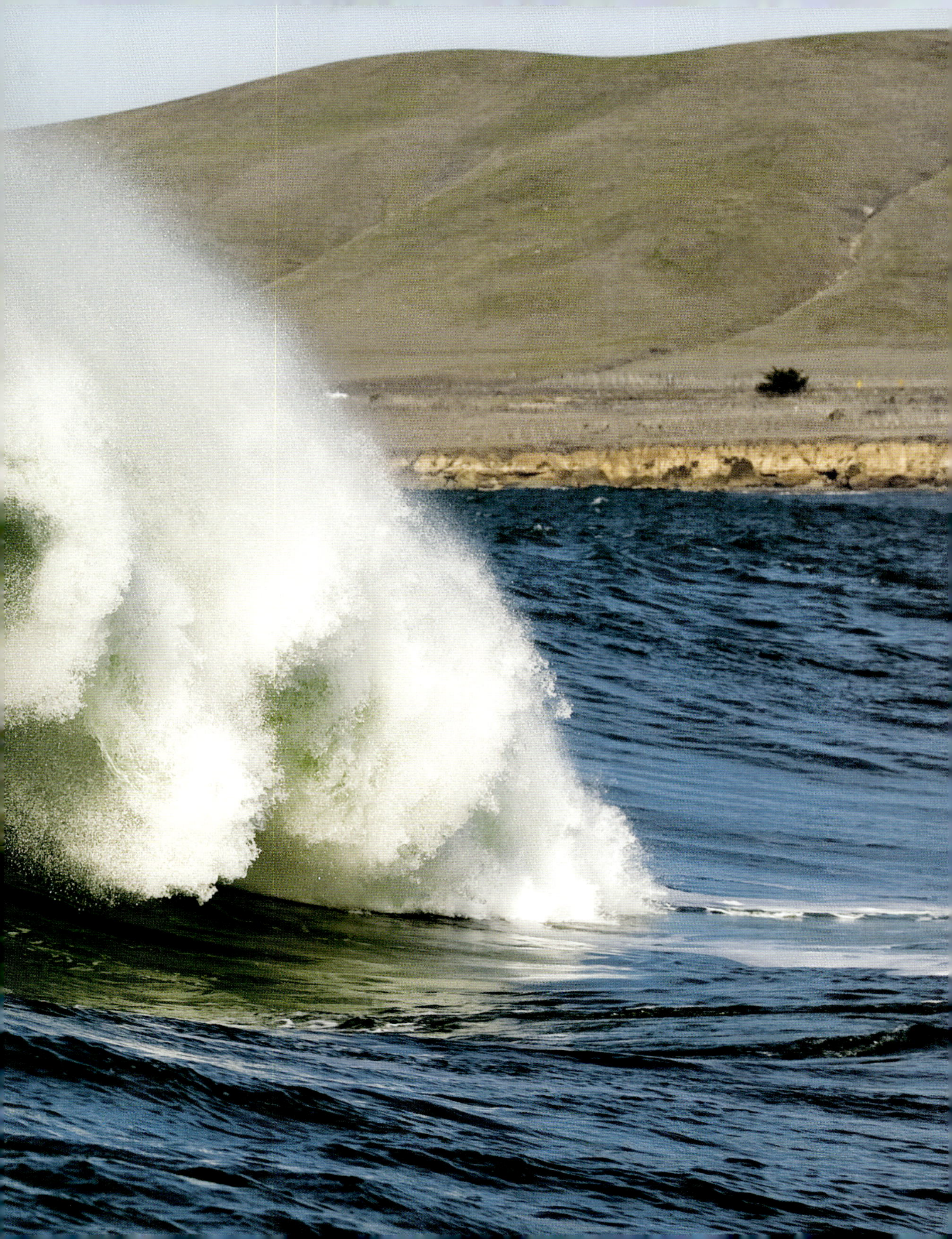

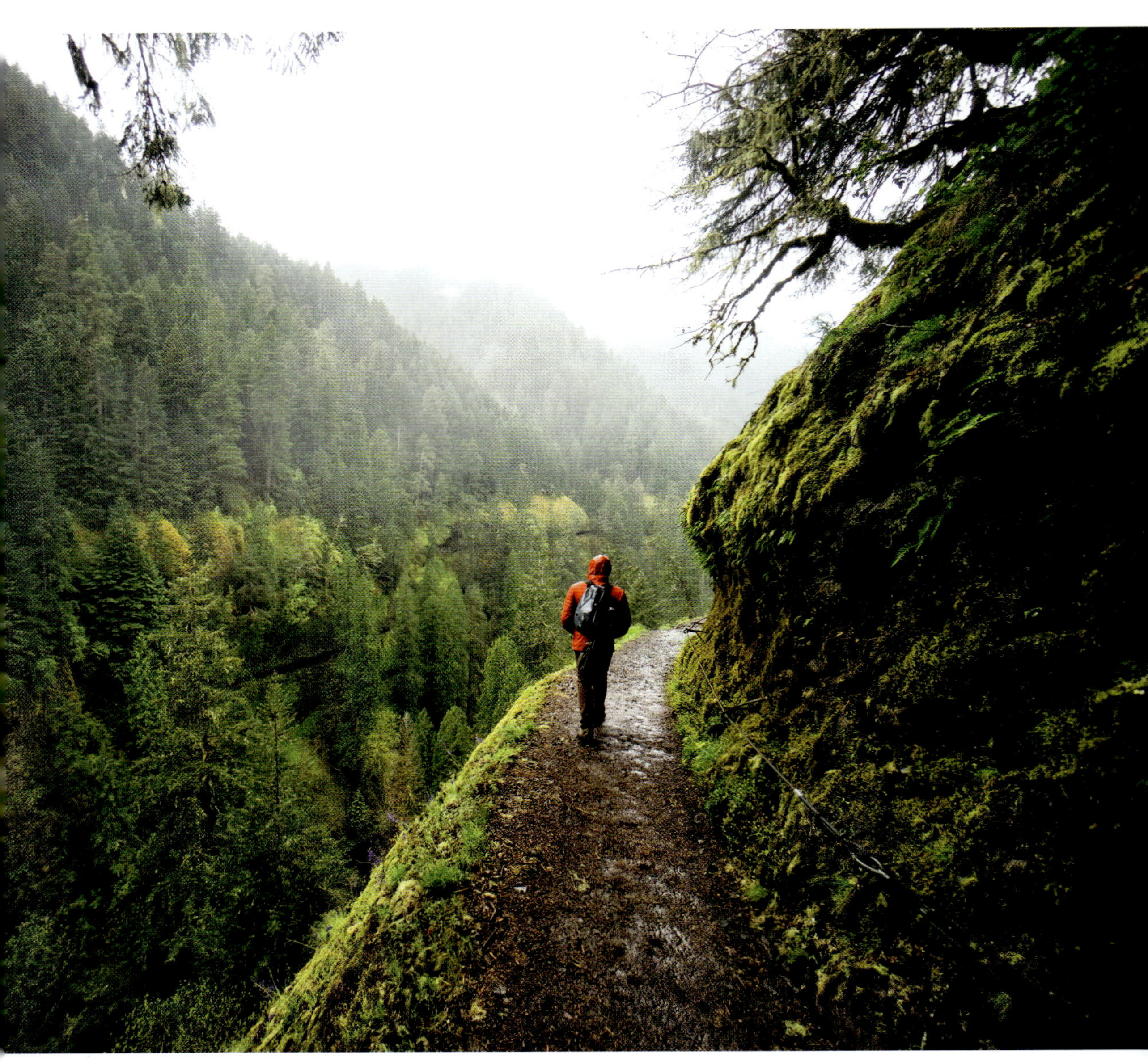

by a human need for instant gratification. I had no time management skills when it came to regulating the new access people had to me, and I found myself getting caught up in the increased demand. I now had an avenue to distribute my older catalog of images, as well as a bridge to my peers and clients. Aside from the visual art I was able to share, I also appreciated being able to create an introspective dialogue about the experiences I was sharing. Each post felt like a journal entry, in which I got increasingly more sure of my voice.

Commercial clients were interested in traditional print campaigns coupled with a social media component. These types of assignments were invigorating for me because the creative control was back in my hands, thus making the need for a middleman creative agency obsolete. Clients were approaching me because they appreciated not only my photography, but also my words and feelings about the places I documented. I could see even then that art and commerce were becoming dangerously intertwined, and I made a pact with myself early on to never promote a product just for the sake of a quick buck. I wanted to create a digital space with the type of quality that could exist for years to come, not one that was inundated with the latest mass-manufactured fad product that would be forgotten a year from now. I tried to think creatively about how I could collaborate with brands to come up with visual narratives that aligned with my core mission, which is to motivate people to get outside and enjoy nature.

Some of my favorite social media assignments were for tourism campaigns, where I was contracted to go to some of my most treasured places. I had a lot of freedom to go and experience cities or national parks in ways I had dreamed of with my friends. These jobs often felt reminiscent of *The California Surf Project*, but through different landscapes and with different copilots.

One of my first forays into working with a tourism client was for the State of Oregon. I had gotten a taste of the wild that existed beyond our Northern California border with Eric in our bus years prior and was anxious to explore. Going into the phone call to discuss creative, I was worried that I might be pressured into projecting a perfect sunny picture of the Oregon coast, even if it poured for eight days straight. Luckily, the tourism board understood my desire to tell an authentic story that was true to my experience. They gave me license to simply explore. So I packed up my trusty Ford Transit Van along with my assistant Preston and my climbing buddy Brian Treitler for the 2,500-mile road trip to the home of The Goonies.

After driving through the night to chase a "blood moon" lunar eclipse, we began our Oregon journey with a snowy sunrise hike to Crater Lake, the deepest in the United States. From there, we packed in way more than two weeks of adventures: rafting the Rogue

263

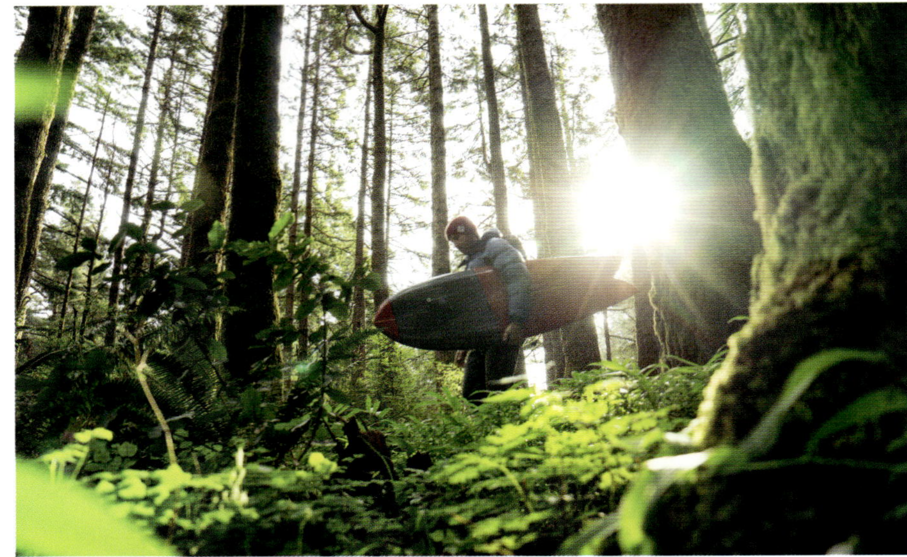

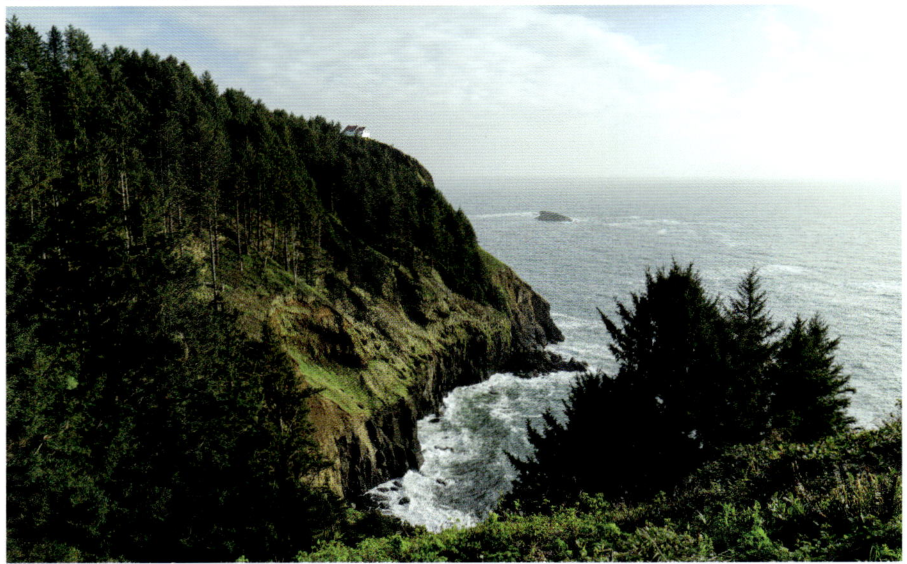

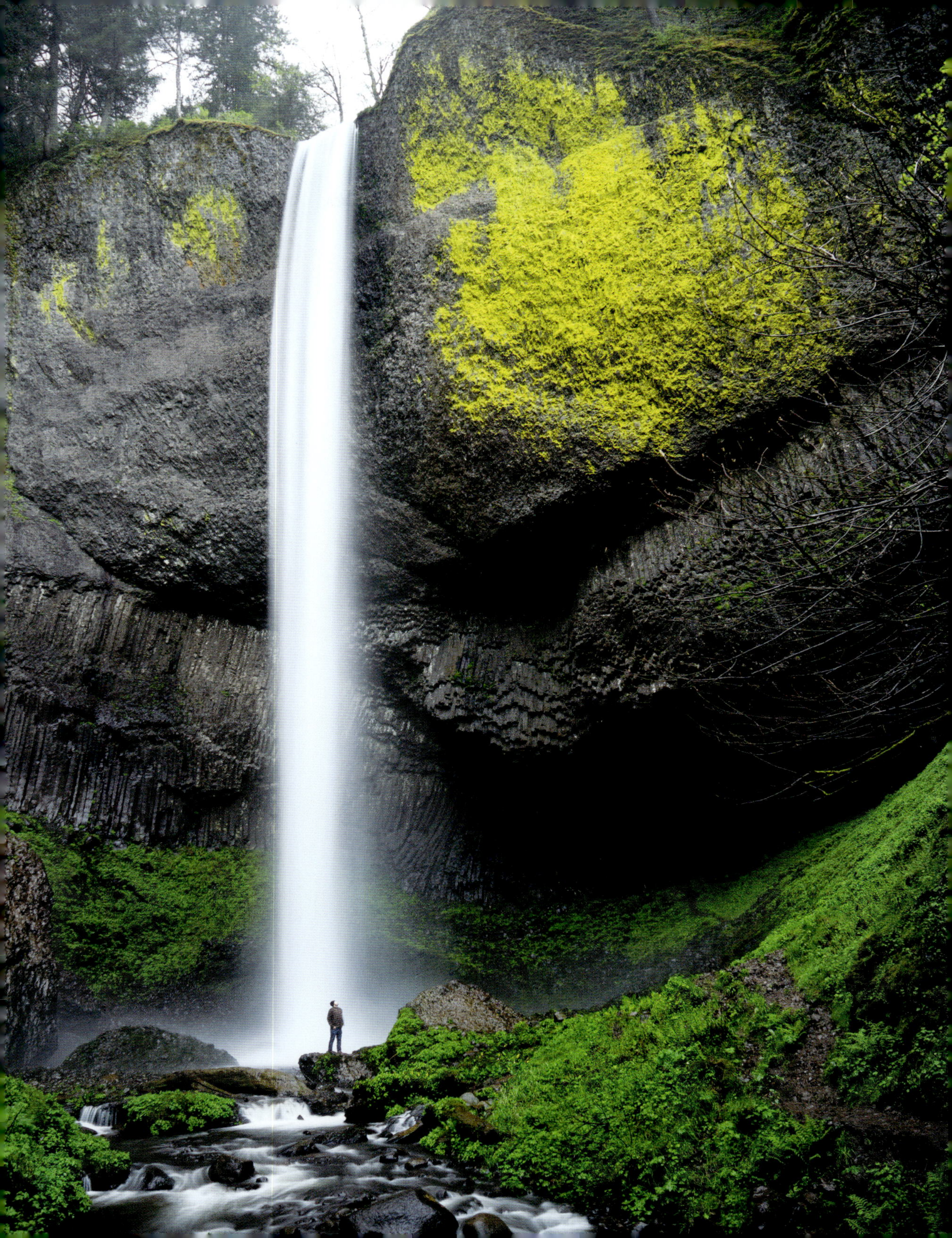

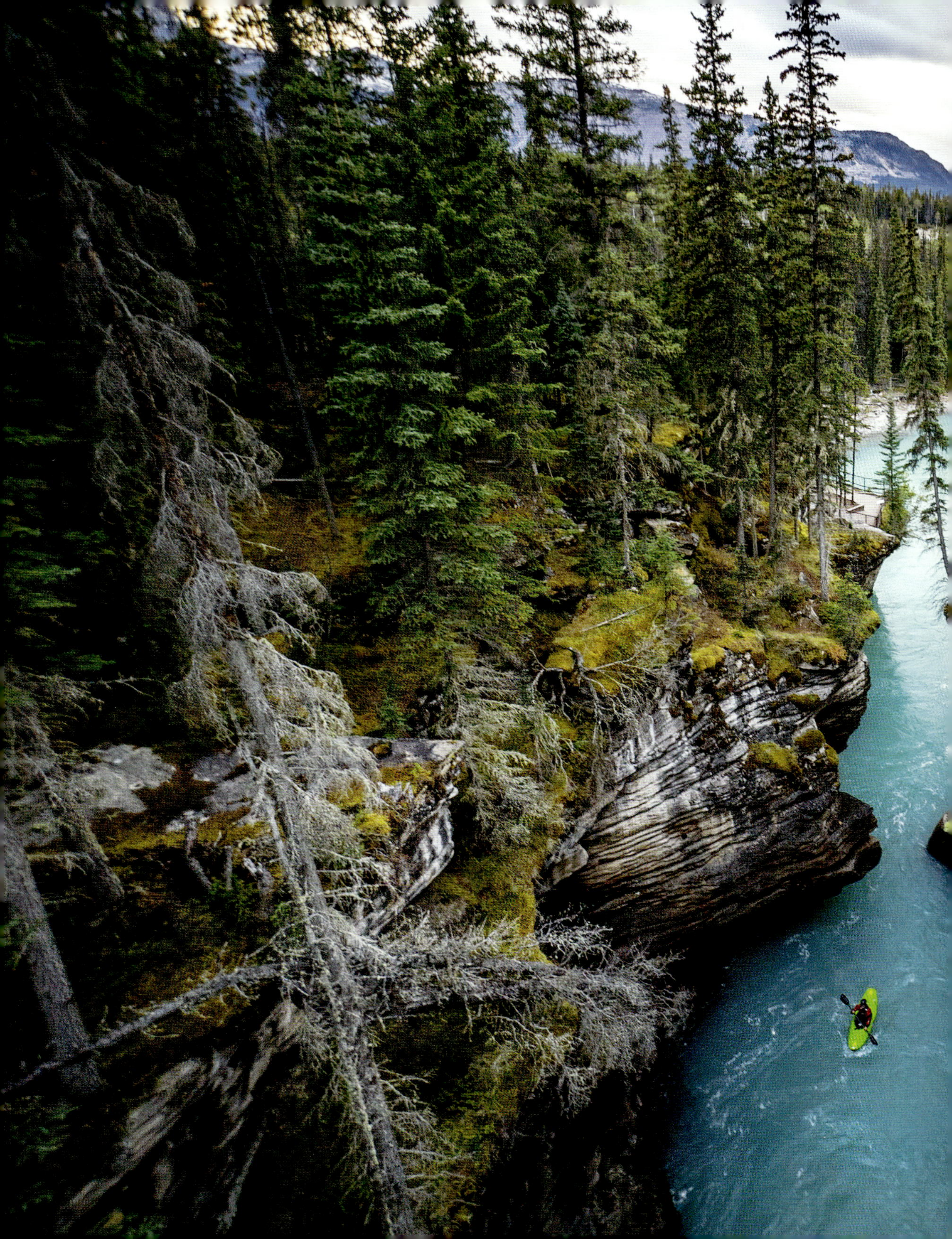

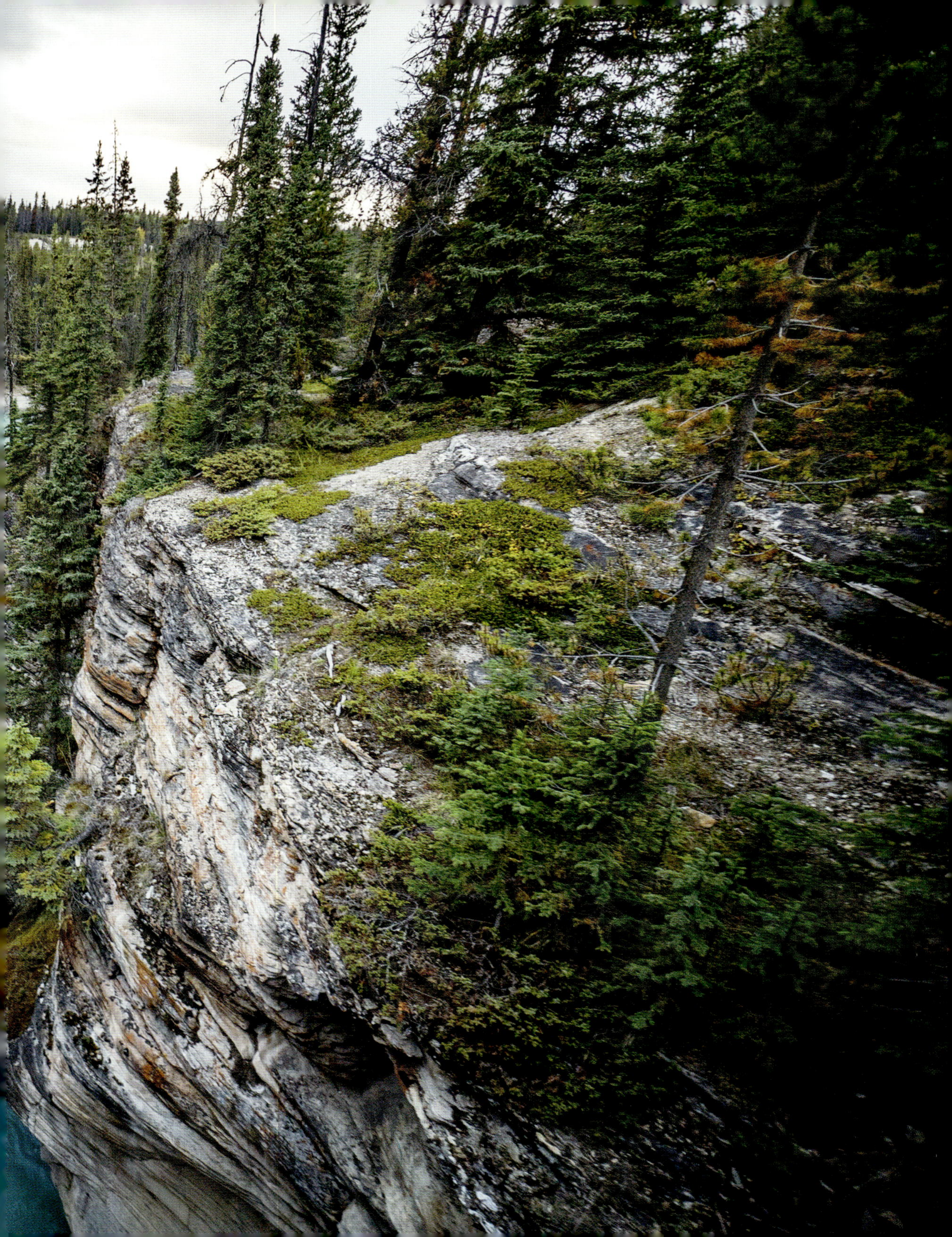

River, climbing at Smith Rock, sleeping in a tree house, tent camping beneath volcanoes, rope swinging into freezing waterways, sandboarding the seaside sand dunes of Florence, staying up until 3:00 A.M. to photograph the night sky, and getting soaked in Pacific coast rain forests, which happened pretty much every day.

Although a lot of the trip was muddy and soggy, it made for a good story about how challenging weather keeps the crowds away, the backdrops moody, and makes the rewards that much sweeter when you finally stumble upon fluorescent leaves and moss set against a soft white waterfall. Or when the clouds finally break and you see a lighthouse, or a rock climber, silhouetted against an indigo sunset. Even without a magazine assignment or commercial brief, I made sure we explored as many crannies of the state as possible and collected nearly as many stories. The Oregon adventure culminated in true Sasquatch country fashion, as we were blindsided by some sort of creature in the middle of the night that totaled the front end of my van.

As the work I did for Travel Oregon circulated, more interest and opportunities came my way from other tourism boards. Excited to be receiving the type of work travel photographers only dream of, I posted most of the commercial tourism photographs I had produced on Instagram. By sharing these projects on social media, I discovered that I wasn't the only one who was passionate about these places.

Along with all those enjoying the vicarious adventure was a tidal wave of viewers questioning my approach and motives. It was no longer just editors and brands I had to answer to anymore, it was an entirely new audience of critics. An audience that never missed when I made a mistake, or a chance to tell me that I should be more responsible. Whether I was sharing a geo-tag (geographical location to a photograph or video) or a photo of a place you're only allowed to shoot with a permit, I was constantly being accused of sharing too much of the wrong information, or not enough of the right information.

The truth is, often when I was shooting these assignments, I had permission to photograph and document areas that aren't typically accessible to the average viewer, while also engaging in activities and sports that aren't typically allowed unless you have that approval. Most everything I did was under

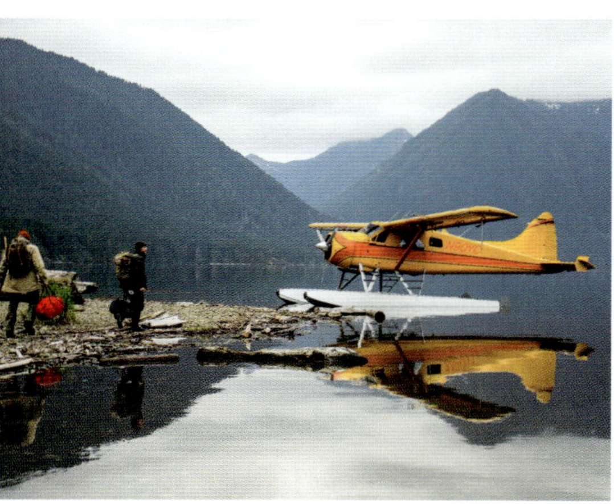

the protective arm of a permit, which assures that any holders are properly experienced and educated in how to operate in the environment there. Whether I was pitching a tent, kayaking an inlet, or building a campfire, I learned the hard way that I had to give an extensive explanation to clarify what was allowed in each area—not an easy thing to squeeze into every Instagram caption.

Not only were my stewardship and responsibility being questioned, but soon my sincerity and authenticity were as well. When contracted for certain assignments, I often had a hefty shot list of required so-called assets and a limited time to complete them. Although I was experiencing genuine adventures, inevitably we would have to re-create certain scenes. It just comes with the territory of commercial work that certain images need to be staged in order to be captured in the right light, or at the right angle, to complete the client's objective by the deadline. But my audience couldn't always tell the difference between commercial and personal work.

Like them, I too grew somewhat tired of the top-of-the-mountain, tent-perched-on-the-overhang clichés, which are a far cry from the gritty, unfiltered moments I was trying to create years earlier for Patagonia. I was probably more sensitive to the remarks, having come from a background where anything less than true photojournalism was unacceptable. And it's true that commercial photography often does blur the boundaries between branding and real life. The biggest lesson for me in the early days of commercial photography was to be clear about how I presented an experience on social media—especially if it relied on permits not available to the public—and to acknowledge if my post was paid for by a client.

Perhaps one of the most difficult criticisms I have had to navigate is the idea that work like mine is responsible for "overtourism." I've seen places that I used to enjoy alone—Roys Peak in New Zealand, Glacier Point in Yosemite, Reynisfjara Beach in Iceland—completely swarmed by people with cameras and mobile phones. The crowds, noise, and trash are certainly a challenging side effect that comes with more tourists, bringing with them a need for more infrastructure to accommodate rehabilitation and regulation. That said, I just can't subscribe to the idea that "Instagram is ruining nature" or that we're "loving places to death."

Nature for me has been a slow burn. The spark started on road trips with my grandparents and grew over time through experience and exposure to wild places. Whether we like it or not, social media has been a gateway drug to nature for many viewers—for people who never took road trips with their grandparents as a kid, for people who have never seen the ocean, for people who have never slept under the stars. It is an elitist attitude to want to privatize the natural world, so only we can enjoy it in seclusion and peace. As a culture, we cannot expect the world to care about these sacred spaces unless we share with people what they are missing.

In the long run, what is it that will ultimately ensure protection for these places—access

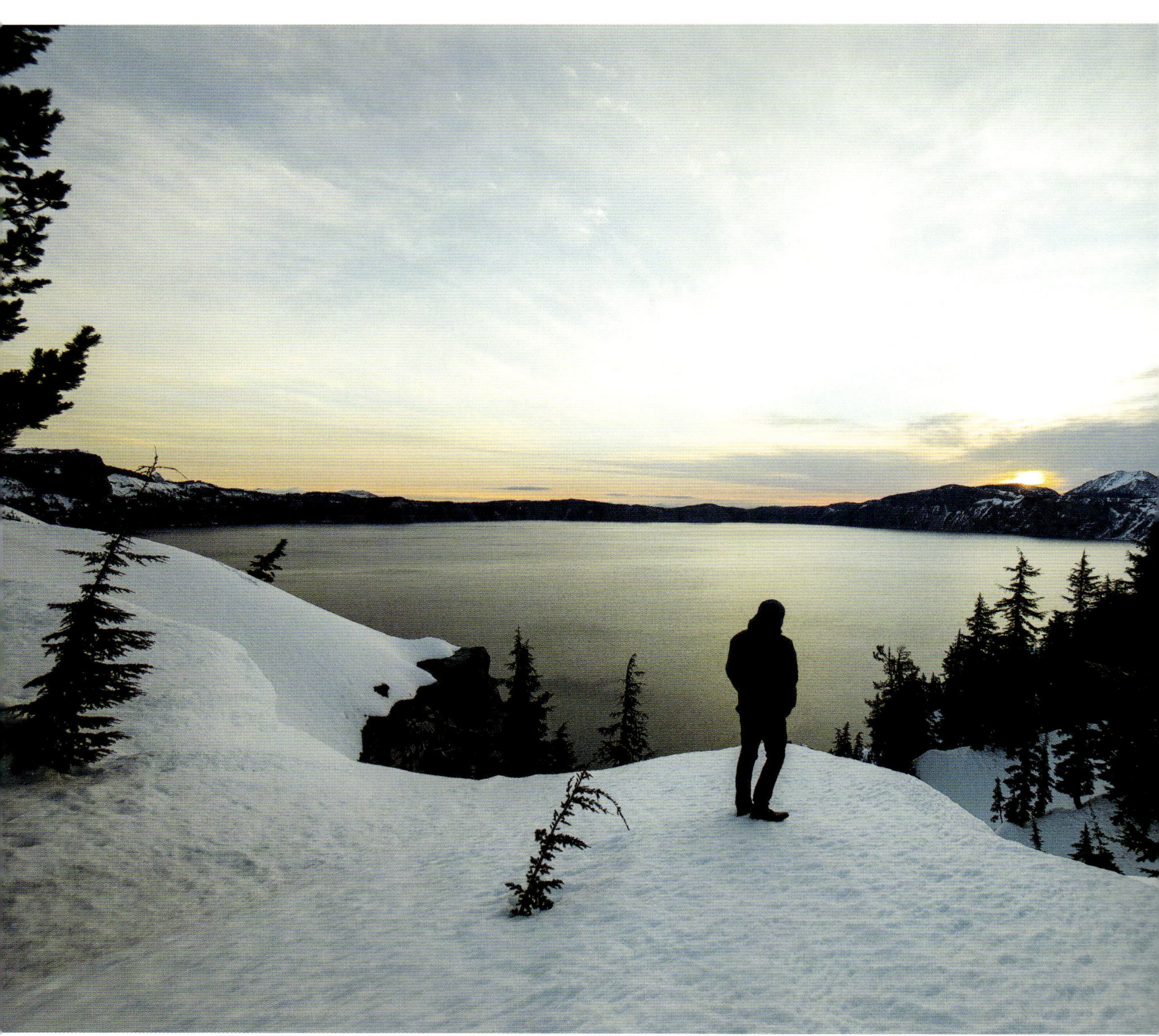

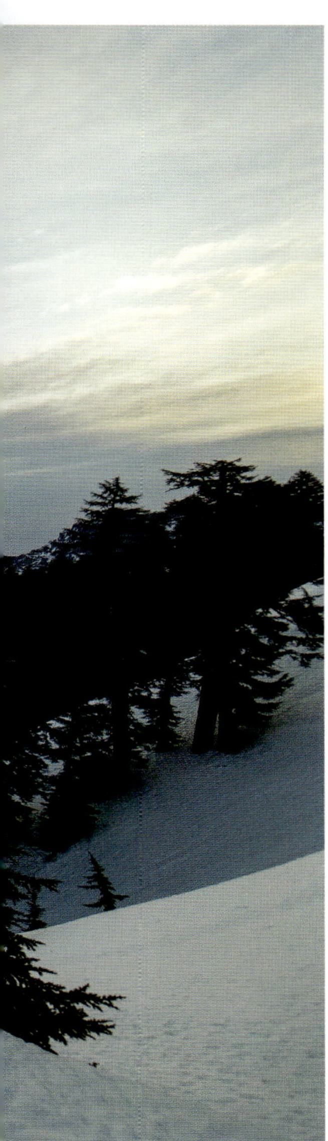

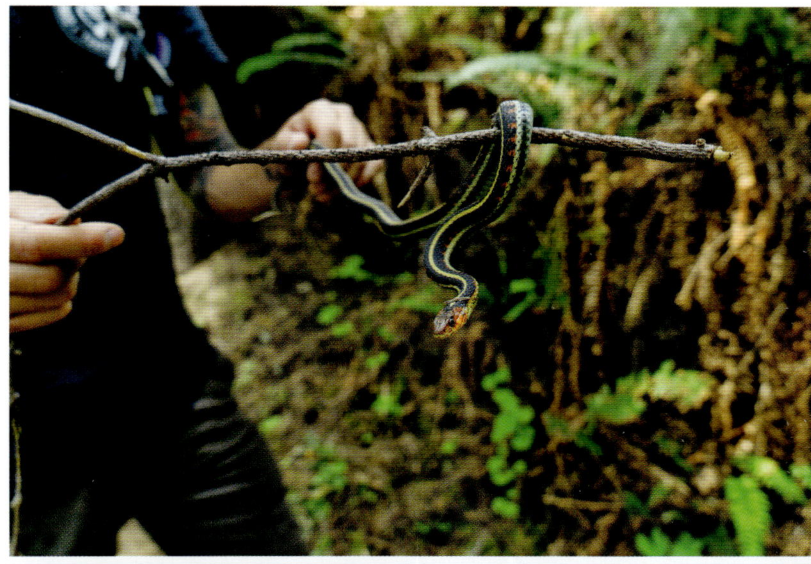

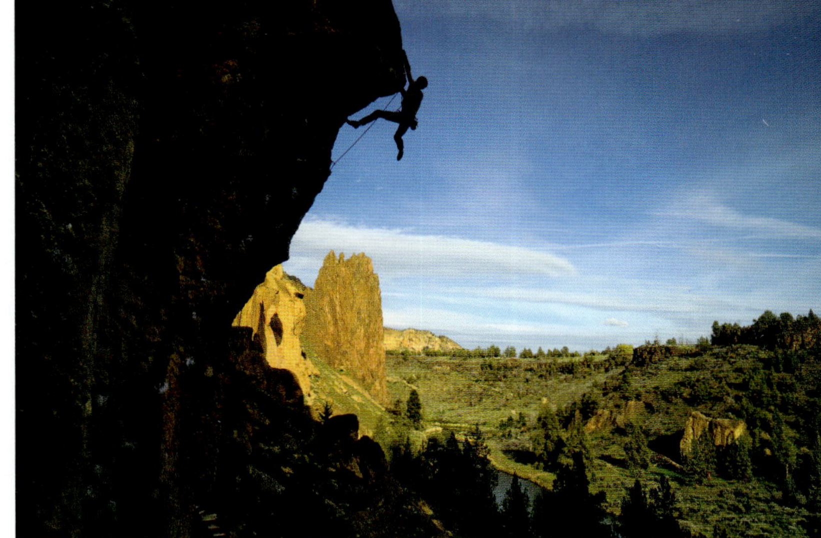

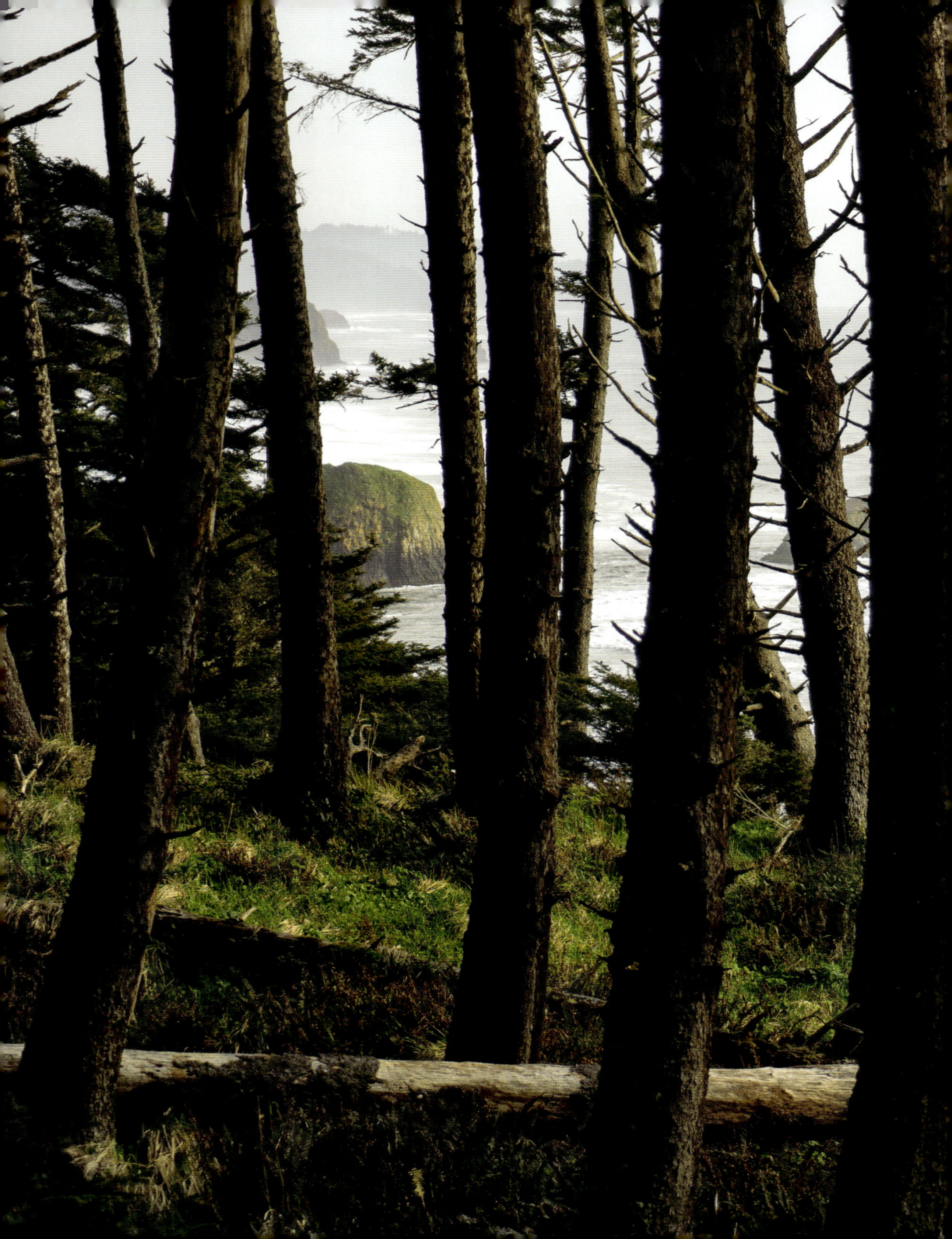

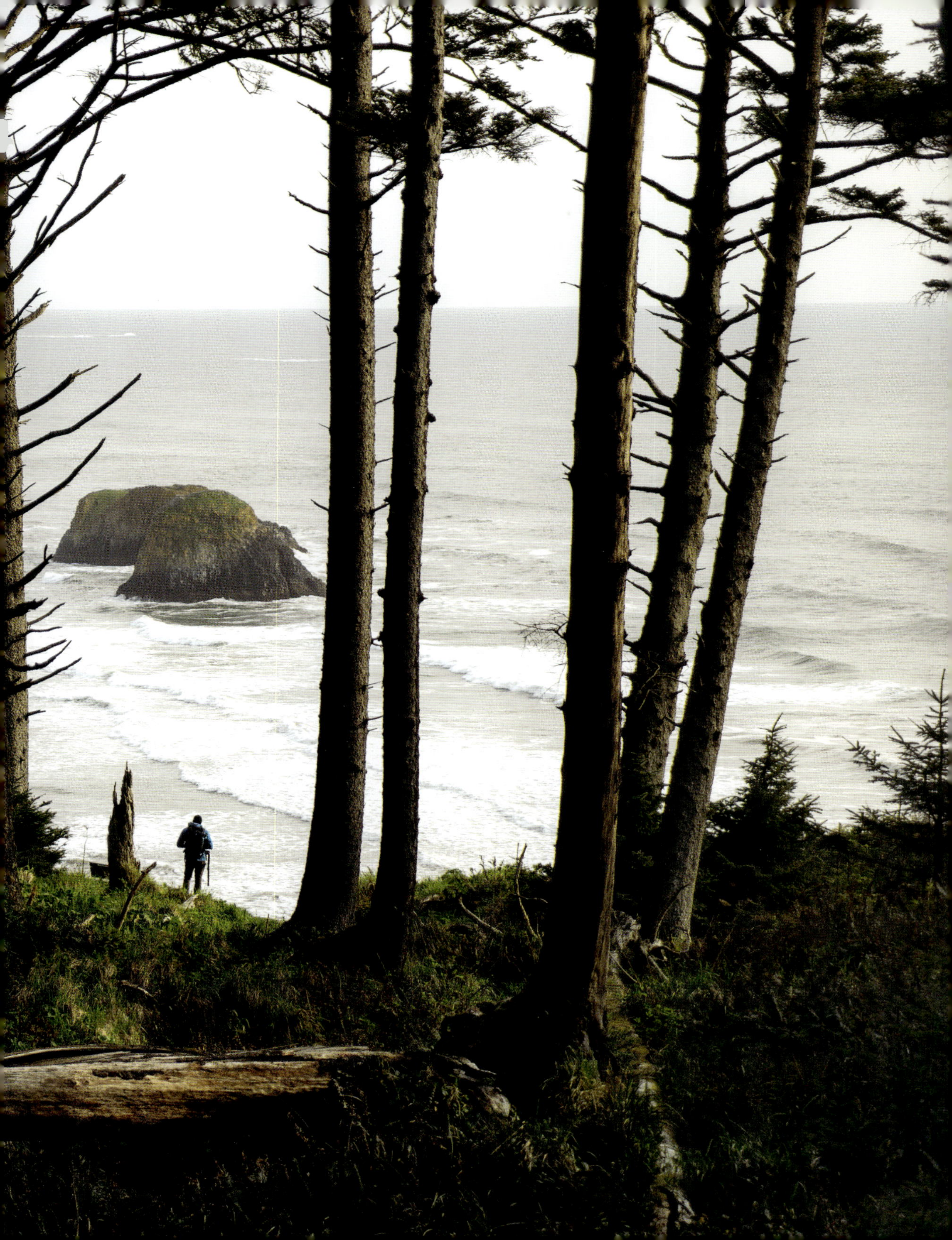

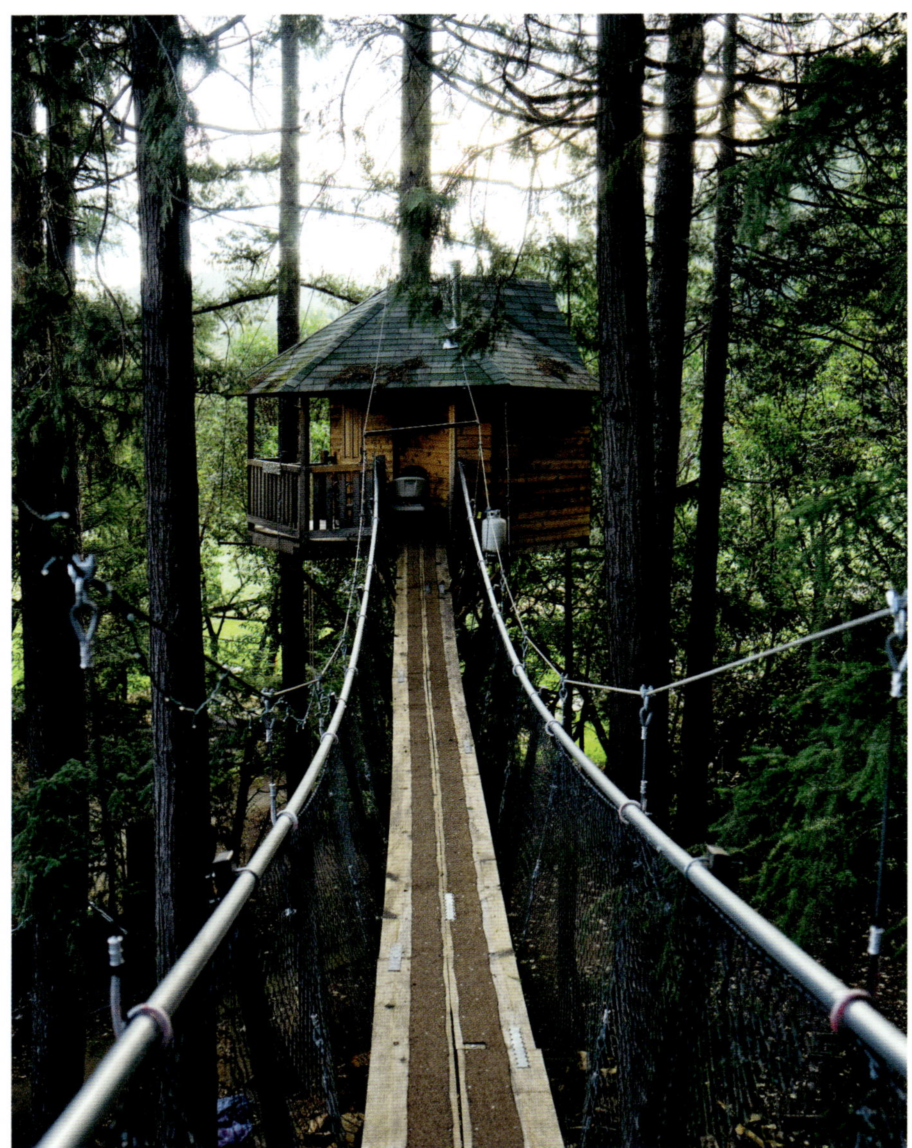

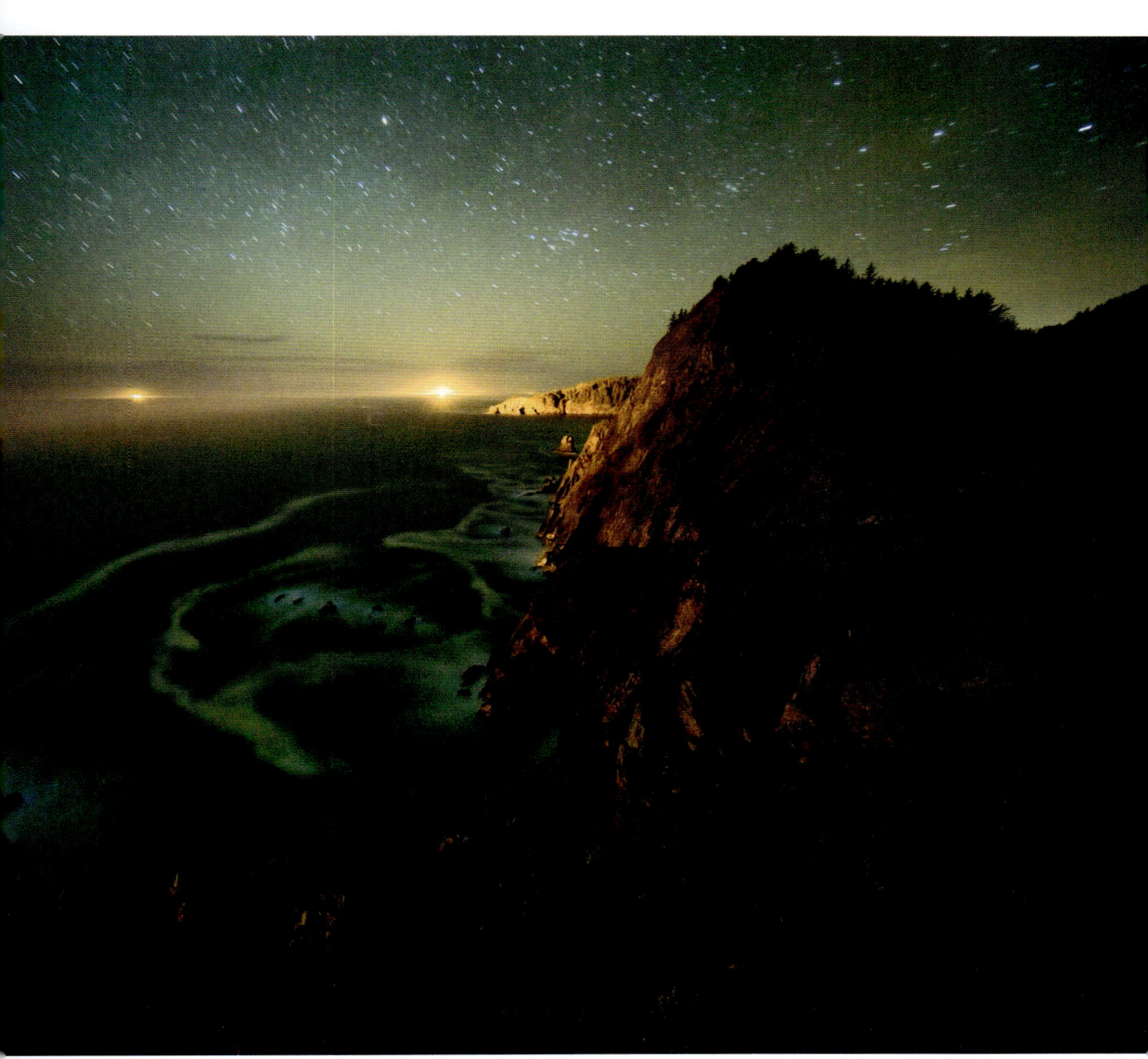

CHRIS BURKARD

WAYWARD

for a select few or access for many? I believe there are also undeniable economic opportunities that tourism brings to remote places, providing much-needed conservation revenue to keep these places healthy and thriving. By sharing sacred spaces, we are opening tourists up to what exists beyond the heavily tagged tourist clickbait. A photo at the rim of the Grand Canyon might lead someone to one day hike farther into that canyon to find a quiet place for reflection just a few miles off the beaten path near the Colorado River.

In many ways, this kind of talk felt a bit like the localism I experienced early in my career. It was just as claustrophobic to have people constantly telling me who should and who should not have access to these places. One thing is for sure: People were no longer just judging my work, they were judging me. And the more avenues I used to share my images, the more scrutiny I came under.

It's also fair to say, the more I shared about myself, the more people wanted to know what made me tick, and this felt like an opportunity. I felt like I had a lot to say, a lot to share. At times, even these new platforms felt limiting. It felt as though things were often lost in translation or never fully expressed. Interestingly, at the height of my angst toward social media, I was granted access to the biggest stage I'd ever stood on. Literally.

In 2015, I got an email with a subject line that read, "TED Speaker Invite." The global TED conference was one of the largest stages in the world, and I was slotted in for a session called "Passion and Consequence" at a TED event in Vancouver, Canada. The overall theme was "Truth and Dare." It certainly felt like a dare—and I had no idea where to start.

TED initially approached me after seeing a short documentary by a digital and print media sales company called SmugMug. The short film, called *Arctic Swell—Surfing the Ends of the Earth*, featured a surf trip I took to Norway. Ironically, I almost turned that opportunity down, since it wasn't a paying job and I was trying to make smarter decisions about when I should and shouldn't leave home. But apparently the video— about how immersing yourself in frigid, untamed landscapes can make you a better person—struck a chord at TED. "Did I have more to say about cold-water surfing?" the email asked.

"Oh, for sure," I said with complete confidence over the phone. "These trips have been the key to self-knowledge, joy, and fulfillment. The pain is in many ways like meditation." Much like most of the biggest breaks I've had in my life, I just went for it, and it paid off. A formal invite followed.

"But what is it that you really want to say?!" longtime family friend and psychotherapist Elizabeth Barrett pried for the tenth time during our writing session. "What have you really learned that is of value?" I hated Elizabeth in that moment—she had hit a nerve. I was only twenty-eight years old. *What the hell did I have to say that was worth sharing*

on the biggest stage I'd likely ever stand on?
I knew I didn't want to take myself too seriously, and I wanted to entertain and make
people laugh, but I also wanted to get to the
root of what my whole career—my "crusade
against the mundane"—had been about.

Now, as I was sitting at Elizabeth's
kitchen island, we had photographs splayed
out for inspiration to help me decipher the
vision for my talk more clearly. One image
in particular—a selfie that commemorated
my nearly hypothermic water session in
Unstad, Norway—symbolized it all for me.
Inside the circular opening of my hooded
wetsuit, my face was red as a tomato, my
eyes were sunken and bloodshot, and in
the corner of my pink puffy lips, you could

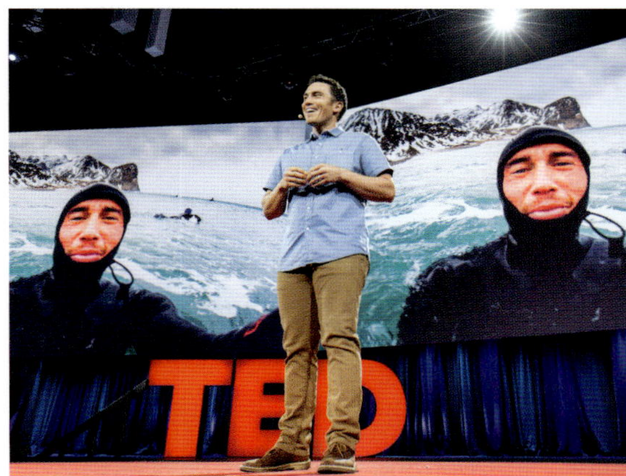

make out the faint lines of a smile. Although that trip didn't produce a cover or significant attention at the time, it's been an experience that continues to show me I didn't
need monetary rewards to deem something successful.

I revised my TED Talk seventeen times. Ultimately, it was my wife, Brea—the person
who knows me best—who helped me nail down the most important line: In life, there
are no shortcuts to joy. Anything that is worth pursuing is going to require us to suffer . . .
just a little bit. That was it, my kernel of truth.

Standing backstage in the red glow of the TED sign, staring out at a dark room that
looked like NASA's Mission Control Center, I felt fear. But just like the anxiety that washed
over me before I went into the water in Norway, I gave it no attention. Before I went out,
I looked at myself in the mirror, reiterated positive affirmations, and tried not to think
about the sea of important faces that would be staring back at me. I was surrounded by
some of the biggest names in technology, entertainment, activism, and design: Bill Gates,
Al Gore, and Monica Lewinsky, to name a few.

When my slideshow turned from tropical waves and crowded beaches to jagged
moonscapes and the northern lights, the audience gasped. When I nailed the speech's
main joke—if shivering is a form of meditation, then I would consider myself a monk—
they laughed right on cue. I anticipated every response and never stopped to correct
or repeat. It was the epitome of preparation and performance. Not a word or pause or
sentiment was out of place, and I smiled all the way to the very last word: *joy.*

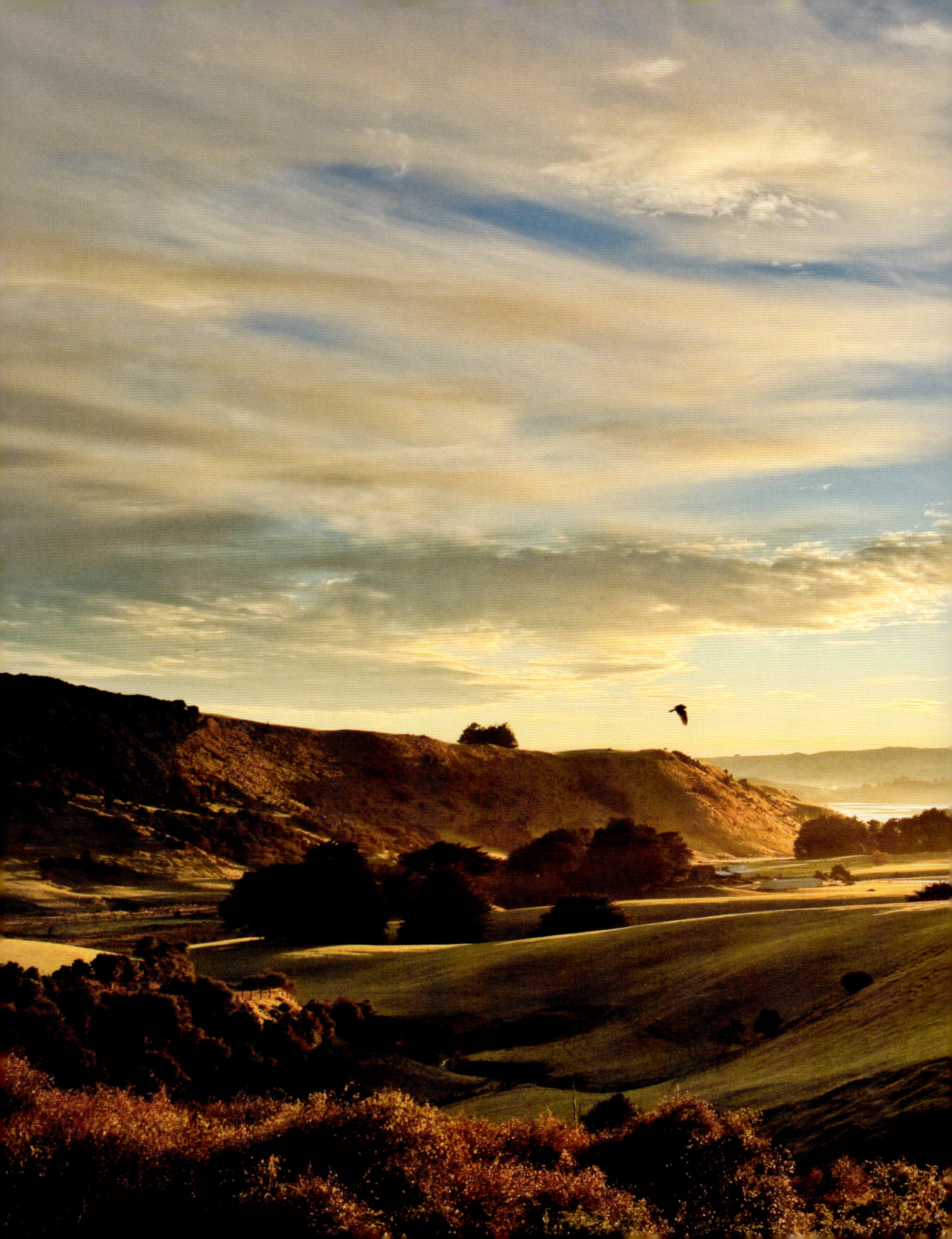

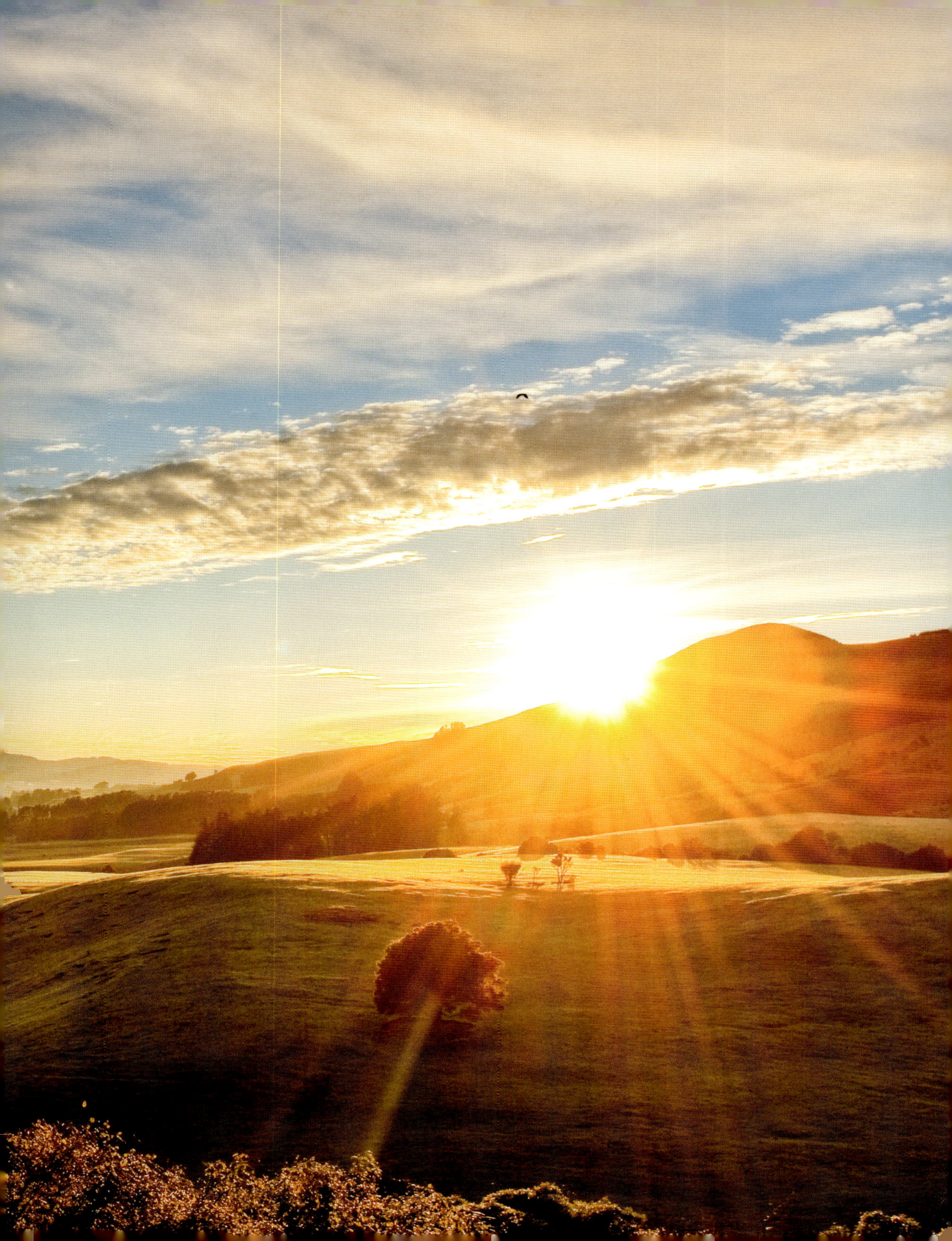

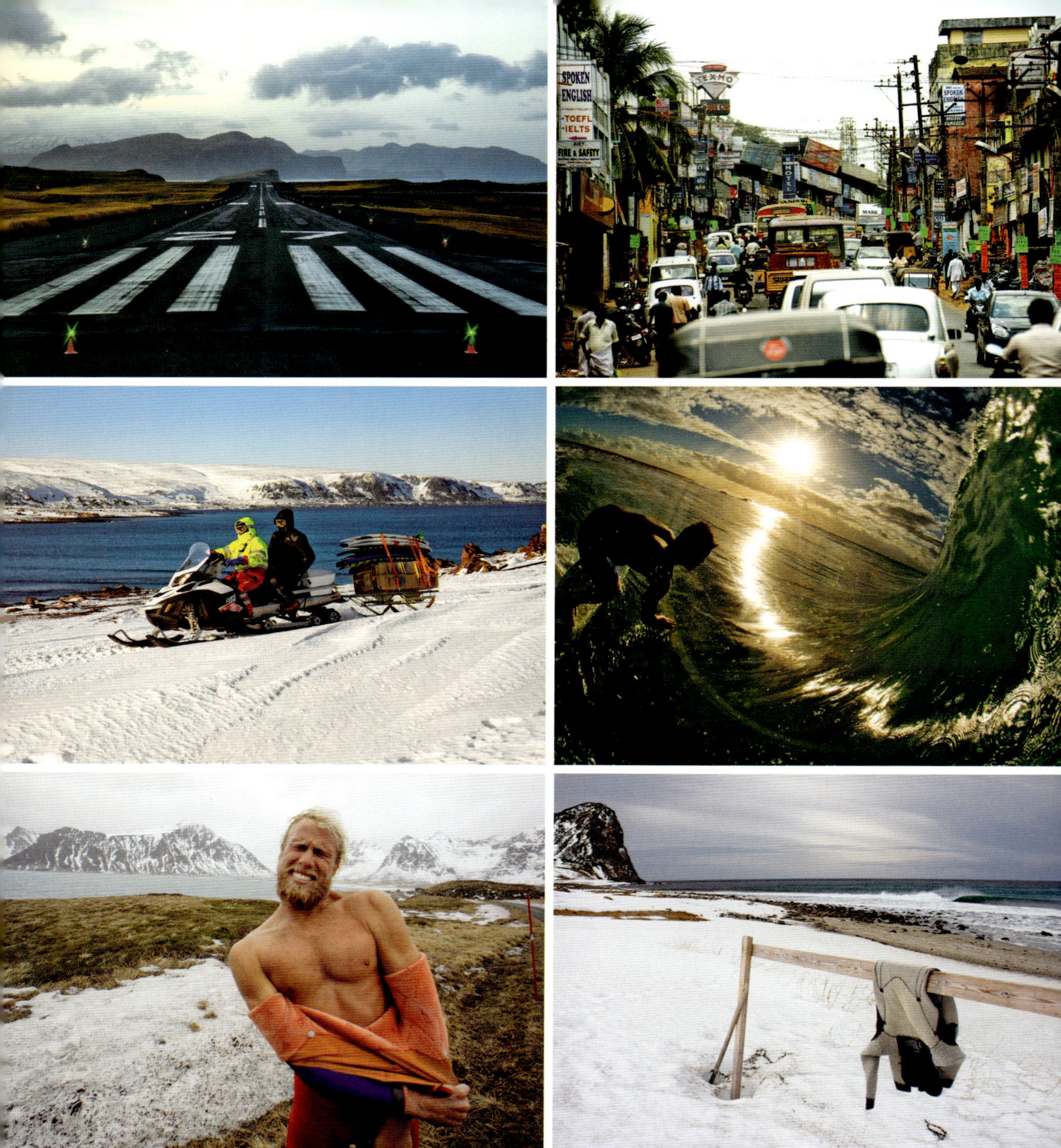

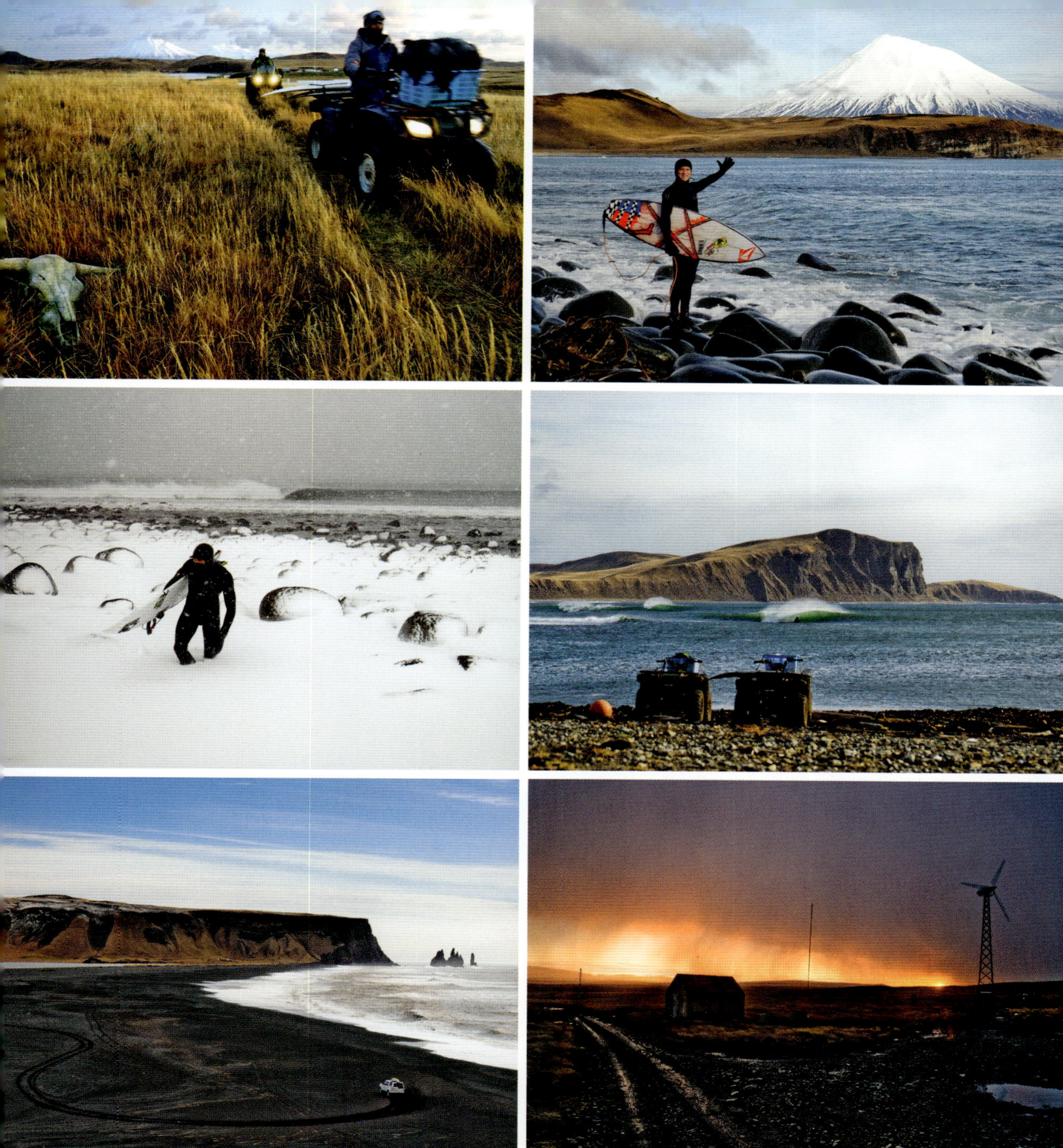

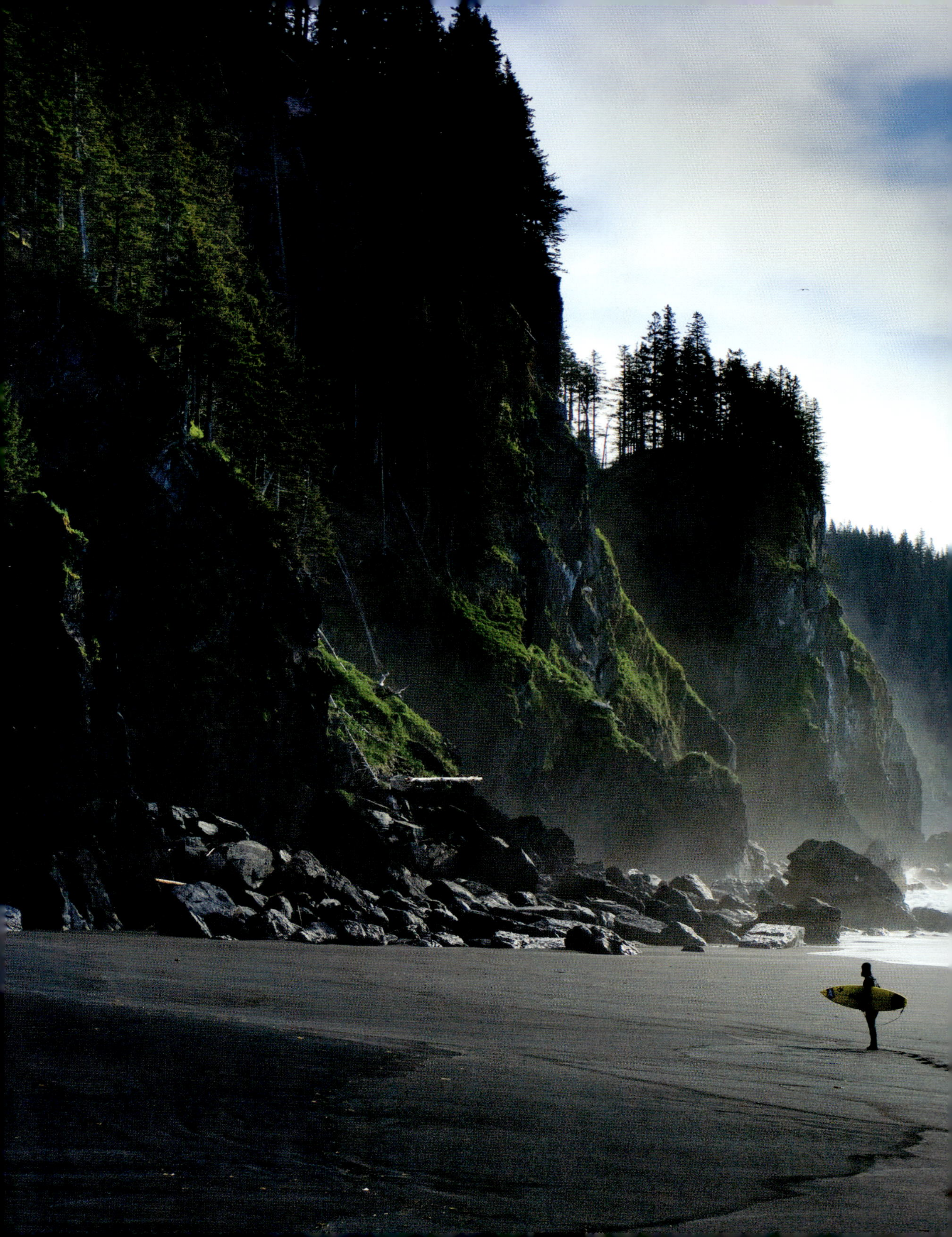

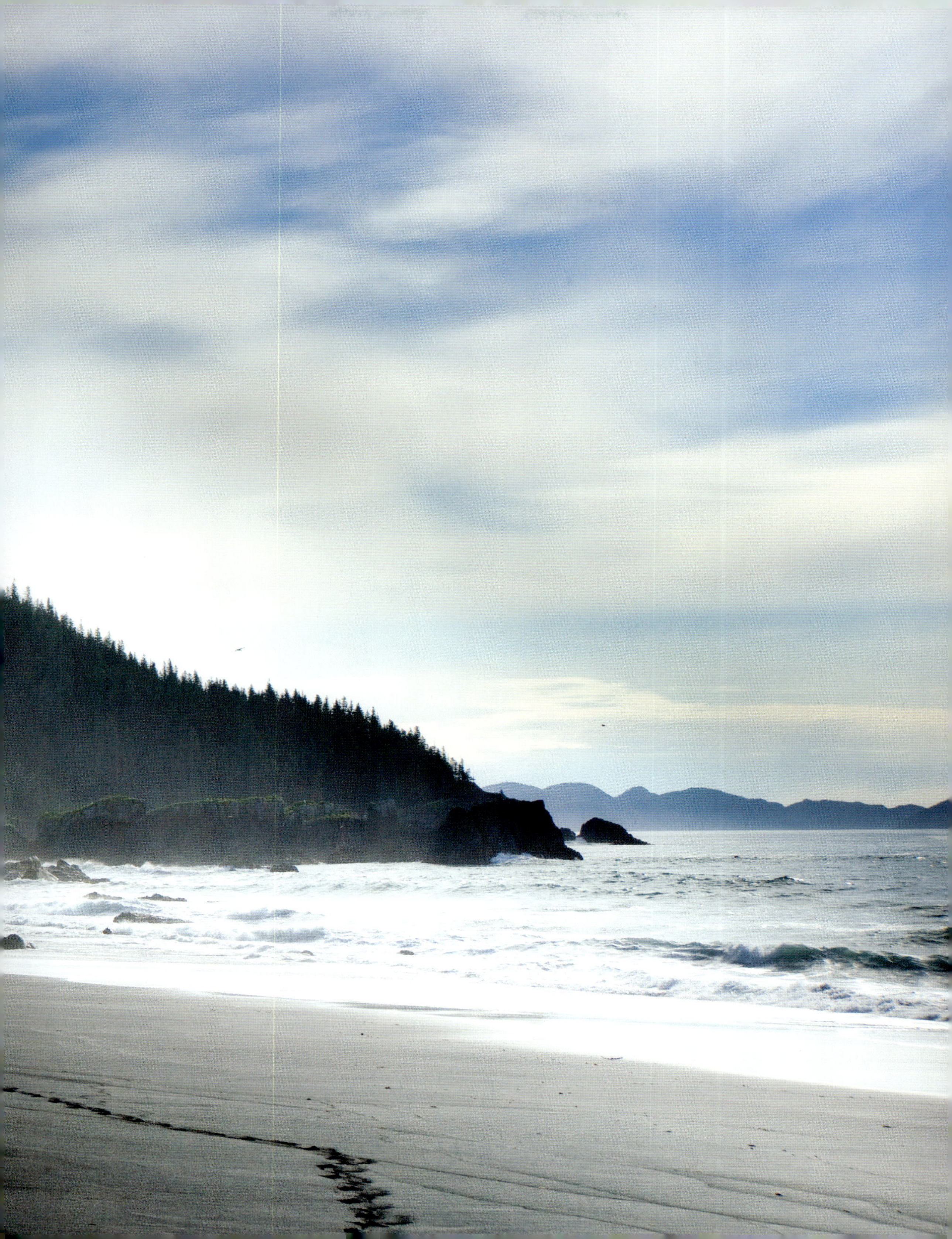

California
Coasting

→

Chris sent me a Facebook message asking if I wanted to do a surf road trip up the Central California coast with Michael Kew and Belinda Baggs. Belinda's one of my favorite longboarders, and I was a big fan of Chris's work, so I thought, *Why not?* I had camped in the area a few times and knew it was a sacred, special place. I was excited to check out some new spots (which we all agreed not to name).

It was April or May, before the June gloom, and I remember it being really dry and warm. There was one session that was completely glassy and sunny, without a single cloud in the sky. Belinda and I took turns catching little peelers and soaking up the mountain backdrop. It was so nice to have one-on-one girl time off the beaten path. That night, we went up to the very top of the ridge and watched the stars come in. We finally had a moment to unwind and talk about our day. We talked about life and traveling on the road. Chris did some time-lapses of us hanging out under the stars.

On our last day, just before sunset, Chris wanted to pull over at a little beach break on the side of the road. It didn't look like much, but we said, "Okay, let's just go for it. The lighting's really pretty." Despite the tiny waves, Chris managed to get this amazing photo of me cross-stepping against the sunset. That's the cool thing about photography. You just need that split second, that one frame, for everything to come together: the lighting, the body language, the camera position. You gotta let the artist do their thing and trust the process. It all pans out.

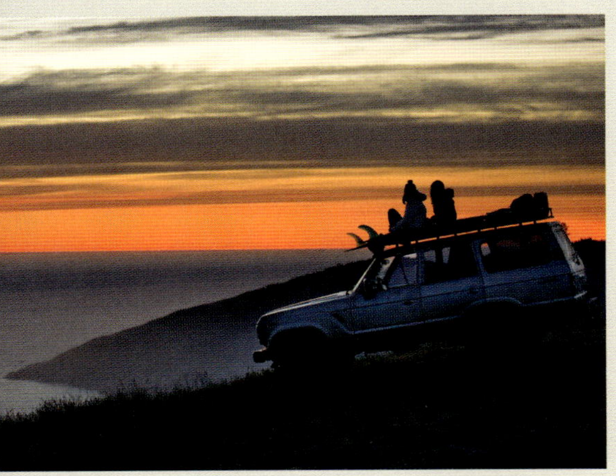

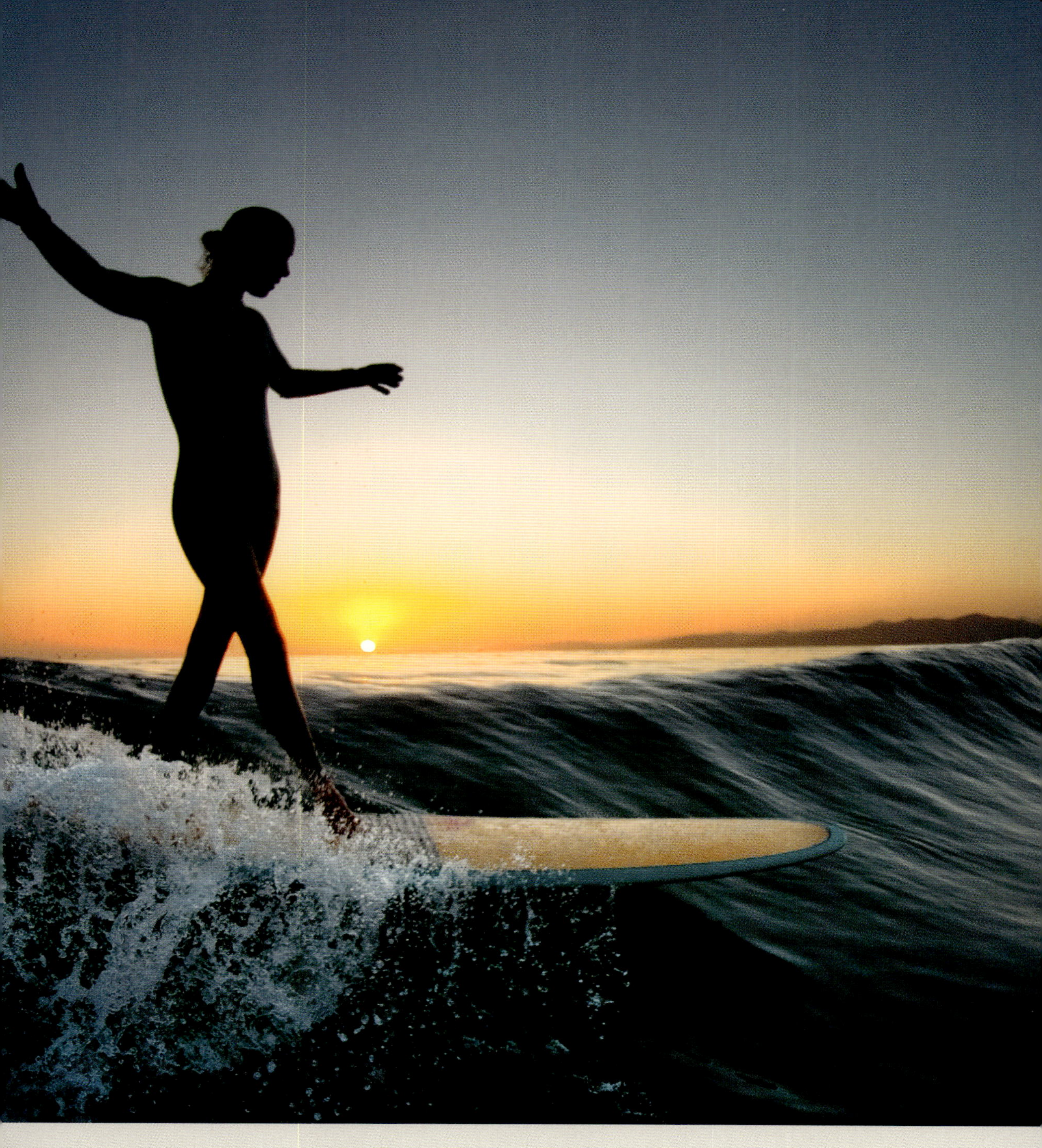
CHRIS BURKARD
WAYWARD

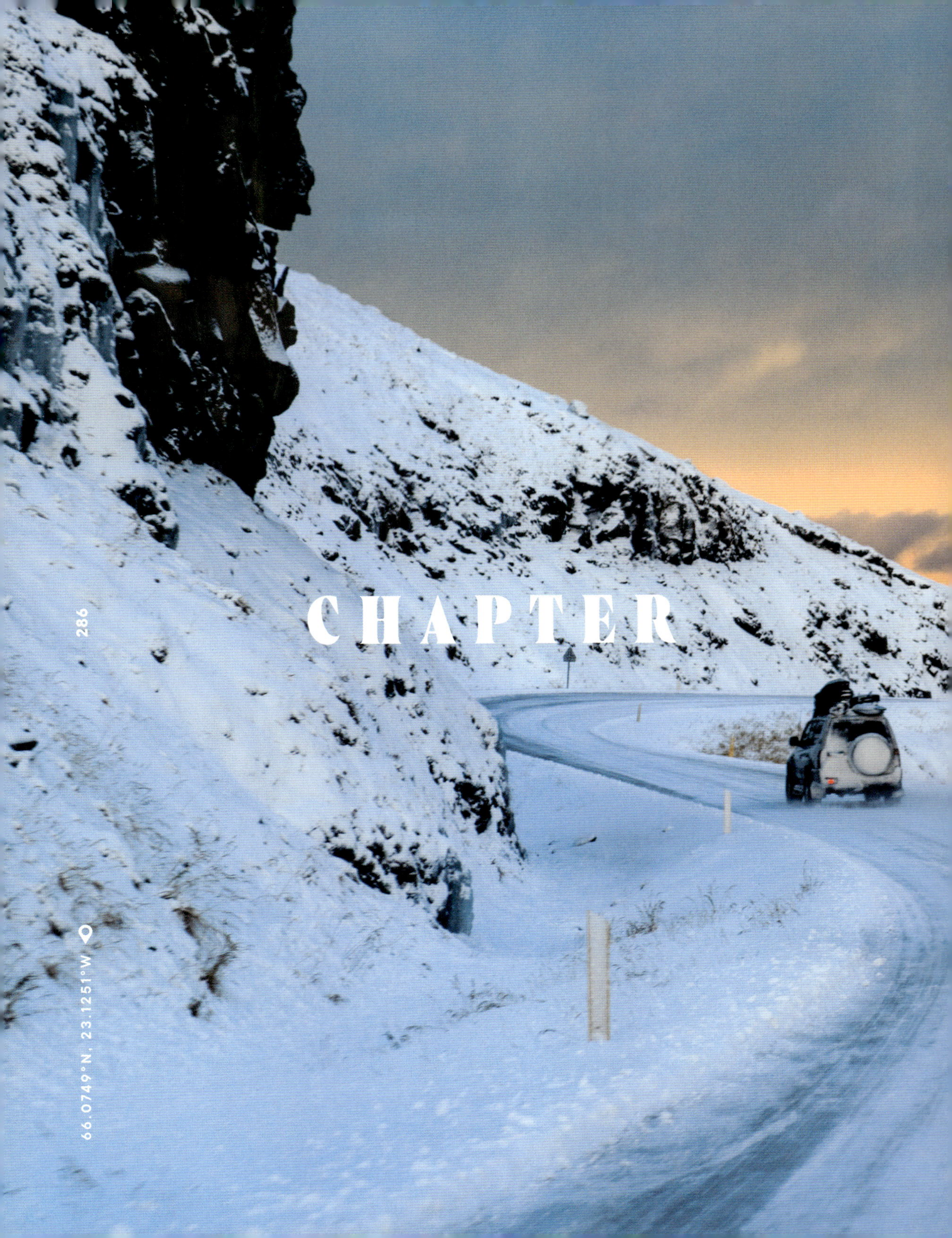

CHAPTER
286
66.0749°N, 23.1251°W

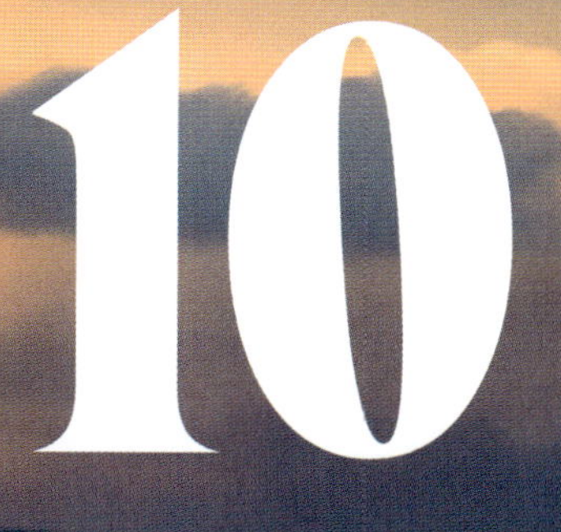

10

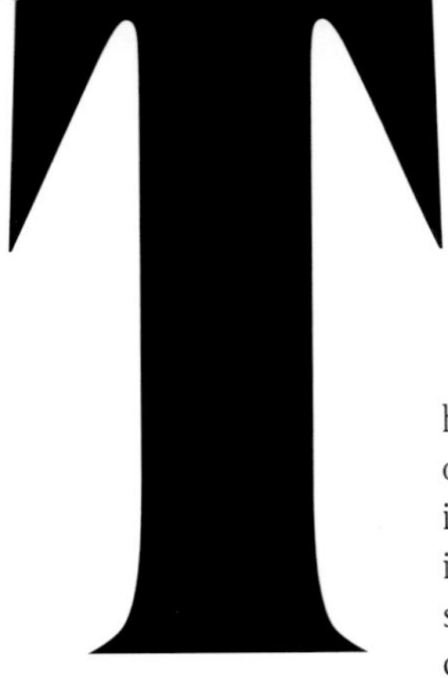

he week before Christmas of 2014, my family was decorating our tree at home without me. I was in Playa del Carmen, Mexico, looking over playback for a short video spot we were filming for a billion-dollar brand. It was the biggest commercial shoot I had ever been on. But I was simply a cog in the machine, just one person among a crew of sixty. The camera was pointed at two models in bathing suits seated on a red surfboard. They stared out at the ocean as if waiting for waves. But it was the Caribbean, so no, there wasn't any surf there.

Someone on the crew mused, "If the client wants a wave, we could just add it to the image in post-production."

I cringed, laughing to myself and thinking, *Oh, so that's all I needed to do all those years searching for perfect waves? Just put them in later using CGI or Photoshop?*

It's funny when you look back and realize certain years just blew by. I got swept away in the busyness of everything, caught up in the idea of success, and somehow along the way I had lost sight of what I had worked so hard to become. When you're moving at a frenzied pace, you don't have the time for self-reflection, and it was only during the months leading up to my TED talk—enduring hours of inadvertent therapy with Elizabeth—that I began to review my life and career. At that point it had become dominated by commercial work rather than the high-stakes expeditions I prided myself on.

In fact, it had been almost two years since my last cold-water adventure to the Aleutian Islands. In many ways that trip was the pinnacle for me. Surfer magazine's editor in chief, Brendon Thomas, even claimed this was the trip that changed his mind about what was possible in cold-water surf, concluding that our story was "probably the most remarkable surf adventure" of his tenure at Surfer magazine. I didn't know how I'd ever top that. Not knowing what was ahead, all I knew was that I longed to be the person shivering in those photos again, seeking out unridden waves at the ends of the earth.

It felt like fate when Ben Weiland and I finally connected on a phone call after being too busy to talk for months. We immediately started bouncing around ideas for a new project in Iceland.

While I always miss my wife and kids when I am away, I've never felt homesick for a place quite like I have for Iceland. It's the only place that has had a strong enough call to keep bringing me back time after time. Since my first transformative visit to Iceland in the spring of 2008, for the Men's Journal article about the surfer Timmy Turner, I knew I'd return often. The place was wild, free, and open, inviting a certain type of traveler to follow their heart as far as it would take them.

On the phone, Ben and I spoke at the rate of rapidly popping kernels; hundreds of potential story lines and possibilities exploded between us. Simply hearing Ben's voice reminded me of why I needed someone like him in my life—he was someone I could dream with. The last time we were in Iceland together we had fantasized about doing a boat trip to surf some remote, mythical waves that our Icelandic friends had hinted at. We knew exactly where we wanted to go and exactly who we wanted to go there with.

The anticipation of these adventures is almost the best part—the rush and excitement over what could be. Though I would once again have to consider the time away from my family. My wife had come to notice that I was at my best as a family man after returning from what she teasingly referred to as "another stupid adventure with your friends." I did indeed always return home happier, and we both knew I needed it. It would be my twenty-seventh trip to the country.

Iceland is never an easy place to surf, but doing so in the dead of winter is, by most accounts, insane. Blankets of snow transform familiar river valleys into indistinguishable monochrome landscapes. Blizzards can blast through without a moment's notice—closing roads, grounding planes, and stranding unsuspecting travelers for days. On the rare occasions when roads are open, driving takes double the time, since you're bracing for snowdrifts, falling rocks, and passing semitrucks that blind you with spray. Add in treacherous swells, below-freezing wind chill, twenty hours of darkness, and *risk* takes on a whole new meaning.

But after twenty-seven trips to Iceland, I had grown fond of the winter there, when the surf is at its most ferocious. The blush of sunrise blends into sunset. For hours of dusky blue, the sun never really rises above the horizon. Endless nights provide ample opportunities to view the elusive northern lights. Winter has always been the time I've felt most alive and connected to the elements.

Traveling in the middle of winter, I knew we would be relying heavily on our Icelandic friends to help navigate the challenging weather and dynamic conditions we soon would be facing. One of the first calls I made was to Erlendur Thor Magnusson, or Elli Thor, as I would come to know him.

I first met Elli during my sixth or seventh trip to Iceland, after coming across his stunning surf photography online. His photos had

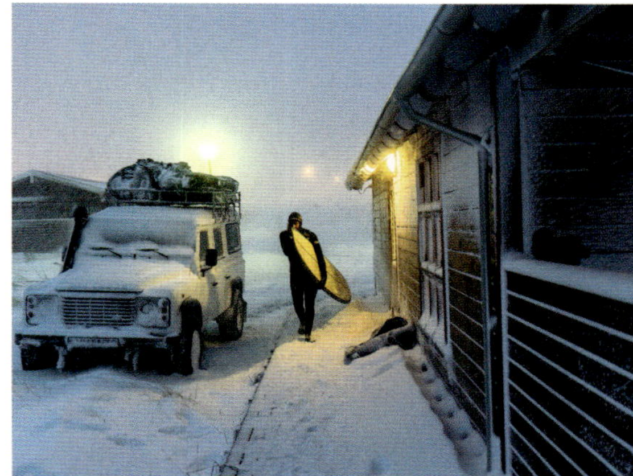

289

a soulful energy that highlighted his ability to capture even the quietest moments. It was obvious he was a silent observer of humans and nature; I immediately respected his craft. I knew there were a handful of local surfers in the country, but I was blown away when I discovered there was an actual surf photographer, who was crazy enough to enjoy the same perspectives I did. Except Elli lived this wild environment every day, while I only briefly enjoyed flings with its ruggedness. Much as I'd done with Ben seven years earlier, I cold-called Elli and asked if we could meet in person. Elli has a striking Viking resemblance and a beard I could only dream of growing. It was extremely rare for me to immediately open up to a stranger, but from the start, he felt like someone I had known forever. We have the same twisted love for cold water and moody beaches, as well as a tireless desire to hunt for waves. Elli and I were destined to be friends, and he has actually become a sort of brother in the years since I first met him.

On our first meeting we shared a long car ride to the northern tip of Iceland, spending most of the seven-hour drive in a constant flow of conversation. Like giddy schoolgirls, we were finishing each other's sentences, making the trip to Mývatn the fastest I'd ever experienced. When two photographers get together, conversation can easily be dominated by photo nerd dialogue, but with Elli, I just loved hearing his stories and talking about life.

Ben and I also invited Sam Hammer, the New Jersey storm surfer who had traveled with me on some of my most influential expeditions to Russia and Norway, as well as my first trip to Iceland in 2008. He had a new daughter on the way, so this would be his last adventure for a while. Next up was Timmy Reyes, a California ripper who lifts everyone up with his childlike stoke. He's surfed everywhere, including Mavericks and Jaws. The cheerful Floridian Justin Quintal rounded out our American talent in the water. I also brought Russell Holliday, who would be my right-hand man, assisting with photography and video.

Perhaps most important to the success of our trip were the other locals on our crew. Heiðar Logi Elíasson, Iceland's first and only professional surfer, has been advancing the sport beyond the sixty-sixth parallel since he was sixteen years old. Ingó Olsen is another

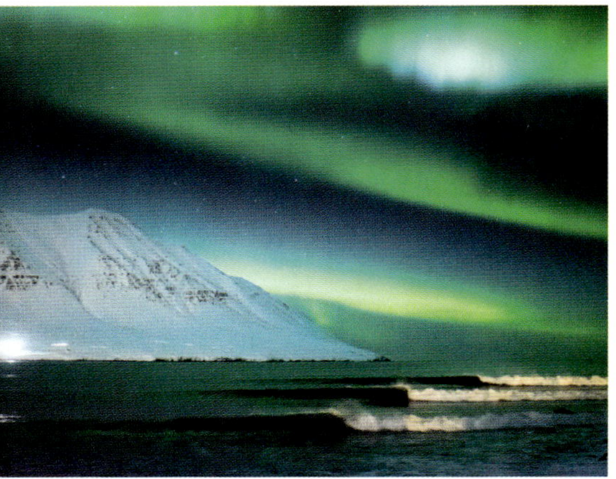

pioneer in these parts, who first found his feet snowboarding for Burton before becoming the surf-addicted founder of the adventure company Arctic Surfers.

I always hoped the people I brought to these wild places would learn to love it as I did. But instead of enticing surfers with empty promises of perfect waves like I used to, I often found brutal honesty was a more successful tactic when gathering the right crew. I never promised world-class waves when I invited people on an unpredictable Arctic surf hunt, but I did guarantee them an adventure they would never forget.

Sure enough, in the countless times I'd visited Iceland, I had never experienced the road conditions we encountered on our way to Ísafjörður and our waiting boat. We battled gusts of snow, sleet, and ice through the dark journey, white-knuckling and willing ourselves to just make it safely. That drive dampened our excitement and sobered us back to the seriousness of our reality.

Finally, we could see our sailboat, the *Aurora*, docked in the harbor, waiting for our arrival. But all well-laid plans flew out the window as soon as our caravan of surfers caught sight of the cresting waves. I called our captain, Siggi, to tell him we would be late. "It's your time to choose to do with what you want," he responded. "Just remember, weather here changes quickly."

That day we ended up scoring what the local surfers called the best waves they had ever experienced in the Arctic. Girthy overhead barrels spiraled along the highway like we were in frozen Western Australia. And to our knowledge, this spot had never been surfed. Everyone surfed until the last drop of sunlight. After braving the savage slab on the side of the highway, which split three surfboards in the span of an hour, we had our name for the wave we had just surfed: "The Sledgehammer."

On our way back to the harbor there was a lot of discussion among the crew about why we were abandoning insane waves for an uncertain excursion out to sea. But the Icelanders understood our insistence. Heiðar, Ingó, and Elli had fantasized about surfing in the far northwest of Iceland for years, imagining crystal clear tubes peeling off sea cliffs that were only accessible by boat. The conditions surfers look for are the same ones sea captains avoid, and we had found the only skipper we could trust to take us there in winter—when most people consider the place a graveyard, not a playground.

"Just don't forget it's midwinter in Iceland, and anything can happen," Captain Siggi warned. "Icelandic seas can be really bad. Things can change very quickly."

The *Aurora* rolled back and forth with the swell. Nine of us were huddled around a small table in the galley, seated beneath black-and-white sailing photos, beat-up wooden skis, and a two-hundred-year-old shotgun. Siggi—Captain Sigurdur Jónsson—had our full attention. A flame danced inside an antique oil lamp, casting a warm glow across

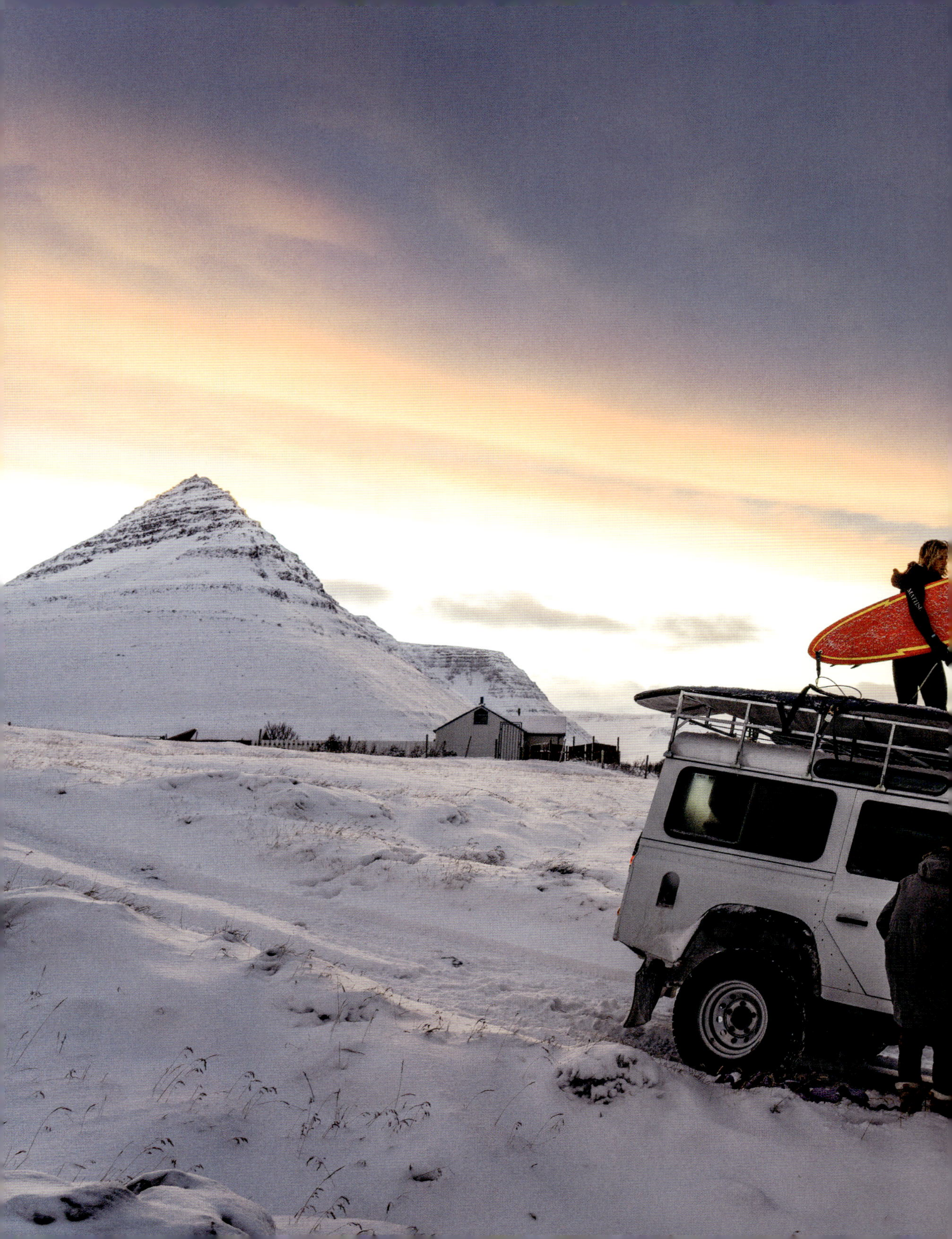

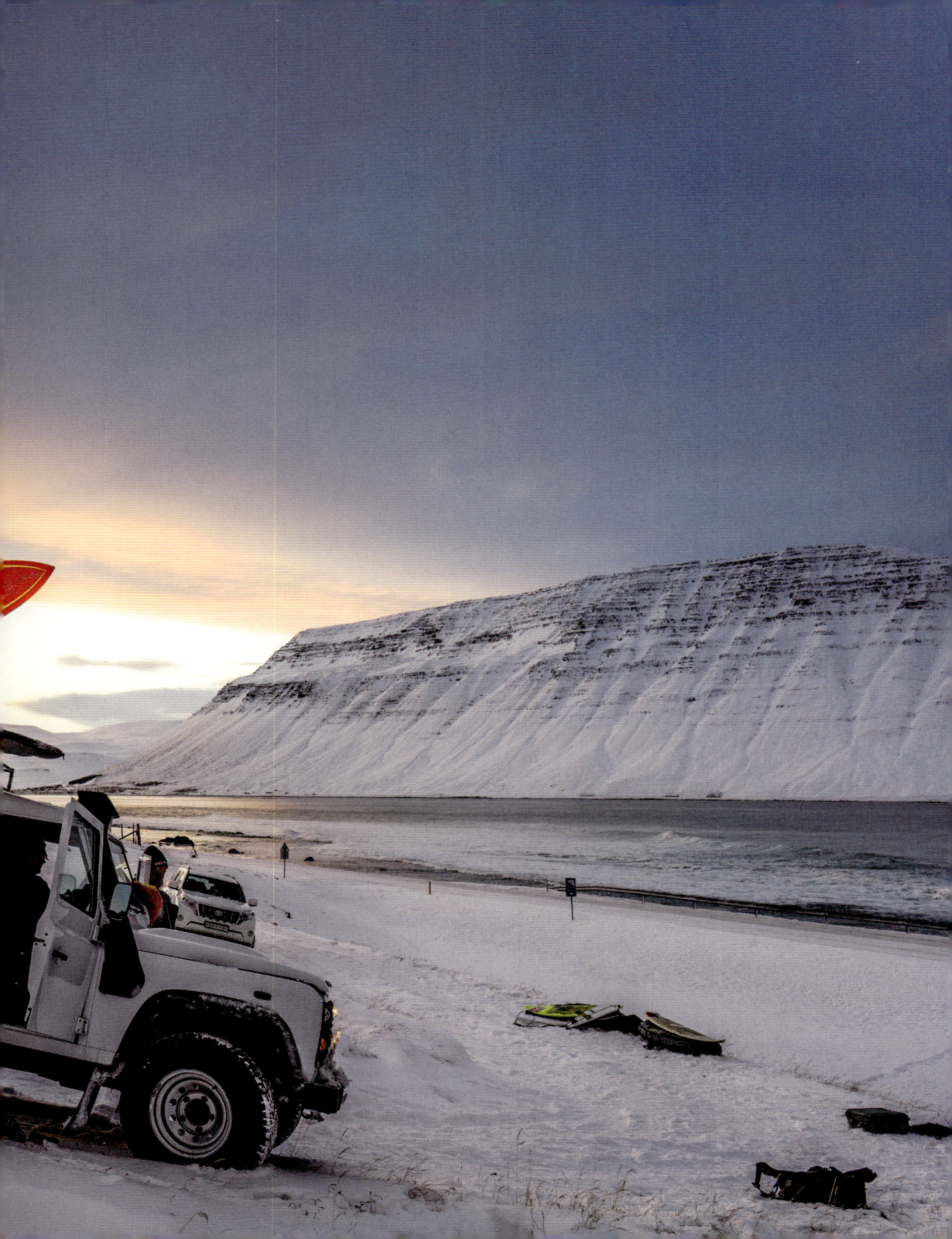

the table. Mugs of tea slid from port to starboard. Our eyes followed Siggi's index finger across a laminated map.

"There's surf at these points," he said, marking imaginary dots on the eastern spikes of Hornstrandir Nature Reserve, the northwestern crest of Iceland that juts up from the Westfjords, which reach out of the Arctic island like a mangled hand.

Despite not publishing in Surfer for a while, I was still a staff photographer and felt the need to produce something worthwhile for them. The magazine assigned us a feature as well as a short film. Ben and I wanted to document the story of Captain Siggi, a seafaring legend with qualities that any filmmaker would dream to highlight in the hero of their story. I first heard about Siggi through backcountry skiers Brody Leven and Camilla Edwards, as well as through another talented Icelandic photographer named Haukur Sigurðsson—who just so happened to be his son. Even legendary surfer Mark "Doc" Renneker had traveled with Siggi on a two-week survey of eastern Greenland, searching for mythical waves. Once Siggi was on my radar, he seemed to keep popping up in conversations.

We thought sharing the perspective of this iconic sea captain might help our audience connect with this wild place on a deeper level. He would easily provide depth and a backbone to the story we had hoped to tell. Surf films have evolved over the years, from hard-core tight action montages to soulful stories of personal transformations that happen on wave-hunting expeditions. There was no guarantee we would score waves where we were headed, but we knew we could structure something meaningful with Siggi at the heart of our adventure.

After finally departing from the dock, we took an overnight crossing and woke up off the coast of the Hornstrandir Nature Reserve, a rhinoceros-shaped landmass of tundra, glacier, and upland walled in by deep fjords and razor-sharp cliffs. It's completely uninhabited, except for a teeming population of seabirds that includes puffin and one of the world's largest packs of Arctic fox. At sea level, there are pods of dolphins, seals, and several species of whale that exist just below the surface. Polar bears have even been known to occasionally float over on Greenland ice drifts.

But that's not what we were looking at from the ice-encrusted railings of Aurora. As we began to stir below deck that morning, we could feel the gentle rolling of the swell beneath us, ramping up our anticipation with every sway. When the sun started to rise, we spotted what we were hoping for as a streak of spray began feathering off the silver sea at the base of a sea cliff just ahead of us.

"There's something that appears to be a wave," Justin said through the fur of his hooded jacket.

"There's definitely a point down there," Heiðar confirmed, with mounting excitement.

The closer we got to shore, the clearer we could see the wave: a smooth left-hander

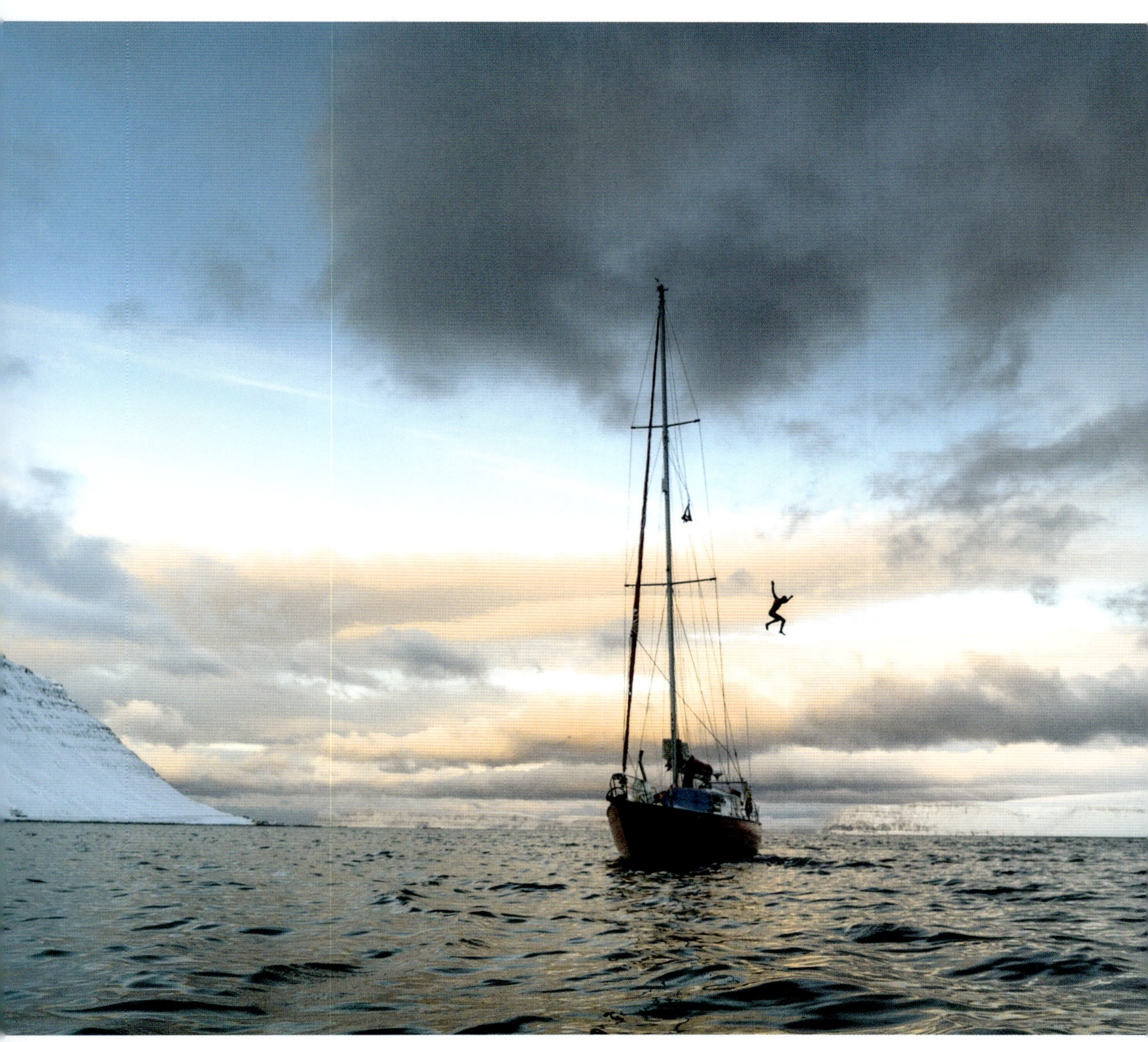

CHRIS BURKARD

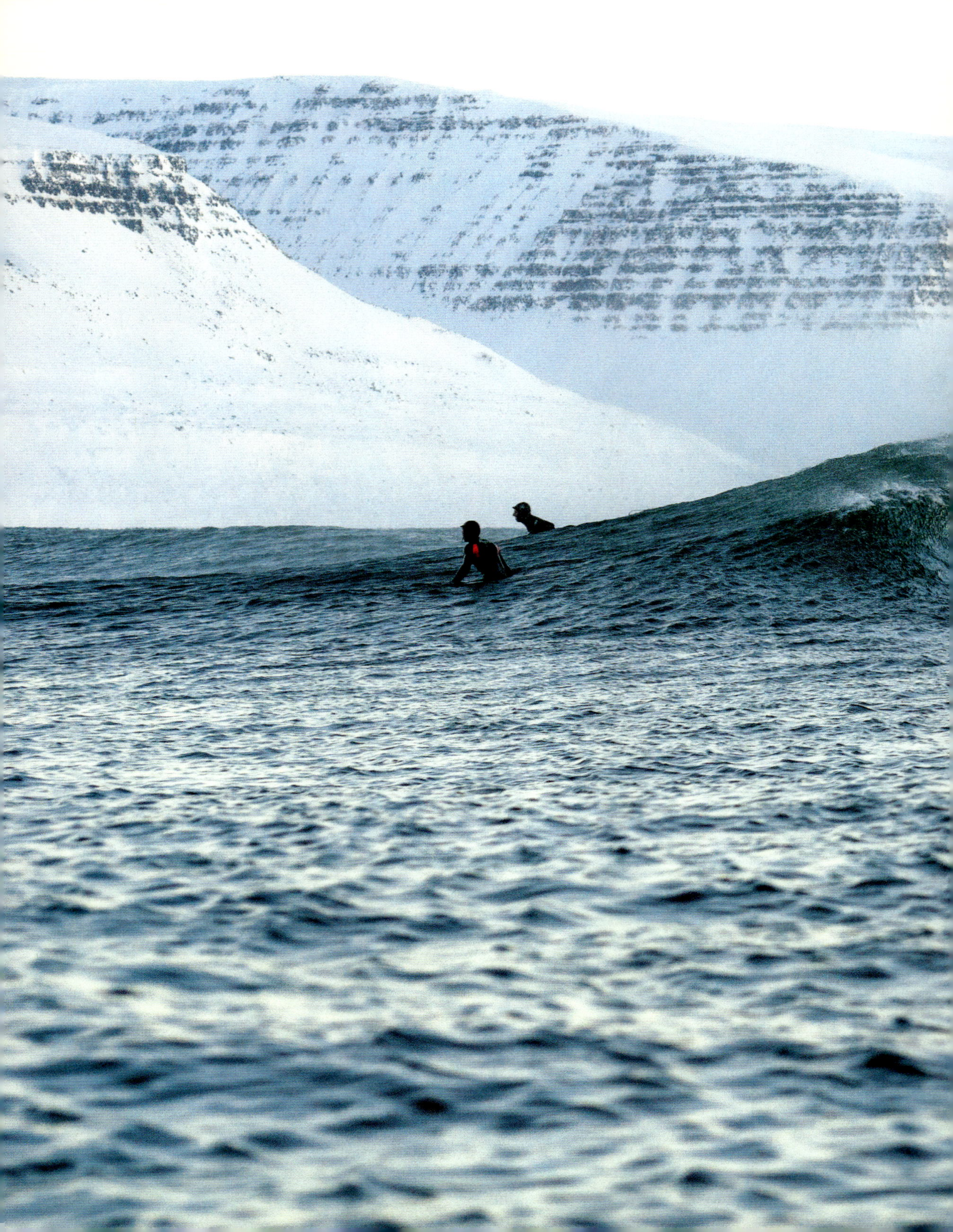

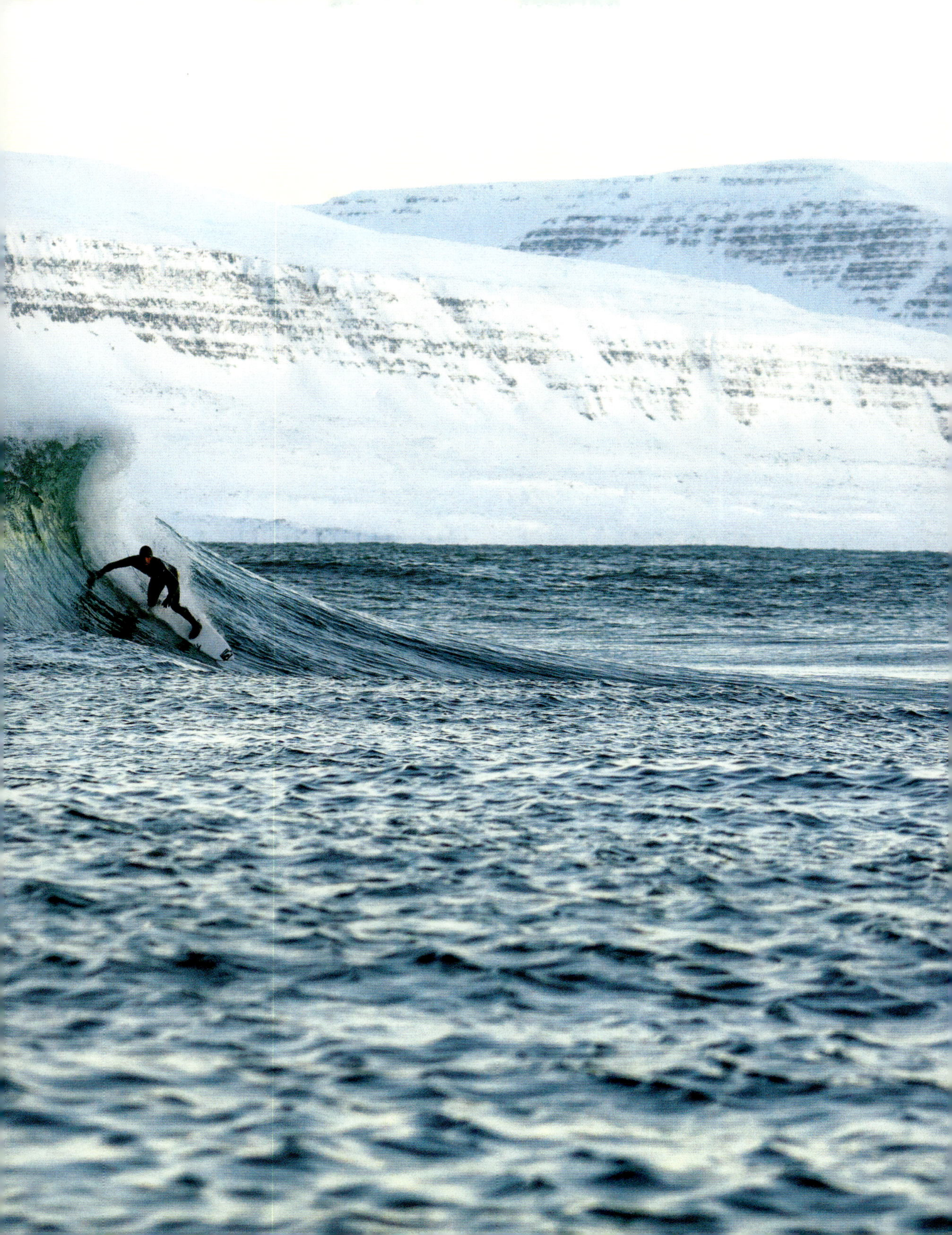

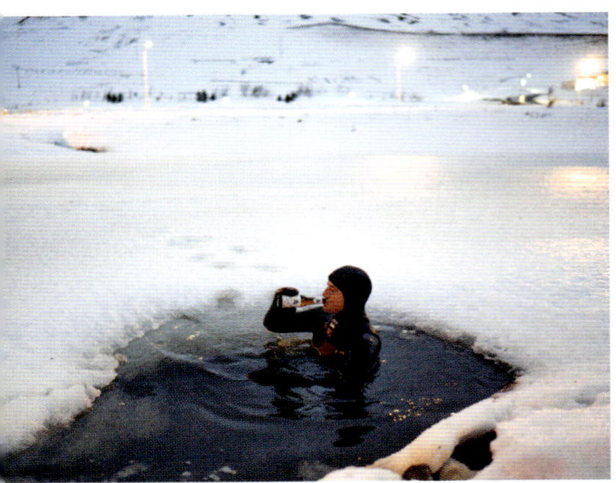

trimming neatly along a bouldery bottom. Russ, Ben, and I tried to quickly load up a Zodiac inflatable boat, preparing to descend upon the wave that was calling to us.

Meanwhile, Siggi was in his command center, listening intently to the local meteorological office for a weather update. While everyone was on deck suiting up to surf and frothing about the possibilities, I went to get an update from Siggi. Walking into the captain's command station, I could hear reports of an ominous incoming storm as Siggi played and replayed its predictions.

I knew my answer even before I asked. "Do we have time to just jump out for a quick twenty-minute session? We've come all this way . . ."

"There's a severe storm coming. It's supposed to hit pretty quickly," Siggi said with calm resolution. Siggi and I matched in our intensities as we both prioritized our responsibilities; I, of course, attempted to persuade him for some wiggle room. His commanding NO was clear. There was sternness in his ice-blue eyes and experience written in his faint wrinkle lines. I knew straightaway that none of my Jedi mind tricks would convince him to let us stay, not even to catch a single wave.

I broke the news: "Guys, we can't go out, we have to turn the *Aurora* around. Siggi wants to be safely tied up in the dock of Ísafjörður before a massive storm hits."

Often when I'm orchestrating a trip, I feel massive amounts of responsibility to ensure everyone's success and happiness. I am the one juggling all the moving parts, making sure they are well-oiled and cared for, and when there's a break in the system, that's usually when my responsibility is acknowledged. If an experience is fruitful, it was luck; if something goes wrong, it's because I didn't prepare for it.

A small part of me died inside as sails started flapping and we raced the dark clouds back to port. They seemed to be moving in on us like an avalanche, but all I could think about was that this trip was finally the one where I may have bit off more than I could chew. "You have to realize you are never in charge," Siggi said to us. "Nature is in charge. But when you submit to her, amazing things can happen." I trusted Siggi and knew that if he was bringing us back, there must have been something huge looming on the horizon.

When we returned to the harbor, the water's surface had frozen into sheets and scales. The temperature must have dropped drastically during our thirty hours away. An icebreaker had to come help carve a path back to Siggi's slip. Uneasiness hovered over us as we tied up the Aurora and unloaded our gear. The air was bitter cold and dead still, holding boat flags limp. But fifteen minutes after we docked, the wind started howling. The promised blizzard turned on as if by the flip of a switch at exactly the moment the meteorological office predicted: 3:15 P.M.

We left the dock and drove our convoy of white SUVs to a cafe in Ísafjörður to check the weather and devise a Plan B. Siggi advised staying in town for the night, but I was worried the highway tunnels might get snowed in and we'd be stuck there for days. I felt like we needed to get moving—and fast. When we sat down at the café and pulled up the weather page, Elli's eyes widened.

"I've never seen these colors before! These are new," he said. "They've added to the scale to accommodate how big the storm is."

That couldn't be right. I looked at the screen and saw a heat map of pink-and-purple streaks. Wind speeds were predicted at 100 to 160 miles per hour. Before I could even process what was imminently headed our way, a TV in the corner of the restaurant caught my attention as it warned people to prepare their homes and boats for a beating. It said the avalanche warning had been raised to the highest level.

"I've never seen anything like this in my life," Ingó said. "The size will make all kinds of spots light up!" he added with excitement.

The Icelanders' eagerness fueled my motivation. If they were willing to go, I was ready to ride into battle with them. There was an area Elli thought might be good once the storm organized itself into waves, but it required a seven-hour journey doubling back the way we had just come, over mountain passes and along sheer cliffs known for avalanches. Yet, it actually didn't take much convincing to leave once we all heard what could be waiting for us.

Ben and I made the final call to continue on, and I took comfort in our cumulative knowledge of the area and the fact that the Icelanders would be leading the way. Everything in life is a calculated risk, and in this case the possible rewards won out. But I'm not gonna lie; I was nervous.

After making a quick phone call to tell Brea I would be out of service for a few hours, we made a final stop at the grocery store, which only intensified our sense of urgency. The place was jammed with frenzied shoppers all rushing to secure their supplies. I watched as locals used their arms to sweep entire shelves full of cans into their shopping carts. As we headed out of town, we noticed we were the only ones going northbound. Everyone else was driving west to their homes to hunker down for the impending apocalypse.

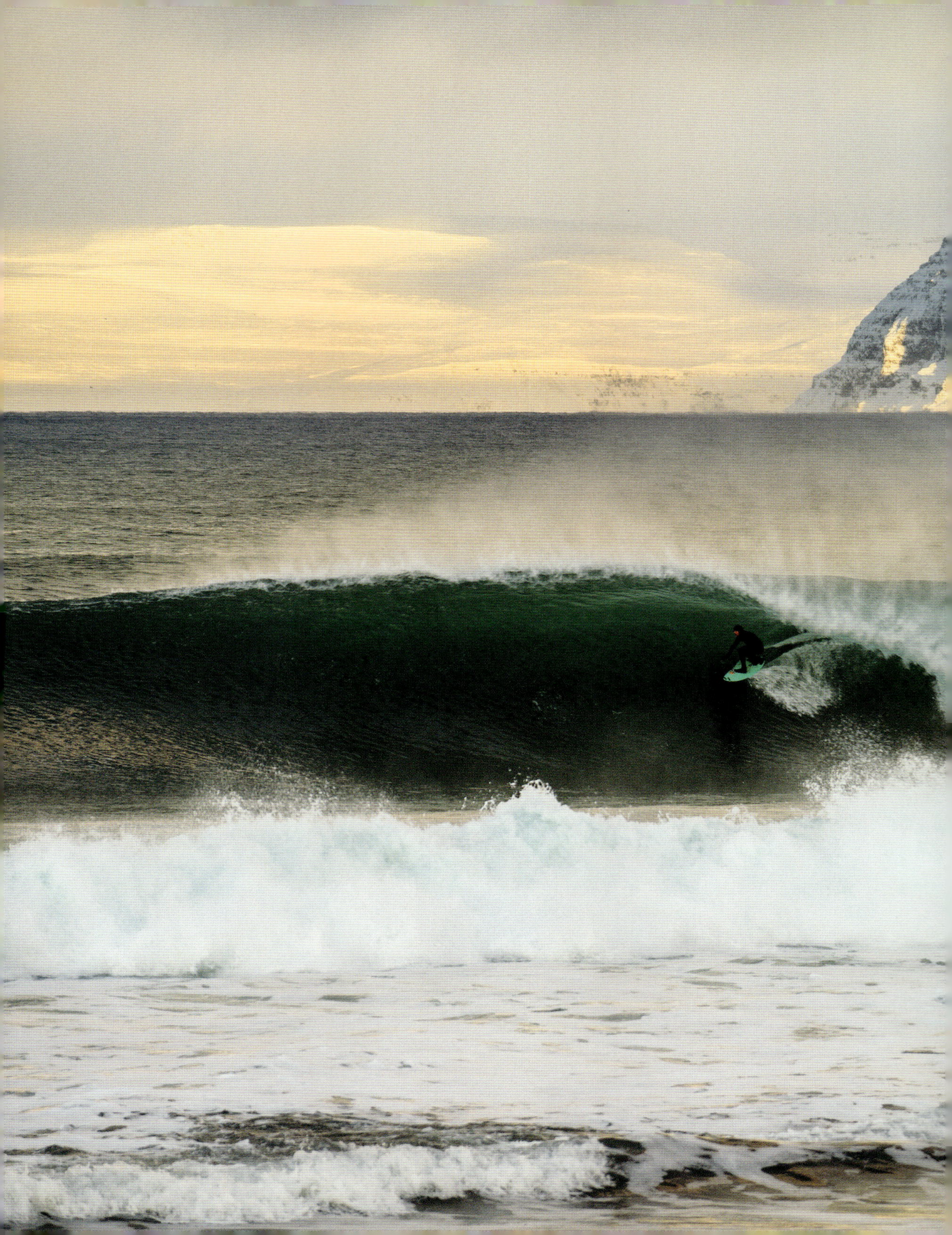

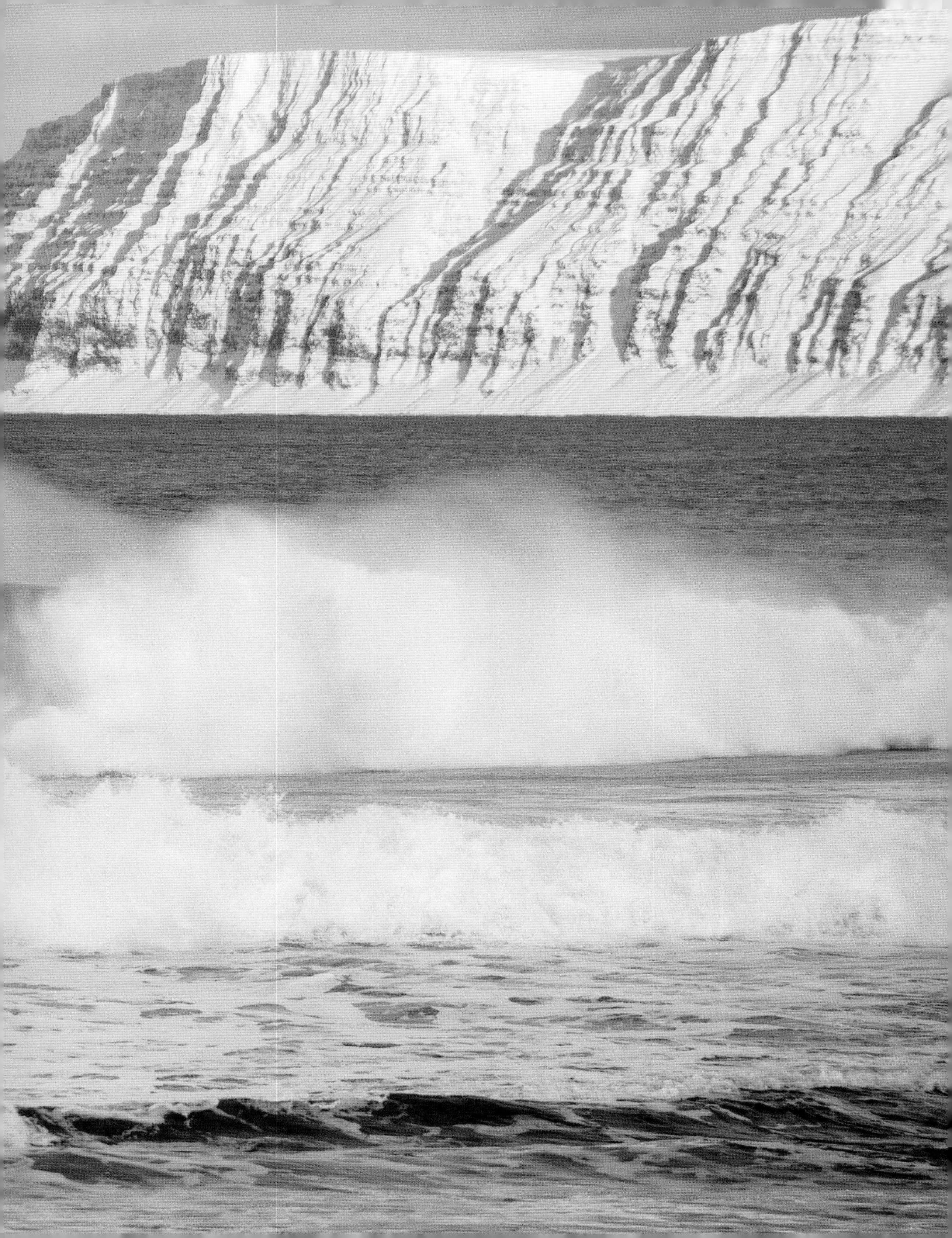

The Icelanders slowly led our convoy up a winding mountain pass. Russ, Ben, and I took the tail end behind Sam, Justin, and Timmy, who plowed a path through thick flurries in their white Defender. A succession of cars had skidded off the road to be engulfed by the storm. It was as if the graveyard of sidelined vehicles were warning us to turn around, but at this point, we had already gone so far that it was safer to keep pushing. There was no guarantee that the route behind us was still passable anyway, so we would be running the risk of being stranded in the middle of the highway if we got stuck trying to head back. A passing semitruck hurled a giant blast against our windshield, leaving us barreled by snow. "Holy shit!" Russ shouted, tightening his grip on the steering wheel.

A mini avalanche then fell from the mountain and slid in front of Elli's rig, which was leading us. Brake lights brightened, the Land Rover slowed, and the guys' tires lost traction as they tried to push through four feet of snow. Our two other cars crawled and spun into the exact same position: stuck. We were somewhere between Ísafjörður and the Troll Peninsula, on a narrow strip of highway, straddling an unstable mountain and a wind-battered drop-off to the sea. Not an ideal place to be sitting ducks.

Our car sat silently inside as the wind roared around us. Unsure of what lay ahead, all I knew was that we couldn't stay here. We had to try to dig ourselves out. I systematically wrapped myself in every layer of clothing I had, pumping myself up to prepare for the cold with each zip of my jacket. In unison, we opened the doors and got blasted by eighty- to hundred-mile-an-hour winds. It was immediate chaos as our headlamps and headlights illuminated horizontal sleet. We shielded our faces with forearms and walked in a slow-motion procession to the car in front of us. Everyone looked like Abominable Snowmen, making it impossible to identify who was who, except for the briefest of moments when I peered out from under my arm and locked eyes with Heiðar. What I saw there was a hesitation that made me worry. Not having time to analyze, I simply yelled over the gale, "We need to do this and get everyone moving!"

Within seconds, Heiðar appeared with a shovel, and we broke off into a frenzy of digging, clearing, rocking, and pushing—starting with the Icelanders' Land Cruiser, which had the highest clearance. Russ and Sam worked on the front tires, while the rest of us convened at the back, ready to push.

"Three, two, one!" I shouted.

We rammed our bodies against the car and unleashed our most primal grunts. Knowing we didn't have enough strength or leverage, I looked up and saw Ben doing what any good filmmaker would do: capturing the whole scene on camera.

"Dude! Right now? Really??" I yelled over the screeching wind.

I still kick myself for forcing him to join us, now knowing that he was capturing some of the most compelling footage of our fiasco. But with Ben by our side, we pushed three more times with increasing intensity, and on our fourth attempt, the car broke loose. Without instruction, we repeated the same maneuver on the second Land Rover and then the third. We all knew what getting stuck in a bad blizzard might mean, freezing and exposed with little to no supplies, but nobody needed to say that. We put all our nerves and adrenaline into the task at hand, performing a self-rescue mission with tactical precision.

Once back on the road, we realized that the farther we went, the worse the conditions became. When I glanced in the rearview mirror, I saw snow blowing so hard that the tire tracks immediately disappeared under a sheet of white behind us. As we continued, we got stuck three more times and mastered our newly learned extraction techniques to choreograph a safe escape.

After fourteen hours on the road, on a route that was supposed to take half the time, we finally arrived at a cabin that was closed for the winter but that Elli had access to. The power was out, but that was the least of our concerns. We made it in one piece. We could sleep. Physically, but even more emotionally drained, we were all grateful to be out of our cars and into the safety of insulated walls.

After a blissful ten hours of sleep, we laid nestled in the refuge of the cabin, wrapped in flannel blankets and still dressed in our clothes from the night before. We all awoke relieved, and almost not believing what we had endured. We started to research road conditions from our phones. The storm had closed the highway in both directions. We wouldn't be going anywhere anytime soon.

Day one in our little cabin haven was a welcome respite from the road. With the power still out, we dined on gas station snacks and even enjoyed a snowball fight. The next day the power returned. On the news, we learned that the storm we had been traveling through wasn't just any storm—it was the worst storm that Iceland had seen in twenty-five years. Incredibly, no deaths or injuries had been reported.

As daylight descended on our third day holed up in a place far too small to contain nine hyperactive men, cabin fever set in. We were restless, uncertain of our options, and it was time to make some tough decisions. Should we stay and see this thing through,

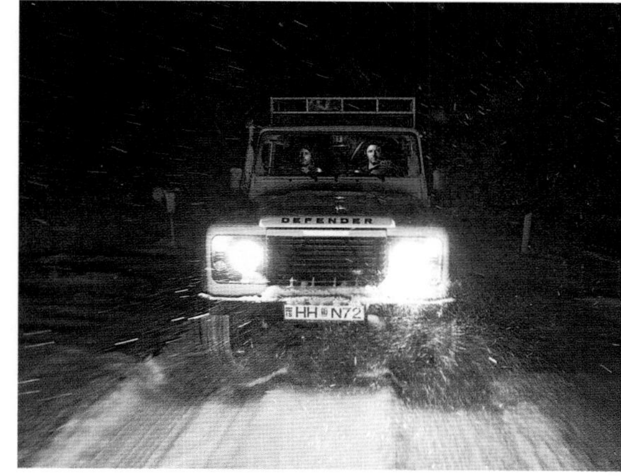

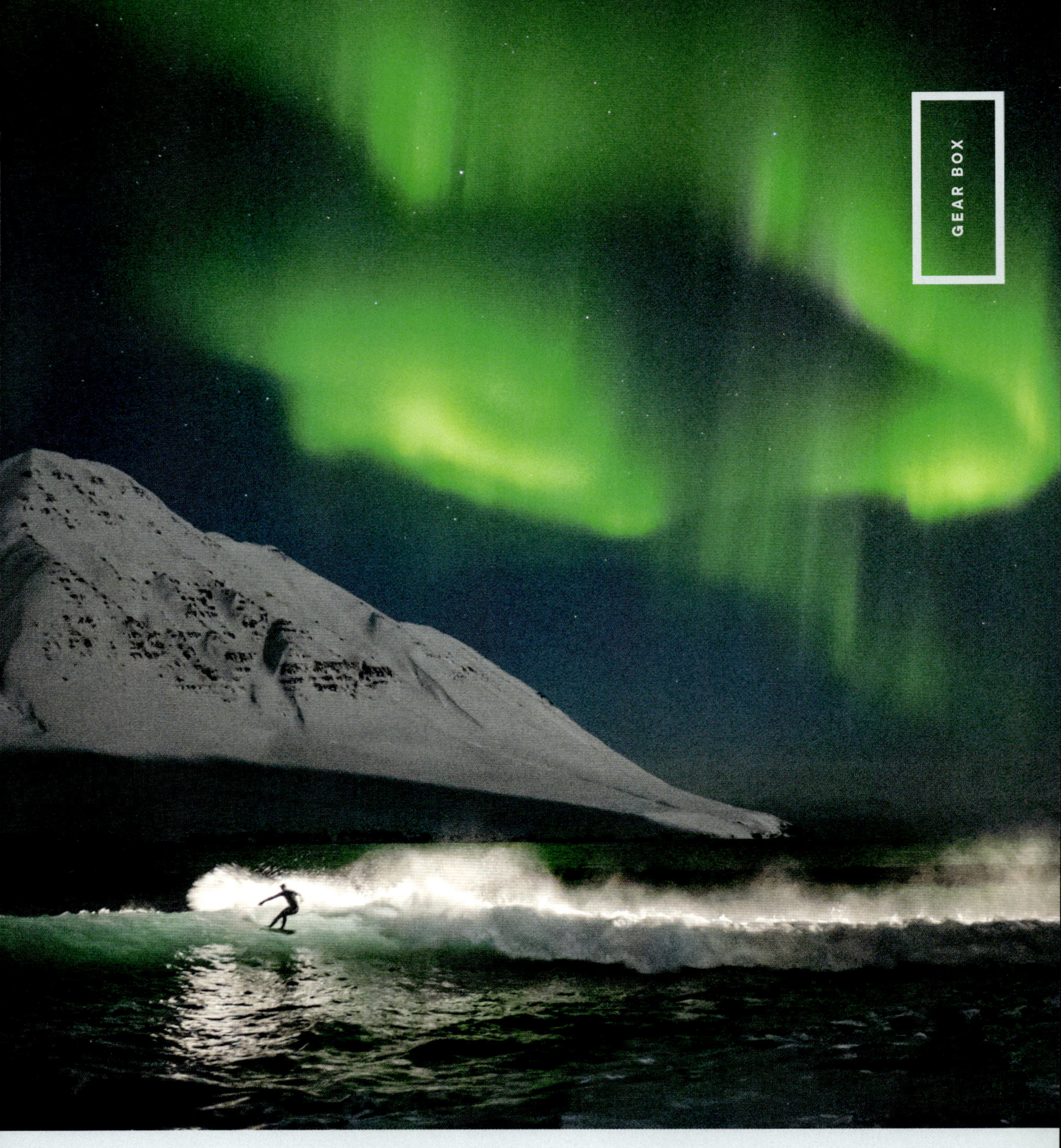
GEAR BOX

Lights of Legends

→ **It's these lights that keep me coming back to** the Arctic. At this point I've been to Iceland more than forty times, and this spectacle—the aurora borealis, as it's called in the north—is one of the main reasons I still feel so drawn to this small island nation. Of course, the people and landscapes lure me back, too, but standing beneath this natural phenomenon is a spiritual experience no matter what your faith is. The first time I witnessed them, along the south coast of Iceland, sleeping on a beach near a campfire, it shook me to my very core. The world I knew was all of a sudden different as I watched something as stable as the night sky take shape and move. It felt . . . out-of-body. A small part of me was even scared for a moment.

In scientific terms, auroras are formed when charged particles are released by the sun, either during eruptions or in an event known as solar wind, which blows five hundred thousand to a million miles per hour. After a couple of days, these particles reach the Earth, where they are caught in its magnetic field, which is strongest at the North and South Poles. The collisions between charged particles and the gasses in our atmosphere result in bursts of light, called photons. An interaction with nitrogen makes the photons gleam pink and purple; oxygen turns them neon green.

But science can go only so far in describing these magical lights. Because of their lively dancing motion, they've long represented the souls of ancestors, and even children, in many cultures around the world. The east Greenland Inuit people believe the aurora borealis reflects the spirits of children who died at birth and are now dancing and spinning in the heavens. In other cultures, the whistling, crackling, and hissing noises that some people claim to hear are just the sounds of our ancestors playing a celestial ball game.

When photographing the northern lights, it's important to use a camera that can handle a high ISO. Another good option is a prime lens with a wide-open aperture, such as Sony's 35-millimeter f1.4. Sony's manual focus assist is also helpful when trying to achieve clarity, allowing you to zoom in and manually adjust the focus ring for the stars in the background. The hardest setting to dial in is the shutter speed, especially when photographing surfers or some other movement amid the aurora. The fastest we could shoot surfing was 1/25th to 1/40th of a second, depending on ambient light, such as the presence of the moon.

If it's your first aurora sighting, I strongly suggest simply taking in the mystical experience without trying to photograph it at all. If you're anything like me, you probably seek outdoor experiences that make you feel small. Well, knowing that auroras are created by particles shot all the way from the sun makes you feel just about as small as you can imagine. Their energy is similar to wave energy, which travels across oceans before releasing the perfect spirals we see from the beach. In the words of our Icelandic captain, Siggi: Auroras are "pointless beauty and performance." Just like surfing. —C.B.

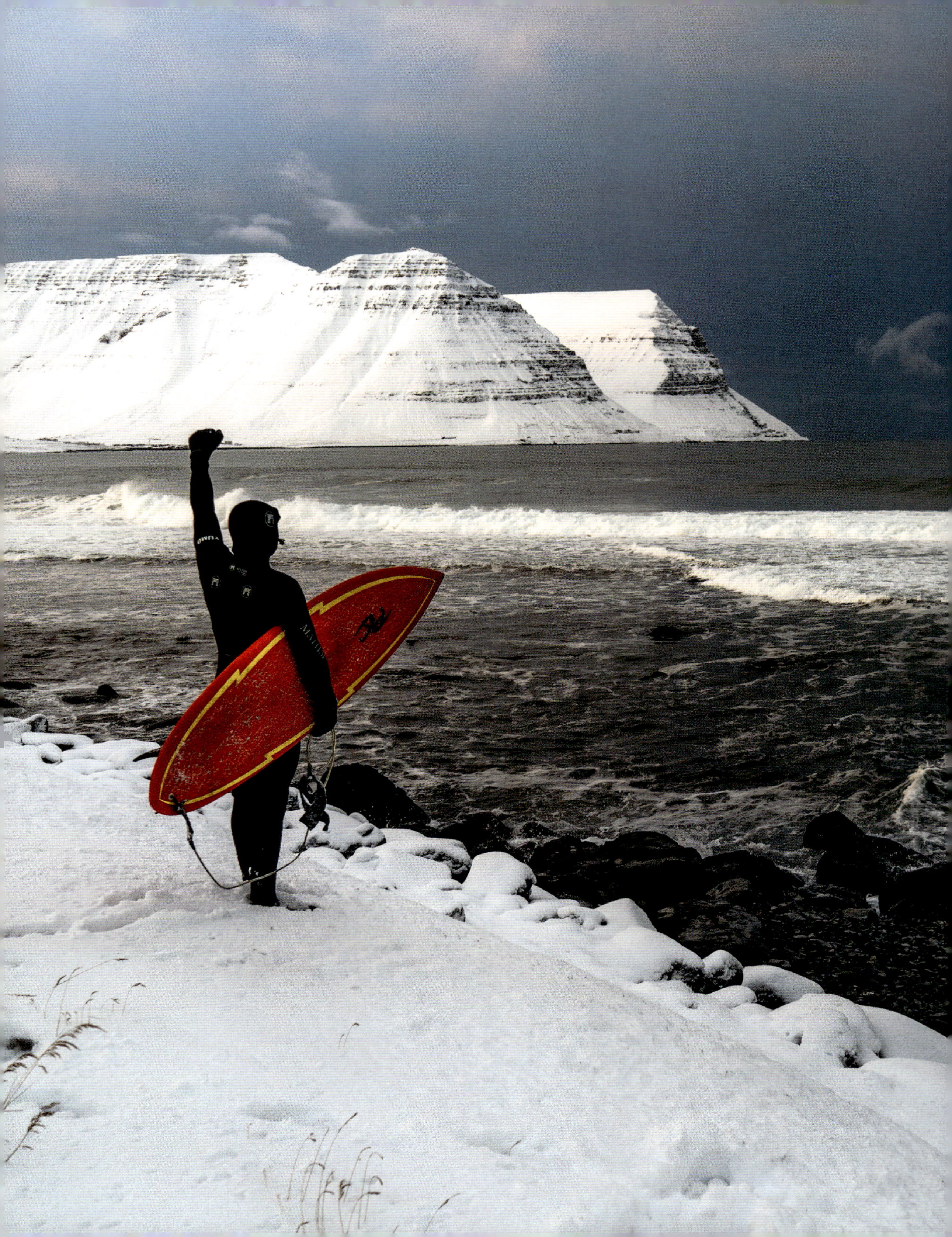

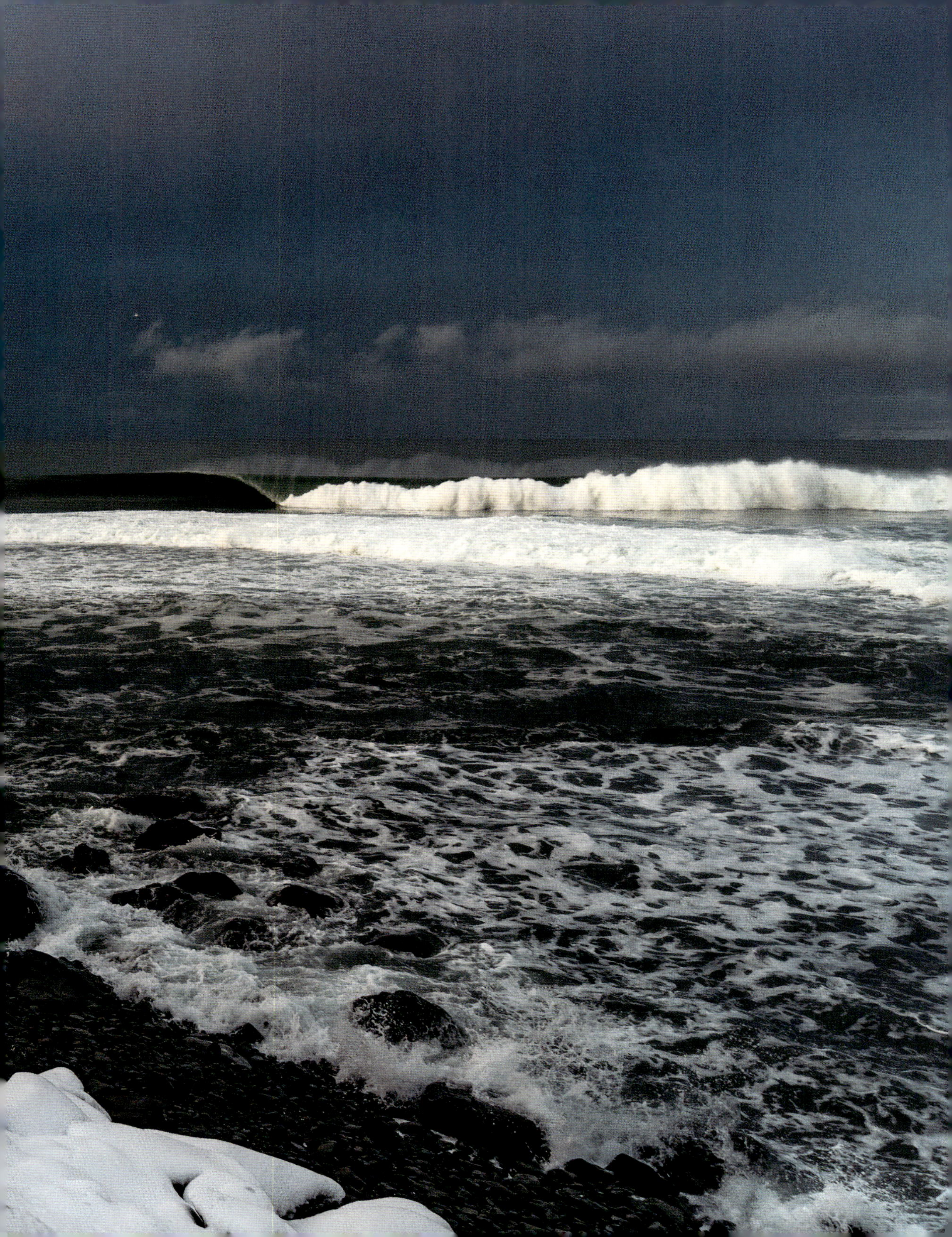

or should we go home? Our scheduled flights were departing the next day out of Keflavík Airport. If we were planning to make them, we would have to leave soon. On the other hand, the Icelanders knew that some of the best swells there arrive on the back sides of big storms, and it felt like we still had unfinished business.

In the midst of our debate, images flashed across our TV screen showing a car smashed by an airborne fence; homes with roofs ripped off; and downed power lines, four hundred in all. The severity of this storm and the carnage that was left in its path were discouraging all of us from staying. But just as I was accepting that our trip was over, the news moved on to updated road conditions. Snowplows had cleared the way to the coast, and the path was laid open before us. We had all the information we needed and now it was time to cast votes. Everyone chose to stay, effectively agreeing that they believed in this mission and what we were trying to accomplish just as much as I did.

When we emerged from the tunnel that led to our northern destination, it was late. But we could still see the glimmer of a point break through the fading light. A procession of swell lines guided us into the fjord. We parked our cars at the edge of the water where freezing air made the ocean smoke. It was night, but the electric-orange gleam of town helped us see the point and the right-hand waves reeling toward a frozen mountain.

Faint green brushstrokes began to appear in the sky: the northern lights.

"Do you think it's bright enough to see out there?" Justin asked.

He and I had talked about trying to surf under the northern lights for years. On our earliest trip together we traveled to the Faroe Islands, where I was with him for his first experience seeing the aurora borealis. Blown away by the scene displayed in front of him, he begged me to take a portrait of him standing under its beauty. The photo immortalized that moment forever and spurred our dream to one day shoot him surfing under the dancing lights. But the swell and aurora had never quite lined up, not to mention that there wasn't equipment capable of capturing that type of low-lit scene at the time.

It's rare to see the northern lights as low on the horizon as they were that night, let alone over the ocean. But there they were, reflecting off white sea spray like fireworks. My Sony a7SII could just pick up the spearmint swirls.

"It actually might happen here," I said.

Justin was ready to attempt a middle-of-the-night wave ride in the Arctic, though he was hoping he wouldn't have to go it alone. Peer pressure had no effect on the rest of the surfers, though, as they all promised support from the shoreline. Sensing Justin was literally and figuratively getting cold feet, I simply reminded him of our dream from years earlier.

The walk down to the water was almost as treacherous as the idea of surfing in the dark, and with the light of my headlamp I had to help Justin navigate ice-blanketed boulders that were guaranteed to break an ankle with even the slightest misstep. Once water started lapping at his feet, there was an extra moment of hesitation between us. We discussed how he would even see what was coming his way, and how he would time the sets. I suggested he just listen for the sets, jump in, and start paddling.

"Chris, all I can see is a white line from the waves where they're crashing. By the time I see that line, it will be too late and I'll be in the impact zone."

Justin had a lot of very valid concerns, but I just couldn't shake the feeling that we were meant to be here, and this moment had arrived for our taking.

"I know it's crazy," I said. "And I'm sorry I'm even asking this of you . . . but when are we ever going to be able to do this again?"

Within minutes he was paddling his longboard over silky black ramps. When a set wave rolled in, he turned his board around and dug into it, popping up, leaning into position, and carving figure eights all the way down the line. Elli looked on in amazement. He of all people knew how rare an aurora-lit surf was. He had never seen it done before. Justin's surf dance seemed like the perfect complement to the mystical energy bursting above his head. Two of the most unpredictable forces on the planet collided here for a brief encounter that we were lucky to be part of.

As it turned out, Justin only caught one wave in the darkness that night. His indiscernible figure blended in with the dark tones of the wave, and although he had successfully surfed under the northern lights, none of us were fully satisfied with the footage. He sat out there shivering for forty minutes, attempting to surf another wave, to no avail. But that night still revealed the perfect cinematic representation of our triumph as a team. This band of brothers had come together to pioneer an experience never documented before. Our time was up. It was already midnight, and we had to leave by 6:00 A.M. in order to be home by Christmas. The entire night simply left us all hungry for more.

That trip sparked a new obsession to somehow properly document the surreal experience of someone surfing under that neon glow. It seemed like a near-impossible task to get clear footage of surfing set against the aurora, a scene that depended on the right wind, swell, tide, air temperature, clarity, and light from the moon. But upon reviewing the imagery back at home, we realized some immediate failures that could be adjusted in order to achieve the documentation we were hoping for.

Two months later our original crew was back in Iceland, along with a few additions. Mike Zeller and Steve Haughelstine from the tenacious production company Sweatpants Media joined the team, bringing with them an impressive background in high-stakes, action-packed filmmaking. We were also joined by the multitalented rock-climbing documentarian duo Renan Ozturk and Taylor Freesolo Rees. Renan is best known for his 2011 ascent of the Shark's Fin route up 20,700-foot Meru Peak in the Himalayas with Jimmy Chin and Conrad Anker, during which he suffered a minor stroke but still summited the

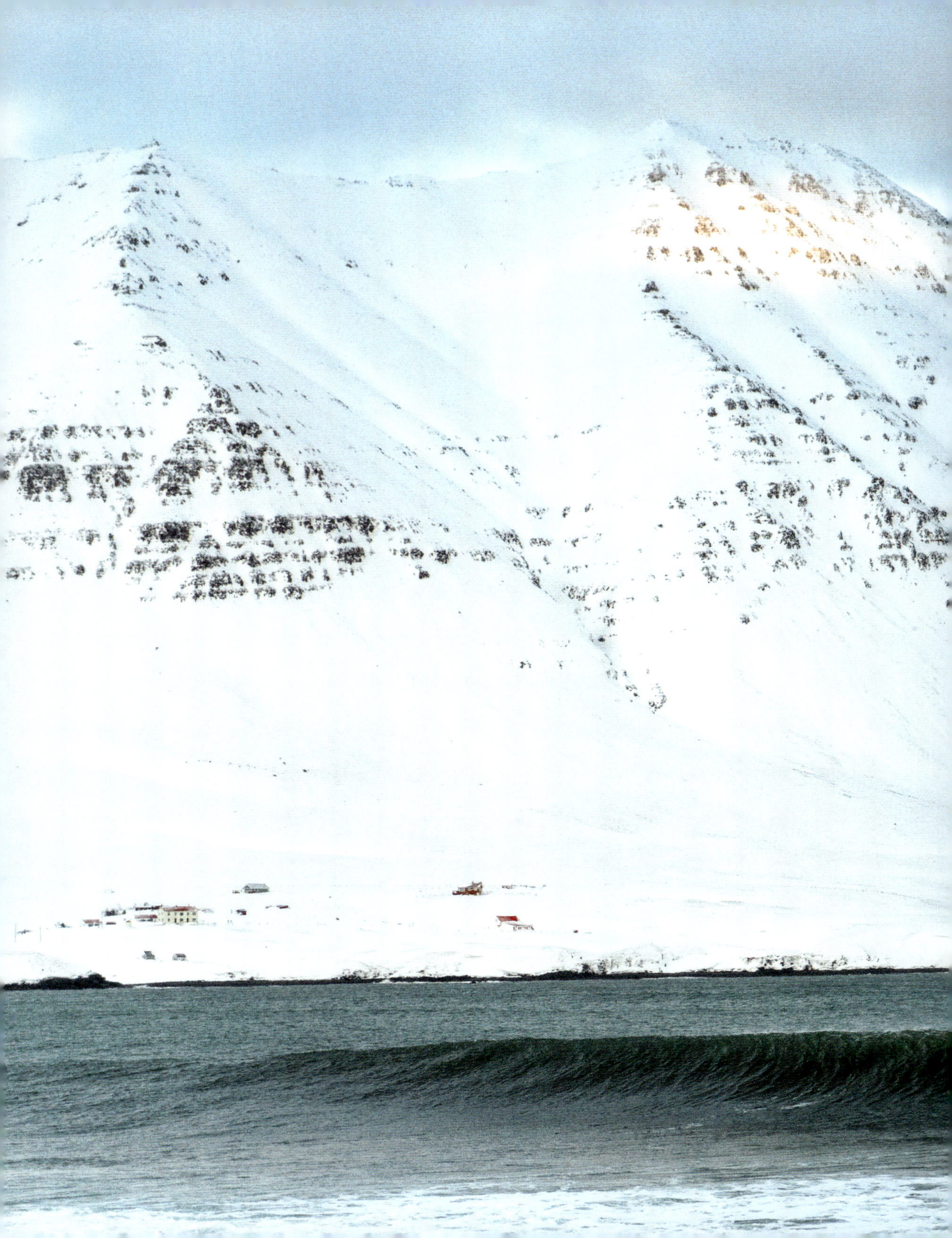

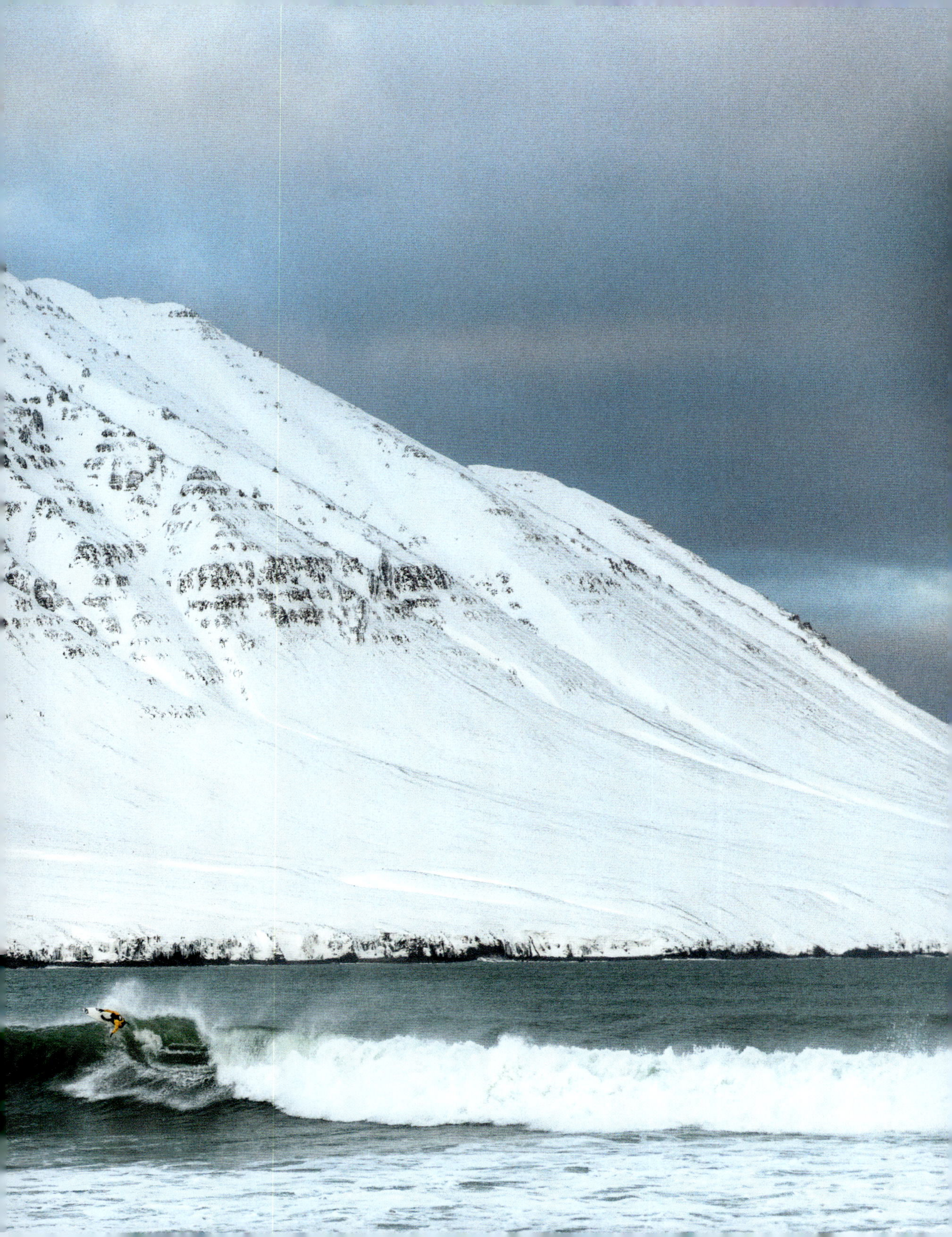

peak. Taylor is a gifted photographer and environmental anthropologist who has coproduced some amazing films with Renan, including *Down to Nothing*, about a leech-infested *National Geographic* expedition to find the highest peak in Myanmar.

We were all using Sony a7S II cameras, which had light sensors that could shoot beyond ISO 20,000—a number that was unheard-of just a few years earlier. We spent hours in our log cabin near the coast, charging batteries and dumping files on hard drives before setting up drones and time lapses to run until the batteries died (which happens a lot faster in the cold). On more than one occasion, the legs of our tripods froze to the shoreline of the icy beach.

Every night Ben and I kept vigilant watch, monitoring the sky for the faintest flicker of color. Whenever we started to see a hint of color, we'd call up the surfers on our walkie-talkies and try to motivate them to freeze their asses off—yet again. No matter how prepared the surfers were with hot water, wool socks, and a heater set to full blast waiting in the car, it took every ounce of strength the guys had to put their weary bodies through that kind of torture night after night. After the coldest sessions, ice crystals would form on their hair and the brims of their wetsuit hoods.

On one of our final nights in Iceland, after days of attempts, we finally had the right conditions. Zero cloud cover and a nearly full moon brought the sky alive. Ben, Russ, and I drove to the beach and immediately saw the potential: the first green wisps of an aurora, three- to four-foot waves, and white lunar light that could make the whole scene complete. The electricity of the moment was palpable.

"Justin, Timmy, do you copy?" I called through the two-way radio. "This isn't gonna last long. We need to shoot it now."

The guys were back at the cabin drinking coffee and whiskey and blasting Lynyrd Skynyrd to pump themselves up, while I was growing more impatient by the minute. I had dreamed of these conditions, and the real possibility of creating the images tied my stomach in knots. The risk of failure was much higher than the chance of success, but those are the kinds of odds I've built my career on. I set up two tripods side by side on the rocks and twisted on two Sony a7SII cameras, one paired with a 50mm lens at an f1.4 aperture, the other with a 35mm at f1.4. Both camera combinations could pick up a surfer backed by snowy mountains and ephemeral lights. Ben took another camera plus a high-powered flashlight up to the point.

When the surfers arrived at the beach, the light show was beginning to really turn on: a vertical blue-green flame started to twist and lick the stars. Overhead, a cat's eye pattern was slowly shifting like a kaleidoscope. Heiðar said this was the best display of the northern lights he'd ever seen, particularly because of where it was located. The light show crested just above the horizon and took a rare position over the ocean.

The guys paddled to the top of the point. Not being able to see a thing in the fluid darkness, Ben illuminated the on-coming waves with a 50,000-lumen turbo flashlight. I tried out different ISOs and shutter speeds—1/15 of a second, 1/25 of a second—until I had clear playback of the surfers and the incredible arena they were performing in. Justin caught the first set on his longboard, riding a high line on the face and producing a white stream off his tail. We couldn't believe it was actually hap-pening. The chorus of everyone watching intensified with hollers and cheers, creating a soundtrack to the emotion we all felt as we witnessed the magic in front of us.

At that end of that magical night in Ice-land, Timmy dropped in for one last run, carving up and down with a force that overpowered his frozen state. His black silhouette looked like a superhero framed by the green wave behind him. Ben and I communicated mainly through hoots at this point, echoing each other's elation.

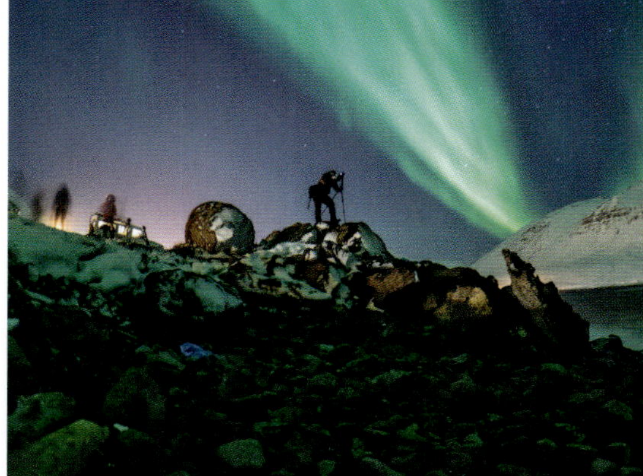

There was no staging the raw emotion we felt. We had worked so hard and put a lot on the line, and despite the odds, we had documented something rare and beautiful that even we hadn't been sure was possible.

To be clear, things going right like this is not really what made me the photographer I am today. My most defining moments and images have more to do with something going right—even perfectly—when all odds are against it. The layers of adversity and the obstacles I overlook to chase a particular image I have in my head are almost comical at times (which is a good thing, since laughter is often all that keeps us going when things get really bad). Things going right at exactly the same moment all seems to be going wrong is magic.

And, while sometimes it's luck, most of the time, success is the result of a ridiculously fine-tuned plan, full of contingencies and split-second decisions. And perhaps that's the part I've gotten really good at. After years of stepping outside my comfort zone, I feel more at home there than I do inside it.

It took me a few years to truly believe my own words spoken on that TED stage, but this experience in many ways cemented what I always knew to be true: In life there are no shortcuts to joy; anything worth pursuing requires us to suffer just a little bit.

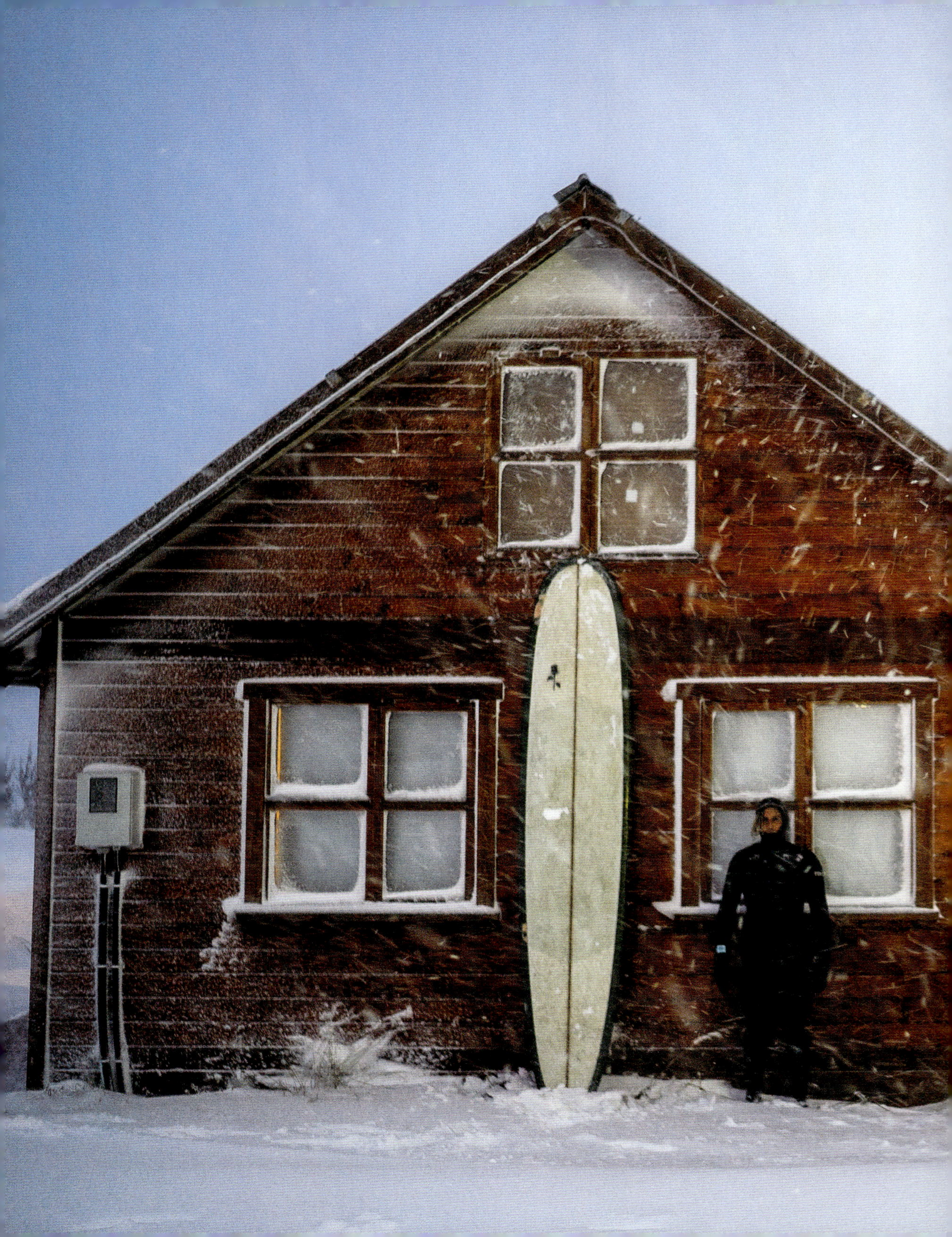

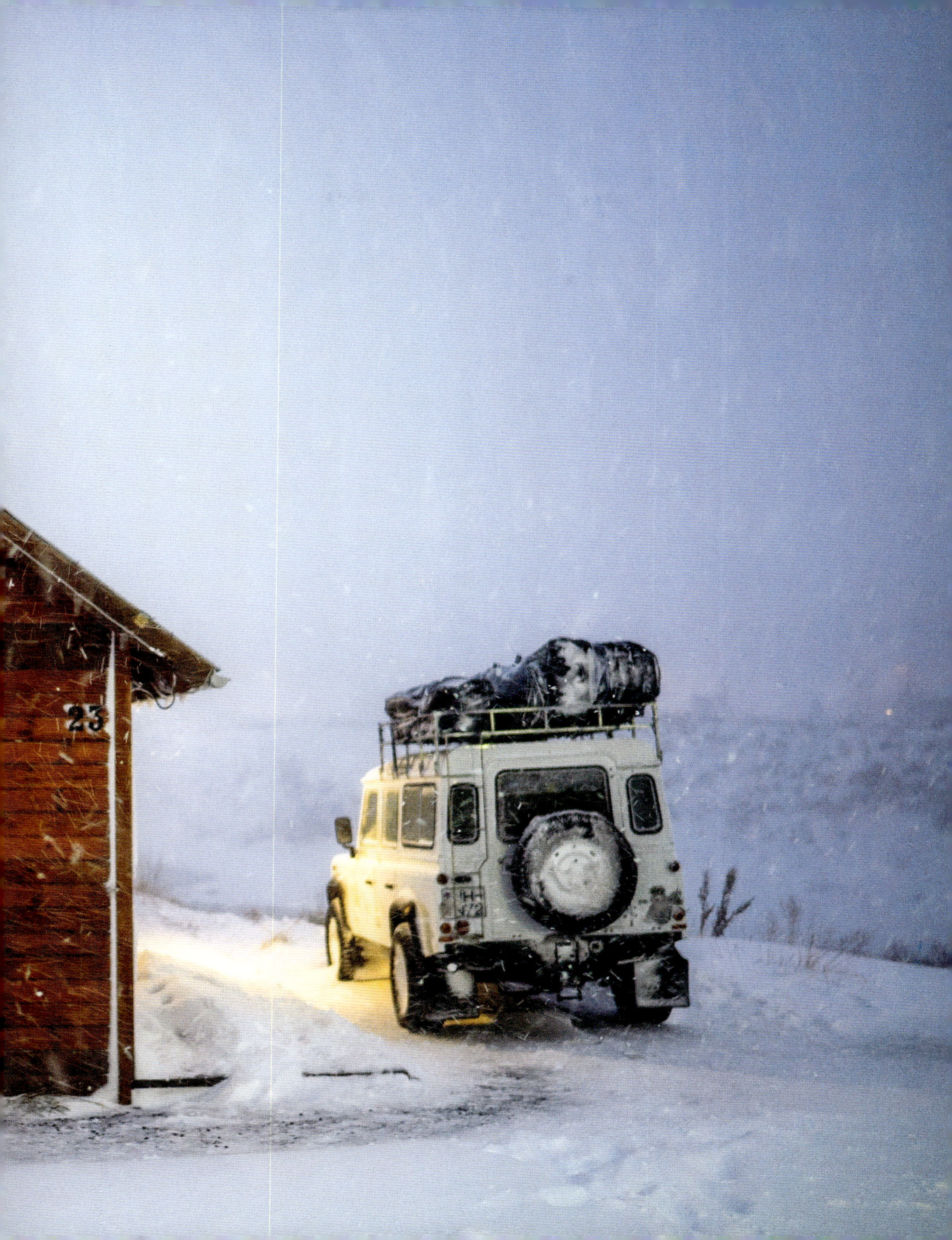
23

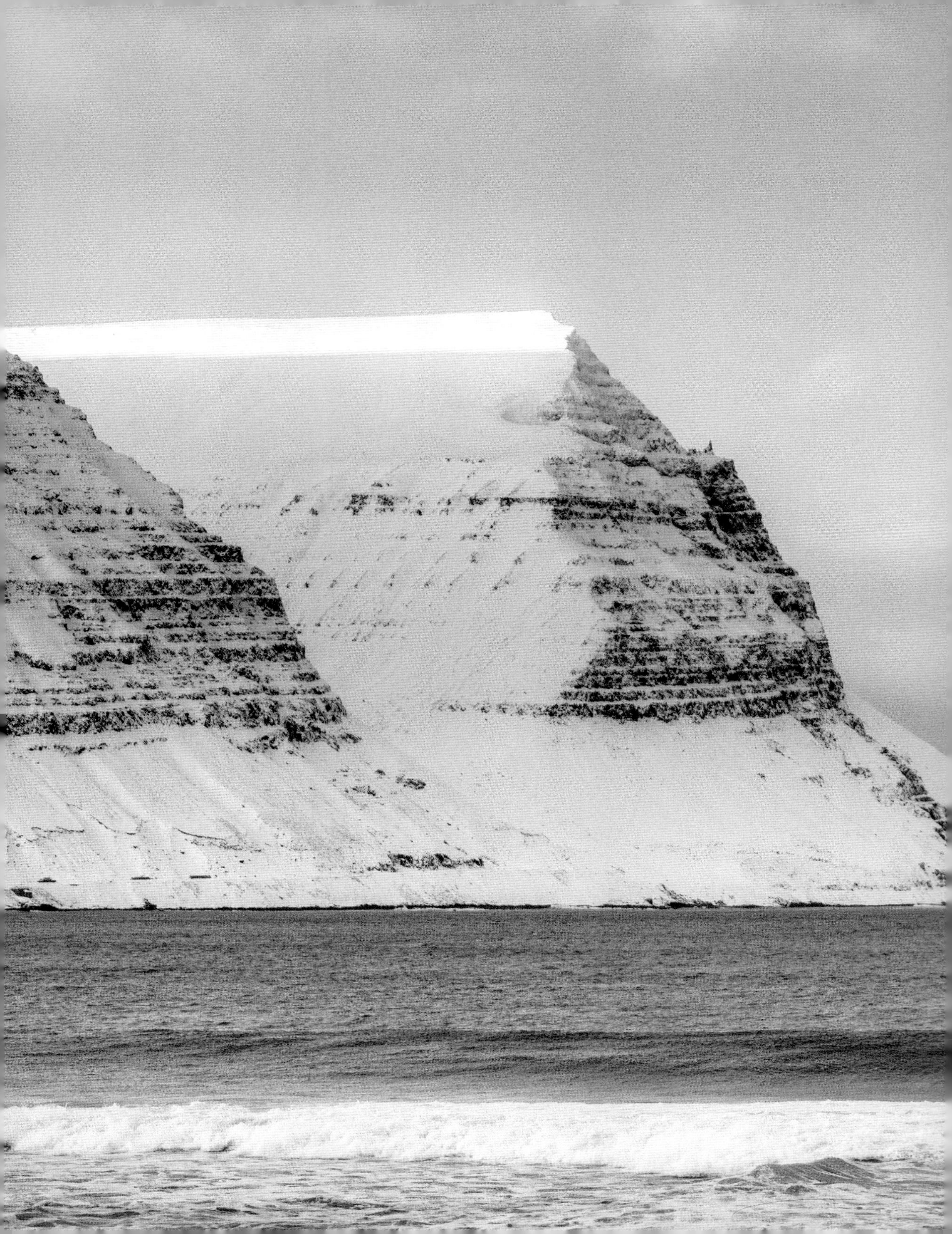

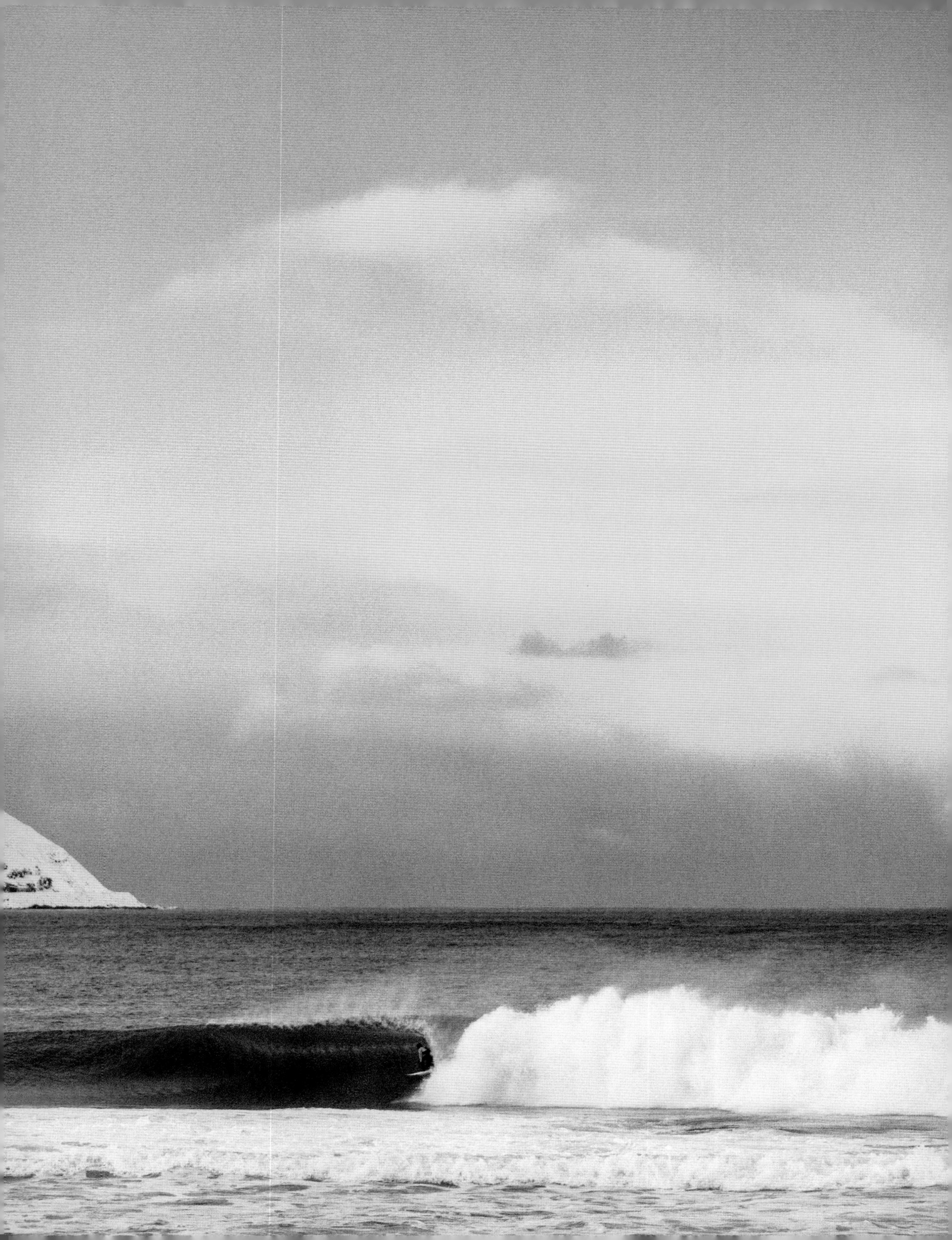

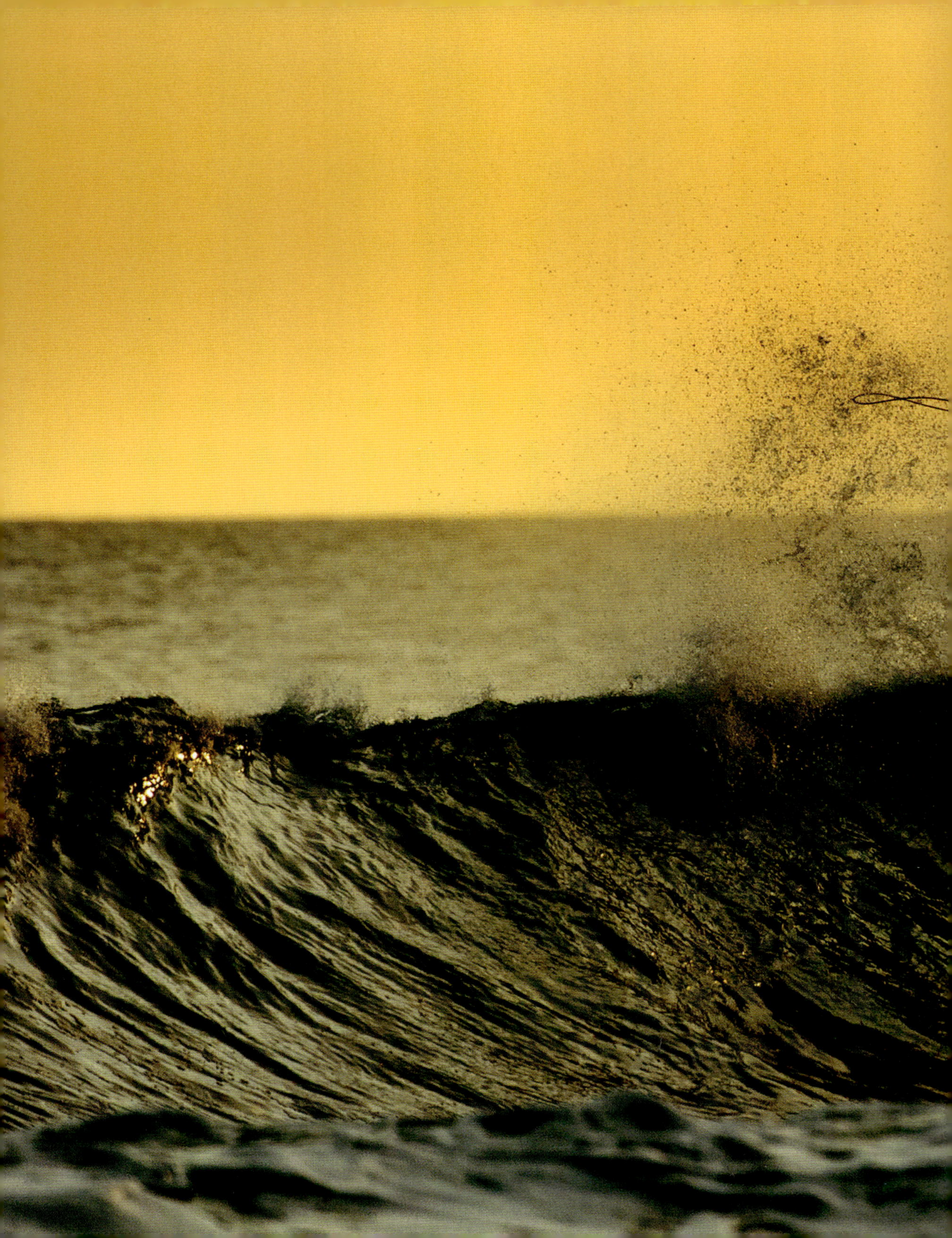

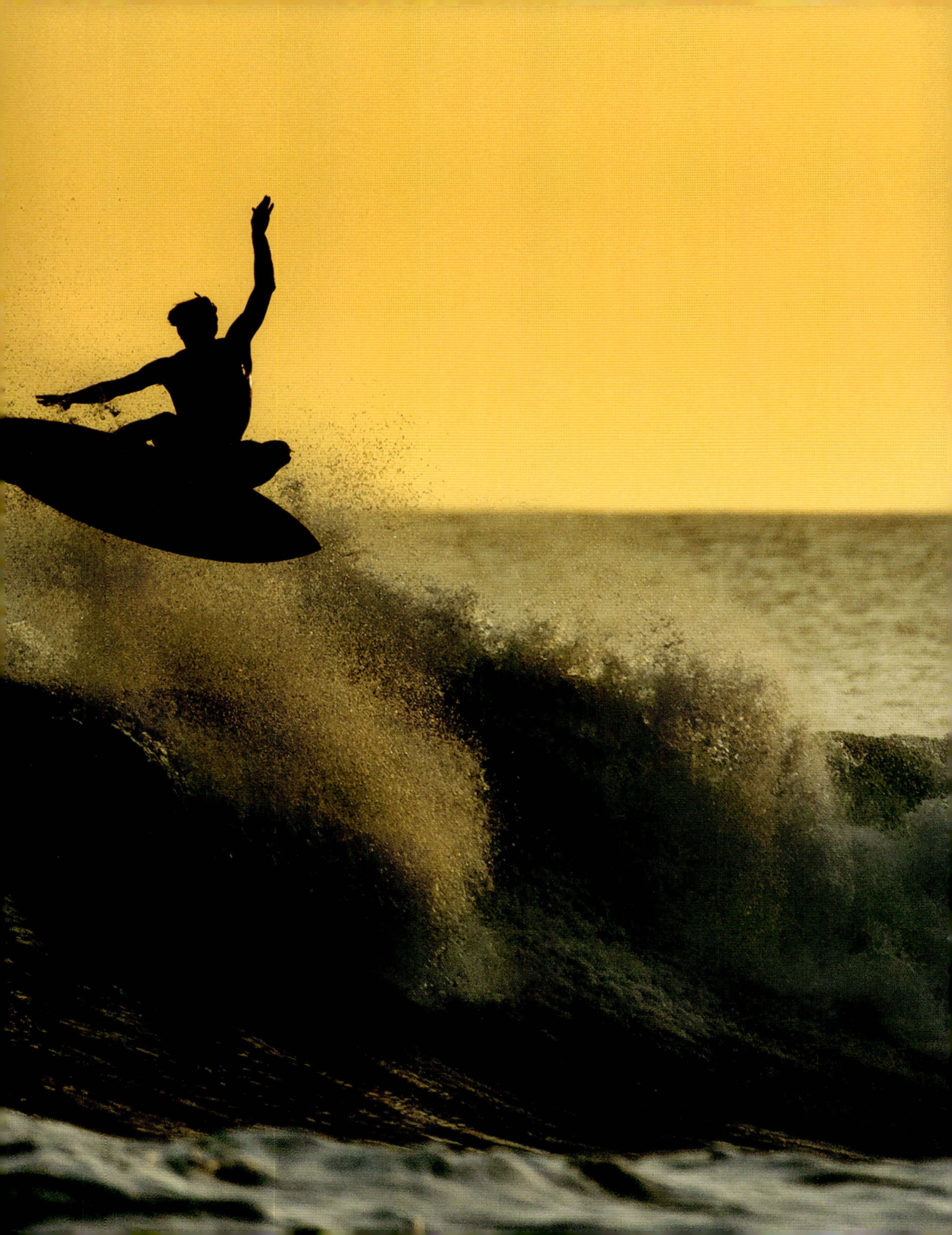

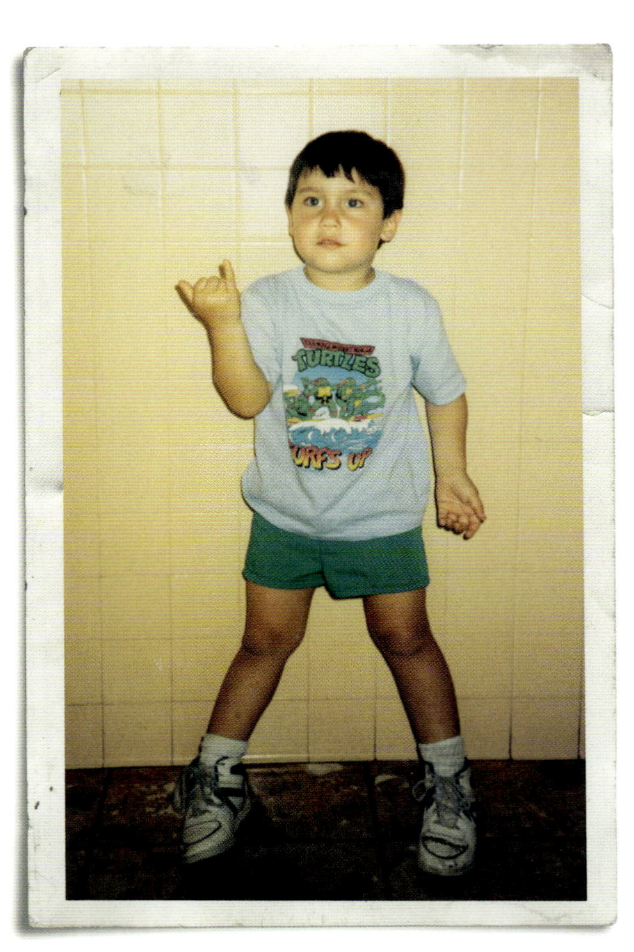

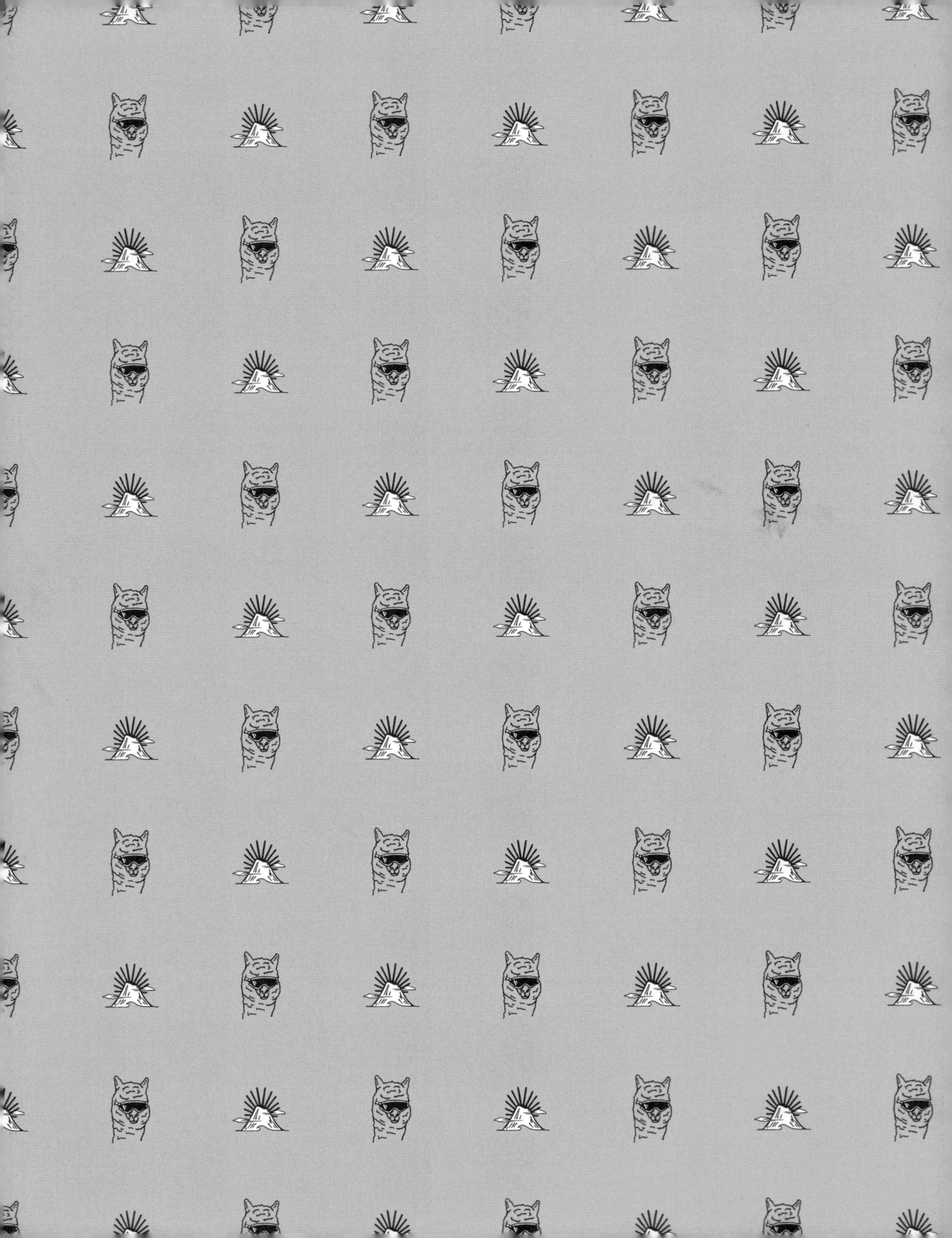